lonely planet

Sweden

Becky Ohlsen
Fran Parnell

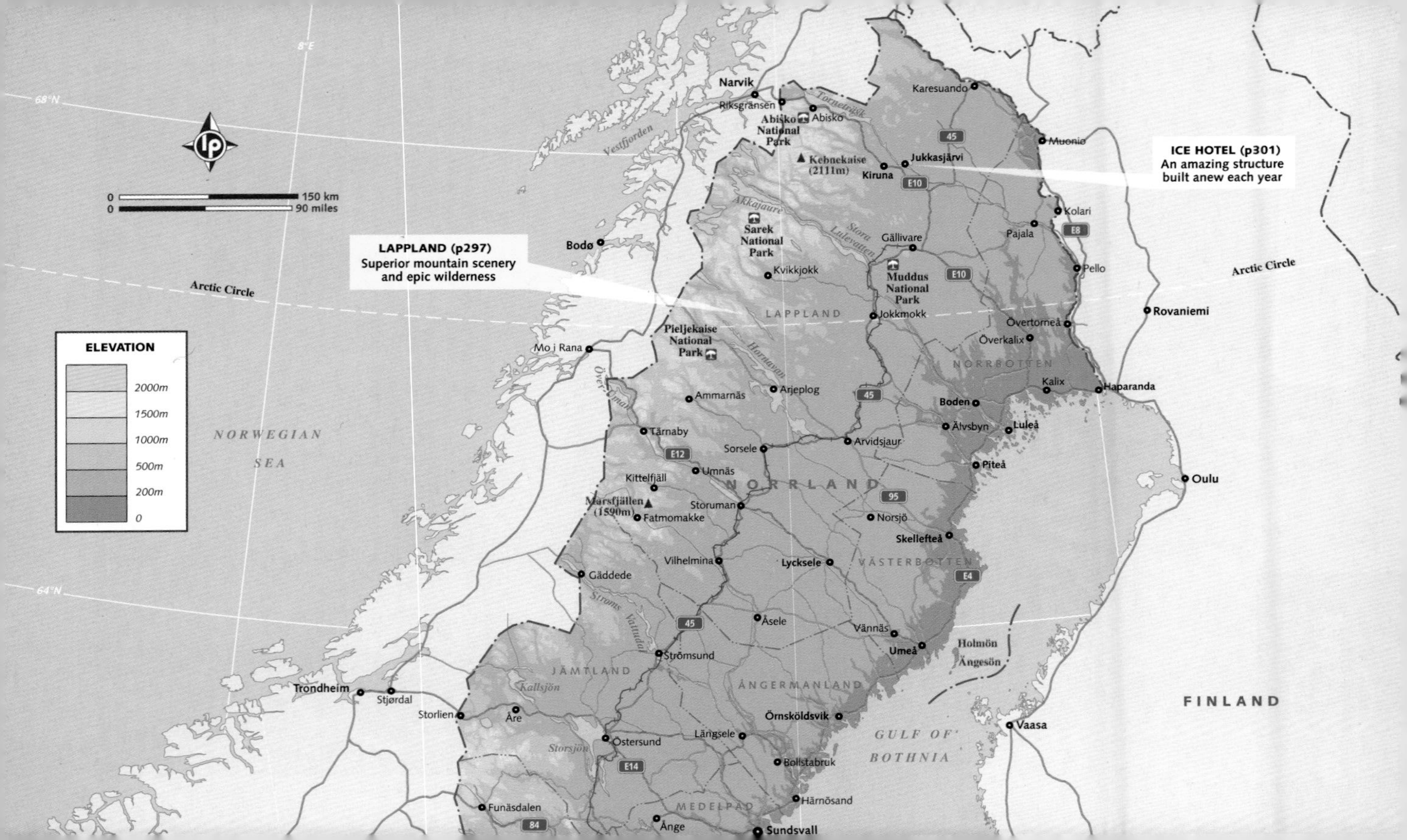
ICE HOTEL (p301)
An amazing structure built anew each year
LAPPLAND (p297)
Superior mountain scenery and epic wilderness
ELEVATION
2000m
1500m
1000m
500m
200m
0
0
150 km
0
90 miles
68°N
64°N
8°E
Arctic Circle
Arctic Circle
NORWEGIAN SEA
GULF OF BOTHNIA
FINLAND
NORRLAND
LAPPLAND
NORRBOTTEN
VÄSTERBOTTEN
JÄMTLAND
ÅNGERMANLAND
MEDELPAD
Narvik
Riksgränsen
Abisko
Abisko National Park
Torneträsk
Karesuando
Muonio
Kebnekaise (2111m)
Jukkasjärvi
Kiruna
Kolari
Pajala
Pello
Akkajaure
Sarek National Park
Stora Lulevatten
Gällivare
Muddus National Park
Kvikkjokk
Bodø
Vestfjorden
Rovaniemi
Jokkmokk
Övertorneå
Överkalix
Pieljekaise National Park
Mo i Rana
Hornavan
Kalix
Haparanda
Ammarnäs
Arjeplog
Boden
Älvsbyn
Luleå
Över-Uman
Tärnaby
Sorsele
Arvidsjaur
Piteå
Oulu
Umnäs
Kittelfjäll
Marsfjällen (1590m)
Fatmomakke
Storuman
Norsjö
Skellefteå
Vilhelmina
Lycksele
Gäddede
Ströms Vattudal
Åsele
Vännäs
Umeå
Holmön
Ängesön
Strömsund
Kallsjön
Trondheim
Stjørdal
Storlien
Åre
Örnsköldsvik
Vaasa
Östersund
Storsjön
Långsele
Bollstabruk
Härnösand
Funäsdalen
Ånge
Sundsvall
E10
E8
E12
E14
E4
45
95
84

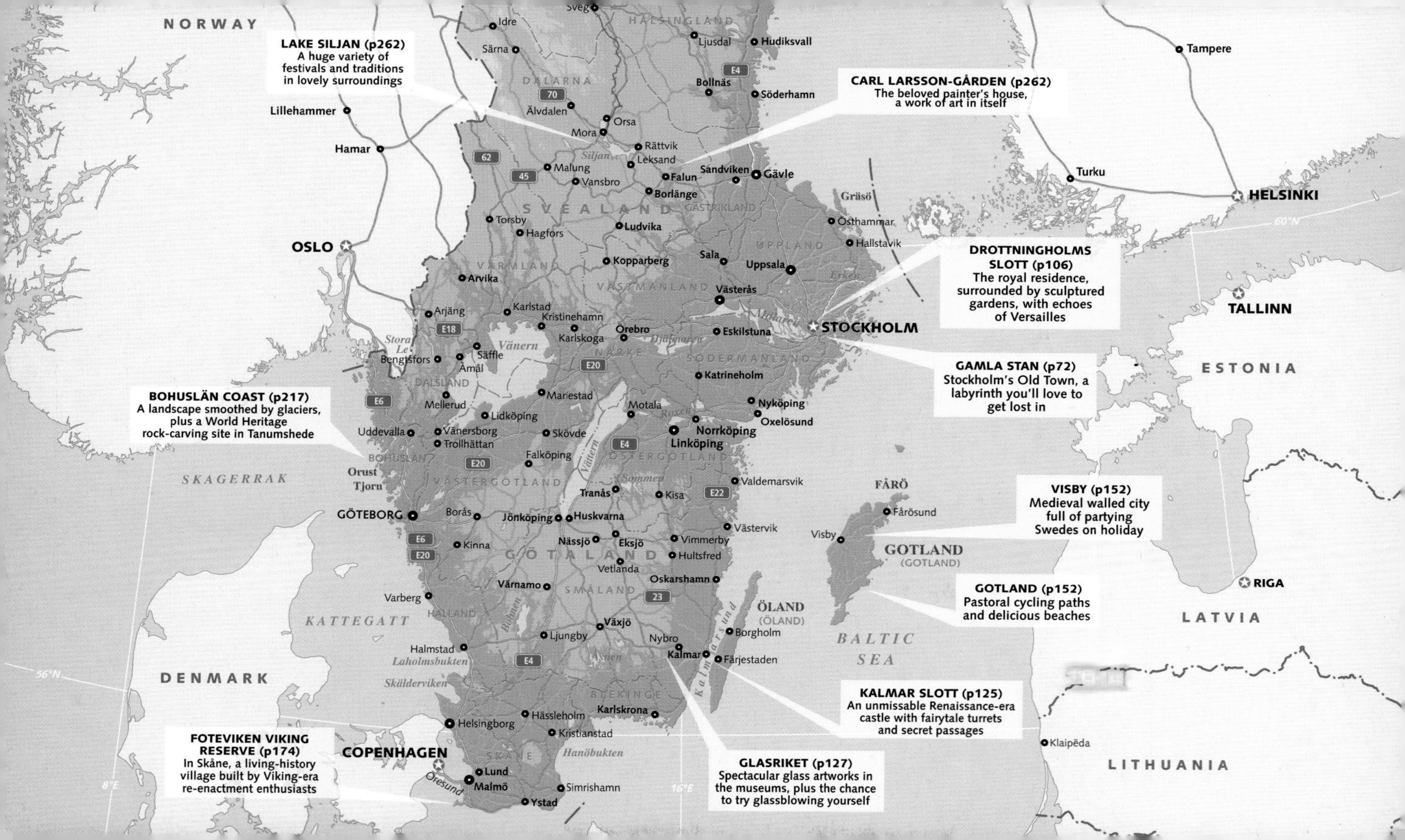

NORWAY
LAKE SILJAN (p262)
A huge variety of festivals and traditions in lovely surroundings
CARL LARSSON-GÅRDEN (p262)
The beloved painter's house, a work of art in itself
DROTTNINGHOLMS SLOTT (p106)
The royal residence, surrounded by sculptured gardens, with echoes of Versailles
GAMLA STAN (p72)
Stockholm's Old Town, a labyrinth you'll love to get lost in
BOHUSLÄN COAST (p217)
A landscape smoothed by glaciers, plus a World Heritage rock-carving site in Tanumshede
VISBY (p152)
Medieval walled city full of partying Swedes on holiday
GOTLAND (p152)
Pastoral cycling paths and delicious beaches
KALMAR SLOTT (p125)
An unmissable Renaissance-era castle with fairytale turrets and secret passages
FOTEVIKEN VIKING RESERVE (p174)
In Skåne, a living-history village built by Viking-era re-enactment enthusiasts
GLASRIKET (p127)
Spectacular glass artworks in the museums, plus the chance to try glassblowing yourself
OSLO
STOCKHOLM
HELSINKI
TALLINN
RIGA
COPENHAGEN
GÖTEBORG
ESTONIA
LATVIA
LITHUANIA
DENMARK
SKAGERRAK
KATTEGATT
BALTIC SEA
SVEALAND
GÖTALAND
GOTLAND
(GOTLAND)
ÖLAND
(ÖLAND)
FÅRÖ
Lillehammer
Hamar
Tampere
Turku
Klaipėda
Idre
Särna
Sveg
Ljusdal
Hudiksvall
Bollnäs
Söderhamn
Älvdalen
Orsa
Mora
Rättvik
Leksand
Malung
Vansbro
Falun
Borlänge
Sandviken
Gävle
Torsby
Hagfors
Ludvika
Kopparberg
Sala
Uppsala
Östhammar
Hallstavik
Gräsö
Arvika
Västerås
Arjäng
Karlstad
Kristinehamn
Karlskoga
Örebro
Eskilstuna
Bengtsfors
Åmål
Säffle
Vänern
Stora Le
Katrineholm
Mariestad
Mellerud
Nyköping
Oxelösund
Motala
Norrköping
Linköping
Lidköping
Vänersborg
Uddevalla
Trollhättan
Skövde
Falköping
Vättern
Orust
Tjorn
Valdemarsvik
Tranås
Kisa
Sommen
Borås
Jönköping
Huskvarna
Västervik
Nässjö
Eksjö
Vimmerby
Hultsfred
Kinna
Vetlanda
Värnamo
Oskarshamn
Varberg
Växjö
Ljungby
Borgholm
Nybro
Kalmar
Färjestaden
Halmstad
Laholmsbukten
Skälderviken
Kalmarsund
Bolmen
Karlskrona
Hässleholm
Helsingborg
Kristianstad
Hanöbukten
Lund
Malmö
Simrishamn
Ystad
Öresund
Mälaren
Hjälmaren
Roxen
Erken
DALARNA
HÄLSINGLAND
GÄSTRIKLAND
UPPLAND
VÄRMLAND
VÄSTMANLAND
NÄRKE
SÖDERMANLAND
DALSLAND
BOHUSLÄN
VÄSTERGÖTLAND
ÖSTERGÖTLAND
SMÅLAND
HALLAND
BLEKINGE
SKÅNE
E4
E6
E18
E20
E22
70
62
45
23
60°N
56°N
8°E
16°E

Destination Sweden

The midnight sun, the snowbound winters, meatballs, herring, Vikings and Volvos, ABBA and the Hives – whatever your pre-existing notions about Sweden may be, a visit to this multifaceted country is bound to both confirm and confound them.

Though you're unlikely to be greeted at the shore by throngs of mead-swilling berserkers in longships, evidence of the Vikings and their pillaging days is easy to find. A stroll through the Swedish countryside will often lead to a picnic on some ancient king's burial mound. Cycling routes frequently pass through fields crowned with ship-shaped stone graves. In cities and alongside roadways, rune stones staunchly declare the historical equivalent of 'Ingmar was here'.

But Sweden's days as a warlike nation are long gone. Instead, its domestic and international policies serve as models of neutrality and consensus-building. This is, after all, the birthplace of the Nobel Peace Prize. Travellers today are more likely to be slayed by visions of pastoral beauty – intense green countryside, impenetrable forests, little red cottages atop remote islands and, everywhere, Sweden's famously clear blue water.

That's not to say all the excitement ended thousands of years ago – far from it. While tradition reigns in places like Dalarna in the Swedish heartland and the Sami territory up north, much of Sweden today buzzes with a more contemporary energy. A wave of immigration in recent years has added spark and variety to the cultural milieu. Urban centres like Stockholm, Göteborg (otherwise known as Gothenburg) and Malmö consistently churn out cultural artefacts for an international audience (think IKEA, H&M, Absolut Vodka). The town of Trollhättan has become Scandinavia's film-making headquarters, with productions by indie darling Lukas Moodysson and Danish *enfant terrible* Lars von Trier. Travellers come to Sweden as much for the flash clubs and ground-breaking new restaurants as they do for wilderness hikes and visits to wooden-horse factories.

In short, try the meatballs and dig the Vikings, but don't stop there – history hasn't.

ANDERS BLOM

Castles & Palaces

ANDERS BLOMQVIST

Marvel at the sheer magnitude of Stockholm's royal palace, Kungliga Slottet (p73)

ANDERS BLOMQVIST

Delve into Swedish history at Gripsholm Slott (p112)

OTHER HIGHLIGHTS

- Enjoy a summer concert in the ruins of Borgholms Slott (p139)
- For a palace with a difference, chill out at the Ice Hotel in Jukkasjärvi in Northern Sweden (p301)
- Stand in awe of Skokloster Slott's (p111) delicate baroque beauty

GRAEME CORNWALLIS

Be spooked in the haunted hallways of Glimmingehus (p181)

Historic Towns

GRAEME CORNWALLIS

Rummage the ruins and visit the well-preserved buildings within the walls of Visby (p152)

Wander the streets of Sigtuna (p111), Sweden's oldest town

VERONICA GARBUTT

OTHER HIGHLIGHTS

- Stroll through the delightful streets and courtyards of Eksjö (p121)
- Learn about Sami culture in Lappstaden (p306), Sweden's best-preserved Sami church village

Relax in the parks and gardens of the 1000-year-old university town of Lund (p171)

ANDERS BLOM(

Islands & Coast

GRAEME CORNWALLIS

Watch the sun set at Langhammarshammaren (p158), Fårö, Gotland

GRAEME CORNWALLIS

Discover picturesque fishing villages on World Heritage–listed Öland (p137)

OTHER HIGHLIGHTS

- Drive along the spectacular Höga Kusten (p282) at the Gulf of Bothnia
- Island-hop to your heart's content in Stockholm's archipelago (p108)
- Enjoy the car-free paradise of the southern archipelago (p215)

ANDERS BLOMQVIST

Spelunk, rock-climb or just soak up the sun on the Kulla Peninsula (p197)

Churches & Cathedrals

Pay your respects at the impressive Riddarholmskyrkan (p74), Sweden's royal necropolis for 700 years

ANDERS BLOMQVIST

CHRISTOPHER WOOD

Gaze up in awe at Scandinavia's largest cathedral (p238) towering over Uppsala

GRAEME CORNW

Meander among Gotland's wealth of medieval churches (p152)

OTHER HIGHLIGHTS

- Meet Finn, the mythological giant, in the crypt of Lund's Domkyrkan (p171)
- See Kalmar's landmark baroque cathedral, Kalmar Domkyrkan (p125)

Rock Carvings & Historic Sites

ANDERS BLOMQVIST

Surround yourself in the mystery of Anundshög's stone ship settings (p248)

ANDERS BLOMQVIST

Goggle at the weird and wonderful Bronze Age rock carvings (p222) on the Tanum plain

OTHER HIGHLIGHTS

- Learn about the Viking legend of Sigurd at Sigurdsristningen (p245)
- Stumble upon the Bronze Age rock carvings in the atmospheric Högsbyn Nature Reserve (p224)

Visit Ales Stenar (p180), Sweden's Stonehenge

ANDERS BLOMQVIST

Activities

ANDERS BLOMQVIST

Get off the roads and explore Sweden by canoe (p56)

Scale Sweden's cliffs (p52) in places like the Kulla Peninsula, Skåne

ANDERS BLOMQVIST

ANDERS BLOMQVIST

Cycle Sweden at your own pace (p53)

OTHER HIGHLIGHTS

- Rug up for a dogsled excursion in Lappland (p55)
- Take to the trails and explore the countryside on horseback (p56)
- Join your fellow twitchers at numerous bird-watchers' towers and nature reserves (p54) across the country

ERNEST MANEWAL

Join the locals and sail through Stockholm's archipelago (p108)

Hike some of Sweden's most famous trails (p48) such as the Skåneleden

ANDERS BLOMQVIST

Brave the white powder at the Riksgränsen ski resort (p303)

CHRISTIAN ASLUND

Cultural Heritage

WAYNE WALTON

Smile at Carl Milles whimsical delights at Stockholm's Millesgården (p82)

OTHER HIGHLIGHTS

- Blow some hot air and create your own glass vase in Glasriket (p127)
- Get inspired to redecorate at the beautiful home of artist Carl Larssons (p262)

Appreciate Sweden's industrial heritage at the Falu Kopparbergsgruva (p260)

ANDERS BLOMQVIST

Step back in time at Skansen (p76), Sweden's largest outdoor museum

ANDERS BLO

Contents

Regional Map Contents

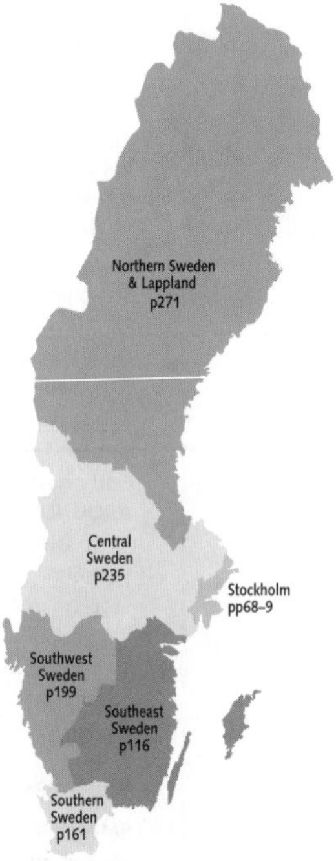

The Authors

BECKY OHLSEN

Stockholm, Northern Sweden & Lappland, Gotland (Southeast Sweden)

Becky has enjoyed travelling in Sweden since she was a little girl visiting her grandparents, when a desperate craving for Swedish chocolate motivated her to learn a few words in her mother's native language. Since then her tastes (and to some extent her vocabulary) have expanded and now include pickled herring in mustard sauce *(senapsill)*, reindeer *(ren)* in tubes and cloudberry *(hjortron)* liqueur. She has an unhealthy fondness for long dark days but also an appreciation for the midnight sun. She's made a meal for dozens of insects while hiking in Norrland and spent enough time exploring the nooks and crannies of Stockholm to know the locations of several free public toilets.

Becky also updated the Destination, Getting Started, Itineraries, Snapshot, The Culture and Food & Drink chapters.

My Favourite Trip

It's about 6 o'clock on a sunny afternoon, and I'm trying, as an adult, to relearn how to ride a bike. ('It's like riding a bike,' they say. Ha!) I've rented a three-gear cruiser that weighs at least 50kg and I'm off to ride the Gotlandsleden (see p24), a bicycle trail that winds through the fields and coastlines of Sweden's favourite holiday island. I decide to head north first, so as not to risk missing Fårö – home of Ingmar Bergman, whom I'm convinced I'll run into by chance. I don't see Ingmar, but I do see some amazing countryside, including dozens of medieval churches and a few spectacular, impossibly quiet beaches. Not a bad way for an old dog to learn a new trick.

FRAN PARNELL

Central Sweden, Southern Sweden, Southwest Sweden, Southeast Sweden

Fran's love of Scandinavia developed while studying for a masters degree in Anglo-Saxon, Norse and Celtic, and she has since been on pilgrimages to as many Viking sites as possible. She gets particularly blown away by Sweden's stone ship settings, and is particularly envious of the folk at the Foteviken Viking Reserve!

Fran also updated the Environment, History, Outdoor Activities, Transport and Directory chapters.

LONELY PLANET AUTHORS

Why is our travel information the best in the world? It's simple: our authors are independent, dedicated travellers. They don't research using just the Internet or phone, and they don't take freebies in exchange for positive coverage. They travel widely, to all the popular spots and off the beaten track. They personally visit thousands of hotels, restaurants, cafés, bars, galleries, palaces, museums and more – and they take pride in getting all the details right, and telling it how it is. For more, see the authors section on www.lonelyplanet.com.

My Favourite Trip

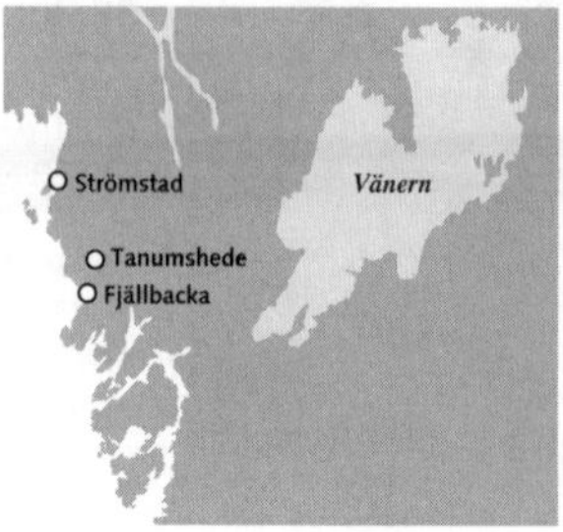

Sweden is filled with so many wonderful places that it's difficult to choose a favourite, but there are some truly idyllic places along the southwestern coast. I would start in Strömstad with a visit to the atmospheric stone ship setting and prehistoric graves, frozen in time and utterly free from crowds. Other ancient mysteries lie a short zip south down the E6: you can't go to this part of the country and not visit the stunning World Heritage rock carvings at Tanumshede. After these silent enigmas, a trip to Ingrid Bergman's favourite holiday village, Fjällbacka, gives you a rousing blast of seaside mayhem: watch the sun setting from the balcony of one of Sweden's most distinctive hotels.

Getting Started

Travel in Sweden is extremely easy, and a bit of advance planning can help preserve your hip pocket. Booking ahead for accommodation and transport within the country will cut costs a lot; and in the major cities, look into discount travel cards before you leave (see p314). Once you arrive, you will find the cities easy to get around and well serviced by public transport, with almost everywhere accessible to wheelchairs.

WHEN TO GO

Despite its northern location in Europe, Sweden isn't as cold as you might expect. The south has a year-round temperate climate and summer can be quite warm in the north. Sweden is at its best during summer and autumn (late May to September), but hikers and campers may wish to avoid the peak of the mosquito season (June and July).

See Climate Charts (p312) for more information.

Due to the country's high latitude, daylight hours are long in summer. Malmö gets 17½ hours of daylight at midsummer, and Sundsvall has constant light during the second half of June, but you have to travel north of the Arctic Circle to experience the true 'midnight sun' – in Kiruna, the sun remains above the horizon for 45 days, from 31 May to 14 July.

Swedes are big on holidays, and even Stockholm shuts down for two or three days around Christmas and midsummer, so plan accordingly. Most Swedes take their vacations from late June to mid-August, so hostels are crowded, but this is also when most hotels offer discounts of up to 50%.

Travel in winter is somewhat restricted and requires some planning as well as serious winter clothing, but there are good opportunities for activities like skiing, dogsledding and snowmobiling. The big cities are in full swing all year, but the smaller towns almost go into hibernation when the temperatures begin to drop (the notable exceptions being popular ski resort towns like Åre, and Jukkasjärvi, home to the Ice Hotel).

COSTS & MONEY

Sweden has a very good standard of living, which means the travel experience is generally high quality but it does tend to be expensive. Careful planning in advance can help reduce costs.

During the low-price summer period (June through until August), if you stay in a midrange hotel (which usually includes a huge buffet breakfast), eat a daily special for lunch and have an evening meal at a moderately

DON'T LEAVE HOME WITHOUT...

- Your ID, passport and visa (if applicable)
- Industrial-strength mosquito repellent in summer
- Good walking shoes
- Layers of warm clothing, just in case
- A swimsuit – again, just in case
- A map of Stockholm's tunnelbana (metro)
- A taste for pickled fish
- A fast-acting liver for *snaps*

TOP TENS

Must-Read Books by Swedish Authors

One of the best ways to get inside the collective mind of a country is to read its top authors. Below is a selection of some of the greatest and most popular works by Swedish authors.

- *The Long Ships,* Frans Gunnar Bengtsson (1954)
- *The Wonderful Adventures of Nils,* Selma Lagerlöf (1906–07)
- *Pippi Longstocking,* Astrid Lindgren (1945)
- *Merab's Beauty,* Torgny Lindgren (1982)
- *The Emigrants* series, Wilhelm Moberg (1949–59)
- *Faceless Killers,* Henning Mankell (1989)
- *Markings,* Dag Hammarskjöld (1963–64)
- *Röda Rummet,* August Strindberg (1879)
- *The Evil,* Jan Guillou (1981)
- *Hash,* Torgny Lindgren (2004)

Favourite Swedish Films

Sweden has long been an important force in the film industry. Listed here are some defining works by Swedish filmmakers.

- *The Seventh Seal,* Ingmar Bergman (1956)
- *I Am Curious: Yellow,* Vilgot Sjöman (1967)
- *All Things Fair,* Bo Widerberg (1995)
- *Lilja 4-Ever,* Lukas Moodysson (2002)
- *Songs from the Second Floor,* Roy Andersson (2000)
- *The Emigrants,* Jan Troell (1971)
- *My Life as a Dog,* Lasse Hallström (1985)
- *Ondskan,* Mikael Håfström (2003)
- *Kops,* Josef Fares (2003)
- *Daybreak,* Björn Runge (2004)

Ten Swedish Festivals

If your trip coincides with one of these important annual festivals, don't miss it – the following list is a good sampling of traditional celebrations throughout Sweden (for more events, see p315).

- Kiruna Snow Festival, late January (p315)
- Vasaloppet, first Sunday in March (p266)
- Valborgsmässoafton (Walpurgis Night), 30 April (p315)
- Swedish National Day, 6 June (p315)
- Midsummer, first Saturday after 21 June (p316)
- Stockholm Jazz Festival, 19–23 July (p86)
- Medieval Week (Visby), early August (p154)
- Stockholm Pride, first week in August (p86)
- Stockholm International Film Festival, mid- to late-November (p86)
- Jokkmokk Winter Market, first Thursday, Friday and Saturday in February (p304)

priced restaurant, you can expect to spend Skr800 per person per day if you're doubling up and Skr1200 if you're travelling alone. Staying in hostels, making your own breakfast, eating the daily special at lunchtime in a restaurant, and picking up supermarket items for dinner will probably cost you Skr350 per day. The cheapest way to visit Sweden is to camp in the woods for free, eat supermarket food, hitchhike and visit only the attractions that have free admission – this will cost less than Skr100 per day. If you stay in commercial camping grounds and prepare your own meals you can squeak by on around Skr250 per person per day. If there are a few of you, sharing car rental for a weekend in order to see some out-of-the-way places is worth considering (some petrol stations offer small cars for as little as Skr200 per day). Self-service pumps that take banknotes or credit cards are slightly cheaper, though many won't accept foreign credit cards.

HOW MUCH?

0.7L bottle of Swedish *brännvin* (vodka) Skr200

Coffee with saffron pancake Skr45

3cm souvenir *Dalahästen* (wooden horse) Skr80

Movie ticket Skr75

Weekend admission to a Stureplan disco Skr150

TRAVEL LITERATURE

Good books on travelling or living in Sweden are few and far between. Mary Wollstonecraft's *A Short Residence in Sweden, Norway and Denmark* records the pioneering feminist author's journey to Scandinavia in 1795 in search of happiness. It's a classic of early English Romanticism and well worth a read.

The reliably hilarious Bill Bryson predictably had an entertainingly difficult time of it in Sweden, as described in two chapters of his European travel book *Neither Here Nor There*.

There are also a couple of good views of Sweden from within, including Selma Lagerlöf's *The Wonderful Adventures of Nils*. This creative account of the country's history and geography is still taught in Swedish classrooms.

Get a taste of a thematic journey in the remotest parts of northern Sweden in Torgny Lindgren's wonderful novel *Hash*. Two odd characters set off on a motorcycle in search of the perfect, life-altering pot of hash *(pölsan)*, a sort of potted-meat dish traditionally prepared in the rural north.

INTERNET RESOURCES

Many Swedish towns and organisations have websites in both Swedish and English (although the English pages are often less detailed). Hotels, restaurants and museums throughout the country can also frequently be found online. The following websites are useful for preplanning:

An introduction to the Sami people (www.itv.se/boreale/samieng.htm) A good place to start learning about the indigenous people of northern Sweden and the issues they face, which include racism and habitat destruction.

Smorgasbord (www.sverigeturism.se/smorgasbord/index.html) A comprehensive website devoted to Swedish culture, industry, history, sports, tourism, environment and more, produced by the nonprofit FÖRST Föreningen Sverigeturism (Swedish Tourism Trade Association).

Sweden.se (www.sweden.se) All kinds of useful information about the country, in a variety of languages.

Swedish Film Institute (www.sfi.se) Loads of information on Swedish films and their significance within and outside the country.

Swedish Institute (www.si.se) The Swedish Institute publishes the best academic information on Sweden in English.

Visit Sweden (www.visit-sweden.com) The official website for tourism in Sweden.

Itineraries

CLASSIC ROUTES

These three suggestions are popular travel routes that take in some of the classic highlights of Sweden. They can be adjusted or mixed-and-matched depending on how much time you have.

AROUND THE CAPITAL & BEYOND **One Week/Start & End in Stockholm**

Start in **Stockholm** (p65), where mandatory attractions include the **Royal Palace**, **Gamla Stan** and **Skansen**. You can cover those in a couple of days if need be, which leaves an evening for enjoying some of the capital city's nightlife – try the clubs around Medborgarplatsen in **Södermalm** (p79). On day three, take a boat tour to the ancient settlement on **Birka** (p107); it's an all-day affair. The next day, check out the spectacular cathedral and palace at **Uppsala** (p236), and, if your schedule allows, peek into the illuminated-manuscripts display at the old university library, **Carolina Rediviva** (p239). Wander around the burial mounds at **Gamla Uppsala** (p238), allowing plenty of time to explore the museum. Spend the rest of the day exploring the adorable village of **Sigtuna** (p111), with its old-fashioned buildings, cute cafés and atmospheric church ruins. If you fancy a drive, head over to **Göteborg** (p200) and explore the **Bohuslän Coast** (p217) for the last couple of days. Alternatively, you could stay put and sample further from the cultural smörgåsbord that is Stockholm.

This trip takes you through some of Sweden's most accessible highlights in and around the capital city.

THE MIDDLE WAY

Two Weeks/Stockholm to Göteborg

Spend the first week as outlined above, checking out **Stockholm** (p65), **Birka** (p107), **Uppsala** (p236) and **Sigtuna** (p111). Then head north towards **Lake Siljan** (p262) to explore the surrounding villages, which are famous for being postcard-pretty and steeped in history. Don't miss the family home of noted Swedish painter Anders Zorn in **Mora** (p266), the town where the world's biggest cross-country ski race, Vasaloppet, ends. Tour a copper mine in **Falun** (p259) such as the World Heritage–listed, Falu Kopparbergsgruva. Stop at **Örebro** (p251) to see the fine castle and to wander through one of Sweden's most beautiful parks before continuing down through the heart of Sweden to **Göteborg** (p200). Spend a day or two in this engaging city, making sure to visit its theme park and taking time to relax and enjoy the atmosphere on the Avenyn. Spend the rest of your trip exploring the craggy coastline and picturesque fishing villages of the **Bohuslän Coast** (p217).

This journey cuts a swath through the belly of the beast, touching on two of the country's best cities and taking in some archetypal Swedish villages.

TIP TO TAIL

One Month/Kiruna to Malmö

This trip is a through-line from the northernmost city in Sweden to just shy of Denmark in the south. Fly in to **Kiruna** (p298), stopping to check out the Ice Hotel if the season is right. Take the train toward Narvik and stop at **Abisko** (p301), a hiker's paradise. Spend a day or two exploring the wilderness, either along the **Kungsleden** or via any of the shorter nearby trails in the area. Expert hikers may opt instead to spend their mountaineering time in the more challenging **Sarek National Park** (p305). From here, head to **Gällivare** (p303) and catch the historic Inlandsbanan railway to **Jokkmokk** (p304), home of probably the best museum to Sami culture anywhere, the **Ájtte** (p304). Continue on the railway through some of the most spectacular scenery in the country, stopping if your schedule allows at **Sorsele** (p306) and **Storuman** (p307) and **Östersund** (p292). From here, rent a car and cruise over to explore the breathtaking scenery of the High Coast, or **Höga Kusten** (p282). Continue southward, aiming towards **Lake Siljan** (p262) and the surrounding villages. Stop to see **Uppsala** and **Gamla Uppsala** (p238) with a detour into **Sigtuna** (p111) on your way to **Stockholm** (p65). The wonderful capital city will hold your attention for as many days as you can devote to it. When it's time to move on, angle southwest toward **Göteborg** (p200), then **Kalmar** (p124) with its enormous and fantastic Renaissance-era castle. Stop at the island town of **Karlskrona** (p133), which is on the Unesco World Heritage List. Wrap things up by exploring the vibrant southern towns of **Lund** (p171) and **Malmö** (p162).

There's a lot of territory to cover in Sweden, but in a full month you can see most of its highlights by following this top-to-bottom route.

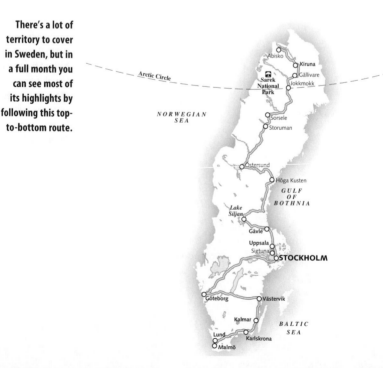

ROADS LESS TRAVELLED

REINDEER GAMES

Five to Seven Days/Start and End in Luleå

From **Luleå** (p288), cruise up to the historic military outpost of **Boden** (p291). Continue heading northwards and cross the Arctic Circle around **Jokkmokk** (p304), which is a Sami cultural centre and home to the excellent **Ájtte museum** (p304). If the weather's in your favour, branch off to **Kvikkjokk** (p305), next-door neighbour to the rugged **Sarek National Park** (p305). Then push on towards **Gällivare** (p303) and up to **Kiruna** (p298). Sweden's northernmost city is worth some exploring on its own, but it also has a charming neighbour in **Jukkasjärvi** (p301), home to the famous Ice Hotel. From here, you could dash over to **Abisko** (p301) for some hiking, or go straight north to the remote village of **Karesuando** (p297), on the Finnish border. Creep along the Sweden–Finland border toward **Pajala** (p292), keeping an eye out for stray Rudolphs – for entertainment, keep a log of the number of reindeer you have to follow at casual trotting speed along major highways. Stop in **Haparanda** (p291) for a picnic or drink with a view over the Gulf of Bothnia, then follow the curve of the coastline back to Luleå.

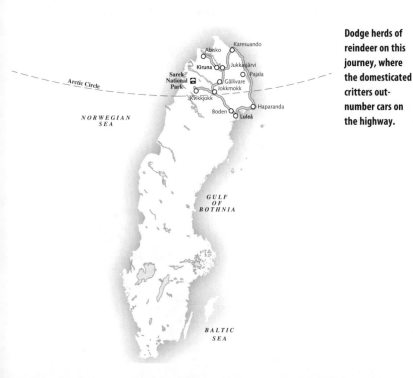

Dodge herds of reindeer on this journey, where the domesticated critters outnumber cars on the highway.

VICIOUS CYCLING

One to Two Weeks/Start and End in Visby

This journey starts directly behind the ferry station in Visby, where you can rent a bicycle and camping equipment at any number of outlets. Once you've got your equipment sorted, head north along the waterfront to catch the Gotlandsleden, the bicycle trail that circumnavigates the island. Follow it to the grotto at **Lummelunda** (p158), then continue northward past Stenkyrka and around to the inlet at Kappelshamn. From here it's an easy morning's ride to Fårösund, where you can stock up on picnic items and catch the free ferry to the islet of **Fårö** (p158). There's a tourist information centre in Fårö town, near another grocery store and café. Take your time circling the islet, stopping at the gravesite of British troops who fought in the Crimean war at **Ryssnäs** (p159) and at any of the beaches or harbours that strike your fancy. Your goal is to reach **Langhammarshammaren** (p158) in time to watch the sunset over the eerie rock formations. Head back to Fårösund, and follow the Gotlandsleden signs southward, stopping first at the **Bungemuseet** (p158). At Slite you can choose to stick to the coastline or head inland through the Kallgateburgs nature reserve; the coastal route is lined with nice beaches, while the inland option passes through some lovely, pastoral countryside. The less ambitious can easily loop back to Visby at this point. The paths converge further south to follow along the coast – don't miss the detour to the Bronze Age cairns at **Uggarderojr** (p159) – and go through **Öja** (p159), where there's a fine church. Then loop around to return through **Burgsvik** (p159). Around Sandhamn you'll have fine views of **Lilla Karlsö** and **Stora Karlsö** (p157). Continue along the bike path northward until you're back in **Visby** (p152). Make sure you leave time at the end of your trip to enjoy the beautiful medieval city itself.

Cycling the Gotlandsleden is an ideal way to see the best of this idyllic island, from sandy beaches to medieval churches.

TAILORED TRIPS

WORLD HERITAGE SITES

Culture hounds might enjoy a quest to see the best of Sweden as defined by Unesco. To start with there's the vast **Laponia area** (p304) in the north, an entire journey's worth of territory on its own. Then, working your way down, there's **Gammelstad Church Village** (p289) in Luleå. The High Coast, or **Höga Kusten** (p282), decorates the coastline from Härnosand up to Örnsköldsvik. In Falun there's the **Falu Kopparbergsgruva** (p260), and nearby are the **Engelsberg Bruk** (p250). In the suburbs of Stockholm you'll find the royal palace and grounds of **Drottningholm** (p104), as well as the unlikely beauty of the architect-designed **Skogskyrkogården** cemetery (p83). Also near the capital is the ancient Viking settlement of **Birka** (p107). Moving south, there's **Tanumshede Rock Carvings** (p222) and the well-preserved naval port of **Karlskrona** (p133). Off the coast are the Hanseatic town of **Visby** (p152) on Gotland, the agricultural landscape of **Southern Öland** (p141). There's also the historic **Varberg Radio Station** (p232) in Grimeton.

ACTIVITIES

Outdoorsy types will be spoilt for choice in Sweden. There's excellent hiking and camping in any number of the country's national parks, especially **Abisko** (p301), as well as the more challenging territory of **Sarek** (p305), and the intermediate **Padjelanta** (p303) and **Skuleskogen** (p283). Closer to Stockholm is the very accessible wilderness of **Tyresta** (p110).

Cycling is another popular activity, and Sweden is well set up for it. The best areas are found in **Skåne** (p160) and **Gotland** (p152); see the cycle tour of Gotlandsleden above for one suggestion.

Wintertime brings another batch of activities to the sporting crowd, most notably alpine skiing in resorts such as **Åre** (p295), **Sälen** (p268), **Hemavan** (p307) and **Riksgränsen** (p302). Cross-country skiing is popular along the hiking trail **Kungsleden** (p49) and other long-distance tracks.

Ice skating is a popular activity for kids and adults alike, and is easy to do on the frozen winter surfaces of **Kungsträdgården** (p84) and other public areas in Stockholm.

Golf is huge in Sweden and there are more than 400 courses to choose from. The most popular options are in the south, but the quirkier choices are up north, including **Björkliden** (p302), near Abisko – home to the country's northernmost course, 240km above the Arctic Circle – and the **Green Line course** (p291) at Haparanda, where playing a round means crossing the Sweden–Finland border four times.

Canoeing and kayaking are popular in a number of rivers and the canals that honeycomb **Stockholm** (p83).

Snapshot

Though it's far from being what anyone would call a country in crisis, Sweden seems to have had its confidence shaken in recent years. After a long and steady history as what most would agree was something of a utopian society, the country famous for its 'middle way' has suddenly faced a number of changes, not just economic but also political and social. The changes have come about because of several modern-day realities such as European Union membership, globalisation and increased immigration. In June 2005 the Swedish government banned smoking in all public places. It's no wonder so many people are looking forward to the day when the EU forces Sweden to relax its strict alcohol policies!

The roots of change are fairly easy to trace. Without generalising too much, it's fair to say that Sweden spent decades as an essentially closed system, with a small population who more or less had similar backgrounds and equal financial standing. The famed Swedish welfare state took care of its citizens 'from erection to resurrection', as the saying goes. Since opening its borders in WWII, Sweden has taken in more immigrants than any other country in Western Europe relative to its population. Over half a million immigrants have come to Sweden from the Middle East, Africa and the Balkans alone. The benefits of this are obvious, but so is the economic impact.

FAST FACTS

Population (estimated July 2005): 9 million

GDP (2004): US$255.4 billion

Inflation rate (2004): 0.4%

Unemployment rate (2004): 5.6%

Area: 449,964 sq km

Life expectancy: men 78.19 years, women 82.74 years

Head of state: King Carl XVI Gustaf

Head of government: Prime Minister Göran Persson (up for election September 2006)

One area in which the impact of immigration is easiest to see is the scarcity of housing, currently a hot-button issue in Sweden. The situation is particularly acute in the capital. According to statistics published by the property-owners organisation Fastighetsägarna, the average income of people living in central Stockholm is 25% higher than that of those who live in the suburbs. The corresponding difference in rent, however, is minimal – at the time of research, rents averaged Skr968 per sq metre in the middle of town, against Skr888 over the city as a whole. But even so the immigrant population is overwhelmingly moving to the suburbs rather than the city centre. The problem, housing experts say, is not so much that newcomers to Stockholm cannot afford central-city housing, but that they don't have the connections required to find the scarce properties available. Whatever the reason, the majority of the immigrant population is relegated to block housing in the suburbs. One unforeseen effect of this is that small centres of vibrant multicultural community life have consequently sprung up in places like Rinkeby and Botkyrka and themselves become destinations for central-city dwellers intent on exploring new cultures and artwork. Cultural centres in the suburbs, are, in fact, where visitors can find some of the most interesting cultural events in the city.

Sweden joined the EU in 1995 with a majority vote, but since then public opinion for the EU has cooled, and in September 2003 voters decided not to trade the krona for the euro.

At the time of writing, 85% of workers in Sweden belonged to a trade union. The unemployment rate was 6.5% of the workforce in August 2005, up from 5.9% a year earlier. The welfare state is the largest employer in the country. The majority party – the Social Democrats, led by Prime Minister Göran Persson, now in his ninth year of office – is already preparing for the September 2006 general election. The Social Democrats are the most successful political party in the world, having been in power for most of the past 73 years. The next election promises to be contentious; heavy campaigning, including televised debates, had already started a full year in advance.

The contest is essentially between four conservative parties on the right, who emphasise job creation through tax cuts (campaign slogans include 'It should be profitable to work'), and the majority left – made up of the Social Democrats, the Greens and the Left Party – who advocate defending Sweden's traditionally high levels of unemployment benefits.

There are, of course, still plenty of utopian aspects to Swedish society. A study by the World Economic Forum found it to be the world's most gender-equal country. In the same study, Sweden came out on top for education, health and wellbeing. Another recent poll showed that nearly 90% of adults in the country read at least one newspaper a day. This would indicate that whatever direction their country goes, it will be the Swedish people, involved and empowered, who take it there.

'There are still plenty of utopian aspects to Swedish society'

History

EARLY HISTORY

Sweden's human history began around 10,000 years ago at the end of the last ice age, once the Scandinavian ice sheet had melted. Tribes from central Europe migrated into the south of Sweden, and ancestors of the Sami people hunted reindeer from Siberia into the northern regions.

These nomadic Stone Age hunter-gatherers gradually made more permanent settlements, keeping animals, catching fish and growing crops. A typical relic of this period (3000 BC to 1800 BC) is the *gångrift*, a dolmen or rectangular passage-tomb covered with capstones, then a mound of earth. Pottery, amber beads and valuable flint tools were buried with the dead. The island of Öland, in southeast Sweden, is a good place to see clusters of Stone Age barrows.

As the climate improved between 1800 BC and 500 BC, Bronze Age cultures blossomed. Their *hällristningar* (rock carvings) are found in many parts of Sweden – Dalsland and Bohuslän are particularly rich areas (see p222). The carvings provide tantalising glimpses of forgotten beliefs, with the sun, hunting scenes and ships being favourite themes. Huge Bronze Age burial mounds, such as Kiviksgraven (p182) in Österlen, suggest that powerful chieftains had control over spiritual and temporal matters. Relatively few bronze artefacts are found in Sweden: the metals had to be imported from central Europe in exchange for furs, amber and other northern treasures.

The Roman historian Tacitus (AD 56–120) first mentions the Svea, a 'militant Germanic race' strong in men, ships and war-gear.

After 500 BC, the Iron Age brought about technological advances, demonstrated by archaeological finds of agricultural tools, graves and primitive furnaces. During this period, the runic alphabet arrived, probably from the Germanic region. It was used to carve inscriptions onto monumental rune stones (there are around 3000 in Sweden) well into medieval times.

By the 7th century AD, the Svea people of the Mälaren valley (just west of Stockholm) had gained supremacy, and their kingdom ('Svea Rike', or Sverige) gave the country of Sweden its name. Birka, founded around 760 on Björkö (an island in Mälaren lake), was a powerful Svea centre for around 200 years. Large numbers of Byzantine and Arab coins have been found there, and stones with runic inscriptions are scattered across the area; see p107 for more details.

VIKINGS & THE ARRIVAL OF CHRISTIANITY

Scandinavia's greatest impact on world history probably occurred during the Viking Age (around 800 to 1100), when hardy pagan Norsemen set sail for other shores. In Sweden, it's generally thought that population pressures were to blame for the sudden exodus: a polygamous society led to an excess of male heirs and ever-smaller plots of land. Combined with the prospects of military adventure and foreign trade abroad, the result was the Viking phenomenon (the word is derived from *vik*, meaning 'bay' or 'cove', and is probably a reference to their anchorages during raids).

The Vikings sailed a new type of boat that was fast and highly manoeuvrable but sturdy enough for ocean crossings, with a heavy keel, up to

TIMELINE

c 10,000 BC
Ice sheets melt and hunters follow reindeer into a newly uncovered Sweden

c 1000 BC
The petroglyph 'The Lovers' is carved into the rocks at Vitlycke, Tanum

16 pairs of oars and a large square sail (the Äskekärr Ship, Sweden's only original Viking vessel, is in Göteborg's Stadsmuseum (p204). Initial hit-and-run raids along the European coast – often on monasteries and their terrified monks – were followed by major military expeditions, settlement and trade. The well-travelled Vikings penetrated the Russian heartland and beyond, venturing as far as America, Constantinople (modern-day Istanbul) and Baghdad.

In Sweden, the Vikings generally cremated their dead and their possessions, then buried the remains under a mound. There are also several impressive stone ship settings, made from upright stones arranged in the shape of a ship. If you're interested in Viking culture, Foteviken (p175) on the southwestern Falsterbo Peninsula is a 'living' reconstruction of a Viking village.

The Vikings by Magnus Magnusson is an extremely readable history book, covering their achievements in Scandinavia (including Sweden), as well as their wild-natured doings around the world.

Early in the 9th century, the missionary St Ansgar established a church at Birka. Sweden's first Christian king, Olof Skötkonung (c 968–1020) is said to have been baptised at St Sigfrid's Well in Husaby (p228) in 1008 – the well is now a sort of place of pilgrimage for Swedes – but worship continued in Uppsala's pagan temple until at least 1090. By 1160, King Erik Jedvarsson (Sweden's patron saint, St Erik) had virtually destroyed the last remnants of paganism.

RISE OF THE SWEDISH STATE

Olof Skötkonung was also the first king to rule over both the Sveas and the Gauts, creating the kernel of the Swedish state. During the 12th and 13th centuries, these united peoples mounted a series of crusades to Finland, Christianising the country and steadily absorbing it into Sweden.

Royal power disintegrated over succession squabbles in the 13th century. The medieval statesman Birger Jarl (1210–66) rose to fill the gap, acting as prince regent for 16 years, and founding the city of Stockholm in 1252.

King Magnus Ladulås (1240–90) introduced a form of feudalism in 1280, but managed to avoid its worst excesses. In fact, the aristocracy were held in check by the king, who forbade them from living off the peasantry when moving from estate to estate.

Magnus' eldest son Birger (1280–1321) assumed power in 1302. After long feuds with his younger brothers, he tricked them into coming to Nyköping castle (p244), where he threw them into the dungeon and starved them to death. After this fratricidal act, the nobility drove Birger into exile. They then chose their own king of Sweden, the infant grandson of King Haakon V of Norway. When Haakon died without leaving a male heir, the kingdoms of Norway and Sweden were united (1319).

The increasingly wealthy church began to show its might in the 13th and 14th centuries, commissioning monumental buildings such as the *domkyrka* (cathedral) in Linköping (founded 1250; see p149), and Scandinavia's largest Gothic cathedral in Uppsala (founded 1285; see p238).

However, in 1350 the rise of state and church endured a horrific setback, when the Black Death swept through the country, carrying off around a third of the Swedish population. In the wake of the horror, St Birgitta (1303–73) reinvigorated the church with her visions and revelations, and founded a nunnery and cathedral in Vadstena, which became Sweden's most important pilgrimage site.

1050s
Unknown Viking scratches runic graffiti onto a statue in Athens

1252
Birger Jarl founds the city of Stockholm

HANSEATIC LEAGUE & THE UNION OF KALMAR

A strange phenomenon of the time was the German-run Hanseatic League, a group of well-organised merchants who established walled trading towns in Germany and along the Baltic coast. In Sweden, they built Visby (p152) and maintained a strong presence in the young city of Stockholm. Their rapid growth caused great concern around the Baltic in the 14th century: an allied Scandinavian front was vital. Negotiated by the Danish regent Margrethe, the Union of Kalmar (1397) united Denmark, Norway and Sweden under one crown.

Erik of Pomerania, Margrethe's nephew, held that crown until 1439. High taxation to fund wars against the Hanseatic League made him deeply unpopular and he was eventually deposed. His replacement was short-lived and succession struggles began again: two powerful Swedish families, the unionist Oxenstiernas and the nationalist Stures, fought for supremacy.

Out of the chaos, Sten Sture the Elder (1440–1503) eventually emerged as 'Guardian of Sweden' in 1470, going on to fight and defeat an army of unionist Danes at the Battle of Brunkenberg (1471) in Stockholm.

The failing Union's death-blow came in 1520: Christian II of Denmark invaded Sweden and killed the regent Sten Sture the Younger (1493–1520). After granting a full amnesty to Sture's followers, Christian went back on his word: 82 of them were arrested, tried and massacred in Stockholm's main square, Stortorget in Gamla Stan (p83), which 'ran with rivers of blood'.

'The brutal Stockholm Bloodbath sparked off a major rebellion under the leadership of Gustav Vasa'

The brutal 'Stockholm Bloodbath' sparked off a major rebellion under the leadership of the young nobleman Gustav Ericsson Vasa (1496–1560). It was a revolution that almost never happened: having failed to raise enough support, Gustav was fleeing for the Norwegian border when two exhausted skiers caught him up to tell him that the people had changed their minds. This legendary ski journey is celebrated every year in the Vasaloppet race (p266) between Sälen and Mora.

In 1523, Sweden seceded from the union and installed Gustav as the first Vasa king: he was crowned on 6 June, now the country's national day.

VASA DYNASTY

Gustav I ruled for 37 years, leaving behind a powerful, centralised nation-state. He introduced the Reformation to Sweden (principally as a fundraising exercise): ecclesiastical property became the king's, and the Lutheran Protestant Church was placed under the crown's direct control.

After Gustav Vasa's death in 1560, bitter rivalry broke out among his sons. His eldest child, Erik XIV (1533–77), held the throne for eight years in a state of increasing paranoia. After committing a trio of injudicious murders at Uppsala Slott (p238), Erik was deposed by his half-brother Johan III (1537–92) and poisoned with pea soup at Örbyhus Slott (p243). During the brothers' reigns, the Danes tried and failed to reassert sovereignty over Sweden in the Seven Years War (1563–70).

Gustav's youngest son, Karl IX (1550–1611), finally had a chance at the throne in 1607, but was unsuccessful militarily and ruled for a mere four years. He was succeeded by his 17-year-old son. Despite his youth, Gustav II Adolf (1594–1632) proved to be a military genius, recapturing southern parts of the country from Denmark and consolidating Sweden's

1350s
The Black Death kills a third of the population

1477
Founding of Scandinavia's oldest university, at Uppsala

control over the eastern Baltic (the copper mine at Falun financed many of his campaigns: see p260). A devout Lutheran, Gustav II supported the German Protestants during the Thirty Years War (1618–48). He invaded Catholic Poland and defeated his cousin King Sigismund III, later meeting his own end in battle in 1632.

Gustav II's daughter, Kristina, was still a child in 1632, and her regent continued her father's warlike policies. In 1654, Kristina abdicated in favour of Karl X Gustav, ending the Vasa dynasty.

For an incredible glimpse into this period, track down Sweden's 17th-century royal warship *Vasa* (commissioned by Gustav II in 1625), now in Stockholm's Vasamuseet (p77).

You can see Erik XIV's bedroom at Kalmar Slott (p125) complete with a secret passage to escape from his brother Johan.

PEAK & DECLINE OF THE SWEDISH EMPIRE

The zenith and collapse of the Swedish empire happened remarkably quickly. During the harsh winter of 1657, Swedish troops invaded Denmark across the frozen Kattegatt, a strait between Sweden and Denmark, and the last remaining parts of southern Sweden still in Danish hands were handed over at the Peace of Roskilde. Bohuslän, Härjedalen and Jämtland were seized from Norway, and the empire reached its maximum size when Sweden established a short-lived American colony in what is now Delaware.

The end of the 17th century saw a developing period of enlightenment in Sweden; Olof Rudbeck achieved widespread fame for his medical work, which included the discovery of the lymphatic system.

Inheritor of this huge and increasingly sophisticated country was King Karl XII (1681–1718). Karl XII was an overenthusiastic military adventurer who spent almost all of his reign at war: he managed to lose Latvia, Estonia and Poland, and the Swedish coast sustained damaging attacks

QUEEN KRISTINA

Queen Kristina (1626–89) lived an eccentric and eventful life. Her father, Gustav II, instructed that the girl be brought up as though she were a prince, then promptly went off and died in battle, leaving his six-year-old successor and his country in the hands of the powerful Chancellor Oxenstierna.

Kristina did indeed receive a boy's education, becoming fluent in six languages and skilled in the arts of war. Childish spats with Oxenstierna increased as she grew older; after being crowned queen in 1644, she delighted in testing her power, defying him even when he had the country's best interests at heart.

Envious of the elegant European courts, Kristina attempted to modernise old-fashioned Sweden. One of her plans was to gather leading intellectuals for philosophical conversation. She's often blamed for the death of Descartes, who reluctantly obeyed her summons only to die of pneumonia in the icy north.

Kristina's ever-erratic behaviour culminated in her abdication in 1654. After handing over the crown to her beloved cousin Karl X Gustav, she threw on men's clothing and scarpered southwards on horseback. Kristina finished up in Rome, where she converted to Catholicism.

Contrary, curious and spoilt, accused of murder and an affair with one of the Pope's cardinals, bisexual, rule-bending Kristina was a fascinating and frustrating character, too huge and colourful to do justice to here. If you want to know more, an excellent biography is *Christina, Queen of Sweden* by Veronica Buckley.

1523
Gustav I becomes the first Vasa king

1628
The royal warship *Vasa* sinks on her maiden voyage

from Russia. Karl XII also fought the Great Nordic War against Norway throughout the early 18th century. A winter siege of Trondheim took its toll on his battle-weary army, and Karl XII was mysteriously shot dead while inspecting his troops – a single event that sealed the fate of Sweden's military might.

King Gustav III wrote his own plays and frequently arrived at formal dinners in fancy dress, to the horror of his more conservative courtiers.

LIBERALISATION OF SWEDEN

During the next 50 years, parliament's power increased and the monarchs became little more than heads of state. Despite the country's decline, intellectual enlightenment streaked ahead and Sweden produced some celebrated writers, philosophers and scientists, including Anders Celsius, whose temperature scale bears his name; Carl Scheele, the discoverer of chlorine; and Carl von Linné (Linnaeus), the great botanist who developed theories about plant reproduction (see p240).

Gustav III (1746–92) curtailed parliamentary powers and reintroduced absolute rule in 1789. He was a popular and cultivated king who inaugurated the Royal Opera House in Stockholm (1782), and opened the Swedish Academy of Literature (1786), now known for awarding the annual Nobel Prize for literature. His foreign policy was less auspicious and he was considered exceptionally lucky to lead Sweden intact through a two-year war with Russia (1788–90). Enemies in the aristocracy conspired against the king, hiring an assassin to shoot him at a masked ball in 1792.

Gustav IV Adolf (1778–1837), Gustav III's son, assumed the throne and got drawn into the Napoleonic Wars, permanently losing Finland (one-third of Sweden's territory) to Russia. Gustav IV was forced to abdicate, and his uncle Karl XIII took the Swedish throne under a new constitution that ended unrestricted royal power.

On his death, it was discovered that Frenchman Jean-Baptiste Bernadotte (king of Sweden for 26 years) had a tattoo that read 'Death to kings!'

Out of the blue, Napoleon's marshal Jean-Baptiste Bernadotte (1763–1844) was invited by a nobleman, Baron Mörner, to succeed the childless Karl XIII to the Swedish throne. The rest of the nobility adjusted to the idea and Bernadotte took up the offer, along with the name Karl Johan. Karl Johan judiciously changed sides in the war, and led Sweden, allied with Britain, Prussia and Russia, against France and Denmark.

After Napoleon's defeat, Sweden forced Denmark to swap Norway for Swedish Pomerania (1814). The Norwegians objected, defiantly choosing king and constitution, and Swedish troops occupied most of the country. This forced union with Norway was Sweden's last military action.

INDUSTRIALISATION

Industry arrived late in Sweden (during the second half of the 19th century), but when it did come, it transformed the country from one of Western Europe's poorest to one of its richest.

The Göta Canal (p146) opened in 1832, providing a valuable transport link between the east and west coasts, and development accelerated when the main railway across Sweden was completed in 1862. Significant Swedish inventions, including dynamite (Alfred Nobel) and the safety match (patented by Johan Edvard Lundstrom; see p116), were carefully exploited by government and industrialists; coupled with efficient steel-making and timber exports, they added to a growing economy and the rise of the new middle class.

1700
Peak of the Swedish empire

1766
Swedish parliament passes the world's first Freedom of the Press Act

However, when small-scale peasant farms were replaced with larger concerns, there was widespread discontent in the countryside, exacerbated by famine. Some agricultural workers joined the population drift from rural areas to towns. Others abandoned Sweden altogether: around one million people (an astonishing quarter of the population!) emigrated over just a few decades, mainly to America.

Although not history textbooks, Vilhelm Moberg's four novels about 19th-century Swedish emigration are based on real people, and bring this period to life. They're translated into English as *The Emigrants*, *Unto A Good Land*, *The Settlers* and *The Last Letter Home*.

The transformation to an industrial society brought with it trade unions and the Social Democratic Labour Party (Social Democrats for short), founded in 1889 to support workers. The party grew quickly and obtained parliamentary representation in 1896 when Hjalmar Branting was elected.

In 1905, King Oscar II (1829–1907) was forced to recognise Norwegian independence and the two countries went their separate ways.

WORLD WARS & THE WELFARE STATE

Sweden declared itself neutral in 1912, and remained so throughout the bloodshed of WWI.

In the interwar period, a Social Democrat–Liberal coalition government took control (1921). Reforms followed quickly, including an eight-hour working day and suffrage for all adults aged over 23.

Swedish neutrality during WWII was somewhat ambiguous: allowing German troops to march through to occupy Norway certainly tarnished Sweden's image. On the other hand, Sweden was a haven for refugees from Finland, Norway, Denmark and the Baltic states; downed allied aircrew who escaped the Gestapo; and many thousands of Jews who escaped persecution and death.

After the war and throughout the 1950s and '60s the Social Democrats continued with the creation of *folkhemmet*, the welfare state. The standard of living for ordinary Swedes rose rapidly and real poverty was virtually eradicated.

MODERN SWEDEN

After a confident few decades, the late 20th century saw some unpleasant surprises for Sweden, as economic pressures clouded Sweden's social goals and various sacks of dirty laundry fell out of the cupboard.

In 1986, Prime Minister Olof Palme (1927–86) was assassinated as he walked home from the cinema. The murder and bungled police inquiry shook ordinary Swedes' confidence in their country, institutions and leaders. The killing remains unsolved, but it seems most likely that external destabilisation lay behind this appalling act. Afterwards, the fortunes of the Social Democrats took a turn for the worse as various scandals came to light, including illegal arms trading in the Middle East by the Bofors company.

The Olof Palme International Center (www.palmecenter.org) has taken up the former prime minister's baton, working for cross-border cooperation.

By late 1992, during the world recession, the country's budgetary problems culminated in frenzied speculation against the Swedish krona. In November of that year the central bank Sveriges Riksbank was forced to abandon fixed exchange rates and let the krona float freely. The currency immediately devalued by 20%, interest rates shot up by a world-record-breaking 500% and unemployment flew to 14%; the government fought back with tax hikes, punishing cuts to the welfare budget and the scrapping of previously relaxed immigration rules.

1832

The Göta Canal opens, linking Sweden's west and east coasts

1930s

The worldwide Depression sparks off plans for the Swedish welfare state

With both economy and national confidence severely shaken, Swedes narrowly voted in favour of joining the European Union (EU), effective from 1 January 1995. Since then, there have been further major reforms and the economy has improved considerably, with falling unemployment and inflation.

The Southeast Asian tsunami on Boxing Day 2004 killed more people from Sweden than from any other nation outside Asia, with almost 600 Swedes still unaccounted for.

Another shocking political murder, of Foreign Minister Anna Lindh (1957–2003), again rocked Sweden to the core. Far-right involvement was suspected – Lindh was a vocal supporter of the euro, and an outspoken critic of both the war in Iraq and Italy's Silvio Berlusconi – but it appears that her attacker had psychiatric problems. Lindh's death occurred just before the Swedish referendum on whether to adopt the single European currency, but didn't affect the eventual outcome: a 'No' vote.

1986

Prime Minister Olof Palme is assasinated as walks home from the cinema

2000

The Öresund Bridge links Sweden and Denmark

The Culture

THE NATIONAL PSYCHE

There's a prevailing view of Swedes as cold and reserved, or at least shy – until the *snaps* comes out, at any rate. Like any stereotype it has some basis in truth, but the national character is, of course, a good deal more complex than popular myth suggests.

Two key concepts that anyone spending a substantial amount of time in Sweden will come to understand are *lagom* and *ordning och reda*. Both are vital components in the mindset of the typical Swedish character. *Lagom* means just right – not too little, not too much. A good example is *mellanöl* (medium ale) – it's not strong, but not as weak as a light ale. An exception to *lagom* is the smorgåsbord.

Ordning och reda connotes tidiness and order, everything in its proper place in the world. A good example is the queuing system; every transaction in all of Sweden requires its participants to take a number and stand in line, which everyone does with the utmost patience. An exception to *ordning och reda* is Stockholm traffic.

Get a two-for-one blast of Swedish culture with Alf Sjöberg's 1951 film version of August Strindberg's play *Miss Julie*, which won the Grand Prix at the Venice Film Festival that year.

LIFESTYLE

Swedes are a friendly sort, though sometimes in a way that strikes outsiders as stiff or overly formal. The handshake is used liberally in both business and social circles when greeting friends or meeting strangers. Introductions generally include full names. *Var så god* is a common phrase and carries all sorts of expressions of goodwill, including 'Welcome', 'Please', 'Pleased to meet you', 'I'm happy to serve you', 'Thanks' and 'You're welcome'. Swedes are generous with their use of 'thank you' *(tack)* to the point that language textbooks make jokes about it.

Most Swedes go on holiday for several weeks in the summer, often in rural or wilderness areas of their own countryside. The *sommarstuga* (summer cottage) is almost *de rigueur* – there are 600,000 second homes in the country.

TRACING YOUR ANCESTORS *Fran Parnell*

Around a million people emigrated from Sweden to the USA and Canada between 1850 and 1930. Many of their 12 million descendants are now returning to find their roots.

Luckily, detailed parish records of births, deaths and marriages have been kept since 1686 and there are *landsarkivet* (regional archives) around the country. The national archive is **Riksarkivet** (☎ 08-737 63 50; www.ra.se; Box 12541, Fyrverkarbacken 13-17, SE-102 29 Stockholm).

SVAR Forskarcentrum (☎ 0623-725 00; www.svar.ra.se; Kägelbacken 6, Box 160, SE-880 40 Ramsele) holds most records from the late 17th century until 1928. You can pay the staff here to research for you (Skr400 per hour) or look for yourself.

Utvandrarnas Hus (Emigrant House), in Växjö, is a very good museum dedicated to the mass departure (see p122). Attached is **Svenska Emigrantinstitutet** (Swedish Emigrant Institute; ☎ 0470-201 20; www.swemi.se; Vilhelm Mobergs gata 4, Box 201, SE-35104 Växjö), with an extensive research centre that you can use (Skr150/200 per half/full day).

Also worth a look is *Tracing Your Swedish Ancestry*, by Nils William Olsson, a free do-it-yourself genealogical guide (40 pages). Get a copy by emailing your name and address to info@swedennewyork.com, or download it from the New York **Consulate-General of Sweden's** website: www.swedeninfo.org/tracing.htm (under Press & Information in the menu).

Sweden has about 105,000km of paved highways – compared to nearly 4 million km in the US.

Traditional folk dress is still seen regularly at midsummer, on Swedish National Day, and for weddings, birthdays and other celebrations. Styles vary depending on the region. The national version was designed in the 20th century: women wear a white hat, yellow skirt and blue sleeveless vest with white flowers on top of a white blouse; men wear a simpler costume of knee-length trousers (breeches), white shirt, vest and wide-brimmed hat.

POPULATION

Sweden's population is relatively small given the size of the country – it has one of the lowest population densities in Europe. Most people are concentrated in the large cities of Stockholm, Göteborg, Malmö and Uppsala.

Most of Sweden's population is considered to be of Nordic stock, thought to have descended from central and northern European tribes who migrated north after the end of the last Ice Age, around 10,000 years ago.

About 30,000 Finnish speakers form a substantial minority in the northeast, near Torneälven (the Torne River). More than 160,000 citizens of other Nordic countries live in Sweden.

Over 20% of Sweden's population are either foreign-born or have at least one non-Swedish parent. Most immigrants have come from other European countries. The largest non-European ethnic group is made up of Middle Eastern citizens, primarily from Iraq, Turkey and Iran. Other countries with a sizeable presence include Poland, Chile and Somalia. There are also an estimated 25,000 Roma.

Sami

Sweden's approximately 17,000 indigenous Sami people (sometimes known by the inappropriate term Lapps) are a significant ethnic minority. These hardy nomadic people have for centuries occupied northern Scandinavia and northwestern Russia, living mainly from their large herds of domestic reindeer. The total population of around 60,000 Sami still forms an ethnic minority in four countries – Norway, Sweden, Finland and Russia. In Sweden, they're mainly found in the mountain areas along the Norwegian border, northwards of mid-Dalarna. The Sami people refer to their country as Sápmi.

As in many countries with an indigenous minority, the history of relations between the Sami and Nordic peoples is often a dark one. Since at least the 1600s, the Sami religious practice of shamanism was denigrated, and *noaidi* (Sami spiritual leaders) were persecuted. Use of the Sami language was discouraged, and Sami children were coerced into school to learn Swedish.

Sami religious traditions are characterised by a relationship to nature. At sites of special power, such as prominent rock formations, people made offerings to their gods and ancestors to ensure success in hunting or other endeavours. Another crucial element in the religious tradition is the singing of the *yoik* (also spelt *joik*), or 'song of the plains'. A *yoik* or *joik* is a traditional song of the Sami folk; an emotion-laden storytelling song. They were briefly banned as part of the suppression of the Sami religion, but are now enjoying a resurgence in popularity.

In the 18th and 19th centuries, the Lutheran Church of Sweden set up schools to educate Sami children in their own language, but from 1913 to 1930 the emphasis changed to providing a basic education in Swedish. Nowadays, Sami education is available in government-run Sami schools or regular compulsory nine-year municipal schools, providing identical schooling to that received by Swedish children but taking into account the Sami linguistic and cultural heritage.

SAMI CULTURAL AREA & DIALECTS

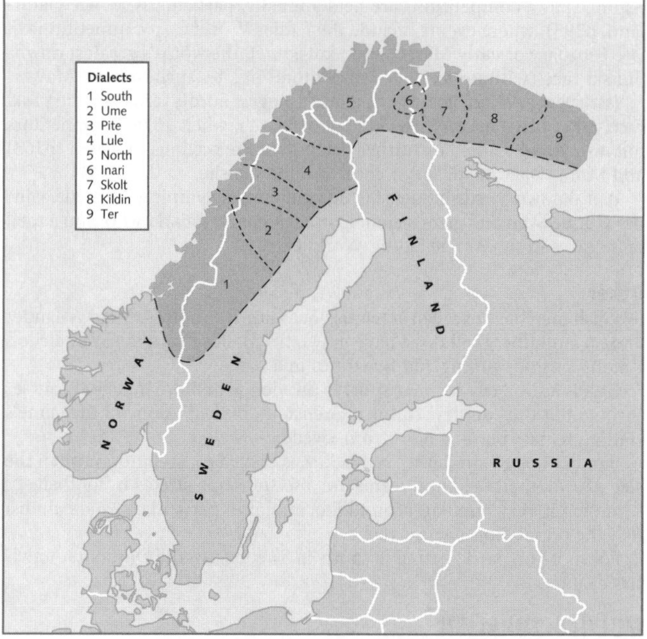

Generally speaking, the Sami in Sweden do not enjoy the same rights as Sami people in Norway and Finland; this is partly because hydroelectric developments and mining activities, that are of great importance to the Swedish economy, have been established on traditional Sami land.

The English-language booklet *The Saami – People of the Sun & Wind*, published by Ájtte, the Swedish Mountain and Saami Museum in Jokkmokk, does a good job of describing Sami traditions in all four countries of the Sápmi region and is available at tourist shops around the area.

Read the news from the underground (mostly in Swedish) at www.sweden.indymedia.org.

SPORT

Football

Football is the most popular sporting activity in Sweden and there are 3320 clubs with over one million members. The domestic season runs from April to early November. The national arena, Råsunda Stadium in Solna, a suburb in Stockholm's northwest, has the capacity to hold 37,000 spectators.

Swedish footballcoach, Sven Göran Eriksson, has achieved fame and notoriety as the head coach of England's national team and for rumours of several scandalous affairs. Perhaps the best-known Swedish football player was Gunnar Nordahl (1921–95), who helped Sweden win gold at the 1948 Olympics, and went on to be the all-time top scorer at AC Milan.

Ice Hockey

There are amateur ice-hockey teams in most Swedish communities. The national premier league, Elitserien, has 12 professional teams; there are also several lower divisions. Matches take place from autumn to late spring, up to four times a week in Stockholm, primarily at Globen arena (see p100).

Skiing

Alpine skiing competitions are held annually, particularly in Åre (Jämtland, p295), where events include the Ladies World Cup competitions in late February or early March, and Skutskjutet, the world's greatest downhill ski race (with up to 3000 competitors) in late April or early May.

Vasaloppet (www.vasaloppet.se), the world's biggest nordic (cross-country) ski race, takes place on the first Sunday in March, when 15,000 competitors follow a 90km route. For further details, see the sections on Sälen (p268) and Mora (Dalarna; p266) or check out the website.

Well-known Swedish skiers include four-time Olympic gold-medal winner Gunde Svan and giant slalom icon Ingemar Stenmark, who won a total of 86 races in the Alpine Skiing World Cup.

Other

Swedish men have excelled at tennis, including Björn Borg, Mats Wilander and Stefan Edberg (all three have now retired). Borg won the Wimbledon Championships in England five times in a row.

Golf is a similarly popular sport in Sweden with more than 400 courses throughout the country. Annika Sörenstam, ranked as one of the game's leading female players, hails from Sweden.

Bandy, though similar to ice hockey, is played on an outdoor pitch the size of a football field and teams are also the same size as in football.

Sailing is very popular, around Stockholm in particular, where almost half the population owns a yacht.

For more on participating in sports in Sweden, see the Outdoors Activities chapter.

MULTICULTURALISM

During WWII, Sweden, which had essentially been a closed society, opened its borders to immigration. For a time, immigrants were expected to assimilate into Swedish society and essentially 'become Swedish', but in 1975 Parliament adopted a new set of policies that emphasised the freedom to preserve and celebrate traditional native cultures. These days some 200 languages are spoken in Sweden, as well as variations on the standard – the hip-hop crowd around Stockholm, for example, speak a vivid mishmash of slang, Swedish and foreign phrases that's been dubbed 'Rinkeby Swedish' after the immigrant-heavy suburb of Rinkeby.

Listen to Swedish radio via the Internet at www.sr.se.

Asians are predicted to constitute one quarter of all foreign-born residents in Sweden in the near future. Many are Muslim, and some disturbing anti-Islamic sentiment has begun to crop up. In 2004, arsonists set fire to the mosque in Malmö, where one quarter of the population is Muslim. As hip-hop artist Timbuktu (himself the Swedish-born son of a mixed-race American couple) told the *Washington Post*, 'Sweden still has a very clear picture of what a Swede is. That no longer exists – the blond, blue-eyed physical traits. That's changing. But it still exists in the minds of some people'.

MEDIA

Domestic newspapers are published only in Swedish, but a wide variety of English-language imports are available at major transport terminals and newsstands – often even in small towns.

Nearly 90% of Swedish adults read at least one daily newspaper and most people subscribe for home delivery. *Dagens Nyheter* is a politically independent paper with a liberal bent, while *Svenska Dagbladet* is the more conservative daily; both are distributed across the country though based in Stockholm. The evening papers (*Aftonbladet* and *Expressen*, the Social

Democrat and liberal papers respectively) also have national coverage. The Swedish government subsidises the second most popular newspaper in a given market, but never more than 3% of the paper's revenue.

RELIGION

Christianity arrived fairly late in Sweden, and was preceded by a long-standing loyalty to Norse gods such as Odin, Thor and their warlike ilk. Some of the outer reaches of Sweden, particularly in the far north, were among the last areas to convert to Christianity in Europe.

According to the country's constitution, Swedish people have the right to practise any religion they choose. Complete separation of church and state took place in 2000; prior to that, Evangelical Lutheranism was the official religion. Since 1994 citizens do not legally acquire a religion at birth but voluntarily become members of a faith. Only about 10% of Swedes regularly attend church services, but church marriages, funerals and communions are still popular.

Astrid Lindgren's Pippi Longstocking might be the best-known book by a Swedish writer; its red-pigtailed heroine is a model of resourcefulness and self-determination. And she can lift up her own horse.

ARTS

Literature

The best known members of Sweden's artistic community have been writers, chiefly the influential dramatist and author August Strindberg (1849–1912), who wrote *Miss Julie* and *The Red Room* among other things, and children's writer Astrid Lindgren (1907–2002). Lindgren's book *Pippi Longstocking* was first published in English in 1950.

During WWII, some Swedish writers took a stand against the Nazis, including Eyvind Johnson (1900–76) with his *Krilon* trilogy, completed in 1943, and the famous poet and novelist Karin Boye (1900–41), whose novel *Kallocain* was published in 1940.

Vilhelm Moberg (1898–1973), a representative of 20th-century proletarian literature and controversial social critic, won international acclaim with *Utvandrarna* (The Emigrants; 1949) and *Nybyggarna* (The Settlers; 1956).

The powerful imagination of Göran Tunström (1937–) is reflected in *Juloratoriet* (The Christmas Oratorio; 1983), which was made into a film, and *Skimmer* (Shimmering; 1996), set in Iceland during Viking times. Other recent authors of note include Torgny Lindgren (1938–), whose magic-realist short stories and novels, such as *Pölsan* (Hash; 2004), are set in his native Norrland, and the popular Henning Mankell (1948–), whose novels feature the moody detective Kurt Wallander.

The poet Carl Michael Bellman is perhaps the dearest to the Swedish soul. Born in Stockholm in 1740, Bellman completed one of his best-known writings, *Fredmans Epistlar* (Fredman's Epistles) at age 30. Greek themes,

Henning Mankell, who created the gloomy detective Kurt Wallander, practically gets his own section in any Swedish bookshop; *Faceless Killers* and *The Dogs of Riga* are among his most influential works.

SELMA LAGERLÖF'S SAGA

Selma Lagerlöf (1858–1940) was an early Swedish literary giant. Two of her best-known works are *Gösta Berlings Saga* (1891) and *Nils Holgerssons underbara resa genom Sverige* (The Wonderful Adventures of Nils; 1906–7). The latter, which is still frequently taught as a geography text in schools, has great character portrayals as well as providing an illuminating portrait of Sweden as a whole.

Lagerlöf was a vocal opponent to the Swedish intellectual and cultural establishment. Despite this, she received the Nobel Prize for Literature in 1909 – the first woman to do so. During WWII she helped several German artists and intellectuals escape the Nazi regime. She donated her Nobel Prize (made of gold) to raise money for Finland's efforts to defend itself against the Soviets. Working for freedom and human rights until the end, Lagerlöf died of a stroke on 16 March 1940.

with references to drunken revelry and Bacchus, the Greek and Roman god of wine, are strong features in this work. Evert Taube (1890–1976), a sailor, author, composer and painter, is known as a latter-day Bellman.

The Swedish Film Institute has loads of information at www.sfi.se, including film reviews, statistics, awards and programmes.

Cinema & TV

Sweden led the way in the silent-film era of the 1920s with such masterpieces as *Körkarlen* (The Phantom Carriage), adapted from a novel by Selma Lagerlöf and directed by Mauritz Stiller. In 1967 came Vilgot Sjöman's notorious *I Am Curious – Yellow*, a political film that got more attention outside Sweden for its X rating. With a few exceptions, one man has largely defined modern Swedish cinema to the world: Ingmar Bergman. With deeply contemplative films like *The Seventh Seal, Through a Glass Darkly* and *Persona*, the beret-clad director explores human alienation, the absence of god, the meaning of life, the certainty of death and other cheerful themes.

More recently, the town of Trollhattan has become a centre of film-making, drawing the likes of wunderkind director Lukas Moodysson, whose *Lilja 4-Ever, Fucking Åmål* and *Tillsammans* have all been both popular and critical hits. Fellow up-and-comer Josef Fares *(Jalla! Jalla!, Kopps)*, who came to Sweden from Lebanon, focuses on themes about the country's growing immigrant communities.

Music

Everyone knows about ABBA, but that's just the tip of the iceberg. Sweden is the third-largest exporter of music in the world, and Swedes buy more recorded music per capita than any other nationality.

Pop bands who actually sing in Swedish are few and far between. Who knew the Caesars ('Jerk It Out') were Swedish? And what about Helena Paparizou, who won the 2005 Eurovision Song Contest for Greece with 'My Number One'? Yep, she's a Swedish citizen.

Other hot names in the pop world are Sahara Hotnights, the Hellacopters, the International Noise Conspiracy and the Shout Out Louds. Late-'90s radio favourites the Cardigans are aiming for a comeback, and recent chart-toppers the Hives are still going strong. Sensitive rockers Dungen are notable for singing lyrics in their native language, although they get just as much attention for lead singer Gustav Ejstes's devastating cheekbones.

Interest in Swedish folk music took off in the 1970s and '80s, thanks mainly to the Falun Folk Music Festival. Traditional Swedish folk music revolves around the triple-beat *polska*, originally a Polish dance. Ethnic folk music includes the Sami *yoik* and a wide range of styles brought to Sweden by immigrants from around the world.

Swedish jazz peaked between the 1920s and '60s. The pianist Jan Johansson (1931–68) succeeded in blending jazz and folk in a peculiarly Swedish fashion. Both Stockholm and Umeå host popular annual jazz festivals.

Although Sweden has never produced a classical composer to match Norway's Edvard Grieg, there has been no shortage of contenders. One of the earliest was Emil Sjögren (1853–1918). He was followed by the Wagnerian Wilhelm Peterson-Berger (1867–1942) and Hugo Alfvén (1872–1960).

Opera flourished after the opening of the Royal Opera House in Stockholm (1782). Opera singer Jenny Lind (1820–87) is known as the 'Swedish nightingale'.

Architecture

Apart from elaborate gravesites, little survives of Bronze Age buildings in Sweden. Several Iron Age relics remain on Öland, including Ismantorp, a fortified village with limestone walls and nine gates.

Excellent examples of Romanesque church architecture dot the country. One of the finest is Domkyrkan (Cathedral) in Lund, consecrated in 1145 and still dominating the city centre with its two imposing square towers.

Gothic styles from the 13th and 14th centuries mainly used brick rather than stone. Some fine examples can be seen at the Mariakyrkan in Sigtuna (completed in 1237) and Uppsala's Domkyrkan, consecrated in 1435.

Gotland is the best place in Sweden to see ecclesiastical Gothic architecture, with around 100 medieval churches on the island.

During and after the Reformation, monasteries and churches were plundered by the crown in favour of wonderful royal palaces and castles like Gustav Vasa's Kalmar Slott and Gripsholm Slott, which has one of the best Renaissance interiors in Sweden.

Magnificently ornate baroque architecture arrived in Sweden (mainly from Italy) during the 1640s while Queen Kristina held the throne. Kalmar Cathedral, designed in 1660, the adjacent Kalmar Rådhus and Drottningholm Slott (1662), just outside Stockholm, were all designed by the court architect Nicodemus Tessin the Elder. Tessin the Younger designed the vast 'new' Royal Palace in Stockholm after the previous palace was gutted by fire in 1697.

The late 19th century and early 20th century saw a rise in romanticism, a particularly Swedish style mainly using wood and brick, which produced such wonders as the Stockholm Rådhus (1916) and Stadshus (City Hall; completed in 1923).

From the 1930s to the '80s, functionalism and the so-called international style took over, with their emphasis on steel, concrete and glass.

'August Strindberg's violently moody seascapes have come to the attention of the art world'

Painting & Sculpture

Carl Larsson, part of an artistic revolution in the 1880s, painted some of the best 19th-century oil paintings in a warm Art Nouveau style. Anders Zorn's portraits of famous Swedes and August Strindberg's violently moody seascapes have also come to the attention of the art world. The nature paintings of Bruno Liljefors are well regarded.

Although there was an initially cautious approach to Cubism, some artists embraced the concepts of surrealist and abstract art, albeit with their own Swedish style, such as the rather bizarre 'dreamland' paintings of Stellan Mörner. Otto Carlsund was the driving force behind early abstract art in Sweden.

More radical art movements in the 1960s and '70s were influenced by diverse sources including far left-wing politics, popular culture, minimalism and pop art.

Carl Milles (1875–1955) is Sweden's greatest sculptor and one of the 20th century's most eminent artists in this field. He once worked as Rodin's assistant and his home in Lidingö, on the outskirts of Stockholm, is a gorgeous museum (p82).

Theatre & Dance

King Gustav III founded the Royal Dramatic Theatre, known as Dramaten, in Stockholm in 1773, and interest in theatre and opera blossomed. Greta Garbo attended the Royal Dramatic Theatre drama school in 1922, and Ingmar Bergman made his directorial debut here in 1951.

In 1773, King Gustav III also founded the Royal Swedish Ballet in Stockholm, the world's fourth-oldest ballet company. Stockholm is home to the House of Dance, the Dance Museum, Kulturhuset and the Dance Centre. Modern dance can also be seen at the Göteborg Opera and the Dance Station in Malmö, with smaller-scale productions performed across Sweden.

Environment

THE LAND

Geography

Sweden occupies the eastern side of the Scandinavian peninsula, and shares borders with Norway, Finland and Denmark (the latter a mere 4km to the southwest of Sweden and joined to it by a spectacular bridge and tunnel).

The surface area of Sweden's (449,964 sq km) is stretched long and thin. Around one-sixth of the country lies within the Arctic Circle, yet Sweden is surprisingly warm thanks to the Gulf Stream: minimum northern temperatures are around –20°C (compared to –45°C in Alaska).

Sweden is a long-drawn-out 1574km from north to south, but averages only about 300km in width.

The country has a 7000km-long coastline, with myriad islands – the Stockholm archipelago alone has an extraordinary 24,000. The largest and most notable islands are Gotland and Öland on the southeast coast, and the best sandy beaches are down the west coast, south of Göteborg.

Forests take up an incredible 57% of Sweden's landscape. The Swedes aren't short of inland lakes either: there are around 100,000 of them in all. Vänern is the largest lake in Western Europe at 5585 sq km. Kebnekaise (2111m), part of the glaciated Kjölen Mountains along the Norwegian border, is Sweden's highest mountain.

Population

Most Swedes live in the flat south of the country, which has an average population density of 35 people per square kilometre. The capital,

LANDSKAP BOUNDARIES

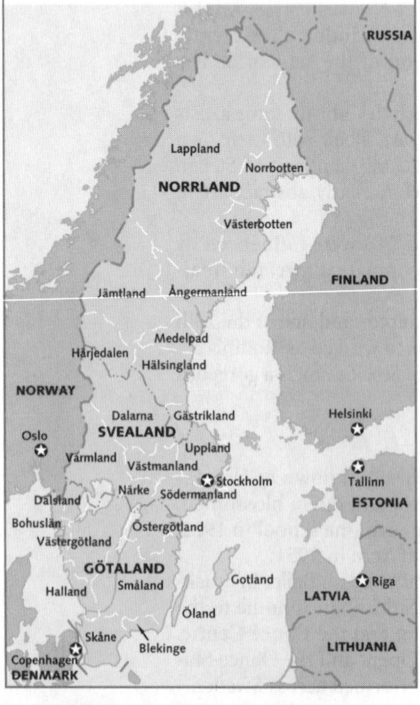

LÄN BOUNDARIES

Stockholm, has 266 people per square kilometre, but in the empty north there are only around nine people per square kilometre.

The 25 historical regions, or *landskap*, are denominators for people's identity and a basis for regional tourist promotion, and are used throughout this book. The 21 counties *(län)* in Sweden form the basis of local government, and these county administrations are responsible for things like regional public transport *(länstrafik)* and regional museums *(länsmuseum)*.

Geology

Between 500 to 370 million years ago, the European and North American continental plates collided, throwing up an impressive range of peaks called the Caledonian Mountains, which were as tall as today's Himalaya. Their worn-down stubs form the 800km-long Kjölen Mountains along the border with Norway.

Parts of Skåne and the islands of Öland and Gotland consist of flat limestone and sandstone deposits, probably laid down in a shallow sea east of the Caledonian Mountains during the same period.

Lake Siljan, in the central south, marks the site of Europe's largest meteoric impact: the 3km-wide fireball hurtled into Sweden 360 million years ago, obliterating all life and creating a 75km ring-shaped crater.

WILDLIFE

Thanks to Sweden's geographical diversity, it has a great variety of European animals, birds and plants.

The fearsome-looking brown bear's favourite food is...blueberries!

Animals

LARGE PREDATORS

Sweden's big carnivores – the bear, wolf, wolverine, lynx and golden eagle – are all endangered species. Illegal hunting carries a maximum prison sentence of four years. Most conflict between human and beast occurs in the Sami reindeer areas: compensation is paid to the Sami whenever predator populations in their lands increase.

Wolves and wolverines are top of Sweden's most endangered list. However, wolf numbers are slowly increasing, and there are now between 70 and 80 of these beautiful creatures in Sweden, mainly in Värmland and Dalarna.

The more solitary wolverine, a larger cousin of the weasel, inhabits high forests and alpine areas along the Norwegian border. Most are in Norrbotten and Västerbotten.

Brown bears were persecuted for centuries, but recent conservation measures have seen numbers increase to around 2000. Bears mostly live in forests in the northern half of the country, but are spreading southwards.

Another fascinating forest dweller is the solitary lynx – the Swedes' favourite endangered species – which belongs to the panther family and is Europe's only large cat. Sweden's 1000 lynx are notoriously difficult to spot because of their nocturnal habits.

Swedish elk are slightly smaller than their closely-related American relatives.

If you have no luck with wildlife in the wild, Grönklitt Bear Park (see p268) has an endangered-animal breeding programme with large and natural-looking enclosures.

OTHER MAMMALS

More than any other animal, the elk (or moose) is the symbol of Sweden. The elk family is the world's largest deer, a gentle knobbly-kneed creature that grows up to 2m tall. Elk are a serious traffic hazard, particularly at night: they can dart out in front of your car at up to 50km/h. For elk-spotting and sausages, visit Sweden's biggest elk park Grönåsens Älgpark (p129).

Around 260,000 domesticated reindeer roam the northern areas, under the watchful eyes of Sami herders.

Hikers encountering lemmings in the mountains may be surprised when these frantic little creatures become enraged and launch incredibly bold attacks. The brown mouselike lemmings (white in winter) are famous for their extraordinary reproductive capacity. Every 10 years or so, the population explodes, resulting in denuded landscapes and thousands of dead lemmings in rivers, lakes, and on roads.

The lemming is the smallest but most important mammal in the Arctic regions – its numbers set the population limits for everything that preys on it.

Musk ox were reintroduced into Norway in the late 1940s and herds have wandered into Sweden, notably in Härjedalen county. Angry adults have a habit of charging anything that annoys them.

Forests, lakes and rivers support beavers, otters, mink, badgers and pine martens. Weasels and stoats are endemic in all counties; northern varieties turn white in the winter and are trapped for their fur (ermine).

Grey and common seals swim in Swedish waters, although overfishing has caused a serious decline in numbers. In 1988 and 2002, thousands of seals were wiped out by the Phocine distemper virus (PDV) after pollution weakened their immune systems. Common dolphins may also be observed from time to time.

BIRDS

Sweden attracts hundreds of nesting species and permanent residents. Some of the best bird-watching sites are the Falsterbo peninsula (p175), Getterön Nature Reserve (p232); Öland, including the nature reserve at its southernmost tip (p141); Tåkern (p152); Hornborgasjön, between Skara and Falköping in Västergötland; and the national parks Färnebofjärden, Muddus and Abisko.

The golden eagle is one of Sweden's most endangered species. It's found in the mountains, and is easily identified by its immense wing span. Another dramatic bird of prey is the white-tailed sea eagle.

Coastal species include common, little and Arctic terns, various gulls, oystercatchers, cormorants, guillemots and razorbills. Territorial arctic skuas can be seen in a few places, notably the Stockholm archipelago and the coast north of Göteborg.

Look out for lovely little goldcrests in coniferous forests. A few spectacular waxwings breed in Lappland, but in winter they arrive from Russia in large numbers and are found throughout Sweden. Grouse or capercaillie strut the forest floor, while ptarmigan and snow buntings are seen above the tree line along the Norwegian border.

For more about bird-watching, read *Where to Watch Birds in Scandinavia* by Johann Stenlund.

Sweden has a wide range of wading and water birds, including the unusual and beautiful red-necked phalaropes, which only breed in the northern mountains. Other waders you're likely to encounter are majestic grey herons (south Sweden), noisy bitterns (south-central Sweden), plovers (including dotterel, in the mountains) and turnstones.

See p55 for information about local ornithological groups.

FISH & CRUSTACEANS

Many marine species have been badly affected by ecological problems in the Baltic (see p47).

Sprats and herring are economically important food sources. Among other marine species, haddock, sea trout, whiting, flounder and plaice are reasonably abundant, particularly in the salty waters of the Kattegatt and Skagerrak, but the cod is heading for extinction due to overfishing.

Indigenous crayfish were once netted or trapped in Sweden's lakes, but overfishing and disease has driven them to extinction.

You can swim, and fish for trout and salmon, in the waters by Stockholm's city centre.

Plants

Swedish flora is typical of that in temperate climates, and includes around 250 species of flowering plants.

In the mountains along the border with Norway, alpine and arctic flowers predominate, including mountain avens, with large white eight-petalled flowers; long-stalked mountain sorrel, an unusual source of vitamin C; glacier crowfoot; alpine aster; and various saxifrages (livelong, mossy, purple, pyramidal and starry).

The limey soils of Öland and Gotland produce rare flowering plants including orchids, all of them protected.

Southern Sweden originally had well-mixed woodland, but much of this has been replaced by farmland or conifer plantations. Northern forests are dominated by Scots pine, Norway spruce and various firs.

Hikers will find a profusion of edible berries, mostly ripe between mid-July and early September. The most popular are blueberries (huckleberries), which grow on open uplands; blue swamp-loving bilberries; red cranberries; muskeg crowberries; and amber-coloured cloudberries. The latter, known as *hjortron,* grow one per stalk on open swampy ground and are a delicacy.

NATIONAL PARKS

Sweden was the first country in Europe to set up a national park (1909). There are now 28 (see below), along with around 2600 smaller nature reserves; together they cover about 9% of Sweden. They're set up by Naturvårdsverket (see p47), which also produces pamphlets about the parks in Swedish and English, and an excellent book *Nationalparkerna i Sverige* (National Parks in Sweden).

Four of Sweden's large rivers (Kalixälven, Piteälven, Vindelälven and Torneälven) have been declared National Heritage Rivers in order to protect them from hydroelectric development.

The right of public access to the countryside *(allemansrätten)* includes national parks and nature reserves; see p54 for more details.

Sweden's National Parks

NORTHERN

Abisko Numerous hiking routes and good accessibility. Northern gateway to the famed Kungsleden hiking track (p49).

Haparanda Skärgård A group of several islands in the far north of the Gulf of Bothnia, with sandy beaches, striking dunes and migrant bird life. Reached by boat from Haparanda.

Muddus Ancient forests and muskeg bogs, plus several deep and impressive gorges, and superb bird-watching opportunities.

Padjelanta High moorland surrounds the lakes Vastenjaure and Virihaure, favoured by a range of Swedish wildlife. The renowned hiking trail, Padjelantaleden, is here (p52).

Pieljekaise Just south of the Arctic Circle, with moorlands, birch forests, flowering meadows and lakes rich in arctic char.

Sarek Sweden's best-loved national park, with wild mountain ranges, glaciers, deep valleys, impressive rivers and vast tracts of birch and willow forest. There's no road access, but experienced hikers can reach the park from the Kungsleden route.

Stora Sjöfallet This park, dominated by lake Akkajaure, has been spoiled by hydroelectric development.

Vadvetjåkka Sweden's northernmost national park. Protects a large river delta containing bogs, lakes, limestone caves and numerous bird species. Access on foot from Abisko.

Four of the national parks in Lappland – Muddus, Padjelanta, Sarek and Stora Sjöfallet – are Unesco World Heritage sites.

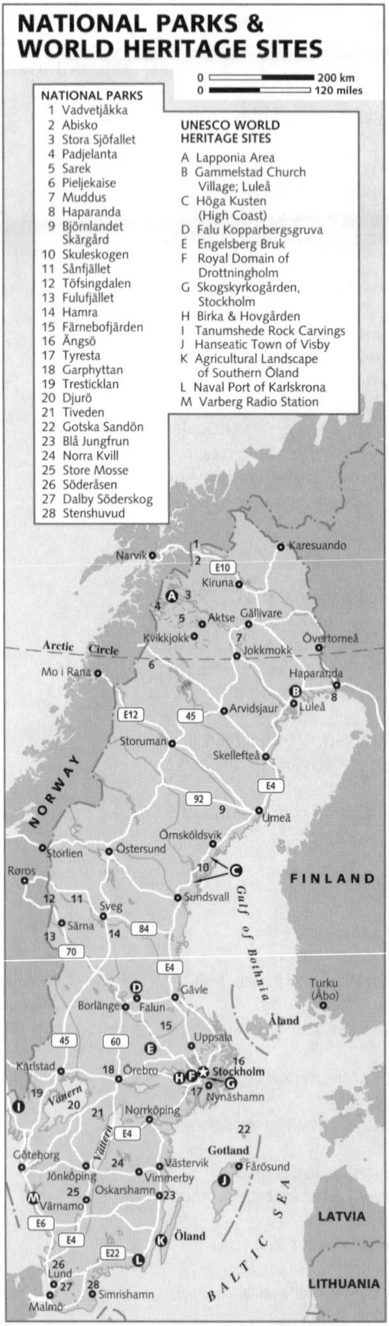

CENTRAL

Björnlandet In the far south of Lappland and well off the beaten track. Natural forest, cliffs and boulder fields.

Färnebofjärden Noted for its abundant bird life, forests, rare lichens and mosses. Good road access to the eastern side.

Fulufjället Sweden's newest national park (2002) contains Njupeskär, the country's highest waterfall at 93m.

Garphyttan A tiny 111-hectare park easily reached from Örebro. Previously cultivated areas have fantastic springtime flower displays.

Hamra Measuring only 800m by 400m, this is a protected area of virgin coniferous forest. Access from a minor road off national road No 45.

Skuleskogen A hilly coastal area with untouched forest, deep valleys, Bronze Age graves, good hiking trails and great sea views. Access from the nearby E4 motorway.

Sånfjället Natural mountain moorland with extensive views. Road and foot access possible from several sides.

Tresticklan An area of natural coniferous forest, with small rift valleys and fine bird life. Access by road from Dals-Ed, in Dalsland.

Tyresta Stockholm's own national park: an extensive forest area with huge 300-year-old pines and interesting rock formations. Easy access by car or bus.

Töfsingdalen Exceptionally wild and remote, with virtually impenetrable boulder fields and pine forest. Must be approached on foot.

Ängsö A tiny island in the northern Stockholm archipelago noted for wonderful meadows, deciduous forest, bird life and spring flowers. Boat access from Furusund.

SOUTHERN

Blå Jungfrun A wonderful island with smooth granite slabs, caves, a labyrinth and great views. Boat access from Oskarshamn.

Dalby Söderskog A forested haven of peace for people and wildlife. Bus access from Lund.

Djurö Bird life and deer on an archipelago of 30 islands in Lake Vänern. Access by private boat only.

Gotska Sandön A beautiful sandy isle featuring dunes, dying pine forest and varied flora and fauna, including unusual beetles. Boats from Nynäshamn and Fårösund.

Norra Kvill A tiny 114-hectare park noted for its ancient coniferous forest, excellent flora and gigantic boulders.

Söderåsen A new park easily reached by road. Contains deep fissure valleys, lush forests and flowing watercourses. Pleasant hiking trails and cycling paths.

Stenshuvud A small coastal park with a great combination of beaches, forest and moorland. Easily reached by road; buses from Simrishamn.

Store Mosse Dominated by bogs with sand dunes, and noted for its bird life and great views. A road runs through the park.

Tiveden Wild hills, forests and lakes, plus extensive boulder fields, beaches and excellent viewpoints. Minor roads and trails pass through it; access from road No 49.

ENVIRONMENTAL ISSUES

Ecological consciousness among Swedes is high, reflected in concern for native animals, clean water and renewable resources. Sweden has a good record when it comes to environmental policies. Industrial and agricultural waste is highly regulated, sewage disposal advanced, greenhouse gas emissions low, and recycling extremely popular.

The North and particularly the Baltic Seas are suffering severe pollution, eutrophication and vast algae blooms, caused partly by nitrogen runoff from Swedish farms. As a result, herring, sprats and Baltic salmon contain high levels of cancer-causing dioxins; they're still being sold in Sweden at the time of writing (with a health warning attached), but will probably be banned by the end of 2006.

Overfishing of these waters is also a huge cause for concern, with cod and Norwegian lobster on the verge of extinction. Fishing quotas may help numbers return.

Some 47% of Sweden's electricity generation comes from hydroelectric sources, mainly dams on large northern rivers. However, there are associated problems, including the displacement of Sami people; landscape scarring; dried-up rivers and waterfalls 'downstream' of the dams; high-voltage power lines sweeping across remote regions; and the depletion of fish stocks, particularly Baltic salmon which cannot return upriver to their spawning grounds. In 1993 the National Heritage Rivers were created to redress this problem.

'Some 47% of Sweden's electricitry comes from hydroelectric sources'

Nuclear power generation has always been a contentious issue in Sweden. At a referendum held in March 1980, the electorate narrowly voted for the phasing-out of the nuclear programme by 2010. One nuclear reactor has shut, but the remaining 10 are unlikely to close by the deadline, because of high costs and no viable alternatives (nuclear power currently provides about 51% of Sweden's electricity generation).

Environmental Organisations

Naturvårdsverket (Swedish Environmental Protection Agency; ☎ 08-698 10 00; www.environ.se; Blekholmsterrassen 36, SE-10648 Stockholm) Government-run central environmental authority, with an extensive and informative website.

Svenska Ekoturismföreningen (Swedish Society of Ecotourism; ☎ 0647-66 00 25; www.ekoturism.org in Swedish; Box 87, SE-83005 Järpen) Promotes environmentally friendly tourism.

Svenska Naturskyddsföreningen (Swedish Society for Nature Conservation; ☎ 08-702 65 00; www.snf.se/english.cfm; Åsögatan 115, Box 4625, SE-11691 Stockholm) Excellent website on current environmental issues.

Outdoor Activities

Sweden has thousands of square kilometres of forest with hiking and cycling tracks, vast numbers of lakes connected by mighty rivers, and a range of alpine mountains – it's ideal for outdoor activities. Most of the information available on the Internet is in Swedish. If you can't read the language, contact the national organisations (listed under individual activities in this section) for the sport you're interested in. Regional and local tourist offices are helpful and staff at outdoor stores can also point you in the right direction.

For organised activity holidays, see p332, check individual destinations in this book, or pick up the booklet *Active Holidays in Sweden* from tourist offices.

HIKING

Hiking is well loved in Sweden and there are thousands of kilometres of marked trails. European Long Distance Footpaths Numbers One and Six run from Varberg to Grövelsjön (1200km) and from Malmö to Norrtälje (1400km), respectively.

Nordkalottleden runs for 450km from Sulitjelma to Kautokeino (both in Norway), but passes through Sweden for most of its route. Finnskogleden is a 240km-long route along the border between Norway and the Värmland region in Sweden. The Arctic Trail (800km) is a joint development of Sweden, Norway and Finland and is entirely above the Arctic Circle; it begins near Kautokeino in Norway and ends in Abisko, Sweden. The most popular route is Kungsleden, and its most beautiful – and busiest – sections are in Lappland.

English-language coverage of hiking and climbing in the Swedish mountains is limited to *Scandinavian Mountains* by Peter Lennon. The Swedish sections aren't very detailed but they're better than nothing.

Many counties have networks of easy walking trails perfect for day hikes, such as sections of the 950km Skåneleden (www.skaneleden.org).

Multiday routes are found in the mountains and forests near the Norwegian border. The best hiking time is during the short snow-free season, between late June and mid-September; conditions are better after early August when the mosquitoes have gone. Overnight huts and lodges are maintained by Svenska Turistföreningen (STF).

Mountain trails in Sweden are marked with cairns, possibly with some red paint. Marked trails have bridges across all but the smallest streams, and wet or fragile areas are crossed on duckboards. Avoid following winter routes (marked by regular poles with red crosses) since they often cross lakes or marshes!

Safety Guidelines

Before embarking on a walking trip, consider the following points to ensure a safe and enjoyable experience:

- Be sure you are healthy and feel comfortable walking for a sustained period.
- Obtain reliable information about physical and environmental conditions along your intended route, and stock up on good maps.
- Be aware of laws, regulations and etiquette regarding wildlife and the environment, including Sweden's *allemansrätten* (right of public access to the countryside: see p54).
- Walk only in regions and on trails within your realm of experience.
- Be aware that weather conditions can change quickly in the Northern Sweden: even in summer, prepare for both cold and warm conditions.

- Ask before you set out about the environmental characteristics that can affect your walk and how local, experienced walkers deal with these considerations.

Equipment

Hikers should be well equipped and prepared for snow in the mountains, even in summer. Prolonged bad weather in the northwest isn't uncommon – Sarek and Sylarna are the most notorious areas. In summer you'll need good boots, waterproof jacket and trousers, several layers of warm clothing (including spare dry clothes), warm hat, sun hat, mosquito repellent (a mosquito head net is also highly advisable), water bottle, maps, compass, and sleeping bag. Basic supplies are often available at huts and most lodges serve meals. If you're going off the main routes you should obviously take full camping equipment – for more information about camping away from the main routes see p54.

Equipment can usually be hired from the STF, but don't rely on this. If you need to replace gear, try the small STF lodge shops or the nationwide chain **Naturkompaniet** (www.naturkompaniet.se). Its a Swedish-only website, but click '*butiker*' and you'll find a list of stores.

'Hikers should be prepared for snow in the mountains, even in summer'

Information

Information in English is scarce – the best source is **Svenska Turistföreningen** (STF; Swedish Touring Association; ☎ 08-463 21 00; www.svenskaturistforeningen.se; Box 25, SE-10120 Stockholm), one of Sweden's largest tour operators. Most of its publications are Swedish-only, however STF staff are generally happy to answer questions and provide information in English over the phone or via email.

For nonmountain walking, address enquiries to **Svenska Gång- och Vandrarförbundet** (SGVF; Swedish Walking Association; ☎ 031-726 61 10; svenskgang@vsif.o.se; Kvibergs Idrottscenter, SE-41582 Göteborg).

MAPS

STF lodges sell up-to-date maps, but it's a good idea to buy them in advance. Try local and regional tourist offices, or buy online or in person at **Kartbutiken** (☎ 08-20 23 03; www.kartbutiken.se; Kungsgatan 74, SE-11122 Stockholm). Maps cost around Skr100 each.

Kungsleden

Kungsleden, meaning 'The King's Trail', is Sweden's most important waymarked hiking and skiing route. Most hikers visit the part that runs for 450km from Abisko (in the north of Lappland) to Hemavan in the south. The route is normally split into five mostly easy or moderate sections. The fifth section has a gap of 188km in STF's hut network, between Kvikkjokk and Ammarnäs. The most popular section is the northern one, from Abisko to Nikkaluokta; Sweden's highest mountain Kebnekaise (2111m) is a glorious extra for this section.

ABISKO TO NIKKALUOKTA

72km to Singi, 86km to Kebnekaise Fjällstation, 105km to Nikkaluokta; 7-8 days; Fjällkartan map BD6

This section of Kungsleden passes through spectacular alpine scenery and is usually followed from north to south. It includes a 33km-long trail from Singi to Nikkaluokta which isn't part of Kungsleden, but which allows an easy exit from the area. An alternative (and much more challenging) start is from Riksgränsen on the Norway–Sweden border; the

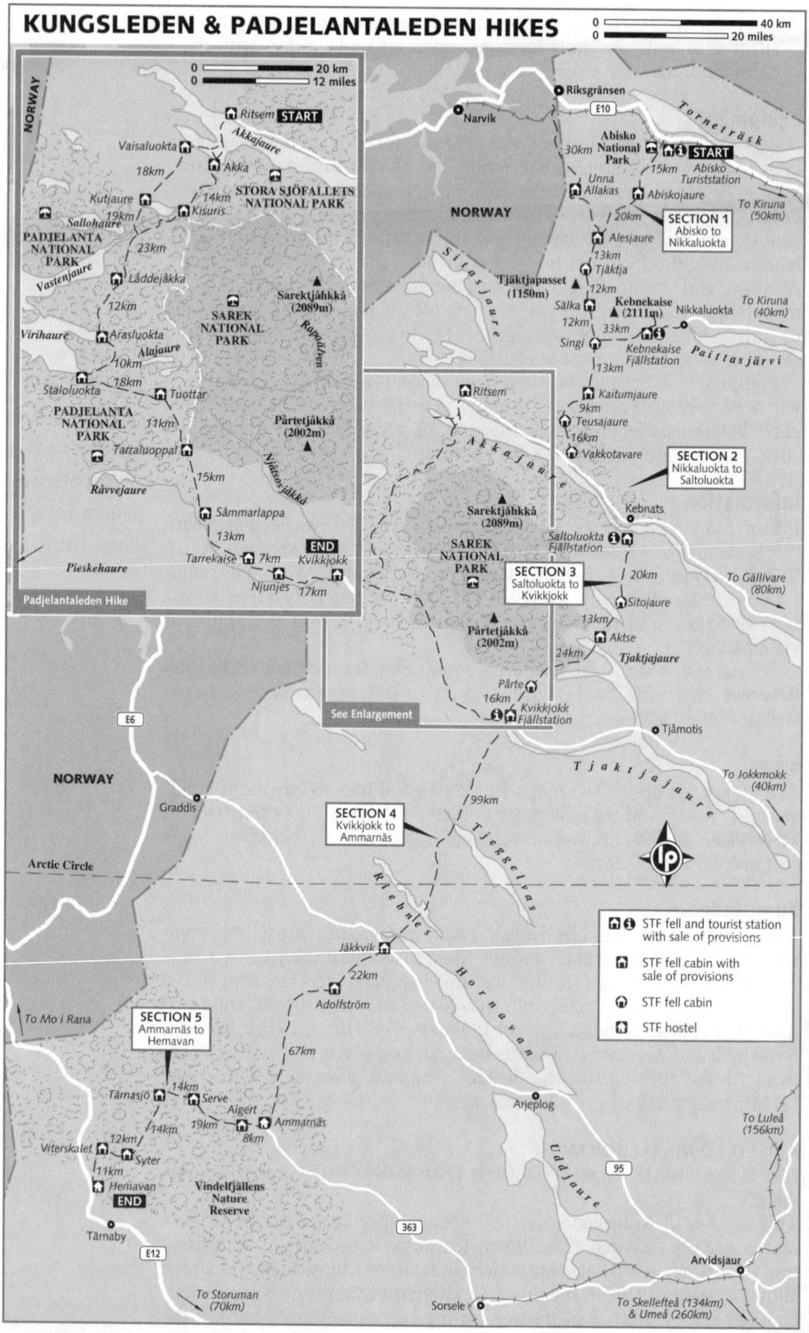

KUNGSLEDEN & PADJELANTALEDEN HIKES
0 40 km
0 20 miles
Riksgränsen
Narvik
E10
Torneträsk
Abisko National Park
START
30km
15km
Abisko Turiststation
Unna Allakas
Abiskojaure
To Kiruna (50km)
NORWAY
20km
SECTION 1
Abisko to Nikkaluokta
Alesjaure
13km
Tjäktja
Sitasjaure
Tjäktjapasset (1150m)
12km
Sälka
Kebnekaise (2111m)
Nikkaluokta
To Kiruna (40km)
12km
33km
Singi
Kebnekaise Fjällstation
Paittasjärvi
13km
Ritsem
Kaitumjaure
9km
Teusajaure
16km
Vakkotavare
Akkajaure
SECTION 2
Nikkaluokta to Saltoluokta
Kebnats
Sarektjåhkkå (2089m)
SAREK NATIONAL PARK
Saltoluokta Fjällstation
SECTION 3
Saltoluokta to Kvikkjokk
20km
To Gällivare (80km)
Sitojaure
13km
Aktse
24km
Tjaktjajaure
Pårtetjåkkå (2002m)
Pårte
16km
Kvikkjokk Fjällstation
See Enlargement
Tjåmotis
E6
Tjaktjajaure
To Jokkmokk (40km)
NORWAY
99km
Graddis
SECTION 4
Kvikkjokk to Ammarnäs
Tjeggelvas
Arctic Circle
Riebnes
Jäkkvik
22km
Adolfström
Hornavan
To Mo i Rana
SECTION 5
Ammarnäs to Hemavan
67km
14km
Tärnasjö
Serve
Aigert
Arjeplog
14km
19km
Ammarnäs
8km
Viterskalet
12km
Syter
Uddjaure
11km
Hemavan
END
Vindelfjällens Nature Reserve
95
To Luleå (156km)
Tärnaby
363
E12
Arvidsjaur
To Storuman (70km)
Sorsele
To Skellefteå (134km) & Umeå (260km)
STF fell and tourist station with sale of provisions
STF fell cabin with sale of provisions
STF fell cabin
STF hostel
0 20 km
0 12 miles
NORWAY
Ritsem
START
Vaisaluokta
Akkajaure
18km
Akka
STORA SJÖFALLETS NATIONAL PARK
Kutjaure
14km
19km
Kisuris
Sallohaure
PADJELANTA NATIONAL PARK
23km
Vastenjaure
Låddejåkkå
Sarektjåhkkå (2089m)
12km
SAREK NATIONAL PARK
Virihaure
Arasluokta
Rapaälven
Alajaure
10km
18km
Staloluokta
Tuottar
PADJELANTA NATIONAL PARK
11km
Pårtetjåkkå (2002m)
Tarraluoppal
15km
Njåtsosjåkkå
Råvvejaure
Såmmarlappa
13km
END
Tarrekaise
7km
Kvikkjokk
Pieskehaure
Njunjes
17km
Padjelantaleden Hike

30km route from there to STF's Unna Allakas is very rocky in places and you'll need to camp en route.

The STF has mountain lodges at Abisko and Kebnekaise, and there are also five STF huts. Many people stop at STF's Kebnekaise Fjallstation for a couple of nights, and some attempt the ascent of Kebnekaise (Sweden's highest mountain) from there – see the following section.

Public transport is available at Abisko, with rail connections to Narvik (Norway), or east to Kiruna and beyond. There are two buses that run daily between Abisko and Kiruna (Skr97, 1½ hours), and also a twice-daily bus service that runs between Nikkaluokta and Kiruna (Skr71, 1¼ hours).

KEBNEKAISE (OPTIONAL)

The hike to the top of Sweden's highest mountain is one of the best in the country and the views of the surrounding peaks and glaciers are incredible on a clear day. In July and August, the marked trail up the southern flanks is usually snow-free and no technical equipment is required to reach the southern top (2111m). To get to the northern top (2097m) from the southern top involves an airy traverse of a knife-edge ice ridge with a rope, ice axe and crampons. The map *Fjällkartan BD6* (Abisko–Kebnekaise) covers the route at 1:100,000, but there's also the very detailed 1:20,000 *Fjällkartan Kebnekaise.*

The trip involves 1900m of ascent and descent. Allow 12 hours, and an extra 1½ hours if you want to include the north top.

True North: The Grand Landscapes of Sweden, by Per Wästberg and Tommy Hammarström, contains stunning images by some of Sweden's top nature photographers.

NIKKALUOKTA TO SALTOLUOKTA

71km from Nikkaluokta to Vakkotavare, 38km from Singi; 5 days; Fjällartan map BD8

The scenery south of Singi is more rounded and less dramatic than the landscape around Kebnekaise. STF has mountain lodges at Kebnekaise and Saltoluokta, and regular huts along the trail. You may have to row yourself 1km across lake Teusajaure (there's an STF boat service in peak season). Everyone takes the bus along the road from Vakkotavare to Kebnats (Skr41), where there's an STF ferry (Skr70 for members, Skr100 non-members) across the lake to Saltoluokta Fjällstation. There's a twice-daily bus service from Ritsem to Gällivare via Vakkotavare and Kebnats.

SALTOLUOKTA TO KVIKKJOKK

73km; 4 days; Fjällkartan map BD10

There are excellent side trips from this section, from Aktse into Sarek National Park, the wildest part of Sweden. Saltoluokta to Kvikkjokk can be completed in four days, but allow six days to include trips into Sarek.

STF has a lodge at Saltoluokta, huts at Sitojaure, Aktse and Pårte, and another lodge in Kvikkjokk.

Sami families run the boat services across the lakes at Sitojaure (☎ 010-261 57 56, ☎ 010-257 52 31 or ☎ 070-274 72 63; Skr100 per trip) and Aktse (☎ 0971-220 22). Kvikkjokk has a twice-daily bus service in summer to Jokkmokk (Skr121) and Murjek train stations (Skr171).

KVIKKJOKK TO AMMARNÄS

188km; 2 weeks; Fjällkartan maps BD14 (north) & BD16 (south)

There are only a few locally-run huts on this section, so you'll need a tent. The more interesting northern part, Kvikkjokk to Jäkkvik (99km), can be completed in five or six days.

Boat services for lake crossings are available at Kvikkjokk, Vuonatjviken (Lake Riebnes) and Saudal (Hornavan). Buses run six days per week (not

Saturday) from Skellefteå to Bodø (Norway) via Jäkkvik, and one to four times daily from Sorsele to Ammarnäs.

AMMARNÄS TO HEMAVAN

78km; 4-5 days; Fjällkartan map AC2

Most of the southernmost section of Kungsleden runs through Vindelfjällens Nature Reserve. The trail is mostly easy, but with a long initial climb.

The STF has hostels at Ammarnäs and Hemavan and five huts en route which all sell provisions.

The Umeå to Hemavan bus runs three or four times daily (only once on Sunday; Skr241, seven hours), and continues to Mo i Rana (Norway; eight hours, once daily).

Padjelantaleden

139km; 8-14 days; Fjällkartan maps BD10 & BD7

The entire Padjelantaleden trail can be hiked in 10 to 14 days. It's generally an easy route, with long sections of duckboards, and all rivers are bridged. The southern section, from Kvikkjokk to Staloluokta (four or five days), is the most popular. At the northern end (by lake Akkajaure), you can start at either STF hut, Vaisaluokta or Akka (the latter is easier). Most of the trail lies in Padjelanta National Park, and all huts in the park are owned by Naturvårdsverket, the Swedish Environmental Protection Agency.

> 'Western Jämtland is one of Sweden's most popular hiking areas'

STF runs the Såmmarlappa, Tarrekaise and Njunjes huts at the southern end of the trail, and the hostel at Kvikkjokk. You can buy provisions at Staloluokta, Såmmarlappa, Tarrekaise and Kvikkjokk.

To reach the northern end of the trail, take the bus from Gällivare to Ritsem (twice daily) and connect there with the STF ferry to Vaisaluokta and Änonjálmme (1.5km north of the Akka STF hut), which runs from midsummer to early September, one to three times daily (Skr140/170 for members/nonmembers). For details of boats from the end of Padjelantaleden to Kvikkjokk (up to three times daily from July to mid-September), call ☎ 0971-210 12. Helicopters (☎ 0971-210 40 or ☎ 0971-210 68) serve Staloluokta from Ritsem or Kvikkjokk daily from midsummer up until early August (Skr750 per flight).

Jämtland

The mountainous part of western Jämtland is one of Sweden's most popular hiking areas. There's a good network of easy to moderate hiking trails served by STF lodges and huts. The most popular route is the 'Jämtland Triangle' (47km), which takes a minimum of three days; allow an extra day for an ascent of the magnificent 1743m-high mountain Sylarna, easily climbed from STF's Sylarna lodge – the route is clearly marked with cairns. The hike runs between STF's Storulvån, Sylarna and Blåhammaren lodges. Sylarna and Blåhammaren don't have road access and Sylarna only has self-catering; meals at Blåhammaren are excellent. The section from Sylarna to Blåhammaren is very marshy and can be quite difficult in wet conditions. Fjällkartan map Z6 covers the area.

See p296 for public transport details.

MOUNTAINEERING & ROCK CLIMBING

Mountaineers head for Sylarna, Helagsfjället, Sarek National Park and the Kebnekaise region.

The complete traverse of Sylarna involves rock climbing up to grade 3. The ridge traverse of Sarektjåhkkå (2089m) in Sarek, the second-highest mountain in Sweden, is about grade 4. There are lots of other glacier and rock routes in Sarek. The Kebnekaise area has many fine climbing routes (grades 2 to 6), including the north wall of Kaskasapakte (2043m), and the steep ridges of Knivkammen (1878m) and Vaktposten (1852m). Ice climbing in the northern regions is excellent, if you can put up with all the darkness and the cold!

For qualified guides, contact **Svenska Bergsguideorganisation** (Swedish Mountain Guide Association; ☎ 098-01 26 56; www3.utsidan.se/sbo; Rymdvägen 11, SE-98145 Kiruna). The website is in Swedish only but under '*medlemmar*' there's a list of guides and their contact details.

Rock climbers can practise on the cliffs around Stockholm and Göteborg – there are 34 climbing areas with 1000 routes around Göteborg, and some 200 cliffs around the capital. Other popular spots are Bohuslän, the Kulla Peninsula (north of Helsingborg), and a newly developed bouldering area, Kjugekull, a few kilometres northeast of Kristianstad. You'll find good climbing walls in Stockholm, Göteborg, Uppsala, Skellefteå and Linköping.

For further information, try the helpful **Svenska Klätterförbundet** (Swedish Climbing Federation; ☎ 08-618 82 70; kansliet@klatterforbundet.com; Lagerlöfsgatan 8, SE-11260 Stockholm).

CYCLING

Sweden is ideal for cycling, with Skåne and Gotland particularly recommended. It's an excellent way to look for prehistoric sites, rune stones and quiet spots for free camping. The cycling season is from May to September in the south, and July and August in the north.

'Cycling is an excellent way to look for prehistoric sites, rune stones and quiet spots for camping'

You can cycle on all roads except motorways (green sign, with two lanes and a bridge on it) and roads for motor vehicles only (green sign with a car symbol). Highways often have a hard shoulder, which keeps cyclists well clear of motor vehicles. Secondary roads are mostly quiet and reasonably safe by European standards.

You can take a bicycle on some *länstrafik* trains and most regional buses (free, or up to Skr50). On the Skåne region's Pågatågen trains, a bike costs the price of a child's ticket. On the Öresund trains (which serve routes between Göteborg–Copenhagen and Kalmar–Alvesta–Copenhagen) you can book a space for your bike on ☎ 0771-75 75 75. Long-distance buses usually don't accept bicycles, and nor does the SJ railway. Bikes are transported free on some ferries, including Vägverket routes.

You can hire bicycles from some campsites, hostels, bike workshops and sports shops; the average price is about Skr100 for a day, or around Skr500 per week (although we have seen costs as high as Skr200 and Skr800 for the same periods of time).

Some country areas, towns and cities have special cycle routes – contact local tourist offices for information and maps. Kustlinjen (591km) runs from Öregrund (Uppland) southwards along the Baltic coast to Västervik, and Skånespåret (800km) is a fine network of cycle routes. The well-signposted 2600km-long Sverigeleden extends from Helsingborg in the south to Karesuando in the north, and links points of interest with suitable roads (mostly with an asphalt surface) and bicycle paths.

Brochures and Swedish-text guidebooks with decent maps are available from **Svenska Cykelsällskapet** (Swedish Cycling Association; ☎ 08-751 6204; www.svenska-cykelsallskapet.se; Torneågatan 10, SE-16406 Kista).

An unusual and very popular cycling activity is *dressin* – also advertised as 'rail pedal trolley', 'cycle trolley' or 'inspection-trolley' rides – where you pedal a wheeled contraption along a disused railway line. Trips cost around

THE RIGHT OF PUBLIC ACCESS

The right of public access to the countryside *(allemansrätten)* is not a legal right, more a common-law privilege. It includes national parks and nature reserves, although special rules may apply. Full details in English can be found on the website www.allemansratten.se.

You're allowed to walk, ski, boat or swim on private land as long as you stay at least 70m from houses and keep out of gardens, fenced areas and cultivated land. You can pick berries and mushrooms, provided they're not protected species. Generally you should move on after one or two nights' camping.

Don't leave rubbish or take live wood, bark, leaves, bushes or nuts. Fires fuelled with fallen wood are allowed where safe, but not on bare rocks (which can crack from the heat). Use a bucket of water to douse a campfire even if you think that it's out. Cars and motorcycles may not be driven across open land or on private roads; look out for the sign *ej motorfordon* (no motor vehicles). Dogs must be kept on leads from 1 March to 20 August. Close all gates and don't disturb farm animals or reindeer. Off-limit areas where birds are nesting are marked with a yellow or red-and-yellow sign containing the words *fågelskydd – tillträde förbjudet.*

If you have a car or bicycle, look for free camping sites around unsealed forest tracks leading from secondary country roads. Make sure your spot is at least 50m from the track and not visible from any house, building or sealed road. Bring drinking water and food, and don't pollute any water sources with soap or food waste.

Above all, remember the mantra: 'Do not disturb, do not destroy'!

Skr450 per day or about Skr1800 a week. The best area in the country to try out this novel experience is Värmland, which has miles of old track: phone ☎ 054 148041 or check out Activities under www.varmland.org for a list of operators.

For further information on cycling, contact your local cycle-touring club.

SKIING

Lift passes and equipment hire are reasonably priced, resorts are well run and facilities are of a high standard. After the spring solstice (21 March), daylight lasts longer than in the Swiss Alps, so you'll get more skiing time out of your pass.

Cross-country (nordic) skiing opportunities vary, but the northwest usually has plenty of snow from December to April (but not much daylight in December and January). Kungsleden and other long-distance tracks provide great skiing. Practically all town areas (except those in the far south) have marked and often illuminated skiing tracks.

From 3 to 18 February 2007, the resort of Åre will be hosting the Alpine Skiing World Championships.

The large ski resorts cater mainly for downhill (alpine and telemark) skiing and snowboarding, but there's also scope for cross-country. For resort reviews in English, visit www.goski.com and www.thealps.com. **SkiStar** (www.skistar.com) manages two of the largest places, Sälen and Åre, and has good information on its website.

The southernmost large resort in Sweden, Sälen (Dalarna), appeals particularly to families, as does Idre, a little further north. Åre, in Jämtland, is great for long, downhill runs (over 1000m descent) and cross-country routes, and is the main party place for young skiers. Nearby ski areas at Duved and Storlien are also good, and less crowded. In Lappland, Hemavan gets fairly busy with spring skiers. Riksgränsen (at the border with Norway on the E10 Kiruna–Narvik road) is the world's northernmost ski resort, and offers interesting options – including heli-skiing and alpine ski touring – from mid-February until late June. Downhill runs at Riksgränsen aren't suitable for beginners.

Take the usual precautions: don't leave marked cross-country or downhill routes without emergency food, a good map, local advice, and proper equipment including a bivouac bag. Temperatures of –30°C or lower (including wind-chill factors) are possible, so check the daily forecasts. Police and tourist offices have information on local warnings. In mountain ski resorts, where there's a risk of avalanche *(lavin)*, susceptible areas are marked by yellow, multilingual signs and buried-skier symbols. Make sure your travel insurance covers skiing.

BOATING & SAILING

Boating and sailing are hugely popular in Sweden. The 7000km-long coastline, with its 60,000 islands, is a sailors' paradise, but look out for the few restricted military areas off the east coast.

Inland, lakes and canals offer pleasant sailing in spring and summer (the canals are generally open for limited seasons). The main canals are the Göta Canal (see p146), the Kinda Canal and the Dalsland Canal. Various companies offer short canal cruises; contact local tourist offices for details. Steamboats and cruisers ply the shores of lakes Vättern and Vänern: see individual town sections for details.

Those with private boats will have to pay lock fees and guest harbour fees (around Skr150 per night, although some small places are free). A useful guide is the free, annual *Gästhamnsguiden* in Swedish, which is published by **Svenska Kryssarklubben** (Swedish Cruising Club; ☎ 08-448 28 80; info@sxk.se;Augustendalsvägen 54, Box 1189, SE-13127 Nacka Strand). It contains comprehensive details of 500 guest harbours throughout the country. It's also available from larger tourist offices and most of the harbours listed.

Svenska Sjöfartsverket (Swedish Maritime Administration; ☎ 011-19 10 00; www.sjofartsverket.se; Huvudkontoret, SE-60178 Norrköping) can send you information on harbour handbooks and sea charts. For charts you can also try **Kartbutiken** (☎ 08-20 23 03; www.kartbutiken.se; Kungsgatan 74, SE-11122 Stockholm).

SKATING

Whenever the ice is thick enough, Stockholm's lake and canal system is exploited by skating enthusiasts seeking the longest possible 'run'. When the Baltic Sea freezes (once or twice every 10 years), fantastic tours of Stockholm's archipelago are possible. The skating season usually lasts from December to March. **Stockholms Skridskoseglarklubb** (Stockholm's Ice Skate Sailing Club; www.sssk.se) has some information in English on its website, but its services are for members only.

Bring a good pair of sunglasses, even if you're visiting in winter, to protect your eyes from glare off snowy surfaces.

DOGSLEDDING & SNOWMOBILE SAFARIS

Organised tours with Siberian huskies pulling your sledge are fairly popular in Lappland, as are excursions on snowmobiles. For further details see the Northern Sweden chapter.

Further south, you can dogsled through the wintry woods of the Dalarna region with **Häst & Vagn** (☎ 0250-55 30 14; hast.vagn@itadventure.se; Torsmo 1646, SE-79491 Orsa); prices are around Skr600/4800/9600 for a half-day/three-day/six-day adventure.

BIRD-WATCHING

There are many keen ornithologists in Sweden, and there are bird-watchers' towers and nature reserves everywhere; see p44 for details of the best bird-watching sites. For further information, contact **Sveriges Ornitologiska Förening** (Swedish Ornithological Society; ☎ 08-612 25 30; www.sofnet.org in Swedish; Ekhagsvägen 3, SE-10405 Stockholm).

HORSE-RIDING

Sweden's multitude of tracks, trails, forests, shorelines and mountains make for some fantastically varied riding. Everything from short hacks to full-on treks are on offer, for around Skr300/500/800 per two hours/half day/full day, on Swedish or Icelandic horses.

For more information see the website www.hastlandet.se, which has comprehensive contact details for approved stables.

Sweden has two indigenous horse breeds: the north Swedish horse and the Gotland pony.

FISHING

There are national and local restrictions on fishing in many of Sweden's inland waters, especially for salmon, trout and eel. Before dropping a line, check with local tourist offices or councils. You generally need a permit, but free fishing is allowed on parts of Vänern, Vättern, Mälaren, Hjälmaren and Storsjön Lakes and most of the coastline.

Local permits for the waters of a *kommun* (municipality) can be bought from tourist offices, sports or camping shops, and some boat or canoe-hire outfits, and typically cost around Skr125 per day. For fishing maps and advice, ask the local tourist office.

Summer is the best fishing time with bait or flies for most species, but trout and pike fishing in southern Sweden is better in spring or autumn and salmon fishing is best in late summer. Ice fishing is popular in winter.

An excellent web resource for fishing in Sweden is www.cinclusc.com/spfguide in Swedish, or contact **Sportfiskeförbundet** (Angling Federation; ☎ 08-704 44 80; info@sportfiskarna.se; Svartviksslingan 28, SE-16739 Bromma).

GOLF

Golf is incredibly fashionable in Sweden. There are over 400 golf courses, open to everyone, and many hotel chains offer golf packages. Courses in the south are often surrounded by rolling farmlands, but things are decidedly weirder in the north – Björkliden, near Abisko, is a golf course 240km above the Arctic Circle, and at the Green Line golf course at Haparanda, playing a round means crossing the Swedish–Finnish border four times. Green fees are around Skr300; for more information, contact **Svenska Golfförbundet** (Swedish Golf Federation; ☎ 08-622 15 00; http://sgf.golf.se; Box 84, Kevingestrand 20, SE-18211 Danderyd).

One in every 16 Swedes plays golf.

CANOEING & KAYAKING

Sweden is a real paradise for canoeists and kayakers (canoes are more common than kayaks). The national canoeing body is **Svenska Kanotförbundet** (Swedish Canoe Federation; ☎ 0155-20 90 80; www.kanot.com; Rosvalla, SE-61162 Nyköping). It provides general advice and produces *Kanotvåg*, a free, annual brochure listing 75 approved canoe centres that hire out canoes (for around Skr250/1300 per day/week).

According to the right of common access, canoeists may paddle or moor virtually anywhere provided they respect the privacy of others and avoid sensitive nesting areas. More good information is available on the Internet at www.kanotguiden.com.

RAFTING

White-water rafting in rubber boats isn't a big activity, since most rivers have low gradients. Localities that do offer the activity include Arvidsjaur on Piteälven (p305); Haparanda on Torneälven (p291); Järpen in Jämtland (one of the best places for rafting in Sweden, see www.jmt.se for more information); and Vindeln, on Vindelälven (p284). You can also go slow-water rafting, especially on Klarälven in Värmland (see p259).

SWIMMING, WINDSURFING & DIVING

Swedish folk need no encouragement to go leaping into lakes, rivers and the sea. The white-sand beaches on the west coast south of Göteborg are some of Sweden's finest. Many campsites have outdoor swimming pools, there are numerous family waterparks, and, for winter, plenty of indoor municipal ones.

Also on the west coast, the area around Varberg (p232) is the premier spot for windsurfing.

There are around 10,000 wrecks lying off Sweden's coastline; those in the Baltic Sea are often in a miraculous state of preservation, thanks to the low salinity of the water. The Kulla Peninsula (p197) also has good diving. Sweden's national diving body **Svenska Sportdykarförbundet** (☎ 08-605 60 00; sportdykning@ssdf.se; Idrottens Hus, SE-12387 Farsta) may be able to help with queries.

Food & Drink

It's fair to say that Swedes are obsessed with food, though they don't have the kind of reputation for it that, say, the French do. Dining, even down to the afternoon coffee break, is ritualised and taken seriously. Food is often considered a means of exploration of other cultures, as well as a celebration of the traditions that hold Swedish society together.

STAPLES & SPECIALITIES

Most folk start the day with a strong cup of coffee. This is usually accompanied by a *frukost* (breakfast) of cereal such as cornflakes or muesli with *filmjölk* (cultured milk) or fruit-flavoured yoghurt. Hotels and hostels offer breakfast buffets of several types of bread, pastries, crispbread and/or rolls, with *pålägg* (toppings) including butter, sliced cheese, boiled eggs, sliced meat and spicy sausage or salami, liver pâté, Kalles caviar (a ubiquitous caviar spread), pickled herring, sliced cucumber, jam and marmalade.

Swedes drink more milk than any other nation in the world, and more coffee than anywhere except Finland.

A hearty lunch has long been a mainstay of the workforce, so it has become institutionalised to a degree – which means it's an affordable and accessible way to get a good solid sampling of typical Swedish cooking. The *dagens rätt* (daily lunch special) includes a main course, salad, beverage, bread and butter, and coffee. Smaller cafés offer lighter versions centred on quiches or salads.

For a lighter lunch yet, head to a *konditori* – an old-fashioned bakery-café where you can get a pastry or a *smörgås* (sandwich), usually very artfully made with greens, shrimp or salmon, boiled eggs, roe and mustard-dill sauce piled onto a slice of bread.

Seafood and meat including game, form the core of the typical Swedish menu – along with the ever-present potato. The word *husmanskost* is used to describe a sort of everyman cuisine: basic, unpretentious, traditional meals like *köttbullar och potatis* (meatballs and potatoes, usually served with lingonberry jam, or *lingonsylt*), *lövbiff och strips* (thinly sliced fried meat and chips/fries) and *pytt i panna* (equivalent to hash: a mix of diced sausage, beef or pork fried with onion and potato and served with sliced beetroot and an egg). Gravadlax or gravlax (cured salmon), caviar, shrimp, and smoked, fried or pickled herring are all popular.

TRAVEL YOUR TASTEBUDS

A lot of the best in Swedish food sounds rather discouraging – pickled herring in mustard sauce, reindeer-cheese cream in a tube, liver paste for breakfast, black-liquorice ice cream. But those brave enough to follow the locals' lead will be treated to some surprisingly good flavour combinations. Lingonberries and cloudberries are two distinctive fruits that add flavour to a number of Swedish dishes. Horseradish and dill are key flavours, too. Pairings of food and beverage are important: there's no crayfish without singing and *snaps;* there's no *sill* (pickled herring) without light ale and strong cheese; there's no coffee without cake – or, heaven forbid, vice versa. The best way to explore the many flavours of Swedish cuisine, from the sublime to the ridiculous, is to make a few trips to a smörgåsbord. This is especially rewarding around the Christmas holidays, but it's an adventure any time of year. Start with the cold-fish plates and work your way to dessert! You're meant to visit the table many times, so take care not to overload.

STOCKHOLM'S TOP FIVE

Here are five places an ambitious diner shouldn't miss while visiting Stockholm, for both atmosphere and food that's the best at what it's trying to be:

- Operakällaren (p94) is famous for its smörgåsbord.
- Eyubi (p94) showcases the sort of bold new cuisine coming from Stockholm's immigrant communities.
- Gondolen (p96) is old-school fancy with an amazing view.
- Östermalms Saluhallen (p97) is a market hall with a huge variety of food stands and restaurants.
- Nystekt Strömming (p95) is the best place in town for fried herring.

DRINKS

Coffee is Sweden's unofficial national drink, but tea is also generally available. *Saft* is cordial commonly made from lingonberries and blueberries as well as orange, apple and grape. Tap water is drinkable everywhere, but sparkling mineral water is common and comes in a wide variety.

Pick up the cookbook *Aquavit and the New Scandinavian Cuisine* by Ethiopian-born Swedish chef Marcus Samuelsson for a taste of what he offers at his Manhattan restaurant. The photos alone look good enough to eat.

Beers are ranked by alcohol content; the stronger the beer, the higher its price and, generally speaking, the more flavour it has. Light beers (*lättöl,* less than 2.25%) and 'folk' beers (*folköl,* 2.25% to 3.5%) account for about two-thirds of all beer sold in Sweden; these can be bought in supermarkets. Medium-strength beer (*mellanöl,* 3.5% to 4.5%) and strong beer (*starköl,* over 4.5%) can be bought only at outlets of the state-owned alcohol store, Systembolaget, or in bars and restaurants.

Swedes generally drink strong beer on special occasions – partly because the everyday beer produced by mass breweries like Falcon, Åbro, Pripps and Spendrups is entirely unremarkable. There are a few good microbrews available in taverns (look for Jämtlands brewery's very good Fallen Angel bitter; Tärnö's Nils Oscar range is good too), and the major producers also tend to bring out decent speciality beers on a limited scale. The large breweries also produce a wide range of drinks from cider to light and dark lagers, porter and stout. Pear and apple ciders are also common, frequently in light-alcohol or alcohol-free versions.

Wines and spirits can be bought only at Systembolaget. Sweden's trademark spirit, *brännvin,* also called *aquavit* (vodka) and drunk as *snaps,* is a fiery and strongly flavoured drink that's usually distilled from potatoes and spiced with herbs.

The family-fun website www.luciamorning.com/todo.html shares instructions for making crafts and snacks related to the winter holidays.

CELEBRATIONS

Certain foods are tied to celebrations and times of the year. The most traditional of these, naturally, is Christmas, when the *julbord,* a particularly elaborate version of the smörgåsbord, comes out. It contains all the usual delicacies – many types of herring, gravlax, meatballs, short ribs, *blodpudding* (blood pudding) etc – as well as seasonal delights like baked ham with mustard sauce, and *Janssons frestelse,* a casserole of sweet cream, potato, onion and anchovy. *Julmust,* a sweet dark-brown soft drink that foams like a beer when poured, and *glögg,* warm spiced wine, are also served around the Christmas holidays. The best accompaniment to a warm cup of *glögg,* available at kiosks everywhere in winter, is a *pepparkaka* (gingerbread cookie).

In summer, when many Swedes are on holiday in the countryside, people tend to dine outdoors. A typical summer lunch consists of various *inlagd sill* (pickled herring) with *knäckebröd* (crispbread), strong cheese like the crumbly *Västerbottens ost,* boiled potatoes, diced chives and cream, plus a finger or two of *snaps* and some light beer 'to help the fish swim down to the stomach'. Midsummer, of course, wouldn't be complete without *sill* (pickled herring) and strawberries. Towards the end of summer, Swedes celebrate (or commiserate) its passing with *Kräftskivor* (crayfish parties) where people wearing bibs and party hats get together to eat *kräftor* boiled with dill, drink *snaps* and sing *snapsvisor* (drinking songs).

25 March is Sweden's official Waffle Day.

In August, noses across the nation crinkle in disgust over or anticipation of *surströmming*, a specially prepared herring that is fermented and tinned and reeks unbelievably when opened – definitely an acquired taste, with plentiful *snaps* being key to the acquisition.

Since pre-Reformation days, split-pea soup and pancakes are traditionally eaten on Thursdays, historically to prepare for fasting on Fridays.

WHERE TO EAT & DRINK

Restaurants are generally open from 11.30am to 2pm or 3pm for lunch, and from 5pm until 10pm for dinner. Cafés, bakeries and coffee shops are likely to be open all day, from 7am or 8am in the morning until at least 6pm.

The website http://scandinaviancooking.com contains articles about Swedish cuisine and recipes for Scandinavian dishes of all kinds.

Tipping is not common in Sweden. A service cost is figured into the bill. If you've had excellent service, a 10% to 15% tip is appropriate.

Quick Eats

Street snacks are the cheapest and most convenient way to fill up in Sweden, particularly in cities but also on beaches, along motorways and in many camping areas. A snack kiosk with a grill is known as a *gatukök* – literally, street kitchen. In the world of Swedish street food, hot dogs reign supreme – the basic model is called a *grillad korv med bröd*, grilled sausage with bread (hot dog in a bun), although you can also ask for it boiled *(kokt korv)*. Brave souls can do a mind-boggling variety of things to the *korv*, chiefly involving rolling it up with any number of accompaniments, from shrimp salad to mashed potatoes to fried onions to coleslaw.

Kebab stands and fast-food windows are almost as common as *korv* carts. Packaged ice-cream treats are another ubiquitous option for quick sustenance on the go.

Self-Catering

Shopping for groceries outside your home country is always illuminating, usually fun and almost inevitably cheaper than eating out. Supermarkets across Sweden have preprepared foods for quick snacks, but making your own meals is easy enough too if you're hostelling or staying in camping grounds with good facilities.

Luleå native and Los Angeles resident Helene Henderson's *The Swedish Table* describes lighter, modern versions of traditional Swedish dishes suitable for catering Hollywood parties, which is how she makes a living.

Supermarkets are easily found in Swedish towns and villages. The main chains are ICA, Konsum and Hemköp (the last often found inside Åhléns department stores). Rimi is another, slightly less common chain.

By law, both the item price and the comparative price per kilogram have to be labelled. Plastic carrier bags usually cost Skr1 at the cashier.

The ideal way to buy produce is through small, rural farm shops or roadside stands. A brochure and website published by **Bo på Lantgård** (☎ 0534-12 07; www.bopalantgard.org) list farms and markets where you can buy fresh produce and smoked fish directly from the folk who raise them.

VEGETARIANS & VEGANS

Vegetarian and vegan restaurants are common; they're easy to find in the major cities, and even in rural areas restaurants generally have one or two vegetarian main-course options on the menu. For this reason we haven't created a separate category for vegetarian listings in this book.

EATING WITH KIDS

Dining with children in Sweden is easy, as they are accepted and catered for even in upscale restaurants.

HABITS & CUSTOMS

Table manners in Sweden are fairly standard for a European country – generally more formal than in the US, but if you follow your host's lead you can't go far wrong.

Should you like to offer a toast, hold up your glass and say *'Skål!'* then nod at each person around the table. The host or hostess should make the first toast (see the boxed text, below).

The classy-looking www.foodfromsweden.com/recipes/has a number of how-to (and why-to) guides to preparing Swedish foods, with gorgeous photography too.

EAT YOUR WORDS

Most people in Sweden speak excellent English and often several other languages, but it's handy, and polite, to be able to order from a Swedish menu. For key phrases and pronunciation guidelines, see p336.

Useful Phrases

Could I see the menu, please?
Kan jag får se menyn? — kan ya for·*se*·a me·*newn*?

Is service included in the bill?
Är serveringsavgiften inräknad? — air ser·*ve*·a·rings aav·yif·*ten* in·*rek*·nad?

I'm a vegetarian.
Jag är vegetarian. — ya air ve·ge·*ta*·ri·an

I don't eat meat.
Jag äter inte kött. — ya *air*·ter *in*·te shert

breakfast	*frukost*	*froo*·kost
lunch	*lunch*	lunfh
dinner	*middag*	*mid*·daa
menu	*meny*	me·*newn*
children's menu	*barnmeny*	baan me·*newn*
wine list	*vinlista*	*veen*·lis·ta
first course/entrée	*förrätt*	fer·*ret*
main course	*huvudrätt/varmrätt*	*hu*·vu·dret/vaam·*ret*
daily special	*dagens rätt* (usually only at lunchtime)	*daa*·gens ret
takeaway	*avhämtning*	*av*·hemt·ning

Food Glossary

BASICS

bröd	brerd	bread
choklad	shoo·*klaad*	chocolate
grädde	*gre*·de	cream
honung	hu·*nung*	honey
ketchup	ke·*choop*	tomato sauce

DOS & DON'TS

On formal occasions, do wait for the host or hostess to welcome you to the table before eating or drinking. Aside from formal *'skåls'*, don't sip from your glass until the host or hostess says, 'Now everyone may drink when he or she likes.' Do wear decent socks when dining in someone's home, as you'll generally be expected to take off your shoes in the foyer. And do bring a small gift, such as a bottle of wine or flowers.

knäckebröd	*kne*·ke·*brerd*	crispbread
matolja	maat·*ol*·yaa	cooking oil
nudlar	*nood*·laar	noodles
ost	oost	cheese
paj	*pa*·ee	pie/quiche
pasta	*paa*·sta	pasta
peppar	*pe*·paar	pepper
pommes frites	pom freets	chips/french fries
ris	rees	rice
salt	saalt	salt
senap	*sen*·nap	mustard
smör	smer	butter
smörgås	*smer*·gors	sandwich
socker	*sok*·ker	sugar
soppa	*sop*·paa	soup
sylt/marmelad	silt/mar·mer·*laad*	jam/marmalade
sås	sors	sauce
yoghurt	*yor*·goort	yogurt
ägg	eg	eggs

VEGETABLES & HERBS (GRÖNSAKER & ÖRTKRYDDOR)

blomkål	*bloom*·kol	cauliflower
bönor	*ber*·*ner*	beans
champinjoner	sham·pin·*yoo*·ner	button mushrooms
dill	dil	dill
gräslök	*gres*·lerk	chives
gurka	*ger*·*ka*	cucumber
haricots verts	*aa*·*ree*·ko·vair	green beans
kryddor	*krew*·*da*	spices
lök	lerk	onion
majs	*ma*·ees	corn
morot	*mo*·rot	carrot
paprika	*pa*·pri·ka	capsicum
persilja	pa·*shil*·ya	parsley
potatis	poo·*ta*·tis	potato
potatismos	poo·*ta*·tis·mus	mashed potatoes
purjolök	*per*·yoo·lerk	leek
rödbetor	*rerd*·*be*·ter	beetroot
rödkål	*rerd*·korl	red cabbage
sallad	*sa*·laad	lettuce
sparris	*sfa*·ris	asparagus
spenat	*spe*·naat	spinach
svamp	svamp	mushrooms
tomat	too·*mat*	tomato
vitkål	*veet*·korl	white cabbage
vitlök	*veet*·lerk	garlic
ärter	*air*·ter	peas

FRUIT (FRUKT)

ananas	*a*·na·nas	pineapple
apelsin	a·pel·*seen*	orange
aprikos	a·pri·kot	apricot
banan	ba·*naan*	banana
blåbär	*blor*·baa	blueberries
citron	si·*troon*	lemon

hallon	hal·*lon*	raspberries
hjortron	*yoor*·tron	cloudberries
jordgubbar	*yoord*·gub·bar	strawberries
lingon	*ling*·on	lingonberries
persika	pa·*shil*·ka	peach
päron	*pe*·ron	pear
smultron	*smul*·tron	wild strawberries
vindruvor	*veen*·dru·ver	grapes
äpple	*e*·ple	apple

MEAT (KÖTT)

and	and	wild duck
anka	*an*·ka	duck
biff	bif	beef/steak
bröst	brerst	breast
entrecote	*un*·tre·kor	steak
filé	fil·*lay*	fillet
fläsk/griskött	*flaisk/gris*·shert	pork
gryta	*grew*·ta	casserole
kalkon	kaal·*kon*	turkey
kalvkött	*kalv*·shert	veal
korv	korv	sausage
kotlett	kot·*let*	chop/cutlet
kyckling	sheek·*ling*	chicken
köttbullar	shert·*bul*·lar	meatballs
köttfärs	*shert*·fash	minced beef
lammkött	*lam·shert*	lamb
lammstek	*lam*·stek	roast lamb
leverpastej	*lee*·ver·pas·*tay*	liver pâté
nötkött	*nert*·shert	beef
oxfilé	*oks*·fil·*lay*	fillet of beef
oxstek	*oks*·stek	roast beef
rådjur	*rord*·yur	venison
renstek	*ren*·stek	reindeer
rostbiff	*rost·bif*	roast beef
skinka	*shing*·ka	ham
älg	*el*·ye	elk

FISH & SEAFOOD (FISK & SKALDJUR)

abborre	*a*·bo·re	perch
forell	fo·*rel*	trout
gädda	*yed·da*	pike
hummer	*hum*·mer	lobster
hälleflundra/helgeflundra	*hal*·le·*flund*·ra	halibut
kaviar	kav·*yaa*	caviar
krabba	*krab*·ba	crab
kräftor	*kref·tor*	crayfish
lax	laaks	salmon
makrill	*mak*·ril	mackerel
musslor	*mus*·ler	mussels
ostron	*oost*·ron	oysters
räkor	*re*·ker	shrimps/prawns
rödspätta	*rerd·spet*·ta	plaice
sill	sil	herring

sjötunga	*sher*·tung·a	sole
strömming	*strer*·ming	Baltic herring
tonfisk	*toon*·fisk	tuna
torsk	torshk	cod
vitling	*vit·ling*	whiting
ål	ol	eel

DESSERTS (DESSERTER/EFTERRÄTTER)

glass	glas	ice cream
kaka	*kaa*·ka	cake
ostkaka	*oost*·kaa·ka	cheesecake
pannkakor	*paan*·kaa·ka	pancakes
småkakor	*smor*·kaa·ka	sweet biscuits/cookies
tårta	*tor*·ta	filled cake
våffla	*vor*·fla	waffle
äppelpaj	*e*·pel·*pa*·ee	apple pie

COOKING STYLES

bakad	*baa*·kad	roasted/baked
friterad	free·*te·rad*	deep fried
gravad	*graa*·vad	cured
grillad	*gril*·lad	grilled
halstrad	hal·*strad*	grilled
kokt	kokt	boiled
marinerad	ma·reen·*nair*·rad	marinated
rökt	rerkt	smoked
stekt	*stekt*	fried
ugnstekt	*ung*·stekt	roasted/baked

DRINKS (DRYCKER)

apelsinjuice	e·pel·*sin*·yoos	orange juice
glögg	glerg	mulled wine
kaffe	*kaf*·fe	coffee
läsk	lesk	soft drink (carbonated)
mjölk	myerlk	milk
saft	saaft	cordial
te	*tay*	tea
varm choklad	*vaam*·shoo·*klaad*	hot chocolate
vatten	*vat*·ten	water
vin (vitt vin/rödvin)	veen (*vit*·veen/*rerd*·veen)	wine (white wine/red wine)
öl	erl	beer

Stockholm

Sweden's capital is one of the most beautiful major cities in the world, a mirage of saffron- and terracotta-coloured buildings shimmering between blue water and bluer skies all summer, or covered with snow and dotted with lights in winter. It's also a vibrant, modern city, famous for producing sleek designs, edgy fashion and world-class nightclubs.

The old town, Gamla Stan, is a compact little maze of cobblestone streets apparently built for small, thin people with very sturdy ankles. The stucco walls of its red, orange and vanilla buildings sag toward each other exhaustedly over countless souvenir shops and ice-cream parlours, while the Royal Palace crowns the tiny island. Just to the south of Gamla Stan is another island neighbourhood, Södermalm, where high waterfront hills are graced by lovely old residences and the main drags are lined with bohemian shops, art galleries and rollicking clubs. On the other side of Gamla Stan is the main city centre, a buzzing metropolis whose boutiques and restaurants can hold their own against just about any big city on the continent.

Surrounding all of this is every Stockholmer's pride and joy – the 24,000 or so rocky islands that make up the archipelago *(skärgård)*.

Stockholmers themselves are almost uniformly polite and friendly, making travel both easy and rewarding. Around 16% of greater Stockholm's 1.2 million people are immigrants, which creates a much more multicultural and diverse cityscape than many travellers might expect. It's certainly not all meatballs, ABBA and Ikea these days!

HIGHLIGHTS

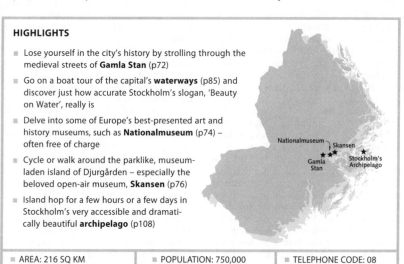

- Lose yourself in the city's history by strolling through the medieval streets of **Gamla Stan** (p72)
- Go on a boat tour of the capital's **waterways** (p85) and discover just how accurate Stockholm's slogan, 'Beauty on Water', really is
- Delve into some of Europe's best-presented art and history museums, such as **Nationalmuseum** (p74) – often free of charge
- Cycle or walk around the parklike, museum-laden island of Djurgården – especially the beloved open-air museum, **Skansen** (p76)
- Island hop for a few hours or a few days in Stockholm's very accessible and dramatically beautiful **archipelago** (p108)

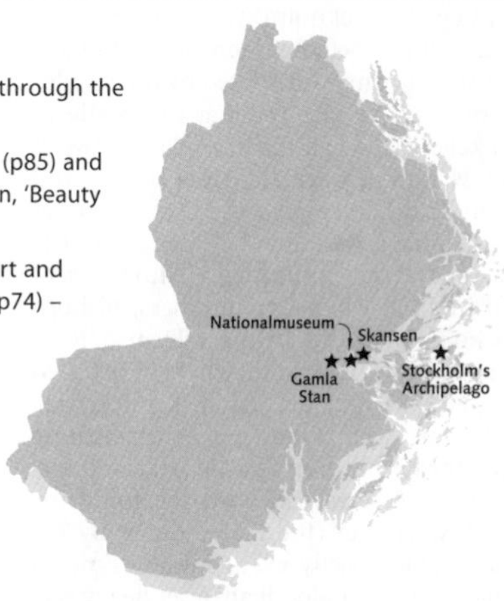

AREA: 216 SQ KM (INNER CITY)	POPULATION: 750,000 (INNER CITY)	TELEPHONE CODE: 08

HISTORY

Swedish political power had been centred around Mälaren lake for centuries, but it was forced to move to the lake's outlet when the rising land made navigation for large boats between the sea and lake impractical. Sweden's most important chieftain in the mid-13th century, Birger Jarl, ordered the construction of a fort on one of the strategically placed islets, where the fresh water entered the sea, and traffic on the waterways was controlled using timber stocks arranged as a fence, or boom. Stockholm, roughly meaning 'tree-trunk islet', may well be named after this boom.

The oldest record of the city consists of two letters dating from 1252. Within a hundred years, Stockholm was the largest city in Sweden, dominated by an impregnable castle (which was never taken by force) and surrounded by a defensive wall. During the period of the Kalmar Union, the king's governor directed affairs from the castle. The city was periodically ravaged by fire until timber buildings with turf roofs were replaced with brick structures. By the late 15th century, the population was around 6000 and Stockholm had become a significant commercial centre. Shipping copper and iron to continental Europe was a lucrative trade that was dominated by German merchants.

In 1471, the Danish king, Christian I, besieged Stockholm while attempting to quell the rebellious Sten Sture, but his 5000-strong army was routed by the Swedes just outside the city walls at the Battle of Brunkeberg (the fighting took place between what is now Vasagatan, Kungsgatan and Sergels Torg). Even after the Danish retreat to Copenhagen, trouble between unionists and separatists continued. Things escalated in 1520 when city burghers, bishops and nobility agreed to meet Danish King Christian II in Stockholm, where he arrested them all at a banquet. After a quick trial, the Swedes were found guilty of burning down the archbishop's castle near Sigtuna, and 82 men were beheaded the following day at Stortorget (the main square by the castle). This ghastly event became known as the Stockholm Bloodbath after heavy rain caused rivers of blood from the bodies to pour down steep alleys descending from the square.

A major rebellion followed and Gustav Vasa finally entered the city in 1523, after a two-year siege. The new king ruled the city with a heavy hand – the role of commerce dwindled and the church was extinguished entirely as royal power grew and the city revolved increasingly around the court. Gustav's son Erik XIV (and later kings) racked up taxation on the burghers to fund wars, but some did well from arms manufacturing and the city's importance as a military headquarters increased. At the end of the 16th century Stockholm's population was 9000, but this expanded in the following century to 60,000, as the Swedish empire reached its greatest extent.

In the 17th century, town planners laid out a street grid beyond the medieval city centre, and Stockholm was proclaimed the capital of Sweden in 1634. Famine wiped out 100,000 people across Sweden during the harsh winter of 1696, and starving hordes descended on the capital. The following year, the original royal castle (Tre Kronor) burned down. In 1711 plague arrived, and the death rate soared to 1200 per day from a population of only 50,000. After the death of King Karl XII, the country, unsurprisingly, stagnated.

In the 18th century, Swedish science and arts blossomed, allowing the creation of institutions and fine buildings. Another period of stagnation followed the assassination of King Gustav III; promised 19th-century reforms never arrived, and bloody street riots were common.

From the 1860s, further town planning created many of the wide avenues and apartment blocks still seen today. The city rapidly industrialised and expanded. In 1912, the Olympic Games were held in Stockholm and by 1915 it was home to 364,000 people.

The next major transformation of the city started in the 1960s, when large 'new towns' sprung up around the outskirts, and extensive 'slum' areas were flattened to make way for concrete office blocks, motorways and other modern developments. The financial and construction boom of the 1980s helped make the city a very expensive place. When that bubble burst due to the 1990s recession, the devalued krona actually helped Stockholm: Swedish tourism grew, and foreign tourists arrived in ever-increasing numbers. The relative easing of licensing restrictions on bars and restaurants, such as hours during which alcohol could be sold, the type of alcohol that was sold and the age of clientele, caused a huge increase in the number of licensed premises and helped create the lively Stockholm you see today.

ORIENTATION

Stockholm is built on islands, except for the modern centre (Norrmalm), a business and shopping hub. At its heart, linked to outlying areas by a network of subways, is the bustling square Sergels Torg. Next door is Centralstationen (the central train station), which is also where all the underground metro (tunnelbana or T) lines meet. The busy tourist office, called Sweden House, is in the eastern part of Norrmalm; it faces the popular park Kungsträdgården.

The triangular island Stadsholmen and its neighbouring islets accommodate Gamla Stan (Old Town), separated from Norrmalm by the narrow channels of Norrström near the royal palace, but connected by several bridges. To the west of this is Mälaren lake.

On the south side of Stadsholmen the main bridge, Centralbron, and the Slussen interchange connect with the southern part of the city, Södermalm, and its spine Götgatan. From its top end the giant stadium, Globen (which looks like a golf ball), is the southern landmark, although you'll cross water again at Skanstull before reaching it.

To the east of Gamla Stan is the pleasant island Skeppsholmen and its little neighbour, Kastellholmen. Further east along Strandvägen and past the pleasure-boat berths at Nybroviken you can cross to Djurgården, with its impressive collection of museums.

Mälaren, the lake west of Gamla Stan, contains many other islands. Also in the city's west, the E4 motorway crosses Stora Essingen, Lilla Essingen and Kungsholmen on its way north. Yet another series of bridges connects Långholmen with the western tip of Södermalm and the southern side of Kungsholmen.

Maps

The free *What's On Stockholm* tourist booklet has good maps, but the folded *Stockholms officiella turistkarta* (Skr25) covers a larger area; both are usually available from tourist offices and hotels. If you're heading for the suburbs, detailed maps of outlying areas can be purchased from tourist offices or map shops. The best available street atlas, *Atlas över Stor-Stockholm* (Kartförlaget; Skr185) in Swedish, covers all of greater Stockholm.

INFORMATION

Bookshops

Akademibokhandeln (Map p80; ☎ 613 61 00; Mäster Samuelsgatan 32) A chain with several locations, good for maps and books in English, including textbooks.

STOCKHOLM IN...

Two Days

Beat the crowds to the labyrinthine streets of **Gamla Stan** (p72) for souvenir shopping and a coffee at **Sundbergs Konditori** (p92). Peek into **Storkyrkan** (p74) and consider a tour of the royal palace, **Kungliga Slottet** (p73), or simply watch the midday changing of the guard. Then wander south to the Söder Heights, which you can climb via the stairs, or by taking the elevator **Katarinahissen** (p82). Most of Stockholm's best nightlife stretches out before you on the island of Södermalm; don't miss **Kvarnen** (p97) or **Mondo** (p99). Spend the next day at **Skansen** (p76), and dine at **Rosendals Trädgårdscafé** (p95).

Four Days

Follow the two-day plan, then take a guided boat tour of **Stockholm's waterways** (p85) for a different perspective. Afterwards, have a drink at **Berns Salonger** (p98), where August Strindberg got the inspiration for his first novel, then stroll over to Skeppsholmen for a peek into the always provocative **Moderna Museet** (p78). Next day, relive Viking history at the **Historiska museet** (p75), then tour the top-notch **Nationalmuseum** (p74). When you get peckish, explore the varied options at **Östermalms Saluhall** (p97). Up for more? Stand in line with Stockholm's elite partygoers at the **Spy Bar** (p99).

STOCKHOLM

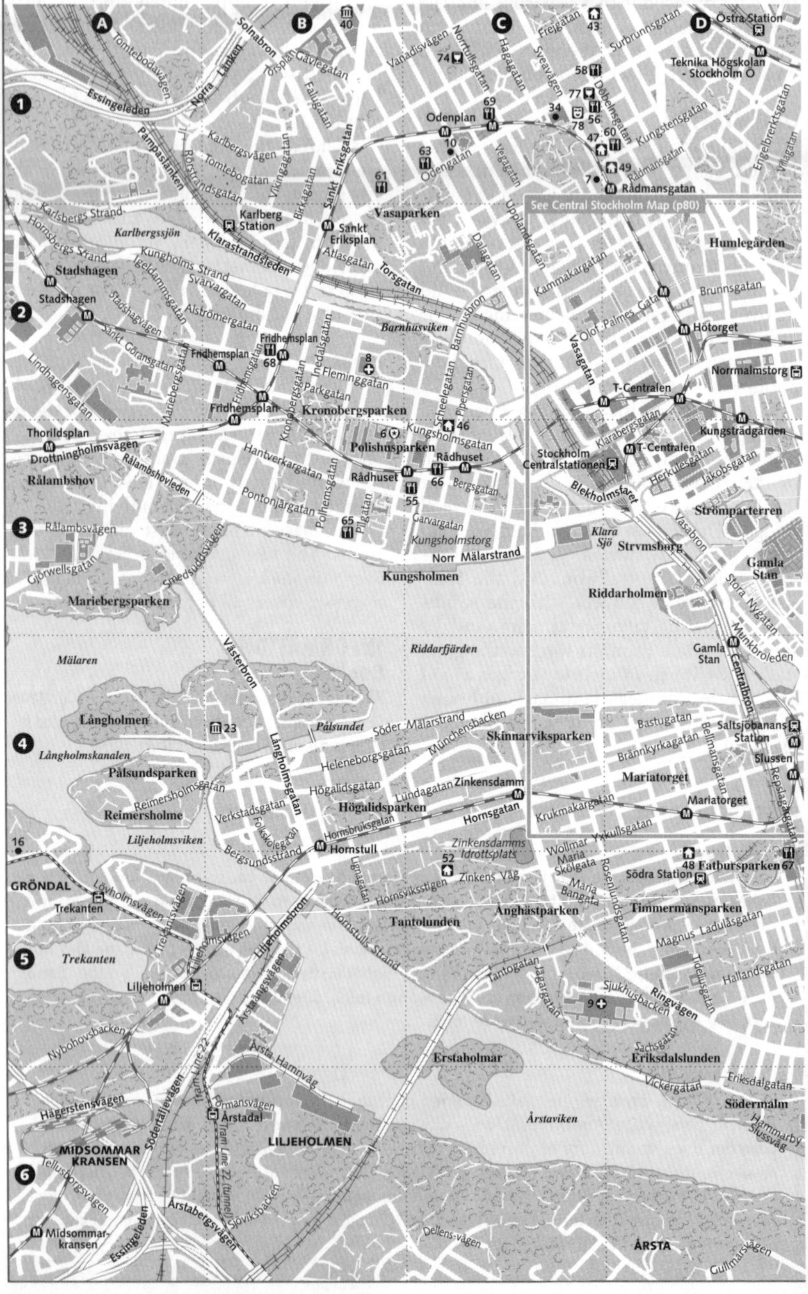

A
B
C
D
1
2
3
4
5
6
Tomtebodavägen
Essingeleden
Norra Länken
Solnabron
Torsplan
Gävlegatan
Vanadisvägen
Norrtullsgatan
Hagagatan
Frejgatan
Sveavägen
Surbrunnsgatan
Östra Station
Tekniska Högskolan - Stockholm Ö
Pampaslänken
Karlbergsvägen
Tomtebogatan
Rörstrandsgatan
Vikingagatan
Birkagatan
Sankt Eriksgatan
Odenplan
Odengatan
Vegagatan
Döbelnsgatan
Kungstensgatan
Rådmansgatan
Engelbrektsgatan
Karlsbergs Strand
Hornsbergs Strand
Karlbergssjön
Karlberg Station
Klarastrandsleden
Sankt Eriksplan
Atlasgatan
Torsgatan
Vasaparken
Dalagatan
Upplandsgatan
See Central Stockholm Map (p80)
Humlegården
Kammakargatan
Brunnsgatan
Olof Palmes Gata
Hötorget
Vasagatan
Normalmstorg
T-Centralen
Kungsträdgården
Stadshagen
Kungsholms Strand
Igeldammsgatan
Svarvargatan
Alströmergatan
Stadshagsvägen
Sankt Göransgatan
Fridhemsplan
Fridhemsgatan
Barnhusviken
Barnhusbron
Inedalsgatan
Fleminggatan
Parkgatan
Kronobergsgatan
Kronobergsparken
Lindhagensgatan
Mariebergsgatan
Scheelegatan
Pipersgatan
Kungsholmsgatan
Thorildsplan
Drottningholmsvägen
Rålambshovsleden
Hantverkargatan
Polishusparken
Rådhuset
Bergsgatan
Stockholm Centralstationen
Klarabergsgatan
Herkulesgatan
Jakobsgatan
Rålambshov
Pontonjärgatan
Polhemsgatan
Pilgatan
Garvargatan
Kungsholmstorg
Blekholmsfaret
Strömparterren
Rålambsvägen
Vasabron
Klara Sjö
Strömsborg
Norr Mälarstrand
Kungsholmen
Gamla Stan
Görwellsgatan
Smedsuddsvägen
Riddarholmen
Stora Nygatan
Mariebergsparken
Riddarfjärden
Munkbroleden
Mälaren
Västerbron
Centralbron
Långholmen
Pålsundet
Söder Mälarstrand
Münchensbacken
Skinnarviksparken
Bastugatan
Saltsjöbanans Station
Långholmskanalen
Bellmansgatan
Brännkyrkagatan
Slussen
Pålsundsparken
Heleneborgsgatan
Högalidsgatan
Långholmsgatan
Mariatorget
Reimersholmsgatan
Lundagatan
Zinkensdamm
Reimersholme
Verkstadsgatan
Högalidsparken
Krukmakargatan
Hornsgatan
Folkskolegatan
Hornsbruksgatan
Yxkullsgatan
Liljeholmsviken
Bergsundsstrand
Hornstull
Zinkensdamms Idrottsplats
Wollmar
Maria Skolgata
Rosenlundsgatan
Fatbursparken
Södra Station
GRÖNDAL
Lövholmsvägen
Lignagatan
Hornsviksstigen
Zinkens Väg
Maria Bangata
Timmermansparken
Trekanten
Trekantsvägen
Liljeholmsbron
Tantolunden
Anghästparken
Magnus Ladulåsgatan
Hornstulls Strand
Tideliusgatan
Hallandsgatan
Liljeholmsvägen
Tantogatan
Jägargatan
Sjukhusbacken
Ringvägen
Liljeholmen
Årstaängsvägen
Nybohovsbacken
Erstaholmar
Eriksdalslunden
Sachsgatan
Tram Line 22
Årsta Hamnväg
Vickergatan
Eriksdalsgatan
Hägerstensvägen
Södertäljevägen
Förmansvägen
Årstadal
Södermalm
Årstaviken
Hammarby Slussväg
MIDSOMMAR KRANSEN
LILJEHOLMEN
Tellusborgsvägen
Tram Line 22 (tunnel)
Sjöviksbacken
Årstabergsvägen
Essingeleden
Midsommarkransen
Dellens-vägen
ÅRSTA
Gullmarsvägen

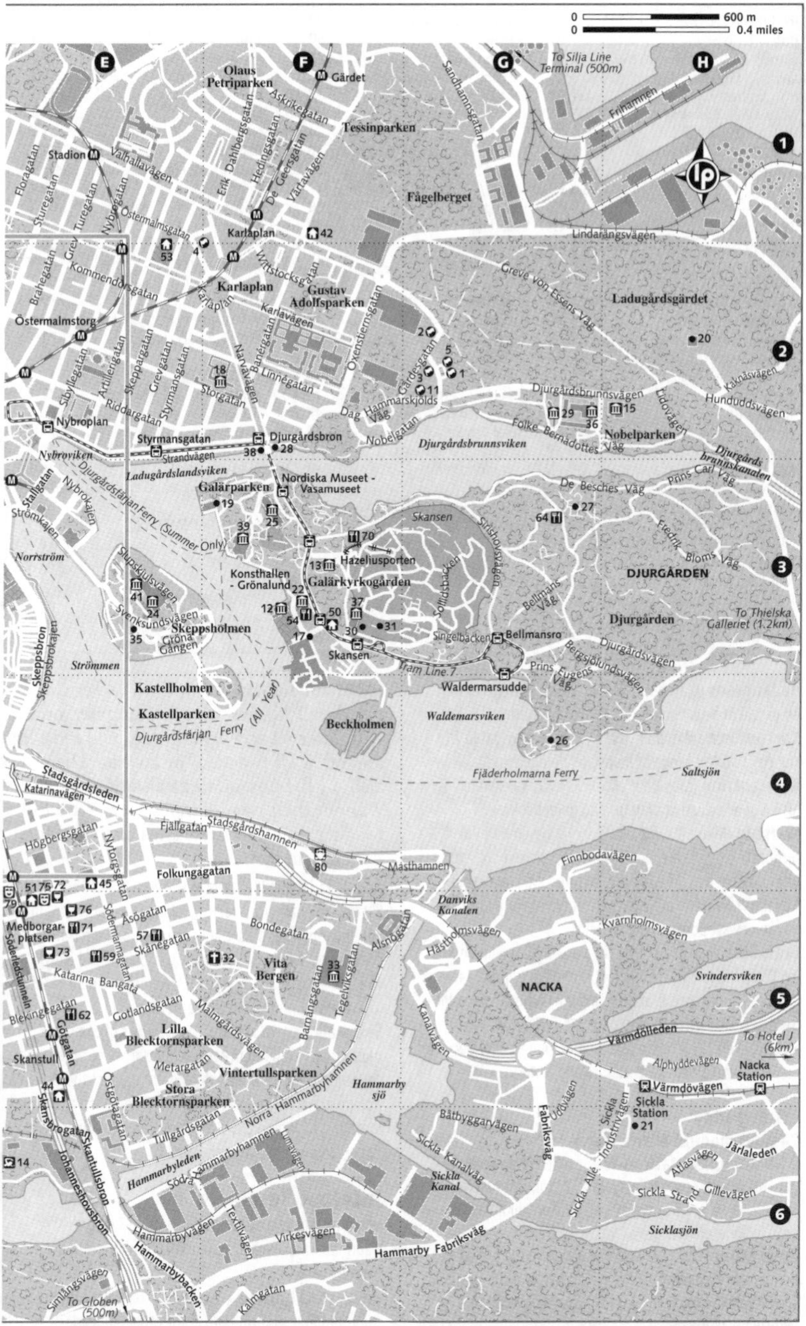
0 600 m
0 0.4 miles
E
F
G
H
1
2
3
4
5
6
Gärdet
To Silja Line Terminal (500m)
Frihamnen
Olaus Petriparken
Askrikegatan
Tessinparken
Sandhamnsgatan
Stadion
Valhallavägen
Floragatan
Sturegatan
Grev Turegatan
Nybrogatan
Erik Dahlbergsgatan
Hedingsgatan
De Geersgatan
Värtavägen
Fågelberget
Östermalmsgatan
Karlaplan
42
53
4
Lindarängsvägen
Kommendörsgatan
Brahegatan
Karlaplan
Wittstocksgatan
Gustav Adolfsparken
Greve von Essens Väg
Ladugårdsgärdet
Östermalmstorg
Karlavägen
Oxenstiernsgatan
20
Sibyllegatan
Artillerigatan
Skeppargatan
Grevgatan
Styrmansgatan
18
Storgatan
Narvavägen
Banérgatan
Linnégatan
Gärdesgatan
2
5
3
1
11
Kaknäsvägen
Hunduddsvägen
Riddargatan
Dag Hammarskjölds Väg
Djurgårdsbrunnsvägen
29
36
15
Lidovägen
Nybroplan
Styrmansgatan
Strandvägen
Djurgårdsbron
38
28
Nobelgatan
Djurgårdsbrunnsviken
Folke Bernadottes Väg
Nobelparken
Djurgårdsbrunnskanalen
Nybroviken
Ladugårdslandsviken
Djurgårdsfärjan Ferry (Summer Only)
Nordiska Museet - Vasamuseet
De Besches Väg
Prins Carl Väg
Stallgatan
Nybrokajen
Galärparken
19
25
Skansen
64
27
Strömkajen
39
70
Sirishovsvägen
Fredrik Bloms Väg
Norrström
Hazeliusporten
13
Konsthallen - Grönalund
Galärkyrkogården
DJURGÅRDEN
Slupskjulsvägen
41
24
22
37
Sollidensbacken
Bellmans Väg
To Thielska Galleriet (1.2km)
Svenksundsvägen
12
54
50
30
31
Djurgården
35
Skeppsholmen
Gröna Gången
17
Singelbacken
Bellmansro
Djurgårdsvägen
Skeppsbron
Skeppsbrokajen
Strömmen
Skansen
Bergsjölundsvägen
Tram Line 7
Prins Eugens Väg
Kastellholmen
Waldermarsudde
Kastellparken
Beckholmen
Waldemarsviken
Djurgårdsfärjan Ferry (All Year)
26
Fjäderholmarna Ferry
Saltsjön
Stadsgårdsleden
Katarinavägen
Fjällgatan
Stadsgårdshamnen
Högbergsgatan
Nytorgsgatan
80
Masthamnen
Finnbodavägen
Folkungagatan
51
75
72
45
79
76
Danviks Kanalen
Medborgarplatsen
71
Åsögatan
Bondegatan
Kvarnholmsvägen
Södermannagatan
57
Skånegatan
Hästholmsvägen
Alsnögatan
73
59
32
Vita Bergen
33
Tegelviksgatan
Svindersviken
Katarina Bangata
NACKA
Söderledstunneln
Blekingegatan
62
Gotlandsgatan
Malmgårdsvägen
Barnängsgatan
Kanalvägen
Götgatan
Lilla Blecktornsparken
Värmdöleden
To Hotel J (6km)
Skanstull
Metargatan
Alphyddevägen
Nacka Station
Vintertullsparken
Hammarby sjö
Värmdövägen
44
Östgötagatan
Stora Blecktornsparken
Norra Hammarbyhamnen
Sickla Station
Uddvägen
Sickla Industriväg
Skansbrogatan
Tullgårdsgatan
Båtbyggarvägen
21
Skantullsbron
Fabriksväg
Järlaleden
14
Johanneshovsbron
Hammarbyleden
Södra Hammarbyhamnen
Lumavägen
Sickla Kanalväg
Atlasvägen
Sickla Allé
Sickla Kanal
Sickla Strand
Gillevägen
Hammarbyvägen
Textilvägen
Virkesvägen
Sicklasjön
Hammarby Fabriksväg
Hammarbybacken
Simlångsvägen
To Globen (500m)
Kalmgatan

INFORMATION
British Embassy......................1 G2
Finnish Embassy......................2 G2
German Embassy......................3 G2
Irish Embassy......................4 E2
Norwegian Embassy......................5 G2
Police Station......................6 B3
RFSL (Gay & Lesbian Organisation)......................7 C1
Sankt Eriks Sjukhus......................8 B2
Södersjukhuset......................9 C5
Tvättomat......................10 C1
US Embassy......................11 G2

SIGHTS & ACTIVITIES
Aquaria Vattenmuseet......................12 F3
Arkitekturmuseet......................(see 24)
Biologiskamuseet......................13 F3
Eriksdalsbadet......................14 E6
Etnografiska Museet......................15 H2
Far & Flyg......................16 A5
Gröna Lund Tivoli......................17 F3
Historiska Museet......................18 F2
Junibacken......................19 F3
Kaknästornet......................20 H2
Klätterverket......................21 H6
Leksaksmuseet......................(see 33)
Liljevalchs Konsthall......................22 F3
Långholmens Fängelsemuseum......................23 B4
Moderna Museet......................24 E3
Nordiska Museet......................25 F3
Prins Eugens Waldemarsudde......................26 G4
Rosendals Slott......................27 G3
Sjöcafé......................28 F2
Sjöhistoriska Museet......................29 G2
Skansen......................30 F3
Skansen Aquarium......................31 F3
Skogens Hus......................(see 37)
Sofia Kyrka......................32 F5
Spårvägsmuseet......................33 F5
Stadsbibliotek......................34 C1
Svensk Form Design Centre......................35 E3
Tekniska Museet......................36 G2
Tobaks & Tändsticksmuseum......................37 F3
Tvillingarnas Sjökrog......................38 F2
Vasamuseet......................39 F3
Vin & Sprithistoriska Museet......................40 B1
Östasiatiska Museet......................41 E3

SLEEPING
Backpackers Inn......................42 F1
Birger Jarl Hotel......................43 C1
Clarion Hotel......................44 E5
Columbus Hotell......................45 E4
First Hotel Amaranten......................46 C3
Hostel Bed & Breakfast......................47 C1
Hotel Tre Små Rum......................48 D5
Långholmen Hotell & Vandrarhem......................(see 23)
Rex Hotel......................49 D1
Scandic Hotel Hasselbacken......................50 F3
Scandic Hotel Malmen......................51 E5
Zinkensdamm Hotell & Vandrarhem......................52 C5
Östra Reals Vandrarhem......................53 E2

EATING
Blå Porten......................54 F3
El Cubanito......................55 C3
Eyubi......................56 C1
Folkhemmet......................57 E5
ICA Baronen......................58 C1
Koh Phangan......................59 E5
Lao Wai......................60 D1
Narknoi......................61 B1
Pelikan......................62 E5
Restaurang Hasselbacken......................(see 50)
Ritorno......................63 C1
Rosendals Trädgårdskafe......................64 G3
Salzer......................65 B3
Spisa Hos Helena......................66 C3
Söderhallarna......................67 D5
Thelins......................68 B2
Tranan......................69 C1
Wärdshuset Ulla Winbladh......................70 F3
Östgöta Källaren......................71 E5

DRINKING
August Bar & Bistro......................72 E5
Bonden......................73 E5
Cliff Barnes......................74 C1
Kvarnen......................75 E5
Soldaten Svejk......................76 E5
Storstad......................77 C1

ENTERTAINMENT
La Habana......................78 C1
Mondo......................79 E5

TRANSPORT
Viking Line Terminal......................80 F4

Hedengrens (Map p80; ☎ 611 51 28; Sturegallerian) An excellent selection of new books in English.

Kartbutiken (Map p80; ☎ 20 23 03; Kungsgatan 74) The city's widest range of maps and guidebooks.

Kartcentrum (Map p80; ☎ 411 16 97; Vasagatan 16) Also a good selection of maps and guidebooks.

Konst-ig (Map p80; ☎ 50 83 15 18; basement, Kulturhuset) A great selection of lush, expensive books on international and Swedish art, architecture and design.

Pressbyrån (Map p80; Centralstationen) For English-language newspapers and paperbacks.

Press Stop Found at a few locations around town – including Drottninggatan 35, Götgatan 31 and Kungsgatan 14 – this is good for both special-interest and international magazines.

Sweden Bookshop (Map p80; ☎ 789 21 31; Slottsbacken 10) A broad selection of high-quality books in English about Sweden, its culture and history.

Emergency

24-hour medical advice (☎ 463 91 00)

24-hour police stations Kungsholmen (Map pp68-9; ☎ 401 00 00; Kungsholmsgatan 37, Kungsholmen); Södermalm (Map p80; ☎ 401 03 00; Torkel Knutssonsgatan 20, Södermalm)

Emergency (☎ 112) Toll-free access to the fire service, police and ambulance.

Larmtjänst (☎ 020-91 00 40) Roadside assistance for vehicle breakdowns.

Internet Access

Nearly all hostels have a computer or two with Internet access for guests, and most hotels offer wi-fi access in rooms. There are also wi-fi hubs in Centralstationen. Those without their own computer have a bit of a tougher time, but there are a couple of Internet cafés in town.

Access IT (Map p80; ☎ 50 83 14 89; Sergels Torg; per hr Skr19; 10am-7pm Tue-Fri, 11am-5pm Sat & Sun) In the basement of Kulturhuset, this space no longer has its own computers, but is a Sidewalk Express point (see below).

Matrix (Map p80; ☎ 20 02 93; Hötorget; per hr Skr35; 10am-6pm) Inside PUB department store.

Sidewalk Express (per hr Skr19) Rows of computer monitors and tall red ticket machines mark out these self-service Internet stations, which seem to roam the city and pop up in new places each week. They're found at various locations, including City Bus Terminalen (2nd floor), and Robert's Coffee, Drottninggatan 33.

Internet Resources

www.alltomstockholm.se Features loads of information on events, restaurants, sports etc; in Swedish only.

www.stockholmtown.com With excellent tourist information in English (and many other languages).

www.visit-stockholm.com A newly updated source for travellers, with nearly 500 pages of information on sights, food, accommodation, shopping and getting out of town.

Laundry

Laundry options are limited – it's best to find a hotel or hostel with facilities. A handy, central laundrette is **Tvättomat** (Map pp68-9; ☎ 34 64 80; Västmannagatan 61; metro T-Odenplan; per load from Skr70; 🕑 8.30am-6.30pm Mon-Fri, 9am-3pm Sat).

Left Luggage

There are three sizes of **left-luggage boxes** (from Skr35-75 per 24hr) at Centralstationen. Similar facilities exist at the neighbouring bus station and at major ferry terminals.

If you have a lost-property inquiry, ask for *tillvaratagna effekter*.

Libraries

Kulturhuset (Map p80; ☎ 50 83 15 08; Sergels Torg; 🕑 11am-7pm Tue-Fri, 11am-5pm Sat & Sun) Has a reading room with international periodicals and newspapers as well as books in various languages.

Stadsbiblioteket (Map pp68-9; ☎ 50 83 11 30; Sveavägen 73; 🕑 9am-9pm Mon-Thu, 9am-7pm Fri, 11am-5pm Sat & Sun, shorter hours in summer) The main city library is just north of the city centre. It's worth a visit if you're into architecture – it's the best example of Stockholm's 1920s neoclassicist style.

Media

The best overall guide for visitors to the capital is the monthly *What's On Stockholm*, available free from tourist offices and many hotels. Tourist offices also carry two separate accommodation guides in English – one for camping, the other for hotels and hostels – both are free. If you can navigate event listings in Swedish, look for *På Stan*, the excellent weekly arts and culture supplement to the daily *Dagens Nyheter* newspaper. Similarly, the free monthly paper *Nöjes-guiden* has listings in Swedish, focusing on youth culture, music, pub and restaurant reviews and entertainment.

Medical Services

Apoteket CW Scheele (Map p80; ☎ 454 81 30; Klarabergsgatan 64) A 24-hour pharmacy.

Sankt Eriks Sjukhus (Map pp68-9; ☎ 672 30 00, 672 31 00 after 8.30pm; Flemminggatan 22; 🕑 8am-9pm) Emergency dental care.

Södersjukhuset (Map pp68-9; ☎ 616 10 00; Ringvägen 52) The most convenient hospital from the city centre.

Money

There are ATMs all over town, including a few at Centralstationen; expect long queues.

The exchange company Forex has about a dozen branches in the capital and charges Skr15 per travellers cheque; the following are some of their handy locations:

Hotellcentralen (🕑 7am to 9pm)

Stockholm Arlanda airport (Terminal 2; 🕑 7am-9pm)

Sweden House (Map pp68-9; ☎ 789 24 90; Hamngatan 27; 🕑 9am to 7pm Mon-Fri, 10am-5pm Sat & Sun)

Post

The always-busy Centralstationen **post office** (🕑 7am-10pm Mon-Fri, 10am-7pm Sat & Sun) keeps the longest hours. You can now buy stamps and send letters at a number of city locations, including newsagents and supermarkets – keep an eye out for the Swedish postal symbol (yellow on a blue background) to indicate that postal services are available at that location.

Telephone

Coin-operated phones are virtually nonexistent and payphones are operated with phone cards purchased from any Pressbyrån location (or with a credit card, although this is ludicrously expensive). Ask for a *telefonkort* for Skr35, Skr60 or Skr100. Local call charges are about Skr3 per minute, while the international rate with a phone card is usually Skr8 to Skr10. For mobile phones, check with your service provider to make sure your network is compatible before assuming the phone will work in Sweden.

Toilets

Public toilets nearly everywhere charge Skr5, and most of them take only a Skr5 coin, so it's handy to keep a few of these with you if you're out sightseeing. (If you're desperate, head for the toilets in one of the city's free museums, or ask nicely at a café or restaurant.)

Tourist Information

Hotellcentralen (Map p80; ☎ 50 82 85 08; Centralstationen; 🕑 24hr) This busy and convenient tourist office is located inside the main train station. You can collect tourist information here as well as reserve hotel rooms and hostel beds (for a fee), buy the Stockholm Package, Stockholm Card or SL Tourist Card, book sightseeing tours and buy maps, books and souvenirs.

Sweden House (Map p80; ☎ 50 82 85 08, www.stockholmtown.se; Hamngatan 27; 🕑 9am-7pm Mon-Fri, 10am-5pm Sat, 10am-4pm Sun) The capital's main tourist office is just off Kungsträdgården across from the NK department store. It has lots of good brochures and can help book hotel rooms, theatre and concert tickets, and packages such as boat trips to the archipelago. There's a Forex currency-exchange counter in the same building.

Travel Agencies

STA (Map p80; ☎ 54 52 66 66; Kungsgatan 30) and the nearby **Kilroy Travels** (Map pp68-9; ☎ 0771-54 57 69; Kungsgatan 4) both specialise in discount youth and student flights.

Universities

Stockholm University (Map p105; www.su.se; T-Universitetet) Founded as Stockholm College with a public lecture series in 1878; up until then, students had to go to Uppsala or Lund to further their studies. The university was taken over by the government in 1960 and it is now among the largest in the country, with around 35,000 students. Most of the university is located 3.5km north of the city centre in Frescati district.

DANGERS & ANNOYANCES

Some parts of the city aren't particularly safe late at night, especially Sergels Torg, Medborgarplatsen (in Södermalm) and Fridhemsplan (on Kungsholmen) when the bars empty around 1am. Visitors should steer clear of night buses at weekends and opt for a taxi instead.

SIGHTS

Swedes really know how to set up a museum, and Stockholm has around 70 of the finest. Many contain world-class treasures, and most are loaded with atmosphere. Best of all, these days several of them are free of charge. Most also have self-guided tours in English and other languages, whether by audiotape or printed brochure.

Stockholm also has 10 royal castles in and around the city, including the largest palace in the world that's still in use, as well as the World Heritage–listed Drottningholm.

The palace and a few other museums and churches are in the Old Town, **Gamla Stan**; the **city centre** has the bulk of the museums, while **Djurgården** hosts the famous outdoor museum Skansen and the Vasa ship museum. Several other worthwhile sights are scattered across the city, but none are too far-flung and they're all easy to reach by public transport.

Gamla Stan

Stockholm began here, and most visitors to the capital do the same. The old town is full of historic buildings that seem to be collapsing towards each other at a glacial pace. Shops and restaurants line its twisted cob-

PENNY-PINCHING PACKAGES

Getting your money's worth out of a visit to Stockholm is a lot easier if you take advantage of one or more discounts offered to tourists. The **Stockholm Card** is available from tourist offices, SL information centres, some museums, some hotels and hostels or online at www.stockholmtown.com. It gives you entry to 75 museums and attractions, travel on public transport (including Katarinahissen, but excluding local ferries, some city buses and airport buses), sightseeing by boat, and parking in certain places. It is valid for 24, 48 or 72 hours and costs Skr260/390/540 (or Skr100/140/190 for accompanying children under 18, maximum two children per adult). To get maximum value, use two 24-hour cards over three days (with a rest day in between) and be sure to note opening hours; for example Skansen remains open until late, whereas royal palaces are only open until 3pm or 4pm.

Students and seniors get discounted admission to most museums and sights without the card, so you'll need to work out if it's cheaper for you to just get a transport pass and pay admission charges separately.

Stockholm à la Carte (from Skr450) is a cut-price package that includes a hotel room and the Stockholm Card. It's available weekends year-round and also throughout the summer (mid-June to mid-August) Its cost depends on the standard of accommodation (prices for central hotels start at around Skr600 per person). Travel agents in other Scandinavian capitals or major Swedish cities can help with arrangements, otherwise contact **Destination Stockholm** (☎ 663 00 80; www.destination-stockholm.com). The website has lots of good information and lists details of the 50-odd hotels involved in the scheme.

blestone streets and stunted alleyways; some of the best are tucked away in vaulted cellars. This island is also, of course, home of the royal palace. The main shopping thoroughfare, Västerlånggatan, is a must, but it's best early in the day or late at night when the flood of tourists lessens. Don't hesitate to veer off onto a parallel alley or linger in one of the quiet squares. Part of the fun of exploring Gamla Stan is getting hopelessly lost in its labyrinth and suddenly emerging onto a bustling square or waterfront view.

KUNGLIGA SLOTTET

The 'new' **Royal Palace** (Map p80; ☎ 402 61 30; www.royalcourt.se; Slottsbacken; adult/child each attraction Skr80/35, combined ticket Skr120/65; most attractions ⏲ 10am-4pm mid-May–Aug, noon-3pm Tue-Sun Sep–mid-May) is one of Stockholm's highlights; it was constructed on the site of the 'old' royal castle, Tre Kronor, which burned down in 1697. The north wing survived and was incorporated into the new palace, but its medieval designs are now concealed by a baroque exterior. The new palace, designed by the court architect Nicodemus Tessin the Younger, wasn't completed until 57 years later. With 608 rooms, it's the world's largest royal castle still used for its original purpose.

The excellent **state apartments**, including the Hall of State and the Apartments of the Royal Orders of Chivalry, are both open to the public (except during state functions, most of which happen in September), with two floors of royal pomp, 18th- and 19th-century furnishings, and portraits of pale princes and princesses. Look for Queen Kristina's silver throne in the Hall of State, and for impressive baroque and rococo designs throughout the rooms.

The Swedish regalia, crowns, sceptres, orbs and keys are displayed at **Skattkammaren** (the Royal Treasury), by the southern entrance to the palace near **Slottskyrkan** (the Royal Chapel). **Gustav III:s Antikmuseum** displays the Mediterranean treasures, particularly sculpture, acquired by that eccentric monarch. At the **Museum Tre Kronor** in the palace basement, you can see the foundations of 13th-century defensive walls and exhibits rescued from the medieval castle during the fire of 1697.

The **Changing of the Guard** takes place in the outer courtyard at 12.15pm Monday to Saturday, and 1.15pm Sunday and public holidays.

HELGEANDSHOLMEN

Though technically separated from Gamla Stan, this little island, in the middle of Norrström, is home to a couple of the most interesting sights in Stockholm. The **Riksdaghuset** (Swedish Parliament; Map p80; ☎ 786 40 00; www.riksdagen.se; admission free; 1hr tours ⏲ 12.30pm & 2pm Mon-Fri late Jun-Aug, 1.30pm Sat & Sun rest of year) consists of two parts; the older front section (facing downstream) dates from the early 20th century, but the other, more modern part contains the current debating chamber. Tours of the building are surprisingly compelling and serve as a primer on the Swedish system of consensus-building government.

Medeltidsmuseet (Medieval Museum; Map p80; ☎ 50 83 17 90; Strömparterren; adult/child Skr60/40; ⏲ 11am-4pm Jul & Aug; 11am-6pm Wed, 11am-4pm Tue & Thu-Sun Sep-Jun), at the other end of the island, is one of the city's most atmospheric museums. While preparing to build a Riksdag car park here in the late 1970s, construction workers unearthed some foundations dating from the 1530s. The ancient walls were preserved as found and a museum was built around them. Faithful reconstructions of typical houses, sheds and workshops transport visitors to medieval Stockholm (though with a better lighting and sound system than they had back then). Also in the museum is the well-preserved, 1520s-era *Riddarsholm* ship.

OTHER SIGHTS

Livrustkammaren (Royal Armoury; Map p80; ☎ 51 95 55 44; Slottsbacken 3; admission free; ⏲ 10am-5pm Jun-Aug, 11am-5pm Tue-Sun & 11am-8pm Thu Sep-May) is part of the palace complex, but it can be visited separately. Best known for displaying Gustav II Adolf's stuffed (and it must be said, somewhat tattered-looking) battle steed, Streiff, the museum covers 500 years of royal history. There's a large collection of royal memorabilia, including suits of armour, countless weapons, five elaborately decorated and colourful carriages, all kinds of ceremonial clothing and the costume Gustav III was wearing when he was assassinated at the opera in 1792.

Kungliga Myntkabinettet (Royal Coin Cabinet; Map p80; ☎ 51 95 53 04; Slottsbacken 6; admission free; ⏲ 10am-4pm) is just across the plaza from the Royal Palace. Here you'll find displays of coins (including Viking silver) and banknotes covering the history of money over the last 2600 years. You'll see the world's oldest coin (from 625 BC), the world's largest coin (a Swedish copper plate weighing 19.7kg) and the world's first banknote (issued in Sweden in 1661).

Stockholm's cathedral, **Storkyrkan** (Map p80; ☎ 723 30 09; admission free; 9am-7pm mid-May–Aug, 9am-7pm Mon-Sat & 9am-5.30pm Sun Sep–mid-May) is next to the Royal Palace; Sweden's monarchs used to be crowned here. The brick-built cathedral dates back to the late 13th century (it's the city's oldest building and was consecrated in 1306), but the exterior is baroque. The ancient and ornate interior contains a life-size statue of St George and his horse confronting the mythical dragon, created by the German sculptor Berndt Notke in 1494. You'll also see the two large royal box pews with crown-shaped canopies and the silver altar. Keep an eye out for posters and handbills advertising musical performances here.

Riddarholmskyrkan (Map p80; ☎ 402 61 30; adult/child Skr20/10; 10am-4pm mid-May–Aug, noon-3pm Tue-Sun Sep 1-18, noon-3pm Sat & Sun Sep 18-30), on the nearby island Riddarholmen, was built by Franciscan monks in the late 13th century. It no longer functions as a church but has been the royal necropolis since the burial of Magnus Ladulås in 1290, and is home to the armourial glory of the Seraphim knightly order. Look for the marble sarcophagus of Gustav II, Sweden's mightiest monarch, and the massed wall plates displaying the coats-of-arms of the knights. There's a guided tour in English at 1pm all open days.

Until 1865, the Swedish parliament met in the 17th-century **Riddarhuset** (House of Nobility; Map p80; ☎ 723 39 90; Riddarhustorget 10; adult/child Skr40/10; 11.30am-12.30pm Mon-Fri), one of the prettiest buildings in the city. These days even the riffraff can visit during the lunch hour. There are 2325 coats of arms belonging to Sweden's nobility on display, and downstairs in the Chancery there's a unique collection of heraldic porcelain.

The **Postmuseum** (Map p80; ☎ 781 1755; Lilla Nygatan 6; adult/child Skr50/free; 11am-4pm Tue-Sun May-Aug, 11am-4pm Tue-Sun & 11am-7pm Wed Sep-Apr), housed in a 17th-century building, describes the history of Sweden's postal service, with displays of Swedish stamps from 1855 to the present day. The philatelic library has 51,000 books on stamps and postal history. There's also a miniature post office for children, a café and a shop. And, of course, you can mail letters, send packages and buy stamps here.

ALFRED NOBEL

Alfred Nobel (1833–96), Swedish chemist, engineer and industrialist, patented a detonator for highly unstable nitroglycerine in 1862. Four years later he made the remarkable discovery that kieselguhr could absorb nitroglycerine safely, but remain an explosive substance. This became known as dynamite and Nobel's factories increased their output 6000-fold over the next 30 years.

As a very wealthy industrialist, Nobel created the annual Nobel Prizes (from 1901) in physics, chemistry, medicine/physiology, literature and peace, to be awarded to those who had benefited humankind the most in the preceding year. A sixth prize, for economics, was added in 1969.

Nobelmuseet (Map p80; ☎ 23 25 06; Stortorget; adult/child Skr50/20; 10am-5pm mid-May–mid-Sep, 11am-5pm Wed-Sun mid-Sep–mid-May, open until 8pm Tue year round), in the Börsen building (the old Stock Exchange), presents the history of the Nobel Prizes and their recipients. It is a great-looking museum, with well-designed exhibitions on the history of the prize, Alfred Nobel himself, and the various recipients over the years. There are also top-notch films on looped display, voice recordings of Nobel Prize acceptance speeches, a travelling collection and several temporary exhibits.

If you happen to be here in summer but long to experience the legendary Scandinavian winter, stop in at the **Ice Gallery** (Map p80; ☎ 790 55 00; Österlånggatan 41; adult/child Skr50/25; 10am-4.30pm Fri-Sun). This small exhibition space has some interesting ice sculptures inspired by the much more elaborate (but winter-only) Ice Hotel in northern Sweden (see p301). The gallery is kept at about –6°C (puffy jackets are provided for visitors).

Central Stockholm

NATIONALMUSEUM

Sweden's largest art museum, the **Nationalmuseum** (Map p80; ☎ 51 95 43 00; www.nationalmuseum.se; Södra Blasieholmshamnen; admission free, extra charge for some temporary exhibits; 11am-8pm Tue & Thu, 11am-5pm Wed, Fri-Sun) houses the national collection of painting, sculpture, drawings, decorative arts and graphics, ranging from the Middle Ages to the 20th century. Some of the art became state property on the death of Gustav III in 1792, making this one of the earliest public museums in the world. There are around 16,000 items of painting and sculpture on display, including magnificent works by artists such as Goya, Rembrandt and Rubens. There are also around 30,000 items of decorative artwork, including porcelain, furniture, glassware, silverware and late-medieval tapestries. In 2000, the museum was the victim of a famous robbery in which art thieves made off with three paintings (two Renoirs and a Rembrandt), all of which have since been recovered. There's an excellent museum shop and a terrace café in the glassed-in Atrium.

HISTORISKA MUSEET

The national historical collection is at this enthralling **museum** (Map pp68-9; ☎ 51 95 56 00; www.historiska.se; Narvavägen 13; admission free; ⏰ 11am-5pm, 11am-8pm Thu Oct-Apr, 10am-5pm May-Sep). A masterpiece of mood and lighting, the Historiska Museet covers 10,000 years of Swedish history and culture (up to 1520), including some archaeological finds from the Viking town, Birka. Don't miss the incredible **Gold Room** in the basement, with its rare treasures. The most astonishing artefact is the 5th-century seven-ringed gold collar with 458 carved figures, weighing 823g. It was found in Västergötland in the 19th century and was probably used by pagan priests in ritualistic ceremonies. Also don't miss the medieval triptychs and altar screens.

STADSHUSET

It looks more like a large church, but the size of **Stadshuset** (Town Hall; map p80; ☎ 50 82 90 58; Hantverkargatan 1; entrance by tour only, adult/child Skr60/30; tours ⏰ 10am, 11am, noon, 2pm & 3pm Jun-Aug, 10am & noon rest of year) is deceptive because it has two internal courtyards. The dominant brown-brick square tower of Stadshuset is topped with a golden spire and the symbol of Swedish power, the three royal crowns. Inside the building, you'll find the beautiful mosaic-lined **Gyllene salen** (Golden Hall), Prins Eugen's own fresco re-creation of the lake view from the gallery, and the hall where the annual Nobel Prize banquet is held. Part of the tour involves walking down the same stairs you'd use if you had won the big prize. Entry is by daily tour only, and these may be interrupted from time to time by preparations for special events. Climb the **tower** (adult/child Skr20/free; ⏰ 10am-4.30pm May-Sep, Sat & Sun in Apr) for a good stair-climbing workout and stellar views of Gamla Stan. In summer a unique feature is that you can dive off the terrace at the edge of the building.

OTHER SIGHTS

Though parts of it are rather graphic, the **Armémuseum** (Map p80; ☎ 788 95 60; Riddargatan 13; admission free; ⏰ 11am-8pm Tue, 11am-4pm Wed-Sun) is an excellent place to see vivid displays of Swedish military history, from the Vikings to the present, with an unidealised – not to say pacifist – bent. There are huge cases of weapons, re-created scenes and sound effects, and disturbingly realistic wax figures forever engaged in historic battles.

A private palace completed in 1898, **Hallwylska Museet** (The Hallwyl Collection; Map p80; ☎ 51 95 55 99; Hamngatan 4; adult/child Skr40/20, living history tours Skr85/50, free admission to 1st-fl state rooms noon-4pm Tue-Sun) is a showcase of eccentricity. Wilhelmina von Hallwyl collected items as diverse as kitchen utensils, Chinese pottery, 17th-century paintings, silverware, sculpture and jewellery. In 1920, she and her husband donated their entire house (including contents) to the nation. The baroque-style great drawing room is particularly impressive and includes a rare, playable grand piano. This delightful museum has guided tours in English at 1pm daily from late June to mid-August; the rest of the year English tours are only at 1pm on Sunday (but you can join one of the more regular tours in Swedish).

The **Vin & Sprithistoriska Museet** (Wine & Spirits Museum; Map pp68-9; ☎ 744 7070; Dalagatan 100; adult/child Skr40/30; ⏰ 10am-7pm Tue, 10am-4pm Wed-Fri, noon-4pm Sat & Sun) might be the only museum in Sweden that offers a new drinking song each week (call ☎ 744 70 75 to hear it). The eccentric museum puts the 'oh' back in alcohol with informative displays on the distilling and filtering process, the strange saga of the Vodka King, the development of Absolut's chic labelling, and best of all, a 'scent organ' that lets you sample each of 55 spices used in traditional *brännvin* and *snaps* recipes. It also has information on Sweden's conservative alcohol policy and what the future might hold. There's a small bar for wine- and liquor-tasting. Take bus 69 from Sergels Torg or walk from T-Odenplan metro station.

The collections in the very attractive **Medelhavsmuseet** (Museum of Mediterranean Antiquities; Map p80; ☎ 51 95 53 80; Fredsgatan 2; admission free; 11am-8pm Tue-Wed, 11am-4pm Thu-Fri, noon-5pm Sat & Sun) include Egyptian, Greek, Cypriot and Roman artefacts. There are decent displays of Islamic art and a small but spectacular gold room, which is unlocked for brief periods by the guard at the front desk – ask politely and you'll be admitted.

The small but evocative **Strindbergsmuseet** (Map p80; ☎ 411 53 54; Drottninggatan 85; adult/child Skr40/free; noon-4pm Tue-Sun) in the Blue Tower, is the well-preserved apartment where the writer and painter August Strindberg (1849–1912) spent his final four years. You'll see the dining room, bedroom, study and his interesting library, which contains some 3000 volumes. There's also a room for temporary exhibits and a bookshop.

At **Musikmuseet** (Map p80; ☎ 5195 5490; Sibyllegatan 2; admission free; 11am-7pm Tue, 11am-4pm Wed-Sun), hands-on displays let you play musical instruments and pretend you're in ABBA after checking out some of the band's original paraphernalia from the 1970s.

Djurgården

The royal park of Djurgården is a must for visitors to Stockholm. The main attractions are Skansen and the extraordinary Vasa Museum, but there are many other interesting places to visit in the park.

Take bus 47 from Centralstationen, or the Djurgården ferry services from Nybroplan or Slussen (frequent in summer); or take the vintage tram from Norrmalmstorg. You can rent bikes by the bridge (see p102), and this is by far the best way to explore the area. Parking is limited during the week and prohibited on summer weekends, when Djurgårdsvägen is closed to traffic.

SKANSEN

The world's first open-air museum, **Skansen** (Map pp68-9; ☎ 442 80 00; www.skansen.se; adult Skr30-80, child free-Skr30, depending on the time of yr; 10am-8pm May, 10am-10pm Jun-Aug, 10am-5pm Sep, 10am-4pm Oct-Apr) was founded in 1891 by Artur Hazelius to let visitors see how Swedes lived in previous times. You could easily spend a day here and still not see it all. Around 150 traditional houses and other exhibits from all over Sweden occupy the attractive hilltop –

AUGUST STRINDBERG

August Strindberg was born in Stockholm in 1849. His mother's death, when he was 13, was an important event in the life of the tortured genius, who was hailed as the 'writer of the people' towards the end of his chaotic life.

Strindberg periodically studied theology and medicine at Uppsala University from 1867 to 1872, but left without a degree. He then worked as a librarian and journalist prior to becoming a productive author, writing novels, plays, poetry, and over 7000 letters. He was also a talented painter of moody scenes.

His breakthrough as a writer came in 1879 with the publication of his novel *The Red Room*. In 1884, Strindberg became notorious after the publication of *Marriage*, a collection of short stories that led to his trial (and acquittal) for blasphemy in the City Court of Stockholm. Much of his work deals with radical approaches to social issues, which didn't go down well with the Swedish establishment.

Strindberg married three times. His first marriage, to Siri von Essen (married 1877, divorced 1891), produced four children. During his stay in central Europe (1892 to 1899), he led an 'artist's life' with the likes of Edvard Munch and Gauguin, and had a short-lived marriage to an Austrian woman, Frida Uhl (married 1893, separated 1894, dissolved 1897), which led to the birth of a daughter. As his instability deepened, Strindberg took an interest in the occult, but the crisis was over upon publication of *Inferno* (1897), an accurate description of his own emotional shambles. After returning to Stockholm in 1899, he married Norwegian Harriet Bosse in 1901 (divorced 1904) and had yet another daughter.

In 1912, Strindberg was awarded an 'Anti–Nobel Prize' (funded by ordinary people from around Sweden) as compensation for not receiving the Nobel Prize for Literature. Although the conservative Swedish Academy basically ignored his work, Strindberg was appreciated by many Swedes and his death, in 1912, was seen as the loss of the country's greatest writer.

it's meant to be 'Sweden in miniature', complete with villages, nature, commerce and industry. The glassblowers' cottage is a popular stop; watching the intricate forms emerge from glowing blobs of liquid glass is so transfixing the museum has set up a mini-amphitheatre there. The Nordic Zoo, with moose, reindeer, wolverines and other native wildlife, is a highlight especially in spring when baby critters scamper around. There's also a petting zoo for kids.

Buildings in the open-air museum represent various trades and areas of the country. Most are inhabited by staff in period costume, often doing handicrafts, playing music or churning butter while cheerfully answering questions about the folk whose lives they are recreating. Part of the pharmacy was moved here from Drottningholm castle; two little garden huts came from Tantolunden in Södermalm. There's a bakery (still operational, serving coffee and lunch), a bank/post office, a machine shop, botanical gardens and Hazelius' mansion, among other things. There are also 46 buildings from rural areas around Sweden, including a Sami camp, farmsteads representing several regions, a manor house and a school. A map and an excellent booklet in English are available to guide you around.

Skansen incorporates a few other museums as well, including the **Tobaks & Tändsticksmuseum** (Tobacco & Matchstick Museum; Map pp68-9; ☎ 442 80 26; 🕑 11am-5pm May-Sep; closed Mon rest of yr), which traces the history of smoking, and the more ecologically oriented **Skogens Hus** (Forestry Information Centre). The **Skansen Aquarium** (Map pp68-9; ☎ 442 8039; adult/child Skr65/35, 🕑 10am-4pm Mon-Fri, 10am-5pm Sat & Sun Sep-May, 10am-6pm Jun & Aug, 10am-8pm Jul) is also good – en route to the fish (including piranhas) you'll walk among the lemurs and see pygmy marmosets, the smallest monkeys in the world.

There are a number of cafés, restaurants and hot-dog stands throughout the park. Carrying water isn't a bad idea in summer. It's not cheating to take the escalator to the top of the hill and meander down from there.

Daily activities take place on Skansen's stages, including folk dancing in summer and an enormous public festival at midsummer. If you're in Stockholm for any of the country's major celebrations (such as Walpurgis Night, Midsummer's Eve, Lucia Festival, Christmas), Skansen is the place to see how Swedes celebrate. See p315 for more information on these events.

VASAMUSEET

A good-humoured glorification of some dodgy calculation, **Vasamuseet** (map pp68-9; ☎ 51 95 48 00; www.vasamuseet.se; adult/child Skr80/free, Wed 5-8pm Skr60; 🕑 9.30am-7pm Jun-Aug, 10am-5pm & 10am-8pm Wed Sep-May) lets you study the lives of 17th-century sailors while appreciating some brilliant achievements in marine archaeology. On 10 August 1628, within minutes of being launched, the top-heavy flagship *Vasa* overturned and went straight to the bottom of Saltsjön. Tour guides explain the extraordinary and controversial 300-year story of its death and resurrection. After being painstakingly raised in 1961, the ship and its incredible wooden sculptures were pieced together like a giant jigsaw. Almost all of what you see today is original.

On the entrance level, there's a model of the ship at scale 1:10 and a cinema that shows a 25-minute film covering topics not included in the exhibitions (in English at 11.30am and 1.30pm daily in summer). There are three other levels of exhibits, including displays of artefacts salvaged from *Vasa*, exhibits on naval warfare and 17th-century sailing and navigation plus sculpture and temporary exhibitions.

The bookshop is worth a visit and there's also a restaurant. Guided tours are in English hourly from 10.30am in summer, and at least twice daily the rest of the year. You'll need a couple of hours to appreciate the place.

GRÖNA LUND TIVOLI

The crowded **Gröna Lund Tivoli** (Map pp68-9; ☎ 58 75 01 00; www.gronalund.com in Swedish; adult/child Skr50/free; 🕑 noon-11pm Sat-Thu, noon-midnight Fri & Sat, May–mid-Sep; noon-11pm most days mid-Jun–mid-Aug) fun park has more than 25 rides, ranging from the easy circus carousel to the terrifying Free Fall, where you drop from a height of 80m in six seconds (there's a lovely, if brief, view over Stockholm at the top). There are lots of places to eat and drink in the park, but whether you'll keep it down is another matter entirely. The Åkbandet day pass gives unlimited rides, or individual rides range from Skr20 to Skr60. Big-name concerts are often staged here in summer. Admission is free for Stockholm Card or 72-hour SL Tourist Card holders.

OTHER SIGHTS

The enormous, impressive **Nordiska Museet** (National Museum of Cultural History; Map pp68-9; ☎ 51 95 60 00; www.nordiskamuseet.se; Djurgårdsvägen 6-16; admission free; 🕑 11am-5pm Jun-Aug, 10am-4pm rest of yr) was also founded by Artur Hazelius. The second-largest indoor space in Sweden, it's housed in an eclectic, Renaissance-style castle. There are notable temporary exhibitions and endless Swedish collections from 1520 to the present day, with a total of 1.5 million items, including the world's largest collection of paintings by August Strindberg. Those who want to delve more deeply into the collection can borrow a free CD player with several hours of English commentary.

The museum hosts several interesting temporary displays, but the high point for visitors is the rare and superb **Sami exhibition** in the basement. Look for the extraordinary 1767 drawing of a Sami castrating a reindeer…with his teeth! There's also a whole section on the various uses of reindeer entrails in both spells and recipes.

The intriguing 'small object exhibition' includes a duchess' silver-lined toilet paper. Other exhibitions include fashion from the 17th to 20th centuries, the table exhibition (running continuously since 1955), Swedish traditions and national costume, and furniture.

Junibacken (Map pp68-9; ☎ 58 72 30 00; adult/child Skr95/70; 🕑 9am-7pm Jul, 10am-5pm Tue-Fri, 9am-6pm Sat-Mon Jun & Aug, 10am-5pm Tue-Fri, 9am-6pm Sat & Sun Jan-May & Sep-Dec) re-creates the fantasy scenes of Astrid Lindgren's children books, stir the imaginations of children and the memories of adults familiar with her characters – chiefly Pippi Longstocking. You'll go on a 10-minute train journey past miniature landscapes, fly over Stockholm observing historical Swedish scenes and traditions, and pass through houses. It's a professional and rather unusual form of entertainment.

Prins Eugens Waldemarsudde (Map pp68-9; ☎ 54 58 37 00; Prins Eugens väg 6; adult/child Skr80/free; 🕑 11am-5pm Tue-Sun), at the southern tip of Djurgården, is a favourite destination for locals, especially in good weather. The palace once belonged to the painter prince, who favoured art over typical royal pleasures. In addition to Eugen's own work, it holds his large collection of Nordic paintings and sculpture. The palace buildings and galleries, connected by tunnels, are surrounded by picturesque gardens and an old windmill, making for a rather idyllic outing.

On the northern side of Djurgården, **Rosendals Slott** (Map pp68-9; ☎ 402 61 30; Rosendalsvägen; adult/child Skr50/25; tours 🕑 noon, 1pm, 2pm, 3pm Tue-Sun) was built as a palace for Karl XIV Johan in the 1820s, and features sumptuous royal furnishings. Admission is by guided tour only. While you're out this way, be sure to stop in the delightful café, which is set among trees and greenhouses and is very popular with the locals.

Thielska Galleriet (Map pp68-9; ☎ 662 58 84; Sjötullsbacken; bus 69 from Centralstationen; adult/child Skr50/free; 🕑 noon-4pm Mon-Sat, 1-4pm Sun), found at the east end of Djurgården, has Ernest Thiel's notable collection of late 19th- and early 20th-century Nordic art, including works by Edvard Munch, Anders Zorn, Bruno Liljefors and Carl Larsson.

Liljevalchs Konsthall (Map pp68-9; ☎ 50 83 13 30; Djurgårdsvägen 60; adult/child Skr50/free; 🕑 11am-5pm Tue-Sun, until 8pm Tue & Thu Sep-May) has four exhibitions a year of contemporary Swedish and international art, including the popular Spring Salon.

Other minor museums around Djurgården include the charmingly dusty, 1893 **Biologiskamuseet** (Museum of Biology; Map pp68-9; ☎ 442 82 15; Hazeliusporten; adult/child Skr30/10; 🕑 11am-4pm Apr-Sep, noon-3pm Tue-Fri & 10am-3pm Sat & Sun rest of yr) and **Aquaria Vattenmuseum** (Map pp68-9; ☎ 660 49 40; Falkenbergsgatan 2; adult/child Skr70/35; 🕑 10am-6pm Jun-Aug, 10am-4.30pm Tue-Sun rest of yr), a pleasant, conservation-themed aquarium.

Skeppsholmen

Moderna Museet (Modern Museum; map pp68-9; ☎ 51 95 52 00; Exercisplan 4; www.modernamuseet.se; admission free; 🕑 10am-8pm Tue-Wed, 10am-6pm Thu-Sun) houses a fine collection of modern art, including paintings, sculpture, videos and photographs. The building itself has recently undergone a renovation (partly due to mould problems) and looks sparkling new. The attached bookstore is heaven for bibliophiles. There's an upstairs restaurant, a tea shop and a chic 1st-floor coffee shop, all rather upscale.

The adjoining **Arkitekturmuseet** (Museum of Architecture; ☎ 58 72 70 00; Exercisplan 4; www.arkitekturmuseet.se; admission free; 🕑 10am-8pm Tue-Wed,

10am-6pm Thu-Sun) is housed in an equally extraordinary space and has displays on Swedish and international architecture, with a permanent exhibition covering 1000 years of Swedish architecture and an archive of 2.5 million documents, photographs, plans, drawings and models. Ask at the information desk about architectural tours of Stockholm.

Across the bridge from Nationalmuseum, **Östasiatiska Museet** (Museum of Far Eastern Antiquities; Map pp68-9; ☎ 51 95 57 50; admission free; ⏲ 11am-8pm Tue, 11am-5pm Wed-Sun) displays ancient and contemporary ceramics, paintings and sculpture. The museum has one of the best collections of Chinese art, stoneware and porcelain in the world, mainly from the Song, Ming and Qing dynasties.

Svensk Form Design Centre (Map pp68-9; ☎ 463 31 34; Holmamiralens väg 2; adult/child Skr20/free; ⏲ noon-7pm Tue-Thu, noon-5pm Fri-Sun) has design exhibitions and a shop. The centre also produces the excellent magazine *Form*, a good primer on current trends and artists, available at newsstands and design shops around town.

Ladugårdsgärdet

The vast parkland of Ladugårdsgärdet is part of the 27-sq-km **Ekoparken** (www.ekoparken.com), the world's first national park within a city. Ekoparken is 14km long and stretches far into the northern suburbs of Stockholm. This section of it, reached by bus 69 from Centralstationen or Sergels Torg, boasts three fine museums and one of the city's most panoramic views.

Sjöhistoriska Museet (National Maritime Museum; Map pp68-9; ☎ 51 95 49 00; Djurgårdsbrunnsvägen 24; admission free; ⏲ 10am-5pm Tue-Sun, until 8:30pm Tue in spring & autumn) has an exhibit of maritime memorabilia and more than 1500 model ships. Displays also cover Swedish shipbuilding, sailors and life on board.

Get your robot fix at **Tekniska Museet** (Museum of Science & Technology; map pp68-9; ☎ 450 56 00; Museivägen 7; adult/child Skr60/30; ⏲ 10am-5pm Mon-Fri, 11am-5pm Sat & Sun), just around the corner from the maritime museum. It has exhaustive exhibits on Swedish inventions and their applications, including everything from motorbikes to mobile phones.

Etnografiska Museet (National Museum of Ethnography; map pp68-9; ☎ 51 95 50 00; Djurgårdsbrunnsvägen 34; admission free; ⏲ 10am-5pm, 10am-8pm Wed) has excellent displays on various aspects of non-European cultures, including several temporary exhibitions each year. The café is a treat, with great music, imported sweets and beverages, and authentically prepared foods from around the world.

About 500m from the museums is the 155m **Kaknästornet** (Kaknäs TV tower; Map pp68-9; ☎ 667 21 80; adult/child Skr30/15; ⏲ 9am-10pm May-Aug, 10am-9pm Sep-Apr), the automatic operations centre for radio and TV broadcasting in Sweden. It opened in 1967 and is still the tallest building in the city. There's a small visitor centre on the ground floor and an **observation deck** and restaurant near the top, both of which provide stellar 360-degree views. There are guided tours at 2pm and 4pm.

Långholmen

This small island in the Mälaren lake once housed a prison, and **Långholmens Fängelsemuseum** (Prison Museum; Map p80; ☎ 668 0500; adult/child Skr25/10; ⏲ 11am-4pm) occupies one of the old building's cells – the rest of the grounds has been converted into a hotel and STF hostel (see p89). The displays here cover 250 years of prison history.

To get to Långholmen, take the metro to Hornstull, then walk along Långholmsgatan. There are some very pleasant picnic and bathing spots on the island.

Södermalm

Known as the quirky, funky island, Söder is home to several galleries, design collectives, secondhand shops, and notable bars and restaurants, as well as some important museums.

Stockholms Stadsmuseum (City museum; Map p80; ☎ 50 83 16 00; Slussen; adult/child Skr60/free; ⏲ 11am-5pm Tue-Sun, 11am-8pm Thu) is housed in the late-17th-century palace of Nicodemus Tessin the Elder, in Ryssgården. Exhibits cover the history of the city and its people, and it's worth a visit once you develop a romantic attachment to Stockholm.

Spårvägsmuseet (Transport Museum; map pp68-9; ☎ 462 55 31; Tegelviksgatan 22; adult/child Skr30/15, incl Leksaksmuseet; ⏲ 10am-5pm Mon-Fri, noon-4pm Sat & Sun), in the Söderhallen transport depot near the Viking Line terminal, has around 40 vehicles, including horse-drawn carriages, Stockholm metro trains, vintage trams and buses.

Newly reopened and sharing an entrance with Spårvägsmuseet, **Leksaksmuseet** (Toy Museum; Map pp68-9; ☎ 641 61 00; Tegelviksgatan 22; ⏲ 10am-5pm Mon-Fri, noon-4pm Sat & Sun) is an

CENTRAL STOCKHOLM

0 300 m
0 0.2 miles

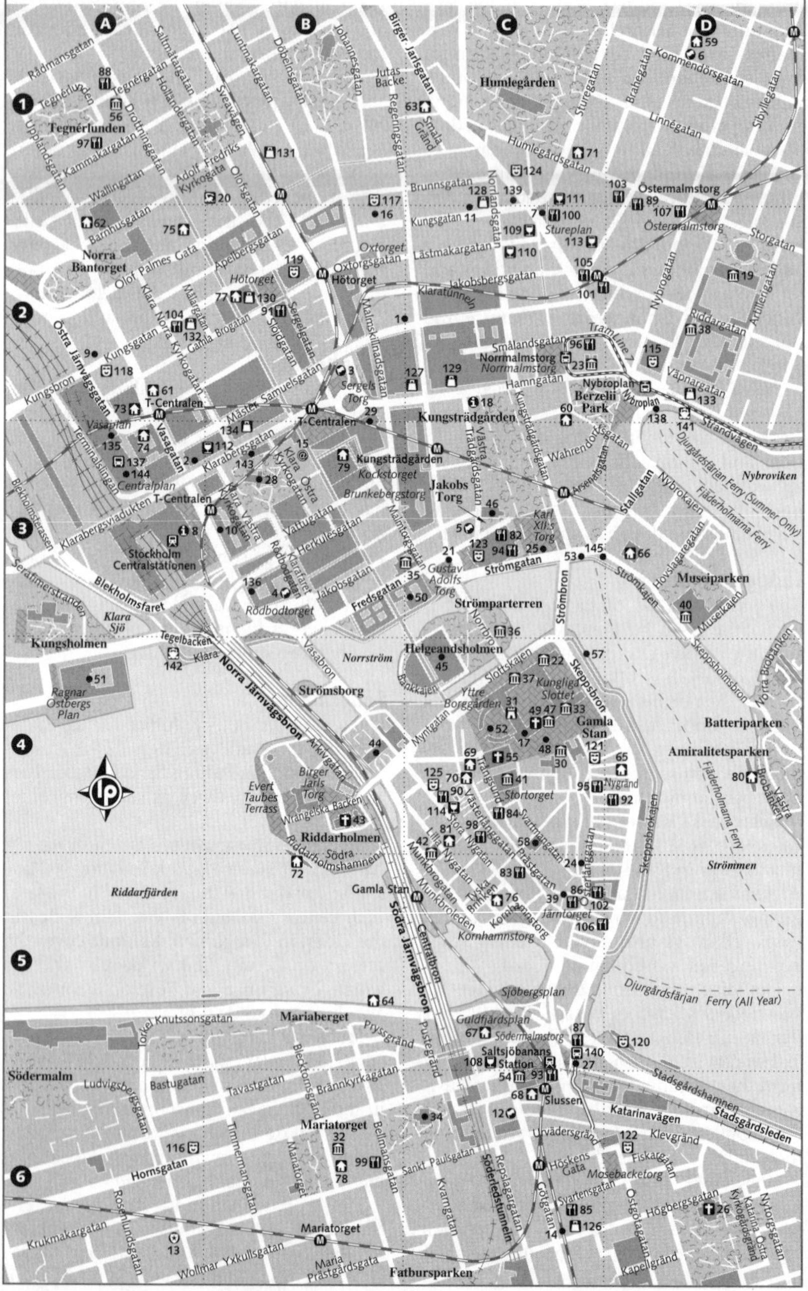

INFORMATION
Access IT .... (see 29)
Akademibokhandeln 1 B2
Apoteket CW Scheele 2 A3
Australian Embassy 3 B2
Canadian Embassy 4 B3
Danish Embassy 5 C3
Forex .... (see 8)
Forex .... (see 18)
French Embassy 6 D1
Hedengrens 7 C2
Hotellcentralen 8 A3
Kartbutiken 9 A2
Kartcentrum 10 B3
Kilroy Travels 11 C2
Konst-ig .... (see 29)
Matrix .... (see 130)
Netherlands Embassy 12 C6
Police Station 13 A6
Post Office .... (see 8)
Press Stop 14 C6
Pressbyrån .... (see 8)
Robert's Coffee 15 B3
STA 16 B2
Sweden Bookshop 17 C4
Sweden House 18 C2

SIGHTS & ACTIVITIES
Armémuseum 19 D2
Centralbadet 20 B1
City Sightseeing 21 C3
Gustav III:s Antikmuseum 22 C4
Hallwylska Museet 23 C2
Ice Gallery 24 C5
Karl XII Statue 25 C3
Katarina Kyrka 26 D6
Katarinahissen 27 C5
Klara Kyrka 28 B3
Kulturhuset 29 B2
Kungliga Myntkabinettet 30 C4
Kungliga Slottet (Royal Palace) 31 C4
Leksaksmuseet 32 B6
Livrustkammaren 33 C4
Maria Magdalena Kyrka 34 C6
Medelhavsmuseet 35 C3
Medeltidsmuseet 36 C3
Museum Tre Kronor 37 C4
Musikmuseet 38 D2
Mårten Trotzigs Gränd 39 C5
Nationalmuseum 40 D3
Nobelmuseet 41 C4
Postmuseum 42 C4
Riddarholmskyrkan 43 B4
Riddarhuset 44 B4
Riksdagshuset 45 C4
Sankt Jakobs Kyrka 46 C3
Skattkammaren 47 C4
Slottsbacken Obelisk 48 C4
Slottskyrkan 49 C4
Sophia Albertina Palace 50 C3
Stadshuset 51 A4
State Apartments Entrance 52 C4
Stockholm Sightseeing 53 C3
Stockholms Stadsmuseum 54 C6
Storkyrkan 55 C4
Strindbergsmuseet 56 A1
Svea Viking 57 C4
Tyska Kyrkan 58 C4

SLEEPING
A&Be Hotel 59 D1
Berns Hotel 60 C2
Central Hotel 61 A2
City Backpackers 62 A2
Crystal Plaza Hotel 63 C1
Den Röda Båten - Mälaren/Ren 64 B5
First Hotel Reisen 65 D4
Grand Hôtel Stockholm 66 D3
Hilton Stockholm Slussen 67 C5
Hotel Anno 1647 .... 68 C6
Lady Hamilton Hotel 69 C4
Lord Nelson Hotel 70 C4
Lydmar Hotel 71 C1
Mälardrottningen 72 B5
Nordic Light Hotel 73 A2
Nordic Sea Hotel 74 A3
Queen's Hotel 75 A2
Rica City Hotel Gamla Stan 76 C5
Rica City Hotel Kungsgatan 77 B2
Rival Hotel 78 B6
Scandic Hotel Sergel Plaza 79 B3
Vandrarhem af Chapman & Skeppsholmen 80 D4
Victory Hotel 81 C4

EATING
Bakfickan 82 C3
Bistro Boheme .... (see 75)
Café Art 83 C5
Chokladkoppen 84 C4
Coop Konsum .... (see 87)
Crêperie Fyra Knop 85 C6
Den Gyldene Freden 86 C5
Franska Matsalen .... (see 66)
Gondolen 87 C5
Grill 88 A1
Grodan Grev Ture 89 D1
Hemköp .... (see 134)
Hermitage 90 C4
Hötorgshallen 91 B2
Källaren Diana 92 D4
Leijontornet .... (see 81)
Nystekt Strömming 93 C6
Operakällaren 94 C3
Pontus in the Greenhouse 95 C4
Restaurant KB 96 C2
Sabai Sabai 97 A1
Siam Thai 98 C4
Soda 99 B6
Sturehof 100 C2
Sturekatten 101 C2
Sundbergs Konditori 102 C5
Tures 103 D1
Verandan .... (see 66)
Vetekatten 104 A2
Vivo T-Jarlen 105 C2
Zum Franziskaner 106 C5
Örtagården .... (see 107)
Östermalms Saluhall 107 D2

DRINKING
Akkurat 108 C5
Berns Salonger .... (see 60)
East 109 C2
Halv Trappa Plus Gård 110 C2
Icebar .... (see 74)
Lydmar Hotel Lounge .... (see 71)
Sturecompagniet 111 C1
Systembolaget 112 B3
Systembolaget 113 C2
Wirströms 114 C4

ENTERTAINMENT
Dramaten 115 D2
Folkoperan 116 A6
Glenn Miller Café 117 B1
Jazzclub Fasching 118 A2
Konserthuset 119 B2
Lady Patricia 120 D5
Mandus 121 C4
Mosebacke Etablissement 122 D6
Operan 123 C3
Spy Bar 124 C1
Stampen 125 C4
Stockholms Stadsteatern .... (see 29)

SHOPPING
DesignTorget .... (see 29)
DesignTorget 126 C6
Hennes & Mauritz 127 C2
Naturkompaniet 128 C1
NK Department Store 129 C2
PUB Department Store 130 B2
Svensk Hemslöjd 131 B1
Svenskt Hantverk 132 A2
Svenskt Tenn 133 D2
Åhléns Department Store 134 B3

TRANSPORT
Arlanda Express Terminal 135 A3
Avis 136 B3
Busstop Ticket Office .... (see 137)
Centralstationen Ticket Office .... (see 8)
Cinderella Batarna .... (see 141)
Cityterminalen 137 A3
Djurgården Boats 138 D2
Silja Line Office 139 C1
Slussen Bus Terminal 140 C5
Statoil .... (see 10)
Strömma Kanalbolaget Boats 141 D2
Strömma Kanalbolaget Boats to Drottningholm & Birka 142 A4
Swebus Express .... (see 137)
Tallink Office 143 B3
Viking Line Office 144 A3
Waxholmsbolaget Office 145 C3
Ybuss .... (see 137)

oversized fantasy nursery full of everything you probably ever wanted as a child, including dolls, model railways, planes and cars. Children will enjoy themselves in the playroom and at the children's theatre.

Head to the northern cliffs of Södermalm for good views and evening walks among the old houses. Some interesting neighbourhoods lie around the **Katarina kyrka** (Map p80), in the park near **Sofia kyrka** (Map pp68–9), around the **Puckeln Shop District** (Hornsgatan) and on Lotsgatan and Fjällgatan, not far from the Viking Line terminal.

You'll get great views from the balcony of **Katarinahissen** (Map p80; ☎ 743 13 95; Slussen; adult/child Skr5/free; 🕑 7.30am-10pm Mon-Sat, 10am-10pm Sun), a lift dating from the 1930s that takes you up 38m to the heights of Slussen. If you prefer, zigzagging wooden stairs also lead up the cliffs to the balcony. At the top is one of the city's best restaurants, Gondolen.

Northern Suburbs

The areas just north of the city centre are full of green, open spaces. Several large parks, spanning from Djurgården in the south, form **Ekoparken** (see p79), the first such protected city area in the world. The less wild, more sculpted **Hagaparken** is also particularly pleasant for walks and bicycle tours and contains some interesting attractions.

MILLESGÅRDEN

Well worth the effort to reach it, beautiful **Millesgården** (Map p105; ☎ 446 75 94; Carl Milles väg 2, Lidingö island; adult/child Skr80/free, 🕑 11am-5pm mid-May-Sep, noon-5pm Tue-Sun Oct–mid-May, until 8pm Thu all yr) was the home and studio of sculptor Carl Milles, an interesting character whose sleek, delicate water sprites and other distinctive sculptures can be seen all over Stockholm. The grounds include a modern gallery for changing exhibitions of contemporary artwork, Milles' elaborately Pompeiian house, and a beautiful outdoor sculpture garden where items from ancient Greece, Rome, medieval times and the Renaissance intermingle with Milles' own work. There's also a museum shop and a café. Take the metro to Ropsten, then bus 207.

NATURHISTORISKA RIKSMUSEET & COSMONOVA

The extensive **Naturhistoriska Riksmuseet** (National Museum of Natural History; map p105; ☎ 51 95 40 40; www.nrm.se; Frescativägen 40; metro T-Universitetet; admission free; 🕑 10am-7pm Tue, Wed & Fri, 10am-8pm Thu, 11am-7pm Sat & Sun) was founded by Carl von Linné in 1739. It's now Sweden's largest museum, packed with hands-on displays about nature as well as whole forests' worth of taxidermied wildlife, dinosaurs, marine life and the hardy fauna of the polar regions.

Adjoining Naturhistoriska Riksmuseet is **Cosmonova** (Map p105; ☎ 51 95 51 30; adult/child Skr75/50, no children under 5 admitted), a combined planetarium and Imax theatre. The diverse topics covered include Everest, Alaska, the oceans and outer space. It screens films on the hour; reservations are recommended.

HAGAPARKEN

Crowning a hilltop at Haga park is the amazing, brightly coloured **Koppartälten** (Copper Tent; map p105; 🕑 dawn-dusk), built in 1787 as a stable and barracks for Gustav III's personal guard. It now contains a café, restaurant and **Haga Parkmuseum** (admission free), with displays about the park, its pavilions and the royal palace, Haga slott (not open to the public).

Gustav III:s Paviljong (Gustav III's Pavilion; ☎ 402 61 30; adult/child Skr50/25 by guided tour only; 🕑 hourly noon-3pm Tue-Sun Jun-Aug) is a superb example of late neoclassical style; the furnishings and décor reflect Gustav III's interest in all things Roman after his Italian tour in 1782.

The charming **Fjärilshuset** (Butterfly House; ☎ 730 39 81; adult/child Skr70/30; 🕑 10am-4pm Tue-Fri, 11am-5:30pm Sat & Sun Apr-Sep, 10am-3pm Tue-Fri, 11am-4pm Sat & Sun Oct-Mar) has an artificial tropical environment with free-flying birds and butterflies. It's a wonderfully incongruous place to visit on a cold winter day.

To reach Hagaparken, take bus 515 from Odenplan to Haga Norra.

ULRIKSDALS SLOTT

Further north is the yellow-painted royal palace **Ulriksdal Slott** (Map p105; ☎ 402 61 30; Ulriksdals Park; guided tours adult/child Skr50/25; tours 🕑 hourly noon-3pm Tue-Sun Jun-Aug; metro T-Bergshamra, then bus 503). This large, early-17th-century building was home to King Gustaf VI Adolf and his family until 1973. Several of their attractive apartments, including the drawing room, which dates from 1923, are open to the public. The **Orangery** (adult/child Skr40/20) contains Swedish sculpture and Mediterranean plants. Queen Kristina's coronation carriage is also on show here.

Southern Suburbs

One of Stockholm's more unusual attractions is **Skogskyrkogården** (Map p105; Söckenvagen; metro to T-Skogskyrkogården; admission free), a cemetery in a peaceful pine woodland setting. The cemetery, designed by the great Gunnar Asplund and Sigurd Lewerentz, is World Heritage–listed in recognition of its unique design and the harmony of function and landscape. The area is dominated by a large granite cross, and there are a number of chapels scattered throughout, this is also where Greta Garbo is buried. It's a pleasant place for a walk.

Fjäderholmarna

These tiny, delightful islands ('Feather Islands') offer an easy escape from the city. They're just 25 minutes away by boat and a favourite swimming spot for locals. As they're located on the eastern side of Djurgården, take one of the **boats** (adult/child Skr75/35 return) that leave from either Nybroplan (half-hourly) or from Slussen (hourly) between May and early September. There are a couple of craft shops and restaurants here, though the main activity is relaxation. The last boats leave the islands at around midnight, making them a perfect spot to enjoy the long daylight hours.

ACTIVITIES

A number of activities are available in and around Stockholm, many of them water-based. Many people head for the coast and the islands of the archipelago (full of good swimming spots) or organise picnics in the parks and gardens. Summer sees both locals and visitors taking advantage of the good weather and long daylight hours to swim, sail, lounge on beaches, hike, walk or bicycle around. In winter, snowy days bring out cross-country skiers. The Tourist office can provide further details.

Swimming

There are indoor and open-air pools as well as a gym at **Eriksdalsbadet** (Map pp68-9; ☎ 50 84 02 50; Hammarby slussväg 8; entry adult/child Skr65/30) in the far south of Södermalm. If you want a relaxing swim in an extraordinary Art Nouveau bathing salon, try **Centralbadet** (Map p80; ☎ 24 24 00; Drottninggatan 88; Skr65-150; 🕒 6am-9pm Mon-Fri, 8am-9pm Sat & Sun), built in 1904. The entrance price includes access to the pool, saunas and gym; treatments, such as massage, are available for an additional fee.

Swimming is also permitted just about anywhere people can scramble their way to the water; look for happy sunbathers clinging to the rocks around Riddarfjärden for a start.

Sailing/Boating

From **Sjöcafé** (Map pp68-9; ☎ 660 57 57; canoes Skr75/300; 🕒 9am-9pm), by the bridge leading to Djurgården, you can rent bikes, in-line skates, kayaks, canoes and rowboats. Opposite is **Tvillingarnas Sjökrog** (Map pp68-9; ☎ 663 37 39; www.tvillingarnas.com in Swedish; Strandvägskajen 27), where you can rent sailing and motorboats in various sizes from April to September. Small boats are available from around Skr350 per hour; larger boats can be rented for a day, weekend or week. You can even rent a 40-foot sailing boat (with or without a skipper).

Cycling

Cycling is best in the parks and away from the busy central streets and arterial roads, but some streets have special cycle lanes (often shared with pedestrians). Bicycles can be rented from **Sjöcafé** (☎ 660 57 57; bicycles per hr/day Skr65/250). Tourist offices can supply maps of cycle routes, see p330 for further information.

Hiking & Climbing

Serious hiking trips in the city are fairly limited, but the parks offer some good walks – the most popular area for short walks is Djurgården. Climbers have better options, with around 150 cliffs within 40 minutes' drive of the city. There's also Sweden's largest indoor climbing centre, **Klätterverket** (Map pp68-9; ☎ 641 10 48; Marcusplatsen 17, Nacka; member/nonmember Skr60/80) next to the J-train Sickla stop, with around 1000 sq metres of artificial climbing.

WALKING TOUR

Stockholm is a compact city, and many of its important historical sights can be visited in a couple of hours on a walking tour.

Starting in the middle at **Centralstationen (1)**, cross Vasagatan and enter the side street Klara Vattugränd. Turn left onto Klara V Kyrkogatan, past the church **Klara kyrka (2)**, where you can get information on all of Stockholm's churches, then turn right onto

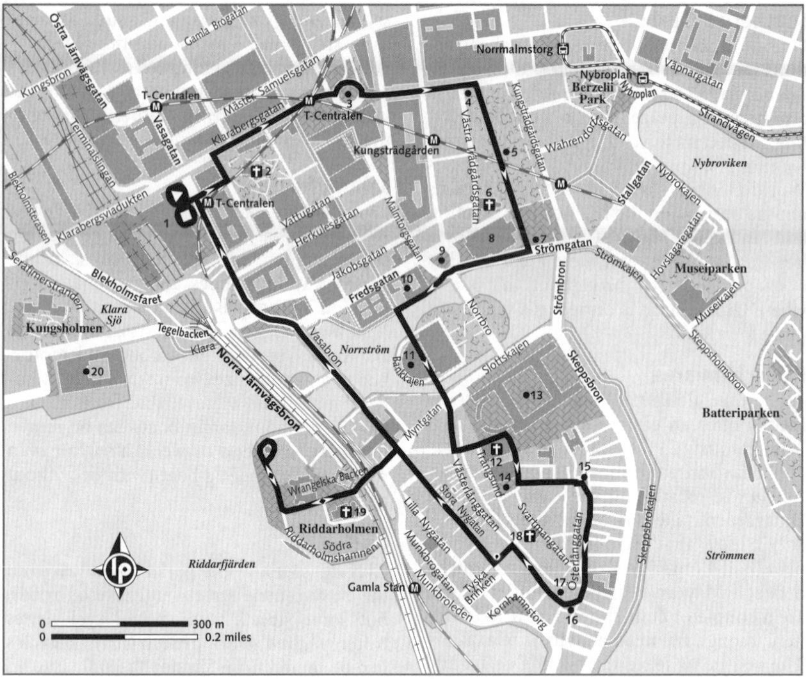

Start/Finish: Centralstationen

Distance: 3.5km

Duration: 2-3 hours

Klarabergsgatan. This is one of Stockholm's main modern shopping streets, lined with designer shops, upscale boutiques and department stores such as Åhléns.

Follow Klarabergsgatan to **Sergels Torg (3)**, where you'll see frenzied commuters, casual shoppers, and possibly a demonstration or a shady deal going down. Regular art exhibitions are held in the basement arena of **Kulturhuset (4)**, which is worth a peek. Continue a short way along Hamngatan before turning right at the tourist office (Sweden House) into the pleasant **Kungsträdgården (5)**. This park, originally the kitchen garden for the Royal Palace, is now a popular spot for relaxing in the sun during the warm half of the year, and ice-skating during the other half. The 17th-century church **Sankt Jakobs kyrka (6)** has an ornate pulpit that's worth a quick look.

Walk through the park to its southern end at **Karl XII:s Torg (7)**, where there's a statue of the warmongering king Karl XII. On your right is **Operan (8)**, the Royal Opera House (opened in 1896) and across the road you'll see the narrow strait Norrström, the freshwater outflow from Mälaren lake. Continue along the waterfront, past Operan and **Gustav Adolfs Torg (9)**, to the grandiose **Sophia Albertina Palace** (**10**; houses the Foreign Ministry), then turn left and cross the Riksbron bridge. Continue across the islet **Helgeandsholmen** (**11**; Island of the Holy Spirit), between the two parts of Sweden's parliament building, **Riksdagshuset**. After crossing over the short Stallbron bridge, you'll arrive on **Stadsholmen**, which is home to the medieval core of Stockholm.

Cross Mynttorget and follow Västerlånggatan for one block, then turn left (east) into Storkyrkobrinken to reach **Storkyrkan (12)**, the city's cathedral and oldest building. Facing the cathedral across the cobbled square is **Kungliga Slottet (13)**, the 'new' Royal Palace (see p73 for more information). Källargränd leads southward to **Stortorget (14)**, where the Stockholm Bloodbath took place in 1520.

Three sides of the square are formed by quaint tenements painted in varying earthy-toned colours; on the fourth side of the square there's **Börsen**, the Stock Exchange and Swedish Academy building, now home to an excellent museum detailing the history of the Nobel prizes and their recipients.

The narrow streets of the eastern half of Gamla Stan still wind along their medieval 14th-century lines and are linked by a fantasy of lanes, arches and stairways. Head east along Köpmangatan to the small square **Köpmantorget (15)** and the oft-photographed statue of St George and the Dragon. Turn right into **Österlånggatan** and follow it past antique shops, art galleries, handicraft outlets and **Den Gyldene Freden**, which has been serving food since 1722, until you reach **Järntorget (16)**, where metals were bought and sold in days long past. From there, keep right and turn into Västerlånggatan, looking out for **Mårten Trotzigs Gränd (17)** by No 81: this is Stockholm's narrowest lane, at less than 1m wide. Follow Prästgatan to the lavishly decorated German church, **Tyska kyrkan (18)**.

Västerlånggatan is lined with shops and boutiques selling souvenirs, and attracts dense crowds, so (unless you're desperate for an ice cream in a waffle cone) follow the quieter parallel street, Stora Nygatan, instead. At Riddarhustorget, turn left (southwest) and cross the short Riddarholmsbron bridge to **Riddarholmen** (Knights Island). The large church **Riddarholmskyrkan (19)** has an iron spire and a basement full of royal corpses. Beyond Riddarholmskyrkan, you'll come to the far side of the island, with great views across the lake to the impressive **Stadshuset** (**20**; Town Hall) and the eastern end of **Kungsholmen** (King's Island). Retrace your steps to Riddarhustorget, then turn left (northwest), cross over Vasabron and continue along Vasagatan back to Centralstationen.

STOCKHOLM FOR CHILDREN

Stockholm is a very child-friendly city. The miniature crowd is welcome in restaurants, museums and most other places their parents go. Of the museums and attractions that cater specifically to children, the can't-miss option is **Skansen** (p76), with its open-air format, petting zoo and glassblowers' workshop. **Nordiska Museet** (p78) has a children's play area in their replica of a historic village. **Junibacken** (p78) takes tykes and their parents into the strange and wonderful world of Pippi Longstocking. **Gröna Lund Tivoli** (p77) is an amusement park on the island of Djurgården, with carnival rides, games and sugary snacks. **Leksaksmuseet** (p79) is full of toys, both to look at and to play with. **Kulturhuset** (p71) is a parent's dream – you can drop off the smallest kids at Rum för Barn, and keep teens entertained with do-it-yourself art projects in the workshop at Lava. **Stadsteatern** (p100) and **Dramaten** (p99) both run children's plays regularly.

TOURS

Stockholm Sightseeing (Map p80; ☎ 58 71 40 20; www.stockholmsightseeing.com) operates frequent cruises from early April to mid-December around the central bridges and canals from Strömkajen (near the Grand Hotel), Nybroplan or Stadshusbron; you will find ticket booths at these departure points. Some of the one-hour tours are free for Stockholm Card holders, but the two-hour tour, Under the Bridges of Stockholm (Skr170), covers more territory and passes under 15 bridges and through two locks, with a recorded commentary in several languages to fill in the history of the areas you pass by.

City Sightseeing (Map p80; ☎ 58 71 40 30; www.citysightseeing.com, Gustav Adolfs Torg) is the land-based sister operation, which runs daily tours of the city departing from Gustav Adolfs Torg between April and early October. There are coach tours of the city (Skr395, 2½ hours) and walking tours around Gamla Stan (Skr90, one hour). There are also combo trips offering sightseeing by coach and boat.

There's a one-hour **English-language guided walk** (🕑 7.30pm Mon, Wed, Thu summer, 1.30pm Sat & Sun Sep-May) through Gamla Stan with an authorised guide. Meet at the Obelisk at Slottsbacken, outside the royal palace; no reservation is needed.

To go back even further in time, take a cruise in a great old wooden ship done up to resemble a Viking longboat. **Svea Viking** (Map p80; ☎ 20 22 23; www.sveaviking.se; adult/child Skr150/50) runs regular 1½ hour sightseeing cruises of the city's waterways and out into the archipelago from midsummer to the end of August. You can't miss the ship, as it's moored outside the Royal Palace.

Stockholm is one of the few cities that allows hot-air balloons to fly over it. Book a tour with **Far & Flyg** (Map p80; ☎ 645 77 00; www.farochflyg.se;

Skr1795 per person; ⌚ May-Sep) for an incredible way to appreciate Stockholm's beauty.

FESTIVALS & EVENTS

There are many festivals, concerts and other happenings on Sergels Torg and Kungsträdgården throughout the summer, and the major museums exhibit temporary exhibitions on a grand scale. *What's on Stockholm* lists daily events.

The biggest events in Stockholm are those celebrated throughout the country, such as Midsummer, Walpurgis Night, Lucia Festival, Christmas and New Year's Eve. See p315 for information on these traditional celebrations, and if you're in Stockholm at the right time, head to Skansen to participate in the festivities.

Lidingöloppet (www.lidingoloppet.se) The world's largest cross-country foot race, with 25,000 to 30,000 participants, is held in late September or early November in Lidingö, on Stockholm's outskirts.

Restaurangernas Dag In early June, Stockholm's restaurants set up tables in central Kungsträdgården and offer food, drinks and entertainment.

Stockholm International Film Festival (www.filmfestivalen.se) A major celebration of important cinema, held in November, the film fest often brings top international directors to town for speaking engagements.

Stockholm Jazz Festival (www.stockholmjazz.com) Held in mid-July, this is one of Europe's premier jazz festivals.

Stockholm Marathon (www.marathon.se) Run in June.

Stockholm Open (www.stockholmopen.se) A major international tennis tournament, held in October.

Stockholm Pride (www.stockholmpride.org) This gay and lesbian event is held annually in early August.

SLEEPING

Whether you choose youth hostels, B&Bs, big-name hotels or boutique digs, you can expect the quality of accommodation in Stockholm to be high. There's little danger you'll turn up to find your bargain-basement room is a fleapit. The trade-off is that it can be an expensive city to sleep in, but there are deals to be found. Most Stockholm hotels offer discounted rates on weekends (Friday, Saturday and often Sunday night) and in summer (from midsummer to mid-August), sometimes up to 50% off the listed price.

The handy booklet *Hotels and Youth Hostels in Stockholm*, available free from tourist offices, lists most hotels and their regular and discount rates. If you need help finding a place to stay, **Hotellcentralen** (Map p80; ☎ 508 285 08; hotels@svb.stockholm.se; inside Centralstationen; ⌚ 24hr) books accommodation for a Skr60 fee (Skr25 for hostels).

A number of agencies, including **Bed & Breakfast Service** (☎ 660 66 54; info@bedbreakfast.se; www.bedbreakfast.se) and **Bed & Breakfast Agency** (☎ 643 80 28; info@bba.nu; www.bba.nu), can arrange apartment or B&B accommodation from around Skr300 per person per night.

Stockholm has HI-affiliated STF hostels (where a membership card yields a Skr45 discount), as well as SVIF hostels and independent hostels (no membership cards required). Many have options for single, double or family rooms. Generally, you'll pay extra to use the hostel's linen; bring your own sleeping sheet to save around Skr50 per night. Many hostels have breakfast available, usually for an additional Skr50 to Skr65.

GAY & LESBIAN STOCKHOLM

The gay scene is well established in Stockholm, although Sweden's famous open-mindedness means people of every sexual orientation are welcome in any bar or club. There is no real 'gay district', although Södermalm is where a large section of the gay population lives and plays. The tourist office publishes a brochure listing popular gay venues, but probably the best source of local information is the free monthly magazine *QX*, found at many clubs, stores and restaurants around town. Its website (www.qx.se) may be more useful as it's more frequently updated.

RFSL (Map pp68-9; ☎ 736 02 12; www.rfsl.se in Swedish; Sveavägen 59), the national organisation for gay and lesbian rights, is a good source of information. In the same building is a gay bookshop, restaurant and nightclub, **Tip Top** (☎ 32 98 00).

Mandus (Map p80; ☎ 20 60 55; Österlånggatan 7) in Gamla Stan is a popular, fun gay-friendly hangout with excellent food. **Häcktet** (☎ 84 59 10; Hornsgatan 82) is a fairly casual lesbian hangout in an old country manor.

The **Lady Patricia** (Map p80; ☎ 743 05 70; Stadsgårdskajen 152), a popular nightclub on board an old battleship, has frequent queer nights and drag shows every Sunday.

SOMETHING SPECIAL

Vandrarhem af Chapman & Skeppsholmen (Map p80; ☎ 463 22 66; www.stfchapman.com; adult Skr155-230, child Skr100, 2-bed room from Skr460, nonmember fee adult/child Skr45/25) The legendary af Chapman is a storied vessel that has done plenty of travelling of its own. It's now well anchored in a superb, quiet location, swaying gently in sight of the city centre off the museum island of Skeppsholmen. Bunks in dorms below decks have a nautical ambience, unsurprisingly. Staff members are friendly and knowledgeable about the city and surrounding areas. Apart from showers and toilets, all facilities are on dry land in the Skeppsholmen hostel, where you'll find a good kitchen with a laid-back common room and a separate TV lounge. Laundry facilities and 24-hour Internet access are available. Stays on the boat are normally limited to five nights from May to September. The boat section of af Chapman will be undergoing repairs from September 2004, so call to find out if it has reopened; meanwhile the adjacent Skeppsholmen hostel is taking up the slack.

Hostels tend to fill up during the late afternoon in peak summer season, so arrive early or book in advance. They can also be busy in May, when Swedish school groups typically visit the capital.

The options below are divided by neighbourhood and price range, then listed in order of author preference. Room prices are for peak season unless otherwise noted.

Gamla Stan

This atmospheric part of town has a few accommodation options that place you right in the thick of the historic Old Town, though budget travellers may be out of luck.

MIDRANGE

Lord Nelson Hotel (Map p80; ☎ 50 64 01 20; www.lord-nelson.se; Västerlånggatan 22; s/d Skr1690-1790/1990-2090, summer & weekend s/d Skr850-1050/1450-1650) Yo-ho-ho, me scurvy barnacles! It's a tight squeeze but this pink-painted, glass-fronted building with the feel of a creaky old ship, is well worth checking into. At just 5m wide, the 17th-century building is Sweden's narrowest hotel. Its nautical theme extends to brass and mahogany furnishings, antique sea-captain trappings and a model ship in each of the small rooms.

Victory Hotel (Map p80; ☎ 50 64 00 00; www.victory-hotel.se; Lilla Nygatan 5; s/d Skr1990-2190/2490-3990, summer & weekend s/d Skr1150-1350/1750-2750) This early 17th-century building is literally full of nautical antiques, grandfather clocks, model ships and art. Most rooms are fairly small, but the museum-like suites are larger. There's also an apartment available for long-term rentals.

Lady Hamilton Hotel (Map p80; ☎ 50 64 01 00; www.lady-hamilton.se; Storkyrkobrinken 5; s/d Skr1790-1990/2290-2490, summer & weekend s/d Skr950-1150/1550-1850) This is old-style luxury (with modern touches where it counts, for example in the bathrooms). The hotel dates back to the 1470s, and is packed with antiques and portraits of Lady Hamilton herself.

Mälardrottningen (Map p80; ☎ 54 51 87 80; www.malardrottningen.se; Riddarholmen; s/d cabins from Skr1100/1220) At one time the world's largest motor yacht, this place offers accommodation in very well-appointed cabins, each with en suite. The cosy vessel, launched in 1924, was previously owned by American heiress Barbara Hutton – it was a gift from her father for her 18th birthday!

Rica City Hotel Gamla Stan (Map p80; ☎ 723 72 50; www.rica.se in Norwegian & Swedish; Lilla Nygatan 25; s/d Skr1695-1895/1945-2045, summer & weekend s/d Skr950-1050/1490-1590) This 17th-century waterfront building has been a hostel and a Salvation Army headquarters. Its 51 rooms are pretty small, and despite the location none have a view of the water, but it's a classy place with unfussy Gustavian décor and good service. The hotel couldn't be better situated for soaking up the history and atmosphere of Gamla Stan; it's also in a prime spot for checking out Södermalm and the city centre.

TOP END

First Hotel Reisen (Map p80; ☎ 22 32 60; reisen@firsthotels.com; Skeppsbron 12; s/d Skr2199/2599, summer & weekend s/d Skr1258/1498) Stockholm's oldest hotel, the Reisen in olden days buzzed with sailors sipping coffee. The eight-storey waterfront building still has a distinct seafaring atmosphere. Rooms in this luxurious hotel feature exposed brick walls and dark wood panelling, wooden floors and sumptuous furnishings.

Central Stockholm

This part of town is the most convenient to Centralstationen, where most visitors first arrive.

BUDGET

City Backpackers (Map p80; ☎ 20 69 20; info@citybackpackers.se; Upplandsgatan 2A; dm from Skr190) The closest hostel to Centralstationen is City Backpackers, and it's a good choice for the clean rooms, friendly staff and excellent facilities including a kitchen, sauna, laundry and free Internet access.

Hostel Bed & Breakfast (Map p80; ☎ 15 28 38; hostelbedandbreakfast@chello.se; Rehnsgatan 21; dm/s/d Skr195/390/430) Near T-Rådmansgatan, north of the city centre, this is a pleasant, informal basement hostel with a kitchen and laundry. There's also a large, backpacker-friendly summer annexe here, with 40 dorm beds (Skr135).

MIDRANGE

Rex Hotel (Map pp68-9; ☎ 16 00 40; www.rexhotel.se; Luntmakargatan 73; s/d Skr900-1450/1450-1690, summer & weekend s/d Skr800-890/990-1090) This new hotel has recently taken shape in a renovated building, dating from 1866. It's comfortable, functional, and beautifully designed without being pretentious, pine floors, natural-tone fabrics and no unnecessary flourishes. And the location is one of Stockholm's most up-and-coming.

Queen's Hotel (Map p80; ☎ 24 94 60; queenshotel@queenshotel.se; Drottninggatan 71A; s/d Skr750-1390/795-1490, summer & weekend s/d Skr750-1250/795-1350) The Queen's Hotel is a pleasant place to stay in the middle of town. It has comfortable rooms with either shared or private facilities in an early 20th-century building on the pedestrian mall. There's also a marble staircase and an antique lift.

Central Hotel (Map p80; ☎ 56 62 08 00; bokning@centralhotel.se; Vasagatan 38; s/d Skr1625/1860, weekends s/d 995/1295) Central Hotel caters primarily to the business traveller, but it has comfortable small rooms, a good location and decent summer discounts, plus a pleasant glass-roofed breakfast area.

TOP END

Nordic Light Hotel (p80; ☎ 50 56 30 00; www.nordiclighthotel.com; Vasaplan 7; s/d Skr2500-3400/2900-3600, weekends s/d from Skr1290/1590, summer s/d from Skr1090/1390) Walking into the Nordic Light means getting an object lesson in modern Scandinavian design. In the rooms, which are equipped to the hilt with all the comforts you'd expect in a top 'design hotel', the typical ocean-view paintings or abstract artwork on the walls have been replaced with individual, specially designed light exhibits, which guests can adjust to suit their mood.

Nordic Sea Hotel (Map p80; ☎ 50 56 30 00; www.nordicseahotel.com; Vasaplan 2-4; s/d Skr1290-3400/2400-3600, summer & weekend s/d from Skr690/1190) This sister hotel to the slightly more upscale and smaller Nordic Light has an impressive 9000L aquarium in the foyer. Its bar is the famous Icebar, built entirely of ice, where you can throw on a parka and mittens and drink chilled vodka concoctions out of little glasses made of ice.

Scandic Hotel Sergel Plaza (Map p80; ☎ 51 72 63 00; www.scandic-hotels.se; Brunkebergstorg 9; s/d from Skr1700/2200, weekends s/d from Skr1150/1250) Situated just off Sergels Torg, this enormous beast of a hotel caters for upscale business travellers, shoppers and the occasional fan of Stalinist architecture. It has more than 400 rooms and impeccable (if you're into that sort of thing) 1980's-era décor.

Rica City Hotel Kungsgatan (Map p80; ☎ 723 72 20; info.kungsgatan@rica.se; Kungsgatan 47; s/d Skr1650-1885/1900-2135, summer & weekend s/d Skr895-995/1345-1445) This will be right up your alley if you're in town to shop. It offers very comfortable rooms in the same block as the PUB department store (where Greta Garbo started her working career). The rooms have burnished wooden floors, tall windows and that typically Scandinavian brand of beautifully crisp, cream-and-beige furnishings in the kind of natural materials that make you feel like you're sleeping in tofu.

Grand Hotel Stockholm (Map p80; ☎ 679 35 00; www.grandhotel.se; Södra Blasieholmshamnen 8; s/d Skr2400-4100/3600-4500) This is where the literati, glitterati and other, more traditional nobility stay when they're in Stockholm. A waterfront landmark, with several exclusive restaurants and a surprisingly comfortable, yet very posh piano bar, this hotel may be the city's most sumptuous lodgings. Some rooms are in the royal Gustavian style, others are intriguing traditional/modern mixes. Room No 701 has a unique tower with a 360 degree view; No 702 is the astounding Nobel Room, where the literature prize-winner stays overnight.

Berns Hotel (Map p80; ☎ 56 63 22 00; www.berns.se; Näckströmsgatan 8; s/d Skr2200-3800/2800-4100) Rooms in this modern hotel, all equipped with CD players, range from 19th-century classical to the latest styles, making the utmost use of marble and lots of dark wood. The attached restaurant and series of bars, dating from 1863, is one of the grandest in the city.

Östermalm

This central neighbourhood is home to most of the city's upscale, exclusive boutiques, many of its finest restaurants, a huge number of excellent museums and some thumping nightlife. There's a good range of accommodation options too, from friendly hostels to top-of-the-line design hotels.

BUDGET

Backpackers Inn (Map pp68-9; ☎ 660 75 15; www.backpackersinn.se; Banérgatan 56; metro T-Karlaplan; dm from Skr130; late-Jun–mid-Aug) The STF Backpackers Inn, located in a fairly modern school building (during the summer holidays only), has 260 beds in seven-bunk classrooms and 40 beds in four-bed family rooms.

Östra Reals Vandrarhem (Map pp68-9; ☎ 664 11 14; www.ostrareal.com; Karlavägen 79; dm from Skr135; mid-Jun–mid-Aug) You'll feel like a naughty orphan sleeping in the austere dorms at this tremendous old-fashioned school building, dating from 1911. Rooms are basic, but common areas are large and comfortable, and have lots of atmosphere, with high ceilings and exposed-brick walls.

MIDRANGE

Birger Jarl Hotel (Map pp68-9; ☎ 674 18 00; www.birgerjarl.se; Tulegatan 8; s/d Skr1695-2150/2040-2450, summer & weekend s/d Skr990-1295/1195-1795) One of Stockholm's flagship design hotels, the Birger Jarl is a constant work-in-progress. Its overall style reflects its origin in the '70s, but each year the hotel brings in new Swedish designers to add or adjust an element of its interior décor. Even the 'standard' rooms are nicely in keeping with the prevailing sleek, modern Scandinavian aesthetic. Whichever room you end up in, it's worth asking if there are others open that you can peek into.

A&Be Hotell (Map p80; ☎ 660 21 00; www.abehotel.com; Grev Turegatan 50; s/d Skr490-790/590-890) Staying in this small, pretty, old-fashioned hotel is like crashing with an elderly aunt – flowery couches, anonymous portraits of the aristocracy, potted plants and lampshades galore. It's comfy but not fussy.

Crystal Plaza Hotel (Map p80; ☎ 406 88 00; www.crystalplazahotel.se; Birger Jarlsgatan 35; s/d Skr1525-1825/2025-2325, summer & weekend rates s/d Skr850-1050/1250-1550) With an impressive eight-storey tower, neoclassical columns and classical-style artwork, this wonderful hotel, housed in an 1895 building, offers both old-fashioned and modern rooms with excellent facilities.

TOP END

Lydmar Hotel (Map p80; ☎ 56 61 13 00; www.lydmar.se; Sturegatan 10; s/d from Skr1500/2400, weekends from Skr1280) Frequented by the seriously hip, this is a 'concept hotel' with the main concept being musical – elevators have 10 choices of soundtrack, touring bands often stay here, and there's live music in the lounge most nights. Rooms are stylishly decorated, and categorized by clothing sizes – from S to XXL – each with its own cutting-edge design. But you won't need to spend too much time there when so much is going on downstairs. The chic lounge is always packed with artistic-looking fashion slaves checking each other out mercilessly.

Djurgården

There's only one hotel on the pretty green island of Djurgården, but it's a doozy.

Scandic Hotel Hasselbacken (Map pp68-9; ☎ 51 73 43 00; hasselbacken@scandic-hotels.com; Hazeliusbacken 20; s/d from Skr1790/2090, weekends from Skr1490) It's hard to imagine a lovelier setting for a stay in Stockholm than this 1925 building on a slope overlooking the amusement park Gröna Lund. The hotel's plush amenities (saunas, satellite TV) and its location on Djurgården round out the luxurious-retreat experience. There's a top-notch restaurant attached, and the lounge has live music most nights.

Långholmen

BUDGET

Långholmen Hotell & Vandrarhem (Map pp68-9; ☎ 668 05 10; www.langholmen.com; hostel dm member/nonmember Skr205/250, children Skr105/130, s cell Skr390/480, 2-bed cell Skr248/293, hotel s/d Skr995-1240/1240-1540, weekend/summer discounts available) Guests at this hotel/hostel, in a former prison on the small island of Långholmen, sleep in bunks in a cell. The friendly, efficient staff members assure you they will not lock you in. There are good kitchen and laundry facilities, and the restaurant serves meals all day. The pun-tastic website talks about the hostel's 'strong convictions' and asserts that it is 'captivating'.

Södermalm

Södermalm, a 15-minute walk or quick subway ride from the Viking Line boats and Centralstationen, is the best bet for interesting budget or midrange accommodation. At the other end of the spectrum, it's also home to the chic new Clarion.

BUDGET

Zinkensdamm Hotell & Vandrarhem (Map pp68-9; ☎ 616 81 00; www.zinkensdamm.com; Zinkens väg 20; hostel dm from Skr185, s without bathroom from Skr440, hotel s/d Skr1240/1540, summer & weekend s/d Skr890/1190) With a foyer that looks like one of those old Main Street façade re-creations you find in cheesy museums, the Zinkensdamm STF is unabashedly about playtime. It's attractive and well equipped – complete with a zany, pink-and-white guest kitchen – and caters for families with kids as well as pub-going backpackers, so it can be crowded and noisy, but that's the trade-off for fun. The hostel breakfast buffet isn't spectacular, but hostellers can buy the much better hotel breakfast.

Den Röda Båten – Mälaren/Ran (Map p80; ☎ 644 43 85; www.theredboat.com; Söder Malärstrand, Kajplats 6; dm Skr195-230, d Skr490-595) 'The Red Boat' is a hotel and hostel on two vessels, Mälaren and Ran. The hostel section is the cosiest of Stockholm's floating accommodations, thanks to lots of dark wood, nautical memorabilia and friendly staff. Hotel-standard rooms are also excellent.

MIDRANGE

Rival Hotel (Map p80; ☎ 54 57 89 00; www.rival.se; Mariatorget 3; s Skr1990-2740, double Skr2290-3040, weekend s/d Skr1190/1340) An exciting place that provides a great example of cohesive design, the Rival is the brainchild of ABBA's Benny Andersson and two other backers. Retro architecture pervades the building. Each room is decorated with posters from great Swedish films and comes with a teddy bear to make guests feel more at home. The complex, which sits at the edge of the lovely, tree-lined Mariatorget, includes a vintage 1940s movie theatre with an adorable foyer which sparkles like a red jewel. There's a good café and bakery adjoining the theatre, and on the opposite side is a nice lounge. The swank cocktail bar is pure over-the-top Art Deco. Several rooms have views over the square.

Hotel Tre Små Rum (Map pp68-9; ☎ 641 23 71; www.tresmarum.se; Högbergsgatan 81; rooms without bathrooms Skr695) Rooms have been added over the years, so the hotel belies its name (Three Small Rooms) and now has seven, but the charm of this quaint 18th-century hotel in a quiet district of Södermalm hasn't been diluted. With its rough-hewn vanilla-coloured walls, Italian-style décor, high ceilings and wooden floors, it's one of the nicest hotels in Stockholm.

Columbus Hotell (Map pp68-9; ☎ 50 31 12 00; www.columbus.se; Tjärhovsgatan 11; s/d Skr950-1250/1250-1550, summer & weekend s/d Skr695-950/895-1250; rooms in budget annex s/d/tr Skr695/895/1095) This highly recommended place is in a quiet part of Södermalm, near T-Medborgarplatsen, and is set around a cobblestone courtyard by a pretty park. As well as the budget rooms (which have TV, telephone and shared bathroom facilities), there are classy hotel-standard rooms.

Hotel Anno 1647 (Map p80; ☎ 442 16 80; www.anno1647.se; Mariagränd 3; s/d Skr1495-1795/1695-2295, summer & weekend s/d Skr850-1295/1050-1595) This historical building has labyrinthine hallways and a range of rooms, most with private modern bathrooms and wooden floors. Some rooms have tiled Swedish stoves, toilets with chains, chandeliers or rococo wallpaper.

TOP END

Clarion Hotel (Map pp68-9; ☎ 462 10 00; www.clarionstockholm.com in Swedish; Ringvägen 98; s/d Skr1895-3645/2545-3845, summer & weekend s/d Skr1195-2595/1595-2895) Entering this hip new hotel in Söder is like walking into a modern-art museum – and in fact the wide ramp leading into the foyer, dotted with stylishly uncomfortable-looking furniture, was modelled on the Tate Modern. The foyer features a huge wall mural and sculptures by Kirsten Ortwed, and the funky lounge bar next to the front desk is full of attractive, well-dressed people. Rooms are furnished with sleek chaise lounges, enormous beds with designer sheets, massive windows and the notable absence of clutter that marks out typically modern Swedish minimalist décor. It's almost too much, but it's unarguably impressive.

Scandic Hotel Malmen (Map pp68-9; ☎ 51 73 47 00; www.scandic-hotels.se, Götgatan 49-51; s/d from Skr1715/2015, weekends from Skr1015) An enormous, unbeautiful box, this functionalist building dating from 1951 is pretty on the inside. Its pleasant rooms feature the clean lines and up-to-date design typical of the Scandic chain, with a major bonus being location – the hotel is smack in the middle of Söder's vibrant nightlife. Its piano bar stays open late, so it can get obnoxiously crowded with drunken louts when nearby bars close.

Hilton Stockholm Slussen (Map p80; ☎ 51 73 53 00; www.hilton.com; Guldgränd 8; s/d from Skr1990, summer & weekend from Skr1450) Perched between the chaotic Slussen interchange and Södermalm's underground highway, Sweden's first Hilton features grand marble staircases and vast, stylish public areas. Rooms are strongly influenced by contemporary design, and foyer furniture is from the Fritz Hansen–Oxford design series.

Kungsholmen

This mostly residential and nontouristy island has one large and high-quality sleeping option.

First Hotel Amaranten (Map pp68-9; ☎ 692 52 00; www.firsthotels.com; Kungsholmsgatan 31; s/d Skr1499-2499/1899-2699; summer & weekend s/d Skr798-1348/1048-1548) The hotel equivalent of a swanky modern office building, this large complex has all the standard comforts. Rooms are decorated with typically Swedish modern design and geared to serve the business traveller; if you've left your laptop at home, you can borrow one from the front desk.

Outlying Areas

BUDGET

If things get desperate in the city, there are more than 20 hostels around the county that can be easily reached by SL buses, trains or archipelago boats within an hour or so. There are also a number of summer camping grounds, which usually offer cheap cabin accommodation as well. Some more options are mentioned in the Around Stockholm section, see p104.

Klubbensborg (Map p105; ☎ 646 12 55; Klubbensborgsvägen 27; beds from Skr180, 6-bed cabin Skr1500) This is a pleasant SVIF hostel in a gorgeous lakeside setting southwest of the city centre. There are several buildings that date from the 17th century, plus a kitchen, laundry, café and summer camping area. The downside is that it's a meandering 1km walk from the closest metro station (T-Mälarhöjden).

Bredäng Camping (Map p105; ☎ 97 70 71; bredangcamping@telia.com; Stora Sällskapets väg; sites Skr175, dm Skr150, 4-bed cabins Skr450; ⏲ mid-Apr-late Oct) This place is 10km southwest of the city centre in a pleasant lakeside location. It's well equipped and has a hostel and cabins. Take the metro to T-Bredäng, then walk 700m. If you're driving, it's well signposted from the E4/E20 motorway.

Hotel Formule 1 (Map p105; ☎ 744 20 44; Mikrofonvägen 30; metro T-Telefonplan; rooms Skr360) The Formule 1 is just about the cheapest option going, with small, uninspiring rooms that accommodate up to three people. Facilities are shared, and it's 4km southwest of town, but who can argue at that price?

TOP END

Hotel J (Map pp68-9; ☎ 601 30 00; www.hotelj.com; Ellensviksvägen 1, Nacka Strand; T-Slussen then bus 404 or 443; s/d Skr1395-2195/1795-2595, summer & weekend from Skr1150) Hotel J is a popular weekend getaway for Stockholmers, and has serious Great Gatsby overtones. The breezy blue-and-white summer house, built in 1912, is named after the boats used in the America's Cup. The scent of good-natured, nonchalant wealth wafts unmistakably through the air here. Rooms are decorated with furnishings by the hip design store R.O.O.M.

EATING

Stockholmers take their food seriously. A meal in an upscale restaurant is treated as a culinary adventure. Most restaurants in the city lean towards providing the dinnertime crowd with a unique experience – not just filling hungry bellies. As much fun as this can be, it also means that finding a casual place to grab a quick bite can be a challenge. If you want a quick, utilitarian meal, your best bet is to visit one of Stockholm's many small cafés. Aside from the beloved Swedish ritual of coffee and cakes, these cafés also serve filling lunches – seafood salads, ham-and-cheese pie (quiche), baguettes filled with salami and brie, and typical Swedish sandwiches *(smörgåsar)*.

The more traditional restaurants in Stockholm specialise in *husmanskost*, or classic Swedish 'plain food.' But the city's increasingly varied cultural makeup means you can also find cuisine from a huge variety of cultures. Leading up to the Christmas holidays – and year-round at a few places –

SOMETHING SPECIAL

Den Gyldene Freden (Map p80; ☎ 24 97 60; Österlånggatan 51; mains from Skr250, 2-/3-course menu Skr418/468, husmanskost Skr96-185; ⏰ dinner Mon-Fri, lunch & dinner Sat until midnight; metro T-Gamla Stan) Once owned by famed Swedish painter Anders Zorn, and now run by the Swedish Academy – the folks responsible for awarding the Nobel Prize for Literature – Den Gyldene Freden (meaning 'the golden peace') is a cornerstone in Stockholm's cultural history. Its three barrel-vaulted cellar dining rooms (two with plasterwork paintings) have been open continuously since 1722. There are few better places in town for classic *husmanskost,* particularly the plate of pickled herring with *Västerbottens ost* (Skr155). There are also traditionally prepared dishes of reindeer, goose, duck and salmon, all with interesting accompaniments such as red wine-dill sauce, mashed pumpkins, mushrooms from local forests, or the Swedish standby, almond potatoes.

you'll find the justifiably famous Swedish smörgåsbord. August and midsummer bring two other beloved Swedish specialities to the table: *surströmming* and crayfish *(kraftor).* The former is incredibly pungent Baltic herring that's been tinned and fermented for up to a year; the latter demands a relatively labour-intensive dining process that tends to shatter inhibitions. Both are acquired tastes and best accompanied by plenty of *snaps.*

Cafés and restaurants usually serve a weekday lunch special (or a choice of several) called *dagens rätt* at a fixed price (typically Skr65 to Skr85) between 11.30am and 2pm Monday to Friday. It's a practice originally supported and subsidised by the Swedish government with the goal of keeping workers happy and efficient all day, and it's still one of the most economical ways to sample top-quality Swedish cooking.

For a quick, inexpensive snack, it's hard to beat a *grillad korv med bröd* – your basic grilled hotdog on a bun – available for Skr10 to Skr20 from carts all over the city.

Gamla Stan

BUDGET

Café Art (Map p80; ☎ 411 76 61; Västerlånggatan 60; sandwiches from Skr35) This barrel-vaulted and brick-lined cellar is a low-key, atmospheric retreat from the Old Town's shopping mayhem. Nestle in for coffee and cake, shrimp salad or a salami-and-brie baguette.

Hermitage (Map p80; ☎ 411 95 00; Stora Nygatan 11; dinner Skr70) This is a welcoming vegetarian restaurant that's well worth a visit. There's a hearty *dagens rätt* available weekdays for Skr65 to Skr75.

Sundbergs Konditori (Map p80; ☎ 10 67 35; Järntorget 83; lunch specials Skr59) This is the oldest bakery-café in Stockholm, dating from 1785, and has a fine early 20th-century-style interior, complete with a copper samovar full of self-serve coffee. The café serves delicious hot sandwiches, pies, omelettes, lasagne and an assortment of to-die-for pastries.

Chokladkoppen (Map p80; ☎ 20 31 70; Stortorget; cakes & snacks Skr30-70) This narrow café, strewn with wax-encrusted candlesticks, has wonderful coffee and cakes, plus outdoor seating on bustling Stortorget – what better way to spend a sunny afternoon? It shifts into a gay-friendly disco in the evening.

MIDRANGE

Zum Franziskaner (Map p80; ☎ 411 83 30; Skeppsbron 44; dagens rätt Skr65, husmanskost Skr92-225; ⏰ closed Sun) Founded in 1421 by German monks, and claiming to be the oldest restaurant in the city, Zum Franziskaner serves German and Austrian beers (bottled) and sausages as well as enormous Swedish *husmanskost* meals. The herring plate with *Västerbottens ost* claims to be an appetizer but is easily meal-sized; the delicious *isterband,* a savoury Swedish country sausage, comes on a vast bed of potatoes in cream sauce. Although the current building dates from 1906, it looks like a museum inside, with well-preserved wooden stalls, ornate cabinets and ceiling artwork.

Källaren Diana (Map p80; ☎ 10 73 10; www.kallarendiana.com; Brunnsgränd 2-4; starters Skr85-185, mains Skr185-285; ⏰ dinner) One of the best ways to brush up on your knowledge of Swedish herring in all its forms is to hit the herring boat (fondly nicknamed the 'Skiff of the Archipelago') in Diana's vaulted cellar rooms. Offered as an appetizer, the ship-shaped *sill* and *strömming* buffet – with dozens of varieties – easily makes a meal, especially with a finger or two of *snaps* with it. The cured reindeer salad (Skr85) is uniquely pungent and satisfying. Diana's turns into a late-night disco at weekends.

Siam Thai (Map p80; ☎ 20 02 33; Stora Nygatan 25; dagens rätt from Skr65, mains Skr95-165; ⏰ closed Sun) The cosy basement restaurant of this vividly decorated place serves up a range of authentic mild to spicy Thai dishes in huge portions.

TOP END

Pontus in the Greenhouse (Map p80; ☎ 23 85 00; Österlånggatan 17; starters Skr215-400, mains from Skr295; ⏰ 11.30am-3pm & 6pm-11pm Mon-Fri, noon-4pm & 5.30-11pm Sat) Just across from the St George monument, this stylish modern restaurant with greenish décor was declared the best in Sweden in 2000 and it deserves the fine reputation. You can eat while seated at a central bar or at regular tables. Courses, including Beluga caviar and Greenhouse canapés, are so pretty to look at you might not want to eat them.

Leijontornet (Map p80; ☎ 14 23 55; Lilla Nygatan 5; starters Skr165-195, mains Skr275-320; 3-/5-course menus Skr420/675; ⏰ 6-10.30pm Mon-Sat, closed Sun) Leijontornet's basement dining room includes the foundations of a 14th-century tower. The brick-vaulted ceilings and candlelight add to the atmosphere, but the furnishings feature modern design. The superb menu, one of the city's finest, includes fish, duck, game and vegetarian dishes. There's also a cheaper, midrange Italian-style *bakfickan* menu. The bar menu offers a few tapas plates (three for Skr125) should you just want to linger over a drink.

Central Stockholm

BUDGET

Vetekatten (Map p80; ☎ 21 84 54; Kungsgatan 55; tea, coffee & snacks from Skr25; ⏰ 7.30am-8pm Mon-Fri, 9am-5pm Sat, noon-5pm Sun) Very grandmother-friendly, the labyrinthine Vetekatten is one of the city's best-known traditional cafés, with lots of small rooms and a great atmosphere. You can also buy baked goods, large sandwiches and cakes to take away.

Ritorno (Map p80; ☎ 32 01 06; Odengatan 80-82; coffee & pastries from Skr25; ⏰ 7am-10pm Mon-Fri, 8am-6pm Sat, 10am-6pm Sun) With scrumptious pastries and a sweet back room that looks like the foyer of an antique movie house that's fallen on hard times, Ritorno is one of the most comfortable cafés in Stockholm. Miniature jukeboxes grace each table (and they actually work!), smoking students glare into textbooks, and punks and pensioners commingle with families.

MIDRANGE

Sabai Sabai (Map p80; ☎ 790 09 13; www.sabai.se; Kammakargatan 44; mains Skr85-179; ⏰ dinner) Friendly and laid-back Sabai Sabai, frequently named as Stockholm's best Thai restaurant, serves great food in an ornate tropical-style interior. The extensive menu includes wok, noodle, curry, fish and seafood dishes. Reservations are recommended.

Tranan (Map pp68-9; ☎ 52 72 81 00; Karlbergsvägen 14; starters Skr55-125, mains Skr95-265; ⏰ dinner until 1am) This stylish, busy place on Odenplan looks like a classic French bistro, with its rustic furniture and checked tablecloths. It's one of the most popular neighbourhood restaurants in Stockholm, constantly recommended by devoted locals. It has an excellent and comprehensive international menu, including a traditional Swedish herring platter. Don't miss the basement bar.

Narknoi (Map pp68-9; ☎ 30 70 70; Odengatan 94; mains Skr121-184; ⏰ lunch & dinner, Sat & Sun dinner only) This award-winning, friendly and unpretentious restaurant is fairly small, with minimalist styles. The mild to hot dishes on the menu include many types of meat and fish, and a less expensive vegetarian selection. Book well in advance.

Bistro Boheme (Map p80; ☎ 411 90 41; Drottninggatan 71A; mains Skr65-175) This place has weird designer furniture (gigantic chairs), huge beer mugs, a tiled bar with loud music, and a beer garden in summer. The menu includes Czech goulash soup and vegetarian lasagne – ask about the all-you-can-eat Sunday soup.

Grill (Map p80; ☎ 31 45 30; www.grill.se; Drottninggatan 89; starters Skr95-195, mains Skr135-285; ⏰ lunch & dinner until 1am, 10pm Sun) This oddly homely restaurant, started by renowned chefs Melker Andersson and Danyel Couet, inhabits a sprawling space that looks like a furniture store, with 10 small dining areas set up like demo living rooms. The menu is arranged by grill type: rotisserie, charcoal, barbecue, etc. Mix and match with Asian table-grilled tuna, BBQ beef brisket, blackened salmon, wood-fired duck, scrumptious desserts – and don't neglect the extensive wine list, also conveniently organis]ed by flavour. The restaurant's service is casual and accommodating.

Lao Wai (Map pp68-9; ☎ 673 78 00; Luntmakargatan 74; mains Skr100-185; ⏰ dinner Tue-Sat) This strictly vegetarian restaurant is heavy on philosophy (it's less a menu than a manifesto) and simple in presentation. In a small white room with simple wooden tables, spices coax miraculous flavours out of various tofu and vegetable combinations.

Restaurant KB (Map p80; ☎ 679 60 32; Smålandsgatan 7; starters Skr95, dagens husmanskost Skr120-150, mains Skr180-250, bar menu Skr75-125; ⏰ 11.30am-midnight Mon-Fri, 5pm-midnight Sat) KB stands for *Konstnärs Bar* – (the artists' bar). On the ground floor of Konstnärs Huset, which provides housing, studio space and classes for artists, the restaurant serves traditional Swedish cuisine in arrangements that highlight each plate's visual beauty. The assorted herring dishes and anything vegetarian or fish-based are highly recommended. The attached bar has wall paintings from 1931.

TOP END

Franska Matsalen (Map p80; ☎ 679 35 84; www.franskamatsalen.se; Grand Hôtel Stockholm, Södra Blasieholmshamnen 8; mains Skr195-485, set menu (incl veg) Skr895-1300; ⏰ 6-11pm Mon-Fri) The ornate French restaurant at the Grand Hôtel fairly wallows in decadence, with elaborate chandeliers, lots of dark wood and deep red carpets. It has been called the best restaurant in Sweden, and the food is spectacular. A twist on beef Wallenberg made with pheasant, a cheese plate with chanterelle-lingonberry chutney, port-braised foie gras with figs, sage-beetroot ravioli, curry apple scallops – are you salivating yet? There's also an extensive French wine list. A smörgåsbord lunch is available 11.30am-3pm weekdays in the hotel's Grand Veranda.

Verandan (Map p80; ☎ 679 35 86; Grand Hotel Stockholm, Södra Blasieholmshamnen 8; breakfast Skr185, mains Skr105-300, buffet Skr315) Less likely to break the bank is Verandan. Here you can enjoy a huge smörgåsbord breakfast, with 124 hot and cold dishes to choose from. There's also a plentiful, traditional lunch buffet (May to September) and dinner buffet (year-round), which includes all the Swedish dishes you have been hankering to try.

Operakällaren (Map p80; ☎ 676 58 00; Jakobs Torg 10; starters Skr275-310, mains Skr380-410, tasting menus from Skr895 (Skr550 veg); ⏰ 5-10pm) The finest place within the Opera House is the century-old Operakällaren, with its fantastic décor, paintings and extravagant furnishings. The gourmet menu, printed in French, includes caviar, fish, hare and pigeon. It's also known as the place to go for the ultimate traditional *julbord* (Christmas smörgåsbord). Men must wear a suit and tie to be admitted. To dine here on weekends, you'll need to book a fortnight in advance, and more around the winter holidays.

Bakfickan (Map p80; ☎ 676 58 08; mains Skr85-125; ⏰ 11.30am-midnight Mon-Sat) With superb service, Art Nouveau decor, stools around the bar and opera-related photos, this little restaurant – the 'back pocket' of Operakällaren – serves gourmet Swedish *husmanskost* at moderate prices. Try the assorted herring, boiled potatoes and crispbread. Look out for opera singers, who tend to eat here after a performance.

Eyubi (Map pp68-9; ☎ 673 52 36; www.eyubi.com in Swedish; Döbelnsgatan 45; mains Skr60-195, meze platter Skr180; ⏰ 5pm-midnight Tue-Thu, 1am Fri & Sat; closed Midsummer-Aug; T-Rådmansgatan) Dramatically situated in a former car park, at the end of a long concrete hallway lined with photos by cutting-edge Stockholm artists, Eyubi makes it clear straightaway that it is no ordinary Mediterranean restaurant. Its classy industrial style and sophisticated menu – where hummus and tabbouleh rub shoulders with saffron-marinated chicken, scampi and lime-orange salmon – draw the trendy and arty from all over the city.

Östermalm

BUDGET

Sturekatten (Map p80; ☎ 611 16 12; Riddargatan 4; cakes & pies Skr15-70, baguettes Skr65; ⏰ 8am-8pm Mon-Fri, 10am-6pm Sat & 11am-6pm Sun) This café looks like a full-grown dollhouse, with three levels and featuring a quaint late-19th-century ambience, with antique chairs, paintings and lamps. This is where the ladies-who-lunch take their mothers-in-law. In summer, if there's room, you can *fika* (a uniquely Swedish word meaning to meet up friends or family to have coffee and cake) in the cute little courtyard.

MIDRANGE

Grodan Grev Ture (Map p80; ☎ 679 61 00; Grev Turegatan 16; lunch Skr95, mains Skr97-202, dinner mains Skr127-219; ⏰ 11.30am-1am Mon-Thu, until 2am Fri & Sat) This huge, sophisticated place includes modern dining areas, a raging cocktail bar and a picture-windowed 18th-century-style room with ornate plasterwork, antique paintings and lighting worthy of Rembrandt. The French-leaning menu includes venison, pike and vegetarian lasagne and is popular with young professional types.

Örtagården (Map p80; ☎ 662 17 28; www.ortagarden.se; Nybrogatan 31, first fl of Östermalms Saluhall Bldg; dagens lunch Skr70, lunch buffet Skr75; ⏰ 10.30am-9.30pm Mon-Fri, 11am-8.30pm Sat, noon-8.30pm Sun) Perched unobtrusively above the food market in Östermalms Saluhall, this vegetarian restaurant offers an extensive buffet at lunch and dinner in a setting reminiscent of a courtyard garden, with fountains and ferns galore.

Sturehof (Map p80; ☎ 440 57 30; Stureplan 2; mains Skr95-330; ⏰ 9am-2am Mon-Fri, noon-2am Sat, 1pm-2am Sun) One of Stockholm's busiest restaurants, particularly in summer when the terrace is perpetually hopping, Sturehof has a modern menu vast enough to satisfy every taste. Fish dishes are recommended, as is the tiny O-bar in the basement.

Tures (Map p80; ☎ 611 02 10; Sturegallerian 10; mains Skr88-165) Highly recommended, this pleasantly dark, red-and-black decorated café sits in the middle of the highbrow Sturegallerian shopping mall. Try the excellent fried herring and *Västerbottens ost*. It's a great place for *fika* or a beer break if your knees get weak while shopping in the mall's exclusive boutiques.

Djurgården

BUDGET

Blå Porten (Map pp68-9; ☎ 663 87 59; Djurgårdsvägen 64; pastries from Skr15, mains Skr65-105; ⏰ 11am-7pm, until 9pm Tue & Thu, longer hr in summer) Best on a sunny day, when you can linger over lunch in the garden, this café next to Liljevalchs Konsthall offers an amazing display of baked goods. The Swedish and international meals are particularly recommended.

MIDRANGE

Rosendals Trädgårdskafe (Map pp68-9; ☎ 54 58 12 70; www.rosendalstradgard.com in Swedish; Rosendalsterrassen 12; cakes & pies from Skr35; ⏰ winter 11am-4pm Tue-Sun, summer 11am-5pm; bus 47, 15 min walk from Djurgårdsbron), Rosendals is an idyllic spot for a fruit pastry and coffee in the summer or a warm cup of *glögg* (mulled wine) and a *lussekatte* (saffron bun) in winter. If the weather is ugly, skulk around the gardens and greenhouses, look moody and pretend you're Strindberg.

TOP END

Restaurang Hasselbacken (Map pp68-9; ☎ 51 73 43 07; www.restauranghasselbacken.com; Hazeliusbacken 20; 2-/3-course menu Skr325/375; ⏰ 1-10pm Mon-Sat late Jun to mid-Aug (restricted menu); otherwise 10am-2pm & 5-10pm Mon-Fri, 1-10pm Sat & 1-9pm Sun) This restaurant, in Scandic Hotel Hasselbacken, serves fine classical Swedish meals with foreign influences in a wonderful jewel box dining room dating from 1923. The menu includes such twists on *husmanskost* as reindeer fillet with *Västerbottens ost* potatoes and morel-currant gravy. There is a superb ceiling and a raised dining area with alcoves and sofas.

Wärdshuset Ulla Winbladh (Map pp68-9; ☎ 663 05 71; www.ullawinbladh.se in Swedish; Rosendalsvägen 8; starters Skr95-140, mains Skr195-290) Named after one of Carl Michael Bellman's lovers, this villa was built as a steam bakery for the Stockholm World's Fair (1897) and now serves fine food in an early 20th-century-style restaurant with a garden setting. The menu features international dishes and traditional Swedish meals, including meatballs and crayfish tails, and it's known for its outstanding herring smörgåsbord.

Södermalm

BUDGET

Nystekt Strömming (Map p80; Södermalmstorg; ⏰ hr vary, generally lunch & dinner) The best place to get fried *(stekt)* herring in all of Stockholm is this unassuming cart outside the metro station at Slussen. Combo plates cost about Skr30 to Skr45, and there are picnic tables outside, perfect for people-watching while you eat.

Soda (Map p80; ☎ 462 00 75; Bellmansgatan 26; ⏰ 8am-8pm Mon-Fri, 10am-7pm Sat & Sun) This is a smoky café full of moody teens and twenty-somethings mooning over their diaries and stealing secret glances at each other. Soda serves coffee American-style in huge green and yellow mugs. It has endearing indie-rock artwork on the walls, and best of all it'll let you read its diaries.

MIDRANGE

Östgöta Källaren (Map pp68-9; ☎ 643 22 40; Östgötagatan 41; mains Skr80-180; ⏰ until midnight) This place has everything to recommend it – a dimly lit romantic atmosphere, friendly service and unpretentious *husmanskost* like Swedish meatballs, *pytt i panna* and all sorts of fish. It's a nice place to linger over a beer or glass of wine.

Pelikan (Map pp68-9; ☎ 55 60 90 90; Blekingegatan 40; mains Skr75-185; ⏰ dinner daily & lunch Sat & Sun; minimum age 23) This well-established place has a unique atmosphere with rooms in three different styles, including a German-style beer hall with monkeys painted on the pillars and ceiling. The food is good – the menu is classic *husmanskost,* and there's usually a vegetarian special on the blackboard.

Koh Phangan (Map pp68-9; ☎ 642 68 65; www.kohphangan.nu in Swedish; Skånegatan 57; mains Skr125-265; ⏰ until 1am) This outrageously kitsch Thai restaurant has to be seen to be believed. It's best at night, when you can enjoy your meal in a real *tuk-tuk* to the accompanying racket of crickets and a tropical thunderstorm. The food is good, but service tends to be sluggish. There's a DJ after 10pm, Tuesday to Sunday.

Creperie Fyra Knop (Map p80; ☎ 640 77 27; Svartensgatan 4; crepes from Skr35, mains Skr60-80; ⏰ dinner Mon-Fri, lunch & dinner weekends) Fyra Knop serves excellent crepes in an intimate, romantic little place, with lots of small rooms tucked away just off the main drag in Söder. A good place for a quiet chat before you hit the clubs down the street.

Folkhemmet (Map pp68-9; ☎ 640 55 95; Renstiernas Gata 30; mains Skr120-198, set menus Skr85/125/215; ⏰ dinner, bar until 1am) Filed under 'only in Sweden' is this madly popular socialist-run bar and restaurant, named after the Social Democratic Party's conception of a welfare state (the name means 'the people's home'). But the food is nowhere near as proletarian as that might imply. The ambitious menu, which changes eight to 10 times a year, features such combinations as red-beet tartlets and asparagus salad with truffle vinaigrette.

TOP END

Gondolen (Map p80; ☎ 641 70 90; www.eriks.se in Swedish; Stadsgården 6; 2-/3-course menu Skr320/395, weekday lunch Skr95-295, dinner Skr255-450; ⏰ lunch & dinner until 1am) This restaurant is top of the heap, both figuratively and literally. With perhaps the most unusual location in Stockholm – it is situated at the top of Katarinahissen, the Slussen elevator built in 1883 – Gondolen offers fantastic views, a dizzyingly patterned wood floor, very comfortable armchairs in the bar and some great fine food. Swedish style dishes such as the herring plate and the warm cloudberries with ice cream are particularly recommended.

Kungsholmen

BUDGET

Thelins (Map pp68-9; ☎ 651 19 00; www.thelinskonditori.se in Swedish; St Eriksgatan 43; coffee & cakes from Skr35; ⏰ 7.30am-7pm Mon-Fri, 9am-5pm Sat & Sun) A traditional, old-fashioned *konditori* with red velvet theatre-style furniture, faux-Parisian white streetlamps sticking up in the middle of the dining area and curtained-off booths in the large back room, Thelins is all charm. Its display case contains some of the best and most beautiful cakes and pastries in Stockholm.

MIDRANGE

El Cubanito (Map pp68-9; ☎ 650 12 38; www.elcubanito.se; Scheelegatan 3; starters Skr60-70, mains Skr125-195; ⏰ dinner, bar until late) This tiny Cuban bar and restaurant's luscious dark wooden floor, pressed-tin bar and decorative ceramic tiles give it the lived-in feel of a stylish old bodega. On the menu are favourites such as *ropa vieja,* fried plantains, tropical chicken and flan for dessert, plus specialities such as *arroz a la Hemingway,* red snapper marinated in cardamom and Cuban approaches to Swedish ingredients, such as fillet of venison in lingon and guava. You can also, of course, get Cuban cigars and a wide selection of rum drinks.

Salzer (Map pp68-9; ☎ 650 30 28; John Ericssonsgatan 6; starters Skr12-150, mains Skr160-220, Sunday brunch buffet Skr150; ⏰ 5pm-midnight Mon-Sat, noon-8pm Sun) The menu at this well-liked *kvarterskrog* (neighbourhood bar) features Swedish and continental choices, including vegetarian. The Swedish country sausage called *isterband,* served over potatoes in a cream sauce, is a favourite dish here. You can also try the local Kungsholmen brew, Lundbergs lager. Prices are lower in the 'Propeller *bakfickan*' so called because John Ericsson, after whom the street is named, invented the propeller.

Spisa Hos Helena (Map pp68-9; ☎ 654 49 26; www.spisahoshelena.se in Swedish; Scheelegatan 18; starters Skr75-100, mains Skr130-200; ⏰ lunch & dinner, closed Sun) This tiny, atmospheric bar and restaurant, with rich red walls and low candlelight, emphasises grilled fish and seafood, as well as offering nouveau twists on traditional meals like beef Rydberg or Swedish meatballs with pickles, lingon and potatoes. The small bar area up front is a warm, cosy place to meet for a drink and one of Helena's homemade truffles (Skr22).

Market Halls

The colourful market halls are excellent places to sample both local and exotic treats.

Östermalms Saluhall (Map p80; Östermalmstorg; www.ostermalmshallen.se in Swedish; 9.30am-6pm Mon-Thu, until 6.30pm Fri & 4pm Sat – until 2pm Sat in summer; T-Östermalmstorg) More upscale than Hötorgshallen, Östermalms Saluhall is excellent for fresh fish and meat, as well as hard-to-find cheeses. The building itself is a Stockholm landmark, designed as a Romanesque cathedral of food in 1885. For a quick lunch, belly up to the bar at Depå Sushi; for more substantial fare, check the extensive *dagens rätt* board at the classy Tysta Mari (Skr60 to Skr85). The pastries at Amandas Brödbod are gorgeous. There's a clean, well-hidden and free toilet in the far corner opposite the entrance.

Hötorgshallen (Map p80; Hötorget; www.hotorgshallen.se; 10am-6pm Mon-Thu, 10am-6.30pm Fri, 10am-4pm Sat, summer 10am-6pm Mon-Fri, 10am-3pm Sat; T-Hötorget) Located in the basement below Filmstaden cinema, Hötorgshallen has several fine specialist food shops selling meat, fish, cheese, groceries, coffee and tea, plus Asian fast-food stands, kebabs and the like. At lunchtime, locals cram themselves into a galley-themed dining nook of Kajsas Fiskrestaurang for huge bowls of *fisksoppa* (fish stew) with mussels and aioli for Skr75 – a treat not to be missed. Outside in the square there's a daily street market with stalls selling flowers, fruits and vegetables and knick-knacks.

Söderhallarna (Map pp68-9; Medborgarplatsen 3; www.soderhallarna.aos.se in Swedish; 10am-6pm Mon-Wed, 10am-7pm Thu & Fri, 10am-4pm Sat; T-Medborgarplatsen) This more modern food hall includes a great vegetarian restaurant, deli, cheese shop, an Asian supermarket and a pub that has live jazz most nights. It's not the most atmospheric place, so plan on enjoying your lunch outdoors on Medborgarplatsen.

Self-Catering

The handiest central supermarket is **Hemköp** (Map p80; Klarabergsgatan 50; 8am-9pm Mon-Fri, 10am-9pm Sat & Sun), in the Åhléns department store. Others include the following:

ICA Baronen (Map pp68-9; Odengatan 40; 8am-10pm; T-Odenplan)

Vivo T-Jarlen (Map pp68-9; inside the Östermalmstorg Tunnelbana station; 7am-9pm Mon-Fri, 10am-7pm Sat, noon-6pm Sun) Enter from Frev Turegatan.

Coop Konsum (Map p80; Katarinavägen 3-7; 7am-9pm Mon-Fri, 9am-9pm Sat & Sun; T-Slussen)

DRINKING

Stockholm's an expensive but stylish place to drink – there are virtually no dives and almost every place has interesting design elements or a stylish atmosphere. Which isn't to say there are no cosy neighbourhood pubs – it's just that in Stockholm, such places look a little more fantastic than usual. You can drink in ornate mansions, monastic cellars, vanilla-lit beer halls or sleek bars with designer lighting, but you'll have some trouble finding a truly boring bar in this city. It seems that almost every decent restaurant and pub in Stockholm has a cool bar attached, and many cafés bring in a DJ of an evening and, *voilà,* another groovy bar is born.

Södermalm is the prime spot for varied nightlife, while Östermalm, especially around Stureplan, is the place to go for the ultrachic discos and mile-long queues.

Mass-market Swedish beers are virtually indistinguishable from one another by flavour, so locals generally order by grade, not brand. The usual order is a *storstark* – which translates to a 'big strong' – if you're not feeling up to a big strong, you can also order a *mellanöl,* or medium beer. Local mega-brew lagers, such as Spendrups, Pripps or Falcon, cost anywhere from Skr35 to Skr52 a pint, and imported beer or mixed drinks can be twice that. The legal drinking age in Sweden is 18 years, but many bars and restaurants impose significantly higher age limits.

Some of the best places to check out include the following.

Soldaten Svejk (Map pp68-9; 641 33 66; Östgötagatan 35) In this crowded, amber-windowed, wooden-floored pub, decorated with heraldic shields, you can get great Czech beer, including the massively popular Staropramen, on tap. There are also simple and solid Czech meals (Skr75 to Skr115); try some of the excellent smoked cheese along with your beer. Be sure to arrive early – there are often long queues for tables.

Kvarnen (Map pp68-9; 643 03 80; Tjärhovsgatan 4; until 3am) A cheerful mixture of Hammarby football fans and Left Party former communists regularly packs Kvarnen, one of the best bars in Söder. The vast beer hall dates from 1907 and seeps tradition. Beyond the scruffy old beerhounds and college boys though, there's a hot dance party in the back room, featuring some of the city's best DJs.

Queues are fairly constant but, for once, justifiable.

Cliff Barnes (Map pp68-9; ☎ 31 80 70; Nortullsgatan 45; ⏰ until 1am Mon-Sat) Named after the loser from the *Dallas* TV soap. People come here to sing along to popular tunes, dance on the tables and get inebriated. It's a hugely popular beer-hall-type place with an outdoor bar in summer.

Wirströms (Map p80; ☎ 21 28 74; Stora Nygatan 13; ⏰ until midnight Mon-Fri, 1am Sat & Sun) This place feels more like a medieval dungeon than an Irish pub – the dark, mysterious, brick-vaulted cellar goes on forever. Arrive early to find a candlelit corner and snuggle in with a pint of Guinness (Skr52). Bar meals and sandwiches (including vegetarian options) are available for Skr75 to Skr95. There's live music in the evenings from Wednesday to Saturday.

Berns Salonger (Map p80; ☎ 56 63 20 00; www.berns.se; Berzelii Park; ⏰ until 1am Mon-Tue, 3am Wed-Thu, 4am Fri & Sat, midnight Sun) With half a dozen bars spread across three levels, this grand mansion of a bar is drenched in history but buzzing with contemporary energy. On the basement level is a popular disco; there's also a wine bar, a cocktail bar, a mirrored bar and a terrace.

Icebar (Map p80; ☎ 50 56 30 00; www.nordichotels.se; inside the Nordic Sea Hotel, Vasaplan 4; admission Skr125; ⏰ until midnight Mon-Sat, 3-9pm Sun) Of course it's silly, but you're intrigued, admit it. Built entirely out of ice; you drink from ice-carved glasses at tables made of ice. The admission price gets you warm booties, mittens, a parka and one drink; refills cost extra, but you'll probably be too cold to want one anyway.

Storstad (Map pp68-9; ☎ 673 38 00; Odengatan 41; ⏰ until 1am Mon-Tue, 3am Wed-Sat) This super-trendy bar is the dictionary definition of Stockholm style, with its bright-white walls, right-angle bar and enormous picture windows. It has a more relaxed vibe than usual, though – this is one of the few places in town where someone might noticeably try to pick you up. DJs play most nights.

Akkurat (Map p80; ☎ 644 00 15; www.akkurat.se in Swedish; Hornsgatan 18; ⏰ until 1am Mon-Sat) Fans of beer should make a point of visiting Akkurat. It has a huge selection of Belgian ales as well as a good range of Swedish-made microbrews, notably the semidivine Jämtlands Bryggeri trio: Heaven, Hell, and Fallen Angel. There's also a vast wall of whiskey, and mussels are on the menu.

August Bar & Bistro (Map pp68-9; ☎ 644 87 00; Folkungagatan 59; ⏰ until 1am) Comfortable, classy and laid-back, this place has become the haven of the Medborgarplatsen area's hipsters who have outgrown Söderkällaren but are tired of waiting to get into Kvarnen. It serves beer, wine and affordable bar food.

Bonden (Map pp68-9; ☎ 641 86 79; Bondegatan 1C; ⏰ until 1am) In this small bar, located by a cow sign outside the door, you'll find a strangely curved ceiling with 19th-century-style light bulbs. It's a nice place to sit and have a quiet chat, but it fills up fast. Next door is the larger, more rock-oriented Bonden Club.

East (Map p80; ☎ 611 49 59; www.east-restaurang.se; Stureplan 13; ⏰ until 3am) The dance floor here gets seriously hopping at night, but there are always a few quiet seats near the bar where you can relax over cocktails, sake and sushi.

Halv Trappa Plus Gård (Map p80; ☎ 611 02 75; Lästmakargatan 3; ⏰ until 3am, closing at 1am Mon-Tue) The back patio here has its own bar and heaters, making it a popular summertime hangout – if you can get in. The classy, labyrinthine bar and chill-out lounges are notoriously well-protected from anything that might seem less than the height of fashion. Dress like the mannequins in the Filippa K windows and try to arrive by 10pm.

Lydmar Hotel Lounge (Map p80; ☎ 56 61 13 00; www.lydmar.se; Sturegatan 10; ⏰ until 1am Sun-Thu, 2am Fri & Sat) If it's not absurdly crowded with attractive young business types, the Lydmar's lounge is a great place to relax with a cocktail and feel incredibly swank.

SYSTEMBOLAGET

The state-owned alcohol monopoly is the only place to buy real booze to take home. A complete listing is given at the back of the price list or on the Internet; the following are a few of the central branches:

Systembolaget (www.systembolaget.se) Grev Turegatan (Map p80; ☎ 611 2270; Grev Turegatan 3; ⏰ 10am to 6pm Mon to Wed, 7pm Thu, 6.30pm Fri, 10am to 2pm Sat); Klarabergsgatan (Map p80; ☎ 21 47 44; Klarabergsgatan 62; ⏰ 10am to 8pm weekdays, 10am to 3pm Sat); Regeringsgatan (Map p80; ☎ 796 98 10; Regeringsgatan 44; ⏰ 10am to 7pm weekdays, 10am to 2pm Sat)

ENTERTAINMENT

Check the local papers (see p71) for up-to-date listings of entertainment events, particularly the Friday *På Stan* section of *Dagens Nyheter* newspaper.

Nightclubs

Going out dancing is a popular pastime for the young and beautiful in Stockholm. The fanciest places have an entry charge of Skr50 to Skr150, but you're likely to spot a local sports celebrity at the bar. For more variety or an alternative to the slick disco scene, try one of the city's many salsa clubs or an indie-rock haven like Mondo.

Sturecompagniet (Map p80; ☎ 611 78 00; www.sturecompagniet.se in Swedish; Sturegatan 4; admission Skr120 after 10pm Fri & Sat; 10pm-5am Wed-Sat) One of the more welcoming clubs in Stureplan, this ornate, high-ceilinged, red-velvet-curtained bar also serves decent food.

Spy Bar (Map p80; ☎ 54 50 37 01; www.thespybar.com in Swedish; Birger Jarlsgatan 20; admission Skr125; 10pm-5am Wed-Sat) Nicknamed 'the Puke' (because spy in Swedish means vomit), this bar is the ice queen of the club scene – you can't help wanting to get in, but you hate it because it won't let you.

La Habana (Map pp68-9; ☎ 16 64 65; Sveavägen 108; until 1am) This Cuban restaurant turns into a crowded salsa bar at night, with limber-legged Swedes and Latinos intermingling over *cuba libres* and *mojitos* in the basement.

Mondo (Map pp68-9; ☎ 673 10 32; Medborgarplatsen 8; until 3am) This newly opened club and cultural centre, in a former school building, puts on unusual, top-notch events every night of the week. It has a bar/restaurant, a large dance floor and music hall, and a tinier club upstairs, plus a gallery and a small movie theatre.

Live Music

Live jazz is extremely popular in the capital and there are a number of excellent venues that show-case it and an annual jazz festival is held in mid-July. All the following clubs have admission charges, which will vary depending on what's featuring on the night.

Glenn Miller Café (Map p80; ☎ 10 03 22; Brunnsgatan 21A; 5pm-midnight Mon-Thu, 5pm-1am Fri & Sat; T-Hötorget, bus 1, 43, 52, 56) This tiny jazz and blues bar draws a faithful, fun-loving crowd to its performances. It's also known for serving excellent, affordable *husmanskost* meals.

Jazzclub Fasching (Map p80; ☎ 21 62 67; www.fasching.se in Swedish; Kungsgatan 63; until 1am Mon-Thu, 4am Fri & Sat; tickets Skr20-200; T-Centralen, bus 1, 47, 53, 69) A world-renowned jazz club, Fasching hosts local artists and unknowns as well as big names in the international jazz world. It's a small, cosy place, with a great view from the balcony but limited standing room.

Stampen (Map p80; ☎ 20 57 93; www.stampen.se; Stora Nygatan 5; 8pm-1am Mon-Wed, until 2am Thu-Sat; tickets Skr100-150; T-Gamla Stan, bus 3, 53, 55, 59, 76) This well-known club in Old Town, with timeworn, quirky décor and a friendly vibe, has blues and some jazz concerts every night; there's a free blues jam featuring local musicians at 2pm on Saturday afternoons.

Mosebacke Etablissement (Map p80; ☎ 55 60 98 90; www.mosebacke.se in Swedish; Mosebacketorg 3; 4pm-1am Mon-Thu, Sun, until 2am Fri & Sat; tickets Skr80-250; T-Slussen, bus 3, 46, 53, 76) Well-known acts of all genres play at the historic Mosebacke, where the sophisticated, regal atmosphere augments any style of music. The outdoor bar here offers a great view of the city.

Concerts & Theatre

Stockholm is a theatre city, with outstanding dance, opera and music performances; for an overview, pick up the free *Teater Guide* from tourist offices. Ticket sales are handled by the tourist office at Sweden House, or you can buy direct from **Biljett-Direkt** (☎ 0771-70 70 70; www.ticnet.se). Tickets generally aren't cheap and they're often sold out, especially for Saturday shows, but you can occasionally get good-value last-minute deals. Operas are usually performed in their original language, while theatre performances are invariably in Swedish.

Konserthuset (Map p80; ☎ 50 66 77 88; www.konserthuset.se; Hötorget; tickets Skr50-350) This venue features classical concerts and other musical events, including the Royal Philharmonic Orchestra.

Operan (Map p80; ☎ 24 82 40; www.operan.se; Gustav Adolfs Torg; tickets Skr135-460) The Royal Opera is the place to go for opera and classical ballet. It also has some bargain tickets in seats with poor views for as little as Skr40, and occasional lunchtime concerts for Skr140 (including lunch).

Folkoperan (Map p80; ☎ 616 07 50; www.folkoperan.se; Hornsgatan 72; tickets Skr250-390) Folkoperan stages unconventional productions of opera and modern ballet that bring the audience close to the stage.

Dramaten (Map p80; ☎ 667 06 80; www.dramaten.se in Swedish; Nybroplan; tickets Skr175-280) The Royal Theatre stages a range of plays in a fantastic Art Nouveau environment.

Stockholms Stadsteatern (Map p80; ☎ 50 62 01 00; Kulturhuset, Sergels Torg; tickets around Skr200) Regular performances are staged here, plus guest appearances by foreign theatre companies.

Globen (☎ 0771-31 00 00; www.globen.se; Globentorget 2; metro T-Globen) This is the big white spherical building (it looks like a giant golf ball) just south of Södermalm. Globen's arenas stage regular big-name pop and rock concerts, as well as sporting events and trade fairs.

Sport

Bandy matches, a uniquely Scandinavian phenomenon, take place all winter at Stockholm's ice arenas. Impromptu ones happen in the square at Medborgarplatsen, while official games are scheduled at Zinkensdamms Idrottsplats.

Zinkensdamms Idrottsplats (☎ 668 93 31; Ringvägen 12-14; Nov-Feb 8am-2pm Tue-Thu, 8am-11pm Sat, 1-4pm Sun; T-Zinkensdamm) Watching a bandy match at Zinkensdamm is great fun. The sport, a precursor to ice hockey but with more players (11 to a side) and less fighting, has grown massively popular since the late-'90s rise of the Hammarby team. There's a round vinyl ball instead of a puck, and the rules are similar to football, except that you hit the ball with a stick instead of kicking it. The season lasts from November to March, meaning it's vital to bring your own thermos of *kaffekask* – a warming mix of coffee and booze.

To really see Swedish sports fans in action, head along to an ice hockey game. Contact **Globen** (☎ 600 34 00; www.globen.se; Arenavägen, Johanneshov; tickets Skr150-200; T-Globen) for details; matches take place here up to three times a week from October to April (tickets cost Skr100 to Skr160). There are regular football fixtures here too.

Impromptu public skating areas spring up during the winter at Kungsträdgården in Norrmalm and in Medborgarplatsen in Södermalm. Skate-rental booths next to the rinks hire equipment for Skr35 to adults, Skr10 for children.

SHOPPING

There's no shortage of gorgeous Swedish design products in Stockholm, but souvenirs, handicrafts or quality Swedish products in glass, wood or pewter are relatively expensive, and some are not easy to cart around or send home. If you make any large purchases, be sure to ask about tax-free shopping.

DesignTorget (www.designtorget.se) Götgatan (Map p80; ☎ 462 35 20; Götgatan 31, Södermalm); Sergels Torg (Map p80; ☎ 50 83 15 20; Basement, Kulturhuset, Sergels Torg B°) Catch the city's cutting-edge new designers before they're famous enough to be unaffordable at a branch of this cooperative décor store; there's a central branch in the basement of Kulturhuset, and one on Söder's main drag.

Hennes & Mauritz (H&M; Map p80; ☎ 796 54 46; Sergels Torg) Heaven for the budget-conscious couture-seeker, H&M specialises in classy Swedish knockoffs of designer clothing.

Svenskt Tenn (Map p80; ☎ 670 16 00; Strandvägen 5) For a taste of Swedish design history that's literally museum-calibre, visit this deluxe shop and be careful not to drool over the beautiful furniture and interior design pieces!

Naturkompaniet (Map p80; ☎ 24 19 96; Kungsgatan 26) If you're gearing up for outdoor activities, this outdoor equipment shop sells a wide selection of gear; there are branches across the city.

A handy place to buy souvenirs is in one of the big department stores – most have basements full of high-quality, typically Swedish gift items to wrap and carry, or ship, home. Good choices include the following places:

NK (Map p80; ☎ 762 80 00; Hamngatan)
PUB (Map p80; ☎ 402 16 11; Drottninggatan 72-6)
Åhléns (Map p80; ☎ 676 60 00; Klarabergsgatan 50)

For smaller shops selling authentic handicrafts, look into **Svensk Hemslöjd** (Map p80; ☎ 23 21 15; Sveavägen 44) and **Svenskt Hantverk** (Map p80; ☎ 21 47 26; Kungsgatan 55).

GETTING THERE & AWAY

Air

The main airport in Stockholm, **Stockholm Arlanda** (☎ 797 60 00; www.lfv.se), is 45km north of the city centre and can be reached from central Stockholm by both bus and express train (see opposite).

Bromma airport (☎ 797 68 74) is 8km west of Stockholm and is used for some domestic flights. **Skavsta airport** (☎ 0155-28 04 00), 100km south of Stockholm, near Nyköping, is also used for domestic flights and some low-cost carriers.

The **SAS** (☎ 020 72 77 27) network serves 27 Swedish destinations from Arlanda, and has international services to Copenhagen,

Oslo, Helsinki and a host of other European cities including Amsterdam, Brussels, Berlin, Dublin, Frankfurt, Geneva, Hamburg, London, Madrid, Manchester, Milan, Moscow, Munich, Paris, Reykjavík, Riga, St Petersburg and Tallinn. The airline also flies directly to Chicago, New York and Bangkok.

Finnair (☎ 020 78 11 00) flies from Stockholm to Turku, Vaasa and Tampere, and several times daily to Helsinki.

Boat

Silja Line (☎ 22 21 40; www.silja.com) runs ferries to Helsinki and Turku. **Viking Line** (☎ 452 40 00; www.vikingline.fi) ferries run to Turku and Helsinki. **Tallink** (☎ 666 60 01; www.tallink.ee) ferries go to Tallinn (Estonia).

Bus

Most long-distance buses arrive and depart from Cityterminalen, which is connected to Centralstationen. Here you'll find the **Busstop ticket office** (☎ 440 85 70; Cityterminalen; 🕑 9am-5.30pm Mon-Fri), which represents the big concerns such as Eurolines and Y-Bussen, along with many of the direct buses to the north.

Swebus Express (☎ 0200 21 82 18; www.swebusexpress.se; 2nd level, Cityterminalen) runs daily to Malmö (9¼ hours), Göteborg (seven hours), Norrköping (two hours), Kalmar (six hours), Mora (4¼ hours), Örebro (three hours) and Oslo (eight hours). There are also direct runs to Gävle (2½ hours), Uppsala (one hour) and Västerås (1¾ hours).

Ybuss (☎ 020 033 44 44; www.ybuss.se in Swedish; Cityterminalen) runs services to Sundsvall, Östersund and Umeå. You'll also find a number of companies running buses from many provincial towns directly to Stockholm. See the relevant destination chapters for details.

Car & Motorcycle

The E4 motorway passes through the city, just west of the centre, on its way from Helsingborg to Haparanda. The E20 motorway from Stockholm to Göteborg via Örebro, follows the E4 as far as Södertälje. The E18 from Kapellskär to Oslo runs from east to west and passes just north of the city centre.

For car hire close to Centralstationen, contact **Statoil** (Map p80; ☎ 20 20 64; Vasagatan 16), or **Avis** (Map p80; ☎ 20 20 60; Vasagatan 10B).

Train

Stockholm is the hub for national train services run by **Sveriges Järnväg** (SJ; ☎ 0771-75 75 75; www.sj.se). and **Tågkompaniet** (☎ 020 44 41 11; www.tagkompaniet.se in Swedish).

Centralstationen (Stockholm C; 🕑 5am-midnight) is the central train station. At the domestic **ticket office** (🕑 7.30am-8pm Mon-Fri, 8.30am-6pm Sat, 9.30am-7pm Sun) there are special ticket windows, where you can purchase international train tickets between 10am and 6pm, Monday to Friday. If your train departs outside these times, you can buy a ticket from the ticket collector on the train.

Direct SJ trains to/from Copenhagen, Oslo and Storlien (for Trondheim) arrive and depart from Centralstationen, as do the overnight Tågkompaniet trains from Göteborg (via Stockholm and Boden) to Kiruna and Narvik; the Arlanda Express; and the SL *pendeltåg* commuter services that run to/from Nynäshamn, Södertälje and Märsta. Other SL local rail lines (Roslagsbanan and Saltsjöbanan) run from Stockholm Östrastationen (T-Tekniska Högskolan) and Slussen, respectively.

In the basement at Centralstationen, you'll find lockers costing Skr35 to Skr75 (depending on size) for 24 hours, toilets for Skr5, and showers (next to the toilets) for Skr25. These facilities are open 5am to midnight daily. There's also a left-luggage office, open daily, and a **lost property office** (☎ 762 25 50; 🕑 10am-6pm Mon-Fri).

Follow the signs to find your way to the local metro (T-bana) network; the underground station here is called T-Centralen.

GETTING AROUND

To/From the Airports

The **Arlanda Express** (☎ 58 88 90 00; tickets from Skr200) train from Centralstationen takes only 20 minutes to reach Arlanda; trains run every 15 minutes from about 5am to midnight. The same trip in a taxi costs around Skr350, but agree on the fare first and don't use any taxi without a contact telephone number displayed. **Taxi Stockholm** (☎ 15 00 00) is one reputable operator.

The cheaper option is the **Flygbuss** service between Arlanda airport and Cityterminalen. Buses leave every 10 or 15 minutes (Skr89, 40 minutes). It's also possible to arrange a connecting **Flygtaxi** (Skr115) to meet you at your Flygbuss stop and take you directly to your door. Tickets for both can be purchased on arrival at the Flygbuss counter at Arlanda airport's main terminal.

Bicycle

Stockholm has a wide network of bicycle paths and in summer you won't regret bringing a bicycle with you or hiring one to get around. The tourist offices have maps for sale, but they're not usually necessary if you have a basic city map already.

Top day trips include Djurgården; Drottningholm (return by steamer); Haga Park or the adjoing Ulriksdal Park or a loop from Gamla Stan to Södermalm, Långholmen and Kungsholmen (on lakeside paths). Trails and bike lanes are clearly marked with traffic signs. Some long-distance routes are marked all the way from central Stockholm: Nynäsleden to Nynäshamn joins Sommarleden near Västerhaninge and swings west to Södertälje. Roslagsleden leads to Norrtälje (linking Blåleden and Vaxholm). Upplandsleden leads to Märsta north of Stockholm, and you can ride to Uppsala via Sigtuna. Sörmlandsleden leads to Södertälje.

Bicycles can be carried free on SL local trains, except during peak hour (6am to 9am and 3pm to 6pm weekdays). They are not allowed in Centralstationen or on the metro, although you'll see some daring souls from time to time.

Sjöcafé (☎ 660 5757; ⌚ 9am-9pm), by the bridge across to Djurgården, rents out bikes for Skr65/250 per hour/day (with options for longer rentals). For about the same price they also rent in-line skates, another good way to get around.

Boat

Djurgårdsfärjan city ferry services connect Gröna Lund Tivoli on Djurgården with Nybroplan and Slussen as frequently as every 10 minutes in summer (considerably less frequently in the low season); a single trip costs Skr20 (free with the SL Tourist Card or a monthly SL card).

Car & Motorcycle

Driving in central Stockholm is not recommended. Small one-way streets, congested bridges and limited parking all present problems; note that Djurgårdsvägen is closed near Skansen at night, on summer weekends and some holidays. Don't attempt to drive through the narrow streets of Gamla Stan.

Parking is a major problem, but there are *P-hus* (parking stations) throughout the city; they charge up to Skr50 per hour, though the fixed evening rate is usually more reasonable. If you do have a car, one of the best options is to stay on the outskirts of town and catch public transport into the centre.

Public Transport

Storstockholms Lokaltrafik (SL; www.sl.se) runs all tunnelbana (T or T-bana) metro trains, local trains and buses within the entire Stockholm county. There is an SL information office in the basement of Centralstationen near the Sergels Torg entrance (open until 11.15pm), which issues timetables and sells the SL Tourist Card and Stockholm Card. You can also call ☎ 600 10 00 for schedule and travel information from 7am to 9pm weekdays, and 8am to 9pm on weekends.

The Stockholm Card (p72 for more information) covers travel on all SL trains and buses in greater Stockholm. The 24-hour (Skr80) and 72-hour (Skr150) SL Tourist Cards are primarily for transport and only give free entry to a few attractions. The 72-hour SL Tourist Card is good value, especially if you use the third afternoon for transport to either end of the county – you can reach the ferry terminals in Grisslehamn, Kapellskär or Nynäshamn, as well as all of the archipelago harbours. If you want to explore the county in more detail, bring a passport photo and get yourself a 30-day SL pass (Skr600, or Skr360 for children age seven to 18 and seniors).

On Stockholm's public transport system the minimum fare costs two coupons, and each additional zone costs another coupon (up to five coupons for four or five zones). Coupons cost Skr10 each, but it's much better to buy strips of tickets for Skr110. Coupons are stamped at the start of a journey. Travelling without a valid ticket can lead to a fine of Skr600 or more. Coupons, tickets and passes can be bought at metro stations, Pressbyrån kiosks, SL railway stations, SL information offices, and from bus drivers.

International rail passes (eg Scanrail, Interrail) aren't valid on SL trains.

BUS

While the bus timetables and route maps are complicated, they're worth studying as there are some useful connections to suburban

STOCKHOLM METRO MAP

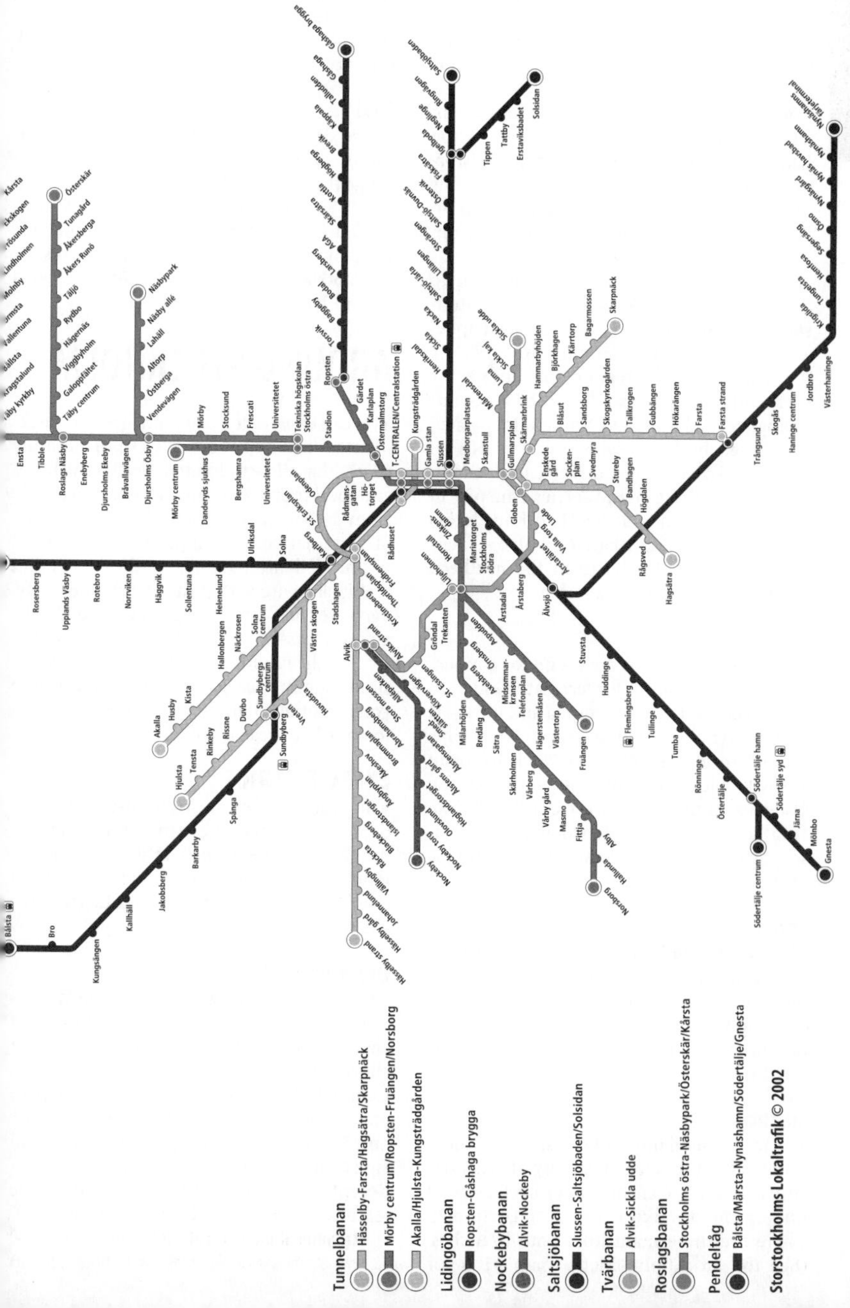

attractions. Ask **SL** (☎ 600 10 00) or any tourist office for the handy inner-city route map *Innerstadsbussar*.

Inner-city buses radiate from Sergels Torg, Odenplan, Fridhemsplan (on Kungsholmen) and Slussen. Bus 47 runs from Sergels Torg to Djurgården, and bus 69 runs from Centralstationen and Sergels Torg to the Ladugårdsgärdet museums and Kaknästornet. Useful buses for hostellers include bus 65, which goes from Centralstationen to Skeppsholmen, and bus 43, which runs from Regeringsgatan to Södermalm.

Inner-city night buses run from 1am to 5pm on a few routes. Most leave from Centralstationen, Sergels Torg, Slussen, Odenplan and Fridhemsplan to the suburbs.

Check where the regional bus hub is for each outlying area. Islands of the Ekerö municipality (including Drottningholm palace) are served by buses with numbers 301 to 323 from T-Brommaplan. Buses to Vaxholm (the 670) and the Åland ferries (the 637 to Grisslehamn and 640 or 631 to Kapellskär) depart from T-Tekniska Högskolan. Odenplan is the hub for buses to the northern suburbs, including Hagaparken.

TRAIN

Local *pendeltåg* trains are useful for connections to Nynäshamn (for ferries to Gotland), to Märsta (for buses to Sigtuna and the short hop to Arlanda Airport) and Södertälje. There are also services to Nockeby from T-Alvik; Lidingö from T-Ropsten; Kårsta, Österskär and Näsbypark from T-Tekniska Högskolan; and to Saltsjöbaden from T-Slussen. SL coupons can be used on these trains, or you can pay on board.

TRAM

The historic **No 7 tram** (☎ 660 77 00) runs between Norrmalmstorg and Skansen, passing most attractions on Djurgården. Separate fees apply for those with a Stockholm Card (adult/child Skr20/10), but the SL Tourist Card is valid.

METRO

The most useful mode of transport in Stockholm is the tunnelbana, run by SL. Its lines converge on T-Centralen, connected by an underground walkway to Centralstationen. There are three main lines with branches. (See the Stockholm Metro map p103 for route details). The blue line has a comprehensive collection of modern art decorating the underground stations, and several stations along other lines are decorated as well, often by famous artists.

Taxi

There's usually no problem finding a taxi, but they're expensive, so check for a meter or arrange the fare first. The flag fall is Skr35, then about Skr7 per kilometre. At night, women should ask about *tjejtaxa,* a discount rate offered by some operators. Reputable firms are **Taxi Stockholm** (☎ 15 00 00), **Taxi 020** (☎ 020 93 93 93) and **Taxi Kurir** (☎ 30 00 00).

AROUND STOCKHOLM

You can explore the county of greater Stockholm with the SL Tourist Card or monthly passes that allow unlimited travel on all buses and local trains. Free timetables are available from the SL office in Centralstationen or the SL terminals at Slussen or Östrastationen.

The delightful islands of the Stockholm archipelago are within easy reach of the city. Ferry services aren't expensive and there's a travel pass available if you want to tour around the islands for a while. On warm and sunny summer days, you could easily believe you're in the south of France rather than in the northern reaches of Europe.

EKERÖ DISTRICT

The pastoral Ekerö district, just 20km west of Stockholm, is home to the fabulous Drottningholm castle as well as several large islands in Mälaren lake, a dozen medieval churches and the Unesco World Heritage site at Birka.

Drottningholm

The royal residence and parks of Drottningholm on Lovön are popular attractions and easy to visit from the capital. If you're not short of time you can cycle out to the palace. Otherwise, take the metro to T-Brommaplan and change to a bus numbered between 301 and 323. If you're driving, there are few road signs for Drottningholm, so get hold of a decent map. The car park is second on the left after crossing Drottningholmsbron.

Strömma Kanalbolaget (Map p80; ☎ 58 71 40 00; www.strommakanalbolaget.com) will take you to

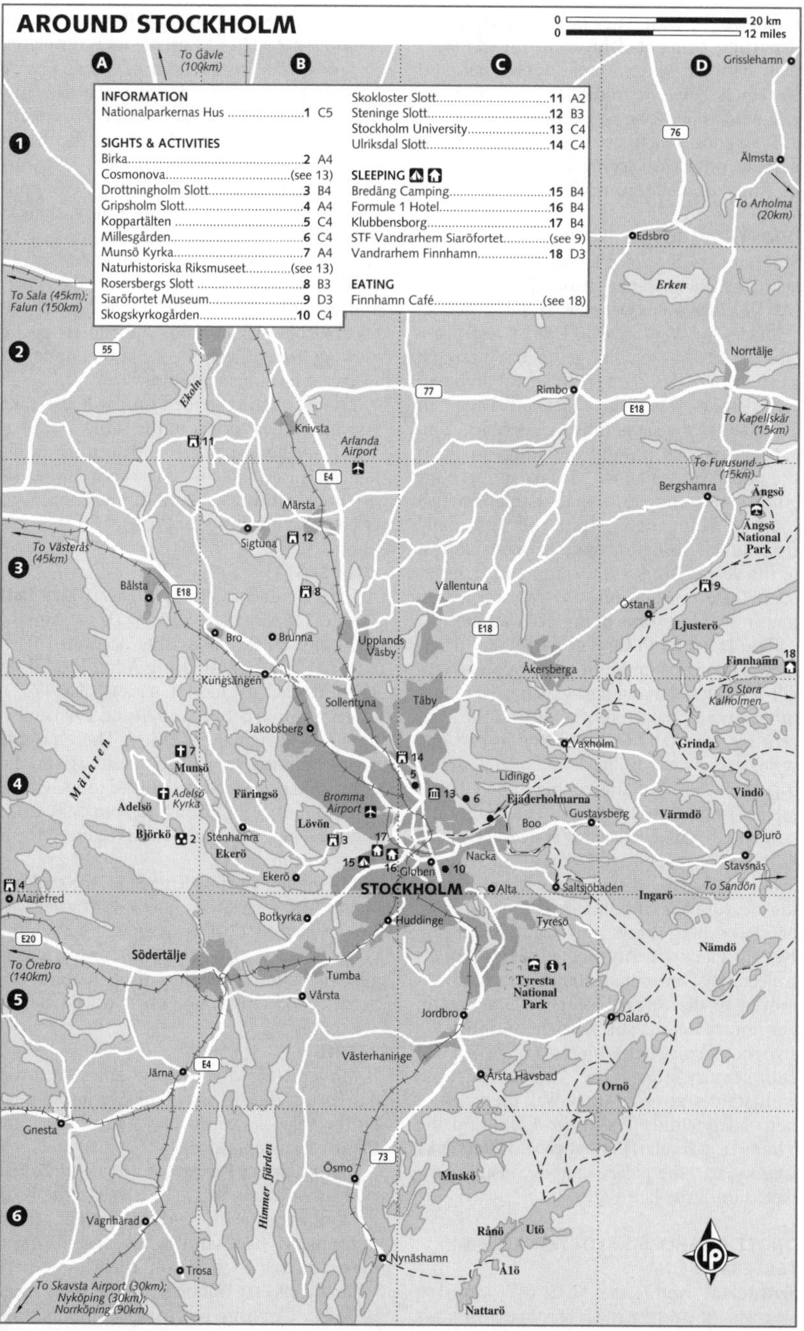
AROUND STOCKHOLM
0 20 km
0 12 miles
INFORMATION
Nationalparkernas Hus 1 C5
SIGHTS & ACTIVITIES
Birka 2 A4
Cosmonova (see 13)
Drottningholm Slott 3 B4
Gripsholm Slott 4 A4
Koppartälten 5 C4
Millesgården 6 C4
Munsö Kyrka 7 A4
Naturhistoriska Riksmuseet (see 13)
Rosersbergs Slott 8 B3
Siaröfortet Museum 9 D3
Skogskyrkogården 10 C4
Skokloster Slott 11 A2
Steninge Slott 12 B3
Stockholm University 13 C4
Ulriksdal Slott 14 C4
SLEEPING
Bredäng Camping 15 B4
Formule 1 Hotel 16 B4
Klubbensborg 17 B4
STF Vandrarhem Siaröfortet (see 9)
Vandrarhem Finnhamn 18 D3
EATING
Finnhamn Café (see 18)
To Gävle (100km)
Grisslehamn
Älmsta
To Arholma (20km)
Edsbro
Erken
To Sala (45km); Falun (150km)
Ekoln
Norrtälje
Rimbo
To Kapellskär (15km)
Knivsta
Arlanda Airport
To Furusund (15km)
Bergshamra
Ängsö
Ängsö National Park
Märsta
Sigtuna
To Västerås (45km)
Bålsta
Vallentuna
Östanå
Ljusterö
Bro
Brunna
Upplands Väsby
Finnhamn
Kungsängen
Åkersberga
To Stora Kalholmen
Sollentuna
Täby
Jakobsberg
Vaxholm
Grinda
Mälaren
Munsö
Lidingö
Adelsö Kyrka
Färingsö
Bromma Airport
Ejäderholmarna
Vindö
Adelsö
Värmdö
Lövön
Gustavsberg
Björkö
Stenhamra
Boo
Djurö
Ekerö
Nacka
Stavsnäs
Globen
Mariefred
Ekerö
STOCKHOLM
Alta
Saltsjöbaden
To Sandön
Ingarö
Botkyrka
Huddinge
Tyresö
Nämdö
To Örebro (140km)
Södertälje
Tumba
Tyresta National Park
Vårsta
Jordbro
Dalarö
Västerhaninge
Järna
Årsta Havsbad
Ornö
Gnesta
Himmer fjärden
Ösmo
Muskö
Vagnhärad
Rånö
Utö
Nynäshamn
Trosa
Ålö
To Skavsta Airport (30km); Nyköping (30km); Norrköping (90km)
Nattarö
55
77
76
E18
E4
E20
73

the palace by boat. They have frequent boats departing from Stadshusbron (Stockholm) daily between May and mid-September, and weekends between mid-September and the end of October (one way/return Skr90/120).

It's a good idea to use the Stockholm Card here, as otherwise seeing everything on the grounds can get expensive.

DROTTNINGHOLMS SLOTT

Still home to the royal family for part of the year, the Renaissance-inspired main **palace** (☎ 402 62 80; www.royalcourt.se; adult/child Skr60/30; 🕒 10am-4.30pm May-Aug, noon-3.30pm Sep, noon-3.30pm Sat & Sun Oct-Apr), with its geometric baroque gardens, was designed by the great architect Nicodemius Tessin the Elder and begun in 1662, about the same time as Versailles. You can either walk around the wings open to the public on your own, or take a one-hour guided tour (no additional charge; English tours at 11am, noon, 1pm and 3pm daily from June to August, reduced schedule rest of the year). Tours are recommended, especially for an insight into the cultural milieu that influenced some of the decorations.

The **Lower North Corps de Garde** was originally a guard room but it's now replete with gilt-leather wall hangings, which used to feature in many palace rooms during the 17th century. The **Karl X Gustav Gallery**, in baroque style, depicts the militaristic endeavours of this monarch, but the ceiling shows battle scenes from classical times. The highly ornamented **State Bedchamber of Hedvig Eleonora** is the most expensive baroque interior in Sweden and it's decorated with paintings that feature the childhood of Karl XI. The painted ceiling shows Karl X and his queen, Hedvig Eleonora. Although Lovisa Ulrika's collection of more than 2000 books has been moved to the Royal Library in Stockholm, her library here is still a bright and impressive room, complete with most of its original 18th-century fittings. The elaborate staircase, with statues at every turn, was the work of both Nicodemius Tessin the Elder and the Younger. Circular **Drottningholms Slottskyrka** (admission free), the palace chapel, wasn't completed until the late 1720s.

DROTTNINGHOLMS SLOTTSTEATER & TEATERMUSEUM

Slottsteater (Court Theatre; ☎ 759 04 06; www.drottningholmsslottsteater.dtm.se; admission by tour adult/child Skr60/40; tours 🕒 hourly 12.30pm-4.30pm May, 11.30am-4.30pm Jun-Aug, 1.30pm-3.30pm Sep) was completed in 1766 on the instructions of Queen Lovisa Ulrika. This extraordinary place was untouched from the time of Gustav III's death (1792) until 1922. It's the oldest theatre in the world still in its original state; performances are held here in summer (see opposite) using 18th-century machinery, such as ropes, pulleys and wagons. Scenes can be changed in less than seven seconds.

Illusion was the order of the day here, and accordingly the theatre makes use of fake marble, fake curtains and papier-mâché viewing boxes. Even the stage was designed to create illusions regarding size.

The interesting guided tour will also take you into other rooms in the same building. You'll see hand-painted 18th-century wallpaper and an Italian-style room *(salon de déjeuner)* with fake three-dimensional wall effects and a ceiling that resembles the sky.

KINA SLOTT

At the far end of the gardens is **Kina Slott** (☎ 402 62 70; adult/child Skr50/25; 🕒 11am-4.30pm May-Aug, noon-3.30pm Sep), a lavishly decorated Chinese pavilion built by King Adolf Fredrik as a birthday gift to Queen Lovisa Ulrika (1753). It was restored between 1989 and 1996 and is now in its original condition. There's a **café** on the premises serving good waffles, and the admission price includes guided tours, which run at 11am, noon, 2pm and 3pm daily from June to August (the schedule is reduced from May to September).

On the slope below Kina Slott, the striking **Guards' Tent** (admission free; 🕒 noon-4pm Jun–mid-Aug) was erected in 1781 as quarters for the dragoons of Gustav III, but it's not really a tent at all. The building now has displays about the gardens and Drottningholm's Royal Guard.

EATING

Bring a picnic with you and enjoy it in the gardens, or dine in one of the two restaurants by the palace. There's also a small kiosk by the driveway entrance.

Drottningholms Paviljongen (☎ 759 04 25; light meals Skr35-100, mains Skr120-185) Close to the boat dock, this café with outdoor seating, serves light meals like sandwiches and heartier mains, as well as coffee and cakes.

Drottningholms Wärdshus (☎ 759 03 08; mains Skr185-230) Opposite the palace grounds, this is a little more upmarket. It offers an extensive menu, with simple *husmanskost* dishes, such as meatballs, from Skr95 and fancier meat and fish mains.

ENTERTAINMENT

Drottningholms Slottsteater (☎ 660 82 25; www.drottningholmsslottsteater.dtm.se; Drottningholm; tickets Skr100-410) This is a beautiful, small 18th-century theatre at the royal palace. It stages opera and ballet productions in summer that are well worth attending.

Ekerö & Munsö

These long and narrow islands in Mälaren lake are joined together and have a main road running most of their length. The free car ferry to Adelsö departs from the northern end of Munsö.

The two churches of Ekerö and Munsö both date from the 12th century. **Munsö kyrka** is an interesting structure with a round-tower and a narrow steeple.

Buses 311 and 312 frequently run out here from T-Brommaplan in Stockholm.

Birka

The Viking trading centre of **Birka** (☎ 56 05 14 45; www.raa.se/birka; 🕑 11am-6pm May-Sep), on Björkö in Mälaren lake, is now a Unesco World Heritage site. It was founded around AD 760 with the intention of expanding and controlling trade in the region. The village attracted merchants and craft workers, and the population grew to about 700. A large defensive fort with thick dry-stone ramparts was constructed next to the village. In 830, the Benedictine monk Ansgar was sent to Birka by the Holy Roman Emperor to convert the heathen Vikings to Christianity and he lived in Birka for 18 months. Birka was abandoned in the late 10th century when Sigtuna took over the role of commercial centre.

The village site is surrounded by a vast graveyard. It's the largest Viking age cemetery in Scandinavia, with around 3000 graves. Most people were cremated, then mounds of earth were piled over the remains, but some Christian coffins and chambered tombs have been found. The fort and harbour have also been excavated. A cross to the memory of St Ansgar can be seen on top of a nearby hill.

The **Birka Museum** (🕑 11am-6pm May-Sep) is excellent. Exhibits include finds from the excavations (which are still proceeding), copies of the most magnificent objects, and an interesting model showing the village as it was in Viking times.

Cruises to Birka run from early May to late September; the round-trip on Strömma Kanalbolaget's *Victoria* from Stadshusbron, Stockholm, is a full day's outing (Skr255). The cruise price includes a visit to the museum and a guided tour in English of the settlement's burial mounds and fortifications. Call ☎ 5871 40 00 for details; boats leave around 9am. Ferries do not run during the midsummer holidays.

Boats also leave from Adelsö (Hovgården) to Birka (Skr95, including museum entry); call ☎ 711 14 57 for details. Summer cruises to Birka depart from many other places around Mälaren, including Mariefred, Södertälje, Strängnäs and Västerås.

VAXHOLM

There's a good reason this pastoral island runs thick with tourists in summer. About 35km northeast of the city, Vaxholm is dotted with the kind of quaint summerhouses kept by the fashionable set in the 19th century. The settlement was founded in 1647, and the oldest buildings are in Norrhamn, a few minutes' walk north of the town hall. There's also interesting architecture along Hamngatan, as well as galleries, boutiques and souvenir shops.

Vaxholm is the gateway to the central and northern reaches of the archipelago. It's a pleasant place with many attractions and a relaxed atmosphere, and it's well worth a visit.

Information

There's a **tourist office** (☎ 54 13 14 80; infp@visitvaxholm.com, www.vaxholm.se; 🕑 10am-6pm Mon-Fri, 10am-4pm Sat & Sun Jun-Aug, 10am-3pm Mon-Fri, 10am-2pm Sat & Sun Sep-May) inside the *rådhus* (town hall), off Hamngatan; look for the onion dome, a product of the *rådhus* rebuilding in 1925. Also on Hamngatan are a bank, supermarkets and other services.

Sights

The construction of **Vaxholm Kastell** (Citadel; ☎ 54 17 21 57; adult/child Skr50/free; 🕑 noon-4pm mid-Jun–mid-Aug), a fortress on an islet just east of the town, was originally ordered by Gustav Vasa in 1544, but most of the current structure dates from 1863. The fortress was attacked by the Danes in 1612 and the Russian navy in 1719. Nowadays, it's home to the National Museum of Coastal Defence and a restaurant-conference centre. The ferry across to the island departs regularly from Söderhamn (the bustling harbour) and the admission price is included in the fare.

The **Hembygdsgård** (☎ 54 13 17 20; Trädgårdsgatan 19; admission free; ⏲ 11am-4pm Sat & Sun May-Aug) preserves the finest old houses in Norrhamn. The **fiskarebostad** is an excellent example of a late-19th-century fisherman's house, with a typical Swedish fireplace. The café here is open daily from May to mid-September.

Sleeping & Eating

Bogesund Vandrarhem (☎ 54 13 22 40; dm Skr210) By a castle 5km southwest of Vaxholm, this is a pleasant, well-equipped STF hostel located in peaceful countryside. Bus 671 stops on the main road about 500m from the hostel.

Waxholms Hotell (☎ 54 13 01 50; info@waxholmshotell.se; Hamngatan 2; s/d from Skr900/1025) Just opposite the harbour front, this hotel is a mixture of Art Nouveau and modern styles. Discounted rooms are available here in July, and on weekends year-round. This grand place is in the centre of the action, and there are restaurants on the premises, including Kabyssen with meals from Skr100 to Skr200 and a popular outdoor terrace.

Moby Dick (☎ 54 13 07 05; Söderhamnsplan 1; meals Skr75-150) On the waterfront, Moby Dick has an extensive menu offering pizza, pasta, salad and more.

Getting There & Away

Bus 670 from the metro station T-Tekniska Högskolan runs regularly to the town.

Waxholmsbolaget (Map p80; ☎ 679 58 30; www.waxholmsbolaget.se) boats sail frequently between Vaxholm and Strömkajen in Stockholm (about 40 minutes). **Strömma Kanalbolaget** (Map p80; ☎ 58 71 40 00; www.strommakanalbolaget.com) sails between Strandvägen and Vaxholm three times daily from mid-June to mid-August (one way/return Skr115/150), and once daily the rest of the year (no services in December and January).

STOCKHOLM ARCHIPELAGO

Ask anyone in Stockholm what one summer activity no visitor should miss, and most will tell you to see the archipelago. With anything between 14,000 and 100,000 islands, depending on whom you ask (the general consensus is 24,000), the archipelago around Stockholm is surprisingly accessible and very rewarding. Every Stockholmer's dream is to own a little red summer cottage on a rocky islet, but visitors can rent them even for short stays, and regular boats offer great opportunities for outings.

Information

For information on cabin and chalet rental in the archipelago, contact **Destination Stockholms Skärgård** (☎ 54 24 81 00; dess.skarg@dess.se, www.dess.se; Lillström, SE-18497 Ljusterö).

For excellent information about the archipelago, in English and other languages, check out www.skargardsstiftelsen.se.

Activities

The biggest boat operator in the archipelago is **Waxholmsbolaget** (Map p80; ☎ 679 58 30; www.waxholmsbolaget.se). Timetables and information are available from its offices outside the Grand Hotel on Strömkajen in Stockholm, and at the harbour in Vaxholm, as well as online. It divides the archipelago into three areas: *Norra Skärgården* is the northern section (north from Ljusterö to Arholma); *Mellersta Skärgården* is the middle section, taking in Vaxholm, Ingmarsö, Stora Kalholmen, Finnhamn, Möja and Sandhamn; and *Södra Skärgården* is the southern section, with boats south to Nämdö, Ornö and Utö.

Waxholmbolaget's Båtluffarkortet pass (Skr300 for five days) gives unlimited rides on its services plus a handy island map.

If your time is short, a recommended tour is the Thousand Island Cruise offered by **Stromma Kanabolaget** (Map p80; ☎ 58 71 40 00; www.strommakanalbolaget.com; Nybrokajen), running daily between late June and mid-August. The full day's tour departs from Stockholm's Nybrokajen at 9.30am and returns at 8.30pm; the cost of Skr900 includes lunch, dinner, drinks and guided tours ashore. The boat pulls in to a number of interesting islands, and there are opportunities for swimming.

Islands

ARHOLMA

Arholma is one of the most interesting islands in the far north of the archipelago. Everything was burnt down during a Russian invasion in 1719. The lighthouse was rebuilt in the 19th century and it's a well-known landmark. It became a popular resort in the early 20th century. It's noted for its traditional village and chapel, and has fine sandy beaches and good swimming from the rocks.

Arholma has a summer café, a shop, a simple camping ground and bike rental. **Vandrarhem Arholma** (☎ 0176-560 18; beds Skr120; yr-round) is a pleasant STF hostel in a renovated barn; advance booking is essential.

You can take bus 640 from Stockholm Tekniska Högskolan to Norrtälje, then 636 to Simpnäs (two to six daily), followed by a 20-minute ferry crossing to the island (Skr30).

ÄNGSÖ

This island, 15km south of Norrtälje, was declared a national park as early as 1909, despite being only 1.5km long and 600m wide. It is characterised by meadows, virgin woodland and magnificent displays of wild flowers (especially in spring). You may also see ospreys, sea eagles and great-crested grebes.

You can't stay overnight in the park, but there are boat trips (from Furusund) and guided walks; contact **Norrtälje tourist office** (☎ 0176-719 90) for current details. Bus 621 runs every hour or two (fewer at weekends) from T-Danderyds sjukhus (Stockholm) to Norrtälje, and buses 632/634 run three or four times daily from Norrtälje to Furusund. Alternatively, there are boats from Stockholm and Vaxholm to Furusund (Skr100).

SIARÖFORTET

The tiny island of Kyrkogårdsön, in the important sea lane just north of Ljusterö (40km due northeast of Stockholm), may be only 400m long but it's one of the most fascinating islands in the archipelago.

After the outbreak of WWI, military authorities decided that the Vaxholm Kastell wasn't good enough and, in 1916, construction of a new fort began on Kyrkogårdsön. This powerful defence facility, Siaröfortet, was never used in anger. Renovated in 1996, it's now open as a **museum** (admission free) and a visit is highly recommended. You'll see the officers' mess, kitchen, sleeping quarters and tunnels, plus two impressive 15.2cm cannons (they're trained on passing Viking Line ferries!) There are no fixed opening times; contact the STF hostel to arrange a tour.

STF Vandrarhem Siaröfortet (☎ 54 24 30 90; beds Skr165; May-Sep) is an excellent STF hostel in the old soldiers' barracks. Canoe hire and breakfast are available; advance booking is recommended.

Waxholmsbolaget ferries to Siaröfortet depart from Strömkajen in Stockholm and sail to Siaröfortet via Vaxholm once or twice daily. The journey takes 1½ hours from Stockholm, or 50 minutes from Vaxholm (Skr100 and Skr90 respectively).

FINNHAMN

This 900m-long island, northeast of Stockholm, has rocky cliffs and a small beach with good swimming opportunities. Finnhamn is fairly trendy, attracting wealthy visitors from Stockholm and beyond. If you want to escape or if accommodation is booked up, you can camp in the woods.

Vandrarhem Finnhamn (☎ 54 24 62 12; inof@finnhamn.nu; dm Skr230; yr-round) is an STF hostel in a large converted warehouse, with boats available to hire. It's the largest hostel in the archipelago; advance booking is essential. The **Finnhamn Café** (☎ 54 24 64 04) serves good meals, and has a lovely view.

You can sail with **Waxholmsbolaget** (Map p80; ☎ 679 58 30) from Strömkajen (Stockholm) to Finnhamn, via Vaxholm, up to five times daily (Skr115, two hours). **Cinderella Båtarna** (Map p80; ☎ 58 71 40 50) also sails here daily from Strandvägen in Stockholm (Skr125).

SANDÖN

Sandön is 2.5km long and has superb sandy beaches that are reminiscent of the Mediterranean on a sunny day. Sandhamn is the northern settlement on the island, but the best beaches are at Trovill, near the southern tip. The wooden houses and narrow alleys of Sandhamn are worth exploring too. However, the island is a popular destination for partygoers and wealthy sailors – many regattas start or finish here. As a result of this, the place is rather expensive and it is best visited just as a day trip. Camping is prohibited.

Sandhamns Värdshus (☎ 57 15 30 51; s/d from Skr550/850) first opened in 1672 and still serves good food. Popular **Dykarbaren** (☎ 57 15 35 54; mains around Skr140) is a fashionable restaurant/bar just 50m from the quay, with lunch specials from Skr75.

Waxholmsbolaget (☎ 679 58 30) sails from Strömkajen to Sandhamn, via Vaxholm, one to four times daily (Skr115, two hours). **Cinderella Båtarna** (☎ 58 71 40 50) do the same run regularly from Strandvägen (Skr125).

Strömma Kanalbolaget (☎ 58 71 40 00) runs tours from Nybroplan to Sandhamn daily between mid-June and mid-August (one way/return Skr130/225), departing at 10am and returning at 6pm (with two hours at Sandhamn). The price includes a one-hour guided walking tour around Sandhamn.

UTÖ

Utö is a delightful island in the southern section of the archipelago – it's 13km long and up to 4km wide. The road and track network make it popular with cyclists.

You can get a reasonable sketch map of the island from the **tourist office** (☎ 50 15 74 10; 10am-4pm Mon-Fri Apr-Sep), found in a small cabin by the guest harbour at Gruvbryggan, also known as Gruvbyn (the northernmost village). When the tourist office is closed, ask at the *värdshus,* which is just up the hill.

Sights & Activities

Most of the sights are at the northern end of the island, near Gruvbryggan. The most unusual is Sweden's oldest iron mine, which opened in 1150 but closed in 1879. The three pits are now flooded – the deepest is Nyköp ingsgruvan (215m). The **mining museum** (opposite the *värdshus*) keeps variable hours, so check locally. The well-preserved, 18th-century **miners' houses** on Lurgatan are worth a look, and the **windmill** (11am-3pm) is fun. The best **sandy beach** is on the north coast, it's a 10 minute walk from the *värdshus* in the direction of Kroka. To see the **glaciated rock slabs** on the east coast, walk for about 20 minutes through the forest towards Rävstavik.

Sleeping & Eating

Open from May to September, the **STF hostel** (☎ 50 42 03 15; receptionen@uto-vardshus.se; Gruvbyggan; dm Skr200), associated with the nearby *värdshus,* is in a former summer house. Reception and meals are at the *värdshus.*

Utö Värdshus (☎ 50 42 03 00; receptionen@uto-vardshus.se; 2-person chalets with breakfast per person low/high season Skr800/1000) This is the only hotel on the island and isn't cheap, but facilities are good and there's the bonus of the on-site **restaurant**, considered the best in the archipelago. Lunch specials are about Skr80, à la carte dinner mains around Skr200. There are also a couple of popular summer bars here.

You may prefer to try the more down-to-earth café **Dannekrogen** (☎ 50 15 70 79), near the Gruvbryggan harbour, or even the bakery and supermarket.

Getting There & Around

The easiest way to reach Utö is to take the *pendeltåg* (commuter train) from Stockholm Centralstationen to Västerhaninge, then bus 846 to Årsta Havsbad. From there, Waxholmsbolaget ferries leave up to a dozen times a day for Utö (Skr65, 45 minutes), but make sure you know whether your boat stops at Spränga or Gruvbryggan first. Ask at the **guest harbour** (☎ 50 15 74 10) about bike hire (from Skr75 per day).

KAPELLSKÄR

Kapellskär is so tiny it can't really even be described as a village – there's little to it except for a camping ground, hostel and large ferry terminal. The coastline, however, is spectacular, dotted with small, still-working fishing villages, and the surrounding countryside is delightfully pastoral. Most people come here for ferry connections to Finland and Estonia; see p328 for details.

There is also a small memorial for the 852 passengers killed in the Estonia ferry disaster of September 1994; it's up the hill across the main road from the ferry terminal.

There's an **STF hostel** (☎ 0176-441 69; Riddersholm; beds Skr140-150; yr-round) off the E18, 2km west of the ferry terminal; you'll need to book in advance if you plan to stay outside of the peak summer season (mid-June to mid-August), and there's no restaurant, so bring your own food.

Viking Line's direct bus from Stockholm Cityterminalen to meet the ferries costs Skr65, but if you have an SL pass, take bus 640 or 644 from T-Tekniska Högskolan to Norrtälje and change to 631, which runs every two hours or so (infrequently at weekends).

TYRESTA NATIONAL PARK

Some of the best hiking and wilderness scenery can be found in the 4900-hectare Tyresta National Park, only 20km southeast of Stockholm. The park, established in 1993, is noted for its virgin forest, which includes 300-year-old pine trees. This is a beautiful area, with rocky outcrops, small lakes, marshes and a wide variety of birdlife, and it's an easy, worthwhile trip if you're looking for a reason to get out of the city and into nature.

At the southwestern edge of the park is **Nationalparkernas Hus** (National Parks Visitors Centre; ☎ 08-745 33 94; adult/child Skr30/15; Tue-Sun). Here you can discover all of Sweden's national parks (28 at the time of research) through exhibitions and slide shows, but be sure to check out the centre itself – it is built in the shape of Sweden, complete with all 41 corners! There are even 'lakes' on the floor, indicated by different stones.

Ask for the national park leaflet in English and the *Tyresta Nationalpark och Naturreservat* leaflet in Swedish, which includes an excellent topographical map at 1:25,000 scale. From the visitors centre there are various trails into the park. *Sörmlandsleden* track cuts across 6km of the park on its way to central Stockholm.

Access to the park is easy. Take the *pendeltåg* to Haninge centrum (also called Handen station) on the Nynäshamn line, then change to bus 807 or 834. Some buses run all the way to the park, others stop at Svartbäcken (2km west of Tyresta village).

SIGTUNA

One of the cutest and most historically relevant villages in the area lies just 40km northwest of Stockholm. Sigtuna, the most pleasant and important historical town near the city, was founded around AD 980. It's the oldest surviving town in Sweden, and the main drag, Storagatan, is probably Sweden's oldest main street.

Around the year 1000, Olof Skötkonung ordered the minting of Sweden's first coins in the town. Ancient church ruins and rune stones are scattered everywhere – there are about 150 runic inscriptions in the area, most dating from the early 11th century, typically located beside ancient roads.

Most of Sigtuna's original buildings were consumed in devastating late-medieval fires, but the main church survived and there are many quaint streets and wooden buildings still following the medieval town plan.

INFORMATION

The friendly **tourist office** (☎ 59 25 00 20; turism@sigtuna.se; Storagatan 33; 10am-6pm Mon-Sat, 11am-5pm Sun Jun-Aug, 10am-5pm Mon-Fri, 11am or noon-3pm Sat & Sun rest of yr) is in an 18th-century wooden house, Drakegården. There are banks and supermarkets nearby, also on Storagatan.

SIGHTS

During medieval times there were seven stone-built churches in Sigtuna, but most have since crumbled. The ruins of the churches of **St Per** and **St Lars** can be seen off Prästgatan. **St Olof church** was built in the early 12th century, but was ruined by the 17th century. The adjacent **Mariakyrkan** (9am-4pm Sep-May, 9am-8pm Jun-Aug) is the oldest brick building in the area – it was a Dominican monastery church from around 1250, but became the parish church in 1529 after the monastery was demolished by Gustav Vasa. There are restored medieval paintings inside and free summer concerts are held weekly.

Sigtuna Museum (☎ 59 78 38 70; Storagatan 55; adult/child Skr20/free; noon-4pm Tue-Sun Sep-May, noon-4pm Jun-Aug) looks after several attractions in the town, all of them on Stora gatan and near the tourist office. **Lundströmska gården** (adult/child Skr10/5; noon-4pm Jun-Aug, noon-4pm Sat & Sun Sep) is an early-20th-century, middle-class home and adjacent general store, complete with period furnishings and goods. **Sigtuna rådhus** (admission free; noon-4pm Jun-Aug, noon-4pm Sat & Sun Sep), the smallest town hall in Scandinavia, dates from 1744 and was designed by the mayor himself. It's on the town square opposite the tourist office. The main museum building has displays of gold jewellery, runes, coins and loot brought home from abroad.

The magnificent private palace **Steninge Slott** (☎ 59 25 95 00), 7km east of Sigtuna, dates from 1705 and was designed by Nicodemus Tessin the Younger. On the guided palace tour (Skr55; noon and 2pm daily in summer), you'll see luxuriously ornate interiors; in the beautiful grounds there is also the excellent **Cultural Centre** (gallery tour Skr75; yr-round). In a converted stone barn dating from the 1870s, you'll find an art gallery, glassworks, a candle-making area, café and restaurant.

Another palace, **Rosersbergs Slott** (☎ 59 03 50 39; tours adult/child Skr50/25; 1am-3pm mid-May–Aug), is on Mälaren lake about 9km southeast of Sigtuna. It was constructed in the 1630s and used as a royal residence from 1762 to 1860; the interior has excellent furnishings from the Empire period (1790–1820) and Queen Hedvig Elisabeth Charlotta's conversation room is quite extraordinary.

Best in a light snow, **Skokloster Slott** (☎ 018-38 60 77; adult/child Skr40/20), around 11km due northwest of Sigtuna (26km by road), is an exceptionally fine whitewashed baroque palace with a fragile beauty unusual in Sweden. It was built between 1654 and 1671 and has impressive stucco ceilings and collections of furniture, textiles, art and arms. There's a small café at the palace. Guided tours run daily from April to October; it's a good idea to call in advance to check times, as the schedule is complicated and ever-shifting.

Skoklosterspelen is a popular medieval festival held at Skokloster Slott. It lasts five days in mid-July and includes around 350 performances, such as tournaments, exhibitions, concerts, 18th-century activities.

The nearby **motor museum** (☎ 018-38 61 06; adult/child Skr50/25; ⏲ noon-4pm May-Sep), adjacent to the *wärdshus* opposite the palace, is one of dozens in Sweden that has a well-preserved collection of vintage cars and motorcycles.

SLEEPING & EATING

Sigtuna Stadshotell (☎ 59 25 01 00; info@sigtunastadshotell.se; Stora Nygatan 3; s/d Skr1600/2150, discounted to Skr1550/2150) The pick of the town's lodgings is the central, newly renovated, Sigtuna Stadshotell. The décor is all pale, sleek and very stylish, and the upmarket restaurant and bar areas have lovely lake views.

Sigtunastiftelsens Gästhem (☎ 59 25 89 00; Manfred Björkquists allé 2-4; s/d Skr800/950) This attractive, imposing place is run by a Christian foundation and looks like a cross between a cloister and a medieval fortress, but rooms are much cosier than that would imply.

Stora Brännbo (☎ 59 25 75 00; Stora Brännbovägen 2-6; s/d from Skr900/1000, discounted to Skr450/650) This is a large hotel and conference centre just north of the town centre.

Tant Brunn Kaffestuga (☎ 59 25 09 34; Laurentii gränd) In a small alley off Storagatan, this is a delightful 17th-century café set around a pretty courtyard. It's well worth seeking out for its home-baked bread and pastries; just watch your head as you walk in, as the roof beams sag rather dangerously.

Farbror Blå Café & Kök (☎ 59 25 60 50; Stora torget 14; mains Skr100-145) This central café, adjacent to the town hall, does a variety of homey dishes, including salads and burgers, as well as cheaper snacks. It's the 'uncle' *(farbror)* to the 'aunt' of Tant Brunn (above); both names are taken from a popular children's story.

GETTING THERE & AROUND

Travel connections are easy from Stockholm. Take a local train to Märsta, from where there are frequent buses to Sigtuna (570 or 575). Bus 883 runs every hour or two from Uppsala to Sigtuna. To get to Rosersbergs Slott, take the SL *pendeltåg* train to Rosersberg, then walk the final 2km to the palace (signposted). For Skokloster, take an hourly SJ train to Bålsta, then the infrequent bus 894.

Strömma Kanalbolaget (☎ 587 140 00; www.strommakanalbolaget.com) offers full-day cruises four times a week from June to August between Stockholm and Uppsala via Sigtuna and Skokloster. The price (from Skr600) includes lunch, dinner and guided tours; with 1¼ hours in Sigtuna and 1¾ hours at Skokloster.

MARIEFRED

☎ 0159

Tiny, lakeside Mariefred is a pretty little village that draws visitors to its impressive castle, Gripsholm Slott.

INFORMATION

Visit the **tourist office** (☎ 297 90; malarturism@strangnas.se, www.mariefred.se; ⏲ Jun-Aug, Mon-Fri Sep-May) and pick up a map and notes (in English) for a self-guided walking tour of the idyllic village centre, with cobblestone streets and many 18th-century buildings.

SIGHTS

Gripsholm Slott (☎ 101 94; adult/child Skr60/30; ⏲ 10am-4pm mid-May–mid-Sep, noon-3pm Sat & Sun mid-Sep–mid-May) is the epitome of castles, with its round towers, spires and drawbridge. It contains some of the state portrait collection, which dates from the 16th century and you can explore the well-decorated rooms.

Originally built in the 1370s, Gripsholm Slott passed into crown hands by the early 15th century. In 1526, Gustav Vasa took over and ordered the demolition of the adjacent monastery. A new castle with walls up to 5m thick was built using materials from the monastery, but extensions, conversions and repairs continued for years. The oldest 'untouched' room is Karl IX's bedchamber, dating from the 1570s. The castle was abandoned in 1715, but it was renovated and extended during the reign of Gustav III (especially between 1773 and 1785). The moat was filled in and, in 1730 and later in 1827, two 11th-century rune stones were found. These stones stand by the access road and are well worth a look; one has a Christian

VISITING ÅLAND

Although there's plenty to keep you busy in Stockholm, you might be interested in catching a boat across Åland (popular with local day-trippers). Technically Finnish, the Åland islands (population 25,400) are unique and autonomous, with their own flag and culture. This goes back to a League of Nations decision in 1921, after a Swedish–Finnish dispute over sovereignty. Åland took its own flag in 1954 and has issued stamps (prized by collectors) since 1984. Both the euro and Swedish krona are legal tender here. A number of Swedish dialects are spoken, and few Ålanders speak Finnish.

Although Åland joined the EU along with Finland in 1995, it was granted a number exemptions, including duty-free tax laws which allowed the essential ferry services between the islands and mainland Finland and Sweden to continue operating profitably.

The islands are popular for summer cycling and camping holidays; there are medieval churches, ruins and fishing villages to explore. The capital (and only town) of Åland is Mariehamn. In summer, it is crowded with tourists but still manages to retain its village flavour and the marinas at the harbours are quite pretty when loaded up with gleaming sailing boats. The main pedestrian street, Torggatan, is a colourful and crowded hive of activity, and there are some fine museums – enough to allow a leisurely day's exploration. Åland's most striking attraction is the medieval castle, Kastelholm, in Sund 20km northeast of Mariehamn. You can only visit on guided tours, which run frequently (in English) from June to August.

For more information visit **Sweden House** (Hamngatan 27, Stockholm), where there's a travel agency, specialising in the islands. The main companies operating between Sweden and Åland (and on to Finland) are **Viking Line** (www.vikingline.aland.fi) and **Silja Line** (www.silja.com), while **Eckerö Linjen** (www.eckerolinjen.fi), **Ånedin Linjen** (www.anedinlinjen.com) and **Birka Cruises** (www.birkacruises.com) operate only between Åland and Sweden. Once on the islands, you can cycle almost anywhere using the bridges or the network ferries.

cross, while the other describes an expedition against the Saracens. The castle was restored again in the 1890s, the moat was cleared and the drawbridge rebuilt.

You can also visit nearby **Grafikens Hus** (☎ 231 60; adult/child Skr50/free; 🕑 11am-5pm May-Aug, 11am-5pm Tue-Sun Sep-Apr), which is a centre for contemporary graphic art and printmaking.

SLEEPING & EATING

STF Vandrarhem Mariefred (☎ 367 00; receptionen.gripsholm@redcross.se; beds Skr190; 🕑 mid-Jun–mid-Aug) This hostel with excellent facilities is only 500m west of the castle in lovely grounds. It's a Red Cross educational centre for most of the year, but during summer break the student lodgings are turned into hostel accommodation.

Gripsholms Värdshus & Hotell (☎ 347 50; info@gripshols-vardshus.se; Kyrkogatan 1; s/d from Skr1400/1600) This place opened in 1609, this is Sweden's oldest inn. This charming and elegant place has 45 individually furnished rooms, full of antiques, and many rooms have great views of the castle. There is also a highly regarded restaurant here, with a beautiful setting and main courses for around Skr250.

Gripsholms Slottscafé (☎ 100 23; meals Skr65-160) In the gardens by the castle, this is a good place for coffee and cake, or for light meals such as quiche, salad or sandwiches.

GETTING THERE & AWAY

Mariefred isn't on the main railway line – the nearest station is at Läggesta, 3km west, with hourly trains from Stockholm. A **museum railway** (☎ 210 06; one way/return Skr40/50) from Läggesta to Mariefred runs on weekends from mid-May to September (daily from midsummer to mid-August), hourly during the day; call to check schedule. Bus 304 runs hourly from Läggesta to Mariefred.

The steamship S/S *Mariefred* (☎ 08-669 88 50) departs from Stadshusbron (Stockholm) for Mariefred, daily from mid-June to mid-August, and weekends only from mid-May to mid-June and mid-August to mid-September (round-trip Skr250). A round-trip ticket from Stockholm, including an SJ train, the museum railway, admission to the castle and S/S *Mariefred*, costs around Skr350 one way and is available at tourist offices.

Southeast Sweden

This superb region has something for everyone: tiny islands, fairytale castles, an epic canal, wonderful medieval towns and a party-hard beach life.

Småland's most famous feature is Glasriket, the 'Kingdom of Crystal', where beautiful glass artworks are produced. Don't miss a mesmerising visit to one of the 'hot shops', where globules of molten glass are twisted and tweaked into wondrous shapes.

Blekinge was the seat of Sweden's 17th-century sea power and the incredible naval city of Karlskrona, now a Unesco World Heritage site, is a singular mixture of brutal fortresses and grandiloquent design.

Most of the superb island of Öland has also made the Unesco list, due to its unique geology, ring forts and Iron Age burial sites. It's also one of Sweden's favourite vacation spots, even the king and queen kick off the cares of state here on their summer holidays.

Östergötland, laced through by the Göta Canal, is home to the small but perky industrial cities of Norrköping and Linköping as well as the lakeside town of Vadstena, one of Sweden's jewels.

Gotland is one of Sweden's richest historical regions with untold numbers of prehistoric sites, Viking rune stones galore, medieval churches and the Unesco-listed walled town of Visby. Throw in endless sandy beaches and you've got yourself a perfect holiday destination.

HIGHLIGHTS

- Admire the military might of **Karlskrona** (p133), a superb naval fortress town
- Check out the Renaissance perfection of **Kalmar's Slott** (p125), a castle right out of a storybook
- Let the kids run wild with Pippi Longstocking at Vimmerby's theme park, **Astrid Lingren's Värld** (p132) or spend a day at the vast **Kolmården zoo** (p143)
- Blow your own glass vase, or buy one made by a master in **Glasriket** (p127)
- Wonder at the windmills, bask on a beach, or get medieval at Eketorp fortress on long, thin **Öland** (p137)
- Climb the hilly streets and prowl the walls of 13th-century **Visby** (p152)
- Take a lazy trip on the **Göta Canal** (p146)

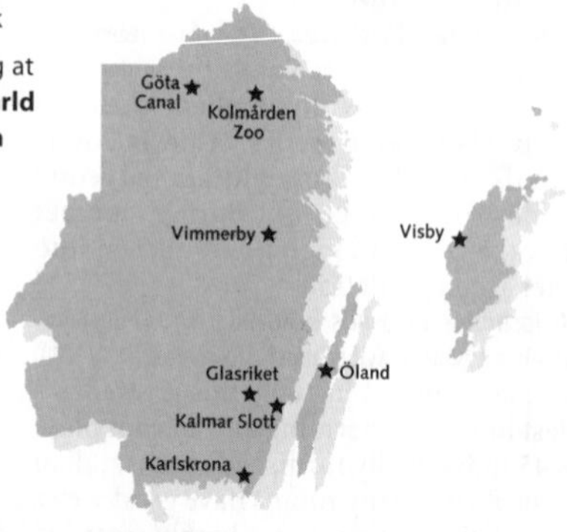

- POPULATION: 1,404,652
- AREA: 49,748 SQ KM
- HIGHEST POINT: STENABOHÖJDEN (327M)

Orientation

Southeast Sweden stretches south along the coast from Stockholm to Skåne and inland as far as Lake Vättern. It incorporates the following *landskap* areas: Småland (including Jönköpings län, Kronobergs län and Kalmar län); the island Öland, off the east coast; Blekinge in the south; Östergötland, the eastern part of Götland, which is split off from the western half by the massive Lake Vättern; and the island of Gotland.

Information

REGIONAL TOURIST OFFICES

Visitors can contact the following for more detailed information on the area:

Blekinge Turism (☎ 0455-30 50 20; www.blekinge turism.com; Ronnebygatan 2, SE-37132 Karlskrona)
Gotlands Turistföreningen (☎ 0498-20 17 00; www .gotland.com; Box 1403, Hamngatan 4, SE-62125, Visby)
Smålands Turism (☎ 036-35 12 70; www.visit -smaland.com; Västra Storgatan 18A, Box 1027, SE-55111 Jönköping)
Turism i Kalmar Län (☎ 0480-44 83 30; www.kalmar .regionforbund.se/turism; Nygatan 34, Box 762, SE-39127 Kalmar)
Turism i Kronoberg (☎ 0470-74 25 70; turism.krono berg@kommun.vaxjo.se; Stationen, Norra Järnvägsgatan, SE-35230 Växjö)
Ölands Turist (☎ 0485-56 06 00; www.olandsturist.se; Turistvägen, Box 74, SE-38621 Färjestaden)
Östsvenska Turistrådet (☎ 011-19 44 73; www .ostgotaporten.com; SE-60181 Norrköping)

Getting Around

There are various small airports scattered through the region, usually with daily direct flights to/from Copenhagen and Stockholm; see individual sections for details.

Year-round ferry services go between Visby on Gotland and both Oskarshamn and Nynäshamn.

Express buses mainly travel along the coast (to Västervik, Oskarshamn, Kalmar and Karlskrona), follow the E4 via Jönköping, or cruise along highway No 33 from Jönköping to Västervik (via Eksjö and Vimmerby). A few express services go through the region's interior; these are operated by **Svenska Buss** (☎ 0771-67 67 67; www.svenskabuss.se) and **Swebus Express** (☎ 0200-21 82 18; www.swebusexpress.se).

The main Malmö to Stockholm railway runs through the region, but you'll have to change to local trains to reach most places of interest. SJ trains run west from Karlskrona to Kristianstad or north from Karlskrona to Kalmar. There are also SJ services from Kalmar to Linköping, and inland routes from Oskarshamn to Nässjö and Kalmar to Göteborg. The Nässjö to Jönköping and Falköping trains are run by **Vättertåg** (☎ 0380-55 44 02).

The following companies provide regional transport links. If you're planning to spend some time here, it's worth enquiring about monthly passes or a *sommarkort,* offering discount travel from midsummer to mid-August. Check also the respective websites for routes, schedules, fares and passes; these sites don't always have information in English, but if you call the telephone numbers listed you'll usually reach someone who can help you in English.

BlekingeTrafiken (☎ 0455-56980; www.blekinge trafiken.se)
Jönköpings Länstrafik (☎ 0771-444333; www.jlt.se)
Kalmar Läns Trafik (☎ 0491-761200; www.klt.se)
Kollektiv Trafiken (☎ 21 41 12)
Länstrafiken Kronoberg (☎ 0771-767076; www .lanstrafikenkron.se)
ÖstgötaTrafiken (☎ 0771-211010; www.ostgota trafiken.se)

SMÅLAND

The region of Småland is one of dense forests, glinting lakes and bare marshlands. Historically it served as buffer zone between the Swedes and Danes; the eastern and southern coasts in particular saw territorial tussles. Today it's better know for the Glasriket (Kingdom of Glass), a sparsely populated area in the central southeast, which is dotted with crystal workshops. Småland is broken up into smaller counties *(läns):* Jönköpings in the northwest, Kronobergs in the southwest, and Kalmar in the east.

JÖNKÖPING & HUSKVARNA

☎ 036 / pop 119,927

Whenever you hear the scratching of matches on sandpaper, spare a thought for Jönköping – birthplace of the safety match. You can visit the restored production area here to learn more about this vital, but little considered, necessity.

Fairytale illustrator John Bauer was inspired by the forests around Jönköping, and the town museum shows off his superb otherworldly drawings of trolls, knights and

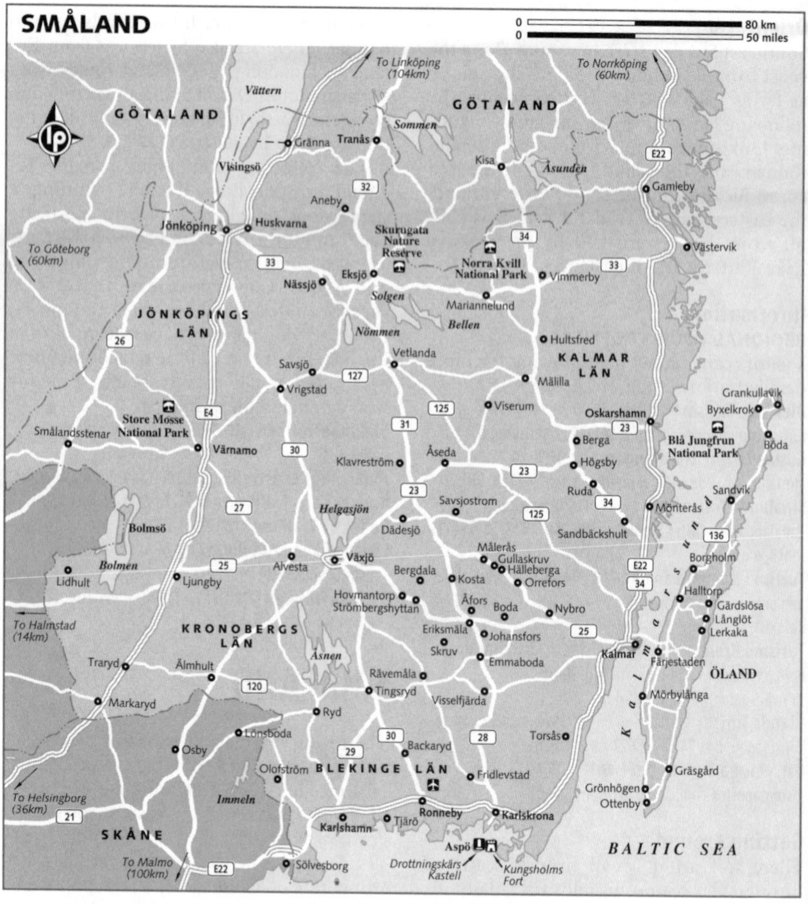

princesses. Other famous sons and daughters include ABBA's Agnetha Fältskog, and indie band The Cardigans.

From Jönköping, at Vättern's southern end, an urban strip stretches 7km eastwards, sucking in Huskvarna, famous for its sewing machines, chainsaws and motorcycles.

Information

The **tourist office** (☎ 10 50 50; www.jonkoping.se; ⌚ 9.30am-7pm Mon-Fri, 9.30am-3pm Sat yr-round & 11am-4.30pm Sun Jun-Aug) is in the Juneporten complex at the train station.

Banks can be found along Östra Storgatan. The large **library** (Dag Hammarskjölds plats), with Internet access and café, is adjacent to the Länsmuseum.

Sights & Activities

JÖNKÖPING

Apparently 'the only match museum in the world', **Tändsticksmuseet** (☎ 10 55 43; Tändsticksgränd 27; adult/under 19yr Skr40/free; ⌚ 10am-5pm Mon-Fri, 10am-3pm Sat & Sun Jun-Aug, 11am-3pm Tue-Sat Sep-May), in an old match factory, deals with this practical Swedish invention. It's quite an eye-opener: the industry was initially based on cheap child labour, workers frequently suffered from repulsive 'phossy jaw', and it was common knowledge that phosphorus matches were good for 'speeding up inheritance and inducing abortions'.

Near the Tändsticksmuseet is the **Radio Museum** (☎ 71 39 59; Tändsticksgränd 16; admission Skr20; ⌚ 10am-5pm Mon-Fri, 10am-1pm Sat, 11am-3pm

Sun Jun–mid-Aug; closed Sun & Mon mid-Aug–May) with a collection of over 1000 radio sets and related memorabilia.

Jönköpings Länsmuseum (☎ 30 18 00; Dag Hammarskjölds Plats; adult/under 18yr Skr40/free; 🕑 11am-5pm Tue & Thu-Sun, 11am-8pm Wed) has collections covering local history and contemporary culture, but the real reason for coming here is to see the haunting fantasy works of artist John Bauer (1882–1918), inspired by Jönköping's countryside.

West of town is the expanse of **Stadsparken**. Its curiosities include the 1458 mounted ornithological taxidermic masterpieces of **Fågelmuseet** (☎ 12 99 83; admission free; 🕑 11am-5pm May-Aug), and the **Friluftsmuseet** (☎ 30 18 00; admission free; 🕑 11am-5pm Jun-Aug) with a charming collection of old buildings.

Snakes, crocodiles, primates and tropical birds fill **Tropikhuset** (☎ 16 89 75; Kompanigatan 8; adult/3-14yr Skr50/30; 🕑 10am-5pm Jun-Aug, 10am-4pm Sep-May), 2km east of town in the A6 Centre. Also here, military history fans will appreciate the **Försvarshistoriska Museum** (☎ 19 04 12; adult/child Skr30/15; 🕑 10am-5pm), which examines 18th- and 19th-century soldiers' lives.

From April to September, visitors can enjoy different **cruises** (☎ 070 637 17 00) on Lake Vättern, aboard the MS *Nya Skärgården*. Evening trips include a buffet dinner and cost around Skr420. The boat departs from Hamnpiren; book at the tourist office.

For waterskiing or boat hire, contact **Marinbod** (☎ 12 04 87; Hamnpiren; 🕑 Jun-early Sep). Waterskiing, wakeboarding and kneeboarding all cost Skr200 per 15 minutes; small motor boats cost Skr250 per three hours or Skr495 for one day.

HUSKVARNA

Square-jawed men going hunting while their wives snuggle up to their sewing machines: the **Husqvarna fabriksmuseum** (☎ 14 61 62; www.husqvarna-museum.nu; Hakarpsvägen 1; adult/12-18yr Skr40/20; 🕑 10am-5pm Mon-Fri, noon-4pm Sat & Sun May-Sep, 10am-3pm Mon-Fri Oct-Apr) conjures up a vivid technicolour 1950s world. The factory began as an arms manufacturer, but diverted into motorbikes, chainsaws, cooking ranges and microwave ovens over the years, and this interesting museum charts the company's rise.

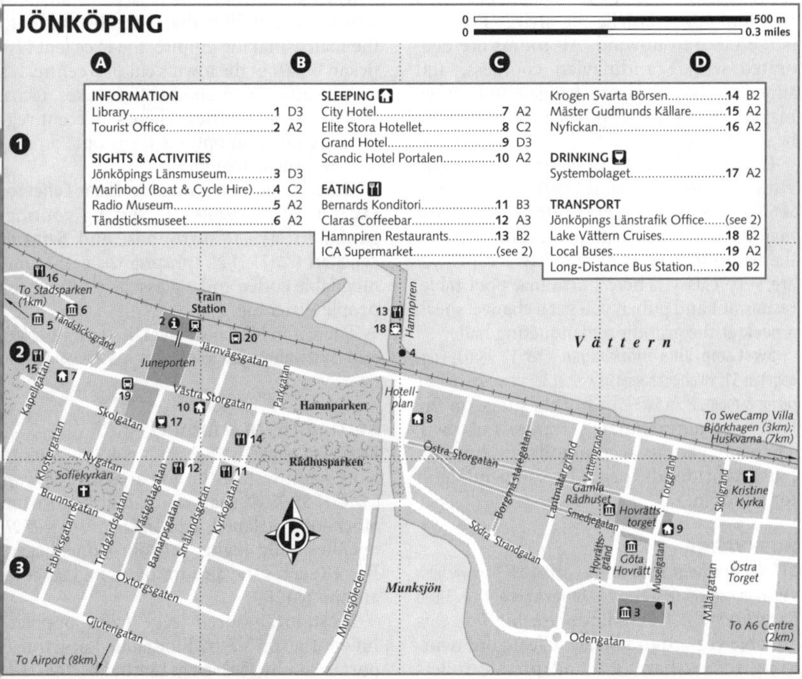

For powerful drama, catch Huskvarna's **Fallens Dag** (Waterfall Day), at the end of August. When darkness falls the floodgates open and a torrential illuminated waterfall is released; contact the tourist office for details.

From Jönköping, take bus 1 to Huskvarna (Skr20), 7km away.

Sleeping

JÖNKÖPING

Grand Hotel (☎ 71 96 00; info@grandhotel-jonkoping.se; Hovrättstorget; s/d from Skr770/930, discounted to Skr490/590) In a stately 17th-century building, this central choice is probably the cheapest in town. Budget, standard and superior rooms are available.

City Hotel (☎ 71 92 80; hotel@cityhotel.nu; Västra Storgatan 25; s/d from Skr895/995, discounted to Skr545/645) Another midrange accommodation option, the friendly family-run City is a step up in quality from the Grand. Rooms are dated but comfortable – those on the top floor have balconies with lake views – and there's a sauna.

Scandic Hotel Portalen (☎ 585 42 00; portalen@scandic-hotels.com; Barnarpsgatan 6; s/d from Skr1290/1490, discounted to Skr790/790; P 💻) One of Scandic's two Jönköping hotels, the stylish Portalen is the place to unwind. All rooms are decorated with Scandinavian coolness, and superiors have private fridges and coffee makers. The hotel also has a large spa with beauty treatments.

Elite Stora Hotellet (☎ 10 00 00; info@jonkoping.elite.se; Hotellplan; s/d from Skr1295/1495, discounted to Skr675/775; P 💻) The Elite is the town's most majestic hotel, with a good location opposite the harbour. Rooms have folksy accents, yet are very classy. There's a sauna, pool table, restaurant and pub; if you get a chance, sneak a peek at the grandiose banqueting hall.

SweCamp Villa Björkhagen (☎ 12 28 63; Friggagatan 31; villabjorkhagen@swipnet.se; sites Skr170-220, cabins & rooms from Skr575) This big site is on the lakeshore, approximately 3km east of town. There are various accommodation options, plus playgrounds, pedal cars and minigolf for children.

HUSKVARNA

STF Vandrarhem Huskvarna (☎ 14 88 70; www.huskvarnavandrarhem.se; Odengatan 10, Huskvarna; 1-/2-/3-bed rm Skr260/340/450) Standards are high at this sizeable year-round hostel. Clean and twinkling rooms have TV and private toilets (except room 37, which is correspondingl cheaper), and breakfast is available (Skr45).

Eating & Drinking

For a seaside vibe and loads of choice hea straight for Hamnpiren (the harbour pier) where you'll find a blur of restaurants wit good lunch specials (around Skr70) an merry crowds gathered for evening meals For cheaper alternatives, try inside the June porten transport/shopping complex.

Krogen Svarta Börsen (☎ 71 22 22; Kyrkogatan 4 mains Skr270-335) Fresh, seasonal ingredient grace the plates at the best dining establishment in town. A great atmosphere, super food and superb service justify the high prices.

Mäster Gudmunds Källare (☎ 10 06 40; Kapellgatan 2; lunch Skr65, dinner mains Skr150-195; 🕑 close Sun summer) This appealing place is in a 17th-century cellar, with beautiful vaulted ceilings, and has good-value lunches (althoug not in summer). Evening mains are mainl meaty and fishy local Swedish dishes, suc as grilled char from Vättern lake, with a few nods to French cuisine.

Nyfickan (☎ 19 06 86; lunch Skr50) In an unusual brick building that once belonged tc the match-making empire, the excellent Nyfickan is part of the town's cultural centre. It's an arty affair with good coffee, cakes, tacos falafel and sandwiches. There's a decent veggie selection, and options for people on gluten- and sugar-free diets.

Other good cafés include **Claras Coffeeba** (☎ 30 01 15; Barnarpsgatan 18), serving gourme *panini* in stylish surrounds; and **Bernards Konditori** (☎ 71 11 21; Kyrkogatan 12), with commendable coffee and a glassed-in terrace for people-watching.

There's an **ICA supermarket** (Juneporten complex) and **Systembolaget** (cnr Skolgatan & Trädgårdsgatan) nearby.

Getting There & Around

Jönköping airport (☎ 31 11 00) is located about 8km southwest of the town centre. **Skyways** (☎ 0771-95 95 00) has daily flights to/from Stockholm Arlanda, and **SAS** (☎ 0770-72 77 27) operates daily flights to/from Copenhagen. Bus 18 serves the airport, or else a taxi costs around Skr180.

Most local buses leave from opposite Juneporten on Västra Storgatan. Local transport is run by **Jönköpings Länstrafik** (☎ 0771-44

43 33; www.jlt.se in Swedish; Juneporten; 7.30am-6pm Mon-Fri); there's an office with information, tickets and passes in Juneporten.

The **long-distance bus station** is next to the train station. There are at least eight daily **Swebus Express** (0200-21 82 18; www.swebusexpress.se) services to Göteborg (Skr120, two hours) and Stockholm (Skr320, 4½ hours); five to Helsingborg (Skr245, three hours) and Malmö (Skr293, 4½ hours); two to Karlstad (Skr265, four hours); and two to Västervik (Skr211, three hours). Svenska Buss runs to Eksjö, Göteborg, Kalmar, Oskarshamn and Stockholm.

Jönköping is on a regional train line; you'll need to change trains in either Nässjö or Falköping to get to or from larger towns.

Taxi Jönköping (34 40 00) is the local taxi company. You can hire bicycles from **Marinbod** (12 04 87; Hamnpiren; per day Skr150; Jun-early Sep).

GRÄNNA & VISINGSÖ

0390

All that's missing from Gränna are Oompa-Loompas. The sweet smell of sugar hangs over the village, and the shops overflow with the village's trademark red-and-white peppermint rock *(polkagris)*. It's a touristy spot with touches of tackiness, but the steep streets, lakeside location and excellent polar exhibition give it a good dose of character.

Across the water and 6km west is the peaceful island of Visingsö. Connected by frequent ferries it's a great place for cycling.

Information

There's a **tourist office** (410 10; www.grm.se; Grenna Kulturgård, Brahegatan 38; 10am-7pm mid-May–Aug, 10am-4pm Sep–mid-May) in central Gränna, and another **tourist office** (401 93; www.visingso.net; 10am-5pm May-Aug, to 7pm late-Jun–mid-Aug, 11am-6pm Mon, 8am-2pm Tue-Fri Sep-Apr) at the harbour in Visingsö.

With ID, you can use the Internet at Gränna **library** (410 15; 10am-7pm Mon-Thu, 10am-1pm Fri), upstairs from the tourist office.

Brahegatan, the main street of Gränna, has a bank and ATM.

Sights

In the same building as the tourist office, **Andréexpedition Polarcenter** (adult/child Skr50/20; 10am-7pm mid-May–Aug, 10am-4pm Sep–mid-May) describes the disastrous attempt of Salomon August Andrée to reach the North Pole by balloon in 1897 (see below). It's riveting stuff, particularly the poignant remnants of the expedition: cracked leather boots, monogrammed handkerchiefs, lucky

BIG TROUBLE IN A SMALL BALLOON

One of Sweden's most famous explorers was Salomon August Andrée, born in Gränna in 1854. He became interested in hot-air ballooning after a visit to America, and eventually bought his own balloon to use for scientific surveys.

In 1895, Andrée announced to the Royal Swedish Academy of Sciences that he intended to fly a 4000km journey over the North Pole, and needed Skr130,000 for the project. Initial scepticism was quashed by the support of explorer Baron Adolf Erik Nordenskiöld (the discoverer of the Northeast Passage), Alfred Nobel and King Oskar.

After one failed attempt, *The Eagle,* with Andrée and two companions aboard, took off on 11 July 1897 from Danskøya, a bleak offshore island near the northwest tip of Svalbard. There was sporadic contact during the first few days – then nothing. The balloon disappeared and its fate wasn't known until 33 years later.

In 1930, the crew of a Norwegian ship discovered the explorers' bodies on Kvitøya, more than 300km east of Danskøya. They were shipped back to Stockholm, with their remaining equipment and rolls of intact camera film. Andrée's diary was also found, documenting their fateful journey.

Three days into its flight, after problems with steering and height control, the balloon had crunched down onto the frozen Arctic Ocean. The explorers salvaged what they could and headed south towards Kvitøya, but lost most of their supplies when an ice floe they were camping on broke up. After three months of living on raw bear meat, seagulls and seals' blood, they reached Kvitøya, where they perished one by one over the next few days; the exact causes of their deaths remain unknown.

SOUTHEAST SWEDEN

amulets, and mustard paper to ward off those polar winds.

But don't be put off by Andrée's ballooning tragedy; for Skr1695 per person you can take a one-hour scenic **hot-air balloon trip** (☎ 305 25; bengt@flyg-ballong.nu) over the area.

Several sweet-makers have kitchens where you can see traditional red-and-white candy being made. One is **Grenna Polkagriskokeri** (☎ 100 39; Brahegatan 39), directly opposite the tourist office, which uses an authentic 19th-century recipe. You can watch porridgey-looking crispbread being produced at **Gränna Knäcke** (☎ 100 57; Brahegatan 43).

Visingsö has a 17th-century **church**, **castle** and **aromatic herb garden**. An extensive network of footpaths and bicycle trails lead through oak woods and at the harbour you can hire bikes (per three hours/one day Skr40/75).

The beautiful lakes of Bunn and Ören, and their dark forests, inspired local artist John Bauer to paint his trolls, princesses and magical pools (see p117). From June to mid-August, you can take a **boat tour** (☎ 510 50; adult/child Skr150/80; 🕑 12.30pm Sat & Sun Jun, 12.30pm Jul–mid-Aug) to the lakes, departing from Bunnströms badplats, 2.5km from Gränna.

Sleeping & Eating

GRÄNNA

The tourist office arranges **private rooms** from Skr140 to Skr250 per person per night (plus Skr100 booking fee).

Gränna Turistbyrås Vandrarhem (☎ 410 10; Bergsgatan 70; dm Skr140; 🕑 mid-Jun–early Aug; Ⓟ) The tourist office administers this SVIF hostel, perched on a hill overlooking town. It's basic, but central and cheap, plus there's a pleasant garden and a few parking spaces up for grabs.

Gyllene Uttern (☎ 108 00; info@gylleneuttern.se; s/d from Skr1150/1395, discounted to Skr750/995; Ⓟ) South of town is imposing Gyllene Uttern, an elegant hotel off the E4. Rooms are simple but masterful, and there are good-value packages including a 'Romantic' weekend option.

Hotell Västanå Slott (☎ 107 00; info@vastanaslott.se; d from Skr1290; 🕑 May-Sep; Ⓟ) This super-stately manor house, about 6km south of town, is a pad for regal relaxation. Per Brahe owned it in the 17th century, although today it's decorated according to its 18th-century past, with chandeliers, dark oil paintings and suits of armour. There are super views over the lake.

Grännastrandens Camping (☎ 107 06; info@grannacamping.se; Hamnen; tent sites/dm Skr160/140, 4-bed cabins from Skr500; 🕑 Jun-Sep) This busy family campsite down by the harbour has a café, shop, minigolf and boat hire.

For a choice of food in a great waterside setting, head down to the harbour (1.5km) where there are restaurants selling Greek, French and Swedish grub (most are open summer only).

Amalias Krog (☎ 100 17; Brahegatan; lunch Skr89, mains Skr100-200) This central joint is a decent eating option, serving no-nonsense food like steaks, salmon and lemon sole in a cool, tiled dining room.

Fiket (☎ 100 57; Brahegatan 57) The pick of Gränna's eateries is this charming bakery-café, selling sandwiches, quiches, salads and *knäckebröd* (crispbread). There's an old jukebox, rock 'n' roll records pepper the walls in kitsch 1950s' style, and there's a breezy balcony at the back.

There are fast-food outlets and a supermarket on Brahegatan.

VISINGSÖ

STF Vandrarhem Visingsö & Pensionat (☎/fax 401 91; info@visingsovandrarhem.se; dm from Skr150, pensionat s/d Skr700/1110; 🕑 Vandrarhem May-Aug) This combined hostel/B&B lies in an oak wood around 3km from the ferry pier. The *vandrarhem* is scattered across three buildings, with a separate kitchen/shower block. The *pensionat* has four cosy rooms with private facilities.

Visingsö Värdshus (☎ 404 96; mains Skr90-130; 🕑 May-Aug) Simple meals, such as grilled chicken, salads, burgers and baked potatoes, are served at this rustic place in the woods. Their speciality is fish from Vättern lake.

Restaurant Solbacken (☎ 400 29; lunch Skr65, mains Skr90-150; 🕑 May-Aug) Local fish also find themselves on the menu at this lively restaurant, pub and pizzeria at Visingsö harbour. There are great views over Vättern from the veranda.

Getting There & Around

Local bus 121 runs hourly from Jönköping to Gränna (Skr55, one hour). Bus 120 runs several times Monday to Friday from Gränna to the mainline train station in Tranås (Skr55, one hour). Daily Swebus Express destinations include Göteborg, Jönköping, Linköping, Norrköping and Stockholm.

The Gränna–Visingsö **ferry** (☎ 410 25) runs every 15 minutes in summer, less frequently the rest of the year. Return tickets for foot passengers are Skr50 per adult, and Skr25 for those between six and 15 years of age; a bicycle is Skr30 and a car with up to five people is Skr230.

EKSJÖ

☎ **0381 / pop 16,571**

Eskjö is one of the most exquisitely preserved wooden towns in Sweden, with buildings in the old town dating back to the 17th century. It's a joy to wander round its lopsided, flower-filled courtyards, and the local museum is a credit to the place.

The **tourist office** (☎ 361 70; www.eksjo.se; Norra Storgatan 29; 8am-8pm Jul–mid-Aug, 10am-6pm Mon-Fri, 10am-2pm Sat rest of yr) can occasionally arrange English-language guided town **tours** (Skr30), and it also has bicycles for hire (per day/week Skr60/225).

Sights

Stroll through the delightful streets and yards of Eksjö, especially those north of Stora Torget. You'll see excellent old buildings at **Fornminnesgårdens Museum** (☎ 148 39; Arendt Byggmästares gatan; admission Skr10; 11am-3pm Mon-Sat mid-Jun–mid-Aug) – some built in the 1620s. Exhibits chart the history of the area from the Stone Age to modern times.

Award-winning **Eksjö Museum** (☎ 361 70; Österlånggatan 31; adult/7-17yr Skr40/20; 10am-5pm Mon-Fri, noon-4pm Sat & Sun Jul & Aug, 1-5pm Tue-Thu, noon-4pm Sat & Sun Sep-Jun) tells the town's story from the 15th century onwards. The top floor is devoted to local Albert Engström (1869–1940), renowned for his satirical cartoons: there's an English translation of the captions. Eksjö was once known as the 'Hussar Town', and the region's long-standing military connections are explored in a fascinating new wing of the museum.

Aschanska gården (☎ 361 70; Norra Storgatan 18) is an interesting 1890s-style house with guided tours at 1pm and 3pm daily July and August (Skr50).

The **Skurugata Nature Reserve**, 13km northeast of Eksjö, is based around a weird 800m-long fissure in the rocks. Its sides tower to 56m, yet in places the fissure is only 7m wide. From the top of the nearby hill, **Skuruhatt** (337m), there are great views of the forests. You'll need your own transport to get here.

The **Höglandsleden** passes through the reserve; ask the tourist office for details of this walking trail and of the **Höglandstrampen cycle route** (booklets in English Skr40).

Sleeping

STF Vandrarhem Eksjö (☎ 361 70; vandrarhem@eksjo.se; Österlånggatan 31; dm/s/d from Skr130/170/330) In the heart of the old town, this *vandrarhem* is based in a supremely quaint wooden building, with a gallery running round the upper floor. Reception is at the tourist office.

Stadshotell (☎ 130 20; info@eksjostadshotell.se; Stora Torget; s/d Skr845/1090, discounted to Skr595/790;) The impressive Stadshotell dominates one edge of the huge 19th-century main square. It has the flashest accommodation in town, with comfortable long-windowed rooms and an elegant restaurant-bar.

Eksjö Camping (☎ 395 00; info@eksjocamping.nu; sites Skr100, 2-/4-bed cabins from Skr200/340) This is a friendly nook by picturesque Husnäsen lake, about a kilometre east of town. There's a restaurant and café, plus minigolf and good swimming. There's also a **hostel** (dm Skr150).

Eating & Drinking

Lennarts Konditori (☎ 61 13 90; Stora Torget) With an outdoor terrace and views of dramatic Stora Torget, this traditional *konditori* is the place to go for cakes, crêpes and quiche.

Restaurang Balkan (☎ 100 20; Norra Storgatan 23; lunch from Skr65, pizzas Skr60, à la carte dishes Skr90-150) The Balkan has a surprising menu of Chinese, Swedish and pizza dishes.

There's a central **Hemköp supermarket** (Österlånggatan) and a **Systembolaget** (Södra Storgatan 4).

Getting There & Around

The bus and train stations are in the southern part of town. The tiny *länståg* (regional train) runs up to seven times daily to/from Jönköping. Local buses run to Nässjö (Skr42, hourly Monday to Friday, six at weekends). Swebus Express runs two buses on the Göteborg–Jönköping–Eksjö–Vimmerby–Västervik route on Fridays and Sundays.

VÄXJÖ

☎ **0470 / pop 76,755**

A venerable old market town, Växjö (pronounced *vak*-choo, with the 'ch' sound as in the Scottish 'loch' – ask a local to demonstrate!), in Kronobergs län, is a very important stop for Americans seeking their

Swedish roots. In mid-August, **Karl Oscar Days** commemorates the mass 19th-century emigration from the area, and the Swedish-American of the year is chosen. There's also a fantastic glass collection in town, plus a little something to stop the kids getting bored…

Information

The **tourist office** (☎ 414 10; www.turism.vaxjo.se; Västra Esplanaden 7; ⌚ 9.30am-6pm Mon-Fri, 10am-2pm Sat & Sun mid-Jun–Aug, 9.30am-4.30pm Mon-Fri rest of yr) shares a building with the **library**, and allows 30 minutes of free Internet access per day. Storgatan is the main pedestrian mall, where you'll find banks and other services.

Sights

Utvandrarnas Hus (Emigrant House; ☎ 201 20; www.swemi.se; Vilhelm Mobergs gata 4; adult/7-16yr Skr40/5; ⌚ 9am-5pm Mon-Fri, 11am-4pm Sat & Sun May-Aug, 9am-4pm Tue-Fri, 11am-4pm Sat Sep-Apr) has scores of intelligent displays on the emigration of over one million Swedes to America (1850–1930). It also includes a replica of Vilhelm Moberg's office and original manuscripts of his famous emigration novels. It's all fascinating stuff, and the centre also has an excellent research facility (open weekdays only, reservations advised) for those tracing their Swedish ancestors.

Next door is **Smålands Museum** (☎ 70 42 00; www.smalandsmuseum.se; Södra Järnvägsgatan 2; adult/under 19yr Skr40/free; ⌚ 10am-5pm Mon-Fri, 11am-5pm Sat & Sun Jun-Aug, closed Mon Sep-May), with a superb exhibition about Sweden's 500-year-old glass industry. Four of the rooms are filled with work from medieval goblets to the most contemporary sculptures, and there's also a great café.

Kids can jump on a spaceship to the Milky Way or create the world's biggest soap bubble at **Xperiment Huset** (☎ 101 25; www.xperiment.se; Lokstallarna; adult/7-16yr Skr75/60; ⌚ 10am-6pm Mon-Fri, 11am-4pm Sat & Sun Jun-Aug, 10am-4pm Tue-Fri, 11am-4pm Sat & Sun Sep-May), a hands-on science and illusion centre.

The impressive twin-spired **Domkyrkan** (Cathedral; ⌚ 9am-5pm) has been struck by lightning and repeatedly ravaged by fire – the latest renovation was in 1995. Inside, there's a fine 15th-century altar and displays of

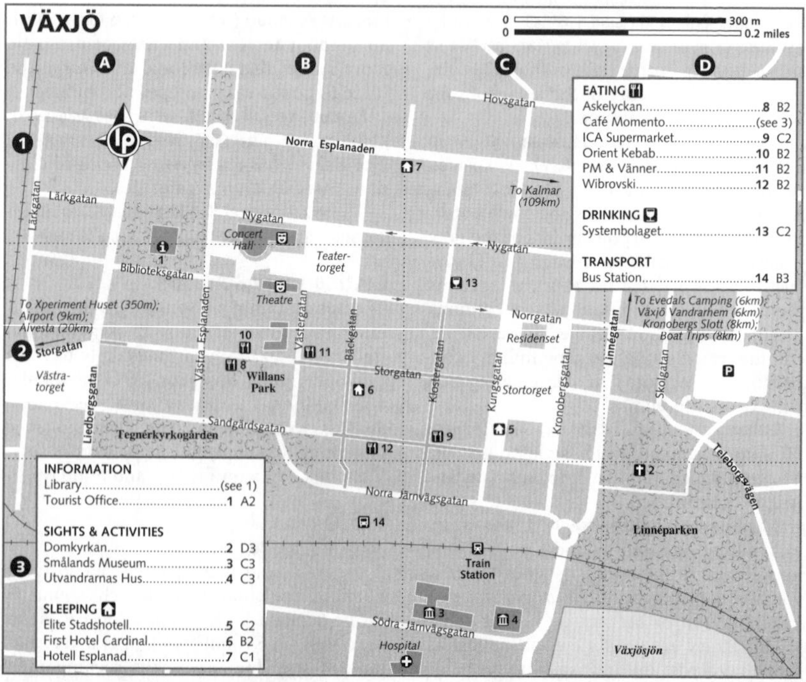

local artwork (in glass, wood and iron). You'll also find a Viking rune stone in the eastern wall.

In 1542, the Småland rebel Nils Dacke spent Christmas in **Kronobergs Slott**, now a ruin. The 14th-century castle is on a small island (reached by footbridge) in photogenic Helgasjön lake, about 8km north of the town. **Boat trips** (☎ 70 42 00; adult/5-12yr Skr125/50; weekends mid-Jun–mid-Aug) on Sweden's oldest steamship, *Thor,* leave from just below the ruins. Take bus 1B from town.

Enquire at the tourist office about guided summer **walking tours** (5.30pm Mon) of town, and also about two-hour summer **sightseeing tours** (☎ 816 84; adult/child Skr55/30) in a red double-decker London bus.

Sleeping

Most of the big chain hotels have a hotel in Växjö.

Växjö Vandrarhem (☎ 630 70; www.vaxjovandrarhem.nu; dm from Skr155; P) Also at Evedal, this former spa hotel dates from the late 18th century. All rooms have washbasins, there's a big kitchen, laundry, and a wonderful lounge in the attic. It's deservedly well loved, so book early. Take bus 1C from town.

Hotell Esplanad (☎ 225 80; Norra Esplanaden 21A; s/d Skr700/800, discounted to Skr470/570; P) The cheapest central accommodation is at the Esplanad, with unfussy, adequate rooms. The lowest-priced have corridor bathrooms.

First Hotel Cardinal (☎ 72 28 00; cardinalhotel@jesab.se; Bäckgatan 10; standard s/d Skr1094/1484, discounted to Skr648/848; P) A jump up in quality, the central Cardinal has 'budget-style' (in a second building round the corner) and more luxurious rooms. There's a sauna, bar and brand-new restaurant.

Elite Stadshotellet (☎ 134 00; info@vaxjo.elite.se; Kungsgatan 6; s/d from Skr1195/1395, discounted to Skr650/775; P) This grand-looking 19th-century building offers a distinctly swish experience. Rooms are large and confident-looking, and there's a popular restaurant and English-style Bishop's Arms pub, serving a good range of food and international beers.

Evedals Camping (☎ 630 34; evedals.camping@telia.com; Evedalsvägen; sites Skr175-215, 4-/6-bed cabins Skr600/700) Evedal is a huge lakeside recreation area, 6km north of the centre, where this campsite is based. You can enjoy the beaches, swimming, canoeing and boating (per hour/day Skr80/200) on Helga lake. There are two restaurants nearby – Restaurang Brunnen, and the more upmarket Evedals Värdshus.

Eating & Drinking

Wibrovski (☎ 74 04 10; Sandgärdsgatan 19; mains Skr145-195; from 6pm Mon-Sat) You can watch fish, lamb and chicken mains being prepared in the open kitchen at this classy restaurant in Växjö's oldest timber house. Retire to the outdoor terrace in fine weather.

PM & Vänner (☎ 70 04 44; Storgatan 24; bar meals Skr65-150, mains Skr190-330; closed Sun) This stylish place is a favourite spot for fashionable locals; the décor is all brushed steel and leather benches, and there are occasional DJs. Dishes steal from all over the world, with Caribbean, Indian, Mexican and African ingredients all popping up.

Café Momento (☎ 391 29; meals around Skr70) Smålands Museum contains this fantastic café. Service is attentive, and there's always an excellent selection of hot and cold gourmet sandwiches, pies, salads, soup, spuds and cakes. In summer, there are tables in the pretty courtyard.

Askelyckan (☎ 123 11; Storgatan 25; closed Sun) Another top lunch spot is this bakery-café, with sandwiches, baguettes, great pastries and a large shady courtyard.

Orient Kebab (☎ 120 32; Storgatan 28; meals around Skr40-60; until 10pm) Don't let the lurid plastic Arabian Nights exterior put you off, inside are decent kebabs, falafel, burgers and pizzas to take away.

There's an **ICA supermarket** (cnr Klostergatan & Sandgärdsgatan; until 8pm Mon-Fri, until 5pm Sat & Sun) and **Systembolaget** (Klostergatan 14).

Getting There & Away

Småland airport (☎ 75 85 00; www.vxo-airport.se) is 9km northwest of Växjö. **SAS** (☎ 0770-72 77 27; www.scandinavian.net) has direct flights to Stockholm Arlanda, **Stockholmsplanet** (☎ 0771-71 72 00; www.stockholmsplanet.com) to Stockholm Bromma, and **European Executive Express** (☎ 0859-36 31 31; www.european.se) flies daily to Copenhagen. Airport bus 50 connects with flights (Skr59), otherwise take a **taxi** (☎ 13500).

Länstrafiken Kronoberg (☎ 0771-76 70 76; www.lanstrafikenkron.se in Swedish) runs the regional bus network, with daily buses to Halmstad, Jönköping and Kosta. Long-distance buses depart from the **station**, next to the train station. Svenska Buss runs one or two services daily to Eksjö (Skr180, 1½ hours), Linköping

(Skr240, 3¼ hours) and Stockholm (Skr340, 6½ hours).

Växjö is served by SJ trains that run roughly hourly between Alvesta (on the main north–south line; Skr39, 15 minutes) and Kalmar (Skr143, 1¼ hours). A few trains run daily directly to Karlskrona (Skr143, 1½ hours), Malmö (Skr240, two hours) and Göteborg (Skr285, three hours).

KALMAR

☎ 0480 / pop 60,649

Kalmar has one of the most spectacular castles in Sweden, with an interior even more perfect than its turreted outside – miss it at your cost. Other excitements in town include Sweden's largest gold hoard, from the 17th-century ship *Kronan,* and picturesque buildings and cobbled streets in the Kvarnholmen area. If you've anything to celebrate, Kalmar's a good place to do it in, with romantic hotels and lively bars.

The short-lived Kalmar Union of 1397, when the crowns of Sweden, Denmark and Norway became one, was agreed to at the castle.

Information

The **tourist office** (☎ 41 77 00; www.kalmar.se/turism; Ölandskajen 9; 9am-9pm Mon-Fri, 10am-5pm Sat & Sun late Jun–mid-Aug, 9am-5pm Mon-Fri, 10am-1pm Sat May & Sep, 9am-5pm Mon-Fri Oct-Apr) sells a good English-language town walking guide, *Wander Round Kalmar by Yourself* (Skr30).

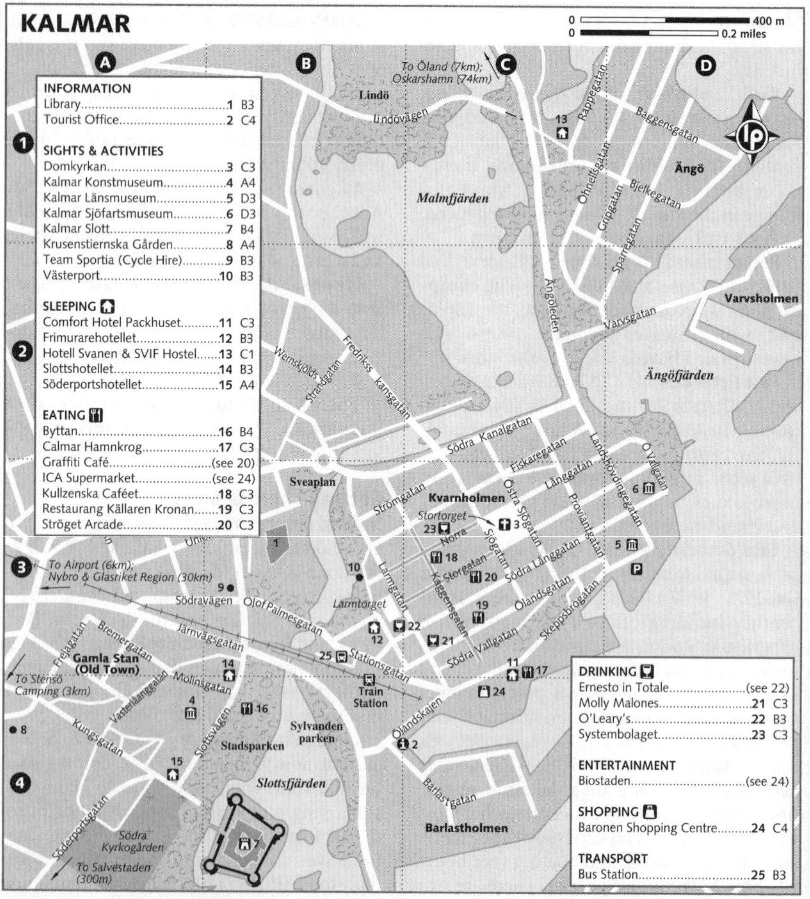

To get free Internet access join the **library** (☎ 45 06 30; Tullslätten 4; ⌚ closed Sun May-Aug) as a temporary member .

You'll find banks and other services on Storgatan.

Sights

KALMAR SLOTT

Fairytale turrets, moat, drawbridge, foul dungeon and secret passages...yes, **Kalmar Slott** (☎ 45 14 90; adult/7-16yr Skr75/20; ⌚ 10am-6pm Jul, 10am-5pm Jun & Aug, 10am-4pm Apr, May & Sep, 11am-3.30pm 2nd weekend of month Oct-Mar) has absolutely everything that a proper castle should. This powerful Renaissance building was once the most important in Sweden, and it's fortified accordingly. It has one of the best-preserved interiors from the period.

King Erik's chamber is a real highlight. Erik's rivalry with his brother Johan caused him to install a secret passage in the loo! There's also a superb suspended ceiling in the **Golden Hall**; eye-boggling wall-to-wall and floor-to-ceiling marquetry in the **Chequered Hall**; an elaborate **bed**, stolen as war booty then carefully vandalised so that no Danish ghosts could haunt it; and a delightful **chapel**, one of Sweden's Most Wanted for weddings.

To find out more, join one of the fascinating **guided tours** (in English at 11.30am & 2.30pm mid-Jun–mid-Aug, plus 3.30pm Jul), included in the admission price. There are also children's activities here in summer; contact the castle for details.

KALMAR LÄNSMUSEUM

The highlight of this **museum** (☎ 45 13 00; www.kalmarlansmuseum.se; Skeppsbrogatan; adult/under 18yr Skr50/free; ⌚ 10am-6pm mid-Jun–mid-Aug, 10am-4pm Mon-Fri, 11am-4pm Sat & Sun mid-Aug–mid-Jun), in an old steam mill by the harbour, are finds from the 17th-century flagship *Kronan*. The ship exploded and sank just before a battle in 1676, with the loss of almost 800 men. It was rediscovered in 1980, and over 22,000 wonderfully preserved items have been excavated so far, including a spectacular gold hoard, clothing, musical instruments and cannon.

OTHER SIGHTS

Aft and slightly to port of the county museum, **Kalmar Sjöfartsmuseum** (☎ 158 75; Södra Långgatan 81; adult/7-12yr Skr30/10; ⌚ 11am-4pm mid-Jun–mid-Sep, noon-4pm Sun mid-Sep–mid-Jun) contains a delightfully eccentric maritime collection, with nautical instruments, bottled ships, foghorns, and things made out of knots and armadillos.

The landmark baroque **Domkyrkan** (Cathedral; Stortorget) was designed by Tessin, King Karl X Gustav's favourite architect. Its sage-green interior is very restful, and there's a spectacular pulpit. To find out more, plug into one of the audiophones by the main door.

Krusenstiernska Gården (☎ 41 15 52; Stora Dammgatan 11; adult/child Skr25/7; ⌚ 1-5pm Mon-Fri Jun-Aug) is a fully furnished, 19th-century middle-class home, 500m from the castle entrance. Tours of the house are on the hour, but entry to the pretty gardens and café is free.

Kalmar Konstmuseum (☎ 42 62 82; Slottsvägen 1D; adult/under 18yr Skr40/free; ⌚ 11am-5pm, to 8pm Thu), near the castle, displays works by well-known Swedish artists like Carl Larsson and Anders Zorn, and houses temporary modern exhibitions.

Västerport was the original point of entry into the city. Nowadays you can watch glass-blowing and pottery-making at the studios here, and buy the results.

Festivals & Events

Historical Kalmar has lots of summery events. One of the biggest is the **Medeltidsfestival & Marknad** (☎ 45 13 74), a medieval festival and market with jousting, music, handicrafts, food and drink. It's held in Salvestaden – a reconstructed medieval village about 500m south of the castle in Kalmarsundsparken – on a weekend in late July. Entry costs Skr80 (family ticket Skr290) per day.

Sleeping

Hotell Svanen (☎ 255 60; www.hotellsvanen.se; Rappegatan 1; dm Skr205, s/d from Skr520/625; P 💻) This 'low-price hotel' is an excellent choice. Its simple rooms are newly restored, with cable TV and private toilets. The **SVIF hostel** is part of the hotel: both share the reception (open all day), kitchen, drinks machines, sauna, foyer, Internet service etc. Svanen is on the island of Ängö, about 1km north of town; walk, or take bus 402.

Slottshotellet (☎ 882 60; www.slottshotellet.se; Slottsvägen 7; s/d from Skr1350/1690, discounted to Skr890/1390; P) The top pick in town is this wonderfully romantic hotel, based in four buildings in a gorgeous green setting near the castle. Most rooms have antique furnishings and are cosy as anything, and some have lovely old Swedish tile stoves. Staff are immensely helpful, and there's also a summer restaurant.

Frimurarehotellet (☎ 152 30; www.frimurarehotellet.com; Larmtorget 2; s/d Skr990/1210, discounted to Skr720/895; 💻) In the heart of the action, this 19th-century building contains spacious rooms full of character with polished wooden floors. The plant-filled lounge is a nice touch, with free tea, coffee and biscuits. There are also cheaper rooms (about Skr200 less) that have showers in the hallway.

Comfort Hotel Packhuset (☎ 570 00; www.hotelpackhuset.se; Skeppsbrogatan 26; s/d Skr1345/1545, discounted to Skr875/1145; P 💻) This chain hotel is based in a converted 18th-century waterfront warehouse that retains its beamed ceilings but is modern in every other way.

Söderportshotellet (☎ 125 01, Slottsvägen 1; s/d Skr495/695; ⏲ mid-Jun–mid-Aug) Söderportshotellet is right outside the castle and offers summertime accommodation in student digs. Rooms are modest yellow-washed affairs; some on the upper floor have castle views. There's a super café-restaurant downstairs that often hosts live jazz and blues.

Stensö Camping (☎ 888 03; www.stensocamping.se; Stensövägen; sites/cabins Skr150/450; ⏲ Apr-Sep) There are family-friendly facilities galore at this campsite, 3km southwest of town, including swimming, boat, canoe and bicycle rental, a restaurant and minigolf. However there's no public transport to the door, buses 401 and 411 stop around 600m away.

Eating

A good area for upmarket dining is the harbour; the view of huge timber yards and cranes is somewhat industrial, but you don't want pretty sailing boats *all* the time…

Calmar Hamnkrog (☎ 41 10 20; Skeppsbrogatan 30; mains Skr130-245) The stylish Hamnkrog serves the best food in town, a combination of Swedish favourites and continental innovations (like grilled swordfish with seafood paella and *gremolata*).

Byttan (☎ 163 60; Stadsparken; lunch Skr70, dinner mains Skr155-195; ⏲ summer) This classy glass-and-steel restaurant is in the park by the castle. It serves classic Swedish dishes, for example herring platters (Skr120), helped down by wonderful views of Kalmar's major attraction.

Restaurang Källaren Kronan (☎ 41 14 00; Ölandsgatan 7; mains Skr100-200; ⏲ closed Mon) Six cellars have been transformed into this high-calibre experience, where a small but select evening menu is served under a snug vaulted ceiling. Mains are mostly meat and fish, but an effort is made for veggies too.

Kullzenska Caféet (☎ 288 82; 1st fl, Kaggensgatan 26; snacks from Skr30) The pick of the town's cafés is this gorgeous maze of genteel 19th-century rooms, with original tiled stoves and furniture. There's a range of sandwiches and cakes (try the great fruit crumbles).

Graffiti Café, (☎ 256 30; Storgatan 24; meals around Skr50; ⏲ closed Sun) Part of the small food hall inside the Ströget arcade, this fast-food café offers salads, baguettes and tasty baked potatoes with a multitude of fillings.

There's also an **ICA supermarket** in the Baronen shopping centre.

Drinking

The following places are popular for food, and also turn into lively drinking spots later in the evening.

Molly Malones (☎ 41 13 44; Lärmgatan 6; meals Skr45-120; ⏲ closed Sun & Mon) This cosy Irish pub serves bar snacks as well as 'authentic' Irish meals (such as steak-and-Guinness pie, and fish and chips).

O'Leary's (☎ 44 09 70; Larmtorget 4; mains Skr140-200) Nearby, this Boston-style sports bar has outdoor seating on the square, and is a crowd-pleaser on summer evenings. Food is of the type that goes well with beer: fajitas, ribs, chicken wings and burgers.

Ernesto in Totale (☎ 200 50; Larmtorget 4; mains Skr90-170; ⏲ until 2am Wed, Fri & Sat) This Italian café, restaurant, bar and nightclub also attracts scores of people, with its *barristas*, extensive menu, after-work promotions, long cocktail list and weekend dancing.

For alcohol, visit **Systembolaget** (Norra Långgatan 23).

Entertainment

The **Biostaden** (☎ 122 44; Skr85) cinema is in the Baronen shopping centre on Skeppsbrogatan.

Getting There & Around

The **airport** (☎ 587 00) is 6km west of town. **SAS** (☎ 0770-72 77 27) flies several times daily to Stockholm and **European Executive Express** (☎ 0859-36 31 31; www.european.se) flies weekdays to Copenhagen. Town bus 20 runs to and from the airport (Skr30).

HERRING À LA GLASSWORKS

In days gone by, glassworks were more than just a workplace – they acted as a focal point for the community, an after-hours gathering spot for workers, hunters and vagrants. They were the place to go to keep warm on long winter evenings, tell stories, make music and enjoy the company of others. Naturally, good food and drink were a vital part of these gatherings – strong *aquavit* (a potent, vodka-like spirit) was shared and food was cooked using the furnaces and cooling ovens. Today visitors to Glasriket can partake in *hyttsill* parties, socialising at long tables and eating food prepared using these traditional methods.

The menu includes salted herring, smoked sausage, bacon and baked potatoes, as well as the regional speciality *ostkaka* (cheesecake). The cost to join a *hyttsill* party is Skr325 (under 10s are free), and the price includes beer, soft drinks and coffee, (*aquavit* costs extra!). Parties are held almost daily from June to August at the larger glassworks of Kosta, Målerås and Orrefors. Contact the regional tourist offices or the glassworks themselves to make a reservation.

All regional and long-distance buses depart from the train station; local town buses have their own station on Östra Sjögatan. Regional buses are run by **Kalmar Länstrafik** (☎ 0491-76 12 00; www.klt.se in Swedish), including buses to Öland.

Four **Swebus Express** (☎ 0200-21 82 18; www.swebusexpress.se) services daily run north to Västervik (Skr130, two hours), Norrköping (Skr220, four hours) and Stockholm (Skr316, 5½ hours); and two services daily run south to Karlskrona (Skr80, 1¼ hours), Karlshamn (Skr110, two hours), Kristianstad (Skr170, three hours), Lund (Skr230, four hours) and Malmö (Skr230, 4½ hours). **Svenska Buss** (☎ 0771-67 67 67; www.svenskabuss.se in Swedish) has four services per week on the same route; journey times and prices are similar. **Silverlinjen** (☎ 0485 261 11; www.silverlinjen.se in Swedish) runs three daily direct buses from Öland to Stockholm (Skr270), calling at Kalmar; reservations are essential.

SJ trains run every hour or two between Kalmar and Alvesta (Skr181, 1¼ hours), where you can connect with the main Stockholm–Malmö line and with trains to Göteborg. There are direct trains running to Linköping up to five times daily (Skr268, three hours), also with connections to Stockholm.

For bicycle hire, contact **Team Sportia** (☎ 212 44; Södravägen 2; per day/week Skr100/400; ⌚ Mon-Sat). **Taxi Kalmar** (☎ 44 44 44) can help you get around town.

GLASRIKET

The **'Kingdom of Crystal'** (www.glasriket.se), with its hypnotic glassblowing workshops hidden in among dense forests, is the most visited area in Sweden outside Stockholm and Göteborg. There are at least 11 glass factories (look for *glasbruk* signs), most with long histories: Kosta, for example, was founded in 1742. The immense popularity of this region is not only with northern Europeans – lots of Americans tour the country tracing their ancestors, many of whom emigrated from this area at the end of the 19th century.

The glassworks have similar opening hours, usually 10am to 6pm Monday to Friday, 10am to 4pm Saturday and noon to 4pm Sunday. Expert glass designers produce some extraordinary avant-garde pieces, often with a good dollop of Swedish humour involved. Factory outlets have substantial discounts on seconds (around 30% to 40% off), and larger places can arrange shipping to your home country.

There's a **Glasriket Pass** (Skr95), which allows free admission into 'hot shops' and museums, and discounts on purchases and *hyttsill* parties; but unless you're intending to go completely glass crazy, it doesn't really add up.

Most of Glasriket is in Kalmar län, with some in Kronobergs län; all parts are covered in this section.

Getting There & Around

Apart from the main routes, bus services around the area are pretty much nonexistent. The easiest way to explore is with your own transport (beware of elk). Bicycle tours on the unsurfaced country roads are excellent; there are plenty of hostels, and you can camp almost anywhere except near the military area on the Kosta–Orrefors road.

Kalmar Länstrafik's bus 139 runs from mid-June to mid-August only and calls at a few of the glass factories. The service operates four times per day on weekdays, once on Saturday, and runs from Nybro to Orrefors and Målerås. Year-round bus services connect Nybro and Orrefors (one weekdays), and Kosta is served by regular bus 218 from Växjö (two or three daily).

Buses and trains run from Emmaboda to Nybro and Kalmar (roughly hourly); trains also run to Karlskrona, Växjö and Alvesta, from where there are direct services to Göteborg and Stockholm.

Nybro

☎ 0481 / pop 19,882

The biggest town in Glasriket, Nybro makes a good base for exploration. It was once an important centre for hand-blown light bulbs(!), and still has two glassworks on its doorstep. Nybro's **tourist office** (☎ 450 85; www.nybro.se; Stadshusplan; 10am-6pm Mon-Fri, 10am-4pm Sat mid-Jun–mid-Aug, 10am-5pm Mon-Fri mid-Aug–mid-Jun) is inside the town hall.

Of the two glassworks, 130-year-old **Pukeberg** (☎ 800 29; www.pukeberg.se; Pukebergarnas väg), just southeast of the centre, is perhaps more interesting for its quaint setting. **Nybro** (☎ 428 81; Herkulesgatan; www.nybro-glasbruk.se) is smaller but also has unusual items, like the range of Beatles glassware.

There's a superior homestead museum **Madesjö Hembygdsgård** (☎ 179 35; adult/child Skr25/5; 10am-5pm Mon-Fri, 11am-5pm Sat & Sun late Jun–Aug), about 2.5km west of town. It's housed inside the 200m-long *kyrkstallarna* (former church stables), and contains an admirable collection, which includes cannonballs, clothing, coffins, carpenters' tools, chainsaws, a classroom, a country shop and a fantastic (ice-) cycle – and they're just the things beginning with 'C'.

Nybro Lågprishotell & Vandrarhem (☎ 109 32; Vasagatan 22; dm Skr150-225, s/d Skr490/740; P) The local STF hostel, near Pukeberg, is clean and comfortable and has a kitchen on each floor as well as a sauna. More expensive 'hotel' rooms have cable TV, nonbunk beds and private showers and toilets. You can rent bicycles.

Stora Hotellet (☎ 519 35; rumsbokning@telia.com; Mellangatan 11; s/d Skr925/1195, discounted to Skr650/850) The town's other option is this dated but reasonable central hotel, by the tourist office. It contains Scandinavia's largest work of art, an impressive 70 sq metre fresco of Nybro's industrial history. The restaurant offers the best choice in town for a meal (pizzas around Skr85).

Joelskogens Camping (☎ 450 86; www.joelskogenscamping.com; Grönvägen 51; site Skr120; May–mid-Sep) Campers should head for this little lakeside ground just out of the centre, with basic facilities (kitchen, laundry, shop) and a small beach area.

SJ trains between Alvesta and Kalmar stop here every hour or two. Regional bus 131 runs to/from Kalmar.

Orrefors

☎ 0481

Founded in 1898, **Orrefors** (☎ 341 95; www.orrefors.se; year-round) is perhaps the most famous of Sweden's glassworks. The huge site holds a factory with glass-blowing demonstrations, museum, impressive gallery and large shop with a shipping service. Orrefors *is* its glassworks and there's little else to the village.

STF Vandrarhem Orrefors (☎ 300 20, 0708 26 78 78; orreforsvandrarhem@tele2.se; Silversparregatan 14; dm/s/d from Skr120/235/320; May-Aug) If you need a lie-down after all the glass-buying, this excellent hostel is located conveniently near the factory. Quaint red houses surround a grassy garden, and the peaceful rooms have proper beds. Breakfast is available on request.

Värdshuset Orren (☎ 300 59; meals around Skr100; 10am-5pm Mon-Fri, 11am-5pm Sat & Sun mid-Jun–mid-Aug, 9am-2pm Mon-Fri mid-Aug–mid-Jun) In the factory grounds, this inn offers good lunches. There's also a kiosk in the glassworks area selling hot dogs and ice cream.

Gullaskruv & Målerås

☎ 0481

Don't miss the glassworks at Gullaskruv, about 6km northwest of Orrefors. Here, Uruguayan-born artist **Carlos R Pebaqué** (☎ 321 17; www.carlosartglass.com) makes utterly extraordinary vases in his one glass oven.

Completely different in scale and style is the large and popular **Mats Jonasson factory** (☎ 314 00; www.matsjonasson.com), 8km further northwest in Målerås, which sells engraved glass animal designs from around Skr200. There's a restaurant serving lunches.

Hallegårdens Vandrarhem (☎ 320 21; Hallegården; per person from Skr175; P) A kilometre or so southeast of Gullaskruv, this super youth hostel is in a tranquil rustic setting. Rooms all have washbasins, and there's a sunny café selling baked potatoes, salads and cakes.

Maleràs Vandrarhem (☎ 311 75; frank.fender@telia.com; Lindvägen 5, Måleràs; per person Skr150; P) Very handy for the Mats Jonasson glassworks, this SVIF hostel is another good place to stay.

For coffee and buns, try the tiny **Café Konditori** (☎ 310 44; Lindvägen 1, Måleràs; closed Sun) attached to Måleràs's bakery.

Kosta

☎ 0478

Kosta is where Glasriket started in 1742. Today the **Kosta Boda** (☎ 503 00; www.kostaboda.se) complex draws in coach loads of visitors, who are all elbows and claws in the vast discount shop. But don't be put off – Sweden even manages to make its tourist traps pleasant places. The two museums contain some amazing creations, there are plenty of glass-blowing demos in the old factory quarters, and there's a good café too.

To see beautiful bandy-legged elk at close quarters, head for **Grönåsens Älgpark** (☎/fax 507 70; www.moosepark.net; 10am-8pm Apr-Nov), Sweden's biggest elk park, located 3km west of town towards Orrefors. You can admire these gentle creatures on a 1.3km walk in the forested enclosure (Skr35). Then, if you wish, you can practise blasting 2D elk shapes made of metal in the shooting range, buy elk sausages to roast on the barbecue outside or purchase an elk-skin baseball cap. And, talking of horror, don't miss the display in the building behind the shop: it's guaranteed that you'll drive 50% slower after you've seen the crumpled metal, glassy eyes and lolling tongue...

Kosta Bad & Camping (☎ 505 17; info@glasriketkosta.se; sites Skr150, cabin from Skr425; Apr-Oct) There are great facilities at this campsite on the edge of Kosta village, including a pool, sauna, shop and boules.

Kosta Värdshus (☎ 500 06; lunch Skr75, s/d Skr420/690) Across the road from the Kosta Boda factory, this hotel/restaurant currently has 10 simple, old fashioned rooms, but big plans are afoot: a new wing with 20 modern rooms is to be built in 2007. The *värdshus* also attracts crowds for its cheap lunches.

For other eating options, try cheerful **Café Kosta** (☎ 502 60) inside the factory's outlet store, with tasty quiches and baked potatoes for around Skr55.

GLASS-BLOWING FUN!

If you feel inspired by Glasriket's top designers, why not have a go at **glass-blowing** (Skr150; most days mid-Jun–mid-Aug) yourself? Several hotshots – Orrefors, Kosta, Pukeberg and Johansfors – risk litigation by allowing you to blow, shape and 'open out' the treacley molten glass. It's the greatest fun, and the endearingly misshapen result will be a source of pride for years to come. Your masterpiece has to cool for two hours before you can take it away.

OSKARSHAMN

☎ 0491 / pop 26,300

Quiet Oskarshamn is useful for its regular boat connections with Gotland, and there are several sights to see while waiting for transport.

The **tourist office** (☎ 881 88; www.oskarshamn.se; Hantverksgatan 18; 9am-6pm Mon-Fri, 10am-3pm Sat, 11am-4pm Sun Jun–mid-Aug, 9-11.30am & 12.30-4.30pm Mon-Fri mid-Aug–May) is in Kulturhuset, along with the **library**, which has free Internet access.

Sights

Upstairs in Kulturhuset, **Döderhultarmuséet** (☎ 880 40; 10am-6pm Mon-Fri & 11am-4pm Sat & Sun Jun–mid-Aug, noon-4pm Tue-Fri, 10am-2pm Sat mid-Aug–May) is well worth a visit. It features the work of local artist, Axel Petersson 'Döderhultarn' (1868–1925), who captured local characters and occasions – weddings, funerals country dances etc – in vigorous and funny wood carvings; around 200 of which are on display. Next door, with the same opening hours, **Sjöfartsmuséet** (☎ 880 45) contains local maritime exhibits.

One admission price (adult/12–20 years Skr35/15) covers entry to both museums.

Blå Jungfrun National Park

Blå Jungfrun (the Blue Maiden), a 1km-long granite island, is known as the 'Witches' Mountain' because, according to tradition, this is where they gather every Easter to meet the devil. The island is a nature reserve loved for its fantastic scenery, gnarled trees, blue hares and bird life, and the curious stone maze, **Trojeborg**.

Between mid-June and August a local **launch** (per adult/7-15yr Skr180/90) departs up to six

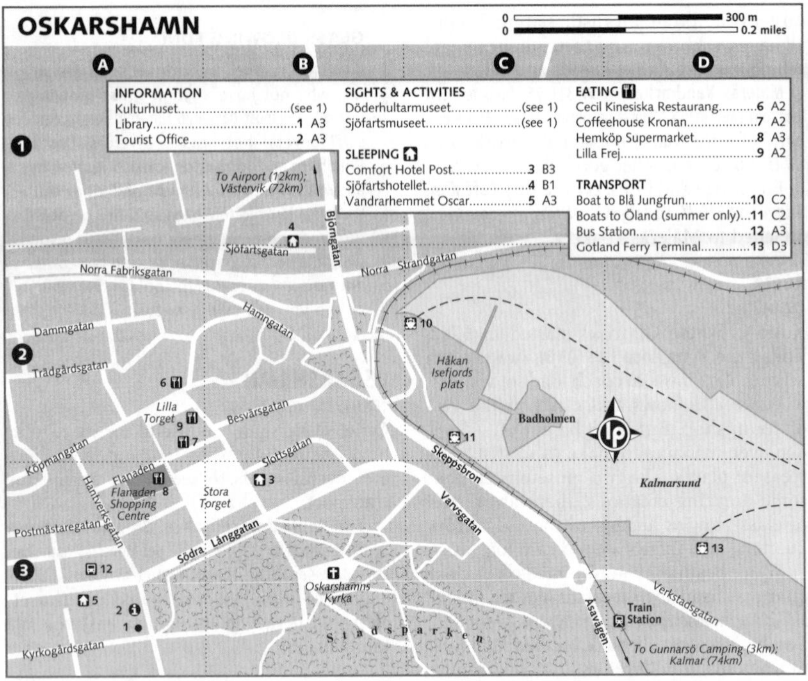

times weekly (usually *not* Mondays) from Brädholmskajen, the quay at the head of the harbour in Oskarshamn, allowing passengers 3½ hours to explore the island. Contact the tourist office for information and bookings.

Sleeping & Eating

Vandrarhemmet Oscar (☎ 158 00; forum@oskarshamn.se; Södra Långgatan 15-17; hostel dm/s/d Skr205/305/410, hotel s/d Skr610/810, discounted to Skr510/675; P) This shiny place, half hotel half hostel, is a brilliant budget option. Rooms have TV, fans and private bathrooms – only the kitchen for self-caterers gives it away as a hostel. It's conveniently placed for travellers, just opposite the bus station.

Sjöfartshotellet (☎ 76 83 00; sjofartshotel@telia.com; Sjöfartsgatan 13; s/d Skr945/1045, discounted to Skr595/695; P) The hotel was created as a sailors' foundation, hence the harbour setting and nautical décor. Its function is still the same today, and sailors have priority, with remaining rooms let to nonnautical guests. Rooms are comfortable, if on the small side, and there's a sauna.

Comfort Hotel Post (☎ 160 60; Stora Torget; s/d Skr1325/1525, discounted to Skr790/990; P) A step up in both price and location is offered at this upmarket hotel on the main square, which also has an interesting history – the hotel was once the grand old post house. The agreeable and ample-sized rooms reflect this past. All prices include an evening buffet, making the discounted prices particularly good value. The hotel's facilities include a sauna, Jacuzzi, restaurant, bar and a cosy lounge.

Gunnarsö Camping (☎ 132 98; Östersjövägen; sites low/high season Skr105/125; May–mid-Sep;) Located 3km southeast of town, this has seaside sites, a heated pool, restaurant, minigolf and other family campsite necessaries. However, it is difficult to get to without a car as public transport connections are very poor.

There are no outstanding restaurants, but there are a couple of pleasant ones. **Lilla Frej** (☎ 843 00; Lilla Torget; lunch Skr70, meals Skr80-160) has modern décor and a varied menu of pizza, pasta, salads, and fish and steak dishes. Just across the square, **Cecil Kinesiska Restaurang** (☎ 187 50; Lilla Torget; dishes Skr89-170) has Chinese cuisine as well as Swedish and even French dishes.

Coffeehouse Kronan (☎ 143 80; Flanaden 6; snacks from Skr45) This is a great lunch spot, with filled baguettes and *panini*, plus tasty cakes and good coffee. In summer there's seating on the bustling pedestrian street outside.

There's a **Hemköp supermarket** nearby in the Flanaden shopping centre.

Getting There & Away

Oskarshamn airport (☎ 332 00) is 12km north of town and **Swedline Express** (☎ 0495-24 90 65) flies twice on weekdays to Stockholm Arlanda.

The bus station is very central, while the train station is on the other side of town, close to the ferry terminal. Long-distance bus services stop at the bus station, but some also stop at the train station (local buses run frequently between the two).

Regional bus services run up to six times daily from Oskarshamn to Kalmar (Skr72, 1½ hours) and Västervik (Skr64, one hour).

Swebus Express has three daily buses between Stockholm and Kalmar that call in at Oskarshamn. Svenska Buss operates four services weekly from Stockholm to Malmö via Oskarshamn, Kalmar and Karlskrona. Regional trains run from Linköping and Nässjö.

Boats to Visby depart from the ferry terminal near the train station, daily in winter and twice daily in summer. There are also boats to Öland leaving from the ferry terminal off Skeppsbron; see p126 for more information.

VÄSTERVIK

☎ 0490 / pop 36,566

Västervik is a popular summer resort on the Baltic Sea, with camera-friendly cobbled streets, buzzing nightlife, sandy beaches just east of town, and 5000 islands on the doorstep. Harried by the Danes in its early years, Västervik grew to become a major shipbuilding centre between the 17th and 19th centuries. Famous sons include former tennis player Stefan Edberg, and Björn Ulvaeus from Abba. Björn often returns in mid-July for **VisFestivalen**, Västervik's 40-year-old folksong festival.

In a striking old Art Nouveau bathhouse, the **tourist office** (☎ 889 00; www.vastervik.se/turist; Strömsholmen; 🕑 10am-7pm Mon-Fri, 10am-5pm Sat & Sun Jul–mid-Aug, 10am-6pm Mon-Fri, 10am-2pm Sat May, Jun & late Aug, 10am-6pm Mon-Fri Sep-Apr) is located on an islet linked by road to the town centre. There's a **library** (☎ 887 77; Spötorget; 🕑 Mon-Fri summer, plus Sat winter) with free Internet access.

Sights & Activities

Västervik is stuffed with beautiful old buildings; ask the tourist office for its first-class town-walk brochure, which leads you round the best. **St Petri Kyrka** is a dramatic mass of spires and buttresses, while the older, calmer **St Gertruds Kyrkan** (Västra Kyrkogatan) dates from 1433 and has taken lightning strikes and riots in its stride. Nearby, **Aspagården** (Västra Kyrkogatan 9), dating from the 17th century, is the oldest wooden house in town. Other old houses from the 1740s can be seen at picture-perfect **Båtmansstugorna** (Båtmansgatan) – former ferrymen's cottages.

Displays at **Kulbackens Museum** (☎ 211 77; adult/under 18yr Skr30/free; 🕑 11am-4pm Mon-Fri, 1-4pm Sat & Sun May-Aug, 11am-4pm Tue-Fri Sep-Apr), just north of the tourist office, cover the history of the town. Also here is **Unos Torn**, an 18m-high lookout tower with fine archipelago views.

Two-hour **archipelago tours** (adult/child Skr130/70) on MS *Freden* depart from Skeppsbron daily from midsummer to the end of August. Make reservations at the tourist office.

Sleeping

The town bursts at the seams in summer, so book accommodation ahead.

Båtmansstugor (☎ 317 67, 194 03; Strömsgatan 42; cottages per person Skr200) This is a collection of delightful 18th-century fishermen's cottages for rent in an atmospheric old part of town. Most cottages sleep four and have their own kitchen, but bathrooms are shared.

Västerviks Stadshotell (☎ 820 00; info@stadshotellet.nu; Storgatan 3; s/d Skr1250/1700, discounted to Skr875/1200; P 💻) Belonging to the Best Western chain, the central Stadshotell has modern, comfortable rooms, sauna and gym, private parking (Skr90 per day), and a restaurant and a popular nightclub on Friday and Saturday nights.

Lysingsbadets (☎ 889 20; lysingsbadet@vastervik.se; low/high season sites Skr120/215, beds Skr140/160, d Skr500/550, cabins from Skr215/365; ♿) This huge, five-star 'holiday village' by the sea (2.5km southeast of town) is a world of its own. Restaurant, golf, a swimming pool, beaches, and boat, bicycle and kayak hire are all available,

ASTRID & PIPPI

If you're a fan of the red-headed, pigtailed strongest girl in the world, you'll already know and revere the name of author Astrid Lindgren (1907–2002). Astrid, a farmer's daughter, was herself an unconventional tomboy, causing scandals in her home town of Vimmerby first by cutting off all her hair as the jazz age dawned, and then by becoming a single mother.

In 1941, Astrid's daughter Karin was stuck in bed with pneumonia, and asked her mother for a story about 'Pippi Longstocking'. The weird name inspired Astrid to invent a stream of stories about that original wild child, an immediate hit with Karin and her friends.

In 1944, Lindgren sprained her ankle and passed the time by writing down the Pippi stories. They were refused for publication, but another book of hers won second prize in a girls' story competition. The next year Lindgren entered a revised Pippi manuscript into another competition, where it won first prize.

This was just the beginning of a prolific career. Lindgren's impressive output included picture books, plays and songs, and her books have been translated into more than 60 languages. She worked in radio, TV and films, was head of the Children's Book Department at her publishers for four years and received numerous honours and awards from around the world.

plus there are extra activities like circus-skill workshops, pony trekking and karaoke evenings. The hostel opens June to August, but cabins and hotel rooms are available year-round. Take local bus 5 (Skr13).

Eating & Drinking

Restaurang Smugglaren (☎ 213 22; Smugglaregränd 1; mains Skr180-230; ⏰ from 6pm summer, shorter hr winter) Tucked down an alley off Strandvägen is the charming Smugglaren, which offers quality food in a cosy wooden building, complete with model ships and paraffin lamps. There's also an outdoor courtyard for summer.

Waterside Fiskaretorget is a hive of activity; there are a number of restaurant-bars located here, and all have outdoor terraces that are especially sought-after on long summer evenings. **Harry's** (☎ 173 00) and the **Brig** (☎ 342 00) are on the square; both open noon to late daily (until 3am Friday and Saturday) in summer, shorter hours during winter. They offer simple bar food, plus an à la carte menu for finer dining, and are great spots to relax over a drink.

Västervik's fast-food speciality is French fries, mashed potato and shrimp salad (Skr20); look out for it at stands along the waterside. **Systembolaget** is on Kvarngatan.

Getting There & Away

Long-distance buses stop outside the train station, at the eastern edge of the town centre. Trains run between Västervik and Linköping up to five times daily (Skr113, 1¾ hours). Daily bus services run every couple of hours to Vimmerby (Skr56, 1¼ hours), Oskarshamn (Skr64, one hour) and Kalmar (Skr112, three hours).

Svenska Buss runs to Stockholm, Kalmar, Karlskrona and Malmö four times per week. On Fridays and Sundays, Swebus Express runs two buses on the Västervik–Vimmerby–Eksjö–Jönköping route.

VIMMERBY

☎ 0492 / pop 15,596

Vimmerby is the birthplace of Astrid Lindgren, and home to one of Sweden's top visitor attractions, a theme park based on the Pippi Longstocking books. Absolutely everything in town revolves around the strongest girl in the world. Even the pretty cobbled town square, Stora Torget, is filled with Pippi entertainments during the summer – there's no escape!

Vimmerby has a busy, helpful **tourist office** (☎ 310 10; www.turism.vimmerby.se; Västra Tullportsgatan 3; ⏰ 9am-8pm late Jun–early Aug, 9am-5pm Mon-Fri rest of year). If you don't know whether Mr Nilsson is a horse or a monkey, **Bokhandeln** (☎ 123 10; Stora Torget 8) sells Pippi books in various languages, including English.

Sights & Activities

Young children and Pippi Longstocking fans should head for **Astrid Lindgrens Värld** (☎ 798 00; www.alv.se; adult/4-15yr/family Skr210/145/640 mid-Jun–mid-Aug; ⏰ 10am-6pm mid-Jun–mid-Aug, 10am-5pm mid-May–mid-Jun & late Aug), on the northern edge of town. Actresses dressed as Pippi (complete with gravity-defying pigtails) sing and dance their way around the 100 buildings and settings from the books – the Swedish kids love it! Prices drop outside peak season, as there are fewer activities and theatre performances. Cars are charged a cheeky Skr20. There's a local bus (Skr18), or it's a 10-minute walk from the centre.

There's a reasonably priced restaurant, a fast-food joint and coffee shops in the park. If you're a dedicated fan, you can stay at the on-site **camping ground** (sites low/high season Skr135/195, 4-bed cabins from Skr495/695; mid-May–mid-Aug).

Older visitors can learn about Lindgren's antiwar and pro-animal-rights stance at **Astrid Lindgren Gården** (798 00; adult/child Skr65/35 or free with admission to theme park; closed Mon & Tue Sep-May), an excellent museum of her life and work. The house is adjacent to the theme park.

If you can't bear to look at those ginger plaits any more, wander down Storgatan where you'll find many of Vimmerby's quaint 18th- and 19th-century wooden houses. There's also **Museet Näktergalen** (76 94 59; Sevedegatan 43; adult/child Skr20/10; noon-5pm Mon-Fri, 10am-2pm Sat mid-Jun–mid-Aug), a small 18th-century house with traditional painted walls and ceilings.

Sleeping & Eating

There's a camping ground at the theme park (see above). There's lots of accommodation in town, much of it offering theme-park packages; ask the tourist office for details.

Vimmerby Vandrarhem (100 20; info@vimmerbyvandrarhem.nu; Järnvägsallén 2; 4-bed rm from Skr500; P) This cheerful newish hostel, based in a fine wooden building, is right near the train station. There are more expensive doubles available, with proper (nonbunk) beds, plus a garden with barbecue.

Ramada Vimmerby Stadshotell (121 00; info@vimstatt.ramadasweden.se; Stora Torget 9; s/d Skr1170/1350, discounted to Skr960/1180; P) You can't miss this dashing pink building on the town square. Rooms aren't anywhere near as grand as the exterior implies, but they're comfortable if small, with cable TV, minibars and the rest. Staff are very friendly, and can make you a picnic hamper (Skr200) for your visit to Astrid Lindgrens Värld. There's a good restaurant.

Konditori Brödstugan (104 21; Storgatan 42; meals around Skr50) One very busy lunch spot is this bakery-café, with a wide choice of quiches, salads, baked potatoes and hot dishes. You may have to lurk for a table.

Getting There & Away

Buses and trains depart from the Resecentrum, downhill past the church from Stora Torget. Swebus Express runs twice on Fridays and Sundays to Eksjö and Jönköping, and in the other direction to Västervik (Skr56, 1¼ hours). Svenska Buss operates daily between Stockholm, Linköping and Vimmerby. After Vimmerby, services continue to either Oskarshamn, Åseda, or Kal mar and Nybro.

Kustpilen trains run several times daily south to Kalmar, or north to Linköping.

BLEKINGE

With its long coastline and safe harbours, Blekinge's past and present are faithfully fastened to the sea. Sweden and Denmark once squabbled over the area, a trump card in power games over the Baltic. Today it's still an important naval zone and parts of the wonderful Unesco site Karlskrona are still under military control. The region's second largest town is Karlshamn, where in the 19th century emigrants boarded ships bound for America. There's watery enjoyment in the fish-filled rivers and lakes, and a stunning southern archipelago to explore at leisure.

KARLSKRONA

0455 / pop 61,137

As you approach Karlskrona, an optical illusion makes it appear to be floating on water – which in a sense, it does; the town has always been a hugely important naval base, dependent on the sea for its survival. In 1998 the entire town was added to the Unesco World Heritage List due to its well-preserved 17th- and 18th-century naval architecture.

After the failed Danish invasion of Skåne in 1679, King Karl XI decided that a southern naval base was needed for better control over the Baltic Sea, and so Karlskrona was created – almost immediately becoming Sweden's third-biggest city. Much of the town is still a military base, so to see certain sights you'll need to book a tour at the tourist office and have ID at the ready.

Information

You'll find ATMs and the post office in the Wachtmeister shopping centre on Borgmästeregatan.

Library (☎ 30 34 65; Stortorget 15-17; 🕑 10am-7pm Mon, Wed & Thu, noon-7pm Tue, 10am-5pm Fri, 10am-1pm Sat) Free Internet access.

Tourist office (☎ 30 34 90; www.karlskrona.se/tourism; Stortorget 2; 🕑 9am-7pm Mon-Fri, 9am-4pm Sat & Sun Jun-Aug, 10am-5pm Mon-Fri, 10am-2pm Sat Sep-May)

Video shop (Admiraltetsgatan 4; per hr Skr29) Internet access.

Sights & Activities

FORTIFICATIONS

The finest attraction is the extraordinary offshore **Kungsholms Fort**, with its curious circular harbour, established in 1680 to defend the town. Four-hour **boat tours** (adult/12-18yr Skr140/70; 🕑 10am & 2.15pm mid-Jun–Aug, plus 3pm & 6.30pm Tue, Thu & Sat Jul) to the fort, including a guided tour of Kungsholm, depart from Fisktorget; book at the tourist office. Another option is the boat operated by **Skärgårdstrafiken** (☎ 783 30), which runs from Fisktorget and circles the fort five times daily from mid-June to mid-August (adult/child Skr80/35); you must inform the tourist office of your visit in advance if you take this second option.

Bristling with cannons, the tower **Drottningskärs kastell** on the island of Aspö was described by Admiral Nelson of the British Royal Navy as 'impregnable' – and it looks it. You can visit it on a **Skärgårdstrafiken boat** (adult/child return Skr80/35; 🕑 Jun-Aug), departing from the end of Östra Köpmansgatan.

MUSEUMS

The striking **Marinmuseum** (☎ 359 30 02; Stumholmen; admission free; 🕑 10am-6pm Jun-Aug, 11am-5pm Tue-Sun Sep-May) is the national naval museum. Inside are reconstructions of a battle deck in wartime, a hall full of fantastic figureheads, piles of model boats, and even some the real thing – such as a minesweeper, a sailing ship and a submarine.

Nearby, the **Konstmuseet** (☎ 30 34 22; Bastionsgatan 8; admission free; 🕑 noon-5pm Tue-Fri, to 7pm Wed, noon-5pm Sat & Sun), once a seamen's barracks, is now a modern art gallery.

The extensive **Blekinge Museum** (☎ 30 49 60; Fisktorget 2; admission free; 🕑 10am-6pm mid-Jun–mid-Aug, 11am-5pm Tue-Sun mid-Aug–mid-Jun) explains the local fishing, boat-building and quarrying trades. The most captivating part is Grevagården, an 18th-century house where each room is filled with thousands of contemporary objects, from thimbles to coffins. There's also a small baroque garden and a pleasant café.

The surprising **Museum Leonardo da Vinci Ideale** (☎ 255 73; Drottninggatan 28) exhibits a private collection of original art, but was closed at the time of writing; phone for information.

OTHER SIGHTS & ACTIVITIES

Stortorget is the town's monumental square, deliberately created to rival the best in Europe. It's dominated by symbols of law and religion: the courthouse; the baroque church **Fredrikskyrkan** (🕑 11am-4pm Mon-Fri, 9.30am-2pm Sat); and **Trefaldighetskyrkan** (Trinity Church; 🕑 11am-4pm Mon-Fri, 9.30am-2pm Sat), inspired by Rome's Pantheon.

Sweden's oldest wooden church is **Amiralitetskyrkan** (☎ 103 56; Vallgatan); outside is the wooden statue **Old Rosenbom**, who raises his hat to charitable visitors.

There's a small Blue-Flag **beach** on Stumholmen. Pick a sunny summer afternoon for a tour around Karlskrona's **archipelago**, made up of an astounding 1650 islands. A three-hour tour costs Skr125/60 per adult/child; contact the Skärgårdstrafiken office at Fisktorget for timetables and information. Enquire at the tourist office about two-hour **guided walks** of the city (adult/12-18yr Skr60/30), held on Saturdays from May to mid-September.

Sleeping

STF Vandrarhem Trossö Karlskrona (☎ 100 20; www.karlskronavandrarhem.se; Drottninggatan 39; dm/s/d Skr125/230/280) Wonderfully friendly, this modern, clean hostel has a laundry, TV room and backyard for kids to play in; parking on the opposite side of the street is free.

STF Vandrarhem Annexe (Bredgatan 16; dm/s/d Skr155/310/375; 🕑 mid-Jun–mid-Aug) There's also this summer-only annexe around the corner; reception is at the main building.

Hotell Siesta (☎ 801 80; info@hotellsiesta.se; Borgmästaregatan 5; budget s/d from Skr615/750, discounted to Skr490/590; P 💻) This decent midrange option is right behind Stortorget. Recently renovated standard rooms are bright and attractive, with green-and-yellow décor. Budget rooms are smaller and older, although they're about to be spruced up.

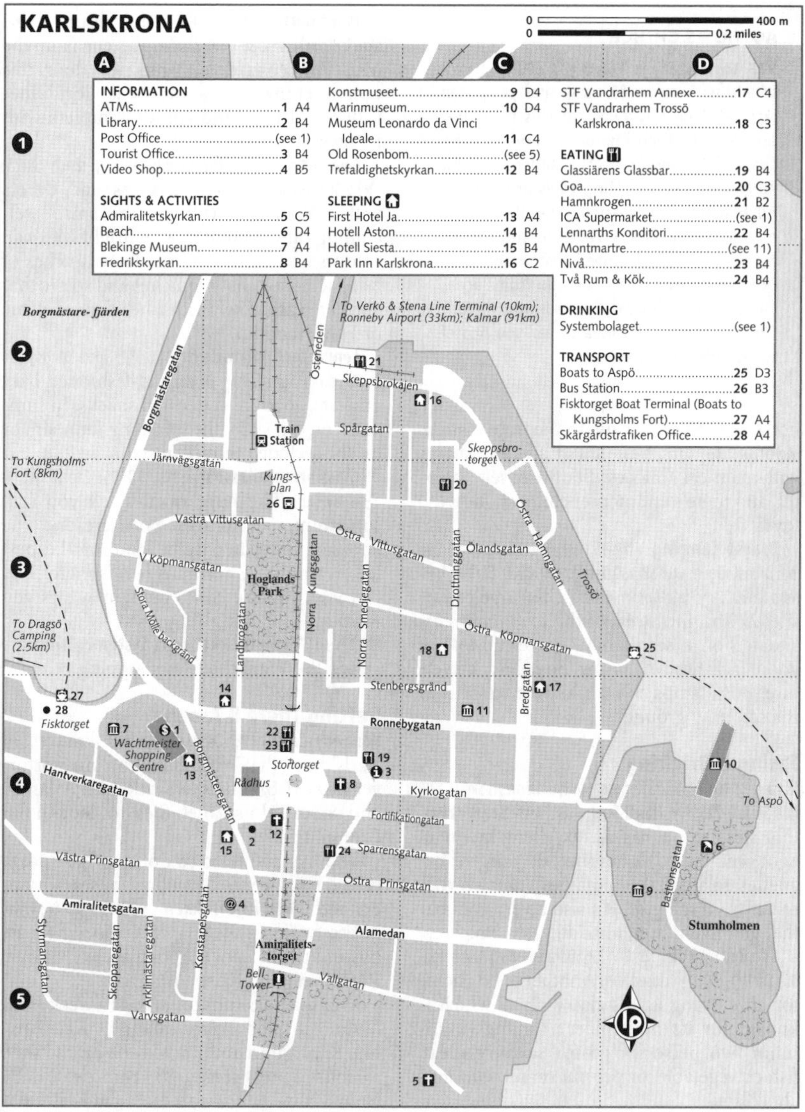

Hotell Aston (☎ 194 70; www.trossohotell.se; Landbrogatan 1; s/d Skr995/1095, discounted to Skr545/645; P 🖳) This is another smart 3rd-floor place, located centrally. There's a sauna and, if you're lucky, you'll get waffles for breakfast.

First Hotel Ja (☎ 555 60; karlskrona.ja@firsthotels.se; Borgmästaregatan 13; s/d Skr1100/1290, discounted to Skr645/795; P) One for shopaholics, this hotel is located inside the Wachtmeister shopping centre. It offers fairly luxurious rooms, which are comfortable and tastefully decorated, plus there's also a sauna, bar and restaurant.

Park Inn Karlskrona (☎ 36 15 00; www.karlskrona.parkinn.se; Skeppsbrokajen; s/d Skr1245/1245, discounted to Skr745/895; P 🖳) The Karlskrona is a business

AUTHOR'S CHOICE

STF Turiststation Tjärö (☎ 600 63; tjaro@stfturist.se; beds Skr280, camp sites per person Skr75; ⏰ early May–early Sep) This place lies on an idyllic island nature reserve, off the coast of Blekinge between Karlshamn and Karlskrona, with walking trails and peaceful beaches. The hostel is highly recommended; breakfast is available and there's a café and fully licensed restaurant, plus boat and canoe hire. Boats run from Järnavik at least six times daily in summer (return Skr80) – it's a good idea to call the hostel to confirm sailing times.

hotel, conveniently close to the train station. Rooms are dark blue, smart and shipshape, with nautical touches. Staff are very helpful, and there's an Internet connection in the foyer.

Dragsö Camping (☎ 153 54; info@dragsocamping.nu; Dragsövägen; sites Skr160, 2-bed cabins from Skr300, hostel d Skr300; ⏰ late Apr–mid-Oct) This large campsite, 2.5km northwest of the town centre, is situated on a scenic bay. There are lots of good facilities, including boat and bicycle hire. Bus 7 stops about a kilometre short of the camping ground.

Eating & Drinking

Nivå (☎ 103 71; Norra Kungsgatan 3; light meals Skr50-120, grill Skr120-225; ⏰ closed Sun) Just off Stortorget, this steakhouse has an excellent menu of light, well-priced dishes (nachos, burgers, baguettes, salads, baked potatoes), plus heartier meals from the grill. It's also a very cool bar that gets lively later, until at least 1am.

Två Rum & Kök (☎ 104 22; Södra Smedjegatan 3; fondue Skr100-200; ⏰ closed Sun) Another good choice for an evening is this classy place, which is known for its magnificent fondue (minimum two persons); go for savoury meat, fish or vegetable, or pig out on scrumptious chocolate.

Hamnkrogen (☎ 803 36; Skeppsbrokajen 18; lunch Skr70, mains Skr79-175) Hamnkrogen is right by the guest harbour, and has outdoor summer seating; it's favoured by people who've just got off the bobbing boats. It offers pizzas, steaks and grills, but if you fancy something spicier, great tandoori dishes, baltis and biryanis are cooked by the restaurant's Indian chef.

Montmartre (☎ 31 18 33; Ronnebygatan 18; pizza Skr65-80, mains Skr80-160) Taking its cue from the Museum Leonardo da Vinci next door, this upmarket pizza restaurant sells Florentine-influenced food and comes complete with its own art gallery.

Goa (☎ 133 70; Drottninggatan 61; lunch Skr75; ⏰ 9.30am-3.30pm Mon-Fri) Veggies and diners with a conscience will love this small, welcoming café, decorated with bright Mexican colours and cacti. It serves tasty lunches of lasagne, soup, salads, quiches and so on, that you can wash down with a healthy smoothie or Fair Trade tea.

Lennarths Konditori (☎ 31 03 32; Norra Kungsgatan 3; ⏰ closed Sun) This is an old-fashioned bakery-café, good for coffee and snacks. In summer you can sit by the splashing fountain, or on the secluded terrace upstairs.

Glassiärens Glassbar (☎ 170 05; Stortorget 4; ⏰ May-Sep) The huge queues tell you that something special is going on here, and true enough, Glassiären sells some of the best ice cream in the northern hemisphere! You can watch waffle cones being made as you wait.

The **ICA supermarket** and **Systembolaget** are inside the Wachtmeister shopping centre.

Getting There & Around

Ronneby airport (☎ 0457-255 90) is 33km west of Karlskrona; the Flygbuss leaves from Stortorget (Skr75). SAS flies to Stockholm Arlanda, and Stockholmsplanet flies to Stockholm Bromma daily.

The bus and train stations are just north of the town centre. Regional buses are operated by **BlekingeTrafiken** (☎ 0455-569 80; www.blekingetrafiken.se). Regular *Kustbussen* (coast buses) operate between Kalmar, Karlskrona, Karlshamn and Kristianstad.

Svenska Buss runs four times a week from Malmö to Stockholm, calling at Kristianstad, Karlshamn and Karlskrona on the way. Swebus Express service 834 runs twice daily from Malmö to Kalmar, calling at Kristianstad, Karlshamn and Karlskrona.

Direct trains run at least 16 times daily to Karlshamn (Skr59, one hour) and Kristianstad (Skr113, two hours), at least six times daily to Emmaboda (Skr69, 40 minutes), and at least a couple of times to Göteborg (Skr388, five hours). Change at Kristianstad or Emmaboda for Malmö and Lund; at Emmaboda for Kalmar.

Stena Line ferries to Gdynia (Poland) depart from Verkö, 10km east of Karlskrona (take bus 6); see p328 for details.

For a taxi, call **Taxi Karlskrona** (☎ 191 00).

KARLSHAMN

☎ 0454 / pop 30,847

With its quaint cobbled streets and old wooden houses, you'd never guess that this quiet town was once so devilish. Alcoholic drinks, tobacco, snuff and playing cards were produced in great quantities here, and it was a major 19th-century smugglers' den! Karlshamn was also the port from where many Swedes left for America. One of Sweden's biggest free festivals, the **Baltic Festival** (Östersjöfestivalen; ☎ 811 16; balticfestival@karlshamn.se) in late July, sees a quarter of a million people roll in for bands, boat races and a carnival parade.

The **tourist office** (☎ 812 13; www.karlshamn.se; Ronnebygatan 1; ⏰ 9am-7pm Mon-Fri, 10am-6pm Sat, noon-6pm Sun mid-Jun–mid-Aug, 9am-5pm Mon-Fri mid-Aug–mid-Jun) can help with information and bookings. Drottninggatan is where you'll find most services.

Sights

The **utvandrar-monumentet** stands in a park by the harbour, commemorating all the America-bound emigrants. The figures on the monument are characters from Vilhelm Moberg's classic work *The Emigrants* – Karl Oscar, looking forward to the new country, and Kristina, looking back towards her beloved Duvemåla. Nearby, you'll find a 300-year-old **fishing cottage** – open summer only.

The 'culture quarter' **Karlshamns Kulturkvarter** (☎ 148 68; Vinkelgatan 8; ⏰ noon-5pm Mon-Fri Jun-Aug, 1-4pm Mon-Fri Sep-May) has interesting information about Karlhamn's tobacco and *punsch*-producing history, and some 18th-century merchants' houses.

Sleeping & Eating

STF Vandrarhem Karlshamn (☎ 140 40; stfturistkhamn@hotmail.com; Surbrunnsvägen 1C; beds Skr165) This hostel is on the eastern side of the town grid, near the train station, and offers good rooms, all with private bathrooms. Kids will love the nearby playground, created by children.

First Hotel Carlshamn (☎ 890 00; carlshamn@firsthotels.se; Varvsgatan 1; s/d Skr1129/1329, discounted to Skr668/868; P 🖳) For high-quality accommodation, walk out of the tourist office and across the road into this upmarket hotel. Cushy rooms are clean-lined and modern, and some have harbour views. There's a sauna, 24-hour bar and a top-quality restaurant too.

Gourmet Grön (☎ 164 40; Östra Piren, Biblioteksgatan 6; tapas/buffet Skr70-150; ⏰ closed Sun) This award-winning waterside restaurant has wonderful lunch-time and evening buffets, with an emphasis on vegetarian food. Nibble on a ciabatta, tapas-style goodies, or inventive spreads with Tunisian, French, Greek and Italian influences.

Köpmannagården (☎ 317 87; Drottninggatan 88; pizzas around Skr70) For cheaper eats, try this pleasant restaurant and pizzeria with its lovely summer courtyard.

Getting There & Away

The bus and train stations are in the north-eastern part of town. For travel information, see the previous section on Karlskrona.

Lisco Line sails daily between Karlshamn and Klaipėda in Lithuania; see p328 for details.

ÖLAND

☎ 0485 / pop 25,000

Like a deranged vision of Don Quixote's, Öland is *covered* in old wooden windmills. Some are spruce, repaired and cherished, others stand forlorn, sails broken and dangling like dead daddy-long-legs. All in all, it's a surreal scene.

At 137km long and 16km wide, Öland is Sweden's smallest province. It's also a hugely popular summer destination for Swedes – even the king and queen have a summer house here. The island gets around two million visitors annually, mostly in July. Around 90% of them flock to the golden shores in the northern half of the island to bask and bathe. If you're looking for more than a beach holiday, it's the south that holds the most surprises. All of Öland, from Färjestaden southwards is a Unesco World Heritage site, designated for its unique agricultural landscape which has been in continuous use from the Stone Age to today.

There are surprisingly few hotels, but you can stay in innumerable private rooms (booked through the tourist offices), at 27

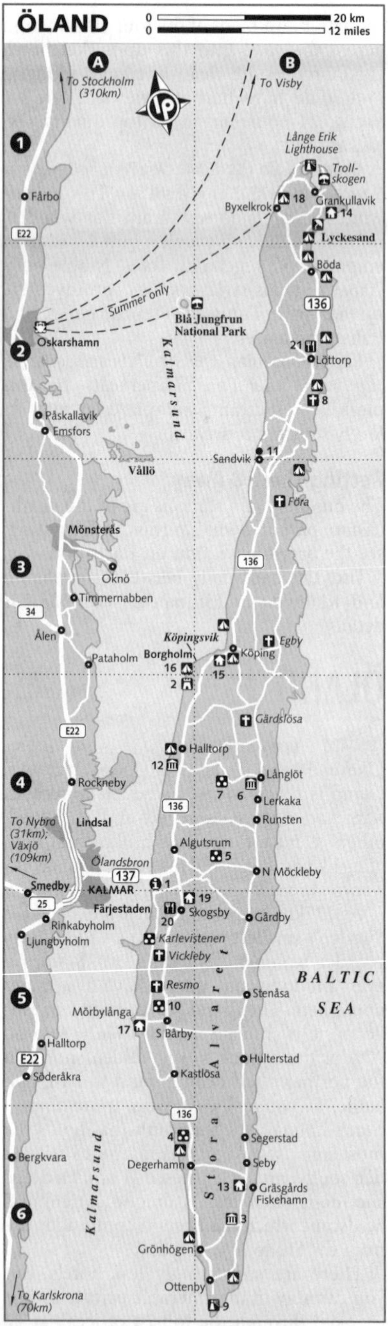

INFORMATION

- Tourist Office....1 A4
- Tourist Office (Borgholm)....(see 16)

SIGHTS & ACTIVITIES

- Borgholms Slott....2 A4
- Eketorp (Ring Fort)....3 B6
- Gettlinge....4 A6
- Gråborg (Ring Fort)....5 B4
- Himmelsberga....6 B4
- Ismantorp Fortress....7 B4
- Källa Kyrka....8 B2
- Långe Jan Lighthouse....9 B6
- Mysinge Hög....10 A5
- Nature Reserve....(see 9)
- Sandvikskvarn....11 B2
- Solliden Palace....(see 2)
- VIDA Museum Konsthall....12 A4
- Ölands Djurpark....(see 1)

SLEEPING

- Ebbas Vandrarhem & Trägårdscafe....(see 16)
- Gammalsbygårdens Gästgiveri....13 B6
- Grankullaviks Vandrarhem....14 B1
- Guntorps Herrgård....15 B3
- Hotell Borgholm....(see 16)
- Kajutan Hotell & Vandrarhem....(see 17)
- Kapelludden Camping & Stugor....16 A3
- Mörby Vandrarhem & Lågprishotell....17 A5
- Neptuni Camping....18 B1
- STF Vandrarhem Ölands Skogsby....19 A5
- Villa Sol....(see 16)

EATING

- Café Restaurang Bojen....20 A5
- Lammet & Grisen....21 B2
- Pubben....(see 16)
- Restaurang Fågel Blå....(see 9)

DRINKING

- Systembolaget....(see 16)

TRANSPORT

- Bus Station....(see 16)

campsites and at least a dozen hostels (book ahead). Camping between midsummer and mid-August can cost up to Skr250 per site. The island has developed a reputation as a foodie's delight, and there are lots of excellent restaurants.

Information

The bridge from Kalmar lands you on the island just north of Färjestaden, where there is a large and well-stocked **tourist office** (☎ 56 06 00; www.olandsturist.com; 8.30am-8.30pm Mon-Sat, 9.30am-7pm Sun Jul, 9am-6pm Mon-Fri, 10am-4pm Sat & Sun May, Jun & early Aug, 9am-5pm Mon-Fri rest of yr; closed late-Dec–early Jan) at the Träffpunkt Öland centre. Staff can book accommodation throughout the island (including cottages and cabins for a Skr75 fee). Model monks and ring forts illustrate the island's history in the **Historium** inside the tourist office, and there's a **Naturum** (Swedish only) for wildlife spotters.

There's also a smaller tourist office in Borgholm (see opposite).

Getting There & Around

BICYCLE

There are no bicycle lanes on the bridge between Öland and Kalmar, so cyclists take their lives into their own hands! Cyclists aren't allowed on the bridge in summer – instead there's a free *Cykelbuss* service to get you across (roughly hourly; enquire at the tourist office in Kalmar).

The following shops hire out bicycles in summer for around Skr100 per day, or about Skr400 a week:

Byxelkroks Cykeluthyrning (☎ 070-579 61 00; Hamnkontoret; Byxelkrok)

ERSA-Cykeluthyrning (☎ 0708-17 75 50; Ekvägen 1; Färjestaden)

Hallbergs Hojjar (☎ 109 40; Köpmangatan; Borgholm)

BOAT

From mid-June to mid-August, MS *Solsund* (☎ 070-621 42 60) sails daily from Byxelkrok (northwest Öland) and Oskarshamn (on the mainland 60km north of Kalmar). One-way tickets cost Skr150/100 per adult/seven-16 years; a car and up to five people costs Skr550, and a bicycle Skr50.

BUS

Silverlinjen (☎ 0485-261 11; www.silverlinjen.se in Swedish) runs three daily direct buses from Öland to Stockholm (Skr270, 6½ hours), calling at Kalmar – reservations are essential.

Buses connect all the main towns on the island from Kalmar, and run every hour or two to Borgholm (Skr48, 50 minutes) and Mörbylånga (Skr32, one hour). A few buses per day run to Byxelkrok and Grankullavik (both Skr88, around 2¼ hours), in the far north of the island. Services to the south are poor, with some improvement from May to August.

BORGHOLM & AROUND

The most happening town on Öland is Borgholm, the 'capital' of the island (it's a small island!). It's a real family place, with every other shop selling flip-flops, plastic octopuses and ice cream. The most dramatic sight is the enormous ruined castle on its outskirts.

The **tourist office** (☎ 890 00; Sandgatan 25; 🕑 9am-5pm Mon-Sat Jul, 9am-5.30pm, 10am-3pm Sat Jun & early Aug, 9am-12.15pm & 1-5.30pm Mon-Fri rest of yr) is at the bus station. Banks and other services are on Storgatan.

Sights

Northern Europe's largest ruined castle, **Borgholms Slott** (☎ 123 33; www.borgholmsslott.se; adult/12-17yr Skr50/20; 🕑 10am-6pm May-Aug, 10am-4pm Apr & Sep), looms just south of town. This epic limestone structure was finally burnt and abandoned early in the 18th century, after being used as a dye works. There's a very good museum inside and a nature reserve nearby. The ruins are a frequent summer concert venue, and there are children's activities between late June and mid-August.

Sweden's most famous 'summer house', **Solliden Palace** (☎ 153 55; adult/7-17yr Skr60/30; 🕑 11am-6pm May–mid-Sep), 2.5km south of the town centre, is used by the royal family. Its exceptional gardens are open to the public and are well worth a wander.

VIDA Museum & Konsthall (☎ 774 40; www.vidamuseum.com; adult/under 15yr Skr40/free; 🕑 10am-7pm Jul, 10am-5pm May, Jun, Aug & Sep, 10am-5pm Sat & Sun only Apr & Oct-Dec) is a strikingly modern museum and art gallery in Halltorp, about 9km south of Borgholm. Its best halls are devoted to two of Sweden's top glass designers.

On the east coast, about 13km southeast of Borgholm, is **Gärdslösa kyrka** (🕑 11am-5pm mid-May–mid-Sep), the best-preserved medieval church (1138) on Öland, with reasonably intact wall and ceiling paintings.

Sleeping

The tourist office can help you find rooms round town.

Ebbas Vandrarhem & Trädgårdscafé (☎ 103 73; rum@ebbas.se; Storgatan 12; lunch Skr75, 2-/4-bed rm Skr530/880; 🕑 May-Sep) Right in the thick of things, Ebbas friendly café has a small STF hostel above it. Five of the agreeable lemon-yellow rooms overlook a big garden, and four the bustling pedestrianised main street. There's a kitchen for self-caterers…or just pop downstairs for a decent choice of hot and cold grub, served until 9pm.

Villa Sol (☎ 56 25 52; www.villasol.nu; Slottsgatan 30; low season s/d from Skr330/500, high season s/d from Skr500/650) Villa Sol has a super garden and small but thoughtfully decorated rooms. Each has a different colour scheme – we like the Yellow Room best, for its sunny feel and private balcony. Prices exclude breakfast, but there is a guest kitchen. Rooms with private bathrooms cost around Skr200 extra.

Guntorps Herrgård (☎ 130 00; www.guntorpsherrgard.se; Guntorpsgatan; s/d from Skr895/1095) This is a delightful old farmhouse east of town. The accommodation is excellent, with either pale romantic rooms, or brash modern black-white-and-red colour schemes. There's the added drawcard of a huge smörgåsbord (Skr175 per person; from 6pm daily) offering superb samples of local dishes.

Hotell Borgholm (770 60; www.hotellborgholm.se; Trädgårdsgatan 15; d Skr990-1595) After a terrible fire in 2004, the Borgholm closed for complete refurbishment. At the time of writing, it had just reopened, shinier and more stylish than ever. Boutique rooms are done out in super-cool Swedish style, all spotlights, sharp lines and serene hues. The owner is Karin Fransson, one of Sweden's best chefs – so, as you can imagine, the restaurant here is first class.

Kapelludden Camping & Stugor (56 07 70; Sandgatan 27; info@kapelludden.se; sites low/high season Skr170/275; 6-bed cabins Skr1220, high season weekly rental only) This beachside campsite is the handiest, just near the tourist office. It's a huge place (some 450 sites) and has five-star, family-oriented facilities, but it can get rowdy in summer.

Eating & Drinking

Nya Conditoriet (100 11; Storgatan 28) This busy old-fashioned bakery-café serves good sandwiches and pastries.

Pubben (124 15; Storgatan 18) There are snacks and light meals here, but mainly people come to this English-style pub for the beer. With genial service and a summery terrace, it's the most heaving bar in town.

There are supermarkets on Storgatan, and a central **Systembolaget** (Östra Kyrkogatan 19).

NORTHERN ÖLAND

At Sandvik on the west coast, about 30km north of Borgholm, **Sandvikskvarn** (261 72; www.sandvikskvarn.com; pizzas from Skr65; noon-8pm May-Sep, to 10pm mid-Jun–mid-Aug) is a Dutch-style windmill and one of the largest in the world. In summer, you can climb its seven storeys for good views across to the mainland. There's a restaurant with old barrels for seats where you can try the local speciality, *lufsa* (baked pork and potato, Skr65); and an adjacent pizzeria.

Källa kyrka, at a little harbour about 36km northeast of Borgholm, off road 136, is a fine example of Öland's medieval fortified churches. The broken **rune stone** inside shows the Christian Cross growing from the pagan tree of life.

Grankullavik, in the far north, has sandy beaches and dense summer crowds; **Lyckesand** is one of the island's best beaches and the strangely twisted trees and ancient barrows at the nearby **Trollskogen** nature reserve are well worth a visit.

Grankullaviks Vandrarhem (240 40, fax 24010; dm from Skr150; May-Sep), a SVIF hostel, is superbly situated on the beachfront and has a kitchen, restaurant and bakery.

Neptuni Camping (284 95; www.neptunicamping.se; Småskogsvägen; sites Skr150, cabins from Skr400) This wild and grassy place is handy for people jumping off the ferry in Byxelkrok, and also has good amenities.

Lammet & Grisen (203 50; Löttorp; from 5pm), 10km south of Böda, is popular for its all-you-can-eat evenings (Skr245), with whole spit-roasted lamb and pork on the menu and live entertainment. The restaurant has recently been renovated, and it's very family-friendly.

Bus 106 runs a route to the north from Borgholm.

WINDMILL MANIA

Once, the little island of Öland had more windmills than Holland! During the 1750s, the wooden mills suddenly became symbols of wealth and power, and every aspiring man-about-town had to have one. Öland's oak forests vanished under the mill-building craze, and soon around 2000 sets of sails were spinning across the island.

By the 1950s, the mills had become obsolete and most fell into disrepair. Nowadays, the 400 or so remaining windmills are recognised as unique historical monuments, and are lovingly restored and tended by local windmill associations.

You'll see two basic types of windmill on Öland: an early style known as 'German' or 'post', where the whole mill was turned into the wind; and later versions known as 'Dutch' or 'tower' windmills, where just the cap revolved.

CENTRAL ÖLAND

Fortresses, a zoo and an excellent farm village are central Öland's biggest sights. The largest settlement is Färjestaden (Ferry

Town), where you can find banks and services; the town rather lost its purpose in life after the bridge was built, although an effort has been made to rejuvenate the old jetty.

Ölands Djurpark (☎ 392 22; admission Skr220; ⏰ 10am-6pm May-Aug, to 8pm mid-Jun–mid-Aug, 11am-4pm Sep) is a zoo, amusement park and water park favoured by families, just north of the bridge near the tourist office. Kids under 1m tall get in for free.

The largest Iron Age ring fort in Sweden, **Gråborg**, was built as the Roman Empire was crumbling. Its monumental walls measure 640m around and are seriously impressive, even though much of the stonework was plundered for later housing. After falling into disuse, the fort sprang back to life around 1200, when the adjacent **St Knut's chapel** (now a ruin) was also built. The Gråborg complex is about 8km east of Färjestaden, just off the Norra Möckleby road; you really need your own transport to get there.

The vast **Ismantorp fortress**, with the remains of 88 houses and nine mysterious gates, is deep in the woods, 5km west of the Himmelsberga museum. It's an undisturbed fortress ruin, clearly showing how the village's tiny huts were encircled by the outer wall (Eketorp, see right, is an imaginative reconstruction of similar remains). The area, just south of the Ekerum–Långlöt road, can be freely visited at any time.

A 17km **hiking trail** leads from Gråborg to Ismantorp fortress.

The best open-air museum on Öland is **Himmelsberga** (☎ 56 10 22; adult/under 15yr Skr55/free; ⏰ 10am-5.30pm mid-May–mid-Aug), a farm village on the east coast at Långlöt. Its quaint cottages are fully furnished. There's hay in the mangers and slippers by the door; it's all so well done you feel as though the inhabitants have just popped out for a minute. There's also a dinky café and a modern art gallery.

STF Vandrarhem Ölands Skogsby (☎ 383 95; info@vandrarhskogsby.se; dm/s/d Skr140/200/280; ⏰ mid-Apr–Sep; P), a charming STF hostel, claims to be Sweden's oldest (it dates from 1934). It's based in a flowery old wooden house, 3km southeast of Färjestaden. The Färjestaden–Mörbylånga bus 103 (Skr18) runs past at least five times daily.

There are a few good eateries at the old jetty in Färjestaden, including **Café Restaurang Bojen** (☎ 310 37; mains Skr90-140; ⏰ from 11.30am Jun-Aug, shorter hr rest of yr), where you can sample fresh fish dishes or try Öland's speciality, *kroppkakor* (potato dumplings stuffed with pork), served with lingonberry jam and cream. There's a large sunny terrace with wonderful views over Kalmarsund.

SOUTHERN ÖLAND

The southern half of the island has made it onto Unesco's World Heritage List. Its treeless, limestone landscape is littered with the relics of human settlement and conflict. Besides linear villages, Iron Age fortresses and tombs, this area is also a natural haven for plants and wildlife.

Birds, insects and flowers populate the unusual limestone plain of **Stora Alvaret**. Birdspotting is best in May and June, which is also when the Alvar's rock roses and rare orchids burst into bloom. The plain occupies most of the inland area of southern Öland, and can be crossed by road from Mörbylånga or Degerhamn.

The ancient grave fields of **Mysinge** and **Gettlinge**, stretching for kilometres on the ridge alongside the main Mörbylånga–Degerhamn road, include burial sites and standing stones from the Stone Age to the late Iron Age. The biggest single monument is the Bronze Age tomb **Mysinge hög**, 4km east of Mörbylånga, from where there are views of almost the whole World Heritage site.

If you can't picture how the ring forts looked in their prime, take a trip to **Eketorp** (☎ 66 20 00; www.eketorp.se; adult/7-14yr Skr70/30; ⏰ 10am-5pm May-Aug, to 6pm Jul–mid-Aug). The site has been partly reconstructed to show what the fortified villages, which went in and out of use over the centuries, were like in medieval times. Children will like the scampering pigs, and the fort is particularly fun when there are re-enactment days – phone for details. Excavations at the site have revealed over 26,000 artefacts, including three tonnes of human bones, some of the finds are on display at the little **museum** inside. There are free **tours** in English at 1pm daily from midsummer to the end of August. The fort is 6km northeast of Grönhögen; there are several buses (summer only) from Mörbylånga.

On the east coast, about 5km north of Eketorp, **Gräsgårds Fiskehamn** is a delightful little fishing harbour. A little further north, there's an 11th-century **rune stone** at Seby, and in Segerstad there are **standing stones**, **stone circles** and over 200 graves.

Öland's southernmost point is a curious place. A **nature reserve** (10am-8pm mid-Jun–early Aug, 11am-4pm Sat & Sun Easter–mid-Jun & late Aug–Sep), almost surrounded by sea, it's popular with families and bird-spotters. Pay Skr50 to park, then you're free to wander round the **Naturum**, snack in the café-restaurant, or climb Scandinavia's tallest lighthouse, **Långe Jan** (42m).

SLEEPING & EATING

Mörby Vandrarhem & Lågprishotell (49393; morby@hotelskansen.com; Bruksgatan; hostel 1-/2-/4-/8-bed rm Skr300/400/600/800, hotel s/d from Skr400/600; May-Aug; P) In the small village of Mörbylånga, this has a mixture of hostel- and hotel-style accommodation. It's great for families, with a nearby park and beaches, and bikes for hire. There's also a restaurant on site.

Kajutan Hotell & Vandrarhem (408 10; kajutan@hotelskansen.com; lunch Skr69, mains Skr100-180, 1-/2-/4-/6-bed room Skr300/400/600/800, hotel s/d Skr690/890) Kajutan is down by Mörbylånga harbour. The new management were revamping the rooms for the 2006 season – although when they'll find time out from the busy bar-restaurant is anyone's guess! Summer lunches, served in a sunny courtyard, are particularly popular.

Gammalsbygårdens Gästgiveri (66 30 51; info@gammalsbygarden.se; s/d Skr600/800; closed Mon & Jan-Feb; P) A graceful country farmhouse on the east coast, 5km north of Eketorp. Rooms (all doubles except one) are individually decor ated, with neat whitewashed walls, a couple have private balconies. The food (mains around Skr160), mostly fish and venison, is also very good – reservations are a must.

Restaurang Fågel Blå (66 12 01; mains Skr90-130; 11am-5pm Jun-Aug, to 10pm Wed & Fri Jul) This super café-restaurant is by the lighthouse in the far south. The sharply designed building offers unparalleled sea views. Scoff à la carte local favourites like venison, herring and *kroppkakor*, or roll up for the twice-weekly evening buffet in July.

There are supermarkets in Mörbylånga, and a Systembolaget.

ÖSTERGÖTLAND

The Göta Canal threads diagonally across Östergötland, with the region's main towns beaded along its banks. These are generally old 19th-century industrial heartlands, full of fascinating architecture, their buildings given new leases of life as heritage centres, restaurants and concert halls. The west of the region, bordered by the mighty Lake Vättern, fits a different pattern. Its flat green countryside is steeped in ancient history, and includes both Sweden's most impressive rune stone and the unmissable medieval town of Vadstena.

NORRKÖPING

011 / pop 124,410

With typical Swedish cleverness and cunning design, Norrköping's closed-down mills and disused canals have been superbly regenerated – like Manchester in England… only beautiful! It's well worth stopping to gaze at the waterfalls, locks and stunning buildings, which now house museums, cafés and a concert hall. Another key attraction is the animal park at Kolmården, some 30km to the northeast.

The industrial development of Norrköping began in the 17th century, but really took off in the late 19th century when textile mills and factories sprang up alongside the swift-flowing Motala ström. Seventy percent of Sweden's textiles were once made in Norrköping, but the last mill closed in the 1970s.

Information

Banks and ATMs can be found along Drottninggatan.

Forex (0200-22 22 20; www.forex.se; Drottninggatan 46; 10am-6pm Mon-Fri, 10am-2pm Sat) Money exchange.

Library (Stadsbiblioteket; Södra Promenaden 105; 8am-8pm Mon-Thu, 8am-6pm Fri, 10am-4pm Sat, noon-4pm Sun) With free Internet access.

Norrköpings Biljard och IT Café (16 34 00; Prästgatan 48; per 25 mins Skr25) Internet access.

Tourist office (15 50 00; www.destination.norrkoping.se; Dalsgatan 16; 10am-6pm Mon-Fri, 10am-2pm Sat & Sun Jul–mid-Aug, shorter hr rest of the yr)

Sights & Activities

Industrilandskapet is the well-preserved industrial area near the river. Pedestrian walkways and bridges lead past magnificent former factory buildings and around the ingenious system of locks and canals. The most thunderous waterfall is **Kungsfallet**, near the islet Laxholmen.

Within the area are several interesting museums, all with free admission. The excellent and unique **Arbetets Museum** (18 98 00;

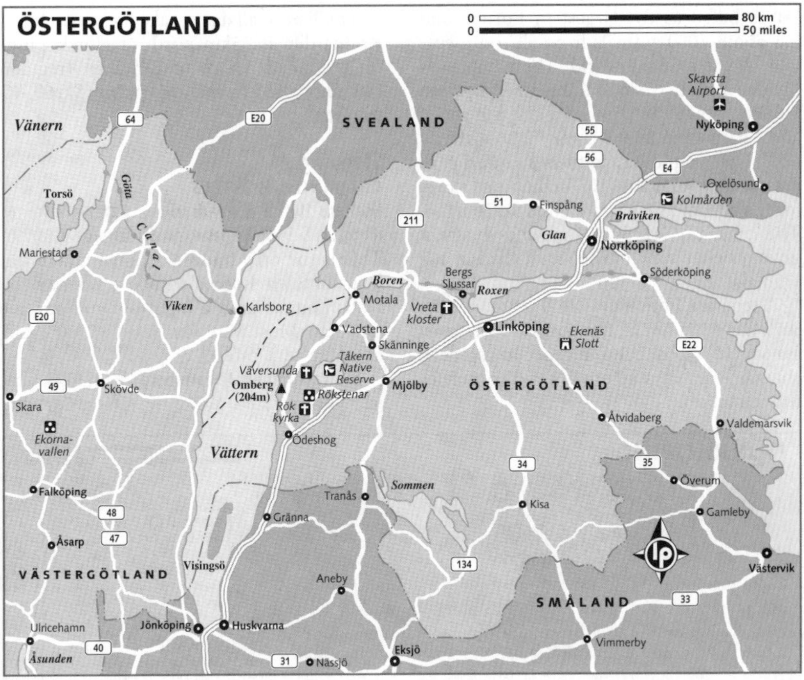

Laxholmen; 11am-5pm) documents working life. There's one permanent display about Alva Carlsson, a typical worker in the former cotton mill, and numerous inventive temporary exhibitions. The seven-sided building, designed in the 1920s, is a work of art in itself – go and see!

Over the bridge, **Stadsmuseum** (15 26 20; Holmbrogränd; 10am-5pm Tue-Fri, 10am-4pm Sat & Sun) delves into the town's industrial past. Some of the machinery is still operational and there's a great café here.

Holmens Museum (12 89 92; 9am-12.30pm Tue & Thu) describes the history of Louis de Geer's paper factory, which was founded in the early 17th century.

A modern addition to the riverside scenery is the extraordinary 1300-seat **Louis de Geer Konserthus** (15 50 30; www.louisdegeer.com; Dalsgatan 15), in a former paper mill. Still containing the original balconies, it's a superb venue which is used for orchestral, jazz and pop concerts.

Other Sights & Activities

Konstmuseum (15 26 00; Kristinaplatsen; adult/under 18yr Skr40/free; noon-4pm Tue & Thu-Sun, noon-8pm Wed mid-Jun–mid-Aug, 11am-5pm Wed & Fri-Sun, 11am-8pm Tue & Thu Sep-May), the large art museum south of the centre, has important early-20th-century works, including examples of modernism and cubism.

For great city views, climb the 68m-high **Rådhustornet** (Town Hall Tower; Drottninggatan; Skr30; 3pm Mon-Fri Jul).

Two kilometres west of the city centre, near the river, are good examples of **Bronze Age rock carvings**, with an adjacent museum, **Hällristningsmuseet** (16 55 45; www.brin.se; Himmelstalund; admission free, guided tours adult/under 18yr Skr30/free; 11am-6pm mid-Jun–Jul, 10am-4.30pm May–mid-Jun & Aug). Guided tours of the rock carvings take place at 2pm in July. Take bus 115 to Riksvägen, then walk the last 500m.

In July, the tiny **vintage tram** No 1 runs a short guided tour through the town centre. It leaves from outside the train station at 5pm and 5.30pm Monday, Wednesday and Friday (Skr40).

Kolmården

Kolmården **zoo** (24 90 00; www.kolmarden.com; 10am-6pm Jul, 10am-5pm May, Jun & Aug, Sat & Sun

Sep) is billed as the largest in Europe and has about 1000 animals from all continents and climates of the world. The complex is divided into two areas: the main **Djurparken** (zoo; adult/4-15yr Skr200/115) with a dolphin show, and **Safariparken** (adult/4-15yr Skr110/80) – if you don't have your own car, there's a safari park **bus tour** (adult/4-15yr Skr30/15). A combined ticket for the zoo and safari park costs Skr260/155. The cable car (Skr80/40) around the park gives a better view of the forest than of the animals.

A separate **Tropicarium** (☎ 39 52 50; adult/4-15yr Skr70/45; 🕑 9am-7pm Jul, 10am-6pm Aug, 10am-4pm or 5pm Sep-Jun) opposite the entrance has spiders, sharks, alligators and snakes and completes the attraction.

You'll need all day to take the zoo in fully. Kolmården is 35km north of Norrköping, on the north shore of Bråviken (regular bus 432 or 433 from Norrköping; Skr60, 40 minutes).

Sleeping

CAMPING & HOSTELS

Hörnans Hotell & Vandrarhem (☎ 16 58 90; cnr Hörngatan & Sankt Persgatan; dm Skr200, s/d Skr385/700) This is the only budget option right in the heart of town. Rooms are above a busy pub-restaurant, so after a night out you haven't far to go. Most were renovated in 2005, and all come with cable TV.

STF Vandrarhem Abborreberg (☎ 31 93 44; abborreberg@telia.com; dm Skr175; 🕑 Apr–mid-Oct; Ⓟ)

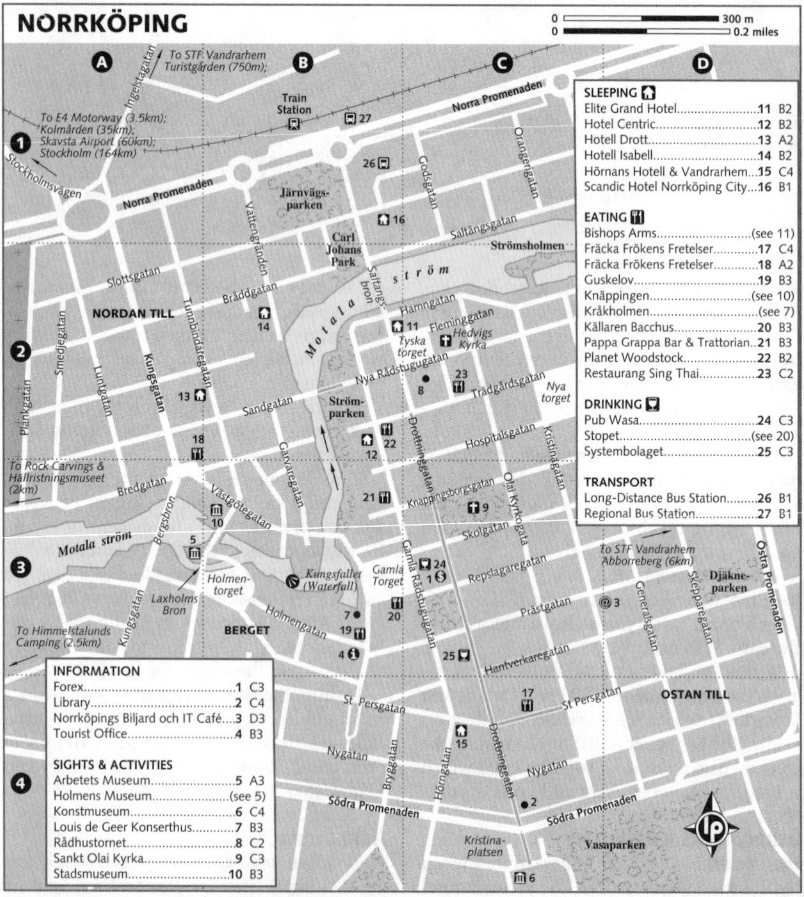

Sweet-toothed hostellers will appreciate this place, with its associated ice-cream parlour. It's beautifully situated in a coastal pine wood 6km east of town, with accommodation in huts scattered through the surrounding park, and is definitely worth the trek. Take bus 111 to Lindö.

Himmelstalunds Camping (☎ 17 11 90; info@norrkopingscamping.com; Campingvägen; sites per night & per person Skr40, cabins from Skr500) This little campsite is on the south bank of Motala ström, approximately 2.5km from the city. It's short on whistles and bells, but there's a small café on site. Public transport is nonexistent.

Also recommended is **STF Vandrarhem Turistgården** (☎ 10 11 60; info@turistgarden.se; Ingelstagatan 31; dm/s/d Skr155/240/340; P), a pleasing little hostel about 800m north of the train station.

HOTELS

Hotell Drott (☎ 18 00 60; www.hotelldrott.com; Tunnbindaregatan 19; s/d Skr695/860, discounted to Skr450/630; P) Staff are very friendly at Hotell Drott. Breakfast includes meatballs(!), light evening meals are an option, and there's also a kitchen for self-caterers. Rooms are old-fashioned but comfy.

Hotel Centric (☎ 12 90 30; info@centrichotel.se; s/d Skr695/825, discounted to Skr450/640; Gamla Rådstugugatan 18; P 💻) There are pleasant large rooms in Norrköping's oldest hotel.

Hotell Isabell (☎ 16 90 82; Vattengränd 7; s/d Skr480/580, discounted to Skr380/480) This is another cheapish hotel, but reception hours are limited, so phone ahead.

Scandic Hotel Norrköping City (☎ 495 52 00; norrkopingcity@scandic-hotels.com; Slottsgatan 99; s/d from Skr890/990, discounted to Skr495/950; P) Near the train station, the Scandic City offers upmarket lodgings, although rooms are more chintzy than usual for this chain. There's a sauna and Jacuzzi, plus a great sun terrace with views over the river.

Elite Grand Hotel (☎ 36 41 00; info.grandhotel@elite.se; Tyska Torget 2; s/d from Skr820/1540, discounted to Skr620/975; P) The top choice in town is this classy hotel, where the stylish foyer area hints at the quality to be found in the hotel's rooms. There's a spa in the cellar, plus a restaurant and a Bishop's Arms pub attached.

Eating & Drinking

Källaren Bacchus (☎ 10 07 40; Gamla Torget 4; lunch Skr63, mains Skr120-220) This popular restaurant and pub has a great garden courtyard in summer. In winter, repair to the vaulted cellar for some snug dining. Steak is a speciality, and there are tasty fish dishes.

Pappa Grappa Bar & Trattorian (☎ 18 00 14; Gamla Rådstugugatan 26; mains Skr120-230; 6pm-1am Mon-Sat) This is an authentic Italian restaurant with an intimate air. There's a full range of antipasto, bruschetta, and meat and fish mains, from vegetarian *tortellini verdi* to rich lobster lasagne. Choose between 120 sorts of grappa while bopping to live weekend DJs.

Guskelov (☎ 13 44 00; Dalsgatan 13; lunch Skr69, mains Skr100-190; 🕑 Tue-Sat from 6pm, plus lunch Mon-Fri winter) With its fancy Art Nouveau front, this is an elegant-looking choice that won't completely break the bank. It's cosy, with a menu of mainly meaty mains, such as burgers, steaks and grills. It turns into a nightclub on Friday and Saturday, with live DJs from all over Sweden.

Restaurang Sing Thai (☎ 18 61 88; Trädgårdsgatan 15; meals Skr95-180; 🕑 noon-10pm) Sing Thai serves a range of quite pricey Thai meals, including curries, satays, seafood and noodle dishes, although the lunch deal is good value at Skr65.

Kråkholmen (☎ 15 50 60; Dalsgatan 15; lunch Skr65; 🕑 11am-3pm Mon-Fri) In summer, Kråkholmen (part of the Louis de Geer Concert Hall) is a fantastic lunch option. You get to sit at a terrace in the industrial area and consume light meals and ice-creams to the sound of the crashing waterfall.

Knäppingen (☎ 10 74 45; www.knappingen.se; Västgötegatan 21; lunch from Skr75; 🕑 closed Mon) The café in the Stadsmuseum makes a refreshing change, offering focaccia, taco, crêpes and better veggie options than boring pasta. In summer, you can sit in a sunny courtyard tucked between several stately old mills.

Fräcka Frökens Frestelser Kungsgatan (☎ 23 88 23, Kungsgatan 43); Sankt Persgatan (☎ 23 96 67; Sankt Persgatan 101) There are two branches of this cool café, offering good coffee, fancy teas (a cup of strawberry-and-cream, anyone?), sandwiches, salads and cakes. Both have outdoor seating areas.

For cheap meals late at night, there's always **Planet Woodstock** (☎ 18 81 11; Gamla Rådstugugatan 11; meals around Skr60; 🕑 until at least 11pm) a slightly grungy place with an extensive menu of bagels, baked potatoes and hot dishes like moussaka and lasagne.

A favourite drinking spot is **Stopet** (☎ 10 07 40; Gamla Torget), an atmospheric cellar pub that fills up after the locals have finished work. Another spot that gets busy after office hours is nearby **Pub Wasa** (☎ 18 26 05; Gamla Rådstugugatan). The **Bishop's Arms** (☎ 36 41 20; Tyska Torget 2), at the Grand Hotel, is a good English-style pub where you can while away an hour or two, sitting outside with a beer and a great view of the river.

The blocks between Drottninggatan and Olai Kyrkogata contain big shopping centres full of chain stores and supermarkets. For alcohol, go to **Systembolaget** (Drottninggatan 50B).

Getting There & Away

Sweden's third-largest airport (Nyköping Skavsta) is 60km away – see p323 for details. To get there take the train to Nyköping, then catch a local bus.

The regional bus station is next to the train station, and long-distance buses leave from a terminal across the road. **Swebus Express** (☎ 0200-21 82 18; www.swebusexpress.se) has very frequent services to Stockholm (Skr110, 2¼ hours) and Jönköping (Skr140, 2½ hours), and several services daily to Göteborg (Skr216, five hours) and Kalmar (Skr170, four hours). **Svenska Buss** (☎ 0771-67 67 67; www.svenskabuss.se in Swedish) runs similar, though less frequent, routes.

Norrköping is on the main north–south railway line, and SJ trains depart every two hours for Stockholm (Skr193, 1½ hours) and Malmö (Skr519, four hours). Kustpilen SJ trains run roughly every two hours, north to Nyköping (Skr75, 40 minutes) and south to Linköping (Skr43, 25 minutes).

Getting Around

Minimum fare on Norrköping's urban transport is Skr20. Trams cover the city and

THE GÖTA CANAL

The Göta Canal is one of the country's biggest attractions as well as its greatest civil engineering feat. Idling along in a boat or cycling the towpaths is a wonderful way to see Götland's countryside.

The canal joins the North Sea with the Baltic Sea, and links the great lakes Vättern and Vänern. Its total length is 190km, although only around 87km is human-made – the rest is rivers and lakes. It was built between 1802 and 1832 by a team of some 60,000 soldiers, and provided a hugely valuable transport and trade link between Sweden's east and west coasts.

There are two sections to the canal: the eastern section from Mem (southeast of Norrköping) to Motala, (north of Vadstena on Vättern); and the western section from Karlsborg (on Vättern) to Sjötorp (on the shores of Vänern). The Göta Canal system is then linked to the sea by the Trollhätte Canal, in Västergötland. Along these stretches of the canal are towpaths, used in earlier times by horses and oxen pulling barges. Nowadays these paths are used by walkers and cyclists, with the occasional canalside youth hostel breaking the journey.

Boat trips are obviously a favourite way to experience the canal. You can go on a four- or six-day cruise of its entire length, travelling from Stockholm to Göteborg (or vice versa) and stopping to enjoy the wayside attractions; see p330 for more information. Alternatively, there are a number of shorter, cheaper boat trips along sections of the canal – any tourist office in the area should be able to advise you. Staff can also tell you about canoeing, cycling or even horse-riding along certain parts.

A good website for information about possible activities and packages on the Göta canal is www.gotakanal.se.

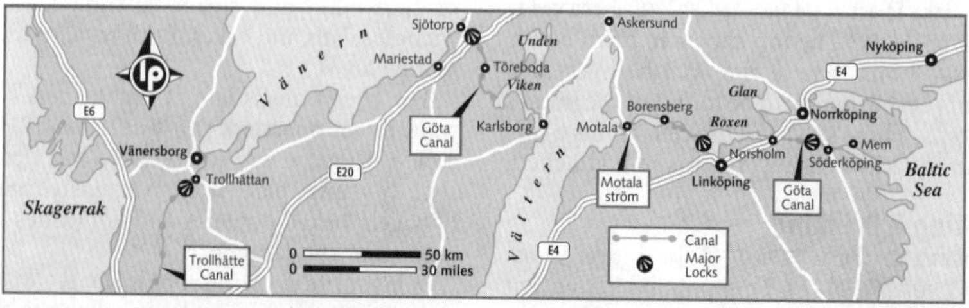

are the quickest option for short hops, especially along Drottninggatan from the train station.

For a taxi, ring **Taxi Norrköping** (☎ 10 10 00).

SÖDERKÖPING

☎ 0121 / pop 14,095

Söderköping, 17km southeast of Norrköping, is a delightful town in which to spend a few hours. Admire its quaint churches and tiny wooden houses, meander the quayside, or use it as the starting place for a trip along the Göta Canal.

Sights & Activities

Staff at the **tourist office** (☎ 181 60; www.soderkoping.se; Margaretagatan 19; 10am-7pm Mon-Fri, 10am-4pm Sat & Sun Jul, 10am-6pm Mon-Fri, 10am-4pm Sat Jun & Aug, 10am-4pm Mon-Fri Sep-May) can help you plan an exploration of the Göta Canal, including cycling or walking along part of it, or cruising some or all of its length.

The quaintest area is **Drothemskvarteren**, where there are two medieval churches. **St Laurentii Kyrkan** is the most impressive, with its ridiculously pointy Gothic spires, wooden-shingled bell tower and 11th-century rune stone. The 14th-century **Drothems Kyrka** is a more homely affair.

If you want to know more about the town's history, visit the little **Stadsmuseum** (☎ 214 84; Gamla Skolgatan 6; admission free; 10am-4pm Jun-Aug, 10am-4pm Mon-Fri Sep-May). Cross the canal from Slussgränd and climb the steps to the top of 78m-high **Ramundberget** for a great view. The town boasts the world's oldest existing **dry dock**, by the canal.

Sleeping & Eating

STF Vandrarhem Mangelgården (☎ 102 13; Skönbergagatan 48; dm Skr160; May-Aug; P) Next door to the camping ground is this STF hostel, in a lovely 18th-century wooden building.

Söderköpings Brunn (☎ 109 00; info@soderkopingsbrunn.se; Skönbergagatan 35; s/d from Skr1375/1800, discounted to Skr1145/1600; P) Söderköping enjoyed a brief spell as a health resort, and you can continue the tradition at this large, luxurious spa, dating from the 1770s and full of old-world class. It offers quality accommodation, pretty grounds and a top-notch restaurant; the company also run Göta Canal boat trips in July.

Korskullens Camping (☎ 216 21; korskullenscamp@hotmail.com; sites Skr140, cabins & chalets from Skr350; mid-May–mid-Sep) This campsite has a pretty set-up just off the E22 motorway southeast of the centre, with green areas, a windmill and a café. Bike hire is also available (per day Skr100).

La Uva (☎ 103 38; Rådhustorget; lunch Skr69, tapas Skr35-80) By the dinky town hall, La Uva is a great Spanish restaurant with around 30 scrumptious snackettes on its tapas menu. There's live jazz and blues music outdoors in summer.

Cafés and restaurants line the canalside. Try **Bondens** (☎ 105 42; Kanalhamnen; meals Skr80-120), a super little creperie with a pleasant woody interior and outdoor seating right by the water.

Getting There & Around

The bus stop is near the tourist office, on the E22. Local buses run once or twice per hour to Norrköping (Skr40, 30 minutes), and Swebus Express runs nine times daily to Jönköping and in the other direction to Stockholm, and three times daily south along the coast to Västervik, Oskarshamn and Kalmar.

Hire bikes at the **B&B Slussen** (☎ 155 46; Slussgränd 10; per day/week Skr100/500), by the canal.

LINKÖPING

☎ 013 / pop 136,912

Linköping is best known for its splendid medieval cathedral, which is definitely worth stopping to admire. It's also infamous for an unhappy historical event, the 'bloodbath of Linköping'. Following the Battle of Stångebro (1598), many of King Sigismund's defeated Catholic army were executed in the town, leaving Duke Karl and his Protestant forces in full control of Sweden.

Linköping is now quite a modern, industrial city (manufacturer Saab is the major employer), but pockets of its past survive in churches, castle, museums and the streets around Hunnebergsgatan and Storgatan.

Information

There are banks and other services around Stora Torget.

Gamer Palace (Drottninggatan 36; per hr Skr19; until at least 8pm) Internet access.

Library (Stadsbiblioteket; ☎ 20 66 03; Östgötagatan 5; 10am-6pm Mon-Fri, 11am-3pm Sat, plus 11am-3pm Sun Sep-Apr) A striking new library, with free Internet access (bring ID) and an excellent café.

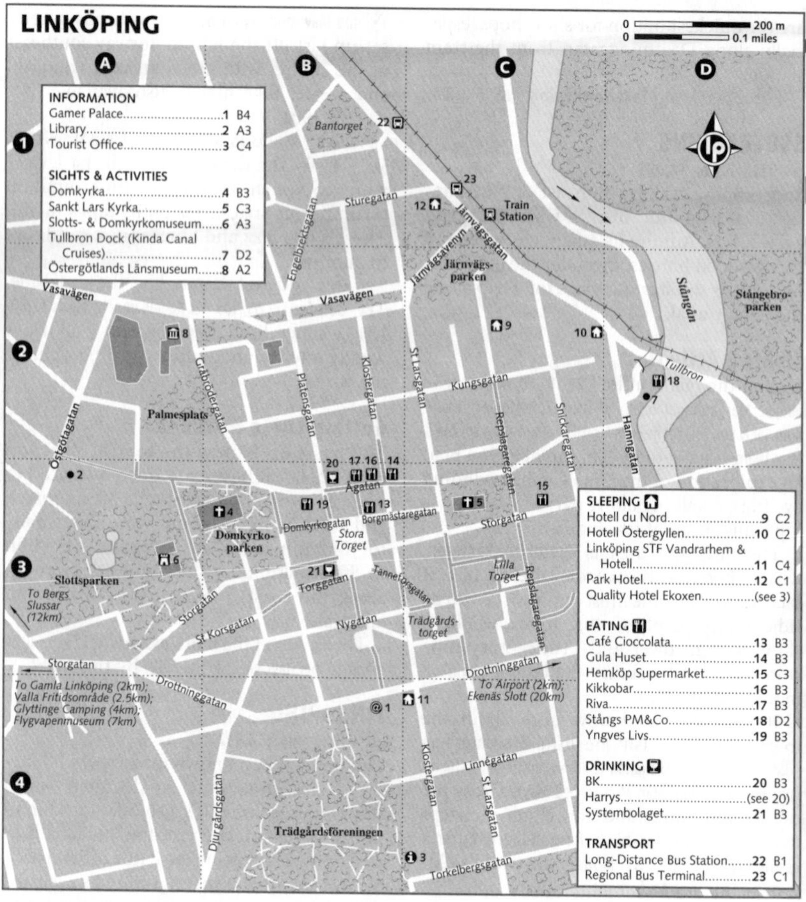

Tourist office (☎ 20 68 35; www.linkoping.se; Klostergatan 68) Inside Quality Hotel Ekoxen. Open 24hr, but staffed only during office hours.

Sights

GAMLA LINKÖPING & VALLA FRITIDSOMRÅDE

The town's best attractions are just outside the centre. Half a million people flock to **Gamla Linköping** (☎ 12 11 10; admission free; bus 202 or 214, Skr20), 2km west of the city. One of the biggest living-museum villages in Sweden, it consists of six streets and around 90 quaint 19th-century houses. These contain about a dozen theme museums (all free, with various opening times), crafty shops and even a small chocolate factory. You can wander among the 19th-century buildings at will.

Just 300m through the forest is **Valla Fritidsområde**, a recreation area with domestic animals, a children's playground, minigolf, a few small museums and many old houses.

KINDA CANAL

Most visitors to Sweden know about the engineering marvel of the Göta Canal, but Linköping boasts its own canal system, the 90km **Kinda Canal**, which opened in 1871. It has 15 locks, including the deepest one in Sweden. Possible cruises include evening sailings, musical outings and wine tasting trips. For a simple day excursion, from late June to early August the **M/S Kind** (☎ 0141-23

3370) leaves Tullbron dock at 10am on Tuesday, Thursday and Saturday, and travels to Rimforsa (adult/6-15yr Skr345/110, return by bus or train included).

OTHER SIGHTS

Made from blocks of hand carved limestone, the enormous **Domkyrka** (9am-6pm) was the country's largest and most expensive church in the Middle Ages. Its foundations were laid around 1250, with its 107m spire and vast interior, it's still astonishing visitors today. Inside, green men stud the ceiling, and there are numerous medieval treasures dating back to the 14th century.

The struggle between church and state is explored in the nearby castle's **Slotts & Domkyrkomuseum** (☎ 12 23 80; adult/under 7yr Skr40/free; noon-4pm Tue-Sun Apr-Sep), where the bolshy, larger-than-life King Gustav Vasa and the last Catholic bishop, Hans Brask, made friends, ate, drank and fell out again. Archaeological finds include two mummified black rats from the bishop's privy!

Just north of the cathedral, **Östergötlands Länsmuseum** (☎ 23 03 00; Vasavägen; adult/child Skr20/10; 11am-8pm Tue, 11am-4pm Wed, Sat & Sun) has a decent European art collection (Cranach's painting of Eden, *Original Sin*, is wonderful, with a smiling Eve twiddling her toes), and Swedish art dating to the Middle Ages.

The concrete floor of **Sankt Lars Kyrka** (Storgatan; 11am-5pm Mon-Fri, 11am-1pm Sat) was built in 1802 above the previous medieval church crypt. Downstairs, you can see 11th-century gravestones and skeletons.

Approximately 7km west of the centre is **Flygvapenmuseum** (☎ 28 35 67; Carl Cederströms gatan; admission free; 10am-5pm Jun-Aug, noon-4pm Tue-Sun Sep-May; bus 213), with exhibits on airforce history and 60 aircraft.

Ekenäs Slott (☎ 771 46; tours Skr80; guided tours on the hr 1-3pm Tue-Sun Jul, Sat & Sun May-Jun & Aug), built between 1630 and 1644, is one of the best-preserved Renaissance castles in Sweden. It has three spectacular towers, a moat, and furniture and fittings from the 17th to 19th centuries. The castle is 20km east of Linköping; you'll need your own transport to get there.

Sleeping

Linköping STF Vandrarhem & Hotell (☎ 35 90 00; www.lvh.se; Klostergatan 52A; dm from Skr190, s/d hotel rooms Skr650/760, discounted weekends to Skr490/590;) A well-swish central hostel with hotel-style accommodation too, mostly with kitchenettes. All rooms have private bathrooms and TVs. It fills up fast, so book ahead.

Hotell Östergyllen (☎ 10 20 75; Hamngatan 2B; s/d from Skr395/550) There's a slight air of peeling paint at this budget hotel not far from the train station, but rooms are comfortable enough. You can pay up to Skr200 extra for a private bathroom.

Hotell du Nord (☎ 12 98 95; www.hotelldunord.se; Repslagaregatan 5; s/d from Skr680/880, discounted to Skr470/620; P) This fuchsia-pink 19th-century building sits in parkland. Rooms are pleasant and light, and you can eat breakfast on the patio in summer.

Park Hotel (☎ 12 90 05; www.fawltytowers.se; Järnvägsgatan 6; s/d Skr890/1090, discounted to Skr590/790; P) Disturbingly billed as Sweden's 'Fawlty Towers', this hotel resembles that madhouse in appearance only. It's actually a smart family-run establishment with clean parquet-floored rooms, on a green piece of land near the train station.

Quality Hotel Ekoxen (☎ 25 26 00; www.ekoxen.se; Klostergatan 68; s/d from Skr1395/1695, discounted to Skr795/995; P) The large Ekoxen has stylish, modern newly renovated rooms. There's a spa and massage centre (including flotation tanks!), and an acclaimed restaurant.

Glyttinge Camping (☎ 17 49 28; glyttinge@swipnet.se; Berggårdsvägen; sites Skr150; May-Sep) This huge campsite, with minigolf and cycle hire, is 4km west of the city centre.

Eating & Drinking

Most places to eat (and drink) are found around the main square or nearby streets, especially along buzzing Ågatan.

Stångs PM&Co (☎ 31 20 00; Södra Stånggatan 1; lunch Skr80, mains Skr215-250; lunch Tue-Fri, from 6pm Tue-Sat, closed lunch Jul) In a 200-year-old warehouse down near the Kinda Canal docks, this is a splendid restaurant with a location to match. The dinner menu is impressive, with old Swedish favourites given snappy new interpretations, and there are frequent evening barbecues in summer.

Riva (☎ 12 95 15; Ågatan 43; mains Skr160-250; from 5pm Mon-Sat) Gourmet pizzas (with toppings such as honey and goat's cheese, or marinated scampi) are baked in big wood-fired ovens at this trendy Italian restaurant.

Kikkobar (☎ 13 13 10; Klostergatan 26; mains Skr130-180) Kikkobar is a cool corner house with

SOUTHEAST SWEDEN

an international menu where 'East meets West' – meaning Western mains like steak and salmon, and plenty of sushi and stir-fry dishes too.

Gula Huset (☎ 13 88 38; Ågatan; lunch Skr69, dinner mains Skr100-200) The courtyard tables are much sought after in summer at the traditional 'Yellow House'. It offers a good-value lunch, plus a long menu featuring pasta, Swedish specialities, and seafood, meat and vegetarian dishes.

BK (☎ 10 01 11; Ågatan 47; tapas around Skr30, mains Skr120-200) It positively heaves on Friday nights. Dabble at the extensive tapas menu, or go for burgers enlivened with mango salsa as the crowds get increasingly raucous.

Harrys (☎ 13 33 90; Ågatan 43) Another lively pub-restaurant with beer-drinking food like spareribs, burgers and burritos.

Café Cioccolata (☎ 13 18 80; Hantverkaregatan 1) A genuine Italian-run café, stylish Cioccolata has a wide range of coffees and filled *panini* or *ciabatta* (around Skr40).

Yngves Livs (☎ 31 88 88; Ågatan 38) A godsend for vegans or anyone with milk allergies, this may be the only café in Sweden to serve vegan lattés! There are crêpes, sandwiches and buns to nibble on too.

The **Hemköp supermarket** on Storgatan has the longest opening hours – until 10pm daily. The Filbytergallerian shopping centre contains a small **Systembolaget** (☎ 27 09 48; Stora Torget).

Getting There & Away

The **airport** (☎ 18 10 30) is only 2km east of town. **Skyways** (☎ 020-95 95 00; www.skyways.se) fly daily direct to Stockholm Arlanda and Copenhagen. There's no airport bus, but **Taxi Linköping** (☎ 14 60 00) charges around Skr130 for the ride.

Regional and local buses, run by **ÖstgötaTrafiken** (☎ 0771-21 10 10; www.ostgotatrafiken.se), leave from the terminal next to the train station; route maps and timetables are available at the information office. Journeys cost from Skr20; the 24-hour *dygnskort* (Skr110) is valid on all buses and local trains within the region. Up to four express buses per day go to Vadstena, otherwise change at Motala.

Long-distance buses depart from a terminal 500m northwest of the train station. Swebus Express runs seven or eight times daily to Jönköping (Skr157, 1½ hours) and Göteborg (Skr271, four hours), and north to Norrköping (Skr65, 40 minutes) and Stockholm (Skr190, three hours).

Linköping is on the main north–south railway line. Regional and express trains run to Stockholm roughly every two hours; express trains go to Malmö. Frequent regional trains run north to Norrköping (Skr43, 25 minutes). Kustpilen SJ trains run every few hours to Norrköping, Nyköping and Kalmar.

Getting Around

Most city buses (Skr20 minimum fare) depart from Centralstationen. For a taxi, ring **Taxi Linköping** (☎ 14 60 00). Bicycle hire is available at **Bertil Anderssons Cykel & Motor** (☎ 31 46 46; Plantensgatan 27).

BERGS SLUSSAR

☎ **013**

Bergs Slussar, 12km northwest of Linköping, is one of the most scenic sections of the Göta Canal – there are seven locks with a height gain of 19m – very impressive in canal terms! The nearby ruin **Vreta kloster**, Sweden's oldest monastery, was founded by Benedictine monks in 1120. It's worth a look, but the adjacent 13th-century **abbey church** is more interesting.

There's a beautifully located **STF Vandrarhem** (☎ 603 30; bergsslussar@sverige.nu; dm Skr185; May-Aug) near the locks, with a café, minigolf and bikes for rent. You'll find a couple of cafés and restaurants out this way, including **Kanalkrogen** (☎ 600 76; meals Skr150-200), with a great range of meals.

Buses 521 and 522 run regularly from Linköping.

VADSTENA

☎ **0143 / pop 7562**

Beautiful Vadstena on Vättern lake is a legacy of both church and state power, and today St Birgitta's abbey and Gustav Vasa's castle compete for the visitor's interest. The atmosphere in the old town (between Storgatan and the abbey), with its wonderful cobbled lanes, evocative street names and wooden buildings, makes Vadstena one of the most pleasing places in Sweden.

Information

The **tourist office** (☎ 315 70; www.vadstena.com; 10am-7pm Jul, 10am-6pm Jun & early Aug, 10am-2pm or 3pm Mon-Fri rest of yr) is inside the castle. Ask for details about town walks and local boat hours. You'll find banks and other services east of the castle, on Storgatan and around Stora Torget.

Sights

Located near the lake, the mighty Renaissance castle **Vadstena Slott** (☎ 315 70; Slottsvägen; adult/7-15yr Skr50/10; 10am-7pm Jul, 10am-6pm Jun & early Aug, 10am-2pm or 3pm Mon-Fri rest of yr) was the family project of the early Vasa kings. The lower floors contain a small historical display. The furnished upper floors are more interesting, but are only open during guided tours (in English at 2pm mid-May–mid-Sep); it's worth going on one if only to visit the chapel, which has an incredible 17-second echo!

The **Sancta Birgitta Klostermuseet** (☎ 100 31; Lasarettsgatan; adult/8-18yr Sk50/20; 11am-6pm Jul, 11am-4pm Jun & Aug) is in Bjälboättens Palats (a royal residence that became a convent in 1384), and tells the story of St Birgitta's rollercoaster life and those of all her saint-and-sinner children. It contains the coffin that she was brought back from Rome in, and there are realistic waxworks in the old nuns' cells.

'Of plain construction, humble and strong', **Klosterkyrkan** (abbey church; admission free; 9am-8pm Jul, 9am-7pm Jun & Aug, 9am-5pm May & Sep) was built in response to one of St Birgitta's visions. After the church's consecration in 1430, Vadstena became *the* top pilgrimage site in Sweden – a trend which is being revived today. Inside are medieval sculptures and some interesting carved floor slabs.

The old courthouse **rådhus**, on the town square, and **Rödtornet** (Sånggatan) both date from late medieval times.

Sleeping

Chain hotels don't get a look-in here; pretty and personal is the rule. Book accommodation well in advance.

STF Vandrarhem Vadstena (☎ 103 02; www.vabostaelle.se/vandrarhem; Skänningegatan 20; dm Skr170; P) This is a lovely big central hostel, with kindly staff, sunny dorms and a large underground kitchen decorated with cheerful red Dala horses. From late August to early June it's essential to book in advance.

27:ans Nattlogi (☎ 765 64; 27ans@va-bostaelle.se; Storgatan 27; s/d from Skr500/650; P) Cool white paint and wooden floors give a calming feel to the six rooms (some with views of Klosterkyrkan). More expensive rooms have private bathrooms. All include breakfast.

Pensionat Solgården (☎ 143 50; Strågatan 3; s/d from Skr540/690; mid-May–Aug) There's a range of uniquely decorated rooms (some with private bathrooms) at this family-run hotel, all with an art/artist connection. They're all *very* different – see the photos at www.pensionat-solgarden.se (Swedish only) to see what takes your fancy.

Vadstena Klosterhotel (☎ 315 30; hotell@klosterhotel.se; s/d from Skr1150/1450; P) History and luxury do a little dance together at this fine hotel in St Birgitta's old convent. The bathrooms are a wee bit dated, but the medieval-style rooms are great, with chandeliers, high wooden beds, indispensable coffee-makers. Most also have stunning lake views.

Vätterviksbadet (☎ 127 30; sites Skr165, simple rooms & cabins from Skr350; May–mid-Sep) This quality campsite is near the lake, 2km north of the town. Its family-friendly amenities include a beach with shallow waters, minigolf, boules, a kiosk and a café.

Eating & Drinking

Restaurant Munkklostret (☎ 130 00; lunch Skr85, mains Skr230-250; from noon in summer, shorter hr winter) The Klosterhotel's excellent restaurant is the best place to eat in town. Seasonal, succulent steak, lamb, game and fish dishes are flavoured with herbs from the monastery garden, and served in the monks' old dormitories. Try a cleansing green-apple sorbet to finish your meal.

Rådhuskällaren (☎ 121 70; Rådhustorget; mains Skr90 to Skr180) This pleasant 15th-century cellar restaurant, under the old courthouse, has simple but filling burger, pasta and fish meals. Its outdoor section is a favourite afternoon drinking spot in summer.

For sandwiches and light meals, visit the open-air café **Hamnpaviljongen** (☎ 310 95) in the park in front of the castle.

The town has a central supermarket, **Coop-Konsum** (Rådhustorget; until 11pm) and **Systembolaget** (☎ 100 36; Hovsgatan 4).

Getting There & Around

See Linköping for regional transport information. Only buses run to Vadstena – take bus 610 to Motala (for trains to Örebro), or bus 661 to Mjölby (for trains to Linköping and Stockholm). **Swebus Express** runs on Fridays and Sundays to/from Stockholm (Skr233, four hours). **Blåklints Buss** (☎ 0142-121 50; www.blaklintsbuss.se in Swedish) runs one service daily from the Viking Line Terminal in Stockholm to Vadstena (Skr160).

Sport Hörnan (☎ 103 62; Storgatan 8; 🕑 9.30am-6.30pm Mon-Fri, 9.30am-2pm Sat) has bikes for rent (per day/week Skr100/300).

AROUND VADSTENA

Rökstenen

Sweden's most famous rune stone, the 9th-century **Rökstenen**, is near the church at Rök (just off the E4 on the road to Heda and Alvastra). It's a monumental memorial stone raised to a dead son. On it is carved the longest runic inscription in the world, an ancient, intricate verse so cryptic that scholars constantly scrap over its interpretation.

There's a small, seasonal **tourist office** (☎ 0142-712 84; 🕑 10am-4pm Jun–mid-Aug, 9am-3pm Mon-Fri, 10am-4pm Sat & Sun May & late Aug) on site. The outdoor exhibition and the stone are open at all times.

Buses are virtually nonexistent, but cycling is a good option, as the scenic flatlands around Vättern lend themselves to the pedal.

Väversunda

The Romanesque 12th-century limestone **Väversunda kyrka**, situated 15km southwest of Vadstena, is a bizarre-looking church, which contains restored 13th-century wall paintings. The adjacent **Tåkern Nature Reserve** attracts lots of different bird species and there's a bird-watcher's tower near the church.

Again, buses are hopeless; a bicycle is by far the best way to explore.

GOTLAND

Gotland is one of the richest historical regions in Sweden, with around 100 medieval churches and an untold number of prehistoric sites, including stone ship settings, burial mounds and the remains of hilltop fortresses. Keep your eyes open for the information boards indicating sites along roadsides.

The island lies nearly halfway between Sweden and Latvia, in the middle of the Baltic Sea, roughly equidistant from the mainland ports of Nynäshamn and Oskarshamn. Gotland is both a region *(landskap)* and a county *(län)*. Visby is the only town, but there are several large, and many small villages. The large island, Fårö, lies off Gotland's northeastern tip and the island national park of Gotska Sandön lies 38km further north. Stora Karlsö and Lilla Karlsö are two small islets just off the western coast.

More good information about Gotland is available on the Internet at www.gotland.net and www.guteinfo.com (in Swedish).

VISBY

☎ 0498 / pop 21,400

The medieval port town of Visby is enough to warrant a trip to Gotland all by itself. A walled city, full of ruined churches and well-preserved buildings both public and residential, the city is a wonder to look at and a delight to get lost in. Its cobbled streets are full of twists and turns and steep hills, with another gorgeous view around

GOTLAND: THE ISLAND OF CHURCHES

Nowhere else in northern Europe are there so many medieval churches in such a small area. There are 92 of them in villages outside Visby; more than 70 still have medieval frescos, and a few also contain very rare medieval stained glass. Visby alone has a dozen church ruins and a magnificent cathedral.

A church was built in most villages during prosperous times from the early 12th century to mid-14th century. After 1350, the money ran out (mainly due to war), and the tradition ended. A lack of funds helped to keep the island in an ecclesiastical time-warp; the old churches weren't demolished, and new ones were never built (until 1960). Each church is still in use, and all those medieval villages still exist as entities.

Most churches are open 9am to 6pm daily from mid-May to late August. Some churches have the old key in the door even before 15 May, or sometimes the key is hidden above the door.

The *Key to the Churches in the Diocese of Visby* is a very useful English-language brochure, which is available free from tourist offices.

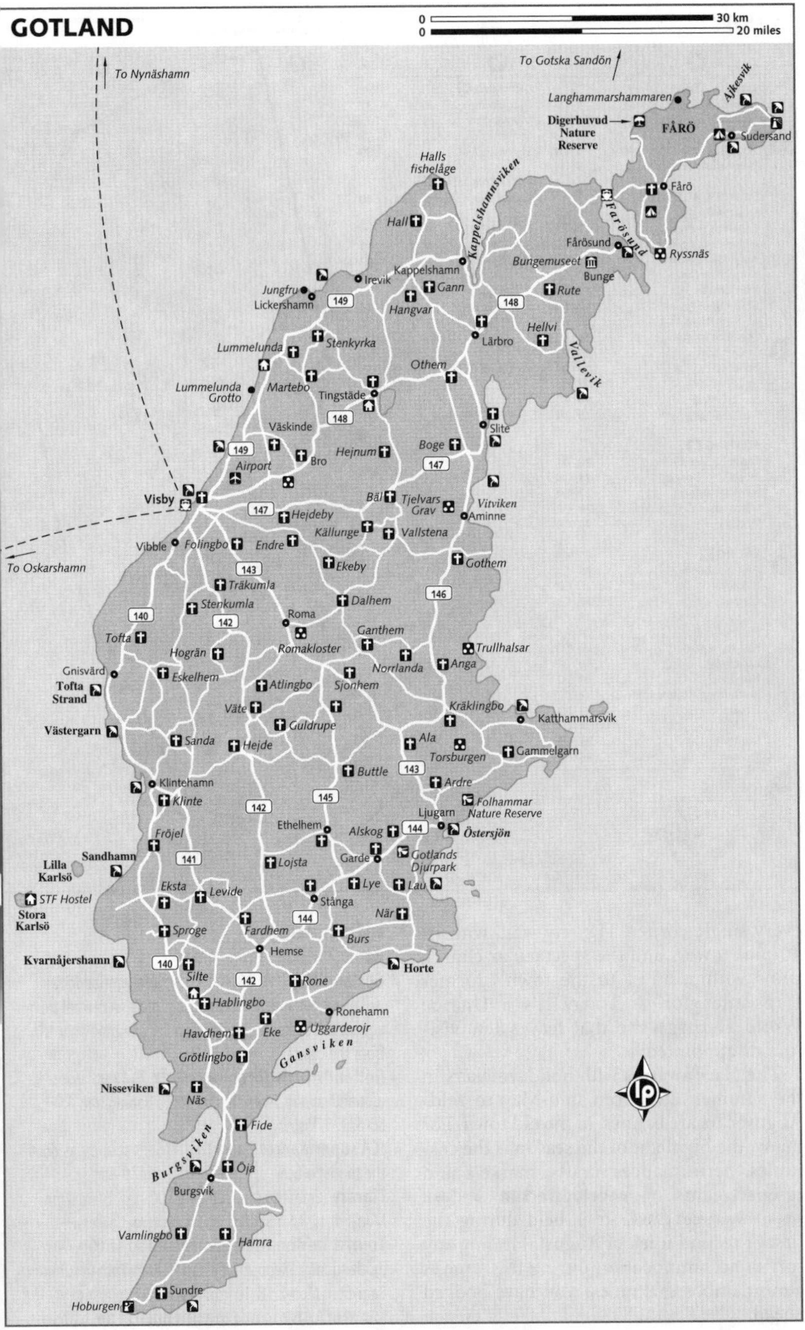

SOUTHEAST SWEDEN

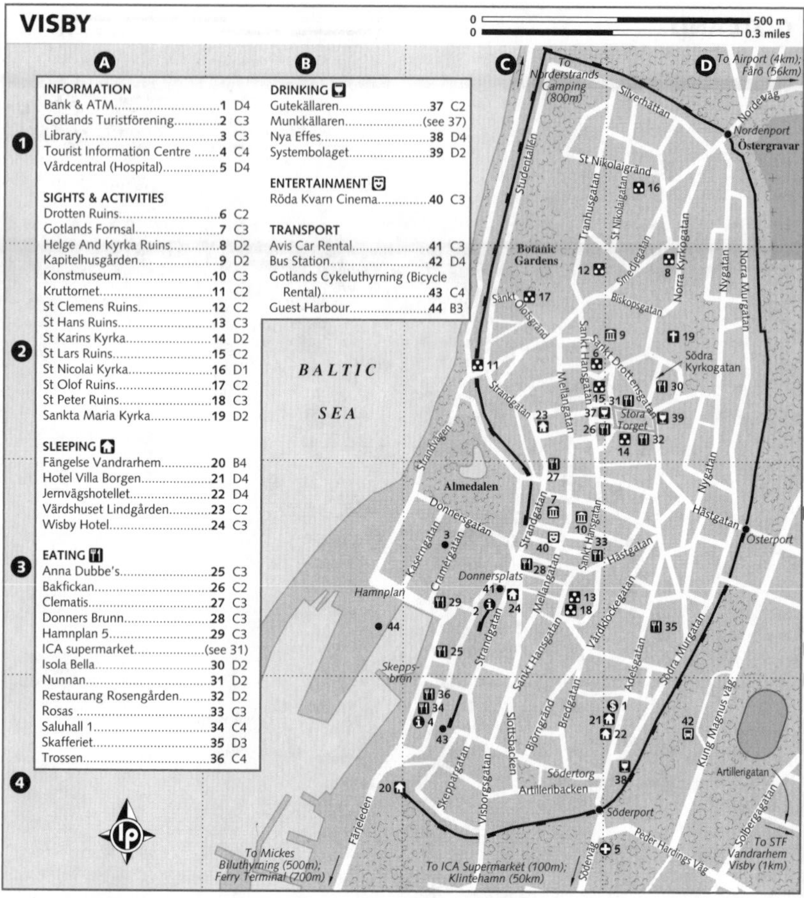

every single corner. The city wall, with its 40-plus towers and the spectacular church ruins within, attest to the town's former Hanseatic glories. Today it's a Unesco World Heritage site that leaves few visitors disappointed.

The place swarms with holidaymakers in the summer, and from mid-May to mid-August cars are banned in the old town. For many, the highlight of the season is the costumes, performances, crafts, markets and re-enactments of **Medeltidsveckan** (Medieval Week; www.medeltidsveckan.com), held during the first or second week of August. Finding any sort of accommodation during this time is almost impossible unless you have booked ahead.

Information

Bank (Adelsgatan) With ATM.

Gotland City (☎ 08-406 15 00; info@gotlandcity.se, www.gotlandcity.se; Kungsgatan 57) A central travel agency in Stockholm, useful if you're planning your trip from the capital.

Gotlands Turistföreningen (☎ 20 17 00; www.gotland.com in Swedish; Box 1403, Hamngatan 4, SE-62125, Visby)

ICA supermarket (Stora Torget) Sells stamps, as does the tourist office.

Library (Cramergatan, ☎ 29 90 00; 10am-7pm Mon-Fri, 12-4pm Sat & Sun) Free Internet access.

Tourist Information Centre (☎ 20 17 00; www.gotland.info; Skeppsbron 4-6; 8am-7pm in summer, 8am-5pm Mon-Fri & 10am-2pm Sat & Sun rest of yr) The tourist office has moved to a new office at the harbour.

Sights & Activities

The town is a noble sight, with its 13th-century wall of 40 towers – be sure to take a few hours and walk around the perimeter (3.5km). Also set aside time to stroll around the Botanic Gardens and the narrow roads and pretty lanes just south of the gardens. Pick up a copy of the booklet *Visby on Your Own* (Skr35, available at the tourist office), which will guide you around the town and give you good snippets of local history. In summer the tourist office also organises two-hour guided walking tours of the town (Skr80), with English-language walks up to four times a week.

The ruins of 10 medieval churches, all located within the town walls, include **St Nicolai Kyrka**, built in 1230 by Dominican monks. The monastery was burned down when Lübeckers attacked Visby in 1525. The **Helge And Kyrka** ruin is the only stone-built octagonal church in Sweden, and it was built in 1200, possibly by the Bishop of Riga; the roof collapsed after a fire in 1611. On Stora Torget, **St Karins Kyrka** has a beautiful Gothic interior and was founded by Franciscans in 1233. The church was extended in the early 14th century, but the monastery was closed by the Reformation and the church fell into disrepair.

The ruins contrast with the old but sound **Sankta Maria kykra** (Cathedral of St Maria; 🕑 8am-5pm Mon-Fri, 8am-6.30pm Sat, 9am-5pm & 6-8pm Sun summer, shorter hr rest of yr). This is an impressive building, with stained-glass windows, carved floor slabs, an ornate carved reredos and wall plaques.

Gotlands Fornsal (☎ 29 27 00; Strandgatan 14; adult/child Skr50/free; 🕑 10am-5pm mid-May–mid-Sep, noon-4pm Tue-Sun mid-Sep–mid-Apr) is one of the largest and best regional museums in Sweden – allow a few hours if you want to appreciate it. Amazing 8th-century, pre-Viking picture stones, human skeletons from chambered tombs, silver treasures and medieval wooden sculptures are among the highlights. **Konstmuseum** (☎ 29 27 75; Sankt Hansgatan 21; adult/child Skr30/10; 🕑 10am-5pm mid-May–mid-Sep, noon-4pm Tue-Sun mid-Sep–mid-May), nearby, is an art museum featuring exhibitions by local, national and international artists.

A number of other interesting ruins are scattered throughout the city centre, each with a brief history on a signboard nearby

Sleeping

Fängelse Vandrarhem (☎ 20 60 50; Skeppsbron 1; dm from Skr150) As hard to get into as it once must have been to get out of, this hostel offers beds year-round in the small converted cells of an old prison. It's in a good location, between the ferry dock and the harbour restaurants, and there's a cute terrace bar in summer. You'll need to reserve well in advance.

Jernvägshotellet (☎ 27 17 07; staff@visbyjernvagshotell.com; Adelsgatan 9; 2-/4-bed rooms from Skr440/800; 🕑 yr-round) You will have to call ahead to book at this place, a small, comfortable and very central hostel with spotless modern facilities.

STF Vandrarhem Visby (☎ 26 98 42; carl.tholin@tjelvar.org; dm from Skr120; 🕑 mid-Jun–mid-Aug) This hostel is southeast of the town centre off Länavägen, in a school residence, and therefore only opens in peak season.

Wisby Hotel (☎ 20 40 00; info@wisbyhotell.se; Strandgatan 6; s/d low season from Skr865/1240, s/d high season Skr1535/1870) Top of the heap in Visby is the luxurious, landmark Wisby, with pillars and vaulted ceilings creating a lovely medieval atmosphere.

Värdshuset Lindgården (☎ 21 87 00; lindgarden.vardshuset@telia.com; Strandgatan 26; s/d low season Skr595/745, s/d high season Skr750/945) This is a good, central option, with rooms set facing a pretty garden beside a popular restaurant. Dine outdoors and listen to music in the courtyard in summer.

Hotel Villa Borgen (☎ 27 99 00; hotell.villaborgen@telia.com; Adelsgatan 11; s/d low season Skr860/970, s/d high season Skr910/1070) This place has pleasant rooms set around a pretty, quiet courtyard, and an intimate breakfast room with French doors and stained glass, that's also a prime spot for people-watching.

Gotlands Resor (☎ 20 12 60; info@gotlandsresor.se; Färjeleden 3) This is a travel agency in Hamnhotellet that books private rooms in Visby – singles/doubles cost around Skr285/425 inside the town walls, or Skr240/380 outside. This agency can also organise cabin rental, provide bike hire and rent camping equipment.

Hamnhotellet (☎ 20 12 50; Färjeleden 3; s/d low season Skr560/600, s/d high season Skr640/760) Hamnhotellet is not far from the ferry terminal and offers uninspiring but cheap (for Visby) hotel rooms.

Norderstrands Camping (☎ 21 21 57; sites low/high season Skr85/145, cabins low/high season from Skr350/550;

⌚ late-Apr–mid-Sep) The closest camping ground is this place by the sea, 800m north of Visby's ring wall (well connected by a walking and cycling path).

Eating & Drinking

There are more restaurants per capita in Visby than in any other Swedish city. Most are clustered around the Old Town squares, on Adelsgatan or at the harbour. Wherever you choose, do not pass up a chance to try the island's speciality – a saffron pancake *(saffranspankaka)* with berries and cream. You'll find it at most coffee shops in Visby and around the island, usually for around Skr45 with coffee.

Donners Brunn (☎ 27 10 90; Donners plats; mains Skr95-235) This is among the finest restaurants in town – *brunn* means 'well' and you'll see it just inside the door. The Swedish and international menu is adventurous and tempting, and there are also cheaper vegetarian and *husmanskost* (home-style fare) options. This restaurant is deservedly popular, so it's wise to book ahead.

Clematis (☎ 21 02 88; Strandgatan 20; ⌚ midsummer–mid-Aug) In summer, visit Clematis, which looks as much like a museum as a restaurant; the medieval atmosphere backs up a menu of food cooked according to medieval recipes. There's also period music and entertainers, including the occasional fire-eater.

Nunnan (☎ 21 28 94; meals Skr80 to Skr180; ⌚ lunch & dinner until 1am) With a menu featuring Greek dishes, Nunnan is an appealing option right on the main square.

Bakfickan (☎ 27 18 07; mains Skr118-218; ⌚ lunch & dinner) The menu at the highly rated Bakfickan features well-prepared fish and seafood – good luck trying to walk past it if you're hungry.

Isola Bella (☎ 21 87 87; Södra Kyrkogatan 20; mains Skr75-185) Between Stora Torget and the cathedral is this narrow place, serving authentic Italian cuisine. There's a thin slice of garden out the back where meals are served in summer.

Nya Effes (☎ 21 06 22; snacks & meals Skr70-145) Be sure to also check out this place, just off Adelsgatan. Full of character, it's a pub-bar built into the town wall, and is a good place for a meal or a drink. There's a simple bar menu, an outdoor courtyard, pool tables and regular live music here in summer.

Rosas (☎ 21 35 14; St Hansgatan 22) This pretty, half-timbered house with a sunny courtyard is an excellent lunch spot, serving baguettes, filled crêpes, baked potatoes and saffron pancakes (all around Skr30 to Skr50).

Skafferiet (☎ 21 45 97; Adelsgatan 38; sandwiches from Skr35) This casual lunch spot has a tempting array of open-faced sandwiches displayed on its counters.

Restaurang Rosengården (☎ 21 81 90) In the shadow of the ruins and facing Stora Torget, this garden restaurant offers weekday lunches of unambitious but filling fare, such as salads and quiches for Skr62, plus evening à la carte dishes from around Skr105.

Hamnplan 5 (☎ 21 07 10; Hamnplan 5) Formerly called Skeppet, this place down by the water is an upmarket restaurant by day and a nightclub by night.

Other hang-outs around the harbour are popular on warm summer days and evenings, including the restaurants **Anna Dubbe's** (pastas from Skr69) and **Trossen** (lunch & dinner from Skr95) and the cheap stalls selling ice cream, sandwiches and pizza inside **Saluhall 1**.

A pair of neighbouring restaurant-bars with seemingly infinite levels of seating, from cellars to balconies, **Gutekällaren** (☎ 21 00 43) and **Munkkälleren** (☎ 227 14 00) are both home to nightclubs popular with the summer crowd.

There is a tiny **ICA supermarket** (Stora Torget) for self-caterers, next-door to Nunnan, or a much larger one on Söderväg, which is south of Söderport. **Systembolaget** (Stora Torget) is central.

Entertainment

For rainy days, there's the **Röda Kvarn cinema** (☎ 21 01 81; Mellangatan 17; tickets Skr80; ⌚ from 5pm).

Getting There & Away

AIR

There are regular **Skyways** (☎ 020-95 95 00; www.skyways.se) flights between Visby and three mainland airports: Stockholm Arlanda, Stockholm Bromma (up to 10 times a day for each airport) and Norrköping (three flights daily on weekdays). Flights between Stockholm and Visby generally cost Skr650 and up, but if your dates are flexible you can get deals from Skr295.

The cheaper local airline is **Gotlands Flyg** (☎ 22 22 22; www.gotlandsflyg.se), with regular flights between Visby and Stockholm Bromma (one to six times daily). Prices start at Skr500 one way; book early for discounts, and inquire after stand-by fares (from Skr350).

The island's **airport** (☎ 26 31 00) is 4km northeast of Visby and is served by buses.

BOAT

Year-round car ferries between Visby and both Nynäshamn and Oskarshamn are operated by **Destination Gotland** (☎ 20 10 20; www.destinationgotland.se). There are departures from Nynäshamn one to five times daily (about five hours, or three by high-speed catamaran). From Oskarshamn, there are one or two daily departures (except Saturday from early November until mid-March) in either direction (four to five hours).

Regular one-way adult tickets for the ferry/catamaran cost Skr228/291, but from mid-June to mid-August there is a far more complicated fare system; some overnight, evening and early-morning sailings in the middle of the week have cheaper fares.

If you want to transport a bicycle it will cost Skr41; a car usually costs Skr317/415, although again in the peak summer season a tiered price system operates. If you hope to take a car on the ferry or catamaran between mid-June and mid-August, it's essential to reserve a place well in advance, as spots fill up quickly with Swedes going on holiday.

Getting Around

There are over 1200km of roads in Gotland, typically running from village to village through the pretty landscape. Cycling on the quiet roads is highly recommended, and bikes can be hired from a number of places in Visby. The forested belt south and east of Visby is useful if you bring a tent and want to take advantage of the liberal camping laws.

Many travel agents and bike-rental places on the island also rent out camping equipment. In Visby, you can hire bikes at about Skr65/325 per day/week from behind Saluhall (on the harbour) or at Österport (down by the outside of the wall). **Gotlands Cykeluthyrning** (☎ 21 41 33), behind Saluhall, also rents tents (Skr75/250 per day/week), or for Skr250 per day (Skr1250 per week) you can hire the 'camping package' – two bikes (or one tandem bike), a tent, a camping stove and two sleeping mats. **Gotlands Resor** (☎ 20 12 60; info@gotlandsresor.se; Färjeleden 3) offers similar packages.

A few companies and service stations offer car hire. A central office in Visby is **Avis** (☎ 21 98 10; godman@gotlandica.se; Donners plats 2), where you can rent a small car from Skr550/3000 per day/week. At the **guest harbour** (☎ 21 51 90) you can also rent cars, motorbikes and mopeds.

Kollektiv Trafiken (☎ 21 41 12) runs buses via most villages to all corners of the island. The most useful routes, that have connections up to seven times daily, operate between Visby and Burgsvik in the far south, Visby and Fårösund in the north (also with bus connections on Fårö), and Visby and Klintehamn. A one-way ticket will not cost you more than Skr59 (although if you take a bike on board it will cost an additional Skr40), but enthusiasts will find a monthly ticket good value at Skr590.

AROUND VISBY

There's not much but forest and farmland until you're at least 10km from Visby. If you're heading northeast, visit the remarkable Bro church, which has several 5th-century picture stones in the south wall of the oratory, excellent sculptures and interior lime paintings.

Heading southeast on road No 143, on your way to Ljugarn, check out the 12th-century Cistercian monastery ruin **Romakloster** (☎ 501 23; adult/child Skr20/free; 🕑 10am-6pm Jun-Aug, & weekends May & Sep), a kilometre from the main road. Summer theatre performances here cost around Skr250 (tickets from Visby tourist office). The 18th-century manor house is also impressive.

Dalhem, 6km northeast of the Cistercian monastery, has a large church with 14th-century stained glass (the oldest in Gotland) and magnificent (albeit restored) wall and ceiling paintings; take note of the scales of good and evil. There's also a historic **steam railway** (☎ 380 43; adult/child Skr40/25; 🕑 11.15am-3.30pm Wed-Thu, Sat & Sun Jun-Aug) and museum in Dalhem.

There's a good range of services in the reasonable-sized town of Klintehamn. From here, you can catch a passenger-only boat to the island nature reserve **Stora Karlsö** (www.storakarlso.com) one to three times daily from May to early September (adult/child return Skr225/110, 30 minutes). You can visit the island as a day trip (with five or six hours ashore), or stay overnight at the hostel (see below).This fairly remote island is home to extensive birdlife including thousands of guillemots and razorbills, there are also impressive cliffs by the lighthouse.

Sleeping & Eating

Pensionat Warfsholm (☎ 24 00 10; warsholm@telia.com; sites Skr85, dm from Skr150, rooms per person with/without bath from Skr440/250) In Klintehamn, this is a hotel, hostel and campground in a pretty waterside spot with a restaurant attached.

STF hostel (☎ 24 05 00; boka@storakarlso.com; dm Skr150) If you want to get away from it all, you can stay on Stora Karlsö at the simple STF hostel. There's a nature exhibit, restaurant and café on the island. Booking ahead is required.

EASTERN GOTLAND

Ancient monuments include the Bronze Age ship setting, Tjelvars grav, 1.5km west of road No 146 (level with Visby), and its surrounding landscape of standing stones, almost all linked with the Gutasaga legends. Gothem church is one of the most impressive in Gotland; the nave is decorated with friezes dating from 1300. Torsburgen, 9km north of Ljugarn, is a partly walled hill fort (the largest in Scandinavia) measuring 5km around its irregular perimeter.

Ljugarn is a small seaside resort, and there are impressive *raukar* formations at Folhammar Nature Reserve, 2km north. Southwest of Ljugarn in the village of Alskog, **Gotlands Djurpark** (☎ 49 35 00; adult/child Skr85/50; 🕑 10am-4pm mid-May–Aug, closed Midsummer Eve) is a small zoo, home to around 40 types of animals, including kangaroos, ostriches and zebras. Southwest of here, the impressive Garde church has four extraordinary medieval lych gates and an upside-down medieval key in the door; the original 12th-century roof can also still be seen.

Sleeping & Eating

STF hostel Ljugarn (☎ 49 31 84; dm from Skr130; 🕑 mid-May–Aug) This place has a fine spot at the eastern end of the Ljugarn village (down by the water).

STF hostel Garda (☎ 49 13 91; gardavh@sverige.nu; dm Skr125; 🕑 Feb-Dec) The hostel in Garde is a series of cabins with three golf courses in the immediate vicinity.

Frejs Magasin (☎ 49 30 11; info@ljugarn.com; s/d Skr450/650, with private facilities Skr700/800) This is a large, central, wooden-built pension, surrounded by green countryside in Ljugarn. It also offers three- and four-bed rooms, and has apartments and cabins available by the week, if you're travelling in a group.

There's a Konsum supermarket in Ljugarn, and some good dining options in summer. **Restaurang Kråkan** (☎ 49 33 71; mains Skr150-200), just off the main road through town, is an upmarket place, and nearby **Bruna Dörren** (☎ 49 32 89; Strandvägen 5; meals from Skr60) is a more casual restaurant and pizzeria with a large outdoor courtyard.

NORTHERN GOTLAND & FÅRÖ

It's hard to imagine a better way to see the area than by cycling up to Fårö and following the bike trails around the little island. There's a **visitors centre** (0498-22 40 22; 🕑 10am-6pm in summer, Sat & Sun rest of yr) with Internet access in Fårö town.

On your way, stop at the **Bungemuseet** (☎ 22 10 18; adult/child Skr70/free; 🕑 10am-4pm mid-May-Aug, 10am-6pm Jul–mid-Aug), an open-air museum with 17th-century houses and picture stones dating from 800. It's near the north-eastern tip, about 1km south of where the ferry connects to Fårö. Across the road is a charming café with some of the best saffron pancakes on the island.

The **grotto** (☎ 27 30 50; adult/child Skr70/50; 🕑 May–mid-Sep) south of Lummelunda is the largest in Gotland. The temperature in the grotto is a cool 8°C, so bring warm clothing. The impressive *raukar* formations at nearby **Lickershamn** are up to 12m high; look out for **Jungfru** (signposted), with its haunting legend. Near the Jungfru trail-head at Lickershamn there's a campground and friendly café serving authentic Thai food (from Skr75) and a hut where you can buy smoked fish (both 🕑 10am-6pm in summer).

The frequent ferry to **Fårö** is free for cars, passengers and cyclists. This island, home to Ingmar Bergman, has magnificent *raukar* formations; watch the sunset at Langhammarshammaren if you can. There are lots of fossils in the rocks by Fårö lighthouse, at the eastern tip of the island. British troops who fought in the Crimean war are buried at **Ryssnäs**, in the extreme south; obey signs posted along roads here, as this area is still used for military training and testing.

Sleeping & Eating

There is a good **STF hostel** in **Lärbro** (☎ 22 50 33; dm Skr150; reception ⏰ 8-11am & 5-10pm), on road No 148 between Visby and Fårösund, open from mid-May to the end of August. It has a gym open to hostel guests for Skr65. There is a beachside **SVIF hostel** (☎ 27 30 43; dm from Skr175) in Lummelunda, signposted from the main road; call ahead if you'll be arriving after 5pm.

There's an ICA supermarket (with an ATM) on the main street near the ferry terminal in Fårösund, and another on Fårö near the tourist office.

GOTSKA SANDÖN NATIONAL PARK

Isolated, triangular-shaped **Gotska Sandön** (www.gotskasandon.com in Swedish), with an area of 37 sq km, is an unusual island, with lighthouses at its three corners, 30km of beaches, sand dunes, pine forest and a church. There is a really good network of trails right around the island.

Camping (sites per person Skr50, beds in basic huts Skr110, cabins from Skr450) near the northern tip is possible; there are basic facilities but you must bring all supplies with you.

Boats (☎ 24 04 50; ⏰ early May–early Sep) run from Fårösund and Nynäshamn three to four times weekly when operating (Skr695/885 return from Fårösund/Nynäshamn, Skr100 for bikes).

SOUTHERN GOTLAND

Hemse is a commercial centre, with good services (such as supermarkets, banks and a bakery), and the smaller village of Burgsvik, further south, is similar.

Öja church dates from 1232 and has Gotland's highest church tower (67m). It has a magnificent cross, and the wall and ceiling paintings are very detailed. Look for the inscribed stone slabs under the covered shelter just outside the churchyard. **Hablingbo** church has three lavishly carved doorways, a votive ship, carved floor slabs and rune stones.

Lojsta has the deepest lakes in Gotland, remains of an early medieval fortress and a fine church. On the eastern coast near Ronehamn, **Uggarderojr** is a huge, late-Bronze Age cairn with nearby traces of settlement. The cairn, probably a navigation marker, is now a long way inland due to post-glacial uplift.

Sleeping & Eating

The Hablingbo **STF hostel** (☎ 48 70 70; vandrarhem@gutevin.se; beds Skr150; ⏰ May-Sep) is next to Gute Vin, a good restaurant and commercial vineyard.

In Björklunda, 2km north of Burgsvik, friendly **Värdshuset Björklunda** (☎ 49 71 90; dm from Skr165, s/d from Skr590/790) is a delightful place reminiscent of a Greek villa, with pretty whitewashed buildings. Meals at the restaurant here are good and reasonably priced.

Southern Sweden

Stimulating to brain, body and soul, the county of Skåne (Scania) lies in the extreme south of the country and has a whirl of wonderful sights and activities. The arty city of Malmö is full of interesting architecture and design, and has picked up some cosmopolitan customs from its big sister across the water, Copenhagen. For charm on a smaller scale, visit the green university town of Lund or meander through the delightful cobbled streets of medieval Ystad. Fans of the Vikings can make a pilgrimage to several fantastic sites, and the region also contains mysterious Bronze Age remains.

Skåne's gently rolling landscape makes you itch to get outdoors, on two feet or two wheels: the Österlen area, with its wandering coastline, waving wheat fields and teeny villages, is particularly enchanting to cycle round. Relax with the children on golden sandy beaches, or get your binoculars ready for some of Sweden's best coastal bird-watching. There are more hostels here than in any other region of the country, so you have no excuse not to get out and about!

Skåne was part of Denmark until 1658 and still retains differences from the rest of Sweden. You can detect it easily in the strong dialect *(skånska)* and the distinctive architecture. Natives of Skåne look more towards Copenhagen than Stockholm, and the record-breaking Öresund bridge has brought Copenhagen even closer.

HIGHLIGHTS

- Ponder the enigma of 'Sweden's Stonehenge', the ship-shaped **Ales Stenar** (p180)
- Talk to real, live Vikings at the excellent (and slightly eccentric) **Foteviken Viking Reserve** (p175)
- Enjoy a continental dining experience in cosmopolitan Malmö's **Lilla Torg** (p167)
- Explore the medieval streets of **Ystad** in the footsteps of fictional crime-fighter Inspector Wallander (p179)
- Travel across an engineering miracle, the **Öresund bridge** (p169)
- Cycle past sweet-smelling orchards, or hike through the coastal nature reserve in mellow **Österlen** (p181)

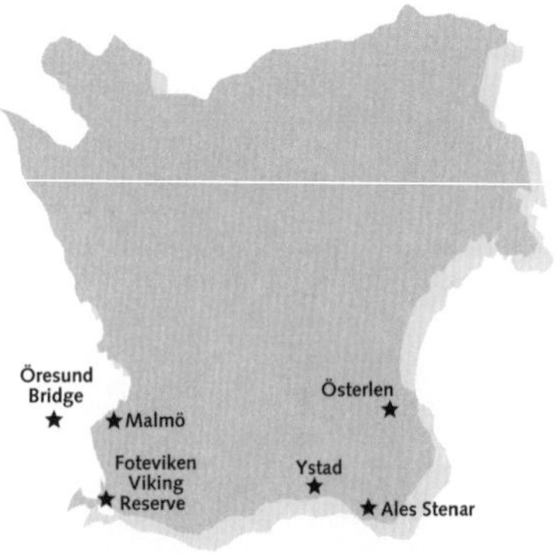

AREA: 11,027 SQ KM	HIGHEST ELEVATION: 212 M	POPULATION: 1,160,919

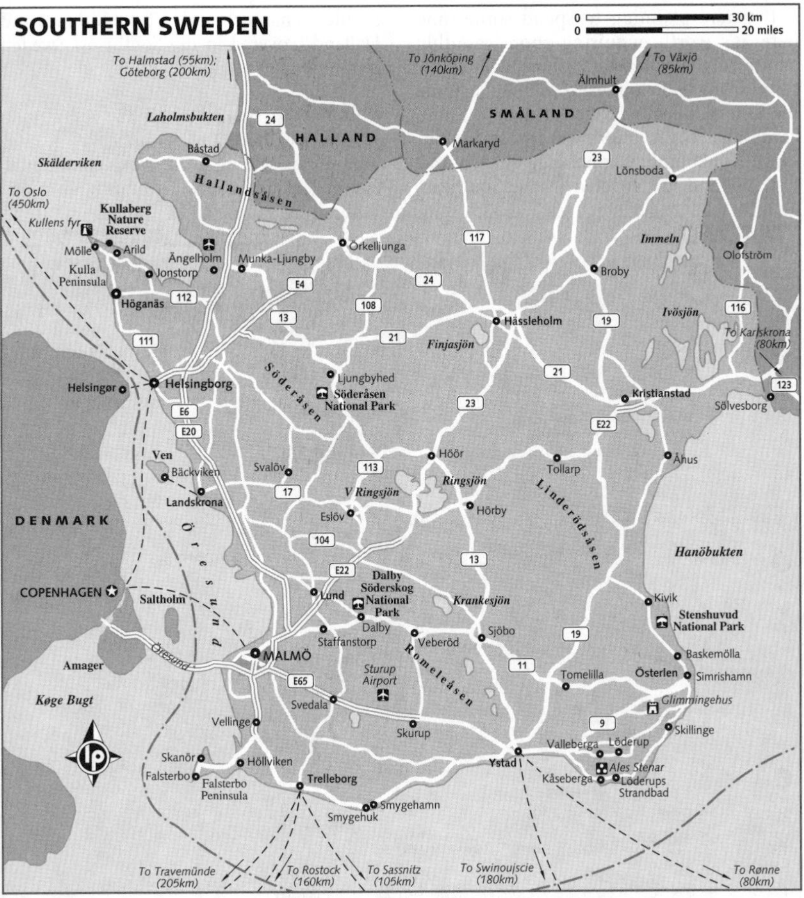

Information

REGIONAL TOURIST OFFICES

There are helpful tourist offices in all major towns. **Position Skåne** (☎ 040-20 96 00; www.skane.com; Stortorget 9, SE-21122 Malmö) dispenses information about the entire region and publishes good brochures and maps.

If you enter the region from Denmark via the bridge over the Öresund, there's a tourist office just off the motorway a few kilometres into the country. This office, called **Skånegården** (☎ 040-34 12 00; Bunkeflov 40), is open daily and can supply information on Malmö, Skåne and the whole of Sweden.

Many of the tourist offices in Skåne stock information for Copenhagen and Denmark for those planning to cross the Öresund.

Getting Around

Public transport in Skåne is efficient and well managed; **Skånetrafiken** (☎ 0771-77 77 77; www.skanetrafiken.skane.se) operates the local bus and train (*Pågatågen*) networks, and there are regular connections to Denmark via the Öresund bridge or the Helsingborg–Helsingør ferry.

An integrated Öresundregionen transport system links trains from Helsingborg via Malmö and Copenhagen to Helsingør. For a round tour of the Öresund or a visit to Copenhagen, the 'Around the Sound' card (Skr249) gives 48 hours unlimited travel on ferries and local trains; this covers transport within Skåne and also along the coast north of Copenhagen.

If you're planning to spend some time here, it's worth enquiring about monthly passes or a *sommarkort*, offering discount travel from midsummer to mid-August: see the Skånetrafiken website for details. These cards also cover public transport in Blekinge, Jönköping, Kronoberg, Örebro and Östergötland (all covered in the Southeast Sweden chapter) and Västergötland and Halland (covered in the Southwest Sweden chapter).

MALMÖ

☎ 040 / pop 269,142

Marvellous Malmö is the most 'continental' of Sweden's cities. It's a vibrant and multi-

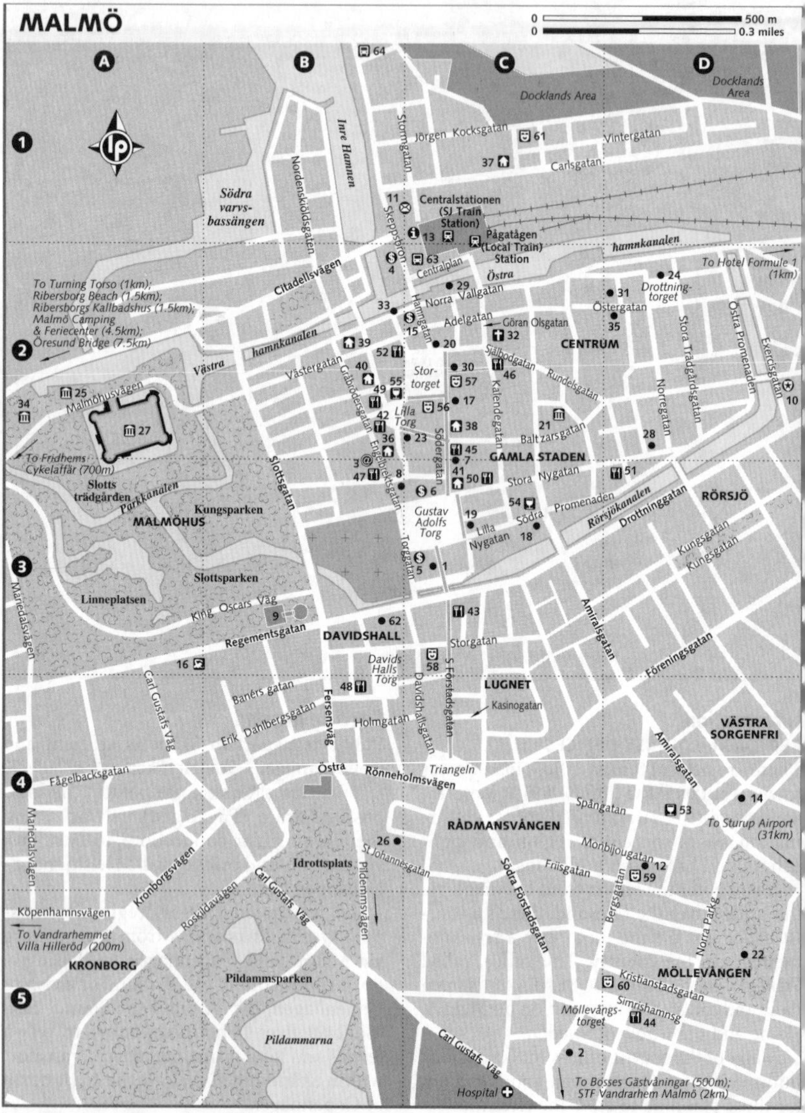

SOUTHERN SWEDEN

cultural place, influenced by Copenhagen across the Öresund and populated by people from 150 nations. Malmö also seems to attract one-off works of architecture and design: the Turning Torso, created by Santiago Calatrava, is the latest wonder, after the jaw-dropping Öresund bridge and tunnel linking Copenhagen and Malmö. On a more personal scale, there are some great modern-art exhibition spaces; and several of the city's half-timbered houses contain unique art and craft galleries. Near these nifty gift shops, the whole of Lilla Torg is a chattering, clinking mass of alfresco diners.

History

Malmö really took off in the 14th century with the arrival of the Hanseatic traders, when grand merchants' houses were built, followed by churches and a castle. The greatest medieval expansion occurred under Jörgen Kock, who became the city's mayor in 1524. The town square, Stortorget, was laid out at that time, and many of the best 16th-century buildings are still standing. After the city capitulated to the Swedes in 1658, Malmö rose in importance as a commercial centre and its castle was strengthened to protect trade.

Nowadays, the 20th century's heavy industries (car and aircraft manufacture, and shipbuilding) have been replaced by smaller companies, particularly in the service, financial and IT sectors. There's also been an upsurge in the number of students living in Malmö (currently around 18,000) with the opening of a new university campus here in the late 1990s.

Orientation

Gamla Staden (Old Town) is the city centre and is encircled by a canal. There are three principal squares here: Stortorget, Lilla Torg and Gustav Adolfs Torg. Malmöhus castle, in its park setting, guards the western end of Gamla Staden. Across the canal on the northern side you'll find the bus and train stations as well as the harbour. South of the city centre, there's a complex network of more modern streets with most interest focused on the square Möllevångstorget. The Öresund bridge is about 8km west of the city centre, served by a motorway which passes south and east of the city.

Information

BOOKSHOPS

Akademibokhandeln (☎ 664 29 90; Södra Tullgatan 3; 🕒 Mon-Sat) Good selection of general books and guidebooks.

Hamrelius (☎ 12 02 88; Södergatan 28) Wide variety of English-language books.

Pressbyrån (Centralstationen; 🕒 until 11pm) Newspapers and international magazines.

INFORMATION

Akademibokhandeln	1	C3
Apotek Gripen	2	C5
Cyberspace Café	3	B3
Fiskehoddorna	(see 34)	
Forex	4	B2
Forex	5	C3
Forex	6	C3
Forex	(see 13)	
Hamrelius	7	C3
Kilroy Travels	8	B3
Malmö Stadsbibliotek (Library)	9	B3
Police Station	10	D2
Post Office	11	C1
Pressbyrån	(see 13)	
RFSL-Malmö	12	D4
Sidewalk Express	(see 13)	
Tourist Office	13	C1
Tvätt-Tjänst i Malmö	14	D4
X-Change	15	C2

SIGHTS & ACTIVITIES

Ak-va-kul	16	A3
Apoteket Lejonet	17	C2
Aquarium	(see 27)	
City Boats Malmö	18	C3
Citytunnelutställningen	19	C3
County Governor's Residence	20	C2
Ebbas Hus	21	C2
Folkets Park	22	D5
Form/Design Center	23	C2
Hedmanska Gården	(see 23)	
Humanitetens Hus	24	D2
Kockska Huset	(see 52)	
Koggmuseet	(see 64)	
Kommendanthuset	25	A2
Malmö Konsthall	26	B4
Malmö Konstmuseum	(see 27)	
Malmöhus Slott	27	A2
Rooseum	28	D2
Rundan Boats	29	C2
Rådhuset	30	C2
St Gertrud Quarter	31	D2
Sankt Petri Kyrka & Krämarekapellet	32	C2
Sightseeing Bus Tours Departure	33	B2
Stadsmuseum	(see 27)	
Teknikens och Sjöfartens Hus	34	A2
Thottska Huset	35	D2

SLEEPING

Clarion Hotel Malmö	36	B2
Comfort Hotel Malmö	37	C1
Hotel Baltzar	38	C2
Hotell Pallas	39	B2
Mäster Johan Hotel	40	B2
Scandic Hotel St Jörgen	41	C3

EATING

Izakaya Koi	42	B2
Konditori Hollandia	43	C3
Krua Thai	44	D5
Krua Thai Takeaway	45	C2
La Empanada	46	C2
Mästerlivs Supermarket	47	B3
Restaurang Davidshall	48	B4
Rådhuskällaren	(see 30)	
Saluhallen	49	B2
Spot	50	C3
Thotts Restaurang	(see 34)	
Vegegården	51	D3
Årstiderna	52	B2

DRINKING

Jeriko	53	D4
Mello Yello	(see 55)	
Moosehead	(see 55)	
Systembolaget	54	C3
Systembolaget	(see 45)	
Victors	55	B2

ENTERTAINMENT

Biograf Spegeln	56	C2
Étage	57	C2
Filmstaden Malmö	58	C3
Kulturbolaget	59	D4
Nyhavn	60	D5
Slagthuset	61	C1

TRANSPORT

Cykelkliniken	62	B3
Local Buses	63	C2
Long-distance Buses	64	B1
Rent-A-Bike	(see 13)	
Statoil Car Hire	(see 4)	
Travelshop	(see 64)	
Turasund	(see 64)	

DISCOUNT CARDS

The discount card *Malmökortet* covers free bus transport, free street parking, free entry to several museums and discounts at other attractions and on sightseeing tours. It's good value at Skr130/160/190 for one/two/three days – the price includes one adult and up to two children under 16. Buy it at the tourist office.

EMERGENCY

Dial ☎ 112 for fire, police or ambulance.

Akutklinik (☎ 33 36 85; entrance 36, Södra Förstadsgatan 101) Emergency ward at the general hospital.

Police station (☎ 20 10 00; Porslinsgatan 6)

INTERNET ACCESS

Cyberspace Café (☎ 611 01 16; Engelbrektsgatan 13; per 30min/1hr Skr20/30; ⏲ 11am-11pm Mon-Fri, 1-11pm Sat & Sun)

Malmö Stadsbibliotek (☎ 660 85 00; Regementsgatan; ⏲ 10am-7pm Mon-Thu, 10am-6pm Fri, 11am-3pm Sat) Free Internet access.

Sidewalk Express (Centralstationen; per hr Skr19)

LAUNDRY

Most hotels, hostels and camping grounds have laundries.

Tvätt-Tjänst i Malmö (☎ 611 70 70; St Knuts Torg 5; ⏲ 8am-5pm Mon-Fri) Closed in July.

LEFT LUGGAGE

There are small/medium/large lockers by platform 4 in Centralstationen for Skr20/25/30 per 24 hours.

MEDICAL SERVICES

You can call the dentist and doctor on duty on ☎ 020-43 44 44.

Apotek Gripen (☎ 19 21 13; Bergsgatan 48; ⏲ 8am-10pm) After-hours pharmacy.

MONEY

Banks and ATMs are found on Södergatan.

Forex (☎ 30 40 31; Centralstationen; ⏲ 7am-9pm) Money exchange, with another branch opposite Centralstationen on Skeppsbron and two more on Gustav Adolfs Torg.

X-Change (☎ 788 88; Hamngatan 1; ⏲ 8am-7pm Mon-Fri, 9am-4pm Sat) Money exchange.

POST

You can buy stamps and post letters from a number of shops and kiosks around town.

Post office (Skeppsbron 1; ⏲ 7am-7pm Mon-Fri) Behind the train station.

TOURIST OFFICES

An excellent source of information on the city can be found on the Internet at www.malmo.com.

Skånegården (☎ 040-20 96 00; www.skane.com; Stortorget 9, SE-21122 Malmö; ⏲ 9am-8pm mid-Jun–mid-Aug, to 6pm early Jun & late Aug, 9am-5pm Mon-Fri, 10am-3pm Sat & Sun Sep-May) On the E20, 800m from the Öresund bridge tollgate. A tourist office designed purely to give information to motorists entering the country from Denmark. Can provide details on Malmö, Skåne and the whole of Sweden.

Tourist office (☎ 34 12 00; www.malmo.se; ⏲ 9am-7pm Mon-Fri, 10am-5pm Sat & Sun Jun-Aug, 9am-6pm Mon-Fri, 10am-2pm Sat & Sun May & Sep, 9am-5pm Mon-Fri, 10am-2pm Sat & Sun Oct-Apr) Inside Centralstationen (train station); it has free Internet hotel-booking service.

TRAVEL AGENCIES

Kilroy Travels (☎ 0771-54 57 69; Engelbrektsgatan 18; ⏲ 10am-6pm Mon-Fri).

Sights & Activities

MALMÖHUS SLOTT

Malmö's castle has an intriguing history, although not much remains of the older citadels built on the site: today, with its red-brick, Functionalist buildings (dating from 1937), it looks more like a factory! Some of the Malmö Museer are based inside the castle (see opposite).

Erik of Pomerania built the first fortress here in 1436, to control the growing medieval town and Öresund shipping. This castle was destroyed between 1534 and 1536 during a popular uprising in Skåne. In the years immediately after the rebellion, King Christian III of Denmark had the castle rebuilt in forbidding late-Gothic and early-Renaissance styles.

The most famous prisoner at Malmöhus Slott (from 1567 to 1573) was the Earl of Bothwell. Bothwell married Mary, Queen of Scots, but was forced to flee from Scotland after she was deposed. On reaching Europe, he was detained by the Danes until his death in 1578.

After the Swedish takeover of Skåne in 1648, the Danes made a futile attempt to recapture the castle in 1677. When peace was restored, interest in the castle waned and most of it became derelict by the 19th century. A devastating fire in 1870 left only the main building and two gun towers intact: these sections were renovated in 1930.

MALMÖ MUSEER

Various museums in and around Malmöhus slott make up the **Malmö Museer** (☎ 34 44 37; www.malmo.se/museer; Malmöhusvägen; combined entry adult/7-15yr Skr40/10, free with Malmökortet; ⏲ 10am-4pm Jun-Aug, noon-4pm Sep-May). There are café-restaurants inside all the museums.

Inside the Castle

The especially interesting **aquarium** has a nocturnal hall (with bats, slow lorris, skinks etc), as well as coral reefs, brightly coloured tropical fish and representatives of local species such as cod and pike. It was being revamped at the time of writing, so should be even better when you visit! The aquarium is associated with the **Naturmuseum** (Natural History Museum), which has typical collections of rocks, stuffed animals and birds.

The galleries of **Malmö Konstmuseum** contain the largest Swedish collection of 20th-century Nordic art, and the **Stadsmuseum** (City Museum) deals with the cultural history of Malmö and Skåne (mostly in Swedish). The **Knight's Hall** has various late-medieval and Renaissance exhibits, such as the regalia of the order of St Knut. The northwest **gun tower** is intact and atmospheric, with cannons pointing in every direction.

On Malmöhusvägen

The excellent **Teknikens och Sjöfartens Hus** is a short distance to the west. It's a technology and maritime museum, with aircraft, vehicles, a horse-drawn tram, steam engines, and the amazing 'U3' walk-in submarine, just outside the main building. The submarine was launched in Karlskrona in 1943 and decommissioned in 1967. Upstairs is a superb hands-on experiment room for kids, which will keep them (and you!) enthralled for ages.

Next door are **Fiskehoddorna** (☎ 12 83 40; ⏲ 6.30am-1pm Tue-Sat), former fishermen's huts where you can buy fresh fish.

The old **Kommendanthuset** (Commandant's House) arsenal is just opposite the castle: it opens for temporary art exhibitions.

Elsewhere in Malmö

Ebbas Hus (☎ 34 44 95; Snapperupsgatan 10; adult/7-15yr Skr10/5; ⏲ noon-4pm Wed & Sat) is the smallest house in Malmö and has been left as it was in the 1920s, when the last occupant lived there.

SANKT PETRI KYRKA

This red-brick Gothic beast is the oldest **church** (Göran Olsgatan; ⏲ 10am-6pm) in the city, built in the early 14th century. The medieval frescoes were whitewashed over by Protestant zealots in 1555, but the original wall-paintings in the **Krämarekapellet** (inside at the rear of Sankt Petri Kyrka) have been successfully restored. There's also a magnificent altarpiece dating from 1611 and a votive ship in the south aisle, dedicated to all who died at sea in WWII. Much of the church has been rebuilt and the 96m tower was constructed in 1890.

ART & DESIGN

The extraordinary **Rooseum** (☎ 12 17 16; www.rooseum.se; Gasverksgatan 22; adult/child Skr40/20, half-price with Malmökortet; ⏲ 2-8pm Wed, noon-6pm Thu-Sun), once the turbine hall of a power station, holds contemporary art exhibitions.

Malmö Konsthall (☎ 34 12 94; St Johannesgatan 7; admission free; ⏲ 11am-5pm, to 9pm Wed), south of the city centre, has vast white display halls where Swedish and foreign artists show off their work.

Another arty place is the **Form/Design Center** (☎ 664 51 50; Lilla Torg 9; admission free; ⏲ 11am-5pm Tue-Fri, 11am-4pm Sat & Sun), in the wonderful courtyarded 16th-century **Hedmanska Gården**, featuring architecture, design and art displays. The surrounding cobbled streets are restored parts of the late-medieval town; the half-timbered houses are now occupied by **galleries** and **boutiques** selling some superb arts and crafts.

UNUSUAL BUILDINGS

In the distant northwest, you may catch sight of the eye-boggling **Turning Torso**, a brand-new apartment block that twists through 90 degrees from bottom to top. Inaugurated at the end of August 2005, it's now Sweden's tallest building at 190m high.

If old edifices are more your style, head for the statue of King Karl X Gustav in the centre of **Stortorget** and look around you (clockwise from the northwestern corner): mayor Jörgen Kock had a stately pile built for himself – **Kockska Huset** (1524) – where Gustav Vasa stayed when he visited the city. It now has a classy restaurant in the vaults beneath. Looking older than it is, the **County Governor's Residence** is a grand, pale, stuccoed masterpiece built in the 19th century but in

Renaissance style. Next door **Rådhuset** (the city hall) was originally built in 1546, but has been altered since then. At the south-eastern corner of the square, **Apoteket Lejonet** was founded in 1571 – it's the city's oldest pharmacy and is still in business, with a dazzling 19th-century interior.

St Gertrud Quarter is just off Östergatan and consists of 19 buildings from the 16th to 19th centuries. Across the road, **Thottska Huset** is the oldest half-timbered house in Malmö (1558). It's been turned into a restaurant, so you can take a look inside.

OTHER SIGHTS

One rather odd attraction is **Citytunnelutställningen** (☎ 32 00 00; www.citytunneln.com; Lilla Nygatan 7; adult/6-17yr Skr40/20, free with Malmökortet; ⌚ 1-5pm Tue-Thu, 1-4pm Fri, 11am-4pm Sat), where you can descend beneath Malmö to look at the drill that's slowly boring a tunnel from Centralstationen to the Öresund Bridge!

Koggmuseet (☎ 33 08 00; www.medeltidsskeppen.se; Skeppsbron 10; adult/7-15yr Skr30/20; ⌚ 11am-4pm mid-May–mid-Sep, 11am-4pm Tue-Sun mid-Sep–mid-May) is a small museum about cogs (14th-century trading vessels), with two beautiful reconstructed **medieval ships** moored outside: boat trips (at noon and 2pm) are included in the admission.

The Red Cross was just setting up **Humanitetens Hus** (☎ 32 65 00; Drottningtorget; admission Skr20; ⌚ noon-4pm Tue, Wed, Fri, noon-8pm Thu) at the time of writing. There's an emphasis on school visits, but it's worth popping in to learn more from these committed folk about their humanitarian work around the world; or to have a cup of coffee at the Fair Trade café.

Small children will enjoy **Folkets Park** (Amiralsgatan 37; ⌚ park 7am-8pm yr-round, attractions noon-7pm May–mid-Aug), geared towards summery family activities, with a miniature farm, fairground rides and **reptile house** (☎ 30 52 37; adult/child Skr50/25; ⌚ 10am-7pm Mon-Fri, noon-7pm Sat & Sun May-Aug, 10am-5pm Mon-Fri, noon-5pm Sat & Sun Sep-Apr).

Activities

Ask the tourist office for the free cycling map *Cykla i Malmö*. See p171 for information about renting bikes.

Aq-va-kul (☎ 30 05 40; Regementsgatan 24; adult/7-17yr/2-6yr/family Skr75/50/30/175; ⌚ 9am-9.30pm Mon & Thu, 9am-8.30pm Tue & Wed, 9am-7.30pm Fri, 9am-5.30pm Sat & Sun) is a water park with heated indoor and outdoor pools, wave machine, a sauna, solarium and even a Turkish bath.

'Malmö's Copacabana' is stretching it, but **Ribersborg** is a lovely long sandy beach backed by parkland, about 2km west of the town centre. Off the beach, at the end of a 200m-long pier, is **Ribersborgs Kallbadshus** (☎ 26 03 66; adult/7-17yr Skr50/35; ⌚ noon-7pm Mon-Fri, 9am-4pm Sat & Sun), an open-air naturist salt-water pool, with separate sections for men and women, and wood-fired sauna dating from 1898.

Scooting round Malmö's canals in a pedal boat is great fun: hire one from **City Boats Malmö** (☎ 0704-71 00 67; Amiralsbron, Södra Promenaden; per 30/60min Skr70/100, 50% discount with Malmökortet; ⌚ mid-Apr–mid-Aug), just east of Gustav Adolfs Torg.

Tours

To experience Malmö by water, visit **Rundan** (☎ 611 74 88; www.rundan.se; adult/5-15yr/family Skr75/40/210), opposite Centralstationen. Depending on the weather, 45-minute boat tours of the canals run regularly from May to September (11am to 7pm mid-June to mid-August, less frequently at other times). Commentary is in Swedish, German and English.

The 1½-hour **sightseeing bus tours** (adult/child Skr100/50, free with Malmökortet) take you to some odd places – like the industrial district and an old limestone quarry! – as well as round parts of the city centre and out to the Öresund bridge; they're good for getting your bearings. The tours run at noon daily (June to August), and guides speak Swedish, English and German. Pick up your ticket first at the tourist office, and the staff will show you where to catch the bus on Norra Vallgatan.

Festivals & Events

The biggest annual event – with 1.5 million visitors! – is the week-long **Malmö Festival** (www.malmofestivalen.se) in mid-August. Most events are free and include theatre, art, singing, music, dance and dragon boat competitions. The opening night is celebrated with a fireworks display and there's a huge crayfish party on Friday in Stortorget. During the week you can get food at a great variety of international stalls. Ask at the tourist office for details.

The 10-day gay and lesbian **Regnbågsfestivalen** (Rainbow Festival) is held in mid-

SOUTHERN SWEDEN

September with a parade, exhibitions, films and parties: contact **RSFL-Malmö** (☎ 611 99 62; malmo@rfsl.se; Monbijougatan 15), Malmö's gay and lesbian centre, for details.

Sleeping

CAMPING, HOSTELS & PRIVATE ROOMS

Private rooms or apartments from about Skr300 per person are available through **City Room** (☎ 795 94; cityroom@telia.com). The agency has no office address but is staffed on weekdays during office hours. Otherwise, contact the tourist office.

Bosses Gästvåningar (☎ 32 62 50; Södra Förstadsgatan 110B; s/d/tr/q from Skr315/450/550/650) The quiet, clean rooms in this central SVIF hostel are like those of a budget hotel, with proper beds, TVs and shared bathrooms. It's run by a serious but very helpful couple, and is close to Möllevångstorget and opposite the town hospital (follow the signs for 'Sjukhuset' if arriving by car).

Vandrarhemmet Villa Hilleröd (☎ 26 56 26; info@villahillerod.se; Ängdalavägen 38; dm Skr190-230) Malmö has a brand-new hostel in the shape of Villa Hilleröd, in a delightful little detached house in the west of the city. Little touches like houseplants keep things looking homely. Arrive in good time, as there's a fee of Skr100 if you appear after 8pm.

STF Vandrarhem Malmö (☎ 822 20; www.malmohostel.com; Backavägen 18; 1-/2-/3-/4-bed r Skr295/370/480/520; s/d Skr285/350; P) The well equipped, if rather large and impersonal, STF hostel is 3.5km south of the city centre, overlooking the E6 (take bus 2 from Centralstationen).

Malmö Camping & Feriecenter (☎ 15 51 65; sibbarps.camping@swipnet.se; Strandgatan 101; low/high season sites Skr150/200, 2-bed cabins Skr290/420) This camp site is by the beach and has a great view of the Öresund bridge. It's about 5km southwest of the centre of town: take bus 12B or 12G from Gustav Adolfs Torg (Skr15).

HOTELS

The tourist office has a free Internet hotel-booking service: follow the links on the website.

Mäster Johan Hotel (☎ 664 64 00; reservation@masterjohan.se; Mäster Johansgatan 13; s/d from Skr1595/2045, discounted to Skr1195/1300; P 💻) Top of the heap is this place, arguably the best hotel in town. Its ultrafresh rooms have beautiful oak floors and snowy-white fabrics, bathrooms have tiles designed by Paloma Picasso, there's a sauna and gym, and a glass-roofed courtyard where you can enjoy the immaculate breakfast buffet. Décor, service, facilities and location are all first-rate.

Scandic Hotel St Jörgen (☎ 693 46 00; stjorgen@scandic-hotels.com; Stora Nygatan 35; s/d from Skr1420/1620, discounted to Skr900/950; P 💻) St Jörgen has all the amenities that you'd expect from this upmarket chain, plus the most charming staff in Malmö! Many of the rooms look out onto Gustav Adolfs Torg; although there are a few weird, windowless, wackily-decorated 'cabin' rooms.

Clarion Hotel Malmö (☎ 710 20; info.malmo@clarion.choicehotels.se; Engelbrektsgatan 16; s/d Skr1495/1790, discounted to Skr790/990; P 💻) Elegant walnut furniture and fittings add a classy touch to the large, bright rooms here. There's also a pleasant restaurant/bar.

Comfort Hotel Malmö (☎ 33 04 40; malmo@comfort.choicehotels.se; Carlsgatan 10C; s/d Skr1250/1395, discounted to Skr699/899; P 💻) Completely overhauled in 2005, this modern hotel (handy for train and ferry) has a clean, new look and very friendly staff. The discounted prices are particularly good, as they include an evening buffet.

Hotel Baltzar (☎ 665 57 00; www.baltzarhotel.se; Södergatan 20; s/d from Skr980/1300, discounted to Skr700/850) A good choice, right in the heart of the city, this imposing listed building has comfortable, antique-furnished rooms. Although it's on a pedestrianised street, you're allowed car access to drop your bags off.

Hotel Pallas (☎ 611 50 77; Norra Vallgatan 74; s/d from Skr395/495) This is a recommended cheapish hotel near the train station. Most rooms are singles; all are fairly simple but lent grace by the lovely 17th-century building. You can pay extra for a huge double room (Skr575); breakfast costs Skr30.

Hotel Formule 1 (☎ 93 05 80; www.hotelformule1.com; Lundavägen 28; rooms Skr330) The bargain basement Formule 1 is 1.5km east of Stortorget. Smallish, functional rooms can sleep up to three people for a flat rate.

Eating

Lilla Torg is a picturesque cobbled square lined with restaurant-bars, all offering great food at similar prices. Their outdoor tables fairly heave in summer with alfresco diners and drinkers: almost like the Mediterranean, if you blank out the blankets and space heaters! For cheaper eats, the area around Möllevångstorget reflects the city's interesting ethnic mix, and there's a swirl of stalls, shops and student-frequented restaurants and bars (although the area can get edgy late at night).

Årstiderna (☎ 23 09 10; www.arstiderna.se; Frans Suellsgatan 3; mains Skr195-310, Swedish menu Skr495; ⏰ 11.30am-3pm & 6pm-midnight Mon-Fri, 6pm-midnight Sat) This is among the most exclusive restaurants in the city, located in the vaulted cellar of Kockska Huset. A sense of excitement is generated by the flaming torches outside, which continues as you descend into the candlelit arches and alcoves. There's a great atmosphere, friendly staff and fine Swedish/continental food – just the place for a romantic dinner.

Rådhuskällaren (☎ 790 20; Stortorget; mains Skr159-189; ⏰ Mon-Sat yr-round, dinner only summer) This is in the 16th-century, barrel-vaulted cellar of the town hall. Rumour has it that two members of the Beatles were turned away in 1967 because they weren't wearing neckties – thankfully things have relaxed a little since then! The food is excellent although the traditional menu (marinated salmon, venison, cloudberry desserts) is quite small.

Thotts Restaurang (☎ 698 48 00; Östergatan 10; mains Skr165-220; ⏰ lunch & dinner) Traditional dishes like grilled rack of wild boar with lingonberries, or cod with langoustine and lobster coulis are served at Thotts; or you can pick at a small selection of tapas (around Skr35) if you're feeling dainty. The restaurant is in a lovely half-timbered house dating from the 16th century. Enter via the SAS Radisson Hotel.

Izakaya Koi (☎ 757 00; Lilla Torg 5; lunch Skr60-75, dinner mains Skr100-150; ⏰ until at least midnight) For something different, try sleek Izakaya Koi, which has won architectural awards for its interior. It serves up quality Japanese cuisine, including highly recommended sushi and sashimi, to Malmö's cosmopolitan crowd.

Restaurang Davidshall (☎ 30 60 08; Erik Dahlbergsgatan 5; tapas Skr40-70, mains Skr110-200; ⏰ lunch & dinner) Modern Davidshall produces contemporary European cuisine, mainly a subtle blending of French and Spanish goodies. There's a long tapas list (garlic bread to green mussels), and classic mains like lamb with Dijon mustard and rosemary.

La Empanada (☎ 12 02 62; Själbodgatan 10; mains Skr45-65; ⏰ closed Sun) This cheap and cheerful place, opposite Sankt Petri Kyrka, is highly recommended for those on a budget. Mainly Mexican dishes (tacos, enchiladas and burritos) are served caféteria-style; it closes in the early evening.

Vegegården (☎ 611 38 88; Stora Nygatan 18; lunch Skr58; ⏰ lunch, dinner Thu-Sun) Veggies and vegans could try this Chinese restaurant, tucked in a quiet corner of the city near the Rooseum. Many of the long list of dishes are soya-based, and there's a warm or cold lunchtime buffet.

Krua Thai (☎ 12 22 87; Möllevångstorget 14; meals around Skr70; ⏰ 11am-4pm Mon, 11am-3pm & 5-10pm Tue-Fri, 1-10pm Sat, 2-10pm Sun) Down the southern end of town is this large, popular and long-standing Thai restaurant. The family have also opened a central takeaway (downstairs, Södergatan 22), for spicy meals on the move.

Spot (☎ 12 02 03; Stora Nygatan 33; mains from Skr60; ⏰ closed Sun) Stylish Spot, an Italian café, sells excellent lunchtime sandwiches, salads, pizzas, and pasta and risotto dishes.

Konditori Hollandia (☎ 12 48 86; Södra Förstadsgatan 8; ⏰ closed Sun) This classic café has the feel of some Victorian lady's parlour! Nibble daintily on salad and sandwiches, or throw the diet in the bin and indulge in one of their delicious patisserie offerings.

Saluhallen (Lilla Torg) For a light meal, snack or picnic, head to the covered market, with food stalls to appeal to every taste (fish, pasta, sushi, kebabs, Chinese dishes and baked potatoes). **Bageri Caféet** (☎ 30 35 13), inside Saluhallen, does filled bagels, baguettes and ciabattas from Skr30.

Self-caterers can buy supplies at the central **Mästerlivs supermarket** (Engelbrektsgatan 15; ⏰ 9am-9pm). The best produce market is on Möllevångstorget, from Monday to Saturday.

Drinking

On Lilla Torg, the absolute coolest places are **Victors** (☎ 12 76 70), **Moosehead** (☎ 12 04 23) and **Mello Yello** (☎ 30 45 25), which stand in a row competing for custom; they're all great spots, with friendly service, outdoor summer seating (you may have to wait for a table), tasty meals, and lots of drinks, from dry white wine to the most lurid of cocktails.

There are numerous bars around Möllevångstorget, which probably appeal to a more studenty crowd, such as **Nyhavn** (☎ 12 88 30), a pub with reasonably priced meals to go along with the beer.

Systembolaget (Södergatan 22) sells beers, wines and spirits.

Entertainment

Malmö has an excellent array of nightlife venues – for up-to-date information pick up the local newspaper *Sydsvenskan* on a Friday, when it contains the listings mag *Dygnet Runt* (which covers Lund as well as Malmö). It's all in Swedish but the club and cinema information is understandable. Alternatively, take the train across to Copenhagen for a huge selection of capital-city delights; trains run every 20 minutes until around 11pm, then hourly until 5am.

NIGHTCLUBS

Bars generally stay open until around 1am, clubs to 3am, 4am or 5am on Friday and Saturday although some bars stay open late during the week; minimum age requirements (20 to 25) vary from venue to venue, and from night to night, so bring some ID. Entry usually costs between Skr50 and Skr100.

Jeriko (☎ 611 84 29; Spångatan 38) Regular performances of jazz, folk and world music.

Kulturbolaget (☎ 30 20 11; Bergsgatan 18) Big-name live-music acts perform here, but even if there's no-one playing, 'KB' has a good bar, nightclub (usually Friday and Saturday), and a highly regarded restaurant.

Étage (☎ 23 20 60; Stortorget 6; Mon-Sat) This central, mainstream club has two dance floors (one of them playing classics and the other playing dance music) and four bars, and quite a large gay clientele.

Slagthuset (☎ 711 12; Jörgen Kocksgatan 7A) The massive (8500-sq-m) 'Slaughterhouse' entertainment complex lies north of the train station. There are restaurants and bars here, and a nightclub (Skr90) until 5am on Friday and Saturday nights, with the latest dance tunes plus hits from the 1970s and '80s.

CINEMAS

There are several cinemas in the city centre; the biggest are these two:

Biograf Spegeln (☎ 12 59 78; Stortorget 29) Hosts alternative selections.

Filmstaden Malmö (☎ 660 20 90; Storgatan 22) Showing Hollywood movies.

Getting There & Away

TO/FROM THE AIRPORT

The regular **Flygbuss** (☎ 669 62 09) runs from Centralstationen to Sturup airport (Skr90, 45 minutes): roughly every 40 minutes on weekdays, hourly on Sunday, six services on Saturday; a taxi should cost no more than Skr400.

AIR

Sturup airport (☎ 613 10 00) is 33km southeast of the city. **SAS** (☎ 0770-72 77 27; www.scandinavian.net) has up to eight nonstop flights to Stockholm

SOUTHERN SWEDEN

BRIDGING THE GAP

In 1995, technology finally caught up with a 100-year-old dream: to build a bridge between Sweden and Denmark Construction began just outside Malmö in October that year, and the Öresund bridge and tunnel opened to traffic in the summer of 2000: you can now drive all the way from Sweden to Germany without using a ferry.

Viewed from the shore, without any surrounding reference points, it's difficult to comprehend the vast scale of the project. Those insignificant-looking central pylons are actually 4km away and are over three times as high as Nelson's Column! It's actually the longest cable-tied road and rail bridge in the world, measuring 7.8km from Lernacken (on the Swedish side, near Malmö) to the artificial island Peberholm, south of Saltholm. After the island, there's a 3km undersea tunnel which emerges just north of Copenhagen airport.

After a slightly shaky start, with less traffic than predicted, bridge usage is increasing: about four million cars drove over it in 2004. Local commuters pay via an electronic transmitter, while tolls for the rest of us are payable by credit card, debit card or in Danish and Swedish currency at the Lernacken toll booths. The crossing isn't cheap – for a motorcycle the price is Skr160, private vehicles (up to 6m) pay Skr285 and private vehicles with trailers, vans or minibuses cost Skr570. If you're travelling between Sweden and Denmark with your own transport, you may want to look at other options (such as ferries between Helsingborg and Helsingør).

Arlanda daily. **Malmö Aviation** (☎ 0771-55 00 10; www.malmoaviation.se) flies a number of times daily to Stockholm Bromma airport. There are also infrequent flights to Antalya, Budapest, Larnaca and Varna. The low-cost carrier **Ryanair** (☎ 0900-202 02 40; www.ryanair.com) flies to Sturup from London's Stansted airport.

Trains run directly from Malmö to Copenhagen's main airport (Skr85, 35 minutes, every 20 minutes), which has a much better international flight selection.

BOAT

Although the Öresund bridge has rendered most of the ferries obsolete, romantics can still travel between Malmö and Copenhagen on the **Turasund** (☎ 17 04 90; www.turasund.se; Skeppsbron 10). A single ticket per adult/4-15 years/bicycle costs Skr65/40/40, and there are three crossings per day (Wednesday to Saturday in May, Monday to Saturday June to early September).

BUS

Local & Regional

The *länstrafik* (public transport network) operates in zones, with a single journey ranging from Skr15 within the city of Malmö to a maximum of Skr84 within the county. The local trains are your best bet for travel to/from the major towns in Skåne; buses are a good option for those towns and out-of-the-way areas not on the train lines.

City buses depart from Centralplan, in front of the train station, and the **Busscentralen** (☎ 43 16 70) office there handles inquiries and sells tickets. Most regional buses leave from the bus station on Spårvägsgatan, while a few go from the section of Norra Vallgatan in front of Centralplan.

Bus 146 is a useful service to the ferries departing from Trelleborg (Skr48, 40 minutes); this service runs once or twice an hour. Another useful service is bus 100 to Falsterbo (Skr48, 50 minutes).

Long-Distance

You can buy tickets for long-distance buses from the **Travelshop** (Malmö Buss & Resecenter; ☎ 33 05 70; www.travelshop.se; Skeppsbron 10), north of the train station by the harbour; buses leave from outside.

Swebus Express (☎ 0200-21 82 18; www.swebusexpress.se) runs two to four times daily to Stockholm (Skr500, 8½ hours), five times to Jönköping (Skr293, 4½ hours) and up to 10 times daily to Göteborg (Skr281, three to four hours); four continue to Oslo (Skr400, 7½ hours). All pass through Lund.

Svenska Buss (☎ 0771-67 67 67; www.svenskabuss.se) runs a service to Stockholm (Skr400, 11 hours) via Karlskrona, on Wednesday, Thursday, Friday and Sunday. There are also one or two services to Göteborg (Skr250, four hours) on Monday, Friday, Saturday and Sunday.

Säfflebussen (☎ 0771-15 15 15; www.safflebussen.se) has nine buses on the Copenhagen–Malmö–Göteborg route per day, with a couple originating from Berlin and continuing on to Oslo.

Eurolines runs services from here to all over Europe – see p327 for details.

There are a few buses heading across the Öresund bridge, but trains are the best option for journeys to Copenhagen and beyond.

CAR & MOTORCYCLE

The E6 motorway runs north–south through the eastern and southern suburbs of Malmö on its way from Göteborg to Trelleborg. The E65 motorway runs east to Ystad, the E22 runs northeast to Lund and Kristianstad, and the E20 goes west across the Öresund bridge (single/return bridge toll Skr285/570, discount with *Malmökortet*) to Copenhagen and north (with the E6) to Göteborg.

Car hire is available at **Statoil** (☎ 12 99 50; Skeppsbron 2), directly opposite Centralstationen. Several of the larger car-hire companies, such as **Avis** (☎ 50 05 15), are represented at Sturup airport.

TRAIN

Pågatågen (local trains) run regularly to Helsingborg (Skr84, one hour), Landskrona (Skr72, 40 minutes), Lund (Skr36, 15 minutes), Simrishamn (Skr84, 1½ hours), Ystad (Skr72, 50 minutes), and other destinations in Skåne (bicycles are half-fare, but are not allowed during peak times, except during mid-June to mid-August). The platform is at the end of Centralstationen and you buy tickets from the machine. International rail passes are accepted.

There's an integrated Öresundregionen transport system which operates trains from Helsingborg via Malmö and Copenhagen to Helsingør. The Malmö to Copenhagen Kastrup airport or Copenhagen central station trips take 20 and 35 minutes, respectively (both journeys Skr87); trains leave every 20 minutes.

X2000 (Skr482, 2¾ hours) and regional (Skr294, 3¼ hours) trains run regularly to/from Göteborg. X2000 (Skr1060, 4½ hours, hourly) and Intercity (Skr675, 6½ hours, infrequent) trains run between Stockholm and Malmö.

Getting Around

Get bus information and buy tickets at the customer service desks in Centralstationen, at Gustav Adolfs Torg and at Värnhemstorget (at the eastern end of Kungsgatan). Local tickets are Skr15 for one hour's travel. The bus hubs are Centralplan (in front of Centralstationen), Gustav Adolfs Torg, Värnhemstorget and Triangeln. *Malmökortet* includes city bus travel.

Car parking in the city is expensive: typical charges are around Skr15 per hour or Skr90 per day (24 hours). Most hotels also charge for parking. Parking in municipal spaces ('Gatukontoret'; ask the tourist office which symbol to look for) is free with *Malmökortet.*

Taxi companies in Malmö have a bad reputation for ripping people off: avoid them if you can, or else don't get into any taxi without arranging a fare with the driver in advance. The tourist office recommends **Taxi Skåne** (☎ 33 03 30) and **Taxi 97** (☎ 97 97 97).

In summer, **Rent-A-Bike** (☎ 0707-49 94 22; www.rent-a-bike.se; per day Skr90) has a handy rental counter inside the tourist office in Centralstationen. Otherwise, try **Fridhems Cykelaffär** (☎ 26 03 35; Tessinsväg 13; per day Skr75) west of the castle, or **Cykelkliniken** (☎ 611 66 66; Regementsgatan 12; per day Skr120).

LUND

☎ 046 / pop 101,423

Lund is a super little place with a 1000-year-old history. Its mighty cathedral, with giants in the crypt and a magical clock, should not be missed; but really the whole town is infused with a mellow charm. Delicious medieval houses are scattered amongst green parks and gardens, and the university adds a quiet buzz of bright young things...though not during the summer holidays when the students go on vacation.

The second-oldest town in Sweden, Lund was founded by the Danes around 1000. It went on to become the seat of the largest archbishopric in Europe after the cathedral was built. Vikings and bishops aside, Lund's modern claim to fame is as the birthplace of the ink-jet printer.

Information

Banks, ATMs and other services can be found along the main street (Stora Södergatan, changing to Kyrkogatan). You can read about the **university** (www.lu.se) online, and www.lund.se is a good website about the town.

Akademibokhandeln (☎ 19 60 00; Storgatan 2; 🕑 10am-6pm Mon-Fri, 10am-3pm Sat) Fantastic university bookshop with a huge selection of foreign-language books.

Forex Bangatan (☎ 32 34 10; Bangatan 8; 🕑 8am-7pm Mon-Fri, 8am-4pm Sat); Västra Mårtensgatan (☎ 14 07 80; Västra Mårtensgatan 6, 🕑 9am-7pm Mon-Fri, 9am-3pm Sat) Two central money-exchange offices.

Library (Sankt Petri Kyrkogatan 6; 🕑 10am-7pm Mon-Thu, 10am-6pm Fri, 10am-3pm Sat) With free Internet access.

Nollett (☎ 70 00 96; Lilla Gråbrödersgatan 2; per hr Skr39; 🕑 10am-midnight Mon-Fri, noon-1am Sat, 1-11pm Sun) Internet access.

Press Stop (Klostergatan 8; 🕑 10am-6pm Mon-Fri, 10am-2pm Sat) Good choice of foreign magazines and newspapers.

Tourist office (☎ 35 50 40; www.lund.se; Kyrkogatan 11; 🕑 10am-6pm Mon-Fri, 10am-2pm Sat & Sun Jun-Aug, 10am-5pm Mon-Fri, 10am-2pm Sat May & Sep, 10am-5pm Mon-Fri Oct-Apr) Helpful tourist office opposite the cathedral.

Sights

DOMKYRKAN

Lund's magnificent Romanesque cathedral, **Domkyrkan** (☎ 35 87 00; 🕑 8am-6pm Mon-Fri, 9.30am-5pm Sat, 9.30am-6pm Sun), with its impressive twin towers, is a must-see. Try to pop in at noon or 3pm (1pm and 3pm on Sunday and holidays) when the marvellous astronomical clock strikes up *In Dulci Jubilo* and the wooden figures at the top whirr into action. Within the crypt, you can find Finn, the mythological giant who helped construct the cathedral, and a 16th-century well carved with comical scenes.

MUSEUMS

The wonderful **Kulturen** (☎ 35 04 00; www.kulturen.com; Tegnerplatsen; adult/child Skr50/free; 🕑 11am-5pm mid-Apr-Sep, to 9pm Jul–mid-Aug, noon-4pm Tue-Sun Oct–mid-Apr), opened in 1892, is a huge open-air museum filling two whole blocks. Its

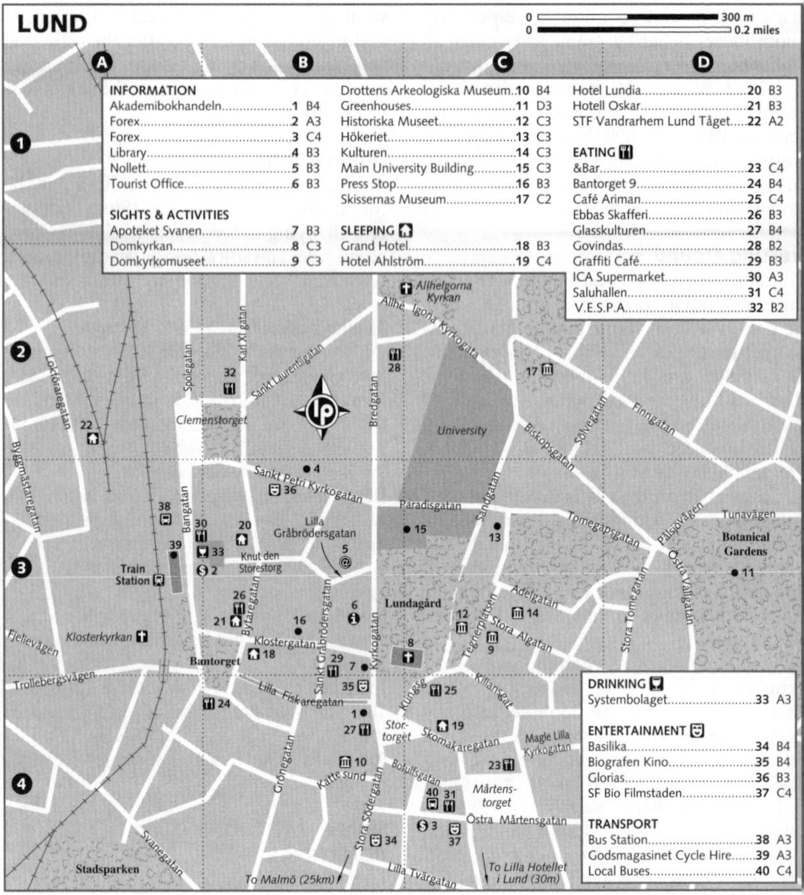

impressive collection of about 30 buildings includes everything from the meanest birch-bark hovel to grand 17th-century houses. There are permanent exhibitions, encompassing Lund in the Middle Ages, old toys, ceramics, silver and glass (among many others), and changing temporary displays. Ask about guided tours in English. There's a popular outdoor restaurant here, outside the museum near several Scanian **rune stones**.

Just behind the cathedral, the rather old-fashioned **Historiska Museet** (☎ 222 79 44; Kraftstorg; Skr30/free; ⏰ 11am-4pm Tue-Fri) has a large collection of pre-Viking Age finds, including a 7000-year-old skeleton. It's joined with the **Domkyrkomuseet**, which explores the history of the church in the area; the rooms filled with countless statues of the crucified Christ are supremely creepy.

The recently refurbished **Skissernas Museum** (Sketch Museum; ☎ 222 72 85; Finngatan 2; adult/under 18yr Skr30/free; ⏰ noon-5pm Tue-Sun) has the world's largest collection of sketches and designs for public artworks, made by Swedish artists and European stalwarts like Matisse, Picasso and Henry Moore.

The underground **Drottens Arkeologiska Museum** (☎ 14 13 28; Kattesund 6) contains the foundations of an 11th-century church, and has a fascinating but grisly collection of skeletons that build a picture of the Middle Ages through their diseases and amputations. The museum was closed at the time of writing: ask the tourist office for reopening details.

There are a number of galleries, plus small, special-interest museums and archives in town, many attached to university departments – enquire at the tourist office.

OTHER SIGHTS

The main **university building**, topped by four sphinxes representing the original faculties, is worth a glance inside.

The 8-hectare **Botanical Gardens** (☎ 222 73 20; Östra Vallgatan 20; admission free; 🕑 6am-9.30pm mid-May–mid-Sep, 6am-8pm rest of yr), east of the town centre, feature around 7000 species. Also on the site are tropical **greenhouses** (admission free; 🕑 noon-3pm).

Take a look inside the charming old-style pharmacy, **Apoteket Svanen** (Kyrkogatan 5), not far from the tourist office. Across the park, **Hökeriet** (☎ 35 04 04; cnr St Annegatan & Tomegapsgatan; 🕑 noon-5pm Tue-Sun) is a tiny old-fashioned general store.

Sleeping

The tourist office can book private rooms from Skr225 per person plus a Skr50 fee.

STF Vandrarhem Lund Tåget (☎ 14 28 20; www.trainhostel.com; Vävaregatan 22; dm Skr135) Children will love the novelty of this hostel, based in old railway carriages in parkland behind the station. The triple bunks and tiny rooms are fine if you're cosying up with loved ones, but a little claustrophobic with strangers; they aren't very soundproof, either.

Hotell Oskar (☎ 18 80 85; www.hotelloskar.com; Bytaregatan 3; s/d Skr980/1350, discounted to Skr700/900) This dinky place in a 19th-century townhouse has smashing rooms filled with sleek Scandinavian designs. It's also well equipped, with DVD players, kettles and stereos. Breakfast is served in lovely Ebbas Skafferi next door.

Hotel Ahlström (☎ 211 01 74; info@hotellahlstrom.se; Skomakaregatan 3; s/d from Skr595/850, discounted to Skr500/650) Lund's oldest hotel is a cheap and friendly option, on a quiet but very central street. Rooms have parquet floors, cool white walls and washbasins (bathrooms are shared). There's no dining room, so breakfast is brought right to your door.

Hotel Lundia (☎ 280 65 00; info@lundia.se; Knut den Stores torg 2; s/d from Skr1395/1795, discounted to Skr795/895) The designers here have gone for a contemporary Scandinavian/Japanese look, leading to sleek but slightly Spartan-looking rooms. There's a stylish brasserie downstairs, serving international cuisine.

Lilla Hotellet i Lund (☎ 32 88 88; lillahotellet@telia.com; Bankgatan 7; s/d Skr930/1130, discounted to Skr730/930; 🕑 closed early Jul-early Aug; P 💻) Rather irritatingly, this little place closes in peak season, but it's a good choice if you're here at other times. The cutesy 19th-century building has cosy rooms with DVD players, and there's a sunny courtyard and guest lounge.

Grand Hotel (☎ 280 61 00; hotel@grandilund.se; Bantorget 1; s/d from Skr1925/2295, discounted to Skr1250/1595; 💻) Lund's most luxurious establishment is the Grand, opened in 1899 and resplendent with gilt and chandeliers. Rooms are on the small side, but decorated in grand style with heavy wooden beds, Persian carpets and cherub wallpaper. It too has an upmarket restaurant on site, and a sauna.

Eating

Grand Hotel (☎ 280 61 00; Bantorget 1; lunch Skr89, dinner mains Skr220-320) The Grand's refined restaurant serves classic menu items like roast venison, wild duck breast and fillets of sole with lobster sauce; the wine selection is equally impressive. The Lund menu features local dishes and/or ingredients; and there's a separate list of veggie creations too.

Bantorget 9 (☎ 32 02 00; Bantorget 9; mains Skr190-250; 🕑 from 6pm Mon-Sat) Another gourmet's delight, with a small but perfectly formed menu. Snuggle down in the cosy candlelight and feast on wild duck and oyster mushrooms, venison in red wine and truffles or a fresh-fish dish. There's a good wine list to oil the evening further.

&Bar (☎ 211 22 88; Mårtenstorget 9; lunch Skr65-79, dinner mains Skr90-210) The fashionable &Bar is relaxed enough to attract a range of people for its lunchtime bagels, salads and specials. À la carte dinner mains are Swedish and international favourites. From 10pm it's a

AUTHOR CHOICE

Ebbas Skafferi (☎ 13 41 56; Bytaregatan 5; lunch Skr65; 🕑 7am-9pm Mon-Fri, 8am-6pm Sat, 9am-8pm Sun) Ebbas is everything you'd want a café to be: worn wooden tables, green plants and flowers, odd bits of artwork, a delightful courtyard, and of course excellent coffee, teas, cakes and lunches (including quiche, risotto, enchiladas and crêpes).

place for cocktails and DJs playing disco, electronica, house, soul and hip-hop (until 2am Thursday to Saturday).

V.E.S.P.A. (☎ 12 71 27; Karl XI gatan 1; pizza Skr65-95; ⌚ lunch & dinner) For pizza and a glass of wine, this shiny-bright Italian bar-restaurant is a good choice; there's outdoor seating in summer.

Café Ariman (☎ 13 12 63; Kungsgatan 2B; snacks around Skr40; ⌚ 11am-midnight Mon, 11am-1am Tue-Thu, 11am-3am Fri & Sat, noon-midnight Sun) This slightly grungy place has a great view of the cathedral, strong coffee and a fine array of café fare along the lines of ciabatta, salads and burritos. It's popular with leftwing students: think nose-rings, dreads and leisurely chess games.

Graffiti Café (☎ 32 82 70; Sankt Gråbrödersgatan 4; meals from Skr40; ⌚ lunch) Part of the Graffiti franchise, selling salads, baguettes and baked potatoes with a disorientating choice of fillings.

Govindas (☎ 12 04 13; Bredgatan 28; lunch Skr60; ⌚ 11.30am-3.30pm Mon-Fri) In a quiet cobbled courtyard filled with trees and shrubs, Govindas is a vegetarian restaurant popular with students.

Saluhallen (Mårtenstorget) The market hall is the spot for reasonably priced food (fresh fish, pasta, burgers, kebabs and croissants), from delicatessen stalls or cheap eateries.

Glasskulturen (☎ 211 00 14; Stortorget 8) On the main square is a gourmet ice-cream shop with long queues in summer.

Self-caterers can stock up at the **ICA supermarket** (Bangatan; ⌚ 8am-10pm) opposite the train station.

Drinking

Glorias (☎ 15 19 85; St Petri Kyrkogatan 9; burgers from Skr90; ⌚ 11.30am-midnight Mon-Wed, 11.30am-1am Thu, 11.30am-3am Fri & Sat, 1-11pm Sun) The waft of booze that hits you in the doorway tells you that eating is secondary here. This often-rowdy, American-style sports bar attracts a young crowd, and has somewhat pricey Cajun-style food and occasional live music. There's dancing until 3am on Fridays and Saturdays.

Basilika (☎ 211 66 60; Stora Södergatan 13) Da yoof love Basilika too: for coffee-drinking, lunch, comedy acts and nightclub (open until 3am weekends).

Systembolaget (Bangatan 10) is near to the ICA supermarket.

Entertainment

Pick up the brochure *i Lund* from the tourist office to find out what's going on in town.

There are several cinemas in Lund, including:

Biografen Kino (☎ 30 30 80; Kyrkogatan 3) Arts cinema.
SF Bio Filmstaden (☎ 0856-26 00 00; Västra Mårtensgatan 12) Mainstream cinema.

Getting There & Away

The regular **Flygbuss** (☎ 0771-77 77 77) runs to Malmö's Sturup airport (Skr90) – see p169.

It's just 15 minutes from Lund to Malmö by train, with frequent SJ and local Pågatågen departures (Skr36). Some trains continue to Copenhagen (Skr127, one hour). Other direct services run from Malmö to Kristianstad and Karlskrona via Lund. All long-distance trains from Stockholm or Göteborg to Malmö stop in Lund.

Long-distance buses leave from outside the train station. Most buses to/from Malmö (except buses to Trelleborg and Falsterbo) run via Lund. See p170 for details.

Getting Around

Stadsbussarna (☎ 35 53 00) local town buses cost Skr12 per ride; the terminal is on Botulfsplatsen, west of Mårtenstorget. Phone **Taxi Skåne** (☎ 33 03 30) for a taxi. To hire a bike, go to **Godsmagasinet** (☎ 35 57 42; Bangatan; ⌚ 6.30am-9.30pm Mon-Fri), a huge bicycle lock-up in the northernmost train-station building.

FALSTERBO PENINSULA

☎ 040

Families and sun-worshippers will love the white-sand beaches at the edges of Falsterbo Peninsula, and ornithologists will enjoy the area's birdlife. The peninsula (30km south of Malmö) also has some real one-off attractions: the unmissable Viking reserve Foteviken, and the weird little amber museum.

The area's major **tourist office** (☎ 42 54 54; www.vellinge.se/turism; Östra Hamnplan 2; ⌚ 10am-6pm Mon-Fri, 10am-2pm Sat & Sun mid-Jun–mid-Aug, 10am-noon & 1-3pm mid-Aug–mid-Jun) is just outside Höllviken, near the lifting bridge. Höllviken is a reasonable-sized town with facilities like banks and supermarkets.

Bärnstensmuseum

Trapped in sticky resin 40 million years ago, insects forage, fight, mate and feed in pieces of amber at the **Bärnstensmuseum** (Ambe

Museum; ☎ 45 45 04; www.brost.se; Södra Mariavägen 4; adult/child Skr10/5; 11am-5pm mid-May–mid-Oct, 11am-5pm Sat & Sun mid-Oct–mid-May). It's small but interesting; movie buffs might like to know that the museum staff acted as advisors to the makers of *Jurassic Park*. Beachcombers may find pieces of washed-up amber in this part of Sweden.

The museum is near the southern edge of Höllviken (just off the coast road towards Trelleborg).

Foteviken

If you mourn the passing of big hairy men in longboats, don't miss one of Sweden's most interesting and unusual attractions, about 700m north of Höllviken. **Vikingareservatet vid Foteviken** (Foteviken Viking Reserve; ☎ 33 08 00; www.foteviken.se; adult/6-15yr Skr60/25; 10am-4pm Jun-Aug, 10am-4pm Mon-Fri May & Sep–mid-Oct) is unique, an excellent 'living' reconstruction of a late-Viking Age village. Entry price includes a highly recommended one-hour guided tour (Swedish, plus English and German if there are enough people); these depart at 11am, 1pm and 2.30pm.

Around 20 authentic reconstructions of houses with reed or turf roofs have been built on the coast, near to the site of the Battle of Foteviken (1134). These belong to various tradespeople; the town's *jarl* (commander of the armed forces), juror and scribe; and the chieftain, whose home has wooden floorboards, fleeces and a Battle of Foteviken tapestry. There's even a shield-lined great hall (the Thinghöll), and a reconstructed warship and lethally powerful war catapult, which you may get to see fired at the end of your tour.

The amazing thing is that this reserve is home to people who live as the Vikings did, eschewing most modern conveniences and following the old traditions, laws and religions – even after the last tourist has left! These modern-day Vikings lead visitors on guided tours through their houses and provide an entertaining and insightful glimpse into Viking times.

If you visit in early June you can witness warrior training and a re-enactment of the 1134 battle; Viking Week is held in late June, and culminates in a Viking market.

There's a reasonable **hostel** (2-bed r Skr350, cottage Skr630) just outside the reserve for visitors.

Falsterbo

Little **Falsterbo Museum** (☎ 47 05 13; falsterbomuseum@mail.bip.net; Sjögatan; adult/7-16yr Skr20/10; 10am-7pm mid-Jun–mid-Aug), at the southern tip of the peninsula, is a pleasing jumble: a small Naturum, old shops and smithies, WWII mines, and the remains of a 13th-century boat.

Falsterbo has a long sandy **beach** that's popular with locals and Malmö holidaymakers. The sandy hook-shaped island of **Måkläppen** is a nature reserve, off-limits to the public from February to October. There are seals and over 50 species of birds, including little terns, Kentish plovers (rare in Sweden) and avocets; in the autumn, between one and three million migrating birds rest their wings here. Near the museum is **Falsterbo Fågelstation** (☎ 47 06 88; birdobs@fbo.pp.se; Sjögatan), a bird observatory which studies these feathery visitors.

Ljungens Camping (☎ 47 11 32; ljungenscamping@telia.com; Strandbadsvägen; sites Skr160; mid-Apr–Sep) This orderly site is a friendly place a couple of kilometres from Falsterbo; amenities include a small crêperie.

Kust Café (☎ 47 38 30; Storgatan 14; snacks from Skr60; 11am-10pm summer) Catering to the fashionable city set is this stylish nautical café, with excellent coffee, ciabattas, salads, pasta and cakes.

Getting There & Away

Bus 100 (Skr48, one hour, every 30 minutes Monday to Saturday, hourly Sunday) runs from Malmö to Falsterbo Strandbad (about 600m east of the Fågelstation).

TRELLEBORG

☎ 0410 / pop 39,477

Trelleborg is the main gateway between Sweden and Germany, with frequent ferries coming and going. It's not really on the tourist trail: if you're arriving in Sweden here, it's probably better to head on for Malmö or Ystad. However, the town will be celebrating its 750th birthday in 2007, so snoop around to see what's worth sticking around for.

Information

Banks and ATMs can be found near Forex and on Algatan.

Internetcafé Gamezone.nu (☎ 415 10; Algatan 66; per hr Skr20) Internet access.

Forex (CB Friisgatan 1; 8am-10pm Mon-Fri, 8am-2pm Sat, noon-5pm Sun) Money exchange.

Library (☎ 531 80; CB Friisgatan 17-19; 10am-6pm Mon-Fri, 11am-2pm Sat) With free Internet access.

Tourist office (☎ 73 33 20; www.trelleborg.se/turism; Hamngatan 9; 9am-7pm Mon-Fri, 10am-6pm Sat, 10am-5pm Sun Jun-Aug, 9am-5pm Mon-Fri Sep-May) Inside the harbour-side complex.

Sights

Quite exciting if you're a Viking fan, **Trelleborgen** (☎ 460 77; admission free) is a 9th-century Viking ring fortress, discovered in 1988 off Bryggaregatan (just west of the town centre). It's built to the same pattern as Danish fortresses of the same era, showing the strong centralised power of Harald Bluetooth at work. A quarter of the palisaded fort and a wooden gateway have been recreated, as has one of the later medieval houses built within the walls (now containing a summer café). There are plans afoot to build a swish museum and a Viking farmhouse.

Trelleborgs Museum (☎ 73 30 50; Östergatan 58; adult/under 8yr Skr20/free; 1-5pm Tue-Sun), just east of the town centre, is housed in an old hospital and covers a wide range of themes, including a 7000-year-old settlement discovered nearby, Viking life, and recent local history.

By the town park, the **Axel Ebbe Konsthall** (☎ 530 56; Hesekillegatan 1; adult/under 8yr Skr20/free; 1-4pm Tue-Sun summer) is a Functionalist building featuring nude sculptures by the native Scanian Axel Ebbe (1868–1941). For a preview, check out the fountain **Sjöormen**, literally 'the sea monster', in the centre of Storatorget.

Sleeping & Eating

The tourist office can book private rooms from Skr300, plus Skr35 booking fee.

Night Stop (☎ 410 70; Östergatan 59; s/d Skr199/299; P) Simple and functional with shared bathrooms, Night Stop is open 24 hours per day and is the cheapest place in Trelleborg to put your head down. It's about 500m from the ferry (turn right along Hamngatan after disembarking), diagonally opposite the museum. Breakfast is an additional Skr40.

Hotell Horizont (☎ 71 32 39; info@horizont.nu; Hamngatan 9; s/d Skr795/995, discounted to Skr650/850; P) The brand-new Horizont has sharp-looking, clean and minimalist rooms, some with harbour views. There's a top-floor restaurant, bar and café, and it's in the same huge building as the tourist office so it's easy to find!

Dannegården (☎ 481 80; office@dannegarden.se; Strandgatan 32; s/d from Skr1092/1428, discounted to Skr644/868; P) Absolutely the most beautiful place in town is this old sea captain's villa. Rooms are luxurious without being over-the-top, there's a high-quality restaurant on the premises, and the gardens are lovely.

Dalabadets Camping (☎ 149 05; Dalabadets Strandväg 2; sites Skr140, 4-bed cabins from Skr350) This is the nearest camping ground, over 3km east. It's a well-equipped place between road No 9 and the beach.

Restaurang & Pizzeria Istanbul (☎ 44 44 44; Algatan 30; mains Skr60-150) This bustling place has a huge menu of pasta, pizza, salad and kebabs, plus more expensive Swedish fish and meat dishes.

Café Vattentornet (☎ 530 70; Stortorget; Mon-Sat) Inside the splendid 58m-high water tower (1912), this is a pleasant ground-floor café selling sandwiches, cakes and other snacks. Its outdoor tables are great for people-watching in summer.

Getting There & Away

Bus 146 runs every half-hour or so between Malmö and Trelleborg's bus station, some 500m inland from the ferry terminals. Bus 165 runs frequently Monday to Friday (four services Saturday and Sunday) from Lund. See p180 for bus travel from Ystad.

For details of international trains from Malmö to Berlin via Trelleborg, see p327.

Scandlines (☎ 650 00; www.scandlines.se) ferries connect Trelleborg to Sassnitz (five daily) and Rostock (two or three daily). **TT-Line** (☎ 562 00; www.ttline.com) ferries and catamarans shuttle between Trelleborg and Travemünde three to five times daily, and between Trelleborg and Rostock up to three times daily. Buy tickets inside the building housing the tourist office (Hamngatan 9). See p329 for full details.

SMYGEHUK

☎ 0410

Thanks to the power of geography – it's Sweden's most southerly point (latitude 55°20'3") – tiny Smygehuk has become something of a tourist magnet, even though its attractions are little, laid-back and low-key.

To the east of the harbour is a summer **tourist office** (☎ 240 53; Jun-Aug) and a café. They're inside **Köpmansmagasinet**, a renovated 19th-century warehouse with local exhibitions of handicrafts and art. Nearby is a huge 19th-century **lime kiln**, evidence of the bygone lime industry; it closed in 1954.

To the west of the harbour, you can scramble to the top of the now-defunct **lighthouse** (17m), dating from 1883, and visit the tiny maritime museum inside **Captain Brinck's Cabin** (admission free; summer). Beware that the opening hours can be are erratic. The lighthouse is managed by the hostel warden, and she opens it if/when she feels like it. There's no admission cost, but donations are vital for its upkeep. Captain Brink's Cabin is run by a pleasant old boy – but when I went, the cabin door was locked, and there was a note stuck on it telling visitors to yell over the wall for him as he was dozing in his garden!

There's a pretty **coastal path**, with good sea views and prolific bird life.

STF Vandrarhem Smygehuk (245 83; info@smygehukhostel.com; dm Skr150; Feb-Nov; P) This is a comfortable, well-equipped hostel in the old lighthouse keeper's residence, next to the lighthouse. You must book beforehand outside of the high season.

There are a few basic eating options at the harbour, including a fast-food kiosk and a fish smokehouse.

The Trelleborg to Ystad bus service (see p180) will take you to Smygehuk.

YSTAD

0411 / pop 26,898

Rambling cobbled streets, evocative street names, and more than 300 half-timbered houses remain in this very picturesque medieval town. It's also the setting for Henning Mankell's best-selling Inspector Wallander crime thrillers, which adds a certain frisson for fans! Another unusual tourist attraction is the annual three-day Military Tattoo in August: rattling drums and military marching create a light-and-sound spectacular.

Ystad was Sweden's window to Europe from the 17th to the mid-19th century, with new ideas and inventions – the first car, bank and hotel – arriving here first. Now the town is a terminal for ferries to Bornholm and Poland, but the port's transitory feel doesn't spread to the rest of Ystad: settle in for a few days to see all the sights.

Information

Banks, ATMs and other services are along Hamngatan.

Forex Cat terminal (8am-6.30pm Mon-Fri, 8am-3pm Sat); Ferry terminal (8am-9.30pm Mon-Fri, 10am-9.30pm Sat & Sun) Money exchange.

Futurezone Internetcafé (106 99; Jennygatan 3; per hr Skr28; 10am-midnight) Internet access.

Library (Surbrunnsvägen 12; 11am-7pm Mon-Thu, 11am-5pm Fri, 10am-2pm Sat) With free Internet access.

Paperback Store (734 14; Stora Östergatan 27) Friendly bookshop selling Henning Mankell's books in English.

Tourist office (57 76 81; www.visitystad.com; St Knuts Torg; 9am-7pm Mon-Fri, 10am-6pm Sat & Sun mid-Jun–mid-Aug, 9am-5pm Mon-Fri rest of yr, plus 11am-2pm Sat mid-May–mid-Jun & late Aug–late Sep) Just opposite the train station.

Sights

Ystad's half-timbered houses are scattered liberally round town, especially on Stora Östergatan. Most are from the latter half of the 18th century, but the façade of the beautiful **Änglahuset** on Stora Norregatan dates from around 1630.

Don't miss the **Sankta Maria Kyrka** (Stortorget; 10am-6pm Jun-Aug, 10am-4pm Sep-May). Ever since 1250, a night watchman has blown his horn through the little window in the church clock-tower (every 15 minutes from 9.15pm to 3am). The watchman was traditionally beheaded if he fell asleep! Some of the interesting features inside include a baroque pulpit (carved in the 1620s) and the pews near the entrance for women who had recently given birth and hadn't yet been churched. **Latinskolan**, next to Sankta Maria Kyrka, is a late-15th-century brick building and is the oldest preserved school in Scandinavia.

Klostret i Ystad (57 72 86; St Petri Kyrkoplan; adult/under 16yr Skr40/free; 10am-5pm Tue-Fri, noon-4pm Sat & Sun Jun-Aug, noon-5pm Tue-Fri, noon-4pm Sat & Sun Sep-May), in the Middle Ages Franciscan monastery of Gråbrödraklostret, features local textiles and silverware, and there's a slide show. The monastery includes the 13th-century deconsecrated St Petri Kyrkan, now used for art exhibitions, which has around 80 gravestones from the 14th to 18th centuries. Included in the same ticket, and with the same opening hours, is the large **Ystads Konstmuseum** (57 72 85; adult/under 16yr Skr40/free), next door to the tourist office, which has a substantial collection of southern Swedish and Danish art.

Charlotte Berlins Museum (188 66; Dammgatan 23; adult/under 16yr Skr10/free; noon-5pm Mon-Fri,

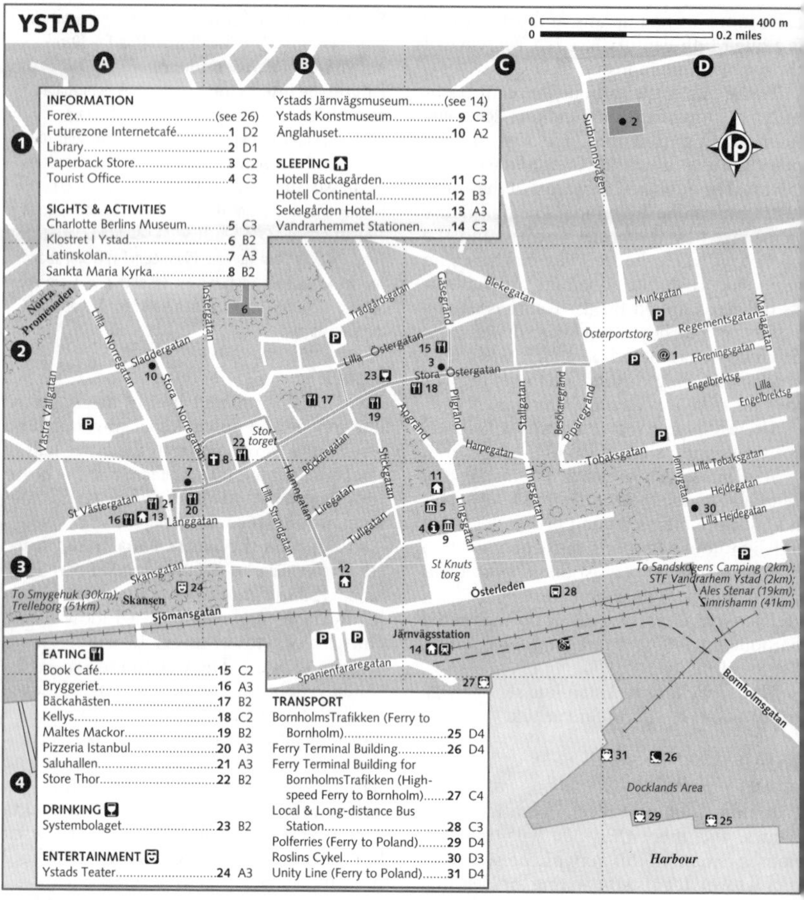

noon-4pm Sat & Sun Jun-Aug) is a small, late-19th-century middle-class home.

Model railway enthusiasts will enjoy **Ystads Järnvägsmuseum** (☎ 130 13; 🕑 11am-7pm Mon-Fri, 1-5pm Sun mid-Jun–mid-Aug), inside the train station, with historic items from the local railway.

Sleeping

Those with their own wheels can choose B&B and cabin options along the scenic coastal roads on either side of Ystad. The tourist office can arrange a B&B from Skr200 per person (plus a Skr40 fee).

STF Vandrarhem Ystad (☎ 665 66; kantarellen@turistlogi.se; Fritidsvägen 9; dm Skr140) In a charming sky-blue building, this pleasant beachside hostel has good facilities for travellers, including bike rental for covering the 2km into the town centre.

Vandrarhemmet Stationen (☎ 0708-57 79 95; ystad.stationen@home.se; dm from Skr185) More convenient is the central SVIF hostel, in the renovated railway building at Ystad train station.

Hotell Continental (☎ 137 00; info@hotelcontinental-ystad.se; Hamngatan 13; s/d from Skr1090/1190, discounted to Skr840/940; P 💻) On the site of the old customs house, this place claims to be Sweden's oldest hotel (it opened in 1829). It's full of old-world charm, with a grand chandeliered foyer and a marble staircase. Recently renovated rooms are fresh, modern and comfortable, and there's a decent bar and restaurant.

Sekelgården Hotel (☎ 739 00; info@sekelgarden.se; Långgatan 18; s/d from Skr695/895) This is a romantic family-run hotel in a magnificent half-timbered house (1793). The rooms take their inspiration from historical styles or people, and there's a sauna and very nice courtyard.

Hotell Bäckagården (☎ 198 48; www.backagarden.nu; Dammgatan 36; s/d from Skr590/720) This is a cosy guesthouse in a 17th-century home one block behind the tourist office. On fine mornings, you can eat breakfast in the lovely walled garden.

Sandskogens Camping (☎ 192 70; info@sandskogenscamping.se; low/high season sites Skr130/160, cabins from Skr380/440; May-Sep) This super-friendly (and super-busy) wooded site is 2km east of Ystad on road No 9 to Simrishamn, across the road from the beach and STF hostel. Bus 572 drives past from town.

Eating & Drinking

Store Thor (☎ 185 10; Stortorget; mains Skr100-200; closed Sun) For an upmarket treat, classy Store Thor is an amazing place in the arched cellar of the old town hall (1572). The décor, food and service are excellent; there are light meals such as tapas, spicy chicken and feta salad, or a gourmet burger, or a selection of grilled meats with a variety of sauces.

Bryggeriet (☎ 699 99; Långgatan 20; lunch Skr65, dinner mains Skr95-195) Another good recommendation is the unique Bryggeriet, a relaxed restaurant and pub in an old brewery. The sunny courtyard is an excellent spot to linger over a well-prepared meal and Ystad Färsköl, a beer brewed on the premises.

Kellys (☎ 123 70; Stora Östergatan 18; lunch Skr60, dinner mains Skr85-105) This place has an excellent international menu; main courses include fish, steaks and curries, with the added bonus of few dishes over Skr100.

Book Café (☎ 134 03; Gåsegränd; closed Sun & Mon) This charming café is well worth seeking out: inside is an inviting living room full of mismatched old furniture and books; outside there's a delightful courtyard. There's good foccacia, pastries and coffee on offer.

Bäckahästen (☎ 140 00; Lilla Östergatan 6; meals from Skr55) There's lots of garden seating at this old-fashioned place in a half-timbered house. Food includes sandwiches and baguettes, and light meals like salads and pastas.

Most budget eating places are on Stora Östergatan, the main pedestrian street, like busy **Maltes Mackor** (☎ 101 30; closed Sun) at No 12, with a great range of sandwiches and rolls. The **Saluhallen** (Stora Västergatan; 8am-9pm), behind the church, is a great central place to stock up on groceries. For alcohol, head to **Systembolaget** (Stora Östergatan 13).

Entertainment

The extraordinary **Ystads Teater** (☎ 57 71 99; Skansgatan; tickets around Skr300) has remained virtually unchanged since opening in 1894 and unusual operas are performed here in late June and July, and also in September and October. Contact the tourist office for details.

SOUTHERN SWEDEN

INSPECTOR WALLANDER'S YSTAD

Fans of crime thrillers probably already know the name of Henning Mankell (1948–), author of the best-selling Inspector Wallander series. The books (10 of which are available in English) are set in the small, seemingly peaceful town of Ystad. The gloomy inspector paces its medieval streets, solving gruesome murders through his meticulous police work…but at a cost to his personal life, which is slowly and painfully disintegrating. The first book is *Faceless Killers;* but it's generally agreed that Mankell really hits his stride in number four, *The Man Who Smiled.*

Exciting times are ahead for aficionados, with 13 new Wallander films, starring Krister Henriksson, either in the bag or being made. If you're in Ystad any time up until autumn 2006, it's quite likely that you'll stumble across a film set or two. You can also tour the places mentioned in Mankell's books, either on a self-guided walk, or with the volunteer fire brigade (Tuesday and Thursday July to mid-August) on a veteran fire engine! Contact Ystad tourist office for details.

Henning Mankell has left Sweden for Maputo, Mozambique. He's still writing, but devotes much of his time to his theatre company and AIDS education work. Find out more at www.henningmankell.com.

Getting There & Away

BOAT

There are daily crossings between Ystad and Swinoujscie by **Unity Line** (☎ 55 69 00; www.unityline.pl) and **Polferries** (☎ 040-12 17 00; www.polferries.se); see p328 for details. The ferry terminal in Ystad is within walking distance of the train station (drivers follow a more circuitous route).

Bornholmstrafikken (☎ 55 87 00; www.bornholmferries.dk) operate frequent ferries and catamarans between Ystad and Rønne, on the Danish island of Bornholm: see p328. Catamarans depart from and arrive at a new terminal directly behind the train station.

BUS

In Ystad, buses depart from outside the train station. To get to Trelleborg (Skr42, one hour), first take bus 303 to Skateholm then transfer to bus 183. The direct bus to Simrishamn (Skr42, one hour) via Löderup and Skillinge runs three to nine times daily. Bus 322 to Skillinge runs via Ales Stenar and Löderups Strandbad three times daily in summer.

SkåneExpressen bus 6 runs to Lund (Skr42, 1¼ hours, hourly weekdays, infrequently on weekends) and bus 4 runs three to nine times daily to Kristianstad (Skr60, 1¾ hours). Local train is the best way to get to Malmö.

TRAIN

There are Pågatågen trains running roughly every hour (fewer on weekends) to/from Malmö (Skr72, 50 minutes). Other local trains run up to 12 times daily to Simrishamn (Skr36, 40 minutes).

Getting Around

There are a handful of local bus services; all depart from outside the tourist office (St Knuts Torg). Try **Taxi Ystad** (☎ 720 00) for a taxi. For bike hire, contact **Roslins Cykel** (☎ 123 15; Jennygatan 11; per day mountain/road bike Skr40/65; 🕒 closed Sun).

AROUND YSTAD

Ales Stenar

Advertised as the Nordic Stonehenge, Ales Stenar has all the mystery of England's monument and none of the money-grabbing greed. This is Sweden's largest stone ship setting, and it's an intriguing attraction. The 67m-long oval of stones, placed in the shape of a boat, was probably constructed around AD 600: why, no-one knows. Limited excavations at the site have revealed no body; it's possible that this wasn't a grave but a ritual site, with built-in solar calendar (the 'stem' and 'stern' stones point towards the midsummer sunset and midwinter sunrise).

It's worth going there to speculate: the enigmatic ship is in the middle of a raised field with an uncannily low and level 360° horizon. However, the area does get swamped by visitors, particularly in summer. There's a tiny **shack** at Kåseberga harbour giving away information about the stones. The harbour car park is chaotic, though: the one just off the main road is better. From either place, the setting is a 1km walk.

Ales Stenar is always open and admission is free. The monument is 19km east of Ystad at Kåseberga, and badly served by public transport: bus 322 from Ystad runs three times daily in summer.

Löderups Strandbad

☎ 0411

With its long stretches of white-sand beaches, the Baltic resort of Löderups Strandbad, 4km east of Ales Stenar, is a decent place for lounging. It can get busy when the Swedish schools are on holiday.

Dag Hammarskjölds Backåkra (☎ 52 60 10; Löderup; adult/under 15yr Skr30/free; 🕒 noon-5pm Jun, 10am-6pm Jul & Aug), about 1km east of Löderups Strandbad, was a summer house acquired by the secretary-general of the UN in 1957. Hammarskjöld was killed in a mysterious plane crash in Zambia four years later; many of his unusual belongings and souvenirs were subsequently moved to this peaceful place to form a memorial museum. The old farmhouse is set in a **nature reserve** of sand dunes, heath and wildflower meadows.

STF Vandrarhem Backåkra (☎ 52 60 80; www.backakra.nu; dm Skr160; 🕒 mid-Apr–Oct; Ⓟ) Beside the main road, this helpful hostel has pleasing rooms, a great garden and bicycles for rent, plus it's within walking distance of the beach. Book ahead in summer

Löderups Strandbad Hotell (☎ 52 62 60; www.loderupsstrandbad.com; s/d high-season Skr620/845, low-season Skr515/740; Ⓟ) Near the camp site, this family hotel is a popular summer spot, with a sauna and restaurant. Cheaper rooms (without bathrooms) are available, and some great cabins, all with sea views (rented by the week only in high season; Skr6495).

Löderups Strandbads Camping (☎ 52 63 11; sites Skr140, cabins from Skr500; ⌚ Apr-Sep) On the edge of the Hagestad Nature Reserve, this is a pleasant spot in a pine forest and next to the beach.

Getting There & Away

See opposite for bus details from Ystad.

ÖSTERLEN

☎ 0414 / pop 19,400

Artists appreciate the soft light of Österlen and have moved here en masse. It's an alluring area full of waving wheat fields, tiny fishing villages and glorious apple orchards, and is well worth exploring if you want a taste of the Swedish countryside. Everything moves at a slow, seductive speed: cycling is the best way of fitting in with the tempo.

Simrishamn

Summer holidaymakers mill around Simrishamn harbour, idly eating ice cream or waiting for the ferry to the Danish island of Bornholm. The rather quaint pastel-coloured houses on **Lilla Norregatan** are worth a look, as is nearby **St Nikolai Kyrka**.

The **tourist office** (☎ 81 98 00; www.turistbyra.simrishamn.se; Tullhusgatan 2; ⌚ 9am-8pm Mon-Fri, 10am-8pm Sat, 11am-8pm Sun Jun–mid-Aug, 9am-5pm Mon-Fri rest of yr) has information on the whole of Österlen. For Internet access, go to P&Ms Coffeehouse (right). Banks and other services are along Storgatan.

SLEEPING & EATING

STF Vandrarhem Simrishamn (☎ 105 40; Christian Barnekowsgatan 10C; dm Skr190) Pick up a map before setting off – this place is quite well hidden, near the town hospital. It's worth seeking out, however; it offers spotless, colourful, modern accommodation with bathroom and TV in every room. Outside June to August, bookings are vital.

Maritim Krog & Hotell (☎ 41 13 60; info@maritim.nu; Hamngatan 31; s/d from Skr900/1100, lunch Skr80, mains Skr170-210) The old blue building by the harbour is a wonderful boutique hotel with very stylish décor (ask for the Herring Room, the pick of the rooms, with balcony and sea views). Also on the premises is an excellent restaurant: unsurprisingly it specialises in creative fish dishes.

Tobisviks Camping (☎ 41 27 78; sites Skr180, cabins from Skr500; ♿) By the beach 2km north of the town centre, this serviceable site is attached to a sports centre and swimming pool.

Kamskogs Krog (☎ 143 48; www.kamskogskrog.se; Storgatan 3; lunch Skr75, dinner mains Skr175-195; ⌚ noon-10pm Jul & Aug, shorter hr rest of yr) Another restaurant putting the emphasis on friendly service, local ingredients and prime preparation is this *krog*, with dishes like seafood casserole, or cod in cider garnished with rosemary. The outside seats on pedestrianised Storgatan are perfect for people-watching.

P&M's Coffeehouse (☎ 149 24; Stortorget 2; ⌚ 10am-9pm summer, shorter hr rest of yr) This huge barn of a café has changing artwork on the walls and an Internet café (per 30 minutes Skr15) hidden in the basement.

GETTING THERE & AROUND

BornholmExpress (☎ 107 00; www.bornholmexpress.se; return ticket adult/under 14yr Skr250/125) started up a new ferry service in 2005 between Simrishamn and Allinge (on the Danish island of Bornholm), running in July only.

SkåneExpressen bus 3 runs every hour or two on weekdays (infrequently on weekends) from Simrishamn (train station) to Kristianstad via Kivik (but it doesn't stop at the Stenshuvud National Park access road). Bus 5 runs every hour or two to Lund on weekdays (infrequently on weekends). See also opposite.

Österlensfågeln is a minibus service that departs from the train station for local destinations (including Kivik, Glimmingehus and Skillinge) every hour or two between 9am and midnight, in July only (Skr20 for a single trip, or Skr60 for a day pass).

Local trains run up to 12 times daily from Simrishamn to Ystad (Skr36, 40 minutes), with connections from Ystad on to Malmö and Lund.

Taxi Österlen (☎ 177 77) can help you get around. **Österlens Cykel & Motor** (☎ 177 44; Stenbocksgatan; per day from Skr50; ⌚ closed Sun), is in the *godsmagasinet* (goods depot) at the train station.

Glimmingehus & Skillinge

The imposing, five-storey **Glimmingehus** (Glimminge castle; ☎ 186 20; adult/7-18yr Skr50/30; ⌚ 10am-

SOUTHERN SWEDEN

6pm Jun-Aug, 11am-4pm Apr, May & Sep), about 5km inland, is the main attraction in these parts. It's scarcely been tinkered with since it was built (some time in the early 1500s), making it one of the best-preserved medieval castles you'll find, with an all-encompassing moat and 11 different ghosts! Guided tours in English are at 2pm daily from July to mid-September (at 2pm weekends in May, June and August). In summer, there's a programme of medieval events and activities: contact the castle for details. The café-restaurant opens for lunch (Skr60-95) between mid-May and August.

The closest settlement to the castle is Skillinge, a reasonably active fishing village. There are a couple of restaurants there, and a fish smokehouse. For lodgings, try picture-perfect **Sjöbacka** (☎ 301 66; info@sjobacka.nu; d from Skr700), 700m west of Skillinge, which offers B&B in a traditional Scanian farmhouse.

For bus information see p180 and p181.

Kivik

Rosy apples and burial cists make a pair of strange but interesting attractions in small, sleepy Kivik (north of Simrishamn).

Kiviksgraven (Kungagraven; ☎ 703 37; admission free; 10am-6pm mid-May–Aug) is Sweden's largest Bronze Age grave, from around 1000 BC. It's an extraordinary shield-like cairn, about 75m in diameter, which used to contain a burial cist and eight engraved slabs. What you see inside today are replicas, as the tomb was looted in the 18th century. There are guided tours in English (at 1.30pm and 3.30pm July to mid-August), which leave from the cinnamon-scented Café Sågmöllan across the stream.

You've 'done' the French vineyards, now how about something new: **Kiviks Musteri** (☎ 719 00; www.kiviksmusteri.se in Swedish; Apr-Sep) is an apple orchard that opens to the public. Visit **Äpplets Hus** (adult/under 12yr Skr40/free), a museum devoted to the myths, history, cultivation and artistry of apples; buy apple juice, cider and apple brandy from the well-stocked shop; or sample the fairly apple-free menu at the restaurant. Kiviks Musteri is a few (signposted) kilometres out of town.

STF Vandrarhem Kivik (☎ 711 95; Tittutvägen; dm Skr195; Mar-Oct) Back in town, this hostel has comfortable accommodation with some sea views, and bikes for rent. The same family also run **STF Vandrarhem Hanöbris** (☎ 700 50; Eliselundsvägen 6; dm Skr190; mid-Jun–mid-Aug) in a distinctive little building higher up the town.

For bus information see p181.

Stenshuvud National Park

Just south of Kivik is this **national park** (www.stenshuvud.se), made up of woodland, marshes, sandy beaches and high headland. Among its more unusual plants and animals are orchids, dormice and tree frogs. There are several fine walks in the area, including the hike up to a 6th-century ruined hill fort. The long-distance path **Skåneleden** (www.skaneleden.org) also runs through the park, along the coast; the best section is from Vik to Kivik (two or three hours).

The **Naturum** (visitor centre; ☎ 708 82; 11am-6pm Jun-Aug, 11am-4pm Sep-May) is 2.5km from the main road. You can arrange a 1½-hour guided tour of the park there, led by its knowledgeable rangers. Tours leave at 10am daily from July to mid-August (Sundays only mid-April to mid-Jun and September to mid-October).

Pretty **Kaffestugan Annorlunda** (☎ 242 86), on the road to the Naturum, serves meals and snacks daily from mid-May to August.

KRISTIANSTAD

☎ 044 / pop 75,592

Kristianstad (pronounced something like krich-*worn*-sta) has a beautiful cathedral and some fine 18th- and 19th-century buildings (amongst the 1970s dross), but a strangely scruffy air overall.

Known as the most Danish town in Sweden, Kristianstad's construction was ordered by the Danish King Christian IV in 1614. Its rectangular street network still follows the first town plan, although the original walls and bastions have long gone. Surprisingly, today's Kristianstad is the region's administrative and political centre, even though it's less than a third the size of Malmö. It's also a major transport hub.

Information

Lilla Torg has banks and ATMs, and the large Domus shopping centre contains the post office. **Kristianstadsdagarna** is an annual, week-long festival, held in early July. The events (in Tivoliparken) include music, dance and a jazz festival.

Game City (☎ 21 27 65; Östra Storgatan 11; per hr Skr15; noon-midnight) Internet access.

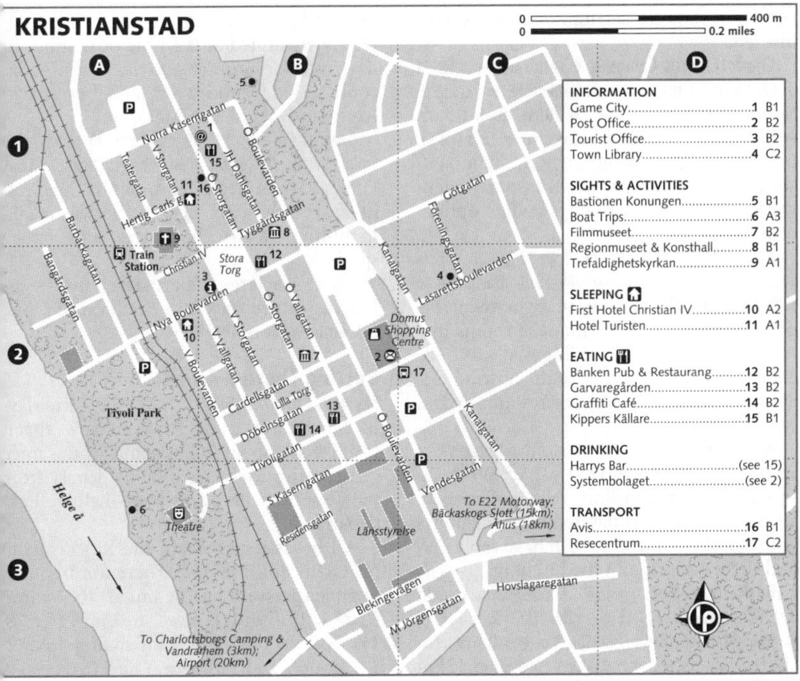

Library (Föreningsgatan 4; 10am-7pm Mon-Fri yr ound, 10am-2pm Sat Jun-Aug, 11am-3pm Sat Sep-May) Vith free Internet access.

Tourist office (☎ 13 53 35; www.kristianstad.se; Stora Torg; 10am-7pm Mon-Fri, 10am-3pm Sat, 10am-2pm Sun mid-Jun–mid-Aug, 10am-5pm Mon-Fri mid-Aug–mid-Jun)

Sights & Activities

Dne of the best Renaissance churches in Scandinavia, **Trefaldighetskyrkan** (Västra Storgatan 5; 8am-4pm) was completed in 1628 when Skåne was still under Danish control. The light-filled interior still has many of its original fittings, including wonderfully carved oak pews, and an ornate marble and alabaster pulpit.

Riverside **Tivoli Park** is a great place for a stroll on summer evenings, or for a waffle or two at the pretty café. For a walking tour round 23 of the town's stately **buildings** (including the Renaissance-style town hall and the restored rampart Bastinonen Konungen), pick up the good free English brochure *Kristianstad at your own pace* from the tourist office.

The **Regionmuseet & Konsthall** (☎ 13 52 45; Stora Torg; admission free; 11am-5pm Jun-Aug, noon-5pm Tue-Sun Sep-May) was originally intended as a palace, but the building ended up being used as an arsenal. It was converted to a museum in 1957, and now contains local history exhibits and art, handicrafts and silverware displays. The café here is perfect for lunch

Swedish film-making began in Kristianstad, so it's appropriate that **Filmmuseet** (☎ 13 57 29; Östra Storgatan 53; admission free; 1-4pm Tue-Fri, noon-5pm Sun Jun-Aug), Sweden's only film museum, is based here.

Naturens Bästa (☎ 61 98 40; www.flodbaten.se) run two-hour **boat trips** (adult/child/family Skr90/50/240) into Kristianstad's unique wetland area, three times daily between May and the middle of September. However, there are several weeks when the boats *don't* run: contact the company or the tourist office to check departures and book tickets.

Sleeping & Eating

The tourist office can arrange private rooms from Skr150 per person plus a Skr40 fee;

otherwise budget accommodation is very limited.

Charlottsborgs Camping & Vandrarhem (☎ 21 07 67; charlottsborg@swipnet.se; Slättängsvägen 98; sites & hostel beds Skr135, cabins from Skr270) is about 3km southwest of the centre (take bus 22 or 23), but we found it to be dirty and the staff rude. If you have private transport, Bäckaskog Slott is a much better budget option; or head for Åhus (see right).

First Hotel Christian IV (☎ 12 63 00; Västra Boulevarden 15; s/d from Skr1260/1510, discounted to Skr660/860; P 💻) The best place in town, this grand hotel offers fine, modern rooms in a turn-of-the-century building that was once a bank. One of the bank vaults now houses a wine cellar; there's also a restaurant and sauna here.

Hotel Turisten (☎ 12 61 50; info@turisten.se; Västra Storgatan 17; s/d Skr795/995, discounted to Skr550/750; 💻) Friendly family-run Turisten has expanded, with 10 new rooms painted in pale colours with smart oak furniture. All have cable TV, and there's a sauna in the building.

Bäckaskogs Slott (☎ 530 20; info@backaskogslott.se; Barumsvägen 113, Kiaby; dm Skr250, s/d from Skr600/900, discounted to Skr550/780; P) This is a charming castle set between two lakes 15km northeast of Kristianstad. It was originally built as a monastery in the mid-13th century and is an impressive place – hostel and hotel accommodation is available in various wings and outhouses. All prices include breakfast, and there's also a moderately priced restaurant. The bus connections aren't great – there are three buses (Skr18, 20 minutes) on weekdays from Kristianstad Resecentrum.

Kippers Källare (☎ 10 62 00; Östra Storgatan 9; mains Skr180-250; 🕓 closed Sun & Mon summer) In a 17th-century arched cellar, this is the most atmospheric restaurant in town. Main courses include vegetarian options. The popular Harrys Bar is on the same premises.

Garvaregården (☎ 21 35 00; Tivoligatan 9; lunch Skr60, meals Skr140-190) This appealing place offers an interesting menu ranging from simple pasta dishes to the super-rich house speciality of lobster-stuffed steak with gorgonzola sauce and potatoes gratin. Enjoy your food in the great outdoor dining area, underneath a crooked 17th-century gallery.

Banken Pub & Restaurang (☎ 10 20 23; Stora Torg; bar meals Skr40-100; 🕓 closed Sun-Tue summer) In an old bank, this restaurant was being completely renovated at the time of writing. Its new interior promises to be cutting-edge cool, serving good beers and bar snacks (club sandwiches, Tex-Mex).

Graffiti Café (☎ 12 59 90; Västra Storgatan; meals around Skr50; 🕓 10am-6.30pm Mon-Fri, 10am-2pm Sat, 11am-5pm Sun) A healthier option is the Graffiti franchise, with excellent budget meals including salads, baguettes and baked spuds.

There's a large supermarket inside the Domus centre on Östra Boulevarden, and **Systembolaget** is also here.

Getting There & Around

Skyways (☎ 0771-95 95 00) flies direct most days to Stockholm from Kristianstad's **airport** (☎ 23 88 50), about 20km south of the town centre. Airport buses (Skr70) depart from the Resecentrum 50 minutes before flight departures.

All buses depart from the Resecentrum on Östra Boulevarden. There are frequent SkåneExpressen buses: bus 1 to Malmö (Skr84, 1½ hours), bus 2 to Lund (Skr78, 1½ hours), bus 3 to Simrishamn (Skr42, 1¼ hours) and bus 4 to Ystad (Skr60, 1½ hours); the latter two services run infrequently on weekends. There are also two to five departures daily to Helsingborg on bus 8. **Svenska Buss** (☎ 0771-67 67 67; www.svenskabuss.se) runs to Malmö, Karlskrona, Kalmar and Stockholm several times weekly.

The train station is across town from the Resecentrum. Trains run daily to Lund (Skr84, one hour) and Malmö (Skr84, 1¼ hours), and many services continue on to Copenhagen (Skr150, two hours). Kustpilen trains run every hour or two to Malmö (with connections at Hässleholm for Helsingborg or Stockholm).

Taxi Kristianstad (☎ 24 62 46) can help you get around. Central car hire is available from **Avis** (☎ 10 30 20; Östra Storgatan 10).

ÅHUS

☎ 044

The small coastal town of Åhus (about 18km southeast of Kristianstad) is a popular summer spot thanks to its long sandy **beach**. The area is also known for its **eels**: the Eel Coast runs south from Åhus, and this delicacy is served up boiled, fried, smoked, grilled or cooked on a bed of straw at restaurants and at autumn Eel Feasts throughout the region.

There's a small **tourist office** (☎ 13 47 77; touristinfo.ahus@kristianstad.se; Järnvägsgatan 7; 🕑 10am-7pm Mon-Fri, 9am-6pm Sat, 10am-2pm Sun mid-Jun–mid-Aug, 10am-5pm mid-Aug–mid-Jun). All the facilities you'll need (bank, supermarket etc) are nearby.

Åhus is the home town of **Absolut Vodka**, and about half a million bottles are produced here every day. The distillery is open to the public on rare occasions in the summer: ask the tourist office for details.

Naturens Bästa (see p183) also run their **boat trips** (adult/child/family Skr60/40/170) from Åhus.

STF Vandrarhem Åhus (☎ 24 85 35; info@cigarrkungenshus.se; Stavgatan 3; dm Skr160-200, hostel s/d from Skr200/320, B&B d from Skr500) Very close to the harbour, this youth hostel/B&B is based in a 19th-century cigar factory. Rooms are newly renovated, and in July there's a tiny waffle hut in the garden!

There are several good dining possibilities down by the harbour.

Bus 551 runs two or three times an hour between Kristianstad and Åhus (Skr24, 24 minutes); it drops you off at the tourist office.

HELSINGBORG

☎ 042 / pop 121,179

Fourteen million passengers per year pass through Helsingborg on their way to/from Denmark: many of them see very little of the town, which is a proper shame. Away from the port and gloomy underground travel centre, there are pedestrian streets and half-timbered houses, a jazzy new waterside art gallery and restaurants, and the ruins of a dramatic castle perched on high.

Helsingborg's position on the Öresund gave it vital strategic importance during the many Swedish–Danish wars, and it was battled over and battered down with depressing regularity. In 1709, the Danes invaded Skåne but were finally defeated the following year in a battle just outside Helsingborg.

Information

First Stop Sweden (☎ 10 41 30; www.firststopsweden.com; Bredgatan 2; 🕑 9am-8pm Mon-Fri, 9am-5pm Sat & Sun Jul & Aug, 9am-6pm Mon-Fri, 9am-2pm Sat & Sun Jun, 8am-5pm Mon-Fri Sep-May) Near the car-ferry ticket booths; dispenses tourist information on the whole country and has an X-Change currency exchange counter.

Knutpunkten complex At the seafront; for currency exchange as well as banks and ATMs. There are also left-luggage lockers here. More banks are on Stortorget.

Library (Stadsbibliotek; Stadsparken) Bring ID to use the free Internet service.

Post office (Stortorget)

Tourist office (☎ 10 43 50; www.helsingborg.se; Rådhuset, Stortorget; 🕑 9am-8pm Mon-Fri, 9am-5pm Sat & 10am-5pm Sun mid-Jun–Aug, 10am-6pm Mon-Fri, 10am-2pm Sat Sep–mid-Jun & 10am-2pm Sun in May)

Sights

TOWN CENTRE

Dramatic steps and archways lead up from Stortorget to the square tower **Kärnan** (☎ 10 59 91; adult/under 16yr Skr20/10; 🕑 11am-7pm Jun-Aug, closed Mon rest of yr), all that remains of the medieval castle. The castle became Swedish property during the 17th-century Danish–Swedish war, and was mostly demolished once the fighting stopped. The tower was restored from dereliction in 1894, and the view from the top (34m) is excellent.

The eye-catching **Dunkers Kulturhus** (☎ 10 74 00; www.dunkerskulturhus.com; Kungsgatan 11; admission adult/under 17yr Skr70/free; 🕑 11am-6pm, to 10pm Tue & Thu), just north of the transport terminals, opened in 2002 and houses a good town museum and temporary art displays (admission includes entry to both), plus a concert hall, restaurant and café. It was created by Danish architect Kim Utzon, son of Sydney Opera House's designer.

Take a stroll along **Norra Hamnen** (the North Harbour) from here to admire the sleek and attractive apartment buildings and restaurant-bars, which are all part of a very successful harbour-redevelopment project.

In the old town, the 15th-century Gothic brick **Mariakyrkan** (☎ 37 28 30; Mariatorget; 🕑 8am-6pm Mon-Fri, 9am-6pm Sat & Sun) has a magnificent interior, including a triptych from 1450 and an ornate pulpit. The outrageous **Rådhuset** (town hall; Stortorget) was completed in 1897 in neo-Gothic style and contains stained-glass scenes illustrating Helsingborg's history.

There are all kinds of small and specialist museums (about the fire brigade, medical

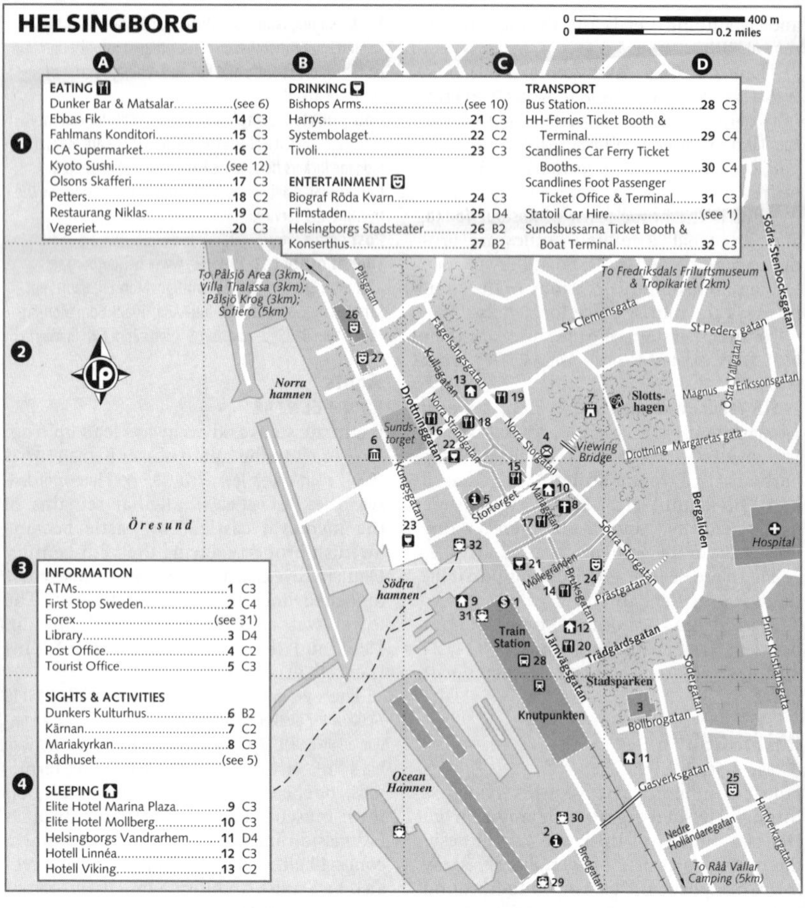

history, sport, schools, military defence) in town: contact the tourist office for details.

FREDRIKSDAL & SOFIERO

Just 2km northeast of the centre is the Fredriksdal area, well worth a visit. Take bus 1 or 7 to the Zoégas bus stop.

One of Sweden's best open-air museums is **Fredriksdals Friluftsmuseum** (☎ 10 45 00; www.fredriksdal.helsingborg.se; off Hävertgatan; adult/under 16yr Skr60/free; 🕑 10am-7.30pm Jun-Aug, 10am-6pm Apr, May & Sep, 11am-4pm Oct-Mar). It's based around an 18th-century manor house, with a street of old houses, children's farm, graphics museum, and extensive grounds. Wildflowers from the area grow in the beautiful botanic gardens, and there's also a grand summer programme of activities and performances in the French baroque open-air theatre. Check the website for current events.

Tropikariet (☎ 13 00 35; Hävertgatan 21; adult/4-12yr Skr60/30; 🕑 11am-4pm Tue-Sun) is a semizoo, with reptile house, aquarium, tiny monkeys and other animals, housed in environments that attempt to recreate their natural habitats. It's just opposite the entrance to Fredriksdal museum.

About 5km north of the town centre (bus 219), **Sofiero** (☎ 13 74 00; www.sofiero.helsingborg.se; Sofierovägen; adult/under 16yr Skr80/free; 🕑 11am-5pm mid-Apr–Sep, to 6pm Jun-Aug) is an impressive former royal summer residence and park with great rhododendrons (best seen when in full bloom in May and June).

SOUTHERN SWEDEN

Sleeping

CAMPING, HOSTELS & PRIVATE ROOMS

The tourist office can organise private rooms for as little as Skr180 per person (without breakfast), but charges a booking fee.

Helsingborgs Vandrarhem (☎ 14 58 50; info@hbgturist.com; Järnvägsgatan 39; dm from Skr185) The only central hostel, this is an excellent modern choice about 200m from Knutpunkten. Reception opens, rather unusually, between 3pm and 5pm.

Villa Thalassa (☎ 38 06 60; www.villathalassa.com; Dag Hammarskjöldsväg; dm from Skr180, d from Skr420; P) This SVIF place is a lovely early-20th-century villa situated in beautiful gardens. Hostel accommodation is in huts, but the hotel-standard rooms (with or without private bathroom) are a cut above if your budget will stretch. The villa is 3km north of the city centre in the Pålsjö area. Bus 219 stops 500m short, at the Pålsjöbaden bus stop.

Råå Vallar Camping (☎ 10 76 80; helsingborg.camping@telia.com; Kustgatan; low/high season sites Skr180/230, cabins Skr550/950; Apr-Oct) About 5km south of the city centre, by Öresund, this is a huge, well-equipped camping ground, with a shop, café and sandy beach. Take bus 1 from the town hall.

HOTELS

Hotell Linnéa (☎ 37 24 00; www.hotell-linnea.se; Prästgatan 4; s/d from Skr935/1085, discounted to Skr740/845) The charming, central Linnéa has friendly management and pretty, personal rooms with wooden floors, crisp bedspreads and antique furniture. It's the pick of the town's midrange offerings.

Hotell Viking (☎ 14 44 20; hotell.viking@helsingborg.se; Fågelsångsgatan 1; s/d from Skr965/1235, discounted to Skr695/895; P) Another inviting hotel, the well-established Viking is on an old and peaceful street but still nicely central. The smart rooms are kept up-to-date: at the time of research Room 15 (Skr1635, discounted to Skr1245) was the flashiest, with its own computer, leather recliners and whirlpool massage bath.

Elite Hotel Mollberg (☎ 37 37 00; mollberg.helsingborg@elite.se; Stortorget 18; s/d from Skr1195/1295, discounted to Skr720/780; P) The main square is dominated by this 19th-century building with its wedding-cake exterior. An understated elegance underpins the rooms, there are excellent facilities, and the restaurant here is one of the best in town.

Elite Hotel Marina Plaza (☎ 19 21 00; reservations.marinaplaza@elite.se; Kungstorget 6; s/d Skr1225/1395, discounted to Skr730/790; P) The Mollberg's sister establishment has modern, luxurious rooms right by the harbour, with a number of restaurants and bars on the premises. You can pay a little extra for sea views.

Eating

Helsingborg has a great selection of restaurants, although a fair few close on Sundays. It's also has a great selection of cafés

Restaurang Niklas (☎ 28 00 50; www.niklas.se; Norra Storgatan 16; mains Skr195-245, 7-course menu Skr795; 6pm-1am Mon-Sat) Niklas is one of Sweden's top TV chefs; he opened his restaurant here in 2000, and it's now a highly feted institution. The menu is influenced by classic Provençale cookery, but the gourmet touches are all his own. If you're going to treat yourself, make it here: just look for the giant iron spoon!

Dunker Bar & Matsalar (☎ 32 29 95; Kungsgatan 11; lunch Skr89, light meals Skr80-140, dinner mains Skr240-300) At the Kulturhus, this is an excellent option: good views, a light and airy interior, and tasty menu items. The restaurant is another gourmet wonder, but there's a cheaper bistro and a good weekend brunch.

Pålsjö Krog (☎ 14 97 30; Drottninggatan 151; mains Skr150-210; from 11.30am Mon-Sat) Near Villa Thalassa hostel, this is a great old seaside inn that has been renovated and turned into an elegant restaurant. There's a lovely veranda and outdoor seating, plus good food choices with the emphasis on fish and seafood.

Olsons Skafferi (☎ 14 07 80; Mariagatan 6; lunch Skr65; 10am-10.30pm Mon-Sat) Olsons is a super little spot, with outdoor seating on the pedestrian square right in front of Mariakyrkan. It doubles as an Italian deli and café, with a rustic look, cheery striped tablecloths and piles of pasta. It's particularly popular at lunchtime.

Vegeriet (☎ 24 03 03; Järnvägsgatan 25; lunch around Skr65; closed Sun) Veggies will rejoice at this place, an appealing veggie café-restaurant with dishes like quiche, lasagne, tortilla and stir-fries; there are also vegan options. However, it usually closes for a month in summer.

Ebbas Fik (☎ 28 14 40; Bruksgatan 20; 9am-6pm Mon-Fri, 9am-4pm Sat) Ebbas is the most fantastic

1950s retro café, complete with jukebox, quiffs and hamburgers made to Elvis's recipe. The extensive café menu also includes (huge) sandwiches, baked potatoes and crazy cakes and buns. It's just perfect – absolutely don't miss it.

Fahlmans Konditori (☎ 21 30 60; Stortorget 11; 🕑 8am-6pm Mon-Fri, 8am-4pm Sat, 11am-5pm Sun) Those with a hatred of rock 'n' roll could turn to Fahlmans, the most traditional of the town's cafés. It's been selling sandwiches and pastries to its customers in genteel surrounds since 1914.

The quickest snacks and a good variety of restaurants are found upstairs in the extensive Knutpunkten complex. Two excellent offerings in the city centre are **Kyoto Sushi** (☎ 12 57 13; Prästgatan 6; lunch Skr59), with a good-value lunch special of nine pieces of sushi and miso soup; and **Petters** (Kullagatan; meals from Skr29), selling hot dogs, baguettes and burgers.

ICA (Drottninggatan 48) is the best centrally-located supermarket.

Drinking

There are lots of good pubs and bars around town, including **Harrys** (☎ 13 91 91; Järnvägsgatan 7) and the **Bishops Arms** (☎ 37 37 77; Södra Storgatan 2), both English-style pubs with a range of beers and comprehensive food menus.

There's a **Systembolaget** on Hästmöllegränd.

Entertainment

Helsingborgs Stadsteater (☎ 10 68 10; Karl Johans gata 1) has regular drama performances, and its neighbour, the **Konserthus** (☎ 10 43 50; Drottninggatan 19), regularly plays host to Helsingborg's Symphony Orchestra. Information and tickets are available from the tourist office.

The **Tivoli** (☎ 18 71 71; Kungsgatan 1) is a popular nightclub with a younger crowd, and there's sometimes live music.

Central **Biograf Röda Kvarn** (☎ 14 50 90; Karlsgatan 7) is Helsingborg's oldest cinema. It shows mostly independent films, but closes from mid-June to mid-August. For mainstream efforts, try the eight-screen **Filmstaden** (Södergatan 19).

Getting There & Away

The main transport centre is the large, waterfront Knutpunkten complex.

BOAT

Knutpunkten is the terminal for the frequent **Scandlines** (☎ 18 63 00; www.scandlines.se) car ferry to Helsingør (adult Skr22, car plus nine people Skr300, free with rail passes). Across the inner harbour, **Sundsbussarna** (☎ 21 60 60) has a terminal with a passenger-only ferry to Helsingør every 30 minutes in summer (Skr22, free with rail passes). There's also a frequent **HH-Ferries** (☎ 19 80 00; www.hhferries.se) service to Helsingør (adult Skr22, car plus nine people Skr265, rail passes not valid).

DFDS Seaways (☎ 24 10 00; www.dfdsseaways.com) runs a ferry every evening to Oslo (from Skr898) from the Sunds terminal. See p329 for more details.

BUS

The bus terminal is at ground level in Knutpunkten. Regional Skånetrafiken buses dominate (see respective destinations for details), but long-distance services are offered by **Swebus Express** (☎ 0200-21 82 18; www.swebusexpress.se), **Svenska Buss** (☎ 0771-67 67 67; www.svenskabuss.se) and **Säfflebussen** (☎ 0771-15 15 15; www.safflebussen.se).

All three companies offer services north to Halmstad and Göteborg (Swebus Express and Säfflebussen services continue to Oslo), and Swebus Express and Svenska Buss operate south to Malmö. Swebus Express and Säfflebussen also run services northeast to Stockholm via Jönköping. Peak fares to Stockholm cost around Skr400 (eight hours), to Göteborg Skr200 (three hours), and to Oslo Skr350 (seven hours).

TRAIN

Underground platforms in Knutpunkten serve both SJ and Pågatågen Kustpilen trains, which depart daily for Stockholm (Skr1081, five hours), Göteborg (Skr280, 2½ to three hours), nearby towns including Lund (Skr72), Malmö (Skr84), Kristianstad (Skr84) and Halmstad (Skr95) as well as Copenhagen and Olso.

Getting Around

Town buses cost Skr15 and run from Rådhuset (town hall). **Bike hire** (per day/week Skr125/500) is available at the tourist office. Call **Taxi Helsingborg** (☎ 18 02 00) for cabs. To hire a car, contact **Statoil** (☎ 18 03 50; Knutpunkten).

(Continued on page 197)

JONATHAN SMITH

Riddarholmen and Riddarholmskyrkan (p74), Stockholm

Historiska Museet (p75), Central Stockholm

JONATHAN SMITH

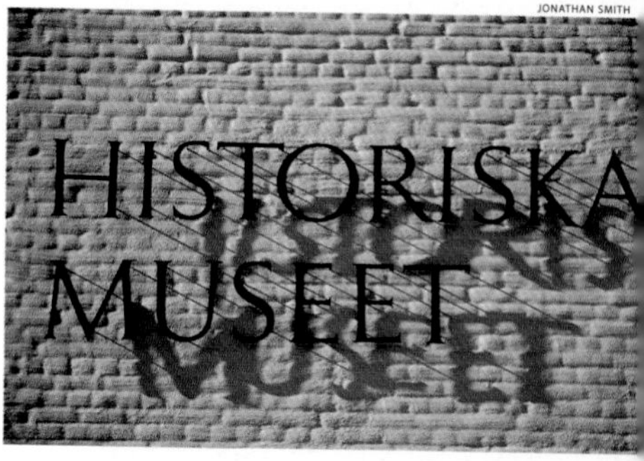

Österlånggatan in Gamla Stan (p72)

JONATHAN SMITH

GRAEME CORNWALLIS

Waterfront houses in Västergötland (p225)

NEIL SETCHFIELD

Patrons at an outdoor café in Göteborg (p200)

Läckö Slott (p227), Lidköping Västergötland

GRAEME CORNWALLIS

Raising the oars as part of midsummer celebrations before church, Rättvik (p264)

ANDERS BLOMQVIST

GRAEME CORNWALLIS

Typical harbour on Lake Mälaren (p246), Västmanland

Skier at Sälen (p268), Dalarna

CHRISTIAN ASLUND

Dalahäst (Dala horse) being painted, Rättvik (p267), Dalarna

ANDERS BLOMQVIST

GRAEME CORNWALLIS

Lake Laitaure, Sarek National Park (p305), Lappland

CHRISTER FREDRIKSSON

Reindeer bull running through wilderness, Lappland (p297)

Views around Häggvik (p282), Höga Kusten, Ångermanland

GRAEME CO

(Continued from page 188)

KULLA PENINSULA

☎ 042

This perfect little peninsula is a rural idyll – with a quietly scandalous nature! It was one of the first resorts to encourage mixed bathing, to the horror of the country. For the last 20 years, the wonderful driftwood sculpture *Nimis,* on the eastern side of the peninsula, has sparked controversy and legal procedures. The area is also known for its ceramics, antiques and tiny fishing villages.

Sights & Activities

Out at the point is Scandinavia's brightest lighthouse, **Kullens fyr**, and the people-magnet **Kullaberg Nature Reserve** (Skr35 road toll) with 11 caves and lots of bird life. The **diving** here is reputedly the best in Sweden: contact the helpful chaps at **Kullen Dyk** (☎ 34 77 14; www.kullendyk.nu; Möllehässle Camping) to go on a dive. You can also go **caving** (☎ 34 70 35) with experienced guides, join a **rock-climbing course** (☎ 34 77 25), indulge in some coastal **fishing**, or strike out on one of several **hiking trails**.

The village of **Mölle** is the main tourist centre, a steep little town with a pretty harbour. Like something from a dream, **Arild** (5km east) is a well-preserved fishing village bursting with roses, hollyhocks, bees and butterflies. Its mini pastel houses cluster round a teeny-tiny harbour, and there are some good coastal nature reserves.

Sleeping & Eating

Accommodation in the area isn't cheap and it fills up fast.

Grand Hotel Mölle (☎ 36 22 30; www.grand-molle.se; Bökebollsvägen 11; s/d from Skr1050/1100; P) You can't miss the Grand, perched high above Mölle with an unusual turreted roof! From the outside, it looks as though it's seen better days, but inside the rooms are done out in modern Scandinavian style with nautical nods (rooms with balconies and sea views are more expensive). There's also a gourmet restaurant on the premises.

Strand Hotell (☎ 34 61 00; www.strand-arild.se; Stora Vägen 42; d from Skr1050; P) This hotel offers charming old-world accommodation in picture-perfect Arild. Four of the elegant rooms in the old building have balconies looking out to sea, and the annexe, opened in 2004, has long thin rooms with terraces and sea views for all. There's also a refined restaurant on the premises.

Möllehässle Camping (☎ 34 73 84; mollehassle@telia.com; low/high season sites Skr150/220, 2-person cabin from Skr600) For budget travellers, this excellent camp site is the best bet. It's 2km southeast of Mölle, and you can rent bikes here for exploring the area (Skr70 per day).

Ellens Café i Ransvik (☎ 34 76 66; Apr-Sep) This traditional place overlooks a popular bathing spot about 1km beyond the Kullaberg toll booth. Enjoy sandwiches, coffee, cake and a swim from the rocks.

Flickorna Lundgren (☎ 34 60 44; May-early Sep) Signposted off the main road between Arild and Jonstorp, this is a huge, well-famous café in a gorgeous garden setting. Grab a huge plate of pastries and your copper kettle, and lose yourself in a cloud of flowers.

Getting There & Away

Bus 219 and 220 run at least hourly from Helsingborg to Höganäs (Skr38, 40 minutes); from there, bus 222 runs every hour or two to Mölle (Skr18, 20 minutes), and the 223 and 224 run to Arild (Skr16, 20 minutes).

Southwest Sweden

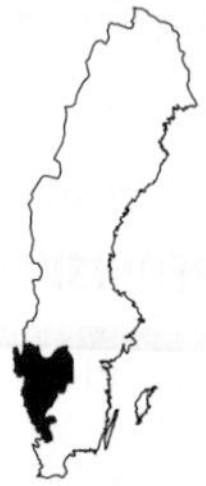

The southwest is Sweden in a nutshell. For big-city living, gorgeous green Göteborg (or Gothenburg in English) offers all the restaurants, culture and theme-park screams you could need. Take advantage of the excellent summer pass and explore every facet of the city for next to nothing.

The rest of the Västergötland region contains a funny old mixture of surprising sights: don't miss Trollhättan, Sweden's film-production capital; Läckö Slott, fairytale castle supreme; and the quiet delights of the Göta Canal, which threads its way across the region.

Facing westwards onto the ocean, the beautiful Bohuslän coastline is a favourite Swedish holiday destination. With its myriad islands, tiny fishing villages and mysterious Bronze Age rock carvings, it manages to retain an enigmatic air in spite of all its adoring visitors.

Europe's third-largest lake, Vänern, strokes the edges of watery, forested Dalsland, a canoeists' paradise and a county for really getting away from the tourist trail. For wilder waves and historical seaside towns, head for Halland. It has clean, sandy Blue Flag beaches and the best windsurfing in Sweden.

HIGHLIGHTS

- Ride till you puke at Sweden's number one attraction, **Liseberg fun park** (p204), in Göteborg
- Puzzle over the weird and wonderful **Bronze Age artwork** (p222) at the Unesco World Heritage site in Tanumshede, Bohuslän
- Enjoy the strange film-set industrial landscape of **Trollhättan** (p226)
- Cruise down the river to the **Nya Älvsborg Fästning** (Nya Älvsborg Fortress; p206) in Göteborg
- Stroll round the picturesque fishing villages of Bohuslän, particularly **Smögen** (p220), **Åstol** (p218) and **Fjällbacka** (p220)
- Catch the waves at **Apelviken** (p232), the country's premier windsurfing beach

AREA: 30,584 SQ KM	HIGHEST ELEVATION: GALTÅSEN (362M)	POPULATION: 1,805,683

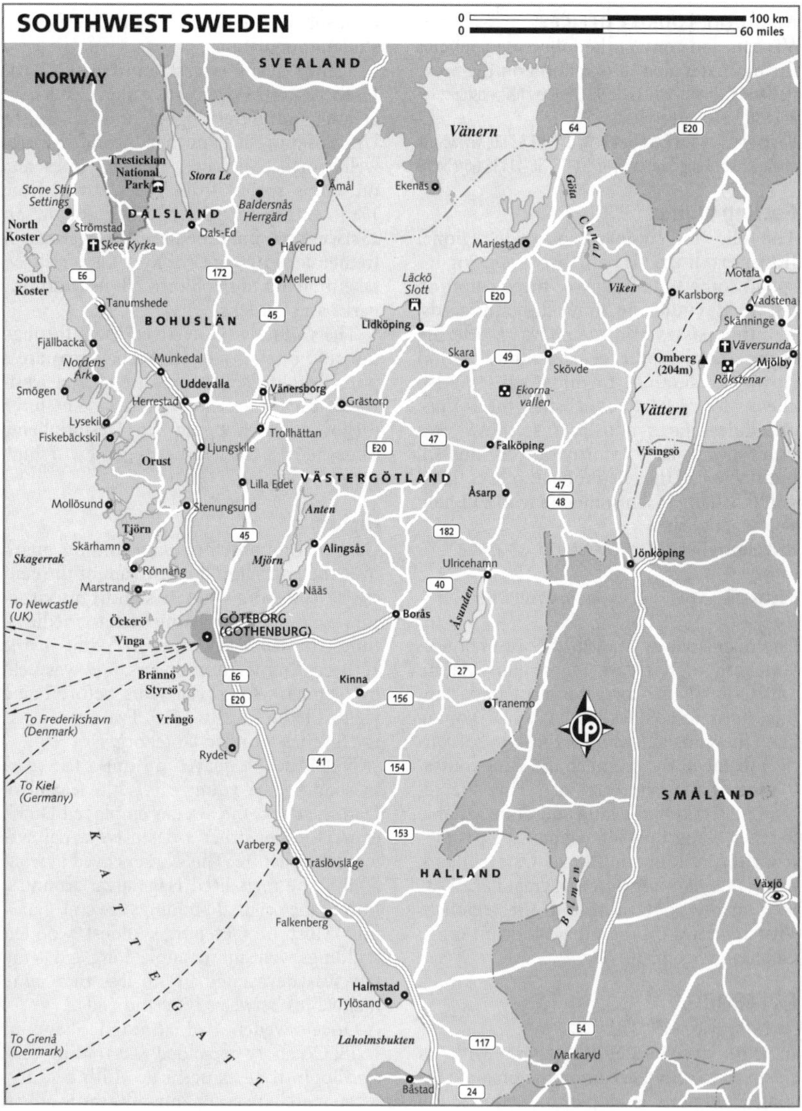

Orientation & Information

Götaland is a large area of Sweden that consists of five different regions or *landskaps:* Bohuslän, Dalsland and Västergötland in the west, Halland in the south, and Östergötland in the east (covered in the Southeast Sweden chapter p142). These regions are grouped together into the three counties or *läns* of Västra Götalands län (taking in Västergötland, Dalsland and Bohuslän), Hallands län and Östergötlands län. Götaland is also the region containing the two largest lakes in Sweden – Vänern and Vättern, which are connected by the Göta canal. The latter lake divides Götaland into two distinct parts.

REGIONAL TOURIST OFFICES

Visitors can contact the following agencies for more detailed information on the area:

HallandsTurist (☎ 035-10 95 60; www.hallandsturist.se; Box 538, SE-30180 Halmstad)

Västsvenska Turistrådet (☎ 031-81 83 00; www.vastsverige.com; Kungsportsavenyn 31-35, SE-41136 Göteborg)

Getting Around

The following companies provide regional transport links. If you are planning to spend some time in any of these counties, it's worth enquiring about discount cards, monthly passes or a *sommarkort*, offering cheap travel in the peak summer period (from midsummer to mid-August). Also check the respective websites for routes, schedules, fares and passes; these sites don't always have information in English, but if you call the telephone numbers listed you'll usually reach someone who can help you in English.

Hallandstrafiken (☎ 0346-486 00, 0771-33 10 30; www.hlt.se)

Västtrafik (☎ 0771-41 43 00; www.vasttrafik.se)

The main railway lines in the west connect Göteborg to Karlstad, Stockholm, Malmö and Oslo. In the east, the most important line runs from Stockholm via Norrköping and Linköping to Malmö. Express buses connect major towns on much the same routes.

One of the best ways of seeing the region is by taking the long and unforgettable journey along the Göta Canal (see p146) – from the rolling country of Östergötland, north of Linköping, into the great Lake Vättern, before continuing into the region of Västergötland on the other side and on to Göteborg. See p330.

SOUTHWEST SWEDEN

GÖTEBORG

☎ 031 / pop 481,410

In expensive Sweden, Göteborg, with its cheap fares, cheap accommodation and fantastic attractions, is a top introduction to the country that shouldn't make your piggy bank turn up its trotters. Göteborg (pronounced something like 'yer-te-bor') is also known by its English name Gothenburg. It is Scandinavia's busiest port and has a continental outlook; its showpiece Kungsportsavenyn boulevard is often nicknamed the 'Champs Élysées', and the comparison is justified (in a low-key Nordic way). The cheerful, relaxed atmosphere is enhanced by the city's large student population.

Scandinavia's largest amusement park, Liseberg, froths over with rollercoasters, ice creams and glittery lights, and the nearby Universeum is another wonder-world well worth exploring. Heritage sites and museums sprout from every street, from 17th-century fortresses to state-of-the-art 21st-century multimedia extravaganzas. A tremendous 10% of Göteborg is green space: take time out to stroll through its charming parks and gardens.

The Göta älv (Göta river) runs through the city: in sunny weather boat trips are a pure delight. You can easily escape westwards on the efficient tram system for a mellow island-hopping trip. Despite being a coastal city, the weather is good with high sunshine levels.

History

Gamla Älvsborg fortress, standing guard over the river 3km downstream of the centre, is Göteborg's oldest significant structure, with portions dating back to medieval times. It was a key strategic point in the 17th-century territorial wars, and was held by Denmark for seven years before being yielded to Sweden in 1619. Two years later, the Swedes founded Göteborg.

Dutch people played an important part in shaping the young city. Still fearful of Danish attack, the Swedes employed Dutch experts to construct a defensive canal system in the centre. The workers lived in what is now the revitalised Haga area: around a fifth of the original buildings are still standing. Most of Göteborg's oldest wooden buildings went up in smoke long ago – the city was devastated by no less than nine major fires between 1669 and 1804.

Once Sweden had annexed Skåne in 1658, Göteborg expanded as a trading centre. Boom-time came in the 18th century, when merchant companies like the Swedish East India Company made huge amounts of wealth. Look around and you'll notice the many grandiose buildings built using the profits of that period.

From the 19th century, shipbuilding was a major part of the city's economy, until the industry totally collapsed in the 1980s. Volvo's first car wheeled out of Göteborg in 1927. It's now one of Sweden's largest companies (although it was taken over by Ford in 1999), and it's estimated that a quarter of the city relies on the company in some way. Today, Göteborg is Sweden's most important industrial and commercial city. Most of Sweden's oil is imported through the vast port.

Orientation

From the centre of the city, Kungsportsavenyn (known simply as 'Avenyn') crosses one of the city's original 17th-century canals (most have been filled in) and leads southeast up to Götaplatsen. The Avenyn is the heart of the city with boutiques, restaurants, galleries, theatres and street cafés. The huge Nordstan shopping centre lies just north of the canal system, opposite the central train station.

The former shipyards and much of the heavy industry (including Volvo) are on the northern island of Hisingen, formed by bifurcation of the Göta älv. Hisingen is reached by road via the monumental Älvsborgs bron (bridge), southwest of the city; by Götaälvbron (north of Centralstationen); and by the E6 motorway tunnel, Tingstadstunneln, northeast of the city centre.

The main E6 motorway, just east of the city centre, runs north–south between Oslo and Malmö.

Information

BOOKSHOPS

Akademibokhandeln Kungsgatan (☎ 15 02 84; Kungsgatan 61; ⌚ 10am-7pm Mon-Fri, 10am-4pm Sat, noon-4pm Sun); Nordstan shopping complex (☎ 61 70 30; Nordstan shopping complex; ⌚ 10am-7pm Mon-Fri, 10am-6pm Sat, 11am-5pm Sun); Vasagatan (☎ 60 96 80; Vasagatan 26-30; ⌚ 10am-6pm Mon-Thu, 10am-4pm Fri, 10am-2pm Sat, closed Jul) The three central branches of Akademibokhandeln offer the best selection of English-language books in the city.

Pocketshop (☎ 10 49 40; Centralstationen; ⌚ 6.15am-9pm Mon-Fri, 7am-8pm Sat, 8.30am-9pm Sun) English-language books.

Press Stop (☎ 15 84 45; Drottninggatan 58; ⌚ 9.30am-6.30pm Mon-Fri, 10am-4pm Sat, noon-3pm Sun) For English-language newspapers and magazines.

Pressbyrån (☎ 15 37 90; Centralstationen; ⌚ 6am-10pm Mon-Fri, 8am-8pm Sat, 8am-10pm Sun) Similar to Press Stop. There is another outlet in Centralstationen open until midnight and a platform kiosk as well.

EMERGENCY

Dial ☎ 112 for fire, police or ambulance in emergency situations only.

Police station (☎ 739 20 00; Ernst Fontells Plats)

INTERNET ACCESS

GameNet (☎ 711 90 16; Viktoriagatan 22; per hr Skr30; ⌚ 1-10pm)

IT Grottan (☎ 778 73 77; Chalmersgatan 27; per hr Skr43; ⌚ 11am-11pm)

Palatset (☎ 13 24 80; Ekelundsgatan 9-11; per hr Skr25; ⌚ until at least midnight) A large bar and billiards hall.

Sidewalk Express (www.sidewalkexpress.se; per hr Skr19) Sidewalk Express computers are found at Centralstationen & the 7-Eleven shop on Vasaplatsen. To log on, buy vouchers from the coin-operated machines and you'll be issued with a username and password.

LEFT LUGGAGE

Luggage **lockers** (small/medium/large Skr20/30/40 for up to 24hr) are available at Centralstationen and the long-distance bus terminal Nils Ericson Terminalen.

GÖTEBORG PASS

The excellent Göteborg Pass discount card is well worth getting, even if all you're going to do is park in Göteborg (which has the most expensive street parking in Sweden, and the most dedicated traffic wardens). You also get free or reduced admission to a bundle of attractions (including Liseberg and the museums), plus free city sightseeing tours, bicycle hire and travel by public transport within the region.

The card costs Skr210/150 per adult/child for 24 hours, Skr295/210 for 48 hours. It's available at tourist offices, hotels and Pressbyrån newsagencies.

Göteborgspaketet is an accommodation package offered at various hotels with prices starting at Skr475 per person per night. It includes the Göteborg Pass for the number of nights you stay. You can book the package in advance over the Internet or telephone the tourist office on ☎ 61 25 00. A variety of more expensive packages includes theatre or concert tickets, casino passes, spa visits etc.

GÖTEBORG (GOTHENBURG)

INFORMATION
Akademibokhandeln....1 F4
Akademibokhandeln....2 F5
Akademibokhandeln....(see 103)
Akuttandvården (Emergency Dentist)....3 G3
Apotek Vasan....(see 103)
Branch Tourist Office....(see 103)
Forex....4 F3
Forex....5 G5
Forex....6 F4
Forex....(see 103)
GameNet....7 F5
IT-Grottan....8 F5
Library....9 G5
Main Tourist Office....10 F4
Palatset....11 E4
Pocketshop....(see 4)
Police Station....12 G4
Post Office....(see 103)
Press Stop....13 F4
Pressbyrån....(see 4)
Sidewalk Express....(see 4)

SIGHTS & ACTIVITIES
Börjessons City Boat Tour....14 F4
Börjessons City Bus Tour....15 F4
Börjessons Cruise....16 F3
Domkyrkan....17 F4
Feskekörka (Fish Church)....18 E4
Götheborgs-Utkiken....19 F2
Hagabadet....20 E5
Hagakyrkan....21 E5
Klippan....22 A6
Konstmuseet....23 G5
Kronhusbodarna....(see 24)
Kronhuset....24 F3
Liseberg....25 H5
Maritiman....26 E3
Masthuggskyrkan....27 C5
Naturhistoriska Museet....28 D6
Oscar Fredriks Kyrka....29 D5
Palmhuset....30 G4
Rosarium....31 G4
Röhsska Museet....32 F5
Sjöfartsmuseet....33 C5
Stadsmuseum....34 E4
Universeum....35 H6
Valhallabadet....36 H5
Varldskulturmuseet....37 H6

SLEEPING
City Hotel....38 G5
Göteborgs Mini-Hotel....39 D5
Göteborgs Vandrarhem....40 H6
Hotel Eggers....41 F3
Hotel Flora....42 F4
Hotel Gothia Towers....43 H5
Hotel Odin Residence....44 G3
Hotel Opera....45 F4
Hotel Royal....46 F4
Hotel Vasa....47 F5
Hotell Barken Viking....48 F3
Linné Vandrarhem....49 D5
Masthuggsterrassens Vandrarhem....50 C5
Radisson SAS Scandinavia Hotel....51 F4
Scandic Hotel Europa....52 F3
Scandic Hotel Rubinen....53 G5
STF Vandrarhem Slottsskogen....54 D6
STF Vandrarhem Stigbergsliden....55 C5
Vanilj Hotel, Kafé & Bar....56 F4

EATING
28+....57 G5
A Hereford Beefstouw....58 D5
Aldardo....59 F4
Andrum....60 F3
Bliss....61 E4
Bombay....62 D5
Brasserie Lipp....63 F4
Brogyllens Konditori....64 F4
Café Garbo....65 F5
Café Kosmos....66 F4
Crepe Van....67 D5
Cyrano....68 D5
Den Lilla Tavernan....69 D6
Espresso House....70 F5
Eva's Paley....71 G5
Fiskekrogen....72 E4
Hemköp Supermarket....(see 103)
Java Kaffebar....73 F5
Joe Farelli's....(see 63)
Kalaya....74 D6
Linnéa....75 G5
Magnus & Magnus....76 E4
Saluhall Briggen....77 D5
Saluhallen....78 F4
Sjöbaren....79 E5
Smaka....80 F5
Solrosen....81 E5
Sushi & Soda....82 D5
Trädgår'n....83 G4

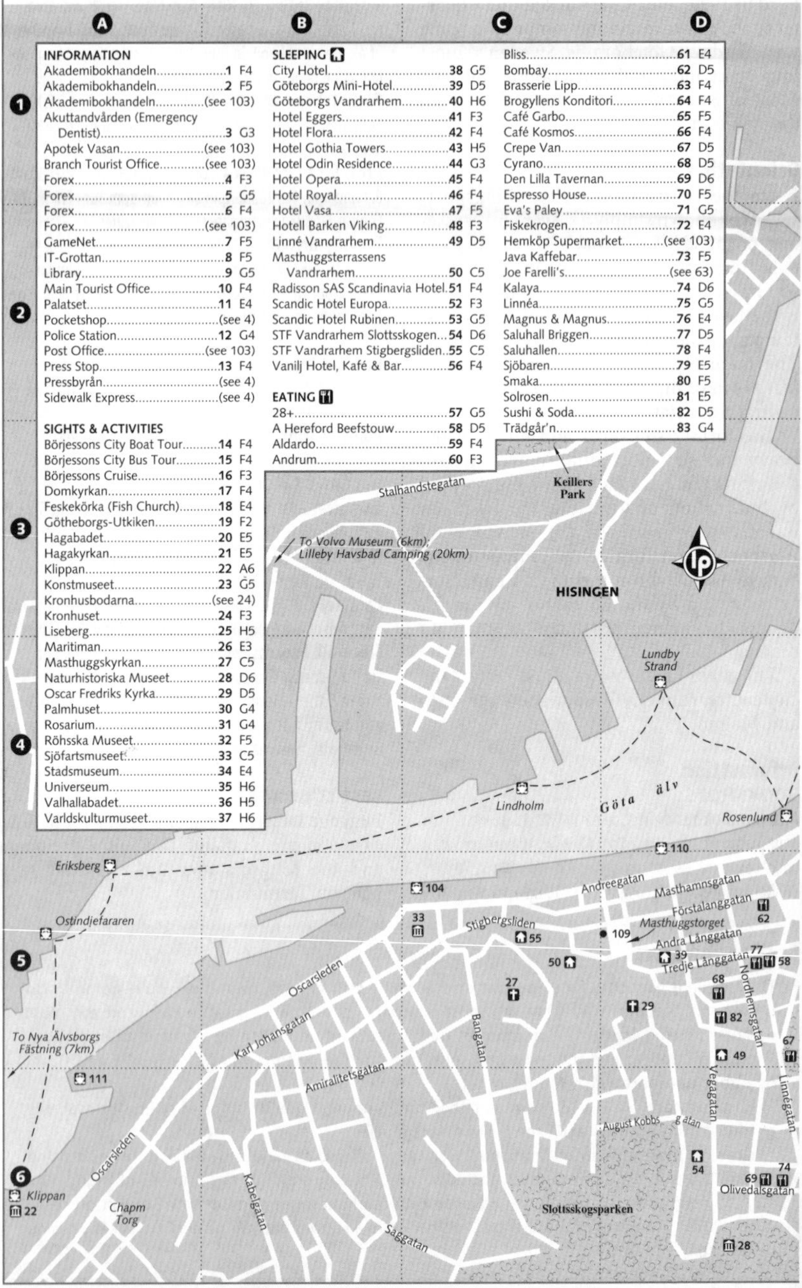

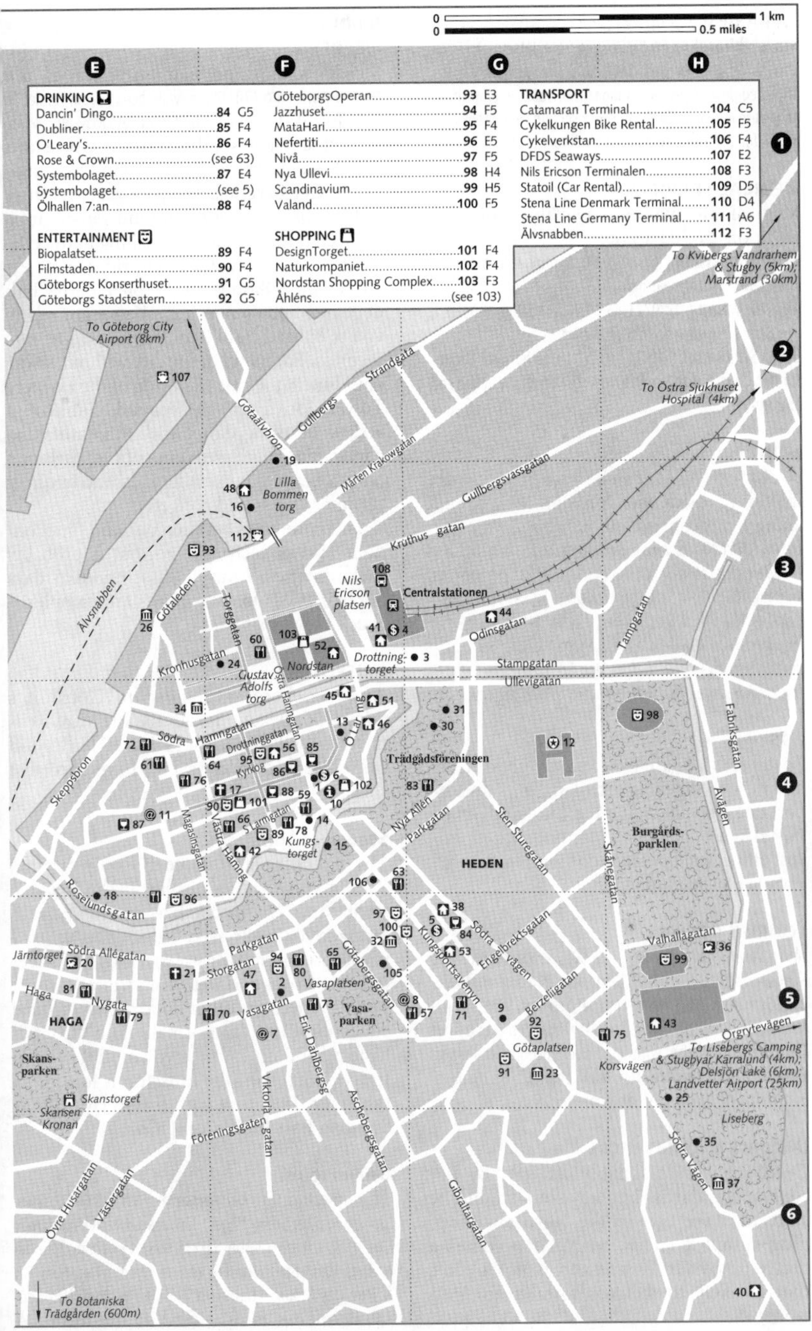

SOUTHWEST SWEDEN

LIBRARIES

Stadsbiblioteket (☎ 61 65 00; Götaplatsen; ⌚ 10am-8pm Mon-Fri, 11am-5pm Sat & Sun) The city library has imported newspapers and magazines, books in English, a good café and a modern computer section (free Internet access for 15/30min without/with library card).

MEDICAL SERVICES

Medical information is available around the clock on ☎ 703 15 00.

Akuttandvården (☎ 80 78 00; Stampgatan 2) For emergency dental treatment.

Apotek Vasan (☎ 0771-45 04 50; Nordstan complex; ⌚ 8am-10pm) Late-night pharmacy.

Östra Sjukhuset (☎ 343 40 00) Large hospital about 5km northeast of the centre, near the terminus at the end of tramline 1.

MONEY

Banks with ATMs can be found everywhere, including inside the Nordstan complex and along Kungsportsavenyn.

Forex (☎ 0200-22 22 20; www.forex.se) Centralstationen (⌚ 7am-9pm Mon-Sat); Kungsportsavenyn 22 (⌚ 9am-7pm Mon-Fri, 10am-4pm Sat); Kungsportsplatsen (⌚ 9am-7pm Mon-Fri, 10am-4pm Sat); Landvetter airport (⌚ 5.15am-9pm Mon-Fri, 5.15am-7pm Sat, 5.15am-10.30pm Sun); Norstan Complex (⌚ 9am-7pm Mon-Fri, 10am-4pm Sat) Foreign exchange office with branches all over the city.

POST

Postal services are now mainly provided by kiosks, newsagents, petrol stations and supermarkets – look for the blue-and-yellow postal symbol.

Post office (Nordstan complex; ⌚ 9am-7pm Mon-Fri, 10am-3pm Sat, noon-3pm Sun)

TOURIST OFFICES

Main tourist office (☎ 61 25 00; www.goteborg.com; Kungsportsplatsen 2; ⌚ 9.30am-8pm mid-Jun–mid-Aug, 9am-5pm Mon-Fri & 10am-2pm Sat Sep-Apr, 9.30am-6pm Mon-Fri & 10am-2pm Sat & Sun May–mid-Jun & end Aug) Central and very busy, with good free brochures and maps.

Branch tourist office (Nordstan complex; ⌚ 10am-6pm Mon-Fri, 10am-5pm Sat, noon-4pm Sun)

Dangers & Annoyances

Göteborg is a reasonably safe city by European standards, but travellers should be alert and take care in the Nordstan shopping complex late at night. It becomes a pretty unsavoury venue and is not a place that is likely to feel comfortable for solo women.

Sights

LISEBERG

Sweden's most popular attraction is this **theme park** (☎ 40 01 00; www.liseberg.se; adult/under 7yr Skr60/free; ⌚ to 10pm or 11pm most days May-Aug, & during Christmas period), southeast of the city centre. Take tram 4 or 5, and enter from Örgrytevägen or Getebergsled. The park gets over three million visitors every year (and sometimes it feels as though they're all visiting at once!).

There are a few fairly big rides – for example, the 90kph wooden rollercoaster Balder, and 2005's new ride Kanonen, where you're blasted from 0 to 75kph in under two seconds. For views of the city without losing your lunch, the ride to the top of the Liseberg Tower, 83m above the ground, climaxes in a slow spinning dance with a breathtaking panorama. There are plenty of carousels and fairytale castles for smaller kids, and frequent summer shows and concerts.

Each ride costs between one and four coupons (Skr15 each) per go, but it probably makes sense to buy a pass (one/two days Skr265/335). Opening hours are complex – check the website.

MUSEUMS

After Liseberg museums are Göteborg's strongest attractions: admission to most is covered by the Göteborg Pass. All have good cafés attached, and several have specialist shops.

Stadsmuseum

The Äskekärr Ship, Sweden's only original Viking vessel, is on display at the **Stadsmuseum** (☎ 61 27 70; Östindiska huset, Norra Hamngatan 12; adult/under 20yr Skr40/free; ⌚ 10am-5pm May-Aug, 10am-5pm Tue-Sun, to 8pm Wed rest of yr), alongside silver treasure troves and weaponry from the same period. There are other good archaeological collections, lots of information on the city's history, and an impressive amount of East Indian porcelain (the museum is located in the huge 18th-century former HQ of the Swedish East India Company).

Universeum

The spectacular **Universeum** (☎ 335 64 50; www.universeum.se; Södra Vägen; low season individual/family Skr110/395, high season Skr135/495; ⌚ 10am-7pm Jul & Aug, 10am-6pm Mon-Fri, to 8pm Wed, 11am-6pm Sat & Sun May & Jun, 11am-6pm Tue-Sun, to 8pm Wed Sep-Apr) is one for families and nature-lovers. A funicular takes you to the top of an indoor mountain, from where you follow the course of a Scandinavian stream down through rivers and lakes to the sea – shark tunnel ahoy! Things take a tropical turn in the absorbing rainforest: birds and butterflies flitter, while more gruesome denizens dwell in Piranha River, Caiman Creek, Anaconda Swamp and Stingray Lagoon.

Röhsska Museet

A carnival of creativity awaits you at **Röhsska Museet** (☎ 61 38 50; www.designmuseum.se; Vasagatan 37; adult/under 20yr Skr40/free; ⏲ noon-8pm Tue, noon-5pm Wed-Fri, 11am-5pm Sat & Sun), Sweden's only art and design museum. Exquisite Chinese and Japanese sculptures and baroque furniture make up the older historical exhibitions. For a huge culture shock, descend to the ultramodern 20th- and 21st-century Scandinavian design section – furniture features strongly, but there's also some outrageous crockery.

Maritiman

Near the opera house north of the centre is the largest floating **ship museum** (☎ 10 59 50; Packhuskajen; adult/7-15yr Skr75/30; ⏲ 10am-6pm May-Aug, 10am-4pm Mar, Apr, Sep & Oct, 10am-4pm Fri-Sun Nov) in the world! It's made up of 19 historical crafts, including fishing boats, a light vessel and a firefighter, linked by walkways. Shinny down into the 69m-long submarine *Nordkaparen*, a throat-tightening glimpse into underwater warfare. Another highlight is the museum's biggest craft, the labyrinthine 121m-long destroyer *Småland*, which saw service from 1952 to 1979. Inside, hunched figures listen to crackling radio messages, and the bunks look just-slept-in – you half expect to meet uniformed sailors in the dim, twisting passages…

There's a lot to see, so allow a couple of hours.

Konstmuseet

The main city art collection is at **Konstmuseet** (☎ 61 29 80; www.konstmuseum.goteborg.se; Götaplatsen; adult/under 20yr Skr40/free; ⏲ 11am-6pm Tue & Thu, 11am-9pm Wed, 11am-5pm Fri-Sun). There are notable works by the French impressionists, Rubens, Van Gogh, Rembrandt, Picasso, and an impressive collection of Scandinavian masters (Bruno Liljefors, Edvard Munch, Anders Zorn, Carl Larsson). Room 22 is particularly distinctive, with its paintings of the uncanny Nordic twilight.

There's also an interesting sculpture hall, the **Hasselblad Center** (☎ 20 35 30) photographic collection, and temporary exhibitions covering the latest in Nordic art.

Outside, Götaplatsen is dominated by the bronze **Poseidon fountain**, which was unveiled to public outcry in 1931. This 7m-high colossus originally had colossal private parts, and the strait-laced citizens of Göteborg demanded some drastic reduction surgery.

Varldskulturmuseet

Opened in 2005, Göteborg's newest and most futuristic museum is **Varldskulturmuseet** (Museum of World Culture; ☎ 63 27 30; www.varldskulturmuseet.se; Södra Vägen 54; admission free; ⏲ noon-5pm Tue, Sat & Sun, noon-9pm Wed-Fri), where ethnography, art and global politics collide in immersive multimedia exhibitions. At the time of writing, themes included: 'Sister of Dreams', on the myths of the Orinoco people; 'No Name Fever', on AIDS; and 'Horizons', stories about Africa. The latter two will run into 2006, to be joined by an exhibition on trafficking.

Sjöfartsmuseet

The main museum of maritime history is **Sjöfartsmuseet** (☎ 61 29 00; www.sjofartsmuseum.goteborg.se; Karl Johansgatan 1; adult/under 20yr Skr40/free; ⏲ 10am-5pm May-Aug, 9am-4pm Tue-Fri, to 8pm Wed, 11am-5pm Sat & Sun Sep-Apr), by Stigbergstorget about 2km west of the city centre. Tram 3, 9 or 11 will get you there. It includes model ships, cannons, a ship's medical room and a large collection of figureheads, such as the vicious-looking *Vinthunden* from the frigate with the same name. The attached **aquarium** (included in the entry fee) has a good selection of Nordic marine life. Outside, the **Sjömanstornet** (Mariner's Tower), topped by a statue of a grieving woman, commemorates the Swedish sailors killed in WWI.

Naturhistoriska Museet

The **Natural History Museum** (☎ 775 24 00; www.gnm.se; Slottsskogen Park; adult/under 20yr Skr60/free; ⏲ 11am-5pm May-Aug, 9am-4pm Tue-Fri, 11am-5pm Sat & Sun Sep-Apr) contains the world's only stuffed blue whale. You could once walk inside its mouth, until an amorous couple were discovered inside and the jaws were firmly shut. As natural history museums go, this is a large and impressive one, with some 10 million specimens of wildlife from around the world. To get there, take tram 1 or 6.

Nya Älvsborgs Fästning

At the mouth of the Göta älv, squat red **Elfsborgs Fortress** has had an interesting history. It was built in the 17th century to defend the young city from Danish attack, and saw action again in the early 18th century during the Great Nordic War. Visitors can see the church built for Karl XII's troops, and the dungeons for when they stepped out-of-line.

The fortress is about 8km downstream from Göteborg. Boat trips and **guided tours** (adult/6-12yr/family Skr110/60/280) are run six times a day from May to August by Börjessons (see opposite). Tours depart from Lilla Bommen harbour, north of the train station. Most are free for holders of the Göteborg Pass.

Volvo Museum

Just celebrating its 10th birthday, the **Volvo Museum** (66 48 14; Hisingen; adult/child Skr30/10; 10am-5pm Tue-Fri, 11am-4pm Sat & Sun Jun-Aug; noon-5pm Tue-Fri, 11am-4pm Sat Sep-May) contains everything from the company's very first car to the most cutting-edge experimental designs – including the first jet engine used by the Swedish Air Force.

The museum is about 8km west of the city centre at Arendal. Fittingly, it's tricky to get to without a car. Take tram 2, 4 or 5 to Eketrägatan, then bus 27.

PARKS

Laid out in 1842, the lovely **Trädgårdsföreningen** (City Park; 365 58 58; Nya Allén; adult/under 17yr Skr15/free; 7am-9pm May-Aug, 7am-6pm or 7.30pm Sep-Apr) is a large protected area off Nya Allén, full of flowers and tiny cafés and popular for lunchtime escapes. It contains Europe's largest **rosarium**, with around 2500 varieties, and the 19th-century **Palmhuset** (41 57 73; adult /under 20yr Skr20/free; 10am-5pm May-Aug, 10am-4pm Sep-Apr). This graceful building is a miniature version of Crystal Palace in London, with five differently heated halls: plant highlights include the camellia collection and the 2m-wide tropical lily pads.

Sweden's largest botanical garden is the **Botaniska Trädgården** (Carl Skottsbergsgatan 22a; admission free; 9am-sunset, greenhouses 10am-5pm), with around 12,000 plant species.

Just across Dag Hammarskjöldsleden, **Slottsskogsparken** (admission free; 24hr) is grea for a stroll. The Naturhistoriska Museet i perched on a hill in the park. There's als **Barnens Zoo** (Children's Zoo; May–early Sep) an **Djurgårdarna**, an animal park with farm animals, elk, deer and other Swedish animal and birds. Feeding time at the seal pond i 2pm daily.

The rocky heights of Ramberget (87m) i **Keillers Park** (Hisingen) give the best view of th city. You can get there on the city bus tou (see opposite), or take a tram to Ramsbergsvallen and walk up.

CHURCHES

Göteborg's churches aren't very old bu they're a better reflection of Swedish architecture than Stockholm's Italian imitations.

The classical **Domkyrkan** (Gustavi Cathedra Västra Hamngatan; 8am-6pm Mon-Fri, 9am-4pm Sa 10am-3pm Sun) was consecrated in 1815 – tw previous cathedrals were destroyed by tow fires. Many of the cathedral's contents ar modern, but there's an 18th-century cloc and reredos. Two other remarkable 19th-century churches are **Hagakyrkan** (731 61 60 Haga Kyrkoplan; 11am-3pm Mon-Thu & Sat) and th neo-Gothic **Oscar Fredriks kyrka** (731 92 50 Oscar Fredriks Kyrkogatan; 8am-4pm Mon-Fri).

One of the most distinctive buildings i Göteborg is **Masthuggskyrkan** (Storebackegatan 9am-6pm summer, 11am-4pm rest of yr), a welcome landmark for sailors and a smashin viewpoint over the western half of the city Completed in 1914, its interior is like a upturned boat.

OTHER SIGHTS

The **Haga district** is Göteborg's oldest suburb and dates back to 1648. In the 1980s an '90s, the area was thoroughly renovated an it's now a pleasing mixture of old and new buildings, independent knick-knack shops and cool cafés.

The red-and-white 'skyscraper' **Göteborgs Utkiken** (15 61 47; Lilla Bommen 1 adult/child Skr20/10 11am-5pm May-Aug, 11am-4pm Sat & Sun Sep-Apr), nicknamed 'The Lipstick' by city-dwellers for obvious reasons, has superior views o the harbour from the top.

The **Klippan precinct** was once a bustle o industry – glassworks, foundries, breweries and salting houses – which has been turned into a picturesque heritage centre. It includes

18th-century sailor's cottages, the remains of Gamla Älvsborgs fort (ransomed from the Danes in 1619), a brewery opened by the Scot David Carnegie (now a hotel), and St Birgittas kapell. Klippan is just off Oscarsleden, about 400m east of Älvsborgsbron – take tram 3 or 9 to Vagnhallen Majorna.

Kronhuset, lying between Postgatan and Kronhusgatan, is the city's oldest secular building, a former arsenal built in Dutch style between 1642 and 1654. It was here that Karl X held the disastrous *riksdag* (parliament) in 1660 – he died while it was in session. **Kronhusbodarna**, just across the courtyard from Kronhuset, consists of several workshops making and selling pottery, silverware, glass and textiles.

The curious **Feskekörka** (☎ 711 35 09; Rosenlundsgatan; 9am-6pm Mon-Fri, 8am-1pm Sat Jun-Aug, closed Mon rest of yr), or 'Fish Church', has nothing remotely to do with ecclesiastical matters – it's a seafood market.

Activities

Cyclists should ask the tourist office for the map *Cykel Karta Göteborg*, which shows the best routes in and around the city. It's divided into three parts (Skr20 each, or Skr50 for all three). See p215 for bike hire.

The best indoor pool is the magnificent and exclusive **Hagabadet** (☎ 60 06 00; Södra Allégatan 3; 6.30am-9.30pm Mon-Thu, 6.30am-8.30pm Fri, 9am-5pm Sat, 10am-6pm Sun). For Skr360 you can swim all day and use the attached sauna, gym and aerobics facilities; between 6.30am and 9am, you can swim for Skr100. There's a Roman bath and all manner of health and beauty treatments if you're feeling travel-weary.

Contained within the vast Valhalla gym/swim/bowling complex is the indoor pool **Valhallabadet** (☎ 61 19 56; Valhallagatan 3; 7am-7pm Mon-Fri, 7am-3pm Sat, 11am-3pm Sun). A swim and sauna costs Skr40, and there's also a relaxing Roman bath here (Skr110).

Outdoor swimming is best in **Delsjön lake**, 6km east of the centre (take tram 5 to Töpelsgatan). You can also hire **canoes** (☎ 40 34 88) and **fish** for pike or perch here: ask the tourist office for tackle shop details, as you'll need a permit.

Bohusleden is an easy walking trail that runs for 360km through Bohuslän, from Lindome (south of Göteborg) to Strömstad, passing just east of the city. You can buy a guide to the route from the tourist offices (Skr45).

For serious **island hopping**, take tram 11 southwest to Saltholmen and you'll have at least 15 different islands to explore – see p215.

There's some good **rock climbing** around Göteborg. Tram 6, 7 and 11 go to Kviberg, close to some of the best climbing, at Utby. Contact **Göteborgs Klätterklubb** (☎ 43 13 86; www.gbgkk.nu in Swedish) for more information.

Tours

Börjessons (☎ 60 96 70; www.borjessons.com) run 50-minute city bus and boat tours (some under the name 'Paddan Sightseeing'). They're a great way to get your bearings and are free with the Göteborg Pass; as are tours to Nya Älvsborgs Fästning. There may be restrictions on times you can go, so check first.

Tour	Frequency	Departs from	Ticket (adult/6-12 yrs)
City Bus Tour	five daily May-Aug	Stora Teatern	Skr120/60
City Boat Tour	from 10am May-Sep	Kungsportsbron	Skr95/60
Nya Älvsborgs Fästning	five to 11am May-Aug	Lilla Bommen	Skr110/60

Börjessons runs tours from Lilla Bommen to **Vinga** (see p216) and around the island of **Hisingen** (adult/6-12yr Skr130/65; 6pm or 7pm Tue-Sun Jul–mid-Aug), amongst others.

Sleeping

Göteborg has several high-quality hostels near the city centre. Most hotels offer exceptional discounts at weekends and in summer.

PRIVATE ROOMS

The tourist office can arrange private rooms from Skr175/225 for a single/double, plus a Skr60 booking fee.

HOSTELS

Most hostels are clustered in the central southwest area, in apartment buildings that sometimes inspire little confidence from the outside, but inside offer accommodation of a very high standard. All are open year-round.

STF Vandrarhem Slottsskogen (☎ 42 65 20; www.sov.nu; Vegagatan 21; dm Skr120-140, s/d Skr260/330; 💻)

Unlike many Swedish hostels, big, friendly Slottsskogen is a cracking place for meeting other travellers. For a small extra payment there's access to a laundry, sauna and sun bed. You can also hire bikes (per day/two days Skr90/160), and the hostel's buffet breakfast (Skr55) is acquiring legendary status. If you're really penny-pinching, you may get an even cheaper bed in one of the inner windowless rooms. Parking spaces can be booked for a fee. Tram 1 or 2 to Olivedalsgatan will get you there.

STF Vandrarhem Stigbergsliden (☎ 24 16 20; vandrarhem.stigbergsliden@telia.com; Stigbergsliden 10; dm Skr120, s/d Skr250/300) In a renovated 19th-century seaman's institute (tram 3, 9 or 11 to Stigbergstorget), this is a hostel with history. Staff are greatly helpful, and besides the usual stuff (big kitchen, laundry, TV room), there's a sheltered yard/garden plus bikes for rent (Skr50 per day).

Masthuggsterrassens Vandrarhem (☎ 42 48 20; www.mastenvandrarhem.com; Masthuggsterrassen 10H; dm/d Skr160/400) If you're looking for a good night's sleep, try this clean, quiet, well-run place. It has good facilities – three lounges, three kitchens and a little library (mostly Swedish books) – and is handy if you're catching an early ferry to Denmark. Take tram 3, 9 or 11 to Masthuggstorget and follow the signs.

Göteborgs Vandrarhem (☎ 40 10 50; www.goteborgsvandrarhem.se; Mölndalsvägen 23; dm Skr150-160, s/d Skr350/370) Nifty for those desperate to get to Liseberg as early as possible! Little extras include a sauna and big sunny terrace. Take tram 4 to Getebergsäng.

Kvibergs Vandrarhem & Stugby (☎ 43 50 55; www.vandrarhem.com; Kvibergsvägen 5; low season 1-/2-/3-/4-bed r Skr250/360/450/580, high season 3-/4-bed r Skr480/600) This recommended SVIF hostel, a few kilometres northeast of the city centre (tram 6, 7 or 11), has super amenities, including sauna, sun beds, laundry, table tennis, two kitchens and two lounges. There are no dorms – instead you rent out the entire room. There are also hotel-style rooms and cabins in the green grounds.

Also recommended:

Göteborgs Mini-Hotel (☎ 24 10 23; www.minihotel.se; Tredje Långgatan 31; dm Skr130-160, d Skr360) Clean and inviting, with renovated rooms and an all-day reception. Breakfast is available June to August.

Linné Vandrarhem (☎ 12 10 60; www.vandrarhemmet-linne.com; Vegagatan 22; dm Skr180, d Skr380) Down the road from Slottsskogen, this SVIF hostel is another good central-ish option.

CAMPING

Lisebergs Camping & Stugbyar Kärralund (☎ 84 0… 00; karralund@liseberg.se; Olbergsgatan 1; low/high seaso… sites with car Skr135/240, cabins & chalets from Skr495/1395… The fun park owns and operates a rang… of accommodation around Göteborg. Thi… camp site is the closest one to town (tram … to Welandergatan); as you'd expect, it's full… geared for families. There are 35 tent sites – unreservable, so turn up early.

Lilleby Havsbad Camping (☎ 56 50 66; Lillebyvägen; low/high season sites t Skr160/190; ⏲ May-Aug… Also part of the Liseberg 'empire', this plac… is by the seaside, 20km west of the city centre in Torslanda. To get there take bus 25 from near Centralstationen to Lillebyvägen, then change to bus 23.

HOTELS

Midrange

Vanilj Hotell, Kafé & Bar (☎ 711 62 20; www.vaniljhotel.entersol.se; Kyrkogatan 38; s/d from Skr895/1095, discounted to Skr595/895; Ⓟ 💻) This is an excellent choice. The owners have made a big effort to make their little hotel, located on a quiet central street, cosy and homelike. Individually decorated rooms (renovated in 2004) range from country checks to Scandinavian cool, and breakfast is served in the lovely café downstairs. Get there early for one of the five parking spaces.

Hotell Barken Viking (☎ 63 58 00; barken.viking@liseberg.se; Gullbergskajen; crew quarters s/d Skr600/850, officer's cabin s/d Skr1195/1495, discounted to Skr895/1095) The *Barken Viking* is a beautiful four-masted sailing ship, converted into a hotel and restaurant and moored near Lilla Bommen harbour. Crew quarters have shared bathrooms and bunks. If you pay extra, you can leave the salty sea dogs behind and promote yourself to an officer's cabin, with proper beds, extra luxuries and private facilities.

Hotel Eggers (☎ 80 60 70; www.hoteleggers.se; Drottningtorget; s/d from Skr1425/1780, discounted to Skr730/1060; Ⓟ 💻) Elegant Eggers was founded as a railway hotel in 1859. Its pleasant rooms are individually decorated, with nods to their Regency-era setting; a good few have private balconies overlooking the bustle of the square. There's also a handy valet parking service (Skr210).

SOUTHWEST SWEDEN

Hotel Vasa (☎ 17 36 30; www.hotelvasa.se; Viktoriagatan 6; s/d from Skr845/995, discounted to Skr625/825; 💻) Hotel Vasa is an attractive, family-run place convenient for the cafés of Vasagatan. There's a courtyard garden, two of the doubles have Jacuzzis, and a nice touch is that each room has a book about Göteborg to leaf through.

Hotel Royal (☎ 700 11 70; www.hotelroyal.nu; Drottninggatan 67; s/d from Skr1045/1295, discounted to Skr790/990; 💻) Göteborg's oldest hotel (1852) has aged very well. The grand entrance has been retained, complete with painted glass ceiling and sweeping staircase, and the agreeable rooms make the necessary 21st-century concessions. It's also blessed with very helpful staff.

City Hotel (☎ 708 40 00; www.cityhotelgbg.se; Lorensbergsgatan 6; s/d without bathroom from Skr495/595, discounted to Skr445/545) The City represents excellent value for such a central hotel (within yards of Sweden's 'Champs Elysées'), and all rooms have recently been renovated. For about Skr300 extra you can have a private bathroom. There's no dining room, so breakfast is brought to your door.

Hotel Opera (☎ 80 50 80; www.hotelopera.se; Norra Hamngatan 38; budget s/d Skr750/895, discounted to Skr495/795, standard s/d Skr1095/1295, discounted to Skr695/895) Conveniently located by the train station and bus terminal. Budget rooms are in an older part of the hotel and are small but adequate, while standard rooms are larger, better decorated, and have extras like desks; all rooms have private bathrooms. Sauna and Jacuzzi are available to all.

Hotel Flora (☎ 13 86 16; www.hotelflora.se; Grönsakstorget 2; s/d Skr475/620, with bathroom Skr990/1195, discounted to Skr650/850) Handily central, not far from the tourist office. It's an old building, slightly battered but comfortable, with a 24-hour reception. Four of the rooms have pleasing river views.

Top-End

Hotel Odin Residence (☎ 745 22 00; www.hotelodin.se; Odinsgatan 6; apt s/d from Skr1495/1895; 💻) Our top pick for space and comfort. This new hotel has fabulous apartments filled with the kind of décor and gadgets you'd kill for at home, and all come equipped with everything you need for a long, happy stay (including a full kitchen, and lounge with TV and stereo). There are cheaper rates for stays of longer than a week.

Hotel Gothia Towers (☎ 750 88 00; info@gothiatowers.com; Mässans Gata 24; s/d from Skr1690/2090, discounted to Skr940/1040; P 💻) Scandinavia's largest hotel is the whopping 23-storey Gothia Towers (take tram 5). Its 704 rooms are stylish and modern, particularly the new 'Design' options: all sharp, clean lines and bathroom windows so you can admire the view from the bath! The sky bar and restaurant Heaven 23, with superb panoramas over the city, are popular with nonguests too.

Radisson SAS Scandinavia Hotel (☎ 758 50 00; Södra Hamngatan 59-65; s/d from Skr1870/1970, discounted to Skr1290/1290; P 💻 🏊) This is one of the most luxurious hotels in Göteborg. Rooms run around a vast atrium (containing shops, bar and restaurant): there's something of a spaceship feel to those looking inwards. Snazzy rooms have beds with light-up Perspex headboards! There's also a health club to help you relax. Breakfast isn't included in the price.

The Scandic chain has several hotels in Göteborg, including:

Scandic Hotel Europa (☎ 751 65 00; europa@scandic-hotels.com; Köpmansgatan 38; s/d Skr1500/1700, discounted to Skr940/990; P 💻 🏊) With 6th-floor pool and sauna area.

Scandic Hotel Rubinen (☎ 751 54 00; rubinen@scandic-hotels.com; Kungsportsavenyn 24; s/d Skr1795/2295, discounted to Skr950/1250; 💻) In the heart of the Avenyn action, with on-site restaurants and cocktail bar.

Eating

Göteborg is awash with sleek and fashionable restaurants. Kungsportsavenyn is lined with restaurant/bars and alfresco eating is the thing when the sun comes out: however, you pay for the privilege of dining on the Avenyn. Vasagatan and Linnégatan have a good choice of restaurants too, but with less big-city pizzazz and often lower prices. Many dining places close on Sundays.

RESTAURANTS

Budget

Andrum (☎ 13 85 04; Östra Hamngatan 19; large/small/mini plate Skr65/50/35; 🕑 11am-10pm Mon-Fri, noon-8pm Sat & Sun) One for the veggies, Andrum does an all-day lunch buffet which is excellent value for money. Choose your plate size, then select from a spread of salads, hot mains and homemade breads. It's simple, tasty, wholesome stuff, and cheerfully recommended.

Bombay (☎ 12 00 39; www.restaurangbombay.com; Andra Långgatan 8; lunch Skr55, mains from Skr70) Bombay is quite a busy lunchtime spot. It does good-value Indian dishes to eat in or take away, with decent tandoori and vegetarian selections.

Solrosen (Kaponjärgatan 4; dinner mains from Skr65; 11.30am-1am Mon-Fri, 2pm-1am Sat) 'Cheap' seems to equate with 'vegetarian' in Göteborg. Another purse-easy choice is 'The Sunflower', a slightly grungy studenty veggie place with great buffets and an all-day special.

Midrange

Trädgår'n (☎ 10 20 90; bokningen@tradgarn.se; Nya Allén; lunch from Skr95, dinner mains Skr145-285; closed Sun) This cool and spacious restaurant, bar and nightclub (until 5am Friday and Saturday) has a summer terrace backing onto the lovely Trädgårdsföreningen park. Lunch here is a treat, with salads, hotplate dishes and four-course meal deals, depending on how hungry you are. In the evening, the restaurant's award-winning chefs rustle up excellent fish and seafood buffets.

Brasserie Lipp (☎ 10 58 30; info@brasserielipp.com; Kungsportsavenyn 8; mains Skr120-240; until at least 1am, closed Sun Oct-Mar) Classic and classy, this French-inspired bar-restaurant has good light meals on its menu, including Caesar salads and club sandwiches, plus more substantial Mediterranean and Asian evening mains. It's also a popular bar, with live DJs on Friday and Saturday nights in summer.

Bliss (☎ 13 85 55; Magasinsgatan 3; lunch Skr74, dinner mains around Skr210; 11.30am-2.30pm Mon-Fri, 6pm-1am or 2am Tue-Sat) Bliss has one of the hippest interiors in Göteborg, with low designer seats, multicoloured fairy lights, and superb food. It's a real night-time joint: if you're not up to a big meal, you can share tapas-style bar snacks and dance to live DJs until late.

Cyrano (☎ 14 30 10; Prinsgatan 7; mains around Skr190; 5-11pm Mon-Fri, 2-11pm Sat, 2-9pm Sun) Squint and you could almost be in Provence. This inviting little French bistro has a warm dark-wood interior and a few outdoor seats. There's an à la carte menu of fish, duck and lamb mains (or frogs' legs in Pernod!), and a larger pizza menu.

Smaka (☎ 13 22 47; info@smaka.se; Vasaplatsen 3; mains Skr120-200; 5pm to 1am or 2am) Smaka serves up wonderful, traditional Swedish *husmanskost* (home cooking) like elk burgers, gravadlax and its speciality, meatballs with mashed potato and lingonberries. Finish off your meal with a cloudberry soufflé, then retire to the lively bar.

Joe Farelli's (☎ 10 58 26; www.joefarelli.com; Kungsportsavenyn 12; pizzas 120-200, mains Skr150-260; noon-1am, to 3am Fri & Sat) A casual Italian-American restaurant-bar, where you can slap ketchup on your US burgers 'n' steaks, or get misty-eyed about the old country with Sicilian-style bruschetta, pizza and pasta. Its Sunday brunch is perfect for soaking up Saturday night's beer.

A Hereford Beefstouw (☎ 775 04 41; www.hereford-beef.com; Linnégatan 5; lunch Skr85, steaks Skr130-350; closed lunch, Sun & Mon in summer) If you're feeling anaemic, this upmarket steakhouse is the answer, offering all manner of meat, including T-bone steaks, veal sirloin and rack of lamb. Solid meals are served on solid African oak tables, and you get a good view of busy Linnégatan as you eat.

Sjöbaren (☎ 711 97 80; Haga Nygata 25; mains Skr100-160; 11am-11pm Mon-Thu, 11am-midnight Fri, noon-midnight Sat, 1-10pm Sun) This cosy place, in the Haga district, serves well-prepared Swedish seafood in a nautical setting (inside) or pleasant courtyard garden. Go for classic dishes like gravadlax, fish soup or seafood pasta.

Den Lilla Tavernan (☎ 12 88 05; Olivedalsgatan 17; mezes Skr30-70, mains around Skr100; from 4pm Mon-Fri, from 1pm Sat & Sun) The Little Tavern is a charming and authentic spot with reasonably priced Greek favourites and a great array of mezes perfect for sharing. There's also musical entertainment of a bazouki nature.

Magnus & Magnus (☎ 13 30 00; magnus@magnusmagnus.com; Magasinsgatan 8; mains Skr155-255; from 6pm Mon-Sat) This modern restaurant draws fashionable crowds with its relaxed atmosphere. Low chairs and handsome tables make it feel more like someone's (swanky) home than a business, and there's a summer courtyard for alfresco dining. Meals are mainly meat and fish, with a tasty range of starters.

Top End

28+ (☎ 20 21 61; Götabergsgatan 28; mains Skr295-365; 6-11pm Mon-Sat) This award-winning gourmet restaurant is a special-occasion place. Thoughtful and intriguing dishes are predominantly fishy, and include smoked mussels with pickled cucumber and baked anglerfish with cherry tomatoes and risotto. For a really exceptional blow-out, go for the seven-course *degustation* fish menu (Skr795). Awkwardly, the restaurant closes from mid-June to late August.

Fiskekrogen (☎ 10 10 05; www.fiskekrogen.com; Lilla Torget 1; mains Skr255-375; ⏰ lunch & dinner Mon-Sat) This is a magnificent fish and seafood restaurant in former East India Company buildings. It has an impressive circular dining room called Blåskajsa, and an equally impressive cellar of over 400 wines.

Linnéa (☎ 16 11 83; info@restauranglinnea.com; Södra Vägen 32; lunch Skr95, mains Skr220-300; ⏰ noon-2pm Mon-Fri, from 5.30pm Mon-Sat) Modern Swedish cuisine is served up at exclusive, intimate Linnéa. Fancy ingredients and some surprisingly homely ones (gooseberries, nettles and lentils) are spun into subtle and succulent meals, beautifully presented on glass plates.

CAFÉS

All of Göteborg's museums have excellent cafés.

Brogyllens Konditori (☎ 13 87 13; Västra Hamngatan 2; snacks Skr25-50; ⏰ closed Sun) Splendid breads, pastries, coffee and cakes are served at this traditional *konditori*. It's swimming in elegance, with grand chandeliers overhead and graceful sculptures scattered around.

Eva's Paley (☎ 16 30 70; Kungsportsavenyn 39; dishes Skr40-60; ⏰ until at least 11pm Mon-Sat) Something of a Göteborg institution, this huge café opens until late every evening and has plenty of outdoor seating in summer. It serves baked potatoes, wraps, meat and veggie pasta, salads and a rainbow of fresh muffins (buy them to take home from the bakery next door).

Café Kosmos (☎ 13 14 00; Västra Hamngatan 20; ⏰ 10am-10pm Mon-Sat, 11am-10pm Sat, noon-10pm Sun) One giant mass of tables (don't expect any privacy), this slick place attracts 20-something crowds. All the usual coffee 'n' café snacks are served up, although one feels the social scene is more important.

Along the leafy Vasagatan boulevard, near the university, there are quite a few cafés. **Java Kaffebar** (Vasagatan 32) is a true student haunt, thick with dreadlocks, dyed hair and nipple rings. It offers cheap bagels and sandwiches to its customers. **Café Garbo** (☎ 774 19 25; Vasagatan 40) and the very trendy **Espresso House** (☎ 397 50; Vasagatan 22) are two coffee houses in the same area, both with large windows and prime people-watching opportunities, plus fashionable café food (Skr30 to Skr60).

QUICK EATS

If you need something quick, the Nordstan shopping complex has loads of fast-food outlets.

Aldardo (☎ 13 23 00; Kungstorget 12; pizza slice from Skr25, pasta from Skr40; ⏰ 10am-6pm Mon-Fri, 10am-2pm Sat, closed mid-Jul–Aug) Right by the tourist office, this busy deli is a recommended spot to pick up authentic Italian fast food – homemade pizza *al taglio* (by the slice) and pasta dishes to go.

Crepe Van (crêpes from Skr20; ⏰ 4-9pm Mon-Thu, 4pm-3am Fri & Sat) Those with a sweet tooth should head to this takeaway van near the McDonald's branch on Linnégatan, also a favourite of 'flushed and clumsy' patrons late on Friday and Saturday.

Sushi & Soda (Prinsgatan 4; ⏰ until 9pm) A sushi takeaway with several branches in the city. This outlet is closest to several of the hostels and serves excellent Japanese lunch deals, including miso soup and 11 pieces of sushi, for around Skr70.

Kalaya (☎ 12 39 98; Olivedalsgatan 13; dishes from Skr60; ⏰ 11am-10pm) Also near the hostel area, Kalaya has authentic Thai noodle and curry dishes.

Alexandras (Kungstorget; ☎ 711 78 78) Located in the central Saluhallen, this place is renowned for its excellent hearty soups and stews (around Skr40), particularly welcoming on a cold day.

SELF-CATERING

Saluhallen (Kungstorget; ⏰ 9am-6pm Mon-Fri, 9am-3pm Sat) This classic old central market hall is the perfect place to put together your picnic pack, with munchables from around the world. It is also full of excellent budget eateries and food stalls.

Saluhall Briggen (Nordhemsgatan 28; ⏰ 9am-6pm Mon-Fri, 9am-2pm Sat) Not as big or as busy as the central Saluhallen, this covered market nevertheless has an array of lunch stalls handy for the hostel district.

Feskekörka (☎ 711 35 09; Rosenlundsgatan; ⏰ 9am-6pm Mon-Fri, 8am-1pm Sat Jun-Aug, closed Mon rest of yr) A market devoted to fresh fish and squamous things, the 'Fish Church' will delight seafood fans.

Hemköp supermarket (Nordstan complex; ⏰ 8am-10pm) Big supermarket in the thick of things.

Systembolaget Kungsportsavenyn (☎ 18 65 24; Kungsportsavenyn 18); Kungsgatan (☎ 711 86 16; Kungsgatan 6) There are various Systembolagets dotted about the place, selling beer, wine and spirits. These are the two most conveniently located in Göteborg.

Drinking

Swedish licensing laws mean that bars must have a restaurant section, although in most cases, it's vice versa – stroll down Kungsportsavenyn and see what takes your fancy. There are also several bars on Järntorget that are currently 'in' drinking spots.

Ölhallen 7:an (☎ 13 60 79; Kungstorget 7) One place that you should check out is this little gem, a well-worn Swedish beerhall that hasn't changed in about 100 years. There's no food, wine or pretension, just beer, and plenty of choices.

Dubliner (☎ 13 90 20; www.dubliner.se; Östra Hamngatan 50B) As authentic an Irish pub as you'll ever find on the continent, the Dubliner has pints of Guinness, bar meals like beef-and-Guinness pie, and live Celtic music every night in summer.

O'Leary's (☎ 711 55 19; Östra Hamngatan 36) Almost opposite is this American-style sports bar with sporting memorabilia plastering the walls, 30 TV screens and bar snacks of the chicken-wing-and-burger variety.

Rose & Crown (☎ 10 58 27; Kungsportsavenyn 6) This is an 'English-style' pub popular with tourists and locals. There's more of a concentration on the restaurant and less on in-your-face drinking than at some other bars.

Dancin' Dingo (☎ 81 18 12; www.dancindingo.se; Kristinelundsgatan 16; until 2am or 3am) Just in case any nationalities are feeling left out, here's an entertaining Australian pub not far off Kungsportsavenyn, with a great if raucous atmosphere.

Entertainment

CLUBS

Most clubs have an age limit of 25 or 27, and there may be an admission charge depending on the night.

Nivå (☎ 701 80 90; Kungsportsavenyn 9; admission free-Skr100; until 3am Wed & Thu, until 4am Fri & Sat) This bar/restaurant metamorphoses into a crowd-pleasing (and crowded) club as the week draws on, with several floors of action. Wednesday night is soul night; other nights are a mix of dancey music, with mellower tunes in the Skybaren.

Valand (☎ 18 30 93; nattklubb@valand.nu; until 3am Wed, until 5am Thu-Sat) Vintage Valand, on the corner of Vasagatan and Kungsportsavenyn, draws a mixed, party-hard crowd. There are various nights – student, R&B, soul, mainstream dance – so check what's on first.

Trädgår'n (☎ 10 20 90; Nya Allén; admission Skr100; until 5am Fri & Sat) With its crazy lasers, huge dance floor and outdoor terrace, this is one of the biggest clubs.

MataHari (☎ 13 69 49; www.gretas.nu; Drottninggatan 35; until 4am Fri & Sat) The nearest thing in Göteborg to a gay club, but welcoming to all, MataHari (part of Gretas Bar & Kök) gets kitschy on Friday and Saturday nights. The minimum age is 20 years.

Nefertiti (☎ 711 15 33; Hvitfeldtsplatsen 6) Supercool Nefertiti near the Fish Church, is a large and well-established venue for live jazz, blues and ethnic music; it also has a nightclub, restaurant and café.

Jazzhuset (☎ 13 35 44; info@jazzhuset.se; Erik Dahlbergsgatan 3) An old jazz club drawing a more mature crowd to its live music sessions, usually Fridays and Saturdays until 3am. In an attempt to snare a younger audience, it also hosts rock and pop bands on Thursdays.

CINEMA, CONCERTS & THEATRE

Check the local events listings for movies and shows or with the tourist office for current schedules and prices.

Göteborgs Stadsteatern (City Theatre; ☎ 61 50 50; www.stadsteatern.goteborg.se; Götaplatsen; tickets from Skr210; closed summer) Stages theatre productions in Swedish.

Göteborgs Konserthus (Concert Hall; ☎ 726 53 00; www.gso.se; Götaplatsen; closed summer) Home to the local symphony orchestra, with some interesting performances.

GöteborgsOperan (☎ 13 13 00; www.opera.se in Swedish; Christina Nilssons gata; tickets Skr100-500) At Lilla Bommen harbour, stages classical and modern ballet and opera and assorted musical performances.

Nya Ullevi (☎ 81 10 20; www.ullevi.se; Skånegatan) An outdoor stadium where huge pop and rock concerts are held.

Scandinavium (☎ 81 10 20; www.scandinavium.se; Valhallagatan 1) An indoor concert venue near Nya Ullevi and run by the same company.

The two biggest cinemas in the centre are the 10-screen **Biopalatset** (☎ 17 45 00; Kungstorget) and **Filmstaden** (☎ 0856-26 00 00; Kungsgatan 35), showing blockbuster movies.

SPORT

Göteborgers are avid sports fans. The city's two biggest stadiums are the outdoor Nya Ullevi (see opposite) for **football** matches, and the indoor Scandinavium (see opposite) where the crowds go wild for **ice hockey**. In August 2006 the European Athletics Championships will be held at the Ullevi stadium.

Shopping

DesignTorget (☎ 774 00 17; Vallgatan 14) A great store showcasing the works (usually quite affordable) of established as well as up-and-coming designers.

Naturkompaniet (☎ 13 51 60; Stora Nygatan 33; Mon-Sat) Sells a wide range of camping and outdoor equipment.

Nordstan shopping complex (☎ 62 39 76) is Sweden's largest mall, with around 150 shops. These include the upmarket department store **NK** (☎ 710 10 00; Östra Hamngatan 42) and cheaper **Åhléns** (☎ 333 4000; Östra Hamngatan 18), both stocking a good range of quality souvenirs.

Göteborg has over 30 art galleries, all with art for sale and free admission. Ask the tourist office for the handy leaflet *Konst i Göteborg*, which has a map showing the city's galleries and design studios.

Getting There & Away

AIR

Twenty-five kilometres east of the city, **Landvetter airport** (☎ 94 10 00; www.landvetter.lfv.se) has up to 30 direct daily flights to/from Stockholm Arlanda and Stockholm Bromma airports (with SAS and Malmö Aviation), as well as a daily service to Umeå and several services per week to Borlänge, Luleå and Sundsvall. See p323 for contact details.

There are also direct flights to European cities including Amsterdam (KLM), Brussels (SN Brussels), Copenhagen (SAS), Frankfurt (Lufthansa and SAS), Helsinki (Finnair, Blue1 and City Airline), London (SAS), Manchester (City Airline), Munich (Lufthansa), Oslo (Wideroe) and Paris (Air France).

Göteborg City Airport (☎ 92 60 60; www.goteborgairport.se), some 15km north of the city at Säve, is used by Ryanair for budget flights to London Stansted, Glasgow and Frankfurt.

BOAT

Göteborg is Scandinavia's largest port and a major entry point for ferries. There are several car/passenger terminals, with ferries to Denmark, Germany, Norway and the UK: for more details see p328.

Nearest to the city centre, the **Stena Line** (☎ 704 00 00; www.stenaline.se) Denmark terminal near Masthuggstorget (tram 3, 9 or 11) has at least seven daily departures for Frederikshavn, with a 50% discount for railpass holders.

Faster and more expensive **SeaCat** (☎ 720 08 00) catamarans to Frederikshavn depart up to three times a day in summer from near Sjöfartsmuseet. Take tram 3 or 9 to Stigbergstorget.

Further west is the Stena Line terminal for the daily car ferry to Kiel (Germany). Take tram 3 or 9 to Chapmans Torg.

DFDS Seaways (☎ 65 06 80; www.dfdsseaways.se) sails twice weekly to Kristiansand (Norway) and Newcastle (UK) from Skandiahamnen on Hisingen (take tram 6 to Frihamnen).

BUS

The bus station, Nils Ericson Terminalen, is next to the train station. There's a **Tidpunkten** (☎ 0771-41 43 00; 7am-10pm Mon-Fri, 9am-10pm Sat, 9am-7pm Sun) office here, giving information and selling tickets for all city and regional public transport within the Göteborg, Bohuslän and Västergötland area.

Eurolines (☎ 10 02 40; www.eurolines.com; Nils Ericsonplatsen) has its main Swedish office at the bus station in central Göteborg. See p326 for details on international bus services offered by the company.

Swebus Express (☎ 0200-21 82 18; www.swebusexpress.se) has an office at the bus terminal and operates frequent buses to most major towns. Services to Stockholm (Skr400, seven hours) run seven to 10 times daily. Other direct destinations include Copenhagen (Skr319, four hours), Halmstad (Skr120, 1¾ hours), Helsingborg (Skr233, three hours), Jönköping (Skr120, two hours), Oslo (Skr250, 3¾ hours), Malmö (Skr281, three hours), and Örebro (Skr281, four hours).

Säfflebussen (☎ 0771-15 15 15; www.safflebussen.se) runs services to Copenhagen (Skr280, 4½ hours, seven daily), Oslo (Skr220, 3¾ hours, seven daily) and Stockholm (Skr320, seven hours, up to four times daily).

Less frequent (usually one to three on Friday and/or Sunday), **Svenska Buss** (☎ 0771-67 67 67; www.svenskabuss.se) runs buses to major towns such as Helsingborg (Skr200, 2½ hours), Malmö (Skr250, four hours) and Oskarshamn (Skr300, 4¾ hours); departures for Stockholm (Skr360, 7¾ hours) via Jönköping (Skr210, 2¼ hours) are daily.

Prices can be considerably lower than those quoted here for advanced bookings or for travel from Monday to Thursday (especially for Swebus Express and Säfflebussen).

CAR & MOTORCYCLE

The E6 motorway runs north–south from Oslo to Malmö just east of the city centre and there's also a complex junction where the E20 motorway diverges east for Stockholm.

International car-hire companies Avis, Europcar and Hertz have desks at Landvetter and Göteborg City airports. For car hire in

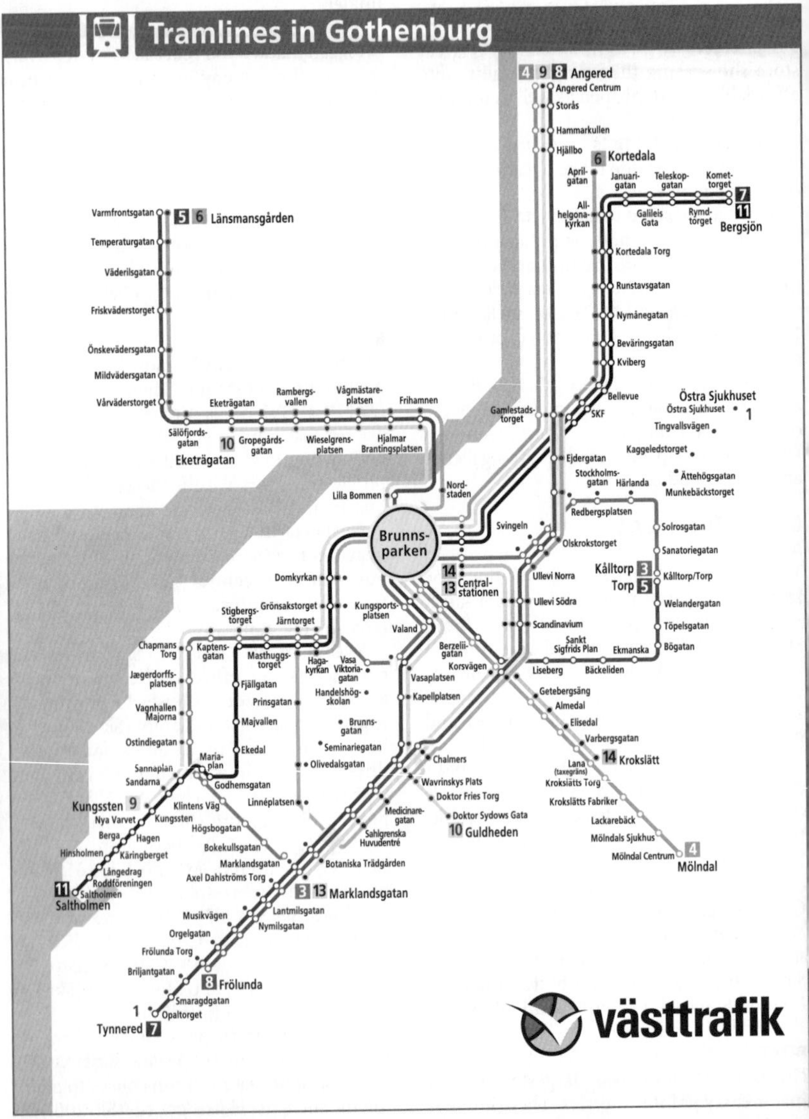

town, contact one of the petrol stations, for example **Statoil** (☎ 85 97 80; Andra Långgatan 46), in the southwestern part of town.

TRAIN

Centralstationen is the oldest railway station in Sweden and is now a listed building. It serves SJ and regional trains, with direct trains to Copenhagen (Skr540, four hours), Malmö (Skr480, 3¼ hours) and Oslo (Skr390, four hours), as well as numerous other destinations in the southern half of Sweden.

Direct Intercity trains to Stockholm depart approximately every two hours (Skr490, five hours), with quicker but more expensive X2000 trains (Skr1110, three hours) also every two hours. Booking your ticket at least a week in advance will bring decent reductions to the prices quoted here.

Overnight trains to the far north of Sweden (via Stockholm) are operated by Tågkompaniet.

Getting Around

TO/FROM THE AIRPORT

Landvetter airport, 25km east of the city, has a frequent Flygbuss service to/from Nils Ericson Terminalen (one-way Skr70, 30 minutes). A taxi from the city centre to the airport will cost around Skr370.

Buses from Göteborg City Airport to Nils Ericson Terminalen leave 50 minutes after flight arrivals. For the return journey, they leave the bus terminal around 2½ hours before flight departures (one-way Skr50, 30 minutes). A taxi should cost around Skr250.

BICYCLE

With the Göteborg Pass, you're entitled to borrow a bike for free from **Cykelverkstan** (☎ 711 97 70; Parkgatan 29): bring some ID. Otherwise try **Cykelkungen** (☎ 18 43 00; Chalmersgatan 19; per day/wk Skr120/500).

PUBLIC TRANSPORT

Buses, trams and ferries run by **Västtrafik** (☎ 0771-41 43 00) make up the city's public transport system; there are Tidpunkten information booths selling tickets and giving out timetables inside **Nils Ericson Terminalen** (🕓 7am-10pm Mon-Fri, 9am-10pm Sat, 9am-7pm Sun), in front of the train station on **Drottningtorget** (🕓 6am-8pm Mon-Fri, 8am-8pm Sat & Sun), and at **Brunnsparken** (🕓 7am-7pm Mon-Fri, 9am-6pm Sat).

Holders of the Göteborg Pass travel free, including on late-night transport. Otherwise a city transport ticket costs adult/child Skr20/10 (Skr40 on late-night transport). Easy-to-use Maxirabatt 100 'value cards' cost Skr100 (from Tidpunkten or Pressbyrån newsagencies) and work out much cheaper than buying tickets each time you travel. A 24-hour Dagkort (day pass) for the whole city area costs Skr50.

The easiest way to cover lengthy distances in Göteborg is by tram. Lines, numbered 1 to 14, converge near Brunnsparken (a block from the train station).

Västtrafik has regional passes for 24 hours/30 days (Skr225/1400) that give unlimited travel on all *länstrafik* buses, trains and boats within Göteborg, Bohuslän and the Västergötland area.

TAXI

One of the larger companies is **Taxi Göteborg** (☎ 65 00 00). Taxis can be picked up outside Centralstationen, at Kungsportsplatsen, and on Kungsportsavenyn. Women travelling alone at night can expect a fare discount.

AROUND GÖTEBORG

Southern Archipelago

☎ 031 / pop 4300

A car-free paradise, the southern archipelago is just a short hop from the busy city. It can get busy in summer, particularly the beaches, but wriggle around and you'll always find a quiet stretch of sand or serene green corner.

There are nine major islands and numerous smaller ones. The largest island is Styrsö, but even that's less than 3km long. Due to previous military restrictions, most of the area was closed to foreigners until 1997; it's now a favourite residential area for wealthy commuters.

Take tram 11 from Göteborg city centre to Saltholmen, from where an excellent 16-destination passenger-only ferry network runs round the islands. The Göteborg Pass is valid, or you can buy a ticket (one-way Skr20) that takes you all the way from central Göteborg to Vrångö; bikes (if there's space available) cost an extra Skr10.

Boats run frequently to Asperö (nine minutes), Brännö (20 minutes) and Styrsö (30 minutes) from around 5.30am to 1am (less frequently at weekends); services to the other islands are more limited.

The best information about the islands is the English-language booklet *Touring the Archipelago*, published by Västtrafik and available from the tourist offices or Tidpunkten booths (see p215).

BRÄNNÖ

pop 790

Car-free Brännö's beaches and outdoor dance floor are its biggest attractions, although it's hard to take your eyes off the local *lastmoped*, bizarre-looking motorised bikes with large trays attached.

The busiest ferry terminal is Rödsten, in the northeast, but ferries also call at Husvik in the southwest. The island's website (www.branno.nu) is in Swedish only.

From the church in the centre of the island, follow the cycle track through the woods towards the west coast. A 15-minute walk from the end of the track leads to a stone causeway and the island **Galterö** – a strange treeless landscape of rock slabs, ponds, deserted sandy beaches and haunting bird calls. You can watch ships of all sizes and colours sail into or out of Göteborg harbour.

On Thursdays from mid-June to mid-August, **Börjessons** (☎ 60 96 70; www.borjessons.com) runs evening cruises from Lilla Bommen harbour to Husvik's **pier dance floor**, where passengers can boogie for a couple of hours before returning to the city. The tour costs Skr130/65 per adult/child; dinner is available on board at an additional cost.

Pensionat Bagge (☎ 97 38 80; www.baggebranno.se; s/d low season Skr330/500, high season Skr390/660) Get away from it all at this simple, friendly place about a kilometre south of the ferry quay; it also offers bike hire.

Brännö Värdshus (☎ 97 04 78; info@brannovardshus.se; Husviksvägen; mains Skr100-210; 🕐 11am-11pm mid-Jun–mid-Aug, 11am-9pm Tue-Sun May, 11am-7pm Thu-Sun rest of yr) With the same owners, the Värdshus has a restaurant, café and bakery and serves excellent meals, including the local speciality *rödspätta* (plaice). There's a grocery shop near the church.

OTHER ISLANDS

Just southeast of Brännö, **Köpstadsö** is a small island with a quaint village of white-painted houses and narrow streets. Transport on the island is even more basic than on Brännö: locals use individually named wheelbarrows, which you'll see neatly parked by the quay!

In the central part of the archipelago, **Styrsö** has two village centres (Bratten and Tången, both with ferry terminals), a mixture of old and modern houses, and a colourful history of smuggling. There's a café and pizzeria at Tången, and a supermarket. A bridge crosses from Styrsö to neighbouring densely populated **Donsö**, with a functioning fishing harbour.

The southern island of **Vrångö** has a good beach for swimming on the west coast, about 10 minutes' walk from the ferry. The northern and southern ends of the island are part of an extensive nature reserve.

Tiny **Vinga**, 8km west of Galterö, has impressive rock slabs and good swimming, and it has been home to a lighthouse since the 17th century. The writer, composer and painter, Evert Taube, was born on the island in 1890 – his father was the lighthouse-keeper. **Borjessons** (☎ 60 96 70; www.borjessons.com) runs full-day tours (adult/6-12 years Skr130/70) from Lilla Bommen (Göteborg) to Vinga via Nya Älvsborg Fästning, daily from mid-July to mid-August.

Marstrand

☎ 0303 / pop 1300

Once a spa town and favourite of the Swedish royal family, Marstrand, with its wooden houses and picturesque island setting, still attracts affluent visitors. It contains Sweden's most popular *gästhamn* (guest harbour), and is *the* weekend destination for boatie types. The village fairly hums with people in summer, but if you don't mind sharing it…well, it's worth sharing.

After disembarking, turn left for the **tourist office** (☎ 600 87; www.marstrand.se; Hamngatan 33; 🕐 9am-6pm Mon-Fri, 11am-5pm Sat, noon-4pm Sun mid-Jun–mid-Aug, 8am-noon Mon-Fri rest of yr). There's no ATM or Systembolaget, so bring wealth and wine with you.

Looming over the village is doughty **Carlstens Fästning** (☎ 602 65; www.carlsten.se; adult/7-15yr Skr60/20; 🕐 11am-6pm mid-Jun–mid-Aug, 11am-4pm Sat & Sun rest of yr), a fortress constructed in the 1660s after the Swedish takeover of Bohuslän; later building work was done by convicts sentenced to hard labour. Its impressive round tower reaches 96m above sea level, and there are smashing archipelago views from the top. Admission includes a guided tour (phone ahead for English-language times), although you can explore by yourself with an audio guide.

Pick up the English-language *Discover Marstrand* brochure (Skr10) from the tourist office and set off for an hour's walk round the island. Buildings of interest include the **town hall**, which is the oldest stone building in the county, and **Maria Kyrka**, dating from the 13th century.

Most of the accommodation options on the island are upmarket.

Marstrands Varmbadhus Båtellet (☎ 600 10; marstrandsvarmbadhus@telia.com; Kungsplan; d/tr/q Skr675/885/1180;) Marstrand's most reasonably priced accommodation is this private hostel, continuing the town's spa tradition with its associated pool and sauna. Turn right after disembarking from the ferry and follow the waterfront for 400m.

Hotell Nautic (☎ 610 30; www.hotellnautic.com; Långgatan 6; B&B s/d Skr850/1100) Located at the northern end of the harbour, the Nautic has bright and simple rooms decked out in blues and creams. A couple have balconies with great sea views.

There are numerous eating options in Marstrand, including cheap fast-food stalls along the harbour.

Marstrands Wärdshus (☎ 603 69; Hamngatan 23; noon-1am Easter-Sep) For fresh seafood in the open air, head for this crustacean restaurant by the harbour. There's a big sunny terrace where you can sit with a G&T and watch the boats sail by.

Bergs Konditori (☎ 600 96; Hamngatan 9; snacks Skr30-60; May-Aug) Follow your nose to this dockside *konditori*, selling fresh bread, cakes, quiches and sandwiches.

From Göteborg you can take bus 312 to Arvidsvik (on Koön) then cross to Marstrand by frequent passenger-only ferry. The complete journey should take about an hour and cost Skr50.

Bohus Fästning

☎ 0303

Survivor of no fewer than 14 sieges, the hulking ruins of **Bohus Fästning** (☎ 992 00; adult/6-16yr Skr30/15; 10am-7pm May-Aug, 11am-5pm Sep, 11am-4pm Sat & Sun Apr) stand on an island in the Nordre älv, near Kungälv. Construction of the fortress was ordered in 1308 by the Norwegian king, to protect Norway's southern border. The building was enlarged over the centuries, becoming one of Sweden's toys at the Peace of Roskilde in 1658. Nowadays, its substantial remains include a remarkable **round tower**. Tourist information for the area is available at the fortress.

STF Vandrarhem & Camping Kungälv (☎ 189 00; info@kungalvsvandrarhem.se; Färjevägen 2, Kungälv; sites Skr130, dm Skr150, 4-bed cabins Skr495; camp site May-mid–Sep) This hostel is in a pleasant riverside setting directly across the road from the fortress. There's also a café here, and you can rent small boats.

The Grön Express bus runs at least every 30 minutes from Göteborg to Kungälv; get off at the Eriksdal stop (Skr40, 25 minutes) and walk the remaining 500m.

BOHUSLÄN

Bohuslän Coast

Some of the finest scenery in Sweden is found along the beautiful Bohuslän Coast. Craggy islands, picturesque fishing villages and the soft western light all create a dreamy magic. It does get very busy in summer with boat- and land-bound tourists, but you'll always find a quiet corner somewhere.

If you're heading north from Göteborg, stop at the **tourist office** (☎ 0303-833 27; www.bastkusten.se; Kulturhuset Fregattan; 9.30am-6pm Mon-Sat, 11am-3pm Sun mid-Jun–mid-Aug, 9am-5pm Mon-Fri rest of yr) in Stenungsund to pick up brochures and especially maps of the surrounding area.

Transport connections are good: the E6 motorway runs north from Göteborg to Oslo via the larger towns of Stenungsund, Ljungskile, Herrestad, Munkedal, Tanumshede and passing close to Strömstad before crossing the Norwegian border. There's a local train service that runs frequently from Göteborg to Strömstad, via much the same towns as the E6 route. Bus connections from these towns to the outlying islands exist, although some aren't terribly frequent. It's an area suited for independent exploration – consider hiring a car or bike in Göteborg so you can enjoy things at your own pace.

TJÖRN & AROUND

☎ 0304 / pop 15,019

A large bridge swoops from Stenungsund (on the Swedish mainland) to the island of **Tjörn** (www.tjorn.se). It's a magnet for artists, thanks to its general prettiness and spangling new watercolour museum; and a fave for sailors, with one of Sweden's biggest sailing competitions, the Tjörn Runt, taking place here in mid/late August.

Skärhamn and **Rönnäng**, in the southwest, are the main settlements on the island and have a few facilities, including a small **tourist office** (☎ 67 10 40; skarhamn@bastkusten.se; Södra Hamnen; 9.30am-6pm Mon-Sat, 11am-3pm mid-Jun–mid-Aug, noon-5pm Mon-Fri, 11am-3pm Sat rest of yr) at Skärhamn.

Skärhamn also contains the impressive **Nordiska Akvarellmuseet** (Nordic Watercolour Museum; ☎ 60 00 80; www.akvarellmuseet.org; Södra Hamnen 6; adult/7-20yr Skr70/10; 11am-6pm Jun-Sep, noon-5pm Tue, Wed & Fri-Sun, noon-8pm Thu Oct-May), a sleek and stylish waterside building housing changing exhibits. There's an award-winning gourmet café and restaurant **Vatten** (☎ 67 00 87) attached; its fish dishes are particularly recommended.

Up the hill is a working smithy, **Smedja Volund** (☎ 67 17 55; info.volund@swipnet.se; Gråskärsvägen 9; 11am-8pm mid-Jun–mid-Aug, noon-5pm Tue-Sun rest of yr), with a café and a studio displaying Bert the blacksmith's unique ironwork; the man himself is often hard at work in the forge.

The Tjörnexpressen bus runs up to eight times weekdays (twice Saturday and Sunday) from Göteborg's bus terminal to Tjörn, calling at Skärhamn, Klädesholmen and Rönnäng. Bus 350 from Stenungsund crosses the island to Rönnäng.

Klädesholmen

The 'herring island' of Klädesholmen, to the far south of Tjörn, is one of the most flawless places on the west coast, although activity is fairly subdued due to the departure of the herring (there were once 30 processing factories here, today reduced to a handful). Find out more at the tiny **herring museum** (☎ 67 33 08; kladesholmens-museum@swipnet.se; Sillgränd 8; adult/child Skr10/5; 3-7pm Jul–mid-Aug), which tells the story of the industry.

Neighbouring **Salt & Sill** (☎ 67 34 80; info@saltosill.com; mains Skr130-300; summer, Wed-Sun rest of yr) has a good choice of main courses, and naturally herring features heavily on the menu.

Åstol

Nearby **Åstol** looks like something from a bizarre dream – this tiny, barren chunk of rock is dotted with rows of white houses that seem to perch on top of each other from the sea. There's not much to do, but for some reason it's utterly loveable. Amble round the car-free streets, admire the views of the other islands, and try the fish at **Åstols Rökeri** (☎ 67 72 60; 11am-midnight mid-Jun–mid-Aug), a fish smokery with summer restaurant attached.

You can reach Åstol by ferry from Rönnäng (Skr30, roughly hourly between 6am and 11.30pm).

Rönnängs Vandrarhem (☎ 67 71 98; Nyponvägen 5, Rönnäng; dm Skr200; P) This SVIF hostel (in Rönnäng, about 1km from the ferry) is good and spacious, with one sizeable kitchen and dorms where you don't have to fight for bag room. The plant-filled terrace is popular for evening meals.

ORUST

☎ 0304 / pop 15,160

Sweden's third-biggest island, **Orust** (www.orust.se) has some breathtakingly pretty fishing villages. It has a thriving boat-building industry, with over half of Sweden's sailing craft made here. A bridge connects Orust to Tjörn, its southern neighbour.

Orust's **tourist office** (☎ 311 40; henan@bastkusten.se; Norra Strandvägen 3; 9.30am-6pm Mon-Sat, 10am-2pm Sun mid-Jun–mid-Aug, 10am-2pm Tue-Sat rest of yr) is in the town of Henån.

There's an outstanding STF hostel, **Tofta gård** (☎ 503 80; www.toftagard.se; low/high season dm Skr170/235, s Skr270/335, d Skr340/470) near Stocken in the island's west, about 5km from the larger village of Ellös. It's located in an old farmhouse and outbuildings in a delightful setting, with good walking, swimming and canoeing nearby. There's also a café and restaurant here in peak season. Reservations are necessary between October and May.

Mollösund

Super-cute **Mollösund**, in the island's southwest, is the oldest fishing village on the Bohuslän coast and is a great place on a sunny day. Artsy-craftsy shops surround a picture-perfect harbour, and there are several gently scenic walking paths.

Mollösunds Hembygdsmuseum (☎ 214 69; admission free; 11am-1pm & 5.30pm-7.30pm late-Jun–early Aug) is in an old fisher-folks house near the water and has exhibits about local life.

Prästgårdens Pension (☎ 210 58; www.prastgardens.se; Kyrkvägen; d from Skr700; P) Slightly inland from the harbour, this is the most delightful little spot. Every room is different: they're high-ceilinged and immaculate, yet retain a homely feel.

Vandrarhem, Café & Restaurant Emma (☎ 211 75; www.caféemma.com; dm Skr220; restaurant ⏲ 11am-midnight mid-Jun–mid-Aug) All things to all people, excellent Emma's is slap on the harbour. The hostel is small and welcoming, and you can rent bikes. The café/restaurant is making a name for itself by serving hearty dishes made from locally sourced and organic ingredients. Specialities are fish soup and exceptional ice cream. Out of season, book for the hostel and phone to check restaurant hours.

Mollösunds Wärdshus (☎ 211 08; Kyrkvägen 9; lunch Skr80, mains from Skr150; low/high season d from Skr850/950) This upmarket 19th-century inn is the place to come for drinks and light lunches in the flowery garden (the restaurant closes for dinner over the summer). There are eight well-turned-out rooms, tastefully decorated with touches of flowers or nautical themes.

There's an ICA supermarket near the harbour.

Bus 375 runs the Uddevalla–Henån–Ellös route around nine times a day Monday to Friday, continuing to Mollösund on six of these journeys (three buses Saturday and Sunday). The Orustexpressen bus runs several times on weekdays direct from Göteborg to Henån; otherwise change in Stenungsund or Lysekil.

LYSEKIL & AROUND

☎ 0523 / pop 14,767

With its air of faded grandeur, the former spa resort of Lysekil feels oddly like an English seaside town. It's low-key, and pampers its summer visitors less than other Bohuslän towns, but there's something pleasing about this more realistic attitude.

The **tourist office** (☎ 130 50; info@lysekilsturist.se; Södra Hamngatan 6; ⏲ 9am-7pm Mon-Sat, 11am-3pm Sun mid-Jun–mid-Aug, phone for times rest of yr) is helpful, and there are good amenities for travellers around town, including banks, supermarkets and **Bogart Video** (☎ 147 13; Rosvikstorg 4; per 30min Skr20; ⏲ 11am-10pm, to midnight summer), a video-rental shop with Internet access.

Sights & Activities

Havets Hus (House of the Sea; ☎ 196 71; www.havetshus.se; Strandvägen 9; adult/5-14yr Skr75/40; ⏲ 10am-4pm mid-Feb–Oct, to 6pm mid-Jun–mid-Aug) is a busy aquarium with sea life from Sweden's only true fjord, which cuts past Lysekil. Wolffish, lumpsuckers, anglerfish…all the cold-water beauties are here.

Lysekil has some interesting architecture dating back to its 19th-century spa days: old bathing huts and **Curmans villor**, the wooden seafront houses built in romantic 'Old Norse' style. Carl Curman was the resort's famous physician, who persuaded visitors that Lysekil's sea bathing was a complete cure-all.

Perched on a hill, the neo-Gothic pink-granite **church** (⏲ 11am-7pm) has some superb paintings and stained glass panes showing local working life.

Out at the tip of the Stångenäs peninsula, the **Stångehuvud Nature Reserve**, with lots of coastal rock slab, has quiet bathing spots and a wooden lookout tower.

Seal safaris (☎ 306 64 02; adult/under 14yr Skr140/70; ⏲ noon, 2pm & 4pm Sun-Thu, noon & 2pm Fri Jul–mid-Aug) lasting 1½ hours leave from near Havets Hus: buy tickets on board. Recommended 4½-hour **boat trips** (adult/child Skr150/75; ⏲ mid-Jun–mid-Aug) to the island of **Käringön** depart once a week in summer.

Passenger-only ferries cross the Gullmarn fjord roughly hourly to **Fiskebäckskil**, where there are cobbled streets, wood-clad houses, a harbour full of boats and a few good restaurants. The interior of the **church** is like an upturned boat, with votive ships and fine ceiling and wall paintings.

Sleeping & Eating

The tourist office can sort out **private rooms** (s/d from Skr285/450) for a booking fee of Skr75.

Strand Vandrarhem & Hotell (☎ 797 51; strand@strandflickorna.se; Strandvägen 1; dm Skr200, hostel s/d Skr250/500, hotel s/d Skr645/790; P) The friendly 'beach girls' run a choice of accommodation not far from Havets Hus. The hostel is a typically good SVIF choice, with hotel-style rooms on offer too; some have sea views.

Havshotell (☎ 797 50; Turistaten 13; s/d Skr895/1395, discounted to Skr795/1195; P) Run by the same folk, this is a more upmarket option than the hostel. It's based in a sensitively renovated turn-of-the-20th-century house, and has characterful rooms all with a seafaring/historical theme.

Siviks Camping (☎ 61 15 28; fax 127 27; sites low/high season Skr140/220; ⏲ mid-May–mid-Sep) Built on large pink-granite slabs by a sandy beach

2km north of town, Siviks is the best camp site in the area, with ample swimming opportunities. Facilities include shop, restaurant, minigolf, dance floor and laundry.

Pråmen (☎ 143 52; Södra Hamnen; lunch Skr95, mains Skr150-250; ⏰ noon-late) You can't miss Pråmen, an atmospheric floating restaurant and bar specialising, understandably, in fish and seafood with the odd meaty main. Crabs, mussels, prawns, halibut, salmon: if it swims, scuttles or sticks to rocks in the sea, it's on the menu.

Café Kungsgatan (☎ 160 01; Kungsgatan 2; lunch Skr70; ⏰ closed Sun) Set back from the seafront, this pleasant café serves homemade lunches: pasta, quiche, salads, hot and cold sandwiches, washed down with all kinds of teas and coffees.

There are a few fast-food places on and around Rosvikstorg and eateries all along the main street.

Getting There & Away

Express bus 840 and 841 run every couple of hours from Göteborg to Lysekil via Uddevalla.

SMÖGEN

☎ 0523

With its waterside boardwalk, rickety fishermen's houses, and steep twisting streets, Smögen is a village out of time – and place. Weirdly, sections of it feel almost southeast Asian – you half expect Jackie Chan to come toppling from one of the almost-stilted houses.

There's a **tourist office** in summer only (☎ 375 44; infor@sostenasturism.se; Torget; ⏰ 10am-8pm Mon-Fri, 11am-7pm Sat & Sun mid-Jun–mid-Aug).

The classic wooden boardwalk **Smögenbryggan** around the harbour is usually packed with visitors – to get peace and quiet, go first thing in the morning or out of season. Fishing boats unload their catches of prawns, lobsters and fish at the harbour, when there's a lively **fish auction** (www.smogens-fiskauktion.com; Fiskhall; ⏰ 8am Mon-Fri, plus 5pm Thu).

Boats (☎ 312 67; Skr50 return) leave for the nature reserve on the nearby island of **Hållö** up to 15 times daily in summer from Smögen harbour.

The **Kon-Tiki Dykcenter** (☎ 374 74; smogen.fkp@kon-tiki.se; Madenvägen 3) does boat dives, PADI courses and hires out kayaks (per three hours/one day Skr150/250).

Makrillvikens Vandrarhem (☎ 315 65; makrillviken@telia.com; Makrillgatan; dm Skr200-250; P) In the former spa bathing house, this is an excellent budget choice – 500m from the boardwalk crowds, and with an old waterside sauna for guest use. There's a small playground, and canoes for hire.

Bryggens Gästhem (☎ 703 91; Madenvägen 2; per person Skr300) Another of Smögen's cheaper options is this 'guesthouse' near the harbour, which has two- to six-bed hostel-style accommodation scattered over three different buildings. A few rooms have balconies with sea views.

Hotel Smögens Havsbad (☎ 668 450; www.smogenshavsbad.se; Hotellgatan 26; low-season Skr1045/1310, high-season s/d Skr1220/1550; P) This hotel had radical surgery just after its 100th birthday: its hideous prosthetic extension is (thankfully for guests) beautiful on the inside, with light Scandinavian-style rooms, many with sea views.

There are plenty of appetising cafés, grill-bars and fish restaurants along Smögenbryggan.

Skärets Krog & Konditori (☎ 323 17; skaret@swipnet.se; Hamnen 1; mains Skr200-285; ⏰ weekends from Easter, daily mid-Jun–mid-Aug) Near the Fiskhall, Skärets has a ground-floor *konditori* serving light meals and yummy cakes. For a quality seafood dinner in classy but cosy surrounds, head upstairs to the restaurant. The fish casserole, flavoured with saffron, is delicious – and there's a fine view of the harbour.

Coffee Room (☎ 308 28; Sillgatan 10; breakfast from Skr39, mains Skr45-80; ⏰ 8am-at least 10pm summer, shorter hr winter) Anyone pining for an English breakfast will sing hallelujahs here over the egg, sausage, bacon, tomato and baked beans. There are also quick and simple lunchtime snacks (*panini*, pasta salads, stir-fries), and evening tapas or barbecues in the airy garden.

Bus 860 and 861 (SmögenExpressen) run regularly from Göteborg to Smögen (around three hours), via Uddevalla, Munkedal, Hunnebostrand and Kungshamn. A couple of the services are direct, otherwise change in one of the towns en route.

FJÄLLBACKA

☎ 0525

Film star Ingrid Bergman spent her summer holidays at Fjällbacka (the main square is named after her). And if it's good enough

NORDENS ARK

Snow leopards, wolves and lynx prowl **Nordens Ark** (☎ 0523-795 90; www.nordensark.se; Åby Säteri; adult/13-17yr/5-12yr/family Skr120/70/55/330; ⌚ 10am-7pm mid-Jun–mid-Aug, 10am-4pm or 5pm rest of yr) a safari park 12km northeast of Smögen and one of the area's big family attractions. It shows off animals and plants from countries with a similar climate to Sweden's, and has breeding programmes for endangered species. Guided tours of the park are available daily in peak season and on weekends the rest of the year (included in entry price). Last admission is two hours before closing.

for Ingrid, it's good enough for us (and half of Sweden). Despite the crowds, Fjällbacka is utterly charming, with its brightly coloured houses squashed between steep cliffs and the rolling sea.

A very helpful **tourist office** (☎ 321 20; Ingrid Bergmanstorg; ⌚ 9.30am-7.30pm mid-Jun–mid-Aug) opens in the summer.

The main attraction is just pottering about, eating ice cream, browsing the trinket shops, or wandering up the cliff or along the Kungsklyftan path. From July to mid-August, there are 1½-hour **island boat trips** (☎ 321 25; info@halsanifjallbacka.se; adult/child Skr100/50; ⌚ noon & 3pm) and two-hour **seal safaris** (adult/child Skr150/75; ⌚ 7pm Thu) departing from the harbour.

Stora Hotellet (☎ 310 03; www.storahotellet-fjallbacka.se; Galärbacken; Jun-Aug s/d/ste from Skr1225/1550/2150, rest of yr Skr1125/1450/1990) One of the most individualistic hotels ever, the incredible Stora Hotellet offers a trip 'around the world in 23 rooms'. It was originally owned by a ship's captain who decorated it with exotic souvenirs. He named each room after his favourite ports and explorers (and girls!), and each tells its own story. The question is, how do you choose which room to book? There's also a restaurant for fine dining.

Oscars II (☎ 322 10; info@fjallbacka.net; Ingrid Bergmanstorg 2; low/high season d Skr850/995, ste Skr1495/1950; restaurant ⌚ until midnight) Another excellent place, Oscars II is a cosy café, bar and brasserie. It has pretty double rooms for rent upstairs, and a suite with its own sunny terrace, lounges and super harbour views.

Badholmens Vandrarhem (☎ 321 50, 0703-28 79 55; per person Skr200) On a teeny little island just off the harbour is this simple hostel, reached by a causeway. Four plain bunk-bedded huts look out to sea, and there's a café, laundry and free sauna for guests nearby.

Bus 875 runs between Göteborg and Strömstad via Hamburgsund and Fjällbacka.

Uddevalla

☎ 0522 / pop 50,068

You may find yourself in Uddevalla, Bohuslän's capital, while waiting for transport connections. It's worth popping into the museum, and the old spa area at Gustafsberg is nice for a swim, but Uddevalla is fairly modern and industrial and there's little reason to linger long. The **tourist office** (☎ 997 20; www.uddevallaforum.se; Kungstorget 4; ⌚ 10am-6pm Mon, 10am-4pm Tue-Fri) can help with information.

Bohusläns Museum (☎ 65 65 00; www.bohusmus.se; Museigatan 1; admission free; ⌚ 10am-8pm Mon-Thu, 10am-4pm Fri-Sun May-Aug, closed Mon Sep-Apr), near the bus station, tells the history of the area from the Stone Age onwards, and has displays on traditional stone, boat-building and fish-preserving industries. There's also an art gallery and restaurant.

STF Vandrarhem Gustafsberg/Uddevalla (☎ 152 00; jan.gustafsberg@telia.com; dm Skr165; ⌚ mid-Jun–mid-Aug) This hostel, based in an old bathing house, is in a wonderful waterside location at the old spa of Gustafsberg, 4km from the centre. There are recreation areas and a café down this way too. The area can best be reached by boat (Skr20) six times daily from the jetty across the river from the museum, or by local bus.

Regional buses and trains run daily to Strömstad (Skr120, 1¼ hours) and Göteborg (Skr110, one hour). **Swebus Express** (☎ 0200-21 82 18; www.swebusexpress.se) runs to Oslo (Skr308, six hours) up to six times daily. Buses drop off and pick up from the bus station on the E6 motorway, rather than in the town centre.

Strömstad

☎ 0526 / pop 11,373

Strömstad is a sparky seaside resort, fishing harbour and spa town, close to the Norwegian border and the old and brand-new Svinesund Bridges. In summer Norwegian tourists pile across to take advantage of

A BEGINNER'S GUIDE TO ROCK CARVINGS

Bohuslän's Bronze Age rock carvings *(hällristningar)* are everywhere, a phenomenal 3000-year-old artistic record of religious beliefs, rites and everyday living. All the carvings are in the open and free to view. An excellent book, *The Rock Carving Tour* (Skr50, from tourist offices/museums in the region), contains thoughtful interpretations and detailed maps showing you how to find the best Bohuslän sites.

The **Tanum plain** is particularly rich in carvings, and the entire 45-sq-km area has been placed on the Unesco World Heritage List. Start your rocky odyssey at **Vitlycke**, within the Tanum area, where you'll find ships, animals, humans and tiny footsteps scattered through the woods. The splendid 22m **Vitlycke Rock** forms a huge canvas for 500 carvings of 'love, power and magic'. These range from simple cup marks to some of Sweden's most famous rock-art images, including the *Lovers,* showing a sacred marriage.

If you're bewildered by the long-armed men, blue whales, sexual imagery and goat-drawn chariots, cross the road to **Vitlycke Museum** (☎ 0525-209 50; www.vitlyckemuseum.se; adult/under 20yr Skr50/free; 10am-6pm Apr-Sep), which has a determined go at explaining them. There are handheld computer guides for hire at extortionate prices, but it's much better to catch the **English tour** (included in museum admission; 3pm), when a knowledgeable human being explains the carvings.

You'll need your own transport to get to Vitlycke. By public transport, the nearest you can get is to Tanumshede, 2.5km north: regional buses on the Göteborg–Uddevalla–Strömstad route stop here. Tanumshede train station is further away still.

Sweden's cheaper prices, lending a particularly lively air to the town's bars.

There are several fantastic Iron Age remains in the area, including one of Sweden's largest ship settings, and some fine **sandy beaches** at Capri and Seläter. Boat trips run to the Koster islands, the most westerly in Sweden and popular for cycling.

The busy **tourist office** (☎ 623 30; www.stromstadtourist.se; Torget; 9am-8pm Mon-Sat, 10am-7pm Sun Jun-Aug, shorter hr Sep-May) is between the two harbours on the main square. Check your email at the **public library** (☎ 193 16; Karlsgatan 17).

SIGHTS & ACTIVITIES

In town, **Strömstads Museum** (☎ 102 75; stromstads.museum@telia.com; Södra Hamngatan 26; adult/child Skr20/free; 11am-4pm Mon-Fri, 11am-2pm Sat) has displays on local themes. One of Sweden's largest and most magnificent **stone ship settings** (admission free; 24hr) lies 6km northeast of Strömstad. It rests in a field full of wildflowers, generally free from other visitors, which makes it a much more personal experience than Ales Stenar (see p180). There are 49 stones in total, with the stem and stern stones reaching over 3m in height; the site has been dated to around AD 400 to 600. Across the road is a huge site containing approximately 40 **Iron Age graves**. Ask at the tourist office or bus station for information on buses, or hire a bicycle (see opposite). Alternatively, there's a lovely walking path from the north of town.

The Romanesque stone **Skee Kyrka** (8am-3pm Mon-Fri Jun-Aug) is about 6km east of Strömstad and has a 10th-century nave. There's also a painted wooden ceiling and an unusual 17th-century reredos with 24 sculptured figures. Nearby, there are **Iron Age graves**, a weird **bell tower** and a mid-Neolithic **passage tomb** (c 3000 BC).

Boat trips (adult/child Skr110/60 return) run from Strömstad's north harbour to the Koster islands (www.kosteroarna.com) roughly every two hours in summer. **North Koster** is hilly and has good beaches. **South Koster** is flatter and better for cycling.

In summer there are also **seal safaris**; ask at the tourist office for times and prices.

SLEEPING & EATING

Crusellska Hemmet (☎ 101 93; Norra Kyrkogatan 12; dm/s/d Skr180/320/400; Mar-Nov; P) Crusellska may sound like a Disney villain, but it's actually an exceptional STF hostel. It feels like a boutique hotel thanks to its drifting white curtains and pale décor, the landing has a comfy seating area with wicker chairs and lounges, the kitchen is big enough for all guests and then some, and there's a peaceful garden out the back. It fills up early, so book ahead.

Hotell Krabban (☎ 142 00; www.hotellkrabban.se; Bergsgatan 15; s/d Skr790/990) 'The Crab' is a small and personal place in the centre of town. Rooms, based in an old wooden building, have a vaguely nautical theme. There are cheaper alternatives (around Skr100 less) if you're happy to share a corridor bathroom.

Strömstad Camping (☎ 611 21; info@stromstadcamping.se; Uddevallavägen; low/high season sites Skr130/160, 2-bed cabins from Skr300/450; May-Sep) In a large, pleasant park at the southern edge of town, the camp site also has 36 shady cabins for rent.

Restaurang Trädgården (☎ 127 24; www.tradgarden.net; Östra Klevgatan 4; lunch Skr119, mains Skr190-260; lunch Mon-Fri, dinner Wed-Sat) Chinking glasses and happy laughter lure you into this busy, bright restaurant. It has a limited but immaculate à la carte menu, where fresh meat and seafood are turned into culinary marvels. There's also a lighter menu of salads, burgers and baked potatoes.

Restaurang Bryggan (☎ 600 65; Ångbåtskajen 6; lunch Skr72, mains Skr115-200; 11am-10pm, shorter hr in winter) Situated in a wonderful place for ocean-gazing, this cosy restaurant is tucked along the little harbour lane behind the tourist office. Dishes are fish- and meat-based, with one veggie option, and you can eat outside in the summer.

Just off the main square, **Laholmens Fisk** (☎ 102 40; Torget) sells seafood baguettes (from Skr40), along with fish fresh off the boats. The **ICA supermarket** (Södra Hamngatan 8) is central, and **Systembolaget** (Oslovägen 7) is a couple of minutes' walk away.

GETTING THERE & AROUND

Buses and trains both use the train station near the southern harbour. The **Swebus Express** (☎ 0200-21 82 18; www.swebusexpress.se) service from Göteborg to Oslo calls here up to six times daily and Strömstadsexpressen runs to Göteborg (Skr200) up to five times daily. Strömstad is the northern terminus of the Bohuståg train system, with around seven trains daily to/from Göteborg (Skr140).

Ferries run from Strömstad to Sandefjord in Norway (see p329).

For a taxi, call **Strömstads Taxi** (☎ 122 00). Car hire is available from **Statoil** (☎ 121 92; Oslovägen 42), bicycles from **Cykelhandlarn** (☎ 607 70; Oslovägen 53; per 1/5 days Skr100/350; May-Aug, closed Sun rest of yr)

DALSLAND

Northern Dalsland is a landscape of long, long lakes, forests and silent towns, and is the place to go if you want to get well away from the tourist trail. You can actually paddle through the wilderness all the way to Norway from sleepy **Dals-Ed** (also known as Ed): contact **Canodal** (☎ 618 03; www.canodal.com; Gamla Edsvägen 4; 2-person canoes Skr180/900 per day/week) for details. The company can supply equipment needed for wilderness camping.

The eastern half of Dalsland is also watery and peaceful, but with more things to see. The scenic **Dalsland Canal** crosses the region, and gets especially interesting (we promise) at Håverud. The canal itself is only 10km long, but it links a series of narrow lakes between Vänern and Stora Le, providing a route 250km long. Not everyone wants to relax on these waterways: a new endurance race, the **Dalsland Kanot Maraton** (www.kanotmaraton.se), sees competitors racing their canoes over a gruelling 55km course here in mid-August.

Håverud

☎ 0530

An intriguing triple transport pile-up occurs at tiny Håverud, where a 32m **aqueduct** carries the Dalsland Canal over the river, and a road bridge crosses above them both.

There's a helpful **tourist office** (☎ 305 80; info@dalslandcenter.com; Dalslands Center) to assist with any enquiries.

The area around the aqueduct is a smashing spot, filled with ambling visitors and the crashing noise of water. Pleasures are simple: visit the Tardis-like **Kanalmuséet** (☎ 306 24; adult/under 15yr Skr30/free; 10am-6pm Jul & Aug, 11am-4pm Jun & Sep) where the history of the canal is told through imaginative displays; sit with a beer and watch boats negotiating the **lock**; or hop on a vessel yourself for various **boat tours** along the canal. These mainly run from July to mid-August, and can be booked at the tourist office; a trip to Upperud costs adult/under 12 years Skr30/20.

STF hostel (☎ 302 75; Museivägen 3; dm Skr150; P) This dinky 1st-floor hostel overlooks the canal. Its attic-like rooms are pleasant but can nevertheless get warm in summer. Outside May to August, bookings are necessary.

Håfveruds Rökeri (☎ 351 31; Dalslands Center; mains Skr150-200; daily summer, weekends rest of yr)

This is a good fish and seafood restaurant, based in an old paper mill with the chains still hanging from the ceiling, which also has chilled-out lockside tables. Sandwiches are served during the day, and there's a delicatessen for self-caterers.

For transport details, see below.

Around Håverud

About 3km south of the aqueduct is **Upperud**, where you'll find the **Dalslands Museum & Konsthall** (☎ 0530-300 98; www.dalslandsmuseum.se; adult/under 12yr Skr40/free; 11am-6pm mid-Jun–mid-Aug, 11am-4pm Wed-Sun mid-Aug–Dec & mid-Mar–mid-Jun). There's a compact permanent display of local art, furniture, ceramics, ironware and Åmål silverware as well as temporary exhibitions. The small sculpture park in the grounds is worth visiting for its eerie installations, hidden amongst the shrubs and trees. Its **Café Bonaparte** (so-called because Napoleon's niece Christine once lived there) is a good place for coffee and snacks.

Another few kilometres south at **Skållerud** is a beautiful 17th-century wooden **church** (☎ 0530-300 14; 8am-6pm Mon-Sat, 9am-6pm Sun May-Sep), with well-preserved paintings and biblical sculptures.

Atmospheric **Högsbyn Nature Reserve**, about 8km north of Håverud near Tisselskog, has woodland walks and a shallow bathing place. Best of all are its impressive Bronze Age **rock carvings** *(hällristningar)*: 50 overgrown slabs feature animals, boats, labyrinths, sun signs, and hand and foot marks. There's a small **museum** (admission by donation; Jun-Aug), and a haunted **café**. You can get here from Håverud on a **boat trip** (☎ 0530-310 97, 0530-304 00; adult/7-14yr Skr140/60; 1pm Jul–mid-Aug) that gives you 45 minutes at the carvings.

Baldersnäs Herrgård (☎ 0531-412 13; admission free; s/d Skr895/1295), 10km further north past the village of Dals Långed, is a lovely manor house and grounds, complete with English garden, swimming spots, restaurant and café, handicraft stalls and a small Naturum. Quality accommodation is offered here too.

Mellerud is on the main Göteborg to Karlstad train line, and Swebus Express buses between Göteborg and Karlstad stop here three times daily in either direction. Local bus 720 runs a circular route to/from Mellerud via Upperud, Håverud and Skållerud.

Åmål

☎ 0532 / pop 12,823

Åmål, the main town in Dalsland, is situated on Lake Vänern. It became infamous after the 1999 release of the Swedish-language film *Fucking Åmål,* which was actually filmed in Trollhättan and was given the very boring title *Show Me Love* for its release to the English-speaking world. The town's biggest event is **Åmåls Bluesfest**, held over the second weekend in July, when Swedish and international artists play and the town drowns in visitors.

The **tourist office** (☎ 170 98; www.amal.se; 8am-7pm Mon-Fri, 9am-6pm Sat, 11am-6pm Sun mid-Jun–mid-Aug, phone for hr rest of yr) is near the guest harbour, and the main street Kungsgatan has all services.

There are a few diversions in the town, but there's no reason for an extended stay – the real attractions are out in the surrounding waterways and forests. The Old Town, around the church **Gamla Kyrkan** (completed in 1669), is a stately collection of 18th-century buildings and worth a quick look. **Åmåls Hembygdsmuseet** (☎ 158 20; Hamngatan 7; adult/child Skr20/free; 1-6pm mid-Jun–Aug, 1-6pm Sat & Sun mid-May–mid-Jun), near the tourist office, is a particularly interesting local museum with three floors of stuff ranging from toys to funeral confectionery.

STF Vandrarhem Åmål (☎ 102 05; lokrantz@home.se; Gerdinsgatan 7; dm Skr140; Apr-Nov) This well-equipped hostel just north of the town centre has nice views over the lake and bikes for hire.

Stadshotellet (☎ 616 10; info@amalsstadshotell.se; Kungsgatan 9; s/d Skr845/1190, discounted to Skr845/890) Central and elegant, the Stadshotell has high-ceilinged, comfortable rooms and helpful staff, plus one of the best restaurants in town, serving mainly Swedish specialities.

Örnäs Camping (☎ 170 97; ornascamping@amal.se; sites from Skr145, cabins from Skr345) This is a large ground on the shore of Lake Vänern, south of the centre. There's a small sandy beach, and bikes and boats are available for rental.

Hamncompagniet (☎ 100 10; Hamngatan 3; lunch Skr70, mains Skr90-170) This flash complex, not far from the tourist office, is a boaties favourite thanks to its proximity to the marina. There's a restaurant, bar and disco, plus lots of outdoor seating by the lake.

SJ trains to Göteborg (Skr156, 1¾ hours) or Karlstad (Skr70, one hour) stop in Åmål up to six times daily. Swebus Express buses follow the same route and call three times a day. The train and bus stations are about a kilometre southwest of the town centre.

VÄSTERGÖTLAND

Vänersborg

☎ 0521 / pop 37,105

Vänersborg, at the southern outlet of Lake Vänern, was once known as 'Little Paris', but it's hard to see why today. The scenic nature reserve/royal hunting grounds outside town are its main attractions, although families may enjoy Skräcklen park, with playgrounds, waffles and some very popular bathing spots.

The **tourist office** (☎ 27 14 00; www.vanersborg.se; 8am-7pm Mon-Fri, 10am-4pm Sat & Sun Jul & Aug, 8am-5pm Mon-Fri Sep-Jun) is at the train station, and banks and other facilities are mostly along Edsgatan.

Vänersborgs Museum (☎ 600 62; Östra Plantaget; adult/under 17yr Skr20/free; noon-4pm Tue, Thu, Sat & Sun yr-round, plus noon-4pm Wed Jun-Aug) is the country's oldest provincial museum and has a remarkable southwest African bird collection along with local exhibits.

Described by Linnaeus as an 'earthly paradise', the **Hunneberg & Hanneberg Nature Reserve** covers two dramatic, craggy plateaus 8km east of town. There are 50km of **walking trails** here that are certainly worth exploring. The deep ravines and primeval forest also make great hiding places for wild elk, and this area has been a favourite royal hunting ground for over 100 years. Three-hour **elk-spotting safaris** (adult/5-16yr Skr240/175; 6.30pm Mon & Thu Jul & Aug) leave from the train station: book tickets at the tourist office.

Kungajaktmuseet Älgens Berg (☎ 27 79 91; www.algensberg.com; adult/child Skr60/30; 10am-6pm Fri-Mon, 10am-8pm Tue-Thu Jul & Aug, 10am-6pm May-Jun, 11am-4pm Tue-Sun Sep-Apr), the royal hunting museum, is at Hunneberg and tells you everything you could ever wish to know about the elk. In summer bus 665 heads out here.

SLEEPING & EATING

Hotell 46:an (☎ /fax 71 15 61; Kyrkogatan 46; s/d Skr595/750, discounted to Skr550/650) This small, family-run place, on a quiet residential street near Skräcklen park, offers six bright and homey rooms. Reception service is limited, so phone before turning up.

Hunnebergs Vandrarhem & Kursgård (☎ 22 03 40; Bergagårdsvägen 9B, Vargön; sites Skr70, dm Skr180; P) In a big old manor house near the cliffs of Hunneberg (7km east of the centre), this is a large, well-equipped SVIF hostel. Camping is permitted in the grounds, and there are bikes for rent. Take the frequent bus 62 from the town square to Vägporten, then walk 500m.

Ronnums Herrgård (☎ 26 00 00; www.ronnums-herrgard.parkinn.se; Vargön; s/d/ste Skr1170/1170/1650; P) Nicole Kidman was a guest at this luxurious mansion, out towards Hunneberg. It's set in gorgeous grounds, the rooms are hugely elegant, and the newly renovated oak-floored suites are particularly special. The hotel frequently has special rates and packages: contact them for details. If you feel like a gastronomic treat, the restaurant is one of the best in the region.

Ristorante Italia (☎ 612 20; Edsgatan 7; lunch Skr65, mains from Skr70; 11.30am-10pm Mon-Thu, 11.30am-11pm Fri, noon-11pm Sat, noon-9pm Sun) Back in town, this is one of a number of busy eateries on the main street. It serves a mixture of Italian and Swedish food, including reasonably priced pizza and pasta, and has outdoor seats in summer.

GETTING THERE & AWAY

Trollhättan-Vänersborgs airport (☎ 825 00; info@fyrstadsflyget.se) lies midway between the two towns. There are around seven direct flights Monday to Friday (one Sunday) to/from Stockholm. Taxis are the only way to access the airport: **Taxi Vänersborg** (☎ 666 00) charge around Skr300 for the trip from Vänersborg. With **Taxi Trollhättan** (☎ 820 00) from Trollhättan, it costs about Skr130.

Local buses run from Torget and long-distance services stop at the train station. Local bus 61, 62 and 65 run roughly half-hourly between Vänersborg and Trollhättan. Express bus 600 runs a couple of times to Trollhättan, continuing to Göteborg.

Säfflebussen (☎ 0771-15 15 15; www.safflebussen.se) has a Göteborg–Trollhättan–Vänersborg–Lidköping–Stockholm service that stops three times daily in Vänersborg. **Swebus Express** (☎ 0200-21 82 18; www.swebusexpress.se) runs three times daily to Göteborg (Skr95, 1½ hours) via Trollhättan, and also north to Karlstad (Skr190, 2½ hours).

SJ trains to Uddevalla (Skr39, 20 minutes) run every one/two hours. Trains to Trollhättan (Skr39, 15 minutes) and Göteborg

HOORAY FOR TROLLYWOOD

In recent years Trollhättan has become home to the Swedish film industry and has earned itself the inevitable nickname 'Trollywood'. A number of Swedish and Scandinavian films have been filmed in and around the town, including Danish producer Lars von Trier's award-winning *Dancer in the Dark* (1999), and *Dogville* (2002), starring Nicole Kidman and Swedish actor Stellan Skarsgård.

Film i Väst (www.filmivast.se) is Trollhättan's large film production company. Check its website for more information, and also ask at the tourist office if you want to know what film sets (and stars) you might stumble across in town.

(Skr119, 1¼ hours) run about every hour (some require a change at Oxnered).

Trollhättan

☎ 0520 / pop 53,154

Trollhättan itself has the air of a surreal filmset: looming warehouses, foggy canals, crashing waterfalls, and a futuristic cable car all give it a bizarre and thrilling edge. The town has really made the most of its industrial heritage, and has plenty of unusual attractions. As well as a three-day **film festival** in mid-August, the town celebrates **Waterfall Days** (www.fallensdagar.se) in mid-July with live bands, fireworks and water-related happenings.

INFORMATION

The excellent **tourist office** (☎ 48 84 72; www.visittrollhattan.se; Åkerssjövägen 10; 10am-6pm mid-Jun–mid-Aug, 10am-4pm Mon-Fri mid-Aug–mid-Jun) is about 1.5km south of the town centre, near the Innovatum. If you want to visit all the attractions, ask for the two-day **Innovatumkortet** (1/2 people Skr130/200, under 16y free on adult ticket; available early Jun–mid-Aug), which includes cable-car trips and museum admissions. It also sells a handy *Guidebook to Trollhättan's Falls & Locks*, which details walking routes in the mazelike industrial areas.

For Internet access, visit the **library** (☎ 49 76 50; Kungsgatan 25; 10am-7pm Mon-Thu, 10am-6pm Fri, 10am-3pm Sat late Aug–mid-Jun, 11am-6pm Mon-Fri mid-Jun-late Aug) or **@Tonis Café** (☎ 141 60; Kungsgatan 19; per 30/60min Skr15/25; noon-9pm).

SIGHTS & ACTIVITIES

Saab Bilmuseum (☎ 843 44; www.saab.com; Åkerssjövägen 10; adult/7-17yr Skr60/30; 10am-2pm & 5-7pm mid-Jun–mid-Aug, phone for winter hr) is a must for car fanatics and fans of Swedish design. The shining white museum contains Saab car models from the first (a sensational 1947 prototype) to the futuristic (experimental designs running on biofuel that know if you're drunk!). There are also videos showing safety tests involving crash-test-dummy elks. You're guided through the museum by electronic handsets (40-minutes' playing time), which contain interesting information in between the irritating Saab advertisements.

Innovatum Kunskapens Hus (☎ 48 84 80; www.innovatum.se; adult/7-19yr/family Skr60/40/130; 10am-6pm mid-Jun–mid-Aug, 11am-4pm Tue-Sun rest of yr), next door to the Saab Bilmuseum, is a fantastic science centre with interactive experiments aimed mainly at children. But don't let that put you off: push the little blighters out of the way and revel in the gyroscopes and whirlpool machines. Why wasn't physics fun like this when we were kids?

In four minutes, the **Innovatum Linbana** (cable car; ☎ 48 84 80; adult/1-19yr Skr40/20; 10am-6pm mid-Jun–mid-Aug, 11am-4pm Sat & Sun mid-Apr–mid-Jun & mid-Aug–Sep) will sweep you over the canal to the hydroelectricity area. Once you're on the far side of the canal, follow the stairs down to the river, where you'll find one of Sweden's most unusual industrial buildings, the potent-looking **Olidan power station**, which supplied much of the country's electricity in the early 20th century. There are three 30-minute tours daily in summer (ask the tourist office for details).

Take a wander southwest to **Slussområde**, a pleasant waterside area of parkland and ancient lock systems. Here you'll find cafés and the **Kanalmuseet** (☎ 47 22 51; Åkersberg; adult/child Skr10/free; 11am-7pm Jun-Aug; noon-5pm Sat & Sun Apr, May & Sep), which describes the history of the canal and contains over 50 model ships.

Northeast near the Hojum power station, witness spectacular cascades when the **waterfall** (3pm Sat & Sun May-Aug, plus 3pm Wed Jul & Aug) is unleashed. Normally the water is diverted through the power stations, but at set times the sluice gates are opened and 300,000L per second thunders through. For an even more remarkable sight, wait for the night-time **illuminated waterfall** (11pm Fri Jul & Aug).

There are also two- to three-hour **canal tours** (per person from Skr180) in summer; enquire at the tourist office for times.

If you can stay awake until it gets dark enough, there's an **open-air cinema** (11pm Thu Jul–mid-Aug) in summer at the Innovatum; most films shown are home-grown Swedish, but it's worth checking the programme for English-language movies.

SLEEPING & EATING

Gula Villan (129 60; trollhattansvandrarhem@telia.com; Tingvallavägen 12; dm Skr135; P) The cheery STF hostel, in a pretty old yellow villa, is about 200m from the train station. You can rent bikes here, and breakfast is available.

Hotell Bele (125 30; www.hotellbele.se; Kungsgatan 37; s/d Skr795/895, discounted to Skr590/690; P) Bele is a central, no-frills option on a pedestrianised street in the heart of town. Accommodation is basic but comfortable, and there's a sauna and solarium for guest use.

Scandic Hotel Swania (890 00; swania@scandic-hotels.com; Storgatan 47; s/d from Skr1430/1630, discounted to Skr890/890; P) For more luxury, head to the upmarket Swania, situated in the old town hall by the canal. Its quality facilities include a restaurant and nightclub.

Grand Café (890 09; light meals Skr80-120, dinner mains Skr170-200) Part of the Swania, this café has a good menu offering light meals (stirfries, salads and mushrooms on toast) to hearty steaks, and prices are more reasonable than the swish décor might have you expect. The bar here is a bustling after-work spot, and the outdoor area is popular in good weather.

Strandgatan (837 17; Strandgatan; mains Skr55-100) One of the best – and busiest – places in town is this trendy bistro serving bagels, quiche, salads and baked potatoes. It's in a fantastic location, with a large canalside seating area in summer.

GETTING THERE & AROUND

See p225 for transport details. To reach the attractions in Trollhättan from the train station or the Drottningtorget bus station, walk south along Drottninggatan, then turn right into Åkerssjövägen, or take town bus 11 – it runs most of the way.

You can rent bikes from **Innovatum Kunskapens Hus** (adult/child/tandem per 3hr Skr40/20/80, per day Skr75/40/140).

Lidköping

0510 / pop 37,241

Lidköping, on Lake Vänern, is bright and cheery. However, many of its finest attractions (like the enchanting castle, Läckö Slott) lie some distance out of town.

The main square, Nya Stadens Torg, is dominated by the **old courthouse** and its tower (actually a replica – the original burnt down in 1960). A previous fire in 1849 destroyed most of the town, but the 17th-century houses around **Limtorget** still stand.

The **tourist office** (200 20; www.lackokinnekulle.se; Bangatan 3; 9am-8pm Mon-Fri, 10am-8pm Sat, noon-6pm Sun mid-Jun–mid-Aug, noon-5pm Mon-Fri rest of yr) is at the train station, and the **public library** (77 00 15; Nya Stadens Torg 5) has free Internet access.

SIGHTS IN TOWN

Rörstrand Fabriksbod (823 46; Fiskaregatan 4; 10am-6pm Mon-Fri, 10am-3pm Sat, noon-4pm Sun) is the second-oldest porcelain factory (still in operation) in Europe. There's a vast shop selling seconds and end-of-lines, so you may snap up some bargains; you can even buy copies of the porcelain used at the Nobel banquets in Stockholm! There's also a small **museum** (Skr20) containing everything from 18th-century faïence to modern creations.

Vänermuseet (77 00 65; Framnäsvägen 2; adult/7-18yr Skr40/20; 10am-5pm Tue-Fri, noon-5pm Sat & Sun) has geological exhibits, including an ancient meteorite and displays about Vänern (the third-largest lake in Europe at 5650 sq km). The most curious item is a 3m-long glass boat.

LÄCKÖ SLOTT

For a fairytale castle fix, get yourself to **Läckö Slott** (103 20; www.lackoslott.se; May-Sep), 23km north of Lidköping near Vänern. It's an extraordinary example of 17th-century Swedish baroque architecture, with cupolas, towers, paintings and ornate plasterwork. The first castle on the site was constructed in 1298, but it was improved enormously by Count Magnus Gabriel de la Gardie after he acquired it in 1615.

The castle now has 240 rooms, with the most impressive being the **King's Hall**, with 13 angels hanging from the ceiling and nine huge paintings depicting the Thirty Years War.

Guided tours (adult/7-15yr/family Skr70/20/160; on the hr 11am-5pm May-Aug, 11am-2pm Sep) lasting 45 minutes give you access to the most interesting rooms; there's an English tour at 3.30pm daily. Otherwise you're free to bimble about in the courtyards and lower floors, which contain a few shops and the castle restaurant, **Fataburen** (lunch Skr110; noon-3pm & 6-9pm mid-Jun–mid-Aug).

In the castle grounds, there's a **café** (lunch Skr80; 11am-6.30pm May-Aug) serving cheaper snacks and a **rental kiosk** (24 98 13; bengtsson@kajakfritid.se; noon-5.30pm mid-Jun–mid-Aug) where you can hire swan-shaped boats (per hour 180) or canoes (per half day from Skr130) for exploring the lake.

Classical music and opera events are held in the courtyard several times a week in July (tickets around Skr320); enquire at Lidköping tourist office.

From mid-June to mid-August, bus 132 runs four to seven times a day from Lidköping to the castle. Car parking costs Skr30.

HUSABY KYRKA & ST SIGFRID'S WELL

Husaby (around 15km east of Lidköping) is inextricably linked to Sweden's history. King Olof Skötkonung, the country's first Christian king, was converted and baptised here by the English missionary Sigfrid in 1008. Olof's royal dunking took place at **St Sigfrid's Well**, near **Husaby Kyrka** (8am-4pm Apr, 8am-8pm May-Sep). A succession of Swedish kings have carved their names into the rocks here.

The church actually dates from the 12th century, but the base of the unusual three-steepled tower may well be that of an earlier wooden structure. An English-language audio guide is available.

There's a small, seasonal **tourist office** (34 32 60; Pilgrimsgården; noon-6pm mid-Jun–mid-Aug) near the church. Bus 106 runs to Husaby, but very infrequently.

KINNEKULLE

The 'flowering mountain' **Kinnekulle** (306m), 18km northeast of Lidköping, is unusually diverse in its geology and plant life. There are numerous short nature trails, or you could explore it on the 45km-long **Kinnekulle vandringsled** (walking trail), which runs past remainders of the old limestone workings. Ask at the tourist office for a map (Skr20). Local trains run to Källby, Råbäck and Hällekis, with access to the trail.

SLEEPING & EATING

STF Vandrarhem Lidköping (664 30; info@lidkopingsvandrarhem.com; Gamla Stadens Torg 4; dm/d Skr140/280) Just a couple of minutes' walk from the train station, this hostel is in a pretty spot in the old town. Standards are high, and the staff are very helpful.

Hotel Läckö (230 00; Gamla Stadens Torg 5; s/d Skr690/890, discounted to Skr590/790) The smiley reception people at this family-run hotel also make you feel very welcome. Comfortable rooms have good high ceilings, and there's the odd quirky touch like the artsy foyer hatstand.

Hotel Stadt (220 85; hotel@stadtlidkoping.se; Gamla Stadens Torg 1; s/d Skr995/1290, discounted to Skr590/790; P) Stadt is the best hotel in town with amenities including restaurant, nightclub and sauna/spa. Rooms are parquet-floored with pristine modern décor and big TVs. At the time of writing, all of the 3rd-floor bedrooms had been newly renovated.

Krono Camping (268 04; www.kronocamping.com; Läckögatan; sites Skr155-200, 2-person cabins Skr395-465;) This is a huge, family-oriented lakeside camping ground, 1.5km northwest of town beside the road to Läckö, where kids can run wild. There's everything you could possibly need: shop, restaurant, laundry, minigolf, boules, sauna, playground, and boat hire.

Café O Bar (270 27; Nya Stadens Torg 4; lunch Skr69, mains Skr150-200) This sleek place, on the main square, is a fashionable restaurant-bar with a good selection of interesting meals, including mushroom risotto or lamb racks with couscous.

Café Limtorget (251 45; Mjölnagården, Limtorget 1; closed Sun) With its rose-filled garden, this is a cute old place well worth seeking out. It serves sandwiches and ciabatta for around Skr40, plus pastries, waffles and other temptations.

There are several other options around Gamla Stadens Torg and the surrounding streets – Källaregatan is fertile ground for cheap pizzerias and grill bars, while Grevgatan has some inviting old cafés.

GETTING THERE & AROUND

Town and regional buses stop on Nya Stadens Torg. Bus 5 runs roughly hourly on weekdays (four Saturday and Sunday) between Trollhättan, Lidköping and Skara.

Säfflebussen (0771-15 15 15; www.safflebussen.se) runs three times daily to Stockholm (via

Örebro; Skr300, 4½ hours) and Göteborg (via Vänersborg and Trollhättan; Skr170, 2½ hours). Länståg trains from Lidköping to Hallsberg or Herrljunga connect with Stockholm and Göteborg services respectively.

Karlsborg

☎ 0505 / pop 6905

Karlsborg is a quiet little town s-t-r-e-e-e-t-c-h-e-d alongside Lake Vättern some 80km east of Lidköping. Amazingly, this peaceful backwater was once intended to be Sweden's capital in times of war, thanks to its beast of a bastion, Karlsborgs Fästning.

The **tourist office** (☎ 173 50; info@karlsborgsturism.se; Ankarvägen 2; 9am-6pm Jul–mid-Aug, 10am-4pm Mon-Fri mid-Aug–Jun) is in an octagonal wooden house between the fort's main entrance and the lake.

Karlsborgs Fästning was one of Europe's largest construction projects. This enormous fortress has a circumference of around 5km, and is so huge that it took from 1820 to 1909 to complete; it was out of date even before it was finished, and was mothballed immediately! Most of the 30-odd buildings inside are original: there's a **military museum** (☎ 854 70; adult/child Skr40/10; 10am-4pm or 6pm mid-May–Aug, 10am-3pm Mon-Fri rest of yr) and a **church**, which has an extraordinary candelabra made from 276 bayonets.

The fortress area is always open. If you want gun smoke, cannon roar and scuttling rats, though, you'll have to book a special-effect **guided tour** (adult/7-12yr Skr80/40; 1pm Jun-Aug) at the tourist office; from midsummer to August, there are up to 12 tours every day. The **Lilla Blå tourist train** (adult/under 12yr Skr80/40; 2pm mid-Jun–mid-Aug) also zips round the centre of the fortress.

Karlsborg is the start/end of the western section of the **Göta Canal** (see boxed text, p146, and p330 for further details).

STF Vandrarhem Karlsborg (☎ 446 00; Ankarvägen 2; dm/d Skr135/300; Jun-Aug; P) Right on the fortress's doorstep, this is used as military accommodation for most of the year. If you can overlook the slightly brusque reception, a good option is to stay here and self-cater (there are supermarkets in the nearby town centre), although there are more sleeping and eating options in town, especially beside the Göta Canal about 2km northwest of the fortress (follow the main road).

A bus runs every hour or two to Skövde, connecting with SJ trains to Göteborg or Stockholm.

HALLAND

Halmstad

☎ 035 / pop 87,929

After roasting themselves on the 6km-long Blue-Flag **beach** at Tylösand (8km east of town), many holidaymakers return to Halmstad's lively bars and clubs at night.

Halmstad was actually Danish until 1645, and served as an important fortified border town. Its street plan was laid out by the Danish King Christian IV after a huge fire wiped out most of the buildings in 1619. He also awarded Halmstad its coat of arms: you'll see the three crowns and three hearts motif dotted all over the place.

The **tourist office** (☎ 13 23 20; www.halmstad.se; 9am-7pm Mon-Sat, 11am-6pm Sun late Jun–mid-Aug, 9am-5pm Mon-Fri rest of yr) is inside Halmstads Slott (castle). Stora Torg and Storgatan have most of the facilities travellers will require, including banks and supermarkets. At the time of writing, a futuristic new **library** (www.huvudbiblioteket.se; Axel Olsonsgata 1) was being built by the river: once it opens in 2006, there should be plenty of free Internet access. Otherwise try **PlaygroundX** (☎ 12 10 90; Storgatan 6; per hr Skr25; 10am-midnight).

SIGHTS & ACTIVITIES

For a small county institution, **Halmstads Museum** (☎ 16 23 00; Tollsgatan; adult/7-15yr Skr40/20; noon-4pm Tue & Thu-Sun, to 8pm Wed) manages to host some good art/design exhibitions. Its modest array of local treasures are displayed with ingenuity: for example, silver hoards and Viking swords are set in cases in the floor, as though just discovered on an archaeological dig.

Halmstad Äventyrsland (☎ 10 84 60; Gamla Tylösandsvägen 1; admission Skr150; 10am-8pm Jul & Aug, shorter hr May, Jun & Sep), lying just out of town, is a theme park for little-ish kids featuring pirates, fairytale characters, dinosaurs, a miniature village, rides and waterslides. A free road train leaves Halmstad roughly every hour from near the corner of Stora Torget and Brogatan; a board tells you the exact departure times.

Another one for families, across the river and downstream from the tourist office, **Tropikcenter** (☎ 12 33 33; Strandgatan; adult/child

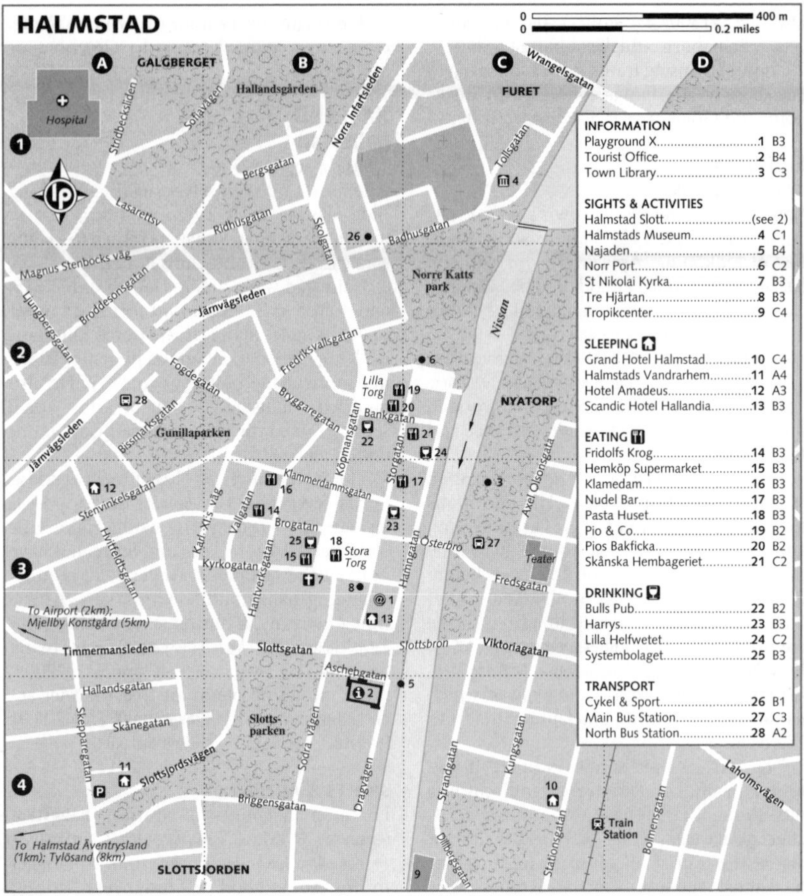

Skr70/40; 10am-6pm Jul, 10am-4pm Aug-Jun) is in the old customs house and shows off tropical birds, fish and reptiles. At both places, kids under 1m tall get in for free.

The museum ship **Najaden** (admission free; 5-7pm Tue & Thu, 11am-3pm Sat Jul & Aug), berthed just outside the castle and built in 1897, was a training ship for the Swedish Royal Navy.

Christian IV built **Halmstad Slott** (open irregularly to guided tours in summer: ask the tourist office for details) and the town walls. The latter were demolished in the 18th century, although fragments like the north gate **Norre Port** remain. Other medieval attractions include the lovely 14th-century church **St Nikolai Kyrka** (8.30am-6pm Jun-Aug, 8.30am-3pm Sep-May), and the half-timbered **Tre Hjärtan** (Three Hearts) building on Stora Torg. In the main square is Carl Milles' sculptural fountain *Europa and the Bull*, and Picasso's *(Woman's Head)* is down by the river.

Mjellby Konstgård (316 19; adult/under 20yr Skr50/free; 1-5pm Tue-Sun mid-Mar-Oct) is 5km from town but worth a trip if you're into modern art – the museum here includes the permanent Halmstad Group exhibition of surrealist and cubist art (labelled in Swedish). Take the irregular bus 330 from the North Bus Station.

Sleeping

IN TOWN

The tourist office can arrange private rooms in town from Skr150 per person (plus booking fee). It's a popular town, and many of the large hotel chains have branches here.

Halmstads Vandrarhem (☎ 12 05 00; halmstad@hallonsten.se; Skepparegatan 23; 2-/4-/5-/6-bed r Skr450/600/725/850; mid-Jun–mid-Aug) This SVIF hostel becomes student digs outside summer. Rooms are slightly battered, with that drawing-pins-in-the-wall look that comes with college accommodation, but they're decent enough and have sofas and desks. There's a spacious garden for evening lounging.

Hotel Amadeus (☎ 16 60 00; www.amadeus.nu; Hvitfeldtsgatan 20; s/d Skr850/1050, discounted to Skr640/840; P) At 65 rooms this isn't a tiny hotel, yet it manages to retain a very personal and welcoming air. Rooms are comfortably mid-market – not old-fashioned but not state-of-the-art, either – and there are budget alternatives (around Skr200 less) if you're counting the pennies.

There's little difference in price or standards at the following two upmarket places, both with sauna, solarium, bar, restaurant and so on:

Grand Hotel Halmstad (☎ 280 81 00; www.grandhotel.nu; Stationsgatan 44; s/d Skr1200/1550, discounted to Skr790/990; P) Handy for the train station, with rooms decorated in a more traditional vein.

Scandic Hotel Hallandia (☎ 295 86 00; hallandia@scandic-hotels.com; Rådhusgatan 4; rm/ste Skr1320/1800, discounted to Skr1090/1320) On the main square with more modern Scandinavian-style accommodation; some rooms have balconies overlooking the river.

IN TYLÖSAND

Hotel Tylösand (☎ 305 00; info@tylosand.se; Tylöhusvägen; d Skr2345, discounted to s/d Skr1295/1395) This is the place to try if you're into the beach, nightclubbing and/or Roxette (it's part-owned by Per Gessle, one half of the Swedish pop duo). It's a large, upmarket complex on the beach, with lots of eating options and summer entertainment happenings; check out the glamorous foyer full of art, and Leifs Lounge nightclub. This is one of the few Swedish hotels where prices go *up* at weekends, although packages are available.

Krono Camping (☎ 305 10; www.kronocamping.se; Kungsvägen 3; sites Skr130-240, cabins from Skr525) A huge and bustling camping ground near the beach, with loads of family-friendly facilities. Avoid holidays such as midsummer, when prices go stratospheric: a whopping Skr840 for three days!

Tylebäck (☎ 19 18 00; info@tyleback.com; Kungsvägen 1; sites Skr220, 1-/2-/3-/4-bed rm Skr260/390/585/780, hotel s/d Skr795/995) Accommodation to suit all pockets – camping, hostel, hotel – is offered at Tylebäck, in a pleasantly rustic location.

EATING & DRINKING

Halmstad is jam-packed with dining spots, pubs and bars, mostly around pedestrianised Storgatan. Alternatively, on summer nights head to the after-beach parties at Tylösand.

Klamedam (☎ 12 40 50; Klammerdammsgatan 21; mains Skr235-265; 6-11pm Mon-Sat) Slide onto suede seats at this exclusive restaurant and prepare for a treat. Dishes are immaculately presented, with mains of mostly fish and meat, and the atmosphere is cultivated and quite romantic.

Pio & Co (☎ 21 06 69; Storgatan 37; mains Skr160-230; from 6pm) Pio's is an award-winning upmarket brasserie. Its extensive menu of quality dishes contains Swedish favourites with a world-flavour twist, such as salmon with sugar-roasted summer veg on couscous.

Pios Bakficka (Lilla Torg; meals under Skr100) Behind Pio & Co is this place, which literally means'Pio's Backpocket'. It's a more casual spot with outdoor seating and a good bar menu.

Fridolfs Krog (☎ 21 16 66; Brogatan 26; meals Skr75-220; from 6pm) Less exclusive and with a wide menu, this is another pleasant place for a fine dinner. There are low-priced pasta options, or more expensive, well-prepared meat and fish meals including bouillabaisse.

Skånska Hembageriet (☎ 21 24 07; Storgatan 40; closed Sun) This is a good old-fashioned bakery with café attached. Sandwiches cost from Skr29, and of course there are lots of freshly baked buns to choose from.

Lilla Helfwetet (☎ 21 04 20; Hamngatan 37; closed Sun) With its funky dancing devil symbol, you can half guess what awaits you in this great converted warehouse near the river. This super-cool restaurant, bar and cocktail lounge transforms into a nightclub on Friday and Saturday nights, when there's partying until 3am.

For something quick, visit hole-in-the-wall **Nudel Bar** (Storgatan; meals incl drink Skr60) or the **Pasta Huset** (pasta Skr29) van on Stora Torg. There's a Hemköp supermarket and a Systembolaget just off Stora Torg.

On the northern part of Storgatan and nearby Lilla Torg are some popular drinking places, including pub-style **Harrys** (☎ 10 55 95; Storgatan 22), with a large outdoor terrace curling round the corner, and the **Bulls Pub** (☎ 14 09 21; Lilla Torg), in a former fire station.

GETTING THERE & AWAY

The **airport** (☎ 12 80 70) is only 2km west of the town centre. Skyways has regular connections to Stockholm's Arlanda airport.

The train station is in the southeastern corner of the town centre, and the bus station is a few blocks away at Österbro. **Swebus Express** (☎ 0200-21 82 18; www.swebusexpress.se) runs buses at least five to seven times daily to Malmö (Skr178, 2¼ hours), Helsingborg (Skr90, one hour), Göteborg (Skr120, 1¾ hours) and Lund. **Svenska Buss** (☎ 0771-67 67 67; www.svenskabuss.se) runs the same routes, at a cheaper price but less frequently. Swebus Express also has a direct twice-weekly service to Jönköping (Skr178, 2¾ hours).

The regular trains between Göteborg (Skr170, 1¼ hours) and Malmö (Skr160, two hours) stop in Halmstad, calling in at Helsingborg (Skr110, one hour) and Varberg (Skr81, 45 minutes).

GETTING AROUND

Local bus 10 runs at least half-hourly to the clubs and beaches at Tylösand (adult/child Skr20/10).

Try **Taxi Halmstad** (☎ 21 80 00) for assistance getting around. You can hire a bike from **Cykel & Sport** (☎ 21 22 51; Norra vägen 11; 10am-6pm Mon-Fri, 10am-1pm Sat) for Skr70/100 per half/full day.

Varberg

☎ 0340 / pop 54,338

This attractive town lies by the side of a 60km stretch of beautiful white-sand beaches: its population consequently triples in the summer months. Varberg's darker side includes its fortress, once used as a prison and now home to an excellently preserved bog body.

The **tourist office** (☎ 887 70; www.turist.varberg.se; Brunnparken; 9.30am-7pm Mon-Sat, 3-6pm Sun late Jun–early Aug, 9.30am-5pm Mon-Fri rest of yr) is located in the centre of town, and most facilities are nearby.

SIGHTS & ACTIVITIES

The **medieval fortress** (☎ 828 30; adult/6-17yr Skr50/10; 10am-5pm mid-Jun– mid-Aug, 10am-4pm Mon-Fri, noon-4pm Sat & Sun rest of yr), with its superb museum, is the main attraction in Varberg. Unusual exhibits include the poor old Bocksten Man, dug out of a peat bog at Åkulle in 1936. His 14th-century costume is the most perfectly preserved medieval clothing in Europe.

Brave the brisk Nordic weather and swim in the striking **Kallbadhuset** (☎ 173 96; adult/under 15yr Skr45/25; mid-Jun–mid-Aug, 1-8pm Wed & 9am-5pm Sat & Sun winter), a bizarre Moorish-style outdoor bathhouse built on stilts above the sea just north of the fort.

Getterön Nature Reserve is just 2km north of the town and has excellent bird life (mostly waders and geese). The reserve has a **Naturum** (visitors centre; ☎ 875 10; Lassavägen 1; 10am-4pm May-Aug; Fri, Sat & Sun Sep-Apr) with good exhibitions.

In 2004, the **Varberg Radio Station** (☎ 67 41 90; Grimeton), about 10km east of Varberg, was added to the Unesco World Heritage List. It was part of the interwar trans atlantic communication network: today it's the only such long-wave radio station left in the world. Admission is by guided tour (on the hour from 11am to 5pm Tuesday to Sunday, July to mid-August): phone ahead to let them know if you'd like an English tour.

Apelviken, just 2km south of Varberg, is Sweden's best place for **windsurfing** and **kitesurfing**. Bring your own kit or rent from **Surfer's Paradise** (☎ 67 70 55; info@surfersparadise.nu; per hr/day Skr80/300; Jun-Aug), which also offers courses: contact them for details.

SLEEPING & EATING

Fästningens Vandrarhem (☎ 887 88; vandrarhem@turist.varberg.se; dm/s/d Skr210/280/470) Within the fortress, this SVIF hostel is one of the finest hostels in Sweden. It offers singles in old prison cells or larger rooms in other buildings.

Hotell Gästis (☎ 180 50; gastis@hotellgastis.nu; Borgmästaregatan 1; s/d from Skr945/1295, discounted to Skr725/1025) This friendly place is highly recommended and probably offers the best value in town in summer. Although it doesn't look like much from the outside, inside it's bright, clean, stylish and colourful, with lots of extras like a library and outdoor terraces, plus guests can rent bikes. All prices include breakfast and a dinner buffet.

Getteröns Camping (☎ 168 85; www.getteronscamping.se; low/high season sites from Skr160/220, cabins & chalets from Skr410/675; ⏰ May–mid-Sep) This well-equipped place is right on a sandy beach on the Getterön peninsula. There are plenty of tent spaces, but it does get busy in high season.

Lundquistska Huset (☎ 143 90; Brunnsparken; mains Skr120-180) When it comes to dining, this upmarket spot near the tourist office offers excellent cuisine, including vegetarian options.

Most cheap restaurants are along the pedestrianised Kungsgatan. **Café Fästnings Terrassen** (☎ 105 81) at the fortress offers the best sea views in town.

GETTING THERE & AROUND

Buses depart from outside the train station; local buses run to Falkenberg, but regular trains are your best bet for places like Halmstad, Göteborg and Malmö.

Stena Line ferries operate between Varberg and the Danish town of Grenå (see p328); the ferry dock is next to the town centre.

Bike hire from **Erlan Cykel** (☎ 144 55; Västra Vallgatan 41) costs from Skr80/350 per day/week. For a taxi try **Varbergs Taxi** (☎ 165 00).

Central Sweden

Like a tastefully arranged towel in a sauna, Svealand drapes itself right across the middle of the country, from the northeastern shore to the western mountains. It's an area strongly associated with Sweden's heritage – it even gave the country its name (Svea Rike, or Sverige). Vikings set out on expeditions from Lake Mälaren, and built their most sacred temple at Gamla Uppsala; rune stones, burial mounds and forts still lie scattered over Uppland.

In the northwest, Dalarna (Dalecarlia) is rich in folk culture and is the home of Sweden's most famous symbol, the brightly coloured wooden *Dalahäst* (Dala horse). On Midsummer's Day, happy hordes of people flock to the country's biggest celebrations, in the town of Leksand.

Svealand is littered with old industrial villages, with perfectly intact 16th- and 17th-century furnaces and forges; they're surprisingly picturesque places, and two of them are unique enough to appear on Unesco's World Heritage List. If you're more of a romantic, head for the region's gorgeous castles: Örbyhus Slott is a particularly fine baroque example.

Svealand's diversity – huge forests, balmy lakes, green meadows and high border mountains – is great news for outdoor types. Try your hand at rafting, canoeing, dogsledding, hiking, canyoning or rock-climbing. Sweden's biggest and best ski resort, at Sälen, explodes with rosy-cheeked skiers once the snows begin to fall.

HIGHLIGHTS

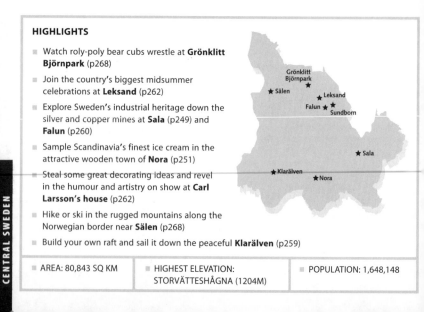

- Watch roly-poly bear cubs wrestle at **Grönklitt Björnpark** (p268)
- Join the country's biggest midsummer celebrations at **Leksand** (p262)
- Explore Sweden's industrial heritage down the silver and copper mines at **Sala** (p249) and **Falun** (p260)
- Sample Scandinavia's finest ice cream in the attractive wooden town of **Nora** (p251)
- Steal some great decorating ideas and revel in the humour and artistry on show at **Carl Larsson's house** (p262)
- Hike or ski in the rugged mountains along the Norwegian border near **Sälen** (p268)
- Build your own raft and sail it down the peaceful **Klarälven** (p259)

- AREA: 80,843 SQ KM
- HIGHEST ELEVATION: STORVÄTTESHÅGNA (1204M)
- POPULATION: 1,648,148

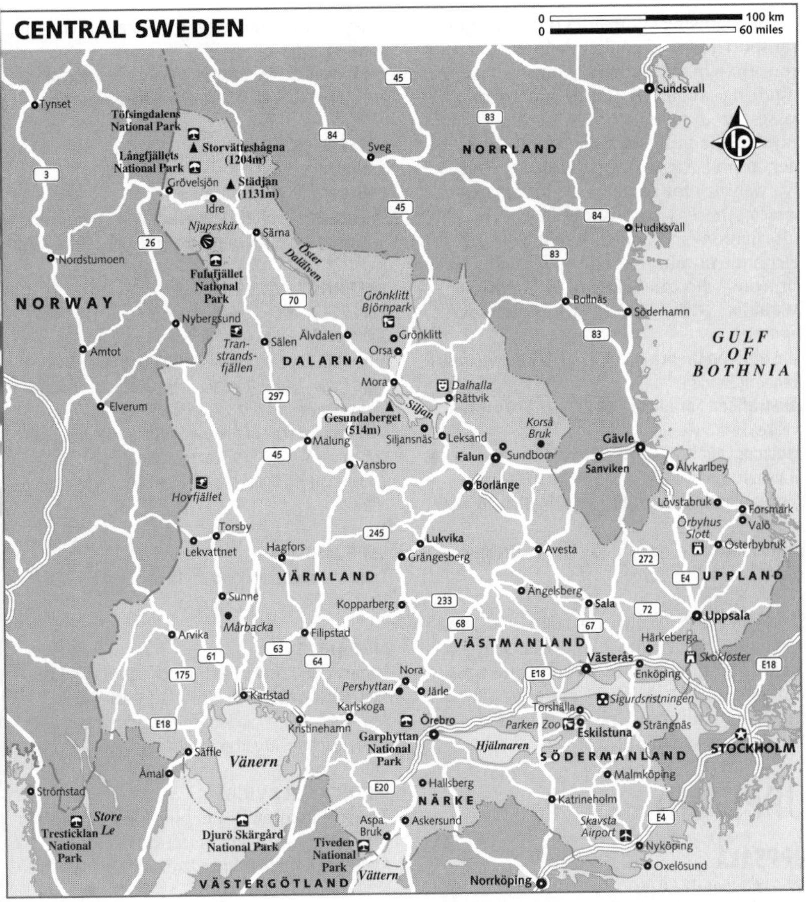

Orientation

Svealand consists of six regions *(landskaps)* and seven counties *(län)*. In the east, there's the regions of Uppland and Södermanland (a.k.a Sörmland), in the middle of the country there's Västmanland and Närke, while the west has Värmland and Dalarna. This book has dealt with the county of Stockholms län in a separate chapter.

Information

REGIONAL TOURIST OFFICES

Visitors can contact the following regional tourist offices for more detailed information on the area.

Sörmlands Turism (☎ 0155-24 59 00; www.sormland.se/turism; Box 58, SE-61122 Nyköping)

Turistinformation Dalarna (☎ 023-640 04; www.dalarna.se; Trotzgatan 10-12, SE-79183 Falun)

Turistrådet Örebro Län (☎ 019-602 70 00; www.orebrolan.se/turism; Eklundavägen 9-15, Box 1613, SE-70116 Örebro)

Uppsala Tourism (☎ 018-727 48 00; www.uppland.nu; Fyristorg 8, SE-75310 Uppsala)

Värmlands Turistråd (☎ 054-14 80 41; www.varmland.org; Drottninggatan 45, SE-65225 Karlstad)

WestmannaTurism (☎ 021-10 38 00; www.vastmanland.se in Swedish; Stora Gatan 40, SE-72187 Västerås)

Getting Around

Express buses connect major towns in southern areas. For the west and north of the region, you'll need to use *länstrafiken* (regional network) services.

The following companies provide regional transport links. If you're planning to spend some time in any of these counties, it's worth inquiring about discount cards, monthly passes or a *sommarkort*, offering cheaper travel in the peak summer period (midsummer to mid-August). Check also the respective websites for routes, schedules, fares and passes; these websites don't always have information in English, but if you call the telephone numbers listed you'll usually reach someone who can help you in English.

Dalatrafik (☎ 0771-95 95 95; www.dalatrafik.se in Swedish)
Länstrafiken Örebro (☎ 0771-22 40 00; www.lanstrafiken.se in Swedish)
Länstrafiken Sörmland (☎ 0771-22 40 00; www.lanstrafiken.se in Swedish)
Upplands Lokaltrafik (☎ 0771-14 14 14; www.upplandslokaltrafik.se in Swedish)
Västmanlands Lokaltrafik (☎ 0774-41 04 10; www.vl.se)
Värmlandstrafik (☎ 0563-532 34; www.kollplatsen.com in Swedish)

SJ (☎ 0771-75 75 75; www.sj.se) trains run along both sides of Mälaren lake. Hallsberg is a major junction and trains continue west to Karlstad and Oslo. There are good services from Stockholm to Uppsala and Mora, and many other destinations.

UPPLAND

UPPSALA

☎ 018 / pop 182,076

There's something of a small, green Amsterdam feel about Uppsala, Sweden's fourth-largest city and one of the oldest – perhaps it's the tranquil waterways, streams of bicycles and young studenty population. Don't miss the spectacular cathedral, dating back to the 15th century, and the Renaissance castle with its impressive history. On the edge of the city, Gamla (Old) Uppsala was once a flourishing 6th-century religious centre where humans were sacrificed to the Norse gods.

Information

BOOKSHOPS

Akademibokhandeln Lundequistska (☎ 13 98 30; Forumgallerian, Dragarbrunnsgatan 43-45; ⏲ 10am-7pm Mon-Fri, 10am-4pm Sat, noon-4pm Sun) The best English-language book selection in Uppsala, upstairs in the shopping centre.
Pressbyrån (Sankt Persgatan 10) Sells foreign newspapers and magazines. Another branch inside the train station.

EMERGENCY

Ambulance (☎ 112)
Police (☎ 16 85 00; Salagatan 18)
University Hospital Emergency Unit (Akademiska Sjukhusets Akutmottagning; ☎ 611 00 00; Sjukhusvägen)

INTERNET ACCESS

Port 22 (Sankt Olofsgatan 32; per hr Skr19; ⏲ 11am-8pm Mon-Fri, 11am-6pm Sat, noon-6pm Sun)
Sidewalk Express (per hr Skr19) Found inside Saffet's, Stora Torget, and at the train station. To log on, buy vouchers from the coin-operated machines.
UNT City Internet Café (cnr Fyristorg & Drottninggatan; per 15mins Skr10; ⏲ 9.30am-5.30pm Mon-Fri, 10.30am-2.30pm Sat) Inside the *Uppsala Nya Tidning* newspaper office.

LEFT LUGGAGE

Train station (small/medium/large lockers per 24hr Skr15/20/25)

LIBRARIES

Library (☎ 727 17 00; Svartbäcksgatan 17; ⏲ 10am-7pm Mon & Wed-Fri, 10am-8pm Tue, 11am-3pm Sat year-round, also 1-4pm Sun Sep-Apr) Offers free Internet access, but bring ID and expect longish waits.

MEDICAL SERVICES

There's an after-hours pharmacy at the hospital (see Emergency section).
Apoteket Kronan (Svartbäcksgatan 8; ⏲ 10am-7pm Mon-Sat)

MONEY

Head to Stora Torget for banks and ATMS.
Forex (☎ 10 30 00; Fyristorg 8; ⏲ 9am-7pm Mon-Fri, 9am-3pm Sat)

POST

A number of central newsagencies also provide postal services.
Post office (Bäverns Gränd 19; 8am-6pm Mon-Fri) Right next to the bus station.

TOURIST INFORMATION

Tourist office (☎ 727 48 00; www.uppsalatourism.se; Fyristorg 8; ⏲ 10am-6pm Mon-Fri, 10am-3pm Sat, also noon-4pm Sun mid-Jun–mid-Aug) Pick up the good *Walking Tour of Uppsala* leaflet, and the listings guide *What's On Uppsala* for the latest entertainment and events.

UPPSALA

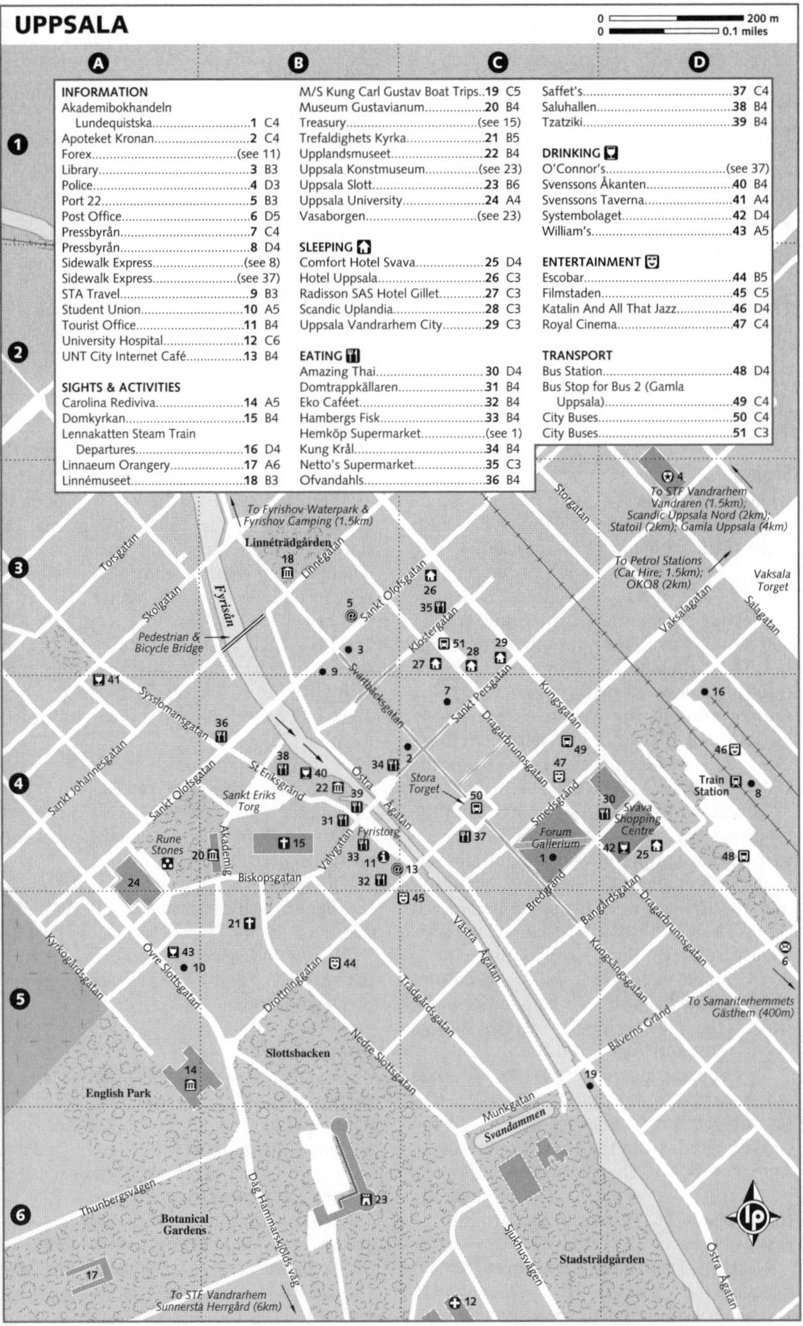

INFORMATION
Akademibokhandeln Lundequistska ... 1 C4
Apoteket Kronan ... 2 C4
Forex ... (see 11)
Library ... 3 B3
Police ... 4 D3
Port 22 ... 5 B3
Post Office ... 6 D5
Pressbyrån ... 7 C4
Pressbyrån ... 8 D4
Sidewalk Express ... (see 8)
Sidewalk Express ... (see 37)
STA Travel ... 9 B3
Student Union ... 10 A5
Tourist Office ... 11 B4
University Hospital ... 12 C6
UNT City Internet Café ... 13 B4

SIGHTS & ACTIVITIES
Carolina Rediviva ... 14 A5
Domkyrkan ... 15 B4
Lennakatten Steam Train Departures ... 16 D4
Linnaeum Orangery ... 17 A6
Linnémuseet ... 18 B3
M/S Kung Carl Gustav Boat Trips .. 19 C5
Museum Gustavianum ... 20 B4
Treasury ... (see 15)
Trefaldighets Kyrka ... 21 B5
Upplandsmuseet ... 22 B4
Uppsala Konstmuseum ... (see 23)
Uppsala Slott ... 23 B6
Uppsala University ... 24 A4
Vasaborgen ... (see 23)

SLEEPING
Comfort Hotel Svava ... 25 D4
Hotel Uppsala ... 26 C3
Radisson SAS Hotel Gillet ... 27 C3
Scandic Uplandia ... 28 C3
Uppsala Vandrarhem City ... 29 C3

EATING
Amazing Thai ... 30 D4
Domtrappkällaren ... 31 B4
Eko Caféet ... 32 B4
Hambergs Fisk ... 33 B4
Hemköp Supermarket ... (see 1)
Kung Krål ... 34 B4
Netto's Supermarket ... 35 C3
Ofvandahls ... 36 B4
Saffet's ... 37 C4
Saluhallen ... 38 B4
Tzatziki ... 39 B4

DRINKING
O'Connor's ... (see 37)
Svenssons Åkanten ... 40 B4
Svenssons Taverna ... 41 A4
Systembolaget ... 42 D4
William's ... 43 A5

ENTERTAINMENT
Escobar ... 44 B5
Filmstaden ... 45 C5
Katalin And All That Jazz ... 46 D4
Royal Cinema ... 47 C4

TRANSPORT
Bus Station ... 48 D4
Bus Stop for Bus 2 (Gamla Uppsala) ... 49 C4
City Buses ... 50 C4
City Buses ... 51 C3

UPPSALA KORTET

This handy little three-day discount card (Skr125) gives free or discounted admission to many of the town's attractions, plus free local bus travel and parking. There are also discounts at participating hotels, restaurants and shops. The card is valid from June to August, and can be bought from the tourist office.

TRAVEL AGENCIES

STA Travel (☎ 020-61 10 10; Sankt Olofsgatan 11)

UNIVERSITIES

Student union (☎ 480 31 00; www.uppsalastudentkar.nu; Övre Slottsgatan 7)

Sights

GAMLA UPPSALA

If you enjoy fresh green countryside buttered thick with pagan history, don't miss Gamla Uppsala, 4km north of the modern city. It's one of Sweden's largest and most important burial sites, containing around 300 mounds from the 6th to the 12th centuries. The earliest and most impressive are the three great **grave mounds** (admission free; 24hr), said to contain the legendary pre-Viking kings Aun, Egils and Adils...although that's unlikely, considering the body from the Östhögen (East Mound) is a woman.

According to breathless reports from the medieval chronicler, Adam of Bremen, a vast golden temple graced Gamla Uppsala in the 10th century. Outside, dog, horse and human sacrifices were strung up in a sacred grove. Thor, Odin and the other Viking gods were displaced when Christianity arrived in 1090, and from 1164, the archbishop of Uppsala had his seat in a cathedral on the site of the present **church** (☎ 0708-56 33 22; 9am-6pm Apr-Sep; 9am-4pm Oct-Mar).

Gamla Uppsala Museum (☎ 23 93 00; www.raa.se/olduppsala; adult/7-18yr Skr50/30; 11am-5pm May-Aug, noon-3pm Wed, Sat & Sun Sep–mid-Dec & Jan-Apr) contains finds from the cremation mounds, a poignant mix of charred and melted beads, bones and buckles. More intact pieces come from various **boat graves** in and around the site.

Nearby is **Friluftsmuseet Disagården** (☎ 16 91 80; admission free, guided tours Skr30; 10am-5pm mid-May–Aug), a 19th-century farming village consisting of 26 timber buildings. Disagården is the focal point for Uppsala's midsummer celebrations.

Just next to the unexcavated flat-topped mound, **Tingshögen** (Court Mound), is **Odinsborg** (☎ 32 35 25; buffet Skr150; 11am-6pm), a restaurant known for its horns of mead and Viking feasts (although daintier refreshments are offered at the downstairs summer café).

If you feel like a peaceful walk, **Erikleden** is a 6km 'pilgrims' path' between the cathedral in Uppsala and the church in Gamla Uppsala. Buses 2 and 110 run daily and are very frequent (between them there's one every 10 minutes Monday to Friday, every 40 minutes at weekends).

UPPSALA SLOTT

Pink and ponderous, **Uppsala Slott** (☎ 727 24 85; admission by guided tour only, adult/6-18yr Skr60/15; in English at 1pm & 3pm Jun-Aug) was built by Gustav Vasa in the 1550s. It contains the state hall where kings were enthroned, and where Queen Kristina abdicated (see boxed text, p31). It was also the scene of a brutal murder in 1567, when crazy King Erik XIV and his guards killed Nils Sture and his two sons, Erik and Svante, after accusing them of high treason. The castle burnt down in 1702, but was rebuilt and took on its present form in 1757.

In the ruins of the death-stained dungeons is a waxworks museum, **Vasaborgen** (☎ 50 77 72; www.vasaborgen.se in Swedish; adult/7-15yr Skr40/20; 10am-4pm May-Aug), where Renaissance scenes and intrigues are brought to life.

The southern wing of the castle houses the **Uppsala Konstmuseum** (☎ 727 24 82; adult/under 19s Skr30/free; noon-4pm Tue-Fri, 11am-5pm Sat & Sun), with five centuries worth of permanent artworks and some interesting temporary exhibitions.

DOMKYRKAN

The Gothic **Domkyrkan** (cathedral; ☎ 18 72 01; www.uppsaladomkyrka.se; admission free; 8am-6pm) dominates the city, just as some of those buried here – including St Erik, Gustav Vasa and the scientist Carl von Linné (see boxed text, p240) – dominated their country.

Gustav's funerary sword, silver crown and shiny golden buttons have been moved to the **treasury** (☎ 18 72 01; adult/child Skr30/free; 10am-5pm Mon-Sat & 12.30-5pm Sun May-Sep, limited hr Oct-Apr) in the cathedral's north tower, where there's also a great display of medieval textiles. Particularly fine are the clothes worn by the three noblemen who were murdered in the castle (see above): they're the only example of 16th-century Swedish high fashion still in existence.

BOTANICAL GARDENS

The excellent **Botanical Gardens** (☎ 471 28 38; www.botan.uu.se; Villavägen 6-8; admission free; 7am-8.30pm May-Aug, 7am-7pm Sep-Apr), below the castle hill, show off over 10,000 different species, and are well worth a wander. Attractions include the 200-year-old **Linnaeum Orangery** (9am-3.30pm Mon-Thu, 9am-2.30pm Fri year-round) and a tropical **greenhouse**, currently undergoing restoration (due to reopen in 2007).

MUSEUMS

With its wonderfully eclectic halls, the **Museum Gustavianum** (☎ 471 75 71; www.gustavianum.uu.se; Akademigatan 3; adult/under 12yr Skr40/free; 11am-4pm Tue-Sun) is the most intriguing of Uppsala's museums. It contains a reconstructed Viking ship burial, Egyptian mummies and Carl von Linné's notebooks, but the most wowing exhibit is the 17th-century **Augsburg Art Cabinet**, containing over a thousand ingenious trinkets, and the vertiginous **anatomical theatre** where executed criminals were dissected.

In the display hall of **Carolina Rediviva** (☎ 471 39 00; Dag Hammarskjölds väg 1; adult/under 12yr Skr20/free; 9am-5pm Mon-Fri, 10am-5pm Sat & 11am-4pm Sun mid-Jun–mid-Aug, 9am-8pm Mon-Fri & 10am-5pm Sat mid-Aug–mid-Jun), the old university library, is the surviving half of the *Codex Argentus* (AD 520), written in silver ink on purple vellum in Gothic.

Upplandsmuseet (☎ 16 91 00; www.upplandsmuseet.se in Swedish; Sankt Eriks Torg 10; free admission; noon-5pm Tue-Sun), in an 18th-century watermill, houses county collections on folk art, music, and the history of Uppsala from the Middle Ages onwards.

Botanists will enjoy **Linnémuseet** (☎ 13 65 40; www.linnaeus.uu.se; Svartbäcksgatan 27; adult/under 16yr Skr25/free; noon-4pm Tue-Sun Jun–mid-Sep), which displays memorabilia linked to Linné's work in Uppsala; and the attached 18th-century **Linnéträdgården** (☎ 471 25 76; adult/under 15yr Skr30/free; 9am-9pm May-Aug, 9am-7pm Sep), Sweden's oldest botanical garden, with more than 1300 species arranged according to Linné's 'sexual system' of classification.

There are also several special-interest museums (on medical history, psychiatry, evolution etc), attached to university departments, with complex opening hours; enquire at the tourist office for details.

OTHER SIGHTS

Trefaldighets Kyrka (9am-5pm) isn't as outwardly impressive as the nearby Domkyrkan, but it has interesting brick vaulting and some 15th-century painted ceilings.

EVERYDAY GODS

Some of the greatest gods of the Nordic world – Tyr, Odin, Thor and Frigg – live on in the English language as the days of the week: Tuesday, Wednesday, Thursday and Friday, respectively.

Tyr was the god of justice, a deity who lost his hand to a giant wolf. The gods tried to trick the wolf, Fenrir, into captivity by challenging him to break an indestructible chain. The wolf was suspicious, but accepted the challenge on condition that one of the gods place a hand in his mouth. Tyr agreed, the gods succeeded in fettering Fenrir, but the furious wolf retaliated by biting off Tyr's right hand.

The most eminent of the Nordic gods was one-eyed Odin, whose eight-legged flying horse, Sleipnir, had runes etched on its teeth. Odin gave up his eye in exchange for wisdom; he also gleaned information from his two ravens Hugin and Munin, who flew daily across the worlds in search of knowledge. As the god of war, Odin sent his 12 Valkyries (battle maidens) to select heroes killed in battle to join him at the palace of Valhalla. He was also the god of poets, a magician and master of runes.

Frigg was Odin's wife, and she's also known as a fertility goddess and the goddess of marriage.

The thunder god, Thor, protected humankind from the malevolent ice giants with his magic hammer, Mjolnir (Thor's-hammer talismans are frequently found in Viking graves). Immensely strong, he would hurl Mjolnir into the clouds to create vast thunderstorms before the hammer came boomeranging back again.

On the lawn by the main **Uppsala University** building (imposing enough to demand a glance inside) are nine typical Uppland **rune stones**.

On 30 April, students dressed in white gather to celebrate the **Walpurgis Festival**. Traditionally, this includes a student boat race on the river at 10am and a run down Carolinabacken at 3pm, as well as various processions and much singing.

Activities

You can ride the narrow-gauge steam train **Lennakatten** (☎ 13 05 00; www.lennakatten.se in Swedish; unlimited day-travel ticket adult/6-15yr/family Skr150/75/300) 33km into the Uppland countryside. Train trips take place up to seven times on Sunday from June to August, and there are also tours on Thursday, Friday and Saturday in July. The trains depart from the Uppsala Östra museum station, behind the main station.

Slow the pace with a boat cruise to the baroque castle of Skokloster. **M/S Kung Carl Gustaf** (☎ 14 48 00; www.kungcarlgustaf.se; return ticket adult/child Skr200/100), a 19th-century ex-steamship, sails Tuesday to Sunday from mid-May to mid-August. Tours leave Islandsbron at 10.30am and return at 4.30pm, allowing 2½ hours at Skokloster. There are also evening river cruises at 7pm Tuesday to Saturday from May to August; the cruise plus buffet and entertainment costs Skr350 per person.

Families with water-loving children should head for **Fyrishov** (☎ 727 49 50; www.fyrishov.se in Swedish; Idrottsgatan 2; adult/3-15yr Skr75/60; 9am-9pm), one of Sweden's largest waterparks with the full complement of slides, Jacuzzis, waterfalls and wave machines.

Sleeping

Uppsala Vandrarhem City (☎ 10 00 08; www.uppsalavandrarhem.se; Sankt Persgatan 16; dm/s/d Skr200/350/480; year-round;) The Vandrarhem City is recommended for its sheer convenience – you really can't stay anywhere more central for these prices. Rooms, all named after famous Uppsala landmarks, are small but decent (although dorms suffer from traffic and level-crossing noise), and there are plenty of toilets and showers to go round.

STF Vandrarhem Sunnersta Herrgård (☎ 32 42 20; info@sunnerstaherrgard.se; Sunnerstavägen 24; dm Skr190, s/d from Skr340/380; Jan–mid-Dec; bus 18 or 20) A pleasant, well-equipped hostel located in a manor house some 6km south of the city centre. It's possible to rent bikes (per day/week Skr50/200), and there's a boat that you can use for free.

STF Vandrarhem Vandraren (☎ 10 43 00; info@vandraren.com; Vattholmavägen 16C; dm Skr210-250, s/d from Skr250/440; mid-Jun–mid-Aug; bus 2, 20, 24 or 54) A student residence for most of the year, this summer hostel 2km north of the city has excellent amenities, including a private bathroom for each room. You can also rent bikes.

Samariterhemmets Gästhem (☎ 10 34 00, fax 10 83 75; Samaritergränd 2; s with/without bathroom Skr570/490 d with/without bathroom Skr840/740, prices discounted by around Skr80) Run by a Christian community, this is a clean, central and inviting guesthouse. Old-style rooms are simply decorated in cool creams, with antique furniture dotted here and there.

CARL VON LINNÉ

He may sound like a complete eccentric – a syphilis doctor who kept monkeys in his back garden –but Carl von Linné (1707–78), or Linnaeus, was a scientific genius. Known as the 'Father of Taxonomy', Linné invented a precise method for ranking minerals, plants and animals. Described in his work *Systema Naturae* the basis of his system is still used today.

Linnaeus believed that by studying the natural world, man could fathom out God's plans. His minute observations led him to devise a classification system of plants (based on their sexual organs) – where one Latin name indicates the genus, and one the species. Some contemporary scientists were appalled at the system's sexual explicitness, but Linnaeus obviously had a sense of humour about it: he named a small and insignificant weed after one of his most vocal critics!

As an inspirational professor at Uppsala university, he packed his pupils off around the globe to bring back samples; two of them even joined Captain Cook's expedition to Australia. Among his other achievements, Linné took Celsius' temperature scale and turned it upside down, giving us 0°C for freezing point and 100°C for boiling point, rather than the other way around.

Hotel Uppsala (☎ 480 50 00; hoteluppsala@profilhotels.se; Kungsgatan 27; s/d from Skr1110/1335, both discounted to Skr700; P 🖳) Newly refurbished in crisp calming birch wood, Hotel Uppsala is great for people who enjoy their snacks: 40 of the rooms have microwaves and fridges.

Scandic Uplandia (☎ 495 26 00; uplandia@scandic-hotels.com; Dragarbrunnsgatan 32; s/d from Skr1325/1640, discounted to Skr915; P ✖ 🖳) Scandic Uplandia is centrally located and recently refurbished, with smart modern rooms.

Scandic Uppsala Nord (☎ 495 23 00; uppsala@scandic-hotels.com; Gamla Uppsalagatan 50; rm from Skr990; P 🖳 ♿) Similar in style but with more in the way of gyms, saunas and solariums, Scandic's other hotel is 2.5km from the city centre on the road to Gamla Uppsala. For guests with a conscience, there are a few 'environmental rooms' where 97% of the contents can be recycled once they're past their best.

Comfort Hotel Svava (☎ 13 00 30; info.co.svava@choicehotels.se; Bangårdsgatan 24; s/d Skr1325/1625, discounted to Skr1125/1380; P ✖) Named after one of Odin's Valkyrie maidens, Hotel Svava, right opposite the train station, is a very comfortable top-end business-style hotel.

Radisson SAS Hotel Gillet (☎ 68 18 00; sales.uppsala@.radissonsas.com; Dragarbrunnsgatan 23; s/d/ste Skr1340/1740/1990, discounted to Skr700/990/1250; P 🖳 ♿) The bathrooms in this smart hotel have just been revamped, and some of the rooms have views of the cathedral (though singles are on the small side). Facilities include a bar, sauna, gym, pool, solarium and ice machines.

Fyrishov Camping (☎ 727 49 60; stugby@fyrishov.se; Idrottsgatan 2; sites Skr130, 4-bed cabins from Skr450; 🕑 year-round; bus 1, 4 or 33 from Dragarbrunnsgatan) This campsite, 2km north of the city, is great for families with waterbabies: it's attached to one of Sweden's largest waterparks.

Eating

RESTAURANTS & CAFÉS

Domtrappkällaren (☎ 13 09 55; info@domtrappkallaren.se; Sankt Eriksgränd 15; lunch from Skr80, dinner mains Skr200-290; 🕑 closed Sun) Previously a prison, this is now a top-notch restaurant set in an atmospheric cellar (lunch is served upstairs). It specialises in gamey dishes and Swedish cooking, such as venison, reindeer and cloudberry soufflé.

Tzatziki (☎ 15 03 33; Fyristorg 4; mezedes Skr49, mains Skr100-140) Tzatziki will supply all your *moussaka* and *souvlaki* needs. There's cosy seating in the 16th-century interior, and in summer the outside tables by the riverside thrum with diners. Service is fast, the food tasty, and there are several veggie options.

Kung Kral (☎ 12 50 90; www.kungkral.se in Swedish; Sankt Persgatan 4; lunch Skr80, mains Skr90-180) In the heart of town, this is perfect for summer lunchtimes, when the umbrella'd seating on Gamla Torget fills with hungry punters. The extensive menu includes burgers, pasta, reindeer, salads and seafood dishes.

Hambergs Fisk (☎ 71 00 50; Fyristorg 8; lunch from Skr80, à la carte mains Skr150-240; 🕑 Tue-Sat) Next to the tourist office is this excellent seafood restaurant, which is especially popular for lunch. Self-caterers may be interested in the attached fresh fish shop.

Amazing Thai (☎ 15 30 10; Bredgränd 14; lunch buffet from Skr60, à la carte dishes Skr90-130) A popular lunch spot thanks to its great-value buffet. The evening menu features a good selection of fragrant stir-fries, noodle dishes and curries.

Ofvandahls (☎ 13 42 04; Sysslomansgatan 3-5; cakes & snacks around Skr40) Something of an Uppsala institution, this classy *konditori* dates back to the 19th century and is a cut above your average coffee-and-bun shop. It's endorsed by no less a personage than the king, and radiates old-world charm.

Eko Caféet (☎ 12 18 45; Drottninggatan 5; snacks Skr50-70) This funky little place with retro and mismatched furniture serves some of the best coffee in town. It does Italian-style wholefood, turns into a tapas bar on Wednesday to Saturday evenings, and frequently hosts live jazz/folk. Things quieten down somewhat in the summer, when it just opens for lunch Monday to Friday.

QUICK EATS & SELF-CATERING

Saffet's (☎ 12 41 25; Stora Torget 1; meals from Skr59) Cheap eats pour from the friers at this central fast-food outlet, serving Tex-Mex, burgers, spuds, kebabs and fish and chips.

Saluhallen (🕑 10am-6pm Mon-Fri, 10am-2pm Sat) Recently rebuilt after a devastating fire, this must now be one of the world's shiniest indoor markets. Stock up on meat, fresh fish, cheeses and fancy chocolates.

There's a central **Hemköp supermarket** (Stora Torget; 🕑 until 10pm) and a branch of the cheaper chain **Netto's** (Klostergatan; 🕑 until 8pm Mon-Fri, 6pm Sat & Sun). For alcohol, **Systembolaget** (Dragarbrunnsgatan 50) is inside the Svava shopping centre.

Drinking & Entertainment

In the evenings, local students converge on the university bars on Sankt Olofsgatan (difficult to get into if you're not an Uppsala student, but worth a go). Or try the bar-restaurants in town.

Svenssons Taverna (☎ 10 09 08; Sysslomansgatan 14) This cool *taverna* has a winning combination of rustic interior and shady outdoor seating area.

Svenssons Åkanten (☎ 15 01 50; Sankt Erikstorg; 🕑 May-Sep) The Tavernas sister venue is equally popular for summer evening drinkies, with a great riverside location near the indoor market.

O'Connor's (☎ 14 40 10; Stora Torget 1) Upstairs from Saffet's is this friendly Irish pub and restaurant (with good pub meals from Skr50). It has live music at least six nights of the week, and a selection of over 70 beers from around the world.

William's (☎ 14 09 20; Övre Slottsgatan 7) In the university quarter, William's is a cosy 'English' pub.

Katalin And All That Jazz (☎ 14 06 80; Godsmagasinet, Östra Station) The excellent Katalin is in a former warehouse behind the train station. It hosts regular live jazz and blues, with occasional rock and pop bands. There's a good restaurant here too.

Escobar (☎ 14 00 40) A popular bar and nightclub which has recently been revamped. At the time of writing, its grand reopening was being eagerly awaited.

Big Hollywood films are screened regularly at the **Royal Cinema** (☎ 13 50 07; Dragarbrunnsgatan 44) and **Filmstaden** (☎ 08 56 26 00 00; www.sf.se in Swedish; Drottninggatan 3).

Getting There & Away

The **Flygbuss** (Bus 801) departs at least twice an hour between 3.15am and midnight for nearby Arlanda airport (Skr80); it leaves from outside Scandic Hotel Uplandia.

Swebus Express (☎ 0200-21 82 18; www.swebusexpress.se) runs regular direct services to Stockholm (Skr65, one hour, at least hourly), Gävle (Skr120, one hour 40mins, two daily), Västerås (Skr90, 1½ hours, eight Monday to Friday, three Saturday and Sunday), Örebro (Skr200, three hours, two to four buses daily) and Falun (Skr190, 3½ hours, two Monday to Saturday, one Sunday). **Svenska Buss** (☎ 0771-67 67 67; www.svenskabuss.se in Swedish) also operates two services on Fridays and Sundays that call at Västerås (Skr60, 1¼ hours), Örebro (Skr120, 2½ hours) and Karlstad (Skr180, 4¼ hours).

There are frequent SJ trains to/from Stockholm (Skr49, 40 minutes). All SJ services to/from Gävle (Skr129, 50 minutes, at least seven daily), Östersund (Skr480, six hours, at least two daily) and Mora (Skr272, 3¼ hours, two daily) also stop in Uppsala.

For car hire, contact **Statoil** (☎ 20 91 00; Gamla Uppsalagatan 48), next to the Scandic Uppsala Nord. There are also three petrol stations with car hire, 1.5km along Vaksalagatan: **OKQ8** (☎ 29 04 96; Årstagatan 5-7) often has good deals.

Getting Around

Upplands Lokaltrafik (☎ 0771-14 14 14; www.ul.se in Swedish) runs traffic within the city and county. **City buses** leave from Stora Torget and the surrounding streets. Tickets cost from Skr20 and give unlimited travel for two hours.

NORTHERN UPPLAND

Centuries-old ironworks and mines dot the green landscape of Northern Uppland. From vast gorges ripped into the ground to spic-and-span forge workers' cottages, the industrial heritage in this area makes for some unique trips. Ask any tourist office for the free booklet *Vallonbruk in Uppland*, or check out www.vallonbruken.nu.

You'll notice the word 'bruk' in many local placenames. A *bruk* is an industrial village that processed raw materials, such as iron ore. Most appeared in the 17th century, and were owned, run and staffed by Dutch and Walloon (Belgian) immigrants. The profits were used to build fine mansions, surrounded by humble workers' homes.

To reach Lövstabruk or Forsmark, take bus 811 from Uppsala to Östhammar (Skr80, 1¼ hours, every 30 minutes Monday to Friday, hourly at weekends), then change to bus 832 (four to eight daily). Bus 823 runs hourly from Uppsala to Österbybruk (Skr60, one hour, at least 10 daily).

Österbybruk

☎ 0295

You'd never guess from its placid air, but Österbybruk and its ironworks were established solely to make munitions for Gustav Vasa's interminable wars. Today the village is a sleepy place, which nevertheless contains most basic facilities (bank, bakery, supermarket, pizzerias etc), and a summer **tourist office** (☎ 214 92; 11am-5pm Jun-Aug).

The pleasant area around the tourist office includes the mansion **Österbybruk Herrgård** (which has summer art exhibitions), **workers' homes** and the world's best-preserved 17th-century **Walloon forge**. Two types of tours are offered: one takes in the grounds of ironworks, the other takes you into the forge and explains its original workings. Both tours are given daily in summer (mid-June to mid-August) and cost Skr40 per adult (free for children).

About 2.5km west, there's the old 100m-deep **Dannemora Gruvor**, once a mine and now a lake. Tours of the mine buildings run at noon and 2pm daily in July, and at weekends in June and August (adult/child Skr50/free). Daredevils can experience the **Gruväventyr** (☎ 207 00; www.gruvaventyr.se in Swedish; Storrymningsvägen 7; admission Skr390; 11am, 1pm, 3pm, 5pm & 7pm Wed-Sun Jul–mid-Aug), an unusual climbing/abseiling/rope-bridge course around the old mine. It's unsuitable for anyone shorter than 1.6m.

The impressive 15th-century castle **Örbyhus Slott** (☎ 214 06; www.orbyhus-slott.com; admission by tour only, adult/12-16yr Skr50/15; 1pm Sat & Sun mid-May–mid-Sep, plus 1pm & 3pm Jul), 10km further west, is where mad King Erik XIV was imprisoned by his brother Johann. Erik was then murdered with a bowl of pea soup laced with arsenic.

Wärdshuset Gammel Tammen (☎ 212 00; info@gammeltammen.se; s/d Skr895/1150, discounted to Skr595/850) This lovely old inn is in one wing of Österbybruk Herrgård, by the ironworks estate. Rooms are cosy and peaceful – some have views over the duck pond – and there's a good restaurant (snacks Skr70, mains Skr150).

Dannemora Vandrarhem (☎ 215 70; Storrymningsvägen 4; beds Skr175; May-Oct) This wee hostel, with 20 beds, is near the Dannemora mine and is based in old mineworkers' houses.

Karins Stallcafé (☎ 401 48; 11am-5pm May-Jul, 11am-4pm Aug) Near the Gammel Tammen, in a former stable, this summer café serves lunches and snacks, set off by chunks of warm homemade bread.

Lövstabruk

☎ 0294

Tiny Lövstabruk (Leufsta Bruk), 24km due north of Österbybruk, is a great example of a mansion with associated factories. In 1627 the Dutchman Louis de Geer came to Lövstabruk, and the mansion was built for his grandson, Charles de Geer, around 1700. The house and its factories were destroyed by a Russian attack in 1719, but everything was rebuilt and iron production continued until 1926.

There is a small **tourist office** (☎ 310 70; 11am-5pm mid-Jun–mid-Aug, 11am-2pm Sat & Sun rest of the yr) next to the church, where you can buy tickets for various one-hour guided tours, including to the mansion (1.30pm); the village and park (noon); and a themed tour, the subject of which changes every year (3.30pm). They all cost Skr50 and run daily from mid-June to mid-August.

Leufstabruks Wärdshus (☎ 311 22; vardshus.lovstabruk@telia.com; budget s/d Skr200/300, historic s/d Skr300/400, with breakfast s/d Skr500/600) This classy inn has options for both lean and bulging wallets. Cheaper hostel-style rooms are in a modern annexe, and the posher accommodation is inside the beautiful 16th-century house. There's also a fine restaurant (mains Skr165 to Skr185), serving everything from coffee and cakes to a full á la carte menu.

Forsmark

☎ 0173

The beautiful surroundings of the **Forsmarksbruk** ironworks are ideal for photographers; it may be an old industrial estate, but its church, manor house, workshops and English gardens, all set around a central pond, are just staggeringly pretty. The **statue** of Neptune in the middle of the pond dates from 1792. There's a seasonal **tourist office** (☎ 500 15; 9am-4pm Jul–mid-Aug) which is staffed until 4pm, but open until 9pm for brochures. These days the main employer in the area is the nearby nuclear power station. An exhibition room adjoining Forsmark tourist office extols the virtues of the plant…with no mention of, for example, the radioactive waste it leaked into the Baltic Sea in June 2005.

The **bruksmuseum** (adult/child Skr20/free; noon-4pm mid-Jun–mid-Aug), with old carriages, sleeping quarters and a factory office, is definitely worth a look, although its opening times can be erratic. **Eldorado** (free; 9am-4pm Mon-Fri, 11.30am Sat & Sun mid-Jun–mid-Aug), a tiny experiment station for kids, has a fantastic rolling-ball machine guaranteed to hypnotise.

Forsmark Wärdshus (☎ 501 00; forsmark.vardshus@telia.com; lunch Skr70, s/d Skr550/750) Friendly staff cope admirably with the hungry coach parties at this lovely old inn. As well as devouring lunch, you can stay in one of the charming rooms (prices include breakfast) overlooking the English park, and rent bicycles (per day Skr100).

SÖDERMANLAND

NYKÖPING

☎ 0155 / pop 49,575

You can easily spend a relaxing summer day or two in Nyköping, checking out its low-key attractions. There's a **tourist office** (☎ 24 82 00; turism@nykoping.se; Stadshuset, Stora Torget; 8am-6pm Mon-Fri, 9am-1pm Sat mid-Jun–mid-Aug, 8am-5pm Mon-Fri rest of yr) inside the rather ugly town hall on the main square. Banks, supermarkets and other services can be found on Västra Storgatan, running west from Stora Torget.

Sights & Activities

The scenic ruined castle **Nyköpingshus** (admission free; 24hr) was the setting for some violent sibling rivalry. In 1317 the king's son, Birger, invited his two brothers, Erik and Valdemar, to a banquet there. When they arrived, he hurled them into the dungeon and threw away the key; they both eventually starved to death. Try to keep your mind free of such gruesome behaviour as you stroll by the tranquil riverside grounds.

You can also visit **Sörmlands Museum** (☎ 24 70 02; adult/under 20yr Skr20/free; 10am-5pm mid-Jun–mid-Aug, 11am-5pm Tue-Sun mid-Aug–mid-Jun) inside the castle. It's made up of the **Kungstornet** (King's Tower), the whitewashed four-storey castle tower; **Gamla Residenset**, the wonderfully recreated old governor's residence; and the neighbouring **Konsthallen**, with interesting art exhibitions and a collection of 19th-century boathouses.

By Stora Torget, there's the old **rådhus**, and **St Nicolai Kyrka**, with a rather splendid pulpit amongst the usual ecclesiastical furnishings. Also of interest are two **rune stones** and the 700 Bronze Age **rock carvings** in Släbroparken, about 2.5km northwest of town.

Take a walk along the river – 'Sweden's longest museum', so the publicity goes. If you fancy a longer hike, the 1000km-long **Sörmlandsleden** (☎ 355 64; www.sormlandsleden.se) passes through town on its meander round the entire county. You can also explore the nearby **archipelago**; inquire at the tourist office.

Sleeping & Eating

Nyköpings Vandrarhem (☎ 21 18 10; Brunnsgatan 2; dm Skr160) This is an 18th-century wooden SVIF hostel, located just outside the castle grounds. It's small and friendly with good facilities.

Comfort Hotel Kompaniet (☎ 28 80 20; Folkungavägen 1; s/d Skr1380/1595, discounted to Skr795/975) Just south of the centre, near the harbour, this has stylishly decorated rooms in a riverside building that was once home to a furniture factory. All prices include a dinner buffet, making the discounted rates particularly good value.

Strandstuviken Camping (☎ 978 10; strandstuviken@hotmail.com; sites Skr140, cabins from Skr375; May-Sep) The nearest camping ground is this family beachside place, with sauna, mini-golf, and canoe and bicycle hire. It's a good 8km southeast of town, though, with no public transport.

Café Hellmans (☎ 21 05 25; Västra Trädgårdsgatan 24; breakfast buffet Skr55, lunch buffet Skr65) This charming place is the nicest spot in town for lunch. As well as good-value buffets, there are bagels and subs from Skr30, plus good coffee and excellent cakes to enjoy in the summer courtyard.

Lotsen (☎ 21 21 03; Skeppsbron; meals Skr80-160; until 2am Wed, Fri & Sat) Summer-opening Lotsen is a casual bar-restaurant down by the harbour. It has good simple meals like pizza, meatballs and burgers, or more upmarket mains like salmon and beef fillet, and there's often live music.

Getting There & Around

Nyköping's **Skavsta airport** (☎ 28 04 00; www.skavsta-air.se), 8km northwest of town, has flights to/from the UK with Ryanair (see p323). Airport buses meet most flights and run to/from Stockholm (Skr130, 80 minutes). Local buses run every 10 minutes from Nyköping to Skavsta (Skr15, 20 minutes); alternatively, a **taxi** (☎ 21 75 00) costs about Skr140.

The bus and train stations are 800m apart on the western side of the central grid. Nyköping is on the regular **Swebus Express** (☎ 0200-21 82 18; www.swebusexpress.se) routes: Stockholm–Norrköping–Jönköping–Göteborg/Malmö, and Stockholm–Norrköping–Kalmar. To get to Eskilstuna, take local bus 701 or 801. SJ trains run every hour or two to Norrköping (Skr75, 40 minutes), Linköping (Skr145, 1¼ hours) and Stockholm (Skr120, one hour). Most X2000 services don't stop in Nyköping.

The tourist office has bikes for rent (per day/week Skr40/200).

ESKILSTUNA

☎ 016 / pop 91,168

Once the murder capital of Sweden, Eskilstuna is now most famous for its zoo, which has had great success in breeding endangered white tigers. There are a number of other things to see, mostly linked to the town's old industries. Twelve kilometres northeast of Eskilstuna is one of the most extraordinary rock carvings in Sweden (see boxed text 'Sigurdsristningen', below).

The **tourist office** (☎ 10 70 00; www.eskilstuna.se in Swedish; Nygatan 15; 9am-6pm Mon-Fri, 10am-3pm Sat & 11am-3pm Sun Jun-Aug, 9am-5pm Mon-Fri Sep-May) dispenses helpful information. You'll find most services around Fristadstorget and the pedestrianised part of Kungsgatan. The central **public library** (☎ 10 13 51; Kriebsensgatan 4; 9am-8pm Mon-Thu, 9am-6pm Fri & 10am-3pm Sat) has free Internet access.

Parken Zoo

One of central Sweden's most popular family attractions is the zoo and amusement park **Parken Zoo** (☎ 10 01 01; www.parkenzoo.se; adult/4-14yr Skr140/100; 10am-6pm Jul–mid-Aug, 10am-4pm mid-Apr–Jun & mid-Aug–early Sep). Animals in the zoo include monkeys, komodo dragons, and some beautiful white tigers who were successfully bred here. It's not a cheap day out though; additional charges are made for: parking (per day Skr40); the **amusement park** (day ticket Skr135; noon-6pm Jul–mid-Aug, noon-4pm mid-May–Jun), which has kiddies' rides and some larger whizzy things; the **reptile house** (adult/child Skr20/10); and the **swimming pool** (adult/7-14yr Skr30/20; 10am-6.30pm late May–mid-Aug).

Parken Zoo is located 1.5km west of the town centre. Bus 1 (Skr19, five minutes) leaves frequently from the train station.

Other Sights

The **Rademachersmedjorna** (Rademacher Forges; ☎ 10 13 71; Rademachergatan; admission free; 11am-4pm Tue-Sun) contain the carefully-conserved 17th-century remnants of Eskilstuna's ironworking past. And the tradition continues: iron-, silver- and goldsmiths all have workshops here.

Faktoriet (☎ 10 23 75; faktoriet@eskilstuna.se; admission free; 11am-4pm Tue-Sun), on the island Strömsholmen, tells the story of Eskilstuna's industrial and cultural heritage. Its mighty steam engines spring into life on the first Sunday of the month (February to November).

At the time of writing, **Konstmuseet's** (☎ 10 13 69) extensive art collection was being relocated to the Munktell area; phone for further details.

In **Torshälla**, 6km north of the town centre, **Brandt Contemporary Glass** (☎ 35 52 30; brandtglass@telia.com; Klockberget; admission Skr30; 11am-4pm Fri & Sat), just behind the church, is a contemporary glass workshop and gallery exhibiting vases and sculptures. The **Ebelingmuséet** (☎ 10 73 05; Eskilstunavägen 5; admission free; noon-4pm Wed-Sun) has bizarre steel sculptures by Allan and Marianne Ebling, and changing temporary exhibitions. The old wooden houses and pretty riverside areas

SIGURDSRISTNINGEN

This exceptionally vivid 3m-long **Viking Age rock carving** (admission free; 24hr; bus 225) tells the story of Sigurd, the greatest hero in Germanic legend. It was the source for Wagner's Ring Cycle, and *The Hobbit* and *Lord of the Rings* also borrow freely from it.

Carved into the bedrock around AD 1000, the carving shows Sigurd killing the snakelike dragon Fafnir (who guards a cursed golden ring). After tasting the dragon's blood, Sigurd is able to understand the language of the birds. They warn of a murderous plot against him, so Sigurd attacks first, chopping off his enemy's head. Also on the stone is Sigurd's horse Grani, a gift from Odin.

The runes in the dragon's body are unrelated to the legend – they explain that a nearby bridge (the abutments can still be seen) was raised by Sigrid in memory of her husband Holmger.

The carving is one of Sweden's finest and worth a detour. It's situated near Sundbyholms Slott and Mälaren lake, 12km northeast of Eskilstuna.

in Torshälla are also worth a look. Take bus 2 or 15 from Eskilstuna to Torshälla (Skr19, 40 minutes).

Sleeping & Eating

STF Hostel Eskilstuna (☎ 51 30 80; vilsta.sporthotell@swipnet.se; dm Skr150, s/d from Skr250/300; ⌚ year-round; bus 12 from Fristadstorget) Lying in the Vilsta nature reserve 2km south of town, this hostel is well provided for – all rooms have en suite and TV. It's part of the Vilsta sport complex, so there are gym, Jacuzzi and sports facilities conveniently to hand.

City Hotell (☎ 10 88 50; www.cityhotell.se; Drottninggatan 15; s/d from Skr899/1155, discounted to Skr575/750) Among the better priced hotels in town is this one, right opposite the train station. Rooms are comfortable, and a few are adorned with wonderful Swedish stoves, giving them a hint of the 19th century.

Sundbyholms Slott (☎ 016-42 84 00; www.sundbyholms-slott.se; s/d from Skr990/1390, ste Skr3250; P 💻) Near Sigurdsristningen, 12km northeast of Eskilstuna. Luxury suites, perfect for a romantic weekend, are available in the tasteful mansion here. If your budget doesn't stretch that far, more prosaic rooms are available in the attached hotel. The castle, by Mälaren lake, not far from the Sigurd carvings, also houses a top-quality restaurant.

Restaurang Tingsgården (☎ 51 66 20; Rådhustorget 2; mains Skr150-220; ⌚ closed Sun) This intimate dining option, inside a wonderful wooden 18th-century house, is a true treat. There's an extensive menu of Swedish favourites, from mussel soup to wild strawberries, and some pleasing nods to international cuisine. In summer, you can sit out on a large deck overlooking the twinkling river.

Café Kaka (☎ 13 10 94; Kyrkogatan 6; meals Skr40-70) Kaka is a funky, upbeat café and meeting place, serving up sandwiches, pasta, salads and the occasional live DJ.

Getting There & Away

The bus station is located 500m east of the train station, beside the river. Local bus 701 goes roughly hourly to Malmköping (Skr43, 45 minutes) and Nyköping (Skr86, two hours). **Swebus Express** (☎ 0200-21 82 18; www.swebusexpress.se) operates up to six buses daily on its Stockholm–Eskilstuna–Örebro route, but trains are best for destinations such as Örebro (Skr102, one hour, every two hours), Västerås (Skr65, 30 minutes, hourly) and Stockholm (Skr118, one hour, hourly).

VÄSTMANLAND

VÄSTERÅS

☎ 021 / pop 131,014

With its cobbled streets, higgledy-piggledy houses and flourishing flower gardens, Västerås' old town is an utter delight. Sweden's sixth-largest city is a place of two halves: head southeast and you'll find modern shopping centres, large industries and sprawling suburbs that bear no resemblance to the teeny lanes and crafty shops you've left behind.

Västerås makes for a pleasant day trip, and is a handy base for exploring Lake Mälaren and important pagan sites nearby.

Information

The **tourist office** (☎ 39 01 00; http://turism.vastmanland.se; Kopparbergsvägen 8; ⌚ 10am-7pm Mon-Fri, 10am-3pm Sat, 10am-2pm Sun mid-Jun–mid-Aug, 9.30am-6pm weekdays, 10am-3pm Sat rest of yr) can help with visitor inquiries for the town and region.

There's a **Forex** (☎ 180080; Stora Gatan 18; ⌚ 9am-7pm Mon-Fri, 9am-3pm Sat) exchange office, banks, ATMs, and most other services visitors will require, along Stora Gatan. The **library** (☎ 39 46 00; Biskopsgatan 2; ⌚ 10am-7pm Mon-Thu, 10am-6pm Fri, 10am-2pm Sat) is opposite domkyrkan (the cathedral) and offers free Internet access. There's also an Internet café, **Galaxies** (☎ 12 54 40; Kopparbergsvägen 27B; per hr Skr45; ⌚ noon-9pm Sun-Thu, noon-10pm Fri & Sat).

Sights

MUSEUMS

The **Konstmuseum** (☎ 16 13 00; Fiskartorget 2; admission free; ⌚ 11am-4pm Tue-Fri & noon-4pm Sat mid-Jun–mid-Aug, 10am-5pm Tue-Fri, 11am-4pm Sat & noon-4pm Sun rest of yr), based in the stately old town hall, devotes its energies to exhibiting contemporary Swedish painters. The permanent collections, with works by artists such as Ivan Aguéli and Bror Hjorth, also get an occasional airing. In the cellar vaults is a decent café, which serves up homemade pies, soups and cakes, and migrates outdoors in summer.

Vallby Friluftsmuseum (☎ 39 80 70; www.vallbyfriluftsmuseum.se; admission free; ⌚ 10am-5pm year-round; bus 10 or 12), off Vallbyleden near the E18 inter-

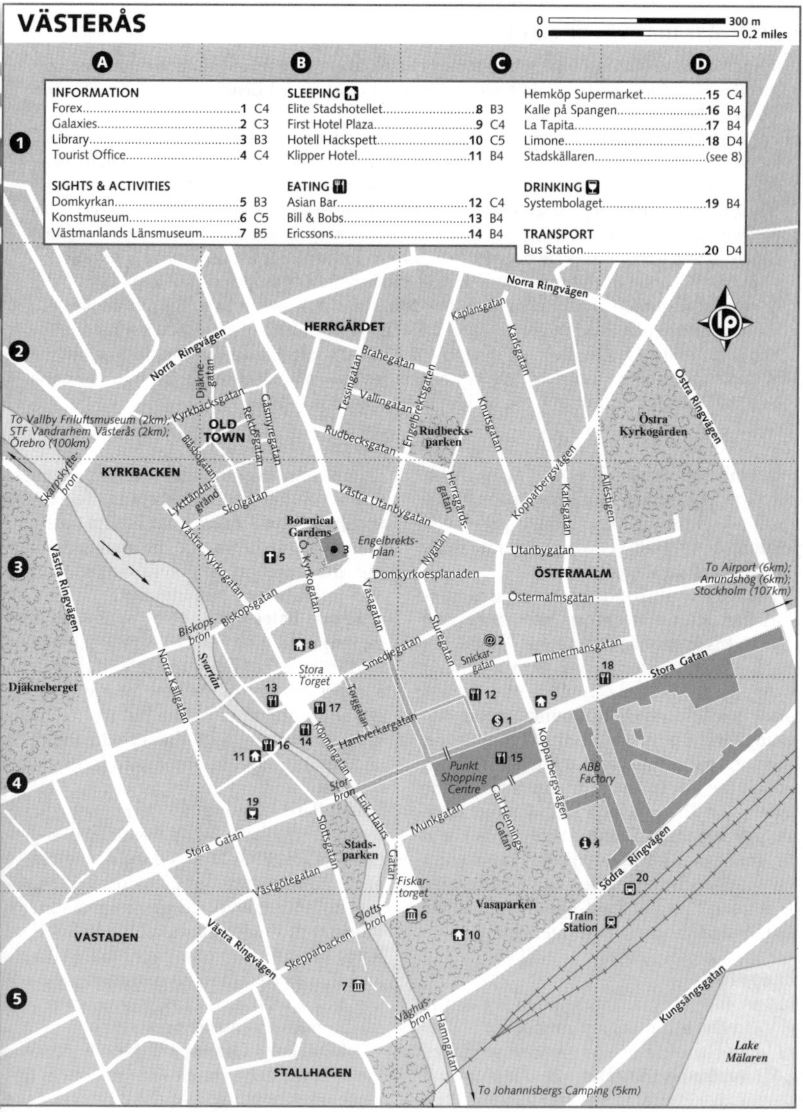

change, 2km northwest of the city, is home to an extensive open-air collection. Among the 40-odd buildings, there's an interesting farmyard and craft workshops.

Västmanlands Länsmuseum (☎ 15 61 00; Slottsgatan), inside Västerås Slottet (manor house), was closed at the time of writing; contact the tourist office for more information.

OTHER SIGHTS

The fine brick-built **Domkyrkan** (Cathedral; Biskopsgatan; 🕑 8am-5pm Mon-Fri, 9.30am-5pm Sat & Sun) was begun in the 12th century, although most of what you see today is late-14th-century work. It contains carved floor slabs, six altar pieces and the marble sarcophagus of crazy King Erik XIV.

ARTY ALTERNATIVE LODGINGS

In addition to Västerås' normal, run-of-the-mill hotels, there are two unique accommodation possibilities in and around town. Both created by local artist Mikael Genberg, they are well worth investigating if you like your lodgings with a twist.

The **Hotell Hackspett**, or Woodpecker Hotel, is a fabulous tree house in the middle of Vasaparken, behind the Konstmuseum. The cabin sleeps only one person and is 13m above the ground in an old oak tree; guests (and breakfast) are hoisted up in a basket! The second of Genberg's fascinating creations is the **Utter Inn**, a small, red, floating cabin in the middle of Mälaren lake, only accessible by boat. The bedroom is downstairs – 3m below the surface – and is complete with glass viewing panels to watch the marine life outside. There's room for two people, and a canoe is provided.

Accommodation in the tree house or lake cabin costs Skr700 per person per night if you bring your own food and bed linen, or the 'deluxe package' (when linen is supplied and you will be delivered food in the evening and breakfast in the morning) is Skr1000 per person. For bookings, contact Mikael Genberg directly (☎ 83 00 23, info@mikaelgenberg.com) or call the Västerås tourist office. Genberg also has a website (www.mikaelgenberg.com); it's in Swedish only, but the pictures will give you an idea of his creations.

Behind the cathedral is the quaint old-town area **Kyrkbacken**, once the student district it is now a wonderfully preserved portion of pre-18th-century Västerås, studded with artisans' workshops.

The city is surrounded by ancient pre-Christian sites. The most interesting and extensive is **Anundshög** (admission free; 24hr), the biggest tumulus in Sweden, 6km northeast of the city. It has a full complement of prehistoric curiosities, such as mounds, stone ship settings and a large 11th-century rune stone. The two main stone ship settings date from around the 1st century. The area is part of the Badelunda Ridge, which includes the 13th-century **Badelunda Church** (1km north) and the 16m-wide **Tibble Labyrinth** (1km south). Ask the tourist office for the handy map *Badelunda Forntids Bygd*. Take bus 12 to the Bjurhovda terminus, then walk 2km east.

Sleeping

Budget travellers will struggle in the centre of Västerås, but there's plenty of choice for middle-of-the-range and top-end spenders.

STF Vandrarhem Västerås (☎ 30 38 00; info.vasteras@quality.choicehotels.se; Svalgången 1, Vallby; dm/s/d Skr205/390/520; year-round;) A couple of kilometres out of town is this recommended (brand-new) hostel, with budget and hotel accommodation. Staff are great, and you can use the sauna and pool for free.

Elite Stadshotellet (☎ 10 28 00; info@vasteras.elite.se; Stora Torget; s/d from Skr1120/1320, discounted to Skr595/795; P) Many of the rooms at the Elite, in a lovely Art Nouveau building, have prime views over the main square – request one if you like people-watching. The décor is tasteful (pale walls, leafy bedspreads and mahogany-style wood), the staff are obliging, and there's a highly regarded restaurant and English-style pub attached.

Klipper Hotel (☎ 41 00 00; niklas@klipperhotel.se; Kungsgatan 4; s/d from Skr595/1190, discounted to Skr595/695; P) The attractive, family-run Klipper has one of the best locations in the city, near the river in the old town. Prices are reasonable, and the comfortable (if smallish) rooms are simple and fresh. Parking costs an extra Skr50 per day.

First Hotel Plaza (☎ 10 10 10; reservations.plaza@firsthotels.se; Karlsgatan 9A; s/d from Skr1269/1469, discounted to Skr588/788;) Bang in the centre of the modern city, this 25-storey skyscraper was built for gravity-defying lounge lizards; it boasts the highest cocktail bar in Sweden! Some rooms have views over Lake Mälaren, and all expected mod cons are here, including a spa with masseurs, sauna, gym and Mediterranean-inspired restaurant.

Johannisbergs Camping (☎ 14 02 79; sites/cabins from Skr80/400; bus 25) The closest campsite is this place, 5km southwest of the city near Lake Mälaren. Facilities include a small swimming area and canoe hire.

Eating & Drinking

La Tapita (☎ 12 10 44; Stora Torget 3; tapas Skr25-65, mains Skr100-185; closed Sun) This Spanish-themed tapas bar and restaurant has a mellow atmosphere, enhanced by Latin music and piles of southern Mediterranean grub.

Nibble an array of tapas, tuck into pasta, fish and meat mains, or share a *paella Valenciana* (Skr166 per person) with a friend.

Stadskällaren (☎ 10 28 00; Stora Torget; mains Skr185-280) In the atmospheric cellar of the Stadshotellet, this restaurant is a great place to treat yourself. Its small but perfectly formed menu is fish- and meat-based, with dishes cooked to perfection in Swedish style.

Limone (☎ 41 75 60, Stora Gatan 4; dishes Skr120-200; closed lunch Jul & Sun year-round) Limone is an elegant, upmarket Italian restaurant, with stylish décor and impressive menu items like *linguini* with crayfish, or grilled veal wrapped in Parma ham.

Bill & Bobs (☎ 41 99 21; Stora Torget 5; meals Skr80-200) A diverse crowd settles down at this casual spot to drink and chatter at the outdoor tables on the main square. Thai chicken and hamburger with bacon bits are a couple of Bill & Bobs' popular 'classic' dishes.

Asian Bar (☎ 18 60 68; Sturegatan 10; lunch Skr60-100; closed Sun) If your saliva starts streaming at words like *teriyaki, ichiban* and *yakitori,* head down to this simple central sushi bar.

Kalle på Spangen (☎ 12 91 29; Kungsgatan 2; meals Skr40-65) This is without doubt the best café in Västerås. It's right by the river in the old part of town, and has several cosy, creaky-floored rooms filled with mismatched furniture and gilt-edged grandfather clocks. Friendly staff serve up a wide selection of coffees, sandwiches, salads, baked potatoes and cakes.

There's a **Hemköp supermarket** (Punkt shopping centre, Stora Gatan) and **Ericssons** (☎ 13 55 12; Stora Torget 3) is an excellent delicatessen for stocking up on picnic supplies. For alcohol, visit **Systembolaget** (Stora Gatan 48).

Getting There & Around

The **airport** (☎ 80 56 00; www.vasterasflygplats.se) is 6km east of the city centre, and is connected by bus L941. Budget carrier **Ryanair** flies here from the UK (see p323 for more details), and SAS flies regularly to Copenhagen (mainly on weekdays).

The bus and train stations are adjacent, on the southern edge of Västerås. Regional buses 65 and 69 run to Sala (one hour, up to eight weekdays, two Saturday and Sunday) as do trains (Skr39, 25 minutes, every two hours). **Swebus Express** (☎ 0200 21 82 18; www.swebusexpress.se) runs to Uppsala (Skr90, 1½ hours, up to six daily), Stockholm (Skr90, one hour 10 minutes, up to nine daily) and Örebro (Skr95, 1½ hours, up to eight daily). **Svenska Buss** (☎ 0771-67 67 67; www.svenskabuss.se in Swedish) also runs routes to Stockholm (Skr70, 1½ hours, one Friday) and Uppsala (Skr70, 1¼ hours, two Friday and Sunday).

Västerås is accessible by hourly trains from Stockholm (Skr91, one hour). Trains to Örebro (Skr102, one hour), Uppsala (Skr100, 1½ hours) and Eskilstuna (Skr65, 30 minutes) are also frequent.

Call **Taxi Västerås** (☎ 18 50 00) to help you get around.

SALA

☎ 0224 / pop 21,554

Sala's silver mine was the source of Sweden's wealth in the 16th and 17th centuries, and a descent into its dank tunnels is a true high (or should that be low?) point of anyone's holiday. The mine quite literally changed the face of the neat town centre; channels and ponds, the source of power for the mines, now weave through and around it, giving a pleasantly watery feel.

The **tourist office** (☎ 552 02; www.sala.se/turism; Stora Torget; 8am-5pm Mon-Fri year-round, plus 10am-2pm Sat May-Sep) is inside the town hall. The free town map is useful if you want to use the walking paths.

Sights & Activities

Sala Silvergruva (☎ 195 41; www.sala.se/salasilvergruva; 11am-5pm May-Aug, noon-4pm Sat & Sun Sep-Apr), about 2km south of the town centre, is the old silver mine area. Above ground, there's a whole weird landscape to explore, made up of chimneys, holes, explosives stores, spoil heaps and engine houses. The listed buildings in the **museum village** contain artists' workshops, a café, a **mine museum** (under construction at the time of writing) and a small Swedish-only **police museum** (adult/child Skr20/10; noon-4pm Jun-Aug), full of rusty knuckledusters.

Under the surface are 20km of galleries, caverns and shafts, into which you can descend on one of several different **mine tours**. The most frequent of these is the informative one-hour **60 Metersturen** (adult/child Skr100/50). There are no set times for English tours – to be certain of catching one, book ahead.

Both village and mine are off the Västerås road. It's a pretty walk along the **Gröna Gången** (Green Walk), which takes you southwest via the parks and the **Mellandammen** pond at Sofielund. Public transport connections aren't good; take the Silverlinjen bus from the train station to Styrars, then walk the remaining 500m.

In the main park in town is **Väsby Kungsgård** (☎ 106 37; vasbykungsgard@glocalnet.net; adult/child Skr20/free; 🕑 1-4pm Mon-Fri year-round), a 16th-century royal farm where Gustav II Adolf (possibly) met his mistress. Excitement for the traveller is confined to the beautifully preserved interiors and 17th-century weapons collection.

Aguélimuseet (☎ 138 20; agueli@sala.se; Norra Esplanaden 7; adult/under 18yr Skr40/free; 🕑 11am-4pm Wed-Sun) exhibits Sweden's largest display of oils and watercolours by local artist Ivan Aguéli (1869–1917). Entry is via the town library.

The houses and courtyard called **Norrmanska Gården** (Norrbygatan) were built in 1736; the area is now home to shops and a café.

Sleeping & Eating

STF Vandrarhem & Camping Sala (☎ 127 30; sites from Skr50, dm Skr125; 🕑 mid-May–Sep, by arrangement outside these months) This haven of tranquillity is in the woods near the Mellandammen pond, 1.5km southwest of the centre. It's a sweet complex with lovely staff and a homely café (🕑 June to August) serving all-day light meals. Walk along Gröna Gången from the bus station, or take the Silverlinjen bus to the water tower and walk the rest of the way.

Hotell Svea (☎ 105 10; Vasbygatan 19; s/d Skr595/695, discounted to Skr495/595) Making a change from huge impersonal chains, friendly 10-roomed Svea puts the emphasis on its personal service. Rooms are old-fashioned but clean and comfortable, and it's exceptionally handy for the train and bus station.

Norrmanska Kök & Bar (☎ 174 73; Brunnsgatan 26; lunch Skr55, dinner Skr80-150; 🕑 11am-2pm Mon & Tue, 11am-10pm Wed & Thu, 11am-1am Fri & Sat) This restaurant, in a rustic 18th-century courtyard, is easily the best place in town for a bite. There's a great array of lunch meals, including pasta, *panini*, baked potatoes and salads. It's a popular evening spot too, with a decent dinner menu.

Värdshuset Gruvcaféet (☎ 195 45; mains Skr79-150; 🕑 11am-5pm May-Aug) If you're out sightseeing at the mine, this charming café, in a wooden building (dating from 1810), does good cakes, sandwiches and hot dishes (pasta, Thai chicken, baked spuds).

Getting There & Around

For transport to and from Västerås, see p249. Going to or from Uppsala, take regional bus 848 (1¼ hours, hourly Monday to Friday, nine buses Saturday and Sunday). Sala is on the main Stockholm to Mora rail line (via Uppsala), with daily trains roughly every two hours (Skr86, 40 minutes).

Ask about bike hire at the tourist office.

ÄNGELSBERG

☎ 0223

Engelsberg Bruk, a Unesco World Heritage site in the tiny village of Ängelsberg, was once one of the most important early-industrial ironworks in Europe. During the 17th and 18th centuries, its rare timber-clad **blast furnace** and **forge** (still in working order) were state-of-the-art technology, and a whole town sprang up around them. Today you can wander round the perfectly preserved estate, made up of a mansion and park, workers' homes and industrial buildings. Guided tours (Skr50) run daily from mid-June to mid-August, and less frequently from May to mid-June and mid-August to mid-September; contact ☎ 131 00 for details.

Ängelsberg is around 60km northwest of Västerås, from where regional trains run every hour or two (Skr98, 45 minutes); from Ängelsberg train station it's a 1.5km walk north to the site.

Nya Servering (☎ 300 18) is not far from Ängelsberg train station and serves food from 11am to 8pm daily. There's a good view from here across to the island Barrön on Åmänningen lake, where the world's oldest-surviving **oil refinery** is located – it was opened in 1875 and closed in 1902.

NORA

☎ 0587 / pop 10,523

One of Sweden's most seductive old wooden towns, Nora sits snugly on the shores of a little lake, clearly confident in its ability to enchant the pants off anyone. Slow your pace and succumb to its cobbled streets and steam trains, mellow boat rides and perfect ice cream.

The helpful **tourist office** (☎ 811 20; nora.turistbyra@nora.se; Stationshuset; 🕑 9am-7pm Mon-Sat & 10am-5pm Sun Jul, 10am-6pm Mon-Sat & 10am-5pm Sun Jun & Aug, 9am-noon & 1-3pm Mon-Fri rest of yr) is at the train station, by the lake. It takes bookings for 11 guided tours (June to August), which either have different themes or take place at a particular attraction. The guided **town walk** (adult/7-14yr Skr60/30) is available in English. Alternatively, buy a brochure (Skr10) for self-guided walks.

Sights & Activities

Trips on the **museum railway** (adult/child return Skr70/35) take you 10km southeast to Järle, or 2.5km west to the excellent old mining village at **Pershyttan**, where there's a guided tour daily at 3pm. The train operates to a complex timetable that includes regular weekend trips from midsummer to mid-August.

The manor house, **Göthlinska Gården**, just off the main square, was built in 1739 and is now a museum featuring furniture, décor and accoutrements from the 17th century onwards; join a summer-only **guided tour** (adult/7-14yr Skr50/25; 1pm Jul-Aug).

Boat trips (070-216 65 24; adult/child return Skr15/5; 10am-6pm Jul & Aug, 10am-6pm weekends mid-May–Jun & early Sep) to the family-friendly island Alntorps ö depart roughly every half hour from the little jetty near the STF hostel. A walk around the island takes about an hour, and there are swimming spots and a café.

Sleeping & Eating

STF Nora Tåghem (146 76; info@norataghem.se; dm Skr120; May–mid-Sep) For novelty value, you can't beat this cheery hostel where bunkbeds are crammed into converted 1930s' railway carriages. All compartments have great views over the lake, and there's a café here which does breakfast, and sandwiches and snacks throughout the day.

Lilla Hotellet (154 00; www.lillahotelletnora.com in Swedish; Rådstugugatan 14; s/d Skr495/760) The charming 'Little Hotel' has a warm and homely feel, with large rooms (some with shared facilities) decorated in 1940s' style. There's a good level of service, and ohh, it's so nice to stay somewhere with a heart and soul.

Nora Stadshotell (31 14 35; norastadshotell@home.se; Rådstugugatan 21; s/d Skr795/850, discounted to Skr595/850) You can't miss this elegant building, planted smack on the main square, although the white-furnitured rooms don't quite live up to the exterior's promise. There are good-value lunch deals (Skr85) at the restaurant, which can be eaten on the airy summer terrace, and á la carte evening mains from Skr150.

Trängbo Camping (123 61; trangbocamping@yahoo.se; sites Skr115; May-Sep) This small campsite is by the lakeside 1.5km north of Nora (there's a lakeshore path for walkers). Amenities are fairly basic, but there's a swimming place and the beach volleyball is popular.

Strandstugan (137 22; Storgatan 1; snacks Skr40-50; summer only) Down by the lake is this delightful red wooden house, set in a flower-filled garden, where you can get coffee, sandwiches, cakes and other home-baked goodies.

Nora Glass (123 32; Storgatan 11; May-Aug) Nora is renowned for its incredible ice cream, made here for over 80 years. You never know what flavours will be available, as three or four different ones are churned out fresh each day, but you DO know that they're worth queuing for.

Self-caterers will find a supermarket on Prästgatan.

Getting There & Around

Länstrafiken Örebro buses run every hour or two to Örebro (Skr47, 40 minutes) and other regional destinations.

Ask the tourist office about bike rental.

NÄRKE

ÖREBRO

019 / pop 126,982

Attractive Örebro has a particularly romantic-looking castle, which is surrounded by a dazzling moat filled with waterlilies (as all such buildings should be). It's certainly a great city to amble round, especially when the weather's fine.

Örebro was built on a prosperous textile industry, and it became a university city in 1998. Most of the city was rebuilt after a devastating fire in 1854.

Information

The busy **tourist office** (21 21 21; www.orebro.se/turism; 10am-6pm Mon-Fri, 10am-4pm Sat & Sun Jun-Aug) is inside the castle.

Banks can be found along Drottning gatan, south of the castle. The **library** (21 10 00; Näbbtorgsgatan) has Internet access, as does **Video Biljard** (611 66 30; Järntorget 6; per 30/60 min Skr20/35; 11am-midnight).

Sights & Activities

The once-powerful **Slottet** (☎ 21 21 21; admission via tours, adult/6-15yr Skr60/20; ⌚ late Jun–mid-Aug) is a magnificent edifice, now used as the county governor's headquarters. Although originally constructed in the late 13th century, most of what you see today is from 300 years later. The outside is far more dramatic than the interior (where the castle's conference business is sadly all too evident). To poke about inside, you'll need to take a tour – there's a historical one at 4.30pm (in Swedish or English, depending on numbers), or a 'Secrets of the Vasa Fortress' option at 2.30pm (in English), which is a slightly toe-curling piece of costumed clowning around. You are allowed unaccompanied into the northwest tower, where there's a small **history exhibition** (admission free; ⌚ 10am-6pm Mon-Fri, 10am-4pm Sat & Sun).

East of the castle, Örebro is blessed with the **Stadsträdgården**, voted Sweden's most beautiful park and great for kids. It stretches alongside the Svartån (the Black River) and merges into the excellent **Wadköping** museum village. The village contains craft workshops, a bakery and period buildings – including Kungsstugan (the King's Lodgings, a medieval house with 16th-century ceiling paintings) and Cajsa Warg's house (home of an 18th-century celebrity chef). You can wander round the village at any time, but the shops, café, exhibitions and museums are open roughly 11am to 4pm (sometimes 5pm) Tuesday to Sunday year-round.

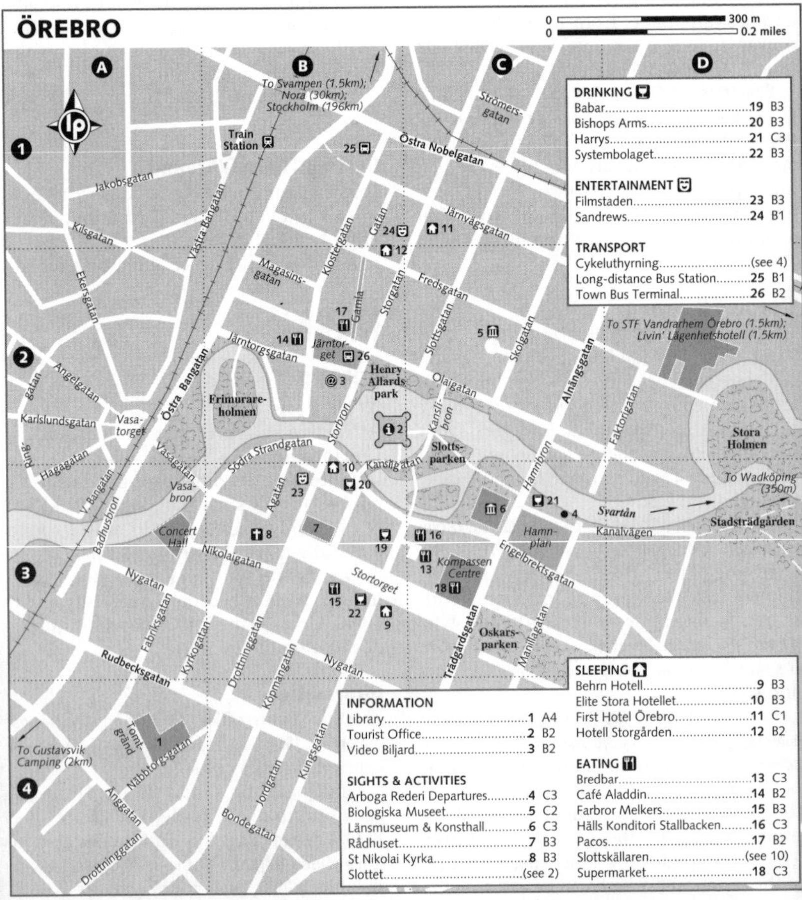

CENTRAL SWEDEN

The **Länsmuseum & Konsthall** (☎ 602 87 00; info@orebrolansmuseum.se; Engelbrektsgatan 3; admission free; 11am-5pm Thu-Tue, 11am-9pm Wed) has permanent artwork grouped into themed rooms, and historical displays about the region (mostly in Swedish).

Many Swedish schools once had private natural history collections, but most were binned in the 1960s. Örebro's **Biologiska Museet** (☎ 21 65 04; adult/under 16yr Skr25/10; 11am-2pm Mon-Fri mid-Jun–mid-Aug), in Karolinska Skolan off Fredsgatan, is a survivor, and is worth a glance for its tier upon tier of stuffed birds.

The 13th-century church **St Nikolai Kyrka** (10am-5pm Mon-Fri, 11am-3pm Sat) has some historical interest: it's where Jean Baptiste Bernadotte (Napoleon's marshal) was chosen to take the Swedish throne. Just opposite, on grand Storgatan, is **Rådhuset** (the city hall); if you're around at the right time, stop to hear the **chimes** (12.05pm & 6.05pm year-round, plus 9pm Jun-Sep), when sculptures representing the city's past, present and future come wheeling out of a high arched window.

The first of Sweden's modern 'mushroom' water towers, **Svampen** (☎ 611 37 35; info@svampen.nu; Dalbygatan 4; admission free; 10am-6pm mid-Jun–mid-Aug, 11am-4pm Sat & Sun rest of yr; bus 11) was built in 1958 and now functions as a lookout tower. There are good views of Lake Hjälmaren and a café at the top.

Arboga Rederi (☎ 10 71 91; info@lagerbjelke.com) offers a number of cruises. Their evening trips on Lake Hjälmaren (Skr240; 7pm) Wednesday to Friday mid-May to September, plus Saturday in July) are popular, and include an onboard shrimp supper.

Sleeping

STF Vandrarhem Örebro (☎ 31 02 40; hepa@hepa.se; Kaptensgatan 1; dm from Skr130; bus 16 or 31; P) This good, but quite well hidden, place lies 1.6km northeast of the train station.

Livin' Lägenhetshotellet (bokning@livin.nu; per night Skr500) The STF hostel also owns this apartment complex next door. Each well-designed flatlet fits up to four people and has a fully equipped kitchen, bathroom and living area. The hostel rents bikes and inline skates.

Hotell Storgården (☎ 12 02 00; www.hotellstorgarden.se; Fredsgatan 11; s/d from Skr680/780, discounted to Skr500/550) It could do with a lick of paint, but this 1st-floor budget hotel is handily central. Rooms, with shuttered windows, are large, airy and have private facilities; the effort stretches to yellowing pads of paper in the desk drawers!

First Hotel Örebro (☎ 611 73 00; www.firsthotels.se; Storgatan 24; s/d Skr1095/1495, discounted to Skr595/795; P) Most of the spacious rooms at this more conventional establishment overlook a quiet,sunny terrace; those on the higher floors have small balconies. Bathrooms have all recently been refurbished and there's a bar selling booze and light meals.

Behrn Hotell (☎ 12 00 95; www.behrnhotell.se; Stortorget 12; s/d Skr995/1295, discounted to Skr645/845; P) Excellently situated on the main square, you get the feeling that the Behrn Hotell goes that extra mile. Rooms are individually decorated and range from medieval-like fittings to clean-cut modern Scandinavian. If you're splashing out, go for a luscious suite, with old wooden beams, chandeliers and Jacuzzi. There's also a spa, and a restaurant which does dinner Tuesday to Friday.

Elite Stora Hotellet (☎ 15 69 00; info.orebro@elite.se; Drottninggatan 1; s/d from Skr1195/1665, discounted to Skr650/795; P) This is the pick of the town's hotels. Many of the sumptuous, newly spruced-up rooms have stunning views of the castle, and offer all the mod cons you'd expect from this upmarket chain.

Gustavsvik Camping (☎ 19 69 50; www.gustavsvik.se; Sommarrovägen; sites Skr130-295, cabins from Skr770; mid-Apr–early Nov; bus 11) This camping facility is 2km south of the city centre. It's huge and family-oriented, with pools, minigolf, a café, and bike rental (Skr60 per day).

Eating

Slottskällaren (☎ 15 69 60; Drottninggatan 1; mains Skr190-220; from 5pm Tue-Sat year-round, plus lunch Mon-Fri Sep-Jun) This upmarket eatery, at the Elite Stora Hotellet, offers fine dining and a good wine cellar. You can nibble beautifully presented meat, fish and veggie dishes in the atmospheric 14th-century vaults, or sit out on the terrace and drink in the glorious castle views.

Bredbar (☎ 31 50 20; Kungsgatan 1; dishes from Skr60) In summer, Bredbar is an ultrapopular place for lunch, thanks to its outdoor seats in a courtyard suntrap. A constant dance of customers swirls in and out for ciabattas, huge bowls of salad and pasta, or hotplate dishes (mostly pasta-based).

Pacos (☎ 10 10 46; Olaigatan 13A; lunch from Skr55, dinner mains Skr100-150; closed Sun) Bright colours, chirpy music and an assortment of well-priced lunchtime specials bring in the diners. Dishes are mainly Tex-Mex food, but pizza and pasta are served, too.

Hälls Konditori Stallbacken (☎ 611 07 66; Engelbrektsgatan 12; meals Skr60) Backing onto the same appealing cobbled courtyard as Bredbar, is this classic old-style café. Sensible light meals (salads, quiche, sandwiches) are on offer, plus there's teetering piles of lurid-coloured creamy cakes and patisseries.

Farbror Melkers (☎ 611 81 99; Stortorget 6; meals around Skr50) If you're more of a modern sort, head instead for this stylish alternative, with good coffee, light meals (sandwiches, baked potatoes), and a large picture window so you can stare out onto the square.

For cheap eats head to **Café Aladdin** (☎ 18 35 30; Klostergatan 11), on slightly grungy Järntorget, which offers pizza, pasta and baked spuds for under Skr40. There's a supermarket in the Kompassen centre on Stortorget.

Drinking & Entertainment

Babar (☎ 10 19 00; Kungsgatan 4; mains Skr130-170) Trendy Babar is a restaurant and bar, fashionable with young, hip student types. It delivers international cuisine, moody lighting and dancey tunes to its customers, and stays open until 2am Wednesday to Saturday for drinking and boogieing (Saturday is over 23s only).

Bishops Arms (☎ 15 69 20; 🕒 until at least midnight) Whether or not you're convinced by the 'authentic English pub' schtick, the bar's outdoor drinking area, with super castle views, is a swinging spot on a summer evening. There are also pub meals here for under Skr100.

Harrys (☎ 10 89 89; Hamnplan; mains Skr80-180; 🕒 from 5pm) Another popular nightspot, Harrys is in a good location down by the river. There's a comprehensive menu of pub meals, live music on a Thursday, and a nightclub on Friday and Saturday.

For take away alcohol head to **Systembolaget** (Stortorget 10).

Örebro's cinemas, both showing mainstream films, are **Filmstaden** (☎ 611 84 00; www.sf se; Drottninggatan 6) and **Sandrews** (☎ 10 44 24; sandrewmetronome.se; Storgatan 19).

Getting There & Away

Long-distance buses, which leave from opposite the train station, run almost everywhere in southern Sweden. From here, **Swebus Express** (☎ 0200-21 82 18; www.swebusexpress.se) has connections to Norrköping, Karlstad and Oslo, Mariestad and Göteborg, Västerås and Uppsala, and Eskilstuna and Stockholm.

Train connections are also good. Direct SJ trains run to/from Stockholm (Skr220, two hours) every hour, some via Västerås (Skr102, one hour); and Göteborg (Skr270, three hours). Other trains run daily to Gävle (Skr242, four hours) and Borlänge (Skr156, 2¼ hours), where you can change for Falun and Mora.

Getting Around

Town buses leave from Järntorget and cost Skr15. **Cykeluthyrning** (☎ 21 19 09), at the Hamn plan boat terminal, rents bikes from May to September from Skr90 per day. For a cab, call **Taxi Kurir** (☎ 12 30 30).

ASKERSUND & AROUND

☎ 0583 / pop 11,477

Askersund, with its quaint little harbour, crooked wooden houses and cobbled square, is often overlooked by travellers, but it's a good place to relax.

The **tourist office** (☎ 810 88; turistbyran@askersund.se; Lilla Bergsgatan 12A; 🕒 10am-7pm mid-Jun–mid-Aug, 10am-12.30pm & 1-4pm Mon-Fri rest of yr), on the main square, has free Internet access (30-minute slots). Ask for information on walking and cycling routes around the lake, and guided tours. Askersund has banks and most other tourist facilities.

Sights

TIVEDEN NATIONAL PARK

Carved by glaciers, this trolls' home and former highwaymen's haunt (about 33km south of Askersund) makes for wonderful wild walking. The park is noted for its ancient virgin forests, which are very rare in southern Sweden, and has lots of dramatic bare bedrock, extensive boulderfields and a scattering of lakes. There's an information centre in the southeastern part of the park (2km from the entrance). The entrance is 5km off the main road (the turn-off is at Bocksjö, on road No 49). There's no public transport to the park.

OTHER SIGHTS

Cool, classical and refined, lakeside **Stjernsund Manor** (☎ 100 04; entry by tour, adult/under 12yr Skr50/free; 🕒 11am, noon, 2pm, 3pm & 4pm mid-May-Aug) contains one of the best-preserved

19th-century interiors in Sweden, with elegant furniture and gilt, glass and velvet fixtures and fittings. There's also an appealing café in the nearby estate manager's old house. The manor is 5km south of town; see the information on M/S *Wettervik*, *below*, for how to get there.

Hembygdsgård (Hagavägen; admission free; exhibitions ⌚ noon-3pm Mon-Fri mid-Jun–mid-Aug) has a collection of old wooden farm buildings, and a childrens' zoo with rabbits, sheep and ducks.

'Boat Harry' runs the small **boat museum** (Hamngatan; adult/child Skr10/free; ⌚ 1-6pm Mon-Fri, noon-4pm Sat & Sun Jul–mid-Aug) at the harbour, with old sailing vessels, motors and model ships.

In July and early August, the **M/S Wettervik** (www.wettervik.se) makes various trips from the harbour, including an excursion to Stjernsund Manor (adult/12-15yr Skr80/40) at 1.30pm and 3pm. To fit in a tour of the house, take the first boat and return on the second (which departs Stjernsund at 3.15pm). Book tours at the tourist office.

Sleeping & Eating

The tourist office can arrange private rooms in the area.

Café Garvaregården (☎ 104 45; info@cafégarvaregarden.com; Sundsgatan; rm Skr700) This desperately lovely B&B in the centre of town is a real find. It offers simple but charming accommodation in an 18th-century house, wrapped around a flower-filled courtyard. There's also an inviting café downstairs.

Aspa Herrgård (☎ 502 10; aspa@edbergs.com; rm from Skr2580, discounted to Skr1495; P 💻) For a true treat, try this luxurious boutique hotel, based in a 17th-century manor house in a comely country setting (17km south of town on road No 49). With its draped beds, flowery cushions and graceful Greek statues, it's the perfect place for a romantic weekend. There's also an exclusive restaurant (non-guests should reserve).

Hotel Ramada Norra Vättern (☎ 120 10; info.norravattern@ramadasweden.se; Klockarbacken; s/d Skr965/1165, discounted to Skr840/840; P) In an unattractive, modern building near the bridge, rooms (off extremely long corridors!) are nevertheless pleasant and well-equipped with minibars, cable TV etc. Staff are friendly, and there's a restaurant here, too.

Wärdshuset Sundsgården (☎ 100 88; Sundsbrogatan 1; lunch Skr65, meals Skr60-180) For dining, the pick of the pile is this fetching old inn. It has a riverside deck so you can sit in the sun and watch the boats sail by, and a selection of good-value light meals (baked potatoes, pasta, salads) for under Skr100.

Husabergsudde Camping (☎ 71 14 35; camping@husabergsudde.se; low/high season sites Skr130/145, cabins from Skr300/330; ⌚ May-Aug) This is a large, lakeside camping ground with top amenities, 1.5km south of town. You can rent canoes and rowing boats (per hour/day Skr30/160) and bikes (per hour/day Skr15/65). There's no public transport to the site.

Café Tutingen (☎ 141 39; Storgatan) This charming café, with its low ceilings, warped old floorboards and mismatched but shapely seating, should be your first choice for coffee and cakes. It does good sandwiches and excellent patisseries, baked on the premises. Best of all is the garden, filled with roses and daisies, and containing the perfect balance of sun and shade.

Getting There & Around

Länstrafiken buses 708 and 841 each run four times on weekdays to Örebro (841 doesn't run in July). Bus 704 runs frequently to the mainline train station at Hallsberg.

Husabergsudde Camping does bike and boat hire.

VÄRMLAND

KARLSTAD

☎ 054 / pop 81,768

Karlstad is the gateway to outdoor activities in Värmland. There are several sights worth seeing in town, and a large student population means that it has a decent restaurant and bar scene.

Sharing the same building as the library, the **tourist office** (☎ 29 84 00; www.karlstad.se; Bibliotekshuset, Västra Torggatan 26; ⌚ 9am-7pm Mon-Fri, 10am-6pm Sat, 11am-4pm Sun mid-Jun–late Aug; 9am-6pm Mon-Thu, 9am-5pm Fri, 11am-4pm Sat late Aug–mid-Jun) has lots of info on both town and county, including fresh-air escapes in the region's forests, and on its rivers and lakes.

Banks and ATMs are along Storgatan. The **library** (☎ 14 85 95; Västra Torggatan 26) has Internet access, as does the **Bogart Nöjesbutik** (☎ 21 21 33; Östra Torggatan 6; per hr Skr35; ⌚ until at least 11pm) video store.

Sights & Activities

Voted Museum of the Year in 2005, the imaginative **Värmlands Museum** (☎ 14 31 00; www.varmlandsmuseum.se; adult/under 20yr Skr40/free; ⏰ 10am-5pm end Jun-end Aug, 10am-5pm Tue & Thu-Sun, 10am-9pm Wed rest of yr) is out on point Sandgrundsudden. Its sensory displays cover local history and culture from the Stone Age to current times, including music, the river, forests and textiles.

For green space and picnics, seek out **Mariebergsskogen** (☎ 29 69 90; mariebergsskogen@karlstad.se; admission free; ⏰ 7am-10pm year-round; bus 1 or 31), a leisure park/open-air museum/animal park in the southwestern part of town (about 1km from the centre).

It's worth popping your head round the door of the 18th-century **cathedral** (⏰ 10am-7pm Mon-Fri, 10am-4pm Sat, 10am-6pm Sun Jun-Aug, 10am-4pm rest of yr), a soothing space with sparkling chandeliers and votive ships. You can visit the small and creepy **old town prison** (Karlbergsgatan 3; admission free; ⏰ 10am-5pm) in the basement of Comfort Hotel Bilan, with original cells, prisoners' letters and a hacksaw found in the post (honest). On the eastern river branch, find **Gamla Stenbron**, Sweden's longest stone bridge at 168m.

From Tuesday to Saturday late June to mid-August, there are regular two-hour **boat cruises** (☎ 21 99 43; adult/child Skr80/50) on Lake Vänern, departing from the harbour behind the train station.

Sleeping

STF Vandrarhem Karlstad (☎ 56 68 40; karlstad.vandrarhem@swipnet.se; dm Skr135, s/d from Skr260/325; ⏰ May–mid-Dec; bus 11 or 32) The hostel is off the E18 motorway at Ulleberg, 3km southwest of Karlstad's centre, and it has good facilities.

Hotell Freden (☎ 21 65 82; www.fredenhotel.com; Fredsgatan 1; s/d Skr480/580, discounted to Skr380/480) One of a number of central hotels opposite the train station, Freden is a simple budget hotel with comfortable rooms and shared bathrooms. Breakfast is not included.

Comfort Hotel Bilan (☎ 10 03 00; bilan@comfort.choicehotels.se; Karlbergsgatan 3; s/d from Skr1250/1550, discounted to Skr790/940; P) The town's old jail cells have been converted into large, bright and cleverly decorated rooms – if it weren't for the display in the basement, you'd never guess the building's history. The added bonus here is that prices include an evening buffet, making discounted rates a particularly good deal.

Elite Stadshotellet (☎ 29 30 00; info.karlstad@elite.se; Kungsgatan 22; s/d from Skr1290/1590, discounted to Skr645/795; P) The elegant Elite is another good upmarket choice, with a lovely riverside location. High-ceilinged rooms give a sense of space and calm, and there are excellent amenities, including a sauna, summer restaurant and English-style pub.

Skutbergets Camping (☎ 53 51 20; www.camping.se/s10; low/high season sites Skr150/205, cabins from Skr375/575; bus 18) This big friendly lakeside ground, 7km west of town, is part of a large sports recreation area, with beach volleyball, a driving range, mini-golf, exercise tracks and a mountain-bike course. There are also sandy and rocky beaches nearby.

Eating & Drinking

Head to the main square, Stora Torget, and its surrounds for good eating and drinking options, most with outdoor summer seating.

Källaren Munken (☎ 18 51 50; restaurang@munken.nu; Västra Torggatan 17; lunch Skr65, mains Skr195-255; ⏰ closed Sun & mid-Jun–mid-Aug) Inspired gourmet meals, like pistachio-baked lamb with artichoke butter, are served up in this elegant but cosy 17th-century vaulted cellar.

Valfrids Krog (☎ 18 30 40; Östra Torggatan; snacks Skr45, mains Skr150-220) This is a relaxed spot for a drink or meal, with light, tapas-style snacks (such as minichorizo, chicken drumsticks and asparagus), and good Swedish and international mains catering to most tastes.

Kebab House (☎ 15 08 15; Västra Torggatan 9; meals from Skr50) Don't be fooled by the name – the Kebab House is a cut above regular fast-food places and serves good-value pizza, kebabs, pasta and salads. In summer, battle your way to one of the popular outdoor tables, in the middle of the busy pedestrianised street.

Rådhuscaféet (☎ 15 29 29; Tingvallagatan 8; meals around Skr50) This café, in one corner of the town hall, is great for watching the world pass by. It serves good coffee, sandwiches and baked potatoes in stately old surroundings.

The **Hemköp supermarket** (☎ 15 22 00; Fredsgatan 4) is inside Åhléns, and **Systembolaget** (☎ 15 56 00; Drottninggatan 26) is close by.

The huge **Ankdammen** (☎ 18 11 10; Magasin 1, Inre Hamn), on a floating jetty at the harbour, is Sweden's largest open-air café and a very popular summer drinking (and eating) spot. Also good for drinks is the **Bishops Arms** (☎ 29 30 20; Kungsgatan 22), with outdoor seating and river views in summer.

Getting There & Around

Karlstad is the major transport hub for western central Sweden. The long-distance bus terminal is at Drottninggatan 43, 600m west of the train station.

Swebus Express (☎ 0200-21 82 18; www.swebusexpress.se) has daily services on a number of routes, including Karlstad–Falun–Gävle, Karlstad–Göteborg, Stockholm–Örebro–Karlstad–Oslo, and Karlstad–Mariestad–Jönköping. **Svenska Buss** (☎ 0771-67 67 67; www.svenskabuss.se in Swedish) runs twice daily on Tuesday and Thursday between Karlstad and Uppsala (Skr190, 4¼ hours), via Örebro and Västerås.

Intercity trains to Stockholm (Skr425, 3¼ hours) run frequently. There are also several daily services to Göteborg (Skr226, three hours) and express services to Oslo (Skr370, three hours).

Värmlandstrafik (☎ 020-22 55 80) runs regional buses. Bus 302 travels to Sunne (Skr68, 1¼ hours, one to five daily) and Torsby (Skr85, two hours, one to three daily). Local trains also operate on this route – prices are the same as for buses.

Free bikes are available from the city's two **Solacykeln booths** Stora Torget (☎ 29 50 29; 🕓 7.30am-7pm Mon-Fri, 10am-3.30pm Sat May-Sep); Outer harbour (🕓 9.30am-5.30pm Mon-Fri, 10am-3.30pm Sat Jun-Aug).

SUNNE

☎ 0565 / pop 13,604

Sunne is the largest ski resort in southern Sweden. In summer, it's a quiet spot with several cultural attractions in the vicinity.

The **tourist office** (☎ 164 00; www.sunne.info; 🕓 9am-9.30pm mid-Jun–mid-August, 9am-5pm Mon-Fri rest of yr) is at the campsite reception building (see right). The town has banks, supermarkets and most other tourist facilities, mainly on Storgatan.

Sights & Activities

The most interesting place in the area is the house at **Mårbacka** (☎ 310 27; www.marbacka.s.se; adult/child Skr60/30; 🕓 11am-3pm mid-May–mid-Jun, 10am-4pm mid-Jun–early Jul & Aug, 10am-5pm Jul, 11am-2pm Sat & Sun Sep), where Swedish novelist Selma Lagerlöf (1858–1940) was born. She was the first woman to receive the Nobel Prize for Literature, and many of her tales are based in the local area. The large kitchen and library where she wrote her books are particularly lovely. Admission is by guided tours only (45 minutes), which leave on the hour – a tour in English is given daily in July at 2pm. Mårbacka is 9km southeast of Sunne; enquire at the tourist office about buses.

Sundsbergs Gård (☎ 103 63; adult/child Skr40/free; 🕓 noon-4pm Tue-Thu & Sat & Sun late Jun–mid-Aug), opposite the tourist office, featured in Lagerlöf's *Gösta Berling's Saga* and now contains a forestry museum, art exhibition, café and manor house with beautiful furnishings.

Flower gardens, a tropical greenhouse and an arboretum will appeal to sedate adults at **Rottneros Park** (☎ 602 95; info@rottnerospark.se; adult/4-15yr Skr120/45; 🕓 mid-May–mid-Sep; bus 302), some 6km south of Sunne. There's also plenty for hyperactive kids – lots of play areas and the tree-top, rope-swinging delights of Sweden's largest climbing forest. Rottneros has its own train station.

The steamship **Freya af Fryken** (☎ 415 90; freja@angbatfreja.nu) sank in 1896, but it was raised and lovingly restored in 1994. Now you can sail along the lakes north and south of Sunne; departures are several times weekly from late June to mid-August, and short trips cost from Skr100 per adult and Skr50 for those between 8 and 15 years. Lunch and dinner cruises are also on the programme.

Ski Sunne (☎ 602 80; www.skisunne.se in Swedish), the town's ski resort, has 10 different descents, a snowboarding area and a cross-country skiing stadium. Or, rattle down the slopes in a wire-caged car in summer, on a **hillrolling** (four descents Skr275; 🕓 11am-4pm Tue-Sat Jul) descent.

Sleeping & Eating

STF Vandrarhem Sunne (☎ 107 88; sunne.vandrarhem@telia.com; Hembygdsvägen 7; dm Skr150) Part of a little homestead museum just north of town, this well-equipped hostel has beds in sunny wooden cabins. There's a futuristic kitchen, airy dining room and outside tables and chairs for alfresco meals. Breakfast is available (Skr50), and bikes can be rented (per day Skr50).

Sunne SweCamp Kolsnäs (☎ 164 00; kolsnas@sunne.se; low/high-season sites Skr130/180, 2-bed cabins Skr290/345, 4-bed cabins Skr395/465; ♿) This is a large, family-oriented camping ground at the southern edge of town, with mini-golf, a restaurant, beach and assorted summer activities, plus bikes, boats and canoes for rent.

Länsmansgården (☎ 140 10; info@lansman.com; s/d from Skr645/820; lunch Skr95, à la carte mains Skr135-240) This historic 'sheriff's house' also features in Lagerlöf's *Gösta Berling's Saga*. It's a picturesque place for a fine lunch or a restful evening in one of the romantic bedrooms, named after the books' characters. The excellent restaurant specialises in very Swedish cuisine, made using fresh local ingredients; dishes include pike pâté, salmon, beef, reindeer and lamb dishes. The mansion is 4km north of Sunne centre, by road No 45 (towards Torsby).

Saffran & Vitlök (☎ 120 09; Storgatan 27; lunch around Skr50; 11am-6pm) This charming café in a cheery blue building serves up baked potatoes, big bowls of salad, two hot lunch options (one meat and one veg), tasty deli items and excellent ice cream.

Köpmangården (☎ 132 50; Ekebyvägen; from noon Tue-Sun) Once a grocer's shop, this is now the town's most popular restaurant and drinking spot. The interior is rather elegant, and there's a large decking area for fine weather.

Strandcaféet (☎ 104 88; Strandpromenaden; mains Skr80-130; summer) In the park is this appealing beach café, with outdoor seating over the water and live music on some summer evenings.

Getting There & Away

Bus 302 runs to Torsby (Skr47, 45 minutes, one to three daily) and Karlstad (Skr68, 1¼ hours, one to five daily). Regional trains to Torsby and Karlstad (one to three daily) are faster than the bus, but cost the same.

TORSBY & AROUND

☎ **0560 / pop 13,086**

Sleepy Torsby, deep in the forests of Värmland, is only 38km from Norway. It's the home town of Sven-Göran Eriksson, coach of England's national football team. The area's history and sights are linked to emigrants from Finland, who settled in western parts of Sweden in the mid 16th century. Spurning Swedish towns, they made for the forests where they built their own distinctive farms and villages.

The **tourist office** (☎ 105 50; www.torsby.se; Gräsmarksvägen 12; 9am-6pm Mon-Fri, 10am-3pm Sat & Sun mid-Jun–Aug, 9am-4pm Mon-Fri Sep–mid-Jun) is a couple of kilometres west of town, on road No 45.

Sights

Torsby Finnkulturcentrum (☎ 162 93; www.finnkulturcentrum.com; Gräsmarksvägen 8; admission Skr20; 11am-4pm mid-Jun–mid-Aug; noon-4pm Tue-Fri rest of yr) has displays describing the 17th-century Finnish settlement of the area, covering smoke-houses, hunting, music and witchcraft. The best bit is the terrace café, with seats overlooking a lulling lake.

The excellent neighbouring **Fordonsmuseum** (☎ 712 10; Gräsmarksvägen 8; adult/under 15yr Skr40/free; 10am-5.30pm mid-Jun–mid-Aug) will appeal to motorheads, with its collection of vintage cars, motorcycles and fire engines.

Hembygdsgården Kollsberg (☎ 718 61; Levgrensvägen 36; adult/child Skr20/free; noon-5pm Jun & Aug, noon-6pm Jul), down beside Lake Fryken, is a dinky homestead museum with a number of old houses, including a Finnish cabin.

One of the best preserved 'Finnish homesteads' in the area is **Ritamäki Finngård** (☎ 502 25; 11am-6pm Jun-Aug), 25km west of Torsby and 5km from Lekvattnet. It was probably built in the late 17th century and was inhabited until 1964, making it the last permanently inhabited Finnish homestead in Sweden. It's surrounded by a nature reserve. Bus 310 goes to Lekvattnet but there is no public transport to Ritamäki.

Activities

There are a number of summer activities and tours in the area, including fishing, canoeing, white-water rafting, rock-climbing, mountain biking, and beaver and elk safaris. Contact the tourist office for information.

Finnskogleden is an easy and well-marked, long-distance path that roughly follows the Norwegian border for 240km – from near Charlottenburg to Søre Osen (in Norway); it passes the old Finnish homestead Ritamäki Finngård. There's a guide book (available from tourist offices, Skr125) that has text in Swedish only, but all the topographical maps you'll need. The best section, Øyermoen to Röjden (or vice versa), requires one or two overnight stops. Bus 311 runs from Torsby to near the border at Röjdåfors (twice daily on weekdays), and bus 310 runs to Vittjärn (twice daily on weekdays), 6km from the border on road No 239.

EXPLORING THE WILDERNESS

Vildmark i Värmland (☎ 140 40; www.vildmark.se) organises outdoor activities in the pristine wilderness of Värmland in summer, including canoe trips (one to six days), beaver-spotting safaris, rock-climbing and rafting.

For a real get-away-from-it-all, back-to-nature experience, try one of their raft trips on the Klarälven. With help, you actually make your own six-person craft from cut logs and lengths of rope. Prices start at Skr500 for a day trip, Skr1840 for five days (four nights) or Skr2190 for eight days (seven nights). If you choose a longer option, you can sleep on board the moored raft, or climb ashore and camp for the night (equipment can be hired at additional cost). You can while away your days fishing, swimming, wildlife spotting and enjoying the serenity. Check out the website for more information.

You can catch boat trips on the **Freya af Fryken** from Torsby (see p257).

Looking like something you might use to smash atoms, the world's longest ski tunnel (1.3km) is due to open here in spring 2006. The **Torsby Ski Tunnel** (Valberget; ⌚ May-Dec) arena will also contain the world's only **indoor biathlon shooting range**. Details had not been finalised at the time of writing: contact the tourist office for further information.

Skiing outdoors is possible from December to Easter, 20km north of Torsby at **Hovfjället** (☎ 313 00; www.hovfjallet.se). There are several ski lifts (up to 542m above sea level) and a variety of runs. Day passes start at Skr215 for adults and Skr180 for 8-15-year-olds. Alpine **ski hire** (☎ 312 55) costs Skr205 per day.

Sleeping & Eating

Hotell Örnen (☎ 146 64; hotell-ornen@telia.com; Östmarksvägen 4; s/d Skr740/890, 1-/2-/3-/4-bed apt Skr890/1100/1310/1520) Cosy Örnen is a pretty lemon-coloured place set behind a white picket fence in the town centre. Newly refurbished Swedish-style rooms are sweet, with flowing curtains, crisp white furniture and folk-art decoration. There are also similar flatlets, with private kitchens.

Torsby Camping (☎ 710 95; info@torsbycamping.se; Bredviken; sites Skr120, cabins from Skr350; ⌚ May–mid-Sep) With its child-friendly beach, playgrounds and mini-golf, this large, well-equipped lakeside ground (4km south of town) is a popular family spot.

There's no shortage of fast-food outlets and pizzerias in the centre. Finer options lie out of town.

Vägsjöfors Herrgård (☎ 313 30; info@vagsjoforsherrgard.com; B&B from Skr310 per person, dm Skr180) Twenty kilometres north of Torsby, by a stunning lake, is this large manor house. B&B rooms are individually decorated so it's a little hard to say what you'll get, but the décor is genteel, and there are hostel beds too. They also serve food, though lunch only (Skr70, noon to 3pm).

Faktoriet (☎ 149 80; Båthamnen; meals around Skr80; ⌚ from noon) By far the most appealing eatery in Torsby is down at the harbour (at the far end of Sjögatan). The view of the harbour is not at all attractive, but this is a cool restaurant with light meals (pasta, baked potatoes, *fajitas*) and a popular bar.

Heidruns Bok- & Bildcafé (☎ 421 26; www.heidruns.se; ⌚ 11am-6pm mid-Jun–mid-Aug) In summer there's live music, poetry and other entertainment at this charming café, run by local poet Bengt Berg. You can feast on books and artwork, or on excellent home-baked cakes! Heidruns is 10km north of Torsby, at Fensbol on road No 45.

Getting There & Away

See opposite for travel information. There are a few buses that run north of Torsby, but generally on weekdays only.

DALARNA

FALUN

☎ 023 / pop 54,994

Falun, which is traditionally the main centre of Dalarna, is synonymous with mining, but don't think grisly thoughts of dark pits and industrial grime – Falu Kopparbergsgruva (Copper Mountain mine) is unique enough to appear on Unesco's World Heritage List and is a fascinating experience. An even more popular attraction is the home of painter Carl Larsson, a work of art in itself and absolutely unmissable.

The **Falun Folkmusik Festival** (www.falufolk.com), with international and regional performers, is held over four days in mid-July; contact the tourist office for tickets.

Information

The **tourist office** (☎ 830 50; www.visitfalun.se; Trotzgatan 10-12; 9am-7pm Mon-Fri, 9am-6pm Sat, 10am-5pm Sun mid-Jun–mid-Aug, 9am-6pm Mon-Fri, 9am-2pm Sat rest of yr) can help with visitor information.

Most services (banks, supermarkets etc) are on or just off Stora Torget. There's Internet access at the **public library** (☎ 833 35; Kristinegatan 15), or at **Falu Biljard Centre** (☎ 282 75; Falugatan 4; per hr Skr30; 1-10pm Mon-Fri, noon-6pm Sat & Sun).

Sights

FALU KOPPARBERGSGRUVA

Falun's copper mine was the world's most important by the 17th century and drove many of Sweden's international aspirations during that period. Today it's on Unesco's World Heritage List and makes for a fascinating day out.

Tradition says that a goat called Kåre first drew attention to the copper reserves, when he rolled in the earth and pranced back to the village with red horns. The first historical mention is in a document from 1288, when the Bishop of Västerås bought shares in the company. As a by-product, the mine produced the red paint that became a characteristic of Swedish houses and Falu Red is still well-used today. The mine finally closed in 1992.

The **mining complex** (☎ 78 20 30; www.kopparberget.com; 10am-5pm May-Aug, noon-4pm Sep, noon-4pm Sat & Sun Oct-Apr; bus 709), to the west of town at the top end of Gruvgatan, contains various sights. Most dramatic is the **Stora Stöten** (Great Pit), a vast hole caused by a major mine collapse in the 17th century. By a miracle, the miners were on holiday that day and no-one was harmed. There are lookouts around the crater edge, and numerous **mine buildings** including a 15m waterwheel and shaft-head machinery.

The **mine museum** (adult/7-18yr Skr40/20) contains everything you could possibly want to know about the history, administration, engineering, geology and copper production of the mine, as well as the sad story of Fat Mats the miner.

You can go on a one-hour tour of the **disused mine** (adult/7-18yr Skr90/45) – bring warm clothing. Prices include museum entry and in high season you shouldn't have to wait more than an hour for an English tour. Between October and April, tours must be booked in advance.

If you get peckish, the pretty café **Gjuthuset** (☎ 132 12), serving coffee, sandwiches and cake, teeters on the edge of the Great Pit. Opposite the main reception is **Geschwornergården Värdshus** (☎ 78 26 16; lunch Skr70), a more stately affair which does excellent hot lunch specials.

OTHER SIGHTS

The World Heritage listing actually encompasses a much larger area than just the Kopparbergsgruva. You can pick up a free brochure, *Discover the Falun World Heritage Site,* which pinpoints all the smelteries, slag heaps and mine estates within a 10km radius of Falun.

Dalarnas Museum (☎ 76 55 00; www.dalarnasmuseum.se; Stigaregatan 2-4; adult/child Skr40/20; 10am-5pm Mon-Fri, noon-5pm Sat & Sun) is a super introduction to Swedish folk art, music and costumes. Selma Lagerlöf's study is preserved here, and there are ever-changing art and craft exhibitions.

A sea of baroque blue-and-gold hits you at **Kristine Kyrka** (☎ 545 70; Stora Torget; 10am-6pm Jun-Aug, 10am-4pm Sep-May), which shows off the riches brought to town by the 17th-century copper trade. Also worth a gander is Falun's oldest building, the late-14th-century **Stora Kopparbergs Kyrka** (☎ 546 00; Kyrkbacksvägen 8; 10am-6pm Jun-Aug, 10am-4pm Sep-May), with brick vaulting and folk-art flowers running round the walls.

If you're feeling energetic, walk up to **Hopptornen** (☎ 835 61; 10am-6pm Sun-Thu, 10am-11pm Fri & Sat mid-May–mid-Aug), the tower and ski jump in the hills behind the town. You can take a lift to the top (Skr20) for a great view.

The Lugnet area in Falun, and the Bjursås area to the northwest, are both winter-sports centres with ski runs, nordic courses and toboggan runs. Also in Lugnet is the **Idrottsmuseum** (☎ 138 24; admission Skr20; 10am-3pm Mon-Fri, 10am-2pm Sat; bus 705 or 713), showcasing local sports.

There are several beautiful old buildings scattered some distance from Falun; if you have time and transport, ask the tourist office for information on Korså Bruk (an excellently preserved former industrial settlement), Svärdsjö Gammelgård (an 18th-century homestead with lots of summer entertainment), Stadisstugan (a house decorated with folk-art Biblical scenes), and Vika Kyrka (with magnificent 16th-century wall paintings and medieval sculptures).

Sleeping

Falu Fängelse Vandrarhem (☎ 79 55 75; info@falufangelse.se; Villavägen 17; dm Skr200) The friendly SVIF hostel is the most central budget option. Accommodation is in the converted cells of an old prison, used for its original purposes up until the mid-1990s.

Hotel Falun (☎ 291 80; Trotzgatan 16; s/d Skr540/740, discounted to Skr490/590; P ☐) There are some good hotel choices right by the tourist office, including this place which has comfortable modern rooms with private toilet and shared shower (or you can pay extra for rooms with full private bathroom).

Park Inn (☎ 70 17 00; www.falun.parkinn.se; Bergskolegränd 7; s/d from Skr1120/1390, discounted to Skr670/790; P ☐) Also located near the tourist office, the Park Inn offers congenial rooms decorated in creams and pale greens. Beds are brand new, and all the bathrooms are due to be renovated in 2005/06. There's a large sunny dining room, plus a bar, sauna and exercise room.

Scandic Hotel Lugnet Falun (☎ 669 22 00; falun@scandic-hotels.com; Svärdsjögatan 51; s/d Skr1295/1595, discounted to Skr840/840; P ☐ ♿) This large, modern building stands out a mile with its ski-jump design. It has heaps of facilities, including a restaurant, bar and even a bowling hall in the basement! The hotel is just east of the centre on road No 80, close to Lugnet.

Lugnets Camping (☎ 835 63; lugnet-anl@falun.se; sites Skr135, simple 2-bed huts from Skr200, cabins Skr600; bus 705 or 713; ♿) This long, thin campsite is 2km northeast of town, in the ski and sports area. Amenities are good: crazy golf, boules and a nearby open-air swimming pool will keep kids amused.

Eating & Drinking

Banken Bar & Brasserie (☎ 71 19 11; Åsgatan 41; basic mains Skr110-145, á la carte mains Skr130-200; ⏲ closed Sun) Based in a former bank, classy Banken has a splendid interior and matching service. The menu includes a *gott & enkelt* (good and simple) category – featuring the likes of burgers and pasta – plus more upmarket 'world cuisine' options.

Två Rum & Kök (☎ 260 25; Stadshusgränd 2; mains Skr190-250; ⏲ Tue-Sat) This restaurant shares the same kitchen as Banken, but it's more exclusive. It's won awards for its gourmet food (dinner only), served in an Art Nouveau interior.

Rådhus Källaren (☎ 254 00; Stora Torget; mains Skr255-275; ⏲ closed Sun) The town hall's atmospheric 17th-century cellars are another good spot for fine (if somewhat overpriced) dining. Dishes are a Swedish-world fusion, focusing on meaty-steaky mains. The bar next door is the place to be seen, and stays open until 2am on Friday and Saturday.

Kopparhattan Café & Restaurang (☎ 191 69; Stigaregatan 2-4; lunch buffet Skr80, eve mains Skr100-150) An excellent choice is this funky, arty café-restaurant, attached to Dalarnas Museum. Choose from upmarket sandwiches (seed bread, brie, roast peppers), soup or a good vegetarian buffet for lunch, and light veggie, fish and meat evening mains. There's an outside terrace overlooking the river, and live music on Friday nights in summer.

Bryggcaféet (☎ 233 30; Fisktorget) Another fab café, Bryggcaféet is a dinky little building which was once the fire station. It serves good coffee and cakes, and has a large decking area by the river.

Lilla Pizzerian (☎ 288 34; Slaggatan 10) For cheap eats, this pizzeria does takeaway and eat-in pizzas and kebabs, with nothing on the menu over Skr55.

Harrys (☎ 79 48 87; Trotzgatan 9-11; ⏲ closed Sun) This pub is entered off Åsgatan, and has everything – pub, restaurant, outdoor area and disco.

For self-caterers, there's a centrally located **ICA supermarket** (Falugatan 1) as well as a **Systembolaget** (Åsgatan 19).

Getting There & Around

Falun isn't on the main train lines – change at Borlänge when coming from Stockholm or Mora – but there are direct trains to and from Gävle (Skr121, 1¼ hours, roughly every two hours).

Swebus Express (☎ 0200-21 82 18; www.swebusexpress.se) has buses on the Göteborg–Karlstad–Falun–Gävle route, and connections to buses on the Stockholm-Borlänge-Mora route.

Regional transport is run by **Dalatrafik** (☎ 0771-95 95 95; www.dalatrafik.se in Swedish), which

'LOVE EACH OTHER, CHILDREN, FOR LOVE IS ALL'

Whatever you do, don't miss the ravishing **Carl Larsson-gården** (☎ 600 53; www.carllarsson.se; Sundborn; Admission by guided tour only, adult/7-17yr Skr90/40; ⌚ 10am-5pm May-Sep, 1pm Mon-Fri Oct-Apr), home of artist Carl Larsson and his wife Karin, in the picturesque village of Sundborn. After the couple's deaths, their early-20th-century home was preserved in its entirety by their children, but it's no gloomy memorial. Lilla Hyttnäs is a work of art, full of brightness, humour and love.

Superb colour schemes, decorations and furniture fill the house: Carl painted portraits of his wife and children everywhere, and Karin's tapestries and embroidery reveal she was as skilled an artist as her husband. Even today, the modern styles in most of the house (especially the dining room) will inspire interior decorators. The **mine master's room** has a beautiful painted ceiling (from 1742) and there's a display of Larsson's collection of **Sami handicraft** in the long passage.

Tours (45 minutes) run almost continuously, but call in advance for times of English tours (alternatively, follow a Swedish tour with an English handbook costing Skr20).

If you like Larsson's work, you can see more at the **Carl Larssons Porträttsamling** (☎ 600 53; Kyrkvägen 18, Sundborn; adult/under 12yr Skr25/free; ⌚ 11am-5pm mid-Jun–mid-Aug), where there are 12 portraits of local worthies.

Bus 64 (Skr34) runs from Falun to Sundborn village (13km).

covers all corners of the county of Dalarna. Tickets cost Skr17 for trips within a zone, and Skr17 extra for each new zone. A 31-day *länskort* costs Skr900 and allows you to travel throughout the county. Regional bus 70 goes approximately hourly to Rättvik (Skr51, one hour) and Mora (Skr85, 1¾ hours).

You can hire bicycles from **Cykel & Fjäll** (☎ 638 62; info@cykelfjall.se; Stora Torget; per day/week Skr90/250; ⌚ closed Sun).

LAKE SILJAN REGION

KABOOOM!! Not a word that would instantly spring to mind as you rest your eyes on the soft forest-and-lake scenery here. But, 360 million years ago, Lake Siljan was the site of Europe's largest meteoric impact. Crashing through the Earth's atmosphere, the giant lump of rock hit Siljan with the force of 500 million atomic bombs, obliterating all life and creating a 75km ring-shaped crater…where you can now paddle canoes in the utmost peace and tranquillity. It's a funny old world.

The area is a very popular summer destination, with numerous outdoor festivals and attractions. Maps of **Siljansleden**, an excellent network of walking and cycling paths extending for more than 300km around Lake Siljan, are available from tourist offices. Another way to enjoy the lake is by boat: in summer, **M/S Gustaf Wasa** (☎ 070-542 10 25; www.wasanet.nu) runs a complex range of lunch, dinner and sightseeing cruises from the main towns of Mora, Rättvik and Leksand. Enquire at any of the area's tourist offices for a schedule.

The big midsummer festival **Musik vid Siljan** (www.musikvidsiljan.se) takes place in venues around the lakeside towns in early July.

Check out the Siljan area website (www.siljan.se) for lots of good information. All the tourist offices in the area have brochures and maps for visitors, and all can help organise accommodation in the region.

Leksand

☎ 0247 / pop 15,504

Leksand's Midsummer Festival is the most popular in Sweden and up to 20,000 spectators watch the maypole being set up on the first Friday evening after 21 June.

The town has a **tourist office** (☎ 79 61 30; leksand@siljan.se; Norsgatan 40; ⌚ 9am-7pm Mon-Fri, 10am-5pm Sat & Sun mid-Jun–mid-Aug, 10am-5pm Mon-Fri rest of yr), and banks and supermarkets, primarily on Sparbankgatan. The **library** (☎ 802 45; Kulturhuset, Kyrkallén) has Internet access.

SIGHTS & ACTIVITIES

Built by a doctor for his young English wife, **Munthe's Hildasholm** (☎ 100 62; www.hildasholm.org; Klockaregatan 5; entry by guided tour, adult/12-16yr Skr70/30, hourly 11am-5pm Mon-Sat 1-5pm Sun Jun–mid-Sep) is a sumptuously decorated early-20th-century mansion, set in beautiful gardens by the lake. Phone ahead for guided tours in English.

Leksands Kyrka (☎ 807 00; ⌚ 9.30am-8pm Jun–mid-Aug, 9.30am-3.30pm rest of yr), with its distinctive onion dome, dates from the early 13th

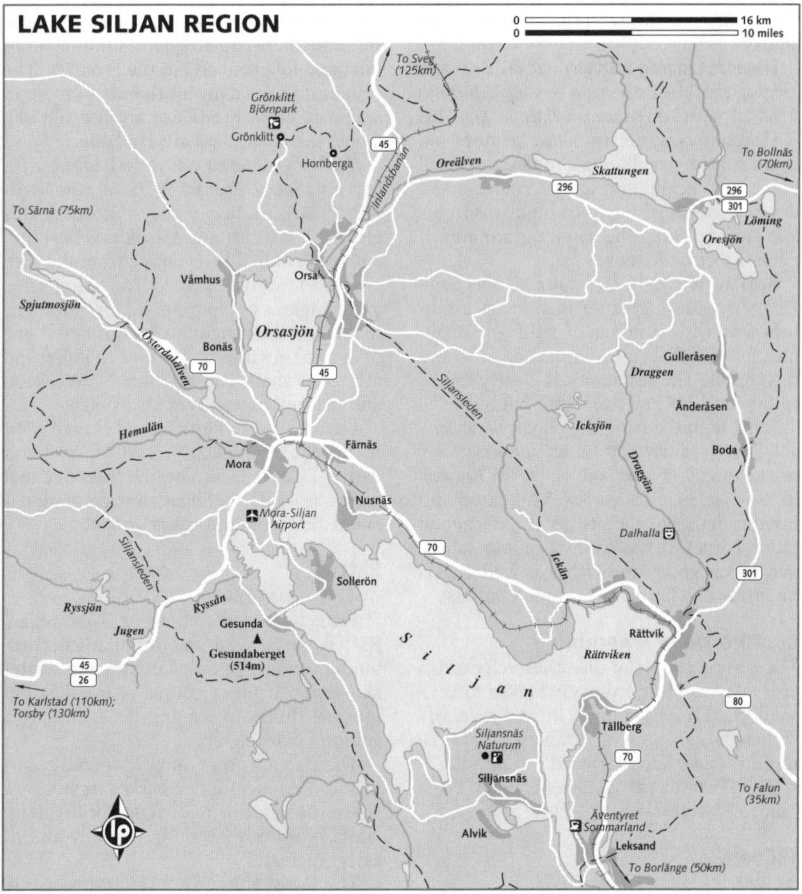

century, but has been extensively renovated and enlarged. The church contains extravagant baroque furnishings.

Families should pick a sunny day and head for **Äventyret Sommarland** (☎ 139 39; admission Skr195, family ticket Skr735; 🕑 10am-5pm Jun & Aug, 10am-6pm Jul; bus 58), a huge waterpark with pools, slides, rides and other amusements, 2km north of Leksand.

Siljansnäs Naturum (☎ 233 00; Siljansnäs; admission free; 🕑 11am-4pm mid-May–Jun, 11am-8pm Jul, 11am-6pm Aug), 14km northwest of Leksand, has information about the meteor and local flora and fauna, with a slightly moth-eaten collection of 50 stuffed animals. The highlight is the 22m-high **viewing tower**, from where you get stunning 360° views around the lake. Bus 84 runs from Leksand to Siljansnäs, from where it's a 300m walk to the Naturum.

SLEEPING & EATING

STF Vandrarhem Leksand (☎ 152 50; info@vandrarhemleksand.se; Parkgården, Källberet; dm Skr130; Ⓟ) It's a little out of the way (2km south of town), but this is a lovely wee hostel, and Dalarna's oldest, with ultracute wooden huts built around a flowery courtyard. Bikes are available for rent (per day Skr70).

Hotell Leksand (☎ 145 70; info@hotelleksand.com; Leksandsvägen 7; s/d Skr740/940; 💻) This is a small, modern and very conveniently situated hotel in the heart of town. Rooms are fairly nondescript, but the folk are friendly and it's not a bad place to lay your head.

Phone first, as the reception doesn't open all day.

Leksands Camping & Stugby (☎ 803 13; leksands.camping.stugby@leksand.se; car & tent low/high season Skr100/115, cabins & chalets from Skr340; bus 58;) This big lakeside campsite has all the facilities you could require – including a restaurant, small beach and neighbouring waterpark – and lies 2km north of town. In high season it's less crowded than the camping grounds at either Mora or Rättvik.

Bygatan 16 (☎ 155 05; Bygatan 16; meals Skr90-190; closed Sun) Bygatan is a smart establishment with a menu of light and main meals, including creative pasta, beef and fish dishes. The restaurant is closely linked to the local hockey team, and has a special 'hockey menu' during the playing season.

Siljans Konditori (☎ 150 70; Sparbanksgatan 5; sandwiches Skr20-45, buffet Skr60-80; 9am-7pm Mon-Fri, 11am-5pm Sat, 11am-2pm Sun) This large and inviting bakery-café sits on the corner of Stora Torget. It has sunny outdoor tables, and serves good sandwiches as well as carnivorous and herbivorous lunch buffets.

GETTING THERE & AROUND

There are a couple of direct intercity trains every day running from Stockholm to Leksand (Skr270, 3¼ hours). Bus 58 regularly connects Leksand with Tällberg (Skr34, 20 minutes) and Rättvik (Skr51, 40 minutes).

The **STF hostel** (☎ 152 50) rents bikes. For a cab, call **Taxi Leksand** (☎ 147 00).

Tällberg

☎ 0247

Tiny Tällberg has a mere 200 residents, yet its eight upmarket hotels and several chic boutiques hint that it's a tourist hotspot. It's certainly an appealing place for lunch and a walk, but unless you're after a romantic countryside escape, it's perhaps better to stay in Rättvik or Leksand and visit for the afternoon. The town's website (www.infotallberg.nu) is in Swedish, but has links to all the hotels.

Klockargården (☎ 502 60; www.klockargarden.com; Siljansvägen 6; s/d/ste from Skr595/990/1590; P) Charm personified, Klockargården is a collection of old timber buildings set around a grassy green courtyard, plus one new wing built in 2004. Each unique room is decorated in a tasteful country style, all the suites have Jacuzzis, and several have trim wooden balconies too. Staff are very helpful, and there are frequent summer craft fairs and folk concerts in the grounds. The restaurant has a daily lunch buffet for Skr95 and à la carte meals are around Skr200. Good-value packages are available.

Åkerblads (☎ 508 00; info@akerblads-tallberg.se; Sjögattu 2; s/d Skr695/1290, lunch Skr125, eve mains Skr195-345; P) Tällberg's oldest hotel is this elegant affair, arranged inside a beautiful collection of buildings dating from the 15th century onwards. There's a relaxation suite, garden tennis and ping-pong for entertainment, and the restaurant is considered one of the region's finest, with a lunch buffet and à la carte main courses nightly. Weekend and half-board packages are available.

Bus 58 between Rättvik and Leksand stops in the village regularly (two to six times daily). Tällberg is also on the train line that travels around Lake Siljan; the train station is about 2km from the village proper.

Rättvik

☎ 0248 / pop 10,864

Stretched along the shores of Lake Siljan, Rättvik is a popular year-round town, combining summery sandy beaches and winter ski slopes. It has a couple of low-key but unusual things to see and do, including a summer bobsleigh run.

There's a full programme of special events in summer, including a **folklore festival** (www.folklore.se) in late July, and a **Classic Car Week** (www.classiccarweek.com in Swedish) in late July and/or early August.

The **tourist office** (☎ 79 72 10; rattvik@siljan.se; Riksvägen 40; 10am-7pm Mon-Fri, 10am-5pm Sat & Sun mid-Jun–mid-Aug, 10am-5pm Mon-Fri rest of yr) is at the train station. Rättvik's facilities include banks and supermarkets on Storgatan, and a **library** (☎ 701 95; Storgatan 2) with Internet access.

SIGHTS & ACTIVITIES

The 725m-long **SommarRodel** (☎ 513 00; info@rattviksbacken.nu; one/three rides Skr45/120; 11am-6pm or 7pm Jun-Aug, closed when raining), a sort of bobsled chute, is lots of fun. You get to hurtle downhill at 35mph, which feels fairly fast so close to the ground.

An enterprising 17-year-old built **Vidablick Utsiktstorn** (adult/5-12yr Skr20/5; 10am-7pm mid-Jun–mid-Aug), a viewing tower about 5km southeast of town, from where there are great panoramas of the lake, a good café and a youth hostel (but unfortunately no public transport).

Scandinavia's longest wooden pier, the impressive 628m **Långbryggan**, runs out into the lake. Other interesting buildings include the 13th-century church and its 87 well-preserved **church stables**, the oldest dating from 1470. The pseudo-rune **memorial** beside the church commemorates the 1520s rising of Gustav Vasa's band against the Danes – the rebellion that created modern Sweden.

The Swedes are mad for them! Get your open-air-museum fix at **Gammelgården** (☎ 514 45; admission free; ⏰ 11am-5pm mid-Jun–mid-Aug), 500m north of the church, which has a good collection of furniture painted in the local style.

Central **Kulturhuset** (☎ 701 95; Storgatan 2; admission free; ⏰ 11am-7pm Mon-Thu, 11am-3pm Fri, 11am-2pm Sat, 1-5pm Sun) houses the library, art exhibitions, and a display describing the Siljan meteor impact 360 million years ago.

The easy **ski slopes** are excellent; there are four lifts and a day pass is Skr200.

Dalhalla (☎ 79 79 50; www.dalhalla.se), an old limestone quarry 7km north of Rättvik, is used as an open-air theatre and concert venue in summer; the acoustics are incredible and the setting is stunning. Tickets usually start at around Skr165 and it's well worth going to see a performance; ask the tourist office for a programme.

SLEEPING

Summer accommodation in Rättvik disappears fast, so it's worth booking ahead – even for campsites. Central places to stay are few and far between.

STF Vandrarhem (☎ 105 66; rattviksparken@rattviksparken.fh.se; Centralgatan; dm Skr150) The well-appointed hostel buildings are clustered round a courtyard in the same park as the campsite here. The large road to one side might bother light sleepers.

Jöns-Andersgården (☎ 130 15; www.jons-andersgarden.se; Bygatan 4; s/d Skr475/600, d with bathroom Skr800; ⏰ mid-Apr–mid-Oct; bus 74; P) Way up on the hill with superb views, beds here are in traditional wooden huts dating from the 15th century. Rooms have all recently been renovated, and there's one great double room that has its own sauna (Skr1100 per night). If you've no transport, the kindly owners will pick you up from the train station by arrangement, and breakfast is included in the price. There's also a very nice Italian café-restaurant on the premises.

Hotell Vidablick (☎ 302 50; vidablick@hantverksbyn.se; Faluvägen; s/d Skr650/1050, discounted to Skr600/850) Vidablick is an excellent choice, with rustic hotel accommodation in grass-roofed huts, some with lake views. The hotel is behind the OKQ8 petrol station on the road to Leksand, about 3km south of town.

Stiftsgården (☎ 510 20; www.stiftsgarden.org; Kyrkvägen 2; s with/without bathroom Skr520/410 d with/without bathroom Skr790/570) This picturesque, church-run place is by the lake, away from the hustle and bustle of town but within walking distance. Rooms are simple but pleasant enough, and breakfast is available for Skr50.

Siljansbadet Camping (☎ 516 91; www.siljansbadet.com; sites low/high season Skr105/185, 4-bed cabins from Skr330/440; ⏰ May-Oct) Near the train station, this campsite is on the lake shore and boasts its own Blue-Flag beach.

Rättviksparken (☎ 561 10; rattviksparken@rattviksparken.fh.se; Furudalsvägen 1; sites low/high season Skr110/150, d Skr325, cabins from Skr425) Another large, bustling campsite, this is by the river off Centralgatan (1km from the train station).

EATING & DRINKING

You might want to head to Tällberg or Mora for a wider choice of restaurants.

Jöns-Andersgården (☎ 130 15; www.jons-andersgarden.se; Bygatan 4; mains Skr135-190; ⏰ Thu-Sun May-Sep; bus 74) If you can stir your stumps and make it up the hill, you'll find this rather sweet restaurant tucked at the top. Dishes such as lemony chicken with *gremolata* potatoes, and *tagliatelle* with truffle oil, bring a taste of Italy to this very Swedish establishment.

Restaurang Anna (☎ 126 81; Vasagatan 3; dishes Skr100-190; ⏰ Tue-Sun) Behind the town hall, this is your best central option for 'finer dining'. It's a good midrange choice, serving Swedish and international dishes, including fish, lamb, pork and reindeer.

Strandrestaurangen (☎ 134 00; ⏰ Jun-Aug) For something a bit different, you could try this beach restaurant. It's really more of a drinking spot though, with live music on Tuesday nights and 'after-beach' parties at the weekend.

The cheapest eateries, like old-style **Fricks Konditori** (☎ 133 36; Stora Torget; sandwiches from Skr35), serving sandwiches, quiche, cakes and coffee, are opposite the train station.

There's a **Systembolaget** (Storgatan), and three supermarkets on the same street.

GETTING THERE & AROUND

Buses depart from outside the train station. Dalatrafik's bus 70 runs regularly between Falun, Rättvik and Mora. A couple of direct intercity trains per day from Stockholm (Skr290, 3½ hours) stop at Rättvik (otherwise you have to change at Borlänge). There are local trains every couple of hours between Rättvik and Mora (Skr65, 25 minutes).

You can hire a bike from **Team Sportia** (☎ 103 33; Storgatan 14, per day/week from Skr100/500). A **taxi** (☎ 510 00) is also an option.

Mora

☎ 0250 / pop 20,083

Mora is spliced with Sweden's historic soul. Legend has it that in 1520 Gustav Vasa arrived here, in a last-ditch attempt to start a rebellion against the Danish regime. The people of Mora weren't interested, and Gustav was forced to put on his skis and flee for the border. After he left, the town reconsidered and two yeomen, Engelbrekt and Lars, volunteered to follow Gustav's tracks, finally overtaking him in Sälen and thereby changing Swedish history.

Today the world's biggest cross-country ski race **Vasaloppet**, which ends in Mora, commemorates this epic chase, and involves 90km of gruelling Nordic skiing. Around 15,000 people take part on the first Sunday in March. In summer, you can walk the route on the 90km **Vasaloppsleden**.

The **tourist office** (☎ 59 20 20; mora@siljan.se; 🕑 10am-7pm Mon-Fri, 10am-5pm Sat & Sun mid-Jun–mid-Aug, 10am-5pm Mon-Fri rest of yr) is at the train station. There are banks, supermarkets and other facilities in town, primarily on Kyrkogatan. The **library** (☎ 267 79; Köpmangatan) has Internet access.

SIGHTS & ACTIVITIES

Even if you have no interest in skiing, you may be pleasantly surprised by the excellent **Vasaloppsmuseet** (☎ 392 25; www.vasaloppet.se; Vasagatan; adult/child Skr30/20; 10am-5pm mid-Jun–mid-Sep, 10am-5pm Mon-Fri mid-Sep–mid-Jun), which really manages to communicate the passion behind the world's largest cross-country skiing event. There's some fantastic crackly black-and-white film of the first race, a display about nine-times winner and hardy old boy Nils 'Mora-Nisse' Karlsson, and an exhibit of prizes. Outside the museum is the race **finish line**, a favourite place for holiday snaps.

Zornmuseet (☎ 59 23 10; www.zorn.se; Vasagatan 36; adult/7-15yr Skr40/2; 🕑 9am-5pm Mon-Sat, 11am-5pm Sun mid-May–mid-Sep, noon-5pm Mon-Sat, 1-5pm Sun rest of yr) celebrates the works and private collections of the Mora painter Anders Zorn (1860–1920), one of Sweden's most famous artists. Many of Zorn's best-known portraits and characteristic nudes are on display here; perhaps most interesting for the foreign visitor are his naturalistic depictions of Swedish life and the countryside.

Next door, the Zorn family house **Zorngården** (☎ 59 23 10; Vasagatan 36; entry & tour adult/7-15yr Skr50/15; 🕑 10am-4pm Mon-Sat, 11am-4pm Sun mid-May–mid-Sep, noon-3pm Mon-Sat, 1-4pm Sun rest of yr) is an excellent example of a wealthy artist's house and reflects Zorn's National Romantic aspirations (check out the Viking-influenced hall). Access to the house is by guided tour (every 15 minutes in summer; phone ahead for English tours).

Tomteland (☎ 287 70; www.tomteland.se; Gesundaberget; individual/family Skr145/525 Jul & Aug, cheaper rest of yr; 🕑 10am-5pm Jul & Aug, shorter hr rest of yr) is where the Swedish Father Christmas lives, so it's naturally popular with Swedish children. Much of the entertainment revolves around children's theatre and storytelling, but there are activities that non-Swedish speakers might enjoy – scary trolls, face-painting, pedal boats, and the chance to see where Santa makes all the toys… It's open year-round, but live events stop out of season, and prices and opening periods shrink; phone first to see what's going on

SLEEPING

STF Vandrarhem Mora (☎ 381 96; info@maalkullann.se; Fredsgatan 6; dm Skr185; Ⓟ) On a quiet backstreet close to the Vasaloppet finish line, this is a small and pleasant youth hostel. Beds are snapped up fast, so book ahead.

Målkull Ann's (☎ 381 90; Vasagatan 19; s/d from Skr550/600; Ⓟ 💻) Hostel proprietor, Ann, also owns this lovely B&B, with cheerful countrified rooms, a sauna and bikes for hire (per day Skr70). Rooms with private bathrooms are a few hundred krona extra.

Hotell Kung Gösta (☎ 150 70; trehotell@telia.com; Kristinebergsgatan 1; dm from Skr130; hotel s/d Skr940/1140, discounted to Skr645/795; Ⓟ 💻 ♿)

THE DALA HORSE

What do Bill Clinton, Elvis Presley and Bob Hope have in common? Answer: they were all given the gift of a Swedish *Dalahäst*. These carved wooden horses are painted in bright colours, and decorated with folk-art flowers. To many people they represent the genuine Sweden, and are a far more powerful symbol than the Swedish flag.

The exact origin of these cheerful ornaments is uncertain. The first written reference comes from the 17th century, when the bishop of Västerås denounced such horrors as 'decks of cards, dice, flutes, dolls, wooden horses, lovers' ballads, impudent paintings', but it's quite likely that they were being carved much earlier. Sitting by the fireside and whittling wood was a common pastime, and the horse was a natural subject – a workmate, friend, and symbol of strength. The painted form that is so common today appeared at the World Exhibition in New York in 1939, and has been a favourite souvenir for travellers to Sweden ever since.

The best known Dala horses come from Nusnäs, 10km southeast of Mora. The two biggest workshops are **Nils Olsson Hemslöjd** (☎ 372 00; www.nohemslojd.se; 🕑 8am-6pm Mon-Fri, 9am-5pm Sat & Sun mid-Jun–mid-Aug, shorter hr & closed Sun rest of yr) and **Grannas A Olsson Hemslöjd** (☎ 372 50; www.grannas.com; 🕑 9am-5pm Mon-Fri, 9am-4pm Sat & Sun mid-Jun–mid-Aug, shorter hr & closed Sun rest of yr), where you can watch the carving and painting, then buy up big at the massive souvenir outlets. Wooden horse sizes stretch from 3cm-high (Skr60) to 50cm-high (Skr2500).

Public transport to Nusnäs isn't great: there are three buses from Mora Monday to Friday only.

Opposite the main train station and handy for travellers, Kung Gösta has standard hotel rooms, recently refurbished, and an indoor swimming pool, sauna and solarium. For budget-minded guests, there's also a hostel annexe, **Kristineberg**, with 10-bed dorms, a self-catering kitchen and separate sauna.

First Hotel Mora (☎ 59 26 50; mora@firsthotels.se; Strandgatan 12; s/d from Skr1145/1345, discounted to Skr748/948; P 💻 ♿) The classiest hotel in Mora is this central and upmarket choice. Rooms are very effective, most combining clean lines, wooden floors and earthy tones with bright folk-art accents. For relaxation, head to the Emma Spa where there are steam rooms and Jacuzzis, plus massage and body treatments.

Moraparken (☎ 276 00; moraparken@mora.se; tent & car Skr140, 2-/4-bed cabins Skr320/455, s/d Skr775/1150, discounted to Skr575/750; P 💻) This place wants for nothing; the campsite and hotel are combined in a great waterside spot, 400m northwest of the church, and both have solid facilities. The purpose-built hotel rooms (all ground floor) are newly renovated, with wooden floors and a sleek modern look. The Vasaloppet track passes through the grounds, and you can hire canoes to splish about on the pond.

EATING

All the hotels mentioned under Sleeping have decent restaurants.

Målkull Ann's (☎ 381 90; Vasagatan; mains Skr145-185) This is a cosy restaurant and café in a smart wooden 19th-century building opposite Vasaloppsmuseet. In summer, light lunches and heartier selections are served on the large balcony, overlooking the lake.

Claras Restaurang (☎ 158 98; Vasagatan 38; lunch Skr75, mains Skr110-190) In the picturesque old town you'll find convivial Claras, with excellent service and a menu of filling staples. Try the wonderful dessert of deep-fried camembert with warm cloudberries.

Mora Kaffestuga (☎ 100 82; morakaffestuga@telia.com; Kyrkogatan 8; meals Skr35-50) For a quick lunch, this spot has a restful grassy garden out the back. On offer are the standard salads, quiches, baguettes etc.

Helmers Konditori (☎ 100 11; Kyrkogatan 10) Next door is another good café-bakery, with homemade bread, sandwiches and cakes.

There are fast-food joints and supermarkets on Kyrkogatan.

GETTING THERE & AROUND

The Mora-Siljan airport is 6km southwest of town on the Malung road. **Skyways** (☎ 0771-95 95 00; www.skyways.se) has three flights to Stockholm Arlanda on weekdays and one on Sunday.

All Dalatrafik buses use the bus station at Moragatan 23. Bus 70 runs to Rättvik and Falun, and buses 103, 104, 105 and 245 run to Orsa. Once or twice daily, bus 170 goes to

Älvdalen, Särna, Idre and Grövelsjön, near the Norwegian border.

Mora is an **SJ** (☎ 0771-75 75 75; www.sj.se) train terminus and the southern terminus of Inlandsbanan (Inland Railway), which runs north to Gällivare (mid-June to mid-August). The main train station is about 1km east of town. The more central Mora Strand is a platform station in town, but not all trains stop there, so check the timetable. When travelling to Östersund, you can choose between Inlandsbanan (Skr347, 6¼ hours, one daily) or bus 245 (Skr255, 5¼ hours, twice daily). For more information on the Inlandsbanan, see p273.

Hire a car in Mora to see the best of the region, especially northwest Dalarna; for smaller budget models try **OKQ8** (☎ 139 58; Vasagatan 1). You can rent a bike at **Intersport** (☎ 59 39 39; Kyrkogatan 7; per day/week Skr100/500).

Orsa & Grönklitt

☎ 0250 / pop 7031

Orsa, 16km north of Mora, puts extra zzzs into the phrase 'sleepy village'. However, it's the place with the most tourist facilities before you get to the area's biggest attraction further north in Grönklitt: the fur, teeth and claws at the wonderful bear park.

The **tourist office** (☎ 55 25 50; orsa@siljan.se; Dalagatan 1; 🕑 mid-Jun–mid-Aug, 10am-5pm Mon-Fri rest of yr) is in Orsa, with banks nearby. Buses 103 and 104 run regularly between Mora and Orsa.

Fat-bottomed roly-poly bear cubs are the star attraction at **Grönklitt Björnpark** (☎ 462 00; www.orsagronklitt.se; adult/6-15yr Skr90/50; 🕑 10am-3pm mid-May–mid-Sep, until 6pm mid-Jun–mid-Aug), 16km from Orsa, an excellent reserve where you can also see lynx, wolves and wolverines. The animals have a lot of space and fairly natural surroundings. The bears are usually fed between 11am and 1pm, when you'll get a great view of them. Summer activities such as fishing, canoeing and elk or beaver safaris can be booked at the park. Bus 118 runs from Mora to Grönklitt, via Orsa (twice daily weekdays, once on Sunday).

In winter, there's a **ski area** (ski passes per day Skr215; 🕑 Dec-Mar) at Grönklitt.

Björnlängan Hostel (☎ 462 00; Grönklitt; 2-/4-bed rm Skr325/425; P) Run by the same people, this private hostel in a low, modern building is up at the bear park. There's no 10-to-a-cubby-hole here: rooms are for two or four people. There's also a sauna for guests.

Orsa Camping (☎ 462 00; www.orsagronklitt.se; Orsa; low/high season sites Skr105/170, cabins per week from Skr2475/4575;) This is a big campsite, beautifully situated on the shores of the lake in Orsa. It's particularly suitable for families, with several playgrounds, a waterslide, canoe hire, crazy golf and a beach to keep the kids happy.

Wärdshuset (☎ 462 31; Grönklitt; lunch Skr95, dinner mains Skr90-150) And yet another piece of the Bear Empire... Also near the park, this inn specialises in pizza, pasta and Swedish buffets (with salmon, prawns, potatoes and all the pickled herring you can stand). In winter, it's the place for aprés-ski drinks.

SÄLEN & AROUND

☎ 0280 / pop 400

Sälen is a tiny spot, way up in the wilds of Dalarna. In summer, the ghost-village offers chilled-out beaver safaris, canoe trips, fishing and horse riding (inquire at the tourist office). As soon as the first snowflakes flutter, though, an amazing transformation occurs: the whole area turns into Sweden's largest and swishest ski resort.

Head first to the Centrumhuset complex, where you'll find a bank, doctor, pharmacy, Systembolaget and most other facilities, including the **tourist office** (☎ 187 00; info@salen.se; 🕑 9am-6pm Mon-Fri, 9am-3pm Sat & Sun Jun-Aug & Dec-Apr, 9am-6pm Mon-Fri, 10am-2pm Sat rest of yr). Opposite the complex are supermarkets and stores where you can rent ski gear in winter, and inline skates, boats and canoes in summer.

Activities

The **ski areas**, with chalets, pubs and nightclubs, are strung out for 20km along the road running through the steep-flanked mountains west of Sälen. There are over 100 lifts, pistes of all degrees, and guaranteed snow from 15 November to April. **Gustav Backen** at Lindvallen is the busiest ski run in Europe; for skiing information visit www.skistar.com. North of Sälen, cheaper and quieter skiing is available at **Näsfjället**.

There's some good **hiking** in the area in summer, mainly north of the road.

Sleeping & Eating

Winter visitors should contact their travel agent or the tourist office for accommodation, or get in contact with **SkiStar** (☎ 0771-84 00 00; www.skistar.com) for packages.

STF Vandrarhem Sälens (☎ 820 40; info@salensvandrarhem.se; dm Skr160) The name's misleading – it's 27km north of Sälen – but if you have your own transport and want to get away from it all, this is the hostel. It's based in a peaceful nature reserve at Gräsheden (near Näsfjället), with some great walks nearby and Kungsleden (see p49) passing 1.5km from the hostel.

Sälens Gästgiveri (☎ 201 85; info@gastis.com; s with/without bathroom Skr550/450 d with/without bathroom Skr650/550; mains Skr110-180) In the village, this place has fairly basic accommodation (you get the idea that the restaurant is more important than the lodgings). Prices given here are for the summer season, winter prices are higher by Skr50 to Skr200 per room. The restaurant is a popular summer choice with a wooden terrace, a well-stocked bar, and a menu ranging from bar snacks and pizzas to substantial steak, pasta and salmon mains.

Inside the Centrumhuset complex there's a delicatessen selling fresh local produce, and an excellent bakery.

Getting There & Around

Bus 95 runs from the ski area to Mora via Sälen, once daily in the ski season (otherwise you have to change buses at Lima). A ski bus tours around the ski area in winter.

IDRE & GRÖVELSJÖN

☎ 0253

The small town of Idre lies close to some beautiful upland wilderness, and there's very good skiing here. The friendly **tourist office** (☎ 200 00; info@idreturism.se; Framgårdsvägen 1; 10am-7pm Mon-Fri, noon-6pm Sat & Sun Jun-Aug, 8am-5pm Mon-Fri Sep-May) has lots of brochures and hiking advice, plus free Internet access. Staff can arrange a variety of activities, including dogsledding, skiing, hiking, canyoning, rock-climbing, boat trips, elk and beaver safaris, horse riding, rafting and canoeing. They can also book accommodation in the area.

Idre Fjäll ski centre (☎ 410 00; www.idrefjall.se; Nov-Apr), 9km east, has three chairlifts, 28 ski-tows and 42 downhill runs – including 11 black runs. Day lift passes are Skr285. There are also 60km of prepared cross-country tracks.

Grövelsjön, 38km northwest of Idre and close to the Norwegian border, lies on the edge of the wild 690 sq km **Långfjällets Nature Reserve**, which is noted for its lichen-covered heaths, moraine heaps and ancient forests. Reindeer from Sweden's southernmost Sami community near Idre wander throughout the area.

Sleeping & Eating

Skiers should contact their travel agent or the tourist office for accommodation packages.

STF Fjällstation Grövelsjön (☎ 59 68 80; grovelsjon@stfturist.se; dm/s/d from Skr240/360/500; Feb-Apr & mid-Jun–Sep) This excellent mountain lodge in Grövelsjön has a wide array of facilities, including a kitchen, spa, shop and outdoor gear hire. The rather good restaurant serves breakfast, lunch and dinner; enquire for half-board and full-board arrangements. This is a big and busy place, with a huge range of tours and activities available.

Sörälvens Fiske Camping (☎ 201 17; www.soralven-camping.com; sites Skr125, cabins Skr480) Sörälven offers rather shadeless camping areas but good cabins, and is popular with the fishing crowd. The campsite is just out of Idre, 2.5km towards Grövelsjön.

There's a supermarket in Idre, and several grills and pizzerias.

Getting There & Away

Dalatrafik bus 170 travels on a route between Mora, Idre and Grövelsjön (2¼ hours from Mora to Idre, 3¾ hours to Grövelsjön). There are three services to Grövelsjön on weekdays, and one or two on weekends.

Northern Sweden & Lappland

It's almost criminal that so few visitors to Sweden make it up to Norrland. Remote wilderness, impenetrable forests and the opportunity for long quiet hikes – the northern part of Sweden is a completely separate experience from the rest of the country. This is the home of the Sami people, northern Scandinavia's indigenous population, whose traditional culture revolves around their herds of domesticated reindeer. You won't have to wait long for a glimpse of the creatures either – on any long stretch of road in the north, you're likely to meet five times as many reindeer as cars.

In Northern Sweden you'll also find Laponia, one of the last great wilderness expanses in Western Europe and a World Heritage–listed site. Its swooping peaks and broad, roadless plains make it heaven for geologists, photographers, hikers and anyone else who loves the idea of standing atop one mountain range to gaze at another across a mighty bog.

All this untamed wilderness makes Norrland and Lappland the places to find Sweden's best outdoor sporting adventures, from dogsledding and nearly year-round skiing, to hiking, camping and canoeing. But the north is most famous as an enormous stage on which the northern lights and midnight sun perform their brilliant tricks. It's also, for the most part, blissfully empty of tourist hordes. It might be a trek to get up here, but it's well worth the effort.

HIGHLIGHTS

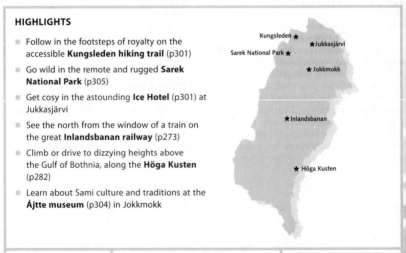

- Follow in the footsteps of royalty on the accessible **Kungsleden hiking trail** (p301)
- Go wild in the remote and rugged **Sarek National Park** (p305)
- Get cosy in the astounding **Ice Hotel** (p301) at Jukkasjärvi
- See the north from the window of a train on the great **Inlandsbanan railway** (p273)
- Climb or drive to dizzying heights above the Gulf of Bothnia, along the **Höga Kusten** (p282)
- Learn about Sami culture and traditions at the **Ájtte museum** (p304) in Jokkmokk

AREA: 242,732 SQ KM	HIGHEST POINT: KEBNEKAISE (2111M)	POPULATION: 1,045,200

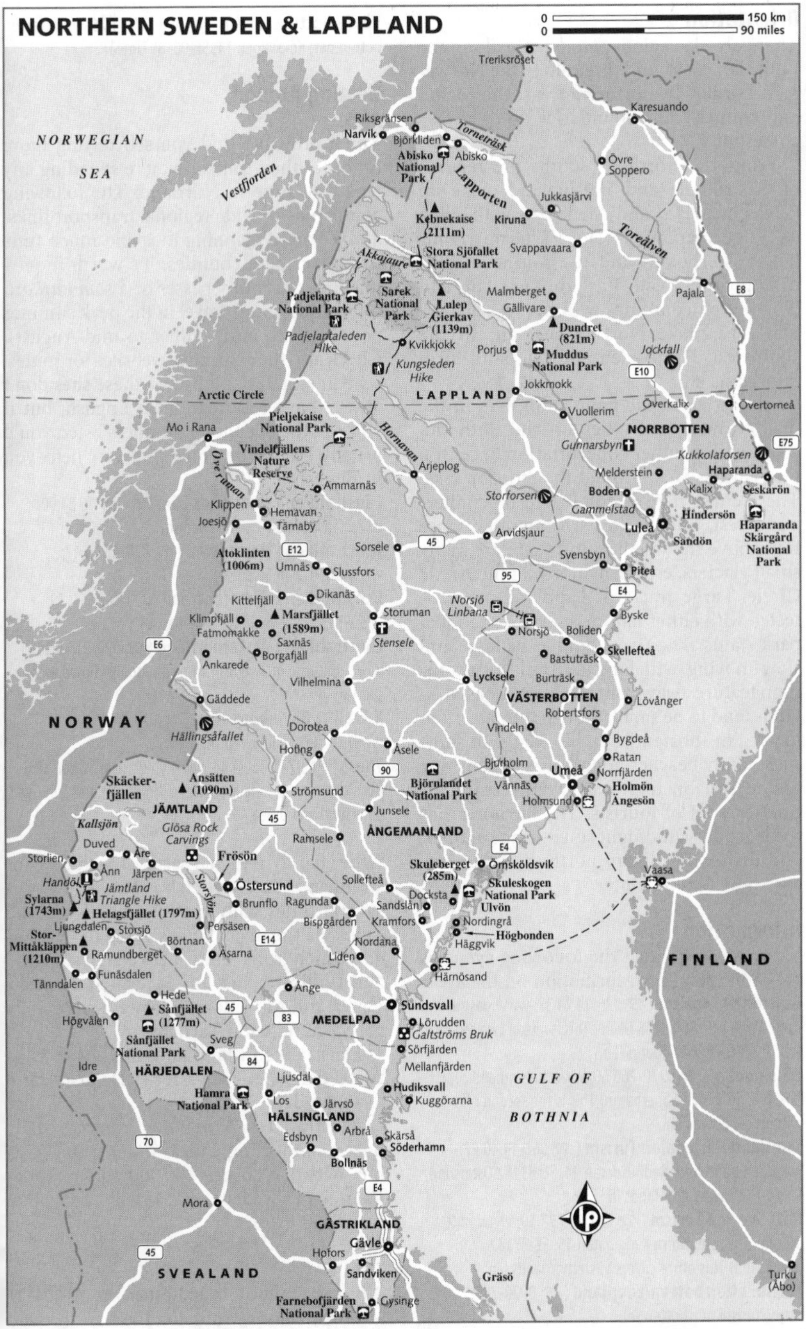
NORTHERN SWEDEN & LAPPLAND
0
150 km
0
90 miles
Treriksröset
Karesuando
Riksgränsen
Narvik
Björkliden
Torneträsk
Abisko National Park
Abisko
NORWEGIAN SEA
Vestfjorden
Övre Soppero
Lapporten
Jukkasjärvi
Kebnekaise (2111m)
Kiruna
Toreälven
Svappavaara
Akkajaure
Stora Sjöfallet National Park
Sarek National Park
Padjelanta National Park
Lulep Gierkav (1139m)
Malmberget
Gällivare
Pajala
E8
Dundret (821m)
Padjelantaleden Hike
Kvikkjokk
Porjus
Muddus National Park
Jockfall
Kungsleden Hike
E10
Arctic Circle
LAPPLAND
Jokkmokk
Överkalix
Övertorneå
Pieljekaise National Park
Mo i Rana
Vuollerim
NORRBOTTEN
Hornavan
Vindelfjällens Nature Reserve
Gunnarsbyn
Kukkolaforsen
E75
Övre Ruman
Arjeplog
Melderstein
Haparanda
Ammarnäs
Kalix
Seskarön
Storforsen
Boden
Klippen
Hemavan
Gammelstad
Hindersön
Joesjö
Tärnaby
Luleå
Haparanda Skärgård National Park
Sandön
Atoklinten (1006m)
E12
Sorsele
45
Arvidsjaur
Umnäs
Slussfors
Svensbyn
Piteå
95
E4
Kittelfjäll
Dikanäs
Norsjö Linbana
Byske
Klimpfjäll
Marsfjället (1589m)
Storuman
Fatmomakke
Saxnäs
Stensele
Norsjö
Boliden
E6
Borgafjäll
Bastuträsk
Skellefteå
Ankarede
Lycksele
Burträsk
Vilhelmina
VÄSTERBOTTEN
Gäddede
Lövånger
Robertsfors
NORWAY
Hällingsåfallet
Dorotea
Vindeln
Bygdeå
Hoting
Åsele
Ratan
90
Bjurholm
Umeå
Norrfjärden
Skäcker-fjällen
Ansätten (1090m)
Björnlandet National Park
Vännäs
Holmön
Strömsund
Holmsund
Ängesön
JÄMTLAND
Junsele
Kallsjön
Glösa Rock Carvings
45
Duved
Ramsele
ÅNGEMANLAND
Storlien
Åre
Frösön
E4
Ånn
Järpen
Skuleberget (285m)
Örnsköldsvik
Vaasa
Handöl
Jämtland Triangle Hike
Östersund
Sollefteå
Skuleskogen National Park
Storsjön
Docksta
Sylarna (1743m)
Helagsfjället (1797m)
Brunflo
Ragunda
Sandslån
Ulvön
Kramfors
Nordingrå
Persäsen
Bispgården
Ljungdalen
Storsjö
Högbonden
Stor-Mittåkläppen (1210m)
E14
Nordana
Ramundberget
Börtnan
Häggvik
Åsarna
Liden
FINLAND
Funäsdalen
Härnösand
Tänndalen
Hede
Ånge
Sånfjället (1277m)
45
Sundsvall
Högvålen
83
MEDELPAD
Lörudden
Galtströms Bruk
Sånfjället National Park
Sveg
Sörfjärden
84
Mellanfjärden
Idre
HÄRJEDALEN
Ljusdal
GULF OF BOTHNIA
Hamra National Park
Hudiksvall
Los
Järvsö
Kuggörarna
HÄLSINGLAND
Arbrå
Skärså
Edsbyn
Söderhamn
70
Bollnäs
E4
Mora
GÄSTRIKLAND
Gävle
45
Hofors
Sandviken
SVEALAND
Gräsö
Turku (Åbo)
Farnebofjärden National Park
Gysinge

Orientation

There are six regions *(landskaps)* along the Bothnian coast, and three along the Norwegian border. In northern areas, the region and county *(län)* boundaries don't always correspond.

From the north to south, the regions of Gästrikland and Hälsingland make up Gävleborgs län, and Medelpad with most of Ångermanland form Västernorrlands län. Västerbotten and the southern third of Lappland create Västerbottens län, and Norrbotten combines with the rest of Lappland to make Norrbottens län. In the southwest, Härjedalen and Jämtland form Jämtlands län.

Almost all of the population lives in the major towns and cities on the Bothnian coast, with another concentration in central Jämtland as well, around the Storsjön lake. The scenery here is dominated by coniferous forest, but the western mountains rise well above the tree line and there are many small glaciers, especially north of the Arctic Circle. Large tracts of Lappland are protected with either nature reserve or national park status. The rivers tend to be large and slow-moving, with long narrow lakes a common feature away from the coast. Coastal islands tend to be small, though they are often located in substantial archipelagos. In summer, sandy beaches, long hours of sunshine and reasonably high water temperatures attract crowds of tourists. The far north has the legendary midnight sun during summer, and the extraordinary northern lights (aurora borealis) in winter.

Information

Visitors can contact the following agencies for more detailed information on the area:

Gästrikland Turism (☎ 026-14 74 37; www.gastrikland.com; Box 1175, SE-80135 Gävle) This is one of two regional tourist offices in Gävleborgs län.

Hälsingetur (☎ 0270-766 60; www.halsingland.com; Box 130, SE-82623 Söderhamn) This is the second office within Gävleborgs län.

Jämtland Härjedalen Turism (☎ 063-14 40 22; www.jamtland.info; Rådhusgatan 44, SE-83182 Östersund) This office covers Jämtlands län.

Mitt Sverige Turism (☎ 0611-55 77 50; www.mittsverigeturism.se; Norra Kyrkogatan 15, SE-87132 Härnösand) This office covers Västernorrlands län.

Turism i Norrbotten/Lappland (☎ 0920-29 35 00; http://turism.norrbotten.se)

VästerbottensTurism (☎ 090-785 71 76; www.vasterbotten.net; Köksvägen 11, SE-90189 Umeå)

Getting Around

BUS

You'll probably find yourself relying more on buses than trains if you're spending any length of time in Norrland. The following companies provide regional transport links, and if you're planning to spend much time in any of these counties, it's worth inquiring about monthly passes or a *sommarkort*, offering discount travel in the peak summer period (from midsummer to mid-August). Check also the respective websites for routes, schedules, fares and passes; these sites don't always have information in English, but if you call the telephone numbers listed you'll usually reach someone who can help you in English.

Länstrafiken i Jämtlands Län (☎ 063-16 84 00; www.lanstrafiken-z.se in Swedish)

Länstrafiken i Norrbotten (☎ 020-47 00 47; www.ltnbd.se in Swedish)

Länstrafiken i Västerbotten (☎ 020-91 00 19, 0950-103 57; www.lanstrafikeniac.se)

Länstrafiken i Västernorrland (☎ 020-51 15 13; www.dintur.se in Swedish) Also commonly known as Din Tur.

X-Trafik i Gävleborgs Län (☎ 020-91 01 09; www.x-trafik.se in Swedish)

Ybuss (☎ 0771-33 44 44; www.ybuss.se in Swedish) Runs express buses daily between Stockholm and Sundsvall, Östersund and Umeå.

Other handy regional services include Länstrafiken i Västerbotten bus 100, which runs several times daily between Sundsvall and Luleå via the major towns along the E4; bus 45, which runs daily between Östersund and Gällivare; and bus 31, which connects Umeå and Mo i Rana (Norway) once daily via Storuman and Tärnaby.

Länstrafiken i Jämtlands län bus 45 runs twice daily between Mora (Dalarna) and Östersund.

Länstrafiken i Norrbotten runs two daily buses connecting Luleå and Kiruna – its bus network covers 100,000 sq km (one-quarter of Sweden), and it will carry bikes for Skr50 extra.

TRAIN

A historic railway, **Inlandsbanan** (☎ 063-10 44 09; www.inlandsbanan.se) runs for 1067km through

INLANDSBANAN

Until the early 20th century, Norrland's rich natural resources had been left largely unexploited. The Inlandsbanan (Inland Railway) was intended to change this, by opening up the northern forests and mountains for colonisation and development.

Digging ditches, excavating gravel, blasting mountains and laying sleepers and rails in an area where there were no roads was no mean feat. For over 30 years, the sleepers continued their inexorable progress northwards, from Kristinehamn in the south to Gällivare in the north – a distance of over 1300km. The Inlandsbanan was the last major undertaking of the Swedish navvies; construction began in 1907 and the project was completed in 1937.

However, by the time the Inlandsbanan was inaugurated, a serious competitor to the train, the car, was already making an impact on Sweden, and soon railway lines were closed in many parts of the country. When it was proposed that even larger stretches of the Inlandsbanan should be closed down, strong protests were heard not only from the regions directly affected, but from all over Sweden. The Inlandsbanan north of Mora is still operating today largely as a result of the wide popular support it received in the face of closure.

If you'd like to know more about the history of the Inlandsbanan and the people who made it happen, visit the Inlandsbanan Museum in Sorsele. A new railway museum with links to the Inland Railway has also been inaugurated in Jamtli in Östersund.

Sweden's interior from Mora to Gällivare via Östersund, Storuman, Arvidsjaur and Jokkmokk (see above). Today it can be covered in either direction by a combination of *rälsbuss* (railcar) and – with some planning – steam train. The journey is popular with tourists and can be done only from late June (just after midsummer) to early August. Travel on the line is slow (the average speed is 50km/h) – it takes seven hours from Mora to Östersund (Skr347) and 15 hours from Östersund to Gällivare (Skr697) – but you can break your journey in any of the small towns en route. Prices are based on a rate of Skr1.08 per km. You can buy tickets for certain legs of the journey, or a special card that will allow you two weeks' unlimited travel on the route (Skr1195); ScanRail cardholders get a 25% discount on this ticket, but not on individual tickets. Interrail pass-holders under 26 can ride on the Inlandsbanan for free. Children over the age of 15 pay half the adult fare; up to two children age 15 and under can ride free with a paying adult.

SJ (☎ 0771-75 75 75; www.sj.se) trains also run as far north as Härnösand; beyond there, you'll need to use trains operated by a different company, **Tågkompaniet** (☎ 020-44 41 11; www.tagkompaniet.se in Swedish).

The Skr13.2 billion, 190km **Botnia Banan** (www.botniabanan.se), a single-track railway being laid from the bridge over Ångermanälven north of Kramfors, via Örnsköldsvik, Husum and Nordmaling to Umeå, will speed travellers along at up to 250km/h and is due to be completed in 2010.

GÄSTRIKLAND

GÄVLE

☎ 026 / pop 92,000

One of Norrland's nicest cities simply to wander around in, Gävle is known as the gateway to the region. It has a distinctly youthful feel, with several parks and plazas thronged with relaxing locals.

There's an old town, with well-preserved wooden buildings and a slightly funkier feel than the centre. To get an idea of the city's character, be sure to stop on the bridge that links the two sections, and look for a signboard telling the tragicomic story of the Gävle Christmas Goat (in English).

Information

The helpful **tourist office** (☎ 14 74 30; turistbyran@gavletourism.se; www.gavle.se/turism; Drottninggatan 9; 10am-7pm Mon-Fri, 10am-4pm Sat, noon-4pm Sun) is not far from the train station.

There are banks and other services all along Drottninggatan and on, or around, the large Stortorget. The public **library** (Slottstorget 1), near the castle, offers free Internet access. For English-language newspapers and magazines go to **Internationell Press** (Södra Kungsgatan 11).

Sights & Activities

The wooden old town of **Gamla Gefle**, south of the city centre, shows what Gävle was like before it was almost completely destroyed by fire in 1869. One of the houses, **Joe Hill-gården** (☎ 61 34 25; Nedre Bergsgatan 28; admission free; 🕑 11am-3pm Tue-Sat Jun-Aug), was the birthplace of the US union organiser who was executed for a murder he didn't commit in Utah, 1915. Some of his poetry forms part of the memorial here.

Berggrenska gården (Kyrkogatan) is the only remaining early-19th-century commercial courtyard in Gävle, and it was lucky to survive the 1869 fire. The nearby **rådhus** (town hall) wasn't so lucky – its present appearance is post-1869, but a town hall has stood on the site since 1628.

The regional **Länsmuseum** (☎ 65 56 00; Södra Strandgatan 20; adult/child Skr40/free; 🕑 noon-4pm Tue-Sun) has an excellent art collection from the 17th century to today, plus displays of local silver and glassware, and historical exhibitions.

You'll find a practical demonstration of forestry and conservation techniques around the parks of **Stadsträdgården** and **Boulognerskogen** (used for open-air music and summer theatre), near the Gävle University campus on Kungsbacksvagen.

The oldest of the churches in Gävle is the **Heliga Trefaldighets kyrka** at the western end of Drottninggatan; it has an 11th-century **rune stone** inside. The buildings of the **castle** on the southern bank of Gävleån are now in administrative use, but there are temporary **art exhibitions** here and a small **prison museum** (tours 🕑 noon-2pm Sun).

From June to August daily **boat tours** (Skr35 each way) run from Södra Skeppsbron to the island of **Limön**, part of the surrounding archipelago. The island has a **nature trail**, a **mass grave** and a **memorial** to the sailors of a ship that was here lost in the early 1800s.

Bönan, 13km northeast of town, is a pretty waterside settlement that's also worth a look; attractions include a fish smokehouse and restaurant. Bus 95 runs out here.

Railway buffs will enjoy the preserved steam locomotives and carriages of the **Järnvägsmuseet** (☎ 14 46 15; Rälsgatan; adult/child Skr40/free; 🕑 10am-4pm Jun-Aug, Tue-Sun rest of yr), the

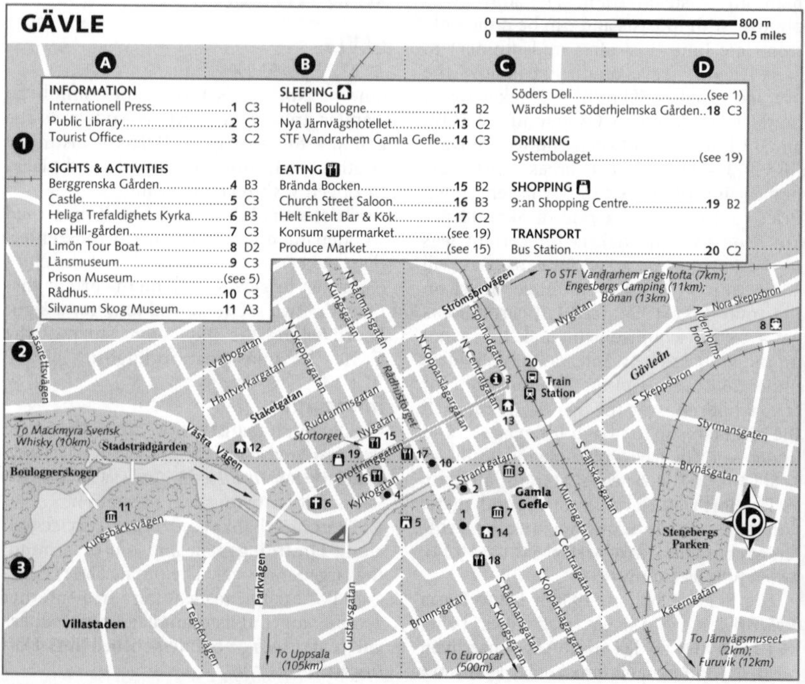

national rail museum, 2km south of the town centre, off Österbågen.

The leisure park and zoo named **Furuvik** (☎ 17 73 00; www.furuvik.se; adult/child Skr120/90, rides Skr10-40, armband Skr150; ⏰ mid-May–Aug), about 12km southeast of Gävle, aims to provide a little of everything; you can behave like a monkey on the amusement rides and then see the real thing at the ape enclosure. From the train station, take frequent bus 838.

A slightly more adult-friendly attraction is the distillery of **Mackmyra Svensk Whisky** (☎ 13 29 79; Bruksgatan 4, Valbo, tours Skr130, whisky tasting from Skr120), established in 1999 as the first Scandinavian malt whisky distillery. It's about 10km west of Gävle and offers regular tours of the distillery (only once a week outside the peak time of late June–August). Inquire at the tourist office for details.

Sleeping

STF Vandrarhem Gamla Gefle (☎ 62 17 45; stf.vandrarhem@telia.com; Södra Rådmansgatan 1; dm from Skr135, s/d Skr260/330) This central place is clean and quiet and set in a homely building around a pleasant courtyard in the old part of town. Bike hire is available, as is breakfast, and there's a good kitchen.

STF Vandrarhem Engeltofta (☎ 961 60; engeltofta@swipnet.se; Bönavägen 118; dm Skr150, s/d from Skr250/385; ⏰ Jun-Aug; bus 95) This STF hostel is in a lovely park setting by the sea, about 6km northeast of the city. Golf and fishing facilities are nearby.

Nya Järnvägshotellet (☎ 12 09 90; s/d from Skr395/525) Just across a public square from the train station, this historic building is also the cheapest hotel in town. The reception and a pub are on the ground floor.

Hotell Boulogne (☎ 12 63 52; Byggmästargatan 1; s/d from Skr395/545) The small and friendly Boulogne is another decent midrange option, although it doesn't look like much from the outside. Some rooms have shared bathroom facilities.

Engesbergs Camping (☎ 990 25; info@engesbergscamping.se; low/high season sites Skr75/100, cabins from Skr350; ⏰ May-Sep; bus 95) This camping ground has clean cabins and characteristically high-quality facilities in a pretty setting by the sea, about 11km northeast of town.

Eating

Brända Bocken (☎ 12 45 45; Stortorget; meals Skr64-149) This fashionable place is right in the heart of the action on the main square. Its outdoor area is a good spot to enjoy a drink with a light meal and do a spot of people-watching.

Helt Enkelt Bar & Kök (☎ 12 06 04; Norra Kungsgatan 3; snacks Skr30-65, meals Skr65-150; ⏰ 4pm-midnight Mon-Thu, 4pm-1am Fri, noon-1pm Sat, 5-11pm Sun) This is a favourite with the locals for its good atmosphere, friendly service and well-priced, unpretentious fare. It has sleek décor but not the prices to match – all but one dish on the menu is under Skr100

Church Street Saloon (☎ 12 62 11; Kyrkogatan 11; meals from Skr70; ⏰ closed Sun) This restaurant-saloon bar has a Wild West theme; it's furnished with antique saddles, Confederate flags and barrels of hooch. The huge menu includes lots of Tex-Mex items.

Söders Deli (Södra Kungsgatan 11; lunches Skr40-75) This tiny but excellent spot, near Internationell Press, serves good coffee and authentic Italian *ciabatta* and pasta.

Wärdshuset Söderhjelmska Gården (☎ 61 33 93; Södra Kungsgatan 2B) This nearby place offers fine food in a great setting – a wooden house dating from 1773 with lots of outdoor seating; *dagens* lunch is Skr75, à la carte meals range from snacks to traditional Swedish dishes and cost from Skr38 to Skr160.

There's a daily **produce market** (Stortorget) and you'll find a **Konsum supermarket** (9:an shopping centre). There's a **Systembolaget** (9:an shopping centre) as well.

Getting There & Away

Numerous long-distance bus services leave from behind the train station (connected by underpass). **Ybuss** (☎ 0200-33 44 44) runs daily to Sundsvall, Umeå and Östersund. **SGS Bussen** (☎ 13 30 30) has two to four daily services to Stockholm. **Swebus Express** (☎ 0200-21 82 18; www.swebusexpress.se) runs to both Uppsala and Stockholm once or twice daily.

SJ trains (☎ 0771-75 75 75) run to Stockholm via Uppsala, and northwards to Sundsvall and beyond; there are up to six X2000 services and several slower trains daily. Other useful direct trains include Gävle to Falun and Örebro.

Local buses leave mainly from around Rådhustorget. **Europcar** (Södra Kungsgatan 62) has car rental. Ask the tourist office about bicycle hire.

GYSINGE

☎ 0291 / pop 36,843

Gysinge, 55km south of Gävle and on the border with Uppland, is known for the fine **Gysinge Bruk** ironworks that operated from 1668 to the early 20th century, and it's a pleasant place for a wander.

There's a small **tourist office** (☎ 210 00; turist.gysinge@sandviken.se; Granövägen 6; 🕓 10am-5pm May-Sep, 10am-5pm Mon-Fri Oct-Apr) where you can rent boats and canoes.

Try your hand at forging at **Krokiga Smedjan** (Crooked Forge; admission free; 🕓 10am-6pm Jun-Aug; noon-5pm Tue-Sun rest of yr), which began operations in 1764; there's also a good **handicraft exhibition**. The traditional **Bagarstugan** still bakes unleavened bread, and is a good place for a coffee and a sandwich. In **Smedsbostaden** (Smith's Cottage; admission free; 🕓 noon-5pm May-Sep) you can experience what local living conditions were like in the late 19th century. **Dalälvarnas Flottningsmuseum** (Museum of River Driving; adult/child Skr20/10; 🕓 noon-5pm mid-Jun–mid-Aug) covers the once crucial, but now defunct, occupation of guiding logs downstream to the sawmills.

Gysinge Wärdshus (☎ 212 00; ysinge@swipnet.se; s/d from Skr950/1250), in the middle of the ironworks area at Gysinge, has very comfortable accommodation plus an excellent restaurant (meals from Skr75).

Bus 49 runs four to six times daily from Gävle to Gysinge.

FÄRNEBOFJÄRDEN NATIONAL PARK

A bird-watcher's favourite national park, Färnebofjärden occupies 260 sq kilometres south of Gysinge, bisected by the river Dalälven. Half-land, half-water, the park has excellent fishing and enough sandy beaches to please those nature-lovers who prefer the type of wildlife typically seen on Swedish beaches in the summer. But primarily the park is known as a bird-watcher's paradise, with ospreys, sea eagles, seven types of woodpecker, Ural owls and capercaillie.

Östa Stugby (☎ 0292-430 04; osta@stugby.com; 6-bed chalet from Skr675 per night; 🕓 yr-round) is in beautiful wilderness near the national park some 30km south of Gysinge. It offers luxurious self-contained six-bed chalets with private beach access, and also hires canoes and boats. There's a signposted 'free beach' near the Stugby – be prepared, however, because what it's free of is clothing.

It's difficult to get here without your own wheels, as there's no public transport to the park. Västmanlands Lokaltrafik bus 71 runs one to six times daily from Heby (connections from Sala) to Tärnsjö (8km from Östa).

HÄLSINGLAND

SÖDERHAMN & AROUND

☎ 0270 / pop 26,731

A small town with a couple of streets of shops and restaurants, and some worthwhile attractions, Söderhamn is known as the town of parks. It was founded in 1620 by Gustav II Adolf.

The **tourist office** (☎ 753 53; info@turism.soderhamn.se; 🕓 8.30am-6pm Mon-Fri, 10am-2pm Sat & Sun) is at the train station, just off the E4 motorway and 1.5km west of the town centre. The town centre has all the main facilities, including banks and supermarkets, mostly along Köpmangatan.

Sights

The history of the town is covered by **Söderhamns Museum** (☎ 157 91; Oxtorgsgatan 5; adult/child Skr25/free; 🕓 noon-5pm Tue-Sun mid-Jun–mid-Aug). Östra Berget hill lies south of the towncentre, with the odd 23m-high tower **Oscarsborg** (admission free; 🕓 11am-5pm Jun-Aug), with a café on top. Reach it by climbing the stairs behind the railroad tracks. Keep a close eye on the clock, too – a sign on the door says anyone left inside when the tower is closed will be locked in!

Ulrika Eleonora Kyrka (🕓 8am-4pm Mon-Fri), just north of the town hall, was designed by Nicodemus Tessin the Younger, and was completed in 1693. **Söderhamns F15 Flygmuseum** (☎ 142 84; adult/child Skr40/20; bus 59; 🕓 10am-5pm Jun-Aug, 11am-3pm Sun Sep-May), located by the airfield, 5km southeast of town, has a collection of old military aircraft.

About 15km northwest of town, **Trönö Gamla Kyrka** (🕓 May-Sep) is a small, well-preserved church of cool grey stone with a wooden belltower that dates from the 12th century. Take bus 67 (two to 11 daily).

Bergviks Industrimuseum (☎ 42 32 80; admission free; 🕓 Tue-Sun), around 16km west of Söderhamn, is a pretty spot with an outdoor café as well as displays about the history of the world's first sulphate factory, opened in

1874. Bus 64 runs to Bergvik every two hours or so.

Skärså, an ideal cycling destination 12km north of Söderhamn, is one of the most beautiful fishing villages in the area. The picturesque red-painted buildings include old boat sheds, houses, summer houses, a restaurant, **museum** (10am–9pm daily in summer) and a good café (Albertina, see below). There's also a fish shop. Take bus 65 (weekdays only).

Sleeping & Eating

First Hotel Statt (☎ 735 70; Oxtorgsgatan 17; s/d from Skr1400) Room 104 at this elegant hotel is supposedly haunted by an old 1800s barman named Karl-Emil; it was the only room left alone during the hotel's otherwise thorough renovation in the late-'90s.

Scandic Hotel Söderhamn (☎ 26 52 00; soderhamn@scandic-hotels.com; Montörsbacken 4; s/d from Skr1200/1500) This is only 300m from the train station and offers good discounted rates, as well as its usual high standard of accommodation.

Mohed Natura Camping (☎ 42 52 33; mohedscamping@glocalnet.net; Mohedsvägen 59; camping per person from Skr100, dm Skr130, cabins from Skr250) This very busy lakeside spot, 11km west of Söderhamn, is a well-equipped camping ground that cohabits with the spotless **STF Vandrarhem** (Jun-Aug) in what looks like an antique school building. You can rent bikes and boats here. Bus 63 and 100 run to Mohed from Söderhamn.

Albertina (☎ 320 10; mains Skr70-150; lunch & dinner until 10pm) Perched above the water in Skärså, with harbour views, this is the nicest place to eat in the area. The menu includes lots of herring and salmon, plus meals for nonfish-lovers too. Adding to the theme, servers are dressed in sailor suits.

Mousquet (☎ 198 97; Köpmangatan 2; dagens lunch Skr60, meals from Skr90; lunch & dinner) This place serves something for everyone, with cheap pub snacks, lots of pizza choices, and seafood, meat and chicken meals.

Kalles Gatukök, opposite Mousquet, is a fast-food outlet that is handy for a quick refuel.

Getting There & Away

Skyways flies from the airfield to Stockholm once or twice on weekdays.

All buses and trains leave from the Resecentrum, at the train station. Ybuss runs daily to Östersund (Skr180, four hours, once or twice daily), Stockholm (Skr180, three to four hours, three daily), Umeå (Skr260, five hours, twice daily) and Uppsala (Skr180, two to 3½ hours, three daily). SJ trains run daily to Hudiksvall, Sundsvall, Härnösand, Gävle and Stockholm.

JÄRVSÖ & AROUND

☎ 0651 / pop 1907

Järvsö is best known for the **Hälsinge Hambon** (www.halsingehambon.x.se), an annual folk dancing contest (with up to 1000 competitors), the final event of which takes place here in early July; look for the statue of dancers by the train station. The sleepy village in the hilly interior of Hälsingland sits at the northern end of a string of lakes that extends from the Bothnian coast at Ljusne, just south of Söderhamn.

There's a **tourist office** (☎ 403 06; Turistvägen 29; mid-Jun–mid-Aug, shorter hr rest of yr) on the main road through town, as well as banks and supermarkets.

Sights

Järvzoo (☎ 411 25; high season adult/child Skr145/90) is a well-stocked, nicely arranged zoo that lets you follow 3km of easy wooden walkways through the forest to observe bears, lynxes, honey buzzards, snowy owls and aggressive wolverines – all in fairly natural surroundings. Its opening hours are complex, but it's generally open from 10am or 11am until 4pm or 5pm June to August, 11am until 2pm or 3pm the rest of the year.

Completed in 1838, **Järvsö Kyrka** (9am-4pm or 5pm) is one of the largest rural churches in Sweden and it has an impressive location on an island in the river. Most of the island is a wooded nature reserve.

The hill, **Öjeberget**, just west of the village, has great views – there's a restaurant on top and you can ski down in winter. Just across the bridge from the church (on the eastern bank of the river), **Stenegård** (☎ 76 73 00; May-Sep, Sat & Sun rest of yr) is an old manor and farm with good handicraft stalls, a café, restaurant and a theatre in an old barn.

Sleeping & Eating

Järvsöbaden (☎ 404 00; info@jarvsobaden.se; s/d from Skr600/800) This friendly hotel, founded as a health farm in 1905, is the best place to stay in town. It's a charming old spread, set in pretty grounds that include a nine-hole golf course, and it has a variety of rooms (some with shared facilities). The restaurant here has a superb lunch smörgåsbord that has to be seen to be believed.

Gästgivars (☎ 416 90; Jon Persvägen 7; dm/s Skr165/215) This small and homely place is near the bridge (follow the signs) and offers very inviting hostel accommodation, plus breakfast for an additional Skr35.

Järvsö Camping (☎ 403 39; sites Skr80, cabins from Skr220) This place is on the main road through the town and offers good facilities.

Järvsö Café & Konditori (☎ 411 11) This is a basic little café down by the train station.

Getting There & Away

Bus 51 runs regularly between Bollnäs and Ljusdal, via Arbrå and Järvsö. Trains run north from Järvsö to Östersund, and south to Gävle and Stockholm.

HUDIKSVALL & AROUND

☎ 0650 / pop 37,048

Hudiksvall is rather adorably nicknamed 'Happy Hudik.' With a well-preserved but small core of old wooden houses (Möljen), and located picturesquely between a lake and a fjord, it's a charming little place to spend a few hours.

The **tourist office** (☎ 191 00; turist@hudiksvall.se, www.hudiksvall.se; mid-Jun–mid-Aug, Mon-Sat rest of yr) is at Möljen, by the harbour. In town, you'll find banks and other services on Storgatan and Drottninggatan. For Internet access, there's a **library** (Storgatan); the **museum** (Storgatan 31; per 30min Skr15) also has computers.

Sights & Activities

The **Hälsinglands Museum** (☎ 196 00; Storgatan 31; admission free; mid-Jun–mid-Aug, Mon-Sat rest of yr) covers local history, culture and art, including the **Malsta Stone** with unusual runic inscriptions. Just southwest of the centre, **Jakobs kyrka** dates from 1672. Parts of **Hälsingtuna Church**, 4km north, were built around 1150, but more extraordinary is the 15th-century **Bergöns Kapell**, 18km due northeast, the oldest fishermen's church in the district.

Attractive **Kuggörarna** is about 30km east of Hudiksvall and is an excellent example of a fishing village (take bus 37, twice daily). The coast shows **raised beaches** caused by post-glacial uplift (still underway) and the forests are growing in boulder-fields. **Mellanfjärden**, 30km north of Hudiksvall, isn't the most photogenic village, but there is a gallery there with displays of local crafts, a summer theatre, a good restaurant and several nature reserves. **Sörfjärden**, 10km north of Mellanfjärden, has an unusual harbour in the river Gnarpsån, and a good sandy beach nearby.

There is a lovely driving route through the fields and farmsteads between lakes **Norrdellen** and **Sördellen**, just west of Hudiksvall. Around the neoclassical **Norrbo Kyrka** there are nine Iron Age graves, church stables from the 1920s and also a mid-18th-century bell tower. **Avholmberget**, just north of Friggesund, is the best viewpoint – you can drive or cycle up it.

Sleeping & Eating

First Hotell Statt (☎ 150 60; Storgatan 36; s/d from Skr1200/1500;) This is the pick of the town's hotels, with central, upmarket lodgings and facilities.

Hotell Temperance (☎ 311 07; Håstgatan 16; dm from Skr150, s/d from Skr550/700) This small, family-run place is between the train station and Jakobs Kyrka and offers simple, comfortable accommodation at reasonable prices.

Malnbadens Camping & STF Hudiksvall (☎ 132 60; info@malnbadenscamping.com; sites Skr115, dm Skr135, cabins Skr400) Four kilometres east of the centre of Hudiksvall, this is a large wooded camping ground that's also home to the pleasant STF hostel, open year-round. Bus 5 runs out here in summer.

Stadt Nöje (lunches Skr59) attached to the First Hotell Statt, this is a stylish and popular restaurant-bar, with good-value lunches plus many appealing à la carte offerings.

Dackås Konditori (☎ 123 29; Storgatan 34, sandwiches from Skr35) This bakery hasn't changed since the 1950s. It has an upstairs café serving sandwiches, plus cakes and pastries to satisfy sugar cravings.

Gretas Krog (☎ 966 00; lunch Skr59, meals Skr130-200) Down on the water behind the tourist office this offers good Swedish dishes, a broad seafood selection and a large, bustling outdoor deck.

Getting There & Away

The bus station is next to the central train station, by the harbour. Ybuss travels daily Gävle (Skr170, 2½ hours, twice daily), Östersund (Skr170, 3½ hours, twice daily), Stockholm (Skr210, five hours, twice daily) and

Umeå (Skr240, five hours, twice daily). SJ trains run to Sundsvall, Gävle, Söderhamn and Stockholm.

MEDELPAD

SUNDSVALL

☎ 060 / pop 93,307

Notable for having managed to rebuild itself in fine style after a devastating fire in 1888, Sundsvall is a confection in pink and tan, with several remarkably pretty buildings of neo-Gothic, neo-Renaissance and neo-baroque architecture. It's a pleasant place to spend a day or two, particularly for those interested in fine dining, as the culinary scene here has a good reputation.

In the first week of July, Sundsvall hosts one of Sweden's largest street festivals (attended by up to 100,000 people), which includes a large musical concert in the centre of town. If you plan to be here then, definitely book accommodation well ahead, and don't count on parking anywhere near the city centre.

Information

Storgatan is the main street, with banks, supermarkets and most facilities.

Forex (Köpmangatan 1) Money exchange.

Public library (Kulturmagasinet, Sjögatan; 🕑 10am-7pm Mon-Thu, 10am-6pm Fri, 11am-4pm Sat, closed Sun) Free Internet access.

Tourist office (☎ 61 04 50; www.sundsvallturism.com; Stora Torget; 🕑 10am-6pm Mon-Fri, 10am-2pm Sat yr-round) Staff have information on activities in the area, plus summer boat tours, and can supply maps detailing galleries in town, or a self-guided pub crawl.

Sights

Kulturmagasinet, on Sjögatan down near the harbour, is a magnificent restoration of some old warehouses. The buildings now contain the town library and **Sundsvall Museum** (☎ 19 18 03; adult/child Skr20/free; 🕑 11am-7pm Mon-Thu, 10am-6pm Fri, 11am-4pm Sat & Sun), which has exhibits of local and natural history, local Iron Age archaeology and geology.

The central church, **Gustav Adolfs kyrka**, is worth a look. There's music here every Wednesday evening in summer.

Up on the hill **Norra Stadsberget** (150m), there is a **viewing tower** as well as a typical **friluftsmuseum** (outdoor museum; admission free), with a collection of local houses. The southern hill, **Södra Stadsberget** (250m), has an extensive plateau that is good for hiking, with trails up to 12km long. There's also free fishing on the **Sidsjön** and several **downhill ski runs** (nordic skiing is also popular). Buses run to either hill once every two hours in summer.

The large island just east of Sundsvall, **Alnö**, has the magnificent **Alnö Gamla Kyrka** (admission free; 🕑 noon-7pm mid-Jun–mid-Aug), 2km north of the bridge (at Vi). The old church, below the road, is a mixture of 12th- and 15th-century styles. The lower parts of the wall paintings were badly damaged by whitewashing in the 18th century, but the upper wall and ceiling paintings are in perfect condition (apart from removal of certain faces by Protestant vandals) and show various biblical scenes. The painting was probably done by one of Albertus Pictor's pupils. Even better is the late 11th-century carved wooden **font** in the new church across the road; the upper part combines Christian and Viking symbolism, while the lower part shows beasts, the embodiment of evil. Take bus 1 to Vi (two or three hourly), then take a Plus bus to the churches (every one or two hours).

For a pleasant excursion, head to **Lörudden**, a picturesque fishing village about 30km southeast of town, with a tiny café and fish smokehouse. There's a beach of flat rocks here, which is perfect for warming up in the sun after a dive into the sea. Take bus 20 south to Njurundabommen, then change to bus 126.

Liden, by the ribbon lake on Indalsälven, is about 46km northwest of Sundsvall on road No 86. **Liden Gamla Kyrka**, completed in 1510, has a lovely location and contains excellent medieval **sculptures** from the 13th, 15th and 16th centuries. There are rather faded wall paintings from 1561, and also a 13th-century crucifix. The view from the **Vättberget**, reached by a 3km unsurfaced road from Liden, is one of the finest in Sweden, and shows the ribbon lake to its best advantage. To reach Liden, take bus 30.

Sleeping

STF Vandrarhem Sundsvall (☎ 61 21 19; stf.vandrarhem.sundsvall@telia.com; Gafelbyvägen; s/d from Skr250/300, dm Skr150-205) The very good STF *vandrarhem* is above the town on Norra Stadsberget, and has both older rooms and more expensive modern rooms with private bath.

The 20-minute walk to the hostel from the city centre is pleasant, but not much fun with heavy bags – a bus runs up here in summer from both the train and the bus stations.

Baltic Hotel (☎ 14 04 40; info.baltic@swedenhotels.se; Sjögatan 5; s/d from Skr1100/1250) Toward the upper end of the accommodation scale is the attractive Baltic, near Kulturmagasinet. It has excellent discounted rates for its bright, modern rooms.

Scandic Hotel Sundsvall City (☎ 785 62 00; sundsvallcity@scandic-hotels.com; Esplanaden 29; s/d from Skr1200/1525) The large and upmarket Sundsvall City has very comfortable rooms, plus lots of facilities on the premises, including a cinema, restaurant and popular pub.

Fläsians Camping (☎ 55 44 75; Norrstigen 15; sites Skr95, cabins from Skr250) This place is near the E4, 4km south of Sundsvall. It's a large, well-equipped and pleasant campground, despite all the industry between it and the city centre. Take bus 2 or 52.

Eating & Drinking

Il Barone (☎ 17 66 04; Kyrkogatan 14; mains Skr180-230, pastas Skr120-150; dinner) Exclusive and sophisticated, Il Barone is a highly regarded restaurant serving authentic Italian cuisine, with risotto and pasta dishes at the lower end of the price scale, plus well-prepared meat and fish meals.

Kajplats 1 (☎ 15 60 06; Hamnplan 1; meals Skr89-225) This place has a hotchpotch of interior

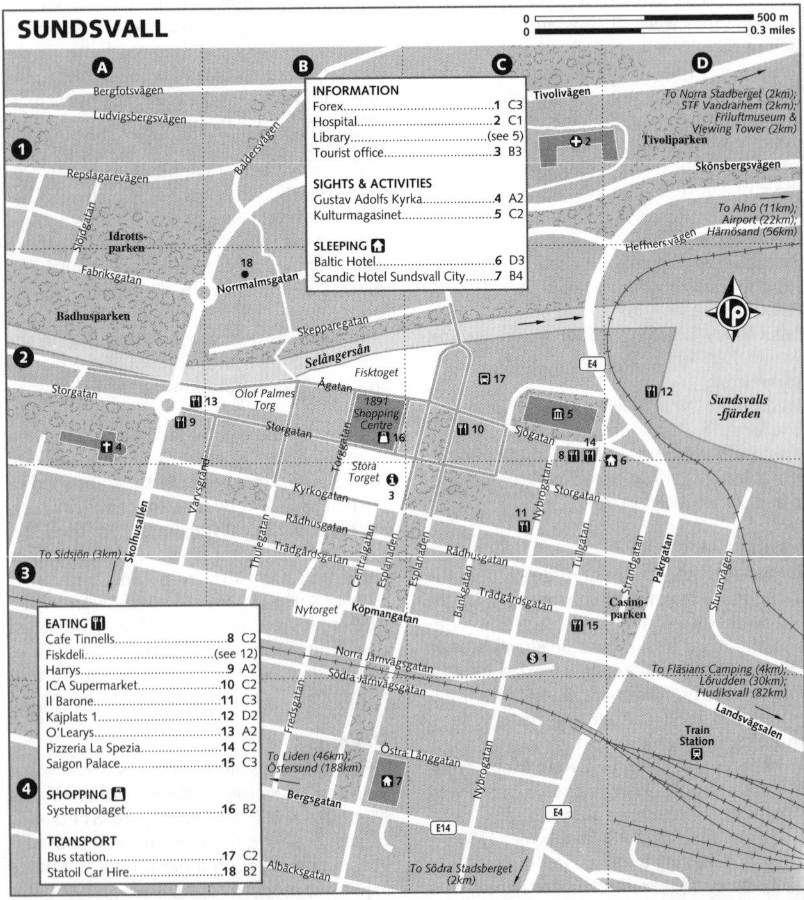

styles (nautical meets opulent Oriental) but it all comes together in a great harbour restaurant-bar, where the emphasis is on fresh fish. Soups and salads are offered for under Skr100, plus there's a selection of tapas plates (around Skr50).

Saigon Palace (☎ 17 30 91; Trädgårdsgatan 5; lunch from Skr65, dishes Skr70-125; ⏰ lunch & dinner) Just slightly off the beaten path, the Saigon Palace has an extensive menu of Chinese, Vietnamese and even Japanese dishes, plus a cheap lunch buffet.

Café Tinells (☎ 561 49; Sjögatan 7; meals Skr40-65) Slick café fare in modern surroundings is offered by Café Tinells, a funky and colourful place with excellent food, including *ciabatta*, salads, baked potatoes, quiche and tempting sugary treats.

Pizzeria La Spezia (☎ 61 12 23; Sjögatan 6) This pizzeria offers very cheap pizza and kebab deals for around Skr45.

There are lots of relatively anonymous, but nevertheless popular, pubs around town, including **Harrys** (☎ 17 55 33; Storgatan 33) and **O'Learys** (☎ 12 41 44; Storgatan 40) opposite each other on Storgatan. Both attract a mixed crowd and offer a range of pub food and drinks.

There's a central **ICA supermarket** (Esplanaden 5) and a **Systembolaget** (1891 shopping centre, Storgatan).

Getting There & Away

The **airport** (☎ 197600) is 22km north of Sundsvall; buses run from the Scandic Hotel and the bus station three to nine times daily (Skr65) to connect with SAS and Skyways flights to Göteborg, Luleå and Stockholm.

All buses depart from the Sundsvall bus station, known as Navet, in the northern part of town near Kulturmagasinet. Ybuss runs daily to Östersund (Skr140, 2½ hours, twice daily), Gävle (Skr190, 3½ hours, twice daily) and Stockholm (Skr220, six hours, three to four daily). Länstrafiken Västerbotten bus 100 runs several times daily to Umeå (3¾ hours), Luleå (eight hours) and most other coastal towns. Prices are set by distance at Skr18 per 7km.

Trains run west to Östersund and south to Söderhamn, Gävle and Stockholm. The station is just east of the town centre, on Köpmangatan.

Statoil (☎ 15 20 70; Norrmalmsgatan 1) offers inexpensive car hire. **Taxi Sundsvall** (☎ 19 90 00) can help you get around.

ÅNGERMANLAND

HÄRNÖSAND

☎ 0611 / pop 25,272

Härnösand, on a narrow strait between the island of Härnön and the mainland, was sacked by the Russians in 1721. It's a small town with a lot going for it, and makes an excellent base for exploring Höga Kusten.

There's a large, well-stocked **tourist office** (☎ 881 40; www.harnosand.se; Järnvägsgatan 2; ⏰ 8am-7pm Mon-Fri, noon-4pm Sat & Sun Jun-Aug, weekdays only rest of yr) outside the town centre, just off the E4; bike rental and free Internet access are available. From here you need to cross Nybron (bridge) to get to the town centre.

The good **Länsmuseet Västernorrland** (☎ 886 00; admission free; ⏰ 11am-5pm), at Murberget (1km north of the tourist office), is a regional museum dedicated to the culture and history of Ångermanland. A self-guided tour on tape (in English) costs Skr20. The open-air museum, **Friluftsmuseet Murberget** (admission free; ⏰ noon-4pm mid-Jun–mid-Aug), adjacent to Länsmuseet Västernorrland, includes a shop, church and school.

The new regional library, **Härnosand Sambibliotek** (⏰ Mon-Sat Aug-Jun), hosts rotating art exhibits and is worth a look for its cutting-edge architecture; the stylish café inside offers a cheap lunch buffet with vegetarian options (from Skr70).

Boat trips taking in the impressive coastal scenery are available in summer, with some routes journeying up to the dramatic Höga Kusten bridge – inquire at the tourist office for details.

The **STF Vandrarhem** (☎ 104 46; vhemmet@harnosandshus.se; Volontärvägen 9-11; dm Skr150; ⏰ mid-Jun–mid-Aug) is 2km east of the train station and offers good amenities. A smaller hostel with brand-new facilities, **Mitti Härnösand** (☎ 741 50; daneb@tiscali.se; Franzengatan 14; ⏰ reception 3-5pm; s/d Skr250/350, 3-/4-bed rooms Skr450/550) is in a restored old building (dating from 1844), directly across the street from the cathedral.

Hotel City (☎ 277 00; hotelcity@kajutan.com; Storgatan 28; s/d Skr790/990) is in the heart of town and has comfortable rooms. Adjacent is the popular restaurant/bar/club, **Kajutan** (☎ 183 00; meals Skr75-250), which offers lunch for Skr65 and a comprehensive menu of snacks, pasta, meat, fish and vegetarian dishes.

The family-run **Mykonos** (☎ 51 18 44; Storgatan; mains from Skr160; ⏲ 2-11pm Tue-Sat) bills itself as a Greek taverna. It looks the part, with fishing nets and maritime knick-knacks everywhere, but the cooking is all gourmet French bistro, and downright spectacular.

The classy restaurant-bar **Apotequet** (☎ 51 17 17; Nybrogatan 3) has its bar area in an old pharmacy, and boasts an attractive patio which is open in summer. It's one of several bars on this street, all of which offer rare bargains on happy-hour drinks.

For souvenirs, pick up some authentic Swedish handicraft at the classy **Svensk Slöjd** (Storgatan 25; ⏲ 10am-6pm Mon-Fri, 10am-3pm Sat), across from Hemköp supermarket.

Länstrafiken Västerbotten bus 100 runs several times daily to Sundsvall, Luleå and points in between. Ybuss runs daily to Gävle (Skr200, 4½ hours, twice daily) and Stockholm (Skr250, six to seven hours, several times daily). Local buses service Sundsvall for train connections to Gävle and Stockholm.

HÖGA KUSTEN

☎ 0613

Some of the most dramatic scenery on the entire Swedish coastline is found here, on the Höga Kusten (meaning the 'High Coast'). The secret to its spectacular beauty is elevation; nowhere else on the coast do you find such a mountainous landscape, with sheer rocky cliffs plunging straight down to the sea, as well as lakes, fjords and islands. The region was recently recognised as a unique area and listed as a Unesco World Heritage site. It has largely been shaped by the combined processes of glaciation, glacial retreat and the emergence of new land from the sea (which continues today at a rate of 0.9m per century). This is a wonderful place for scenic drives, but the narrow twisty roads can make it difficult for whoever's stuck behind the wheel.

Höga Kusten stretches from north of Härnösand to Örnsköldsvik, and either place makes a handy base for exploration. Tourist offices in both towns can help you with information on exploring the region by bus, car or on an organised tour. There is also a regional **tourist office** (☎ 504 80; www.hogakusten.com) serving the area; it's located inside Hotell Höga Kusten, just north of the spectacular E4 suspension bridge over Storfjärden. Here you can pick up information on attractions and accommodation options in the tiny villages along the coast. The information area is crowded with brochures and open all year, and the desk is staffed from 10am to 6pm June to August. There's also useful information on the Internet at www.turistinfo.kramfors.se.

Unfortunately, there's little public transport in the area. Buses cruise along the E4 Hwy, but don't make it into the villages, and as a result this area is virtually impossible to explore thoroughly without your own set of wheels. That's unless, of course, you wish to walk the **Höga Kustenleden**, a 127km hiking trail stretching from Veda in the south, through Kramfors, and finishing near Örnsköldsvik, with shelters and cabins situated along its length. Ask the tourist office for the map and guide book (Skr80). It's also very easy to walk smaller sections of the trail as day or half-day trips.

In addition to the striking landscapes, the other major attractions of the region are the many well-preserved **fishing villages** – the pick of them being Barsta, Bönhamn and Norrfällsviken – and the lovely offshore **islands**, especially Högbonden and Ulvön; for transport information see opposite.

Ulvön is worth a visit for the view from the hill, **Lotsberget** (100m), though the charming main village can be spoiled by the large tour groups who line up to see the tiny, 17th-century **chapel**. Also worth checking out are **Hembygdsgården**, a 19th-century house with furnishings, and **Sandviken**, a 17th-century village at the northern end of the island.

Norrfällsviken is a picture-perfect half-circle of red-and-white fishing huts, lining a narrow inlet. There's a hilltop chapel from 1649 (the key is kept next to the door), and the friendly **Fisk Restaurang** (☎ 0613-211 42; fish plates Skr70-120; ⏲ 10am-10pm) sells smoked fish to take away, as well as more substantial meals in its cosy wood-panelled restaurant-pub. At 9pm it turns into a karaoke bar!

Back on the mainland, you'll find the bizarre **Mannaminne** (☎ 202 90; admission Skr40; ⏲ Jun-Sep; Sat & Sun Oct-Nov & Apr-May), near Häggvik. Built around a broken, rusting piece of farm equipment, this is an eccentric collection of just about everything, from subjects as diverse as farming, emigration and technology. It also offers accommodation (see below), and the attached café is famous for its rendition of fried herring and potatoes;

customers get a discount on museum admission. Walk up the steep hill behind the museum for the best view in the area (35 minutes return).

Friendly **Skuleberget Naturum** (☎ 401 71; admission free; ⏰ Jun-Aug, shorter hr rest of yr), by the E4 north of Docksta, has exhibitions and lots of information on the area. The steep mountain, **Skuleberget** (285m), soars above the Naturum, where you can ask about hiking routes, the chairlift (Skr60/40) on the other side, and rock-climbing routes (grades II to III).

Skuleskogen National Park, a few kilometres northeast, contains varied and magnificent scenery, including **Slåtterdalskrevan**, a 200m-deep canyon. The park is signposted from the E4, and the Höga Kustenleden walking trail passes through it.

Sleeping & Eating

Hotell Höga Kusten (☎ 72 22 70; s/d Skr845/1095, discounted to Skr500/750) You'll wake up on top of the world if you stay at this place, the large hotel just off the E4 next to the bridge. There's also a café here serving coffee as well as snacks, and a restaurant with basic meals from Skr85.

Vandrarhem Högbonden (☎ 230 05, 420 49; dm from Skr195; ⏰ May-Oct) This is a relaxing getaway on the island of Högbonden, reached by boat from Bönhamn and Barsta. There's a kitchen here, and a café open in summer. You'll need to book well in advance.

STF Vandrarhem Docksta (☎ 130 64; kustlada@telia.com; sites Skr100, dm/cabins from Skr120/300; ⏰ yr-round; ♿) This attractive and busy hostel is actually 3km south of Docksta at Skoved, right along the Höga Kustenleden (High Coast Trail). It has a party atmosphere and good facilities, including a restaurant and an outdoor stage for summer concerts.

Mannaminne (☎ 202 90; info@mannaminne.se; s/d from Skr350/550) The aforementioned eccentric open-air museum, near tiny Häggvik, also offers B&B accommodation and cottages.

Kustgårdens Vandrarhem (☎ 212 55; dm Skr130), in Norrfällsviken, is operated by the nearby **Brittas Restaurang** (☎ 212 55; low/high season cabins from Skr800/950; ♿), a popular summer complex consisting of a restaurant and pub, plus self-contained cabins.

Delightful Norrfällsviken has a very good **camping ground** (☎ 213 82; sites Skr120, cabins from Skr350). The area surrounding the Naturum at Skuleberget is well set up for outdoor enthusiasts, with a **camping ground** (☎ 130 64; sites Skr90, cabins from Skr295, rooms from Skr200), a restaurant, and shops selling outdoor gear.

There are supermarkets in Ullanger, Nordingrå, Docksta and Mjällom.

Getting There & Around

Bus 217 runs one to six times daily between Nordingrå, the bridge and Kramfors. Other than that, you'll need to walk, cycle or drive yourself around the area. Länstrafiken Västerbotten bus 100 runs along the E4.

Ferries to Högbonden (☎ 0706-81 82 84; adult/child return Skr80/40) go from Barsta (every two hours 9.30am–5.30pm, returning 45 minutes later, mid-June–mid-August) and from Bönhamn (every two hours 9.45am–5.45pm mid-June–mid-August). **Ferries to Ulvön** (☎ 0613-105 50, 13000; adult/child return Skr150/50; ⏰ Jun-Aug) leave from Ullånger (9.30am), Docksta (10.15am) and Mjällomslandet (10.45am), arriving at 11.30am and returning at 3pm from Ulvöhamn.

ÖRNSKÖLDSVIK

☎ **0660 / pop 54,945**

Most famous within Sweden for being the town that produced the handsome ice hockey star Peter 'Foppa' Forsberg, Örnsköldsvik is the largest town in Ångermanland. It's a fine base for exploring the High Coast, but otherwise doesn't demand a lengthy stay.

There's a helpful **tourist office** (☎ 881 00; www.ornskoldsvik.se; inside Paradisbadet; ⏰ 9am-6pm Mon-Fri, 10am-2pm Sat & Sun Jun-Aug). There are banks around Storatorget, and the **library** (Lasarettsgatan 5) offers Internet access.

Walk up **Varvsberget** (80m) for a good view of the town; it's south of the centre – some 275 steps lead up from Modovägen.

Örnsköldsviks Museum (☎ 886 01; Läroverksgatan 1; adult/child Skr20/free; ⏰ noon-4pm mid-Jun–mid-Aug, Tue-Sun rest of yr) covers 9000 years of local history and includes a section on the Sami. The impressive-looking **Rådhuset Konsthall** (☎ 886 08; Rådhusgatan 1; adult/child Skr20/free; ⏰ noon-4pm Tue-Sun) features local art exhibitions.

Gene Fornby (☎ 53710; adult/child Skr60/30; ⏰ noon-5pm Jul–mid-Aug), About 5km south of the centre is an interesting reconstruction of an Iron Age farm, complete with actors and a wide range of activities, from baking to iron working. Guided tours run at

12.30pm, 2pm and 3.30pm. Take bus 21 to Geneåsvägen, then walk to the farm, or ask at the tourist office about the regular direct bus service from town.

Sleeping & Eating

STF Vandrarhem (☎ 702 44; Högsnäsgården, Högsnäs 99; dm/cabins from Skr130/230; 🕑 yr-round) This place is in a lovely setting 9km west of town, just off the E4. Take bus 40 or 412.

Strand City Hotell (☎ 106 10; Nygatan 2; s/d from Skr595/850, discounted to Skr450/550) In the town centre, this place offers decent midrange accommodation.

First Hotel Statt (☎ 26 55 90; Lasarettsgatan 2; s/d from Skr1520/1402, discounted to Skr702/852) The First Hotel Statt is a more upmarket option, with facilities typical of a high-end chain hotel.

Café Galleri M (☎ 168 60; Storgatan 8; lunch Skr59; 🕑 lunch & dinner Mon-Fri, lunch Sat, closed Sun) This is a pleasant little café and a good spot for lunch, with a small adjacent art gallery.

Mamma Mia (☎ 147 00; Storgatan 6; meals Skr60-200) Nearby Mamma Mia has an extensive menu of Italian food, including pizza and pasta dishes under Skr100.

Restaurang Varvberget (☎ 844 80; lunch Skr65) On top of Varvberget, this place does typically Swedish food and a good weekday lunch special, which you can enjoy along with great views.

Down by the harbour you'll find some good dining options, including the excellent **Fina Fisken** (☎ 150 05; meals Skr85-170), serving local fish dishes in a fine atmosphere.

Getting There & Away

Länstrafiken Västerbotten runs bus 100 along the E4 several times daily – south to Sundsvall (2½ hours), north to Umeå (three hours) and Luleå (six hours).

VÄSTERBOTTEN

UMEÅ

☎ 090 / pop 106,000

With the vibrant feel of a college town (it has some 22,000 students), Umeå can be a welcome return to urbanity after a stay in the barren north. It's one of the fastest-growing towns in Sweden and an agreeable place to hang out, wind down or stock up for an outdoor adventure.

Information

Forex (Renmarkstorget) Near the tourist office.

Library (Rådhusesplanaden 6A) Internet access.

Naturkompaniet (Rådhusesplanaden 7) Outdoor gear is sold here.

Press Stop (Victoria Gallerian shopping centre) International magazines sold.

Tourist office (☎ 16 16 16; umeturist@umea.se, www.umea.se/turism; Renmarkstorget 15; 🕑 8am-7pm Mon-Fri, 10am-4pm Sat, noon-4pm Sun mid-Jun–mid-Aug; Mon-Fri rest of yr) A central place that can help you with visitor inquiries.

Sights & Activities

Gammlia, 1km east of the town centre, has several museums and shouldn't be missed. Attractions include the cultural/historical exhibits and Sami collections of the regional **Västerbottens Museum** (☎ 17 18 00; admission free), the modern art museum, **Bildmuseet**, and the **Maritime Museum**. The surrounding **Friluftsmuseet**, featuring old houses and staff wearing period clothes, is also worth a look. The museums are open daily June to August (closed Monday for the rest of the year).

Holmön, which calls itself the sunniest place in Sweden, is a 15km-long offshore island with a **boat museum** (adult/child Skr20/free; 🕑 Jun-Aug) and a collection of traditional craft, plus a good quayside restaurant and swimming beaches. In July there's a rowboat race to Finland, which is only 36km away. Free ferries depart two to three times daily from Norrfjärden, 26km northeast of Umeå (bus 118 or 119, Skr32).

The island of **Norrbyskär**, 40km south of Umeå, is another worthwhile destination. It has an interesting history – a sawmill community was built up here from nothing in less than 10 years, only to disappear just as suddenly 10 years later. There is a museum as well as other attractions; buses run to and from Umeå to Norrbyn, to connect with ferries – inquire at the tourist office for times.

There are a number of activities in the surrounding area, many of them based at **Vindeln**, 54km northwest of Umeå. Adventures on offer include fishing, white-water rafting, jet-boating and canoeing on the local rivers, plus horse riding and a variety of walking trails (from two hours to three days). The tourist office can help you to organise these. Bus 16 connects Vindeln and Umeå.

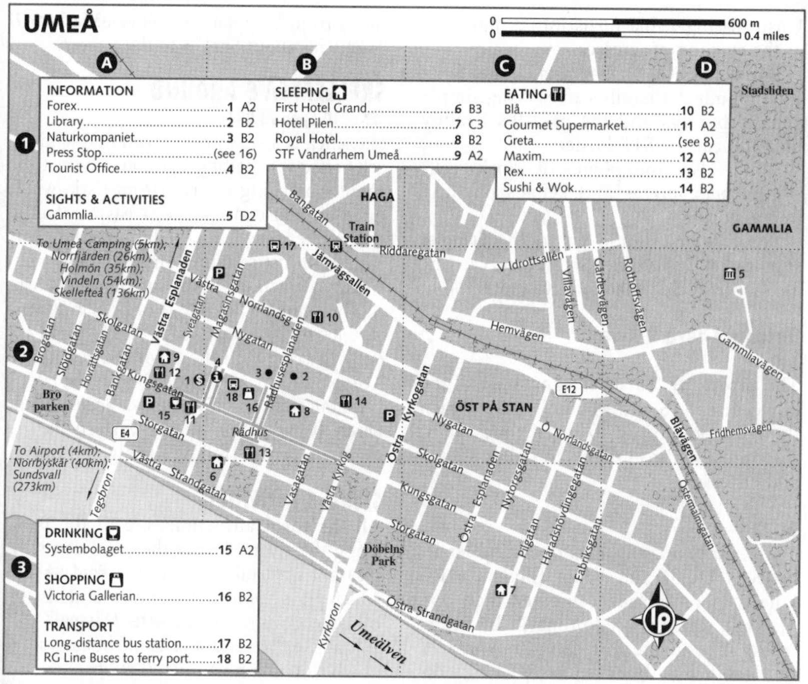

Sleeping

STF Vandrarhem Umeå (☎ 77 16 50; info@vandrarhemmet.se; Västra Esplanaden 10; dm from Skr130) This busy and efficient (if rather Dickensian) youth hostel is one of the few in the region that's actually occupied by youths. It's in a great location, a residential neighbourhood mere steps from the town centre.

First Hotel Grand (☎ 77 88 70; umea.grand@firsthotels.se; Storgatan 46; s/d from Skr900/1100) This is the oldest hotel in Umeå, and it has good service and friendly staff.

Hotel Pilen (☎ 14 14 60; Pilgatan 5; s/d Skr550/750) This is a comfortable, family-run place in a quiet area some 600m from the town centre.

Royal Hotel (☎ 10 07 30; hotelroyal@telia.com; Skolgatan 62; s/d from Skr850/1200) The Royal Hotel offers good accommodation in the heart of town and has an excellent restaurant.

Umeå Camping (☎ 70 26 00; umea.camping@umea.se; sites Skr125, basic huts from Skr200, cabins & chalets from Skr265) This well-equipped camping ground is 5km northeast of the town centre and just off the E4; take bus 2, 6 or 9 (Skr16).

Eating & Drinking

Greta (☎ 10 07 35; Skolgatan 62; mains Skr130-250) Upmarket, stylish Greta at the Royal Hotel offers well-prepared Swedish and international dishes, with especially good fish and seafood.

Rex (☎ 12 60 50; Rådhustorget; mains Skr100-200) This place, at the back of the town hall, offers an excellent cocktail list and a menu of favourites served up in bright and breezy surrounds.

Sushi & Wok (☎ 14 19 00; Vasaplan; lunch Skr65, meals Skr90-150) This is a sleek restaurant and bar serving good Asian dishes, including sushi.

Lottas Krog (☎ 12 95 51; Nygatan 22; mains Skr85-225) This is a friendly pub-restaurant with an extensive menu featuring something for everyone – from fish and chips or a veggie burger to chicken tandoori or even a fillet of wild boar.

Blå (☎ 13 23 00; Rådhusesplanaden 14; meals Skr75-130) This is a large, shiny, trendy place, with a nightly all-you-can-eat Thai buffet in winter and a regular menu of fashionable fare like risotto, gnocchi and baked salmon.

Unsurprisingly, Blå turns into a nightclub as the evening progresses.

Maxim (☎ 13 82 83; Kungsgatan 47; meals Skr35-65) is a budget-friendly café serving simple kebabs, burgers and the like. It's handily located near the STF hostel.

You'll also find plenty of kiosks selling burgers, pizzas and kebabs on busy Rådhustorget.

Self-caterers should go to the **Gourmet supermarket** (Renmarkstorget 5A) and you can buy alcohol from **Systembolaget** (Kungsgatan 50A).

Getting There & Away

AIR

The **airport** (☎ 71 61 00) is 4km south of the city centre. SAS and Malmö Aviation each fly to Stockholm up to seven times daily; there are also direct flights to Luleå, Kiruna and Östersund.

BOAT

There are two companies operating ferries between Umeå and Vaasa (Finland); RG Line is more passenger-oriented than Botnia Link, which is used primarily by freight trucks. A bus to the port leaves from near the tourist office an hour before RG Line's departures; see p328 for contact information.

BUS

The long-distance bus station is directly opposite the train station. Ybuss runs services south daily to Gävle and Stockholm, via the coastal towns of Sundsvall, Örnsköldsvik, Härnösand, Hudiksvall and Söderhamn.

Umeå is the main centre for **Länstrafiken i Västerbotten** (☎ 020-91 00 19; www.ltnbd.se), the regional bus network that covers over 55,000 sq km. Direct buses to Mo i Rana (Norway) run once daily, but buses going as far as Tärnaby run up to four times a day. Other daily destinations include Östersund, Skellefteå and Luleå.

TRAIN

Tågkompaniet trains leave daily from Umeå, to connect at Vännäs with the north–south trains between Stockholm and Boden and Luleå; from Boden there are connections to Kiruna and Narvik (Norway).

Getting Around

Local buses leave from Vasaplan on Skolgatan. The No 80 **Flybuss** (☎ 14 11 90) departs regularly from Vasaplan, or call **Umeå Taxi** (☎ 77 00 00) – it's about Skr125 to the airport.

SKELLEFTEÅ & AROUND

☎ 0910 / pop 73,000

Skellefteå is a very pretty town that lends itself perfectly to getting an ice-cream treat and sauntering along the riverfront park, where open-air museums make it easy to feel as if you're engaged in an educational activity instead of just relaxing. There are also a few worthy attractions in the surrounding area.

The **tourist office** (☎ 73 60 20; http://turistinfo.skelleftea.se; Trädgårdsgatan 7; ⏰ mid-Jun–mid-Aug, Mon-Fri rest of yr) is in the town centre, just off Torget, the main square. Banks are along Nygatan, and there's Internet access at the **library** (Viktoriaplatsen), in the eastern part of the town centre (follow Kanalgatan east).

Sights & Activities

All the town attractions are in the parks along the river, west of the town centre. A pleasant walk takes you to the **Nordanå park**, which plays home to the cultural and historical collections of the **Skellefteå Museum** (☎ 73 55 10; admission free) and several old houses, some of which contain handicraft shops.

West of Nordanå is **Bonnstan**, a unique housing precinct with 392 preserved 17th-century wooden houses – many of them still inhabited in summer. Further west, there is the small island of Kyrkholmen (which has an excellent café) and an early-16th-century **church**. You'll find a 13th-century wooden **Madonna** inside, as well as an adjacent storehouse for tithes (dating from 1674). Cross the river on **Lejonströmsbron**, Sweden's longest wooden bridge, built during the year 1737. Jumping off the bridge in hot weather is not strictly endorsed, but it's certainly not unheard of.

The recommended gold-mine museum, **Bergrum Boliden** (☎ 58 00 60; adult/child Skr20/10; ⏰ 10am-5pm Jun-Aug; bus 204 or 205), 35km west of Skellefteå, has interesting multimedia displays covering geology and mining.

The tiny settlement of Örträsk, around 80km west of Skellefteå (north of Norsjö), has **Norsjö Linbana** (☎ 0918-210 25; adult/child Skr250/100; ⏰ tours at 1pm midsummer–mid-Aug, by appointment rest of yr), the world's longest cable-car ride (13km). Previously used for iron-ore transport, you can now board it to glide silently over the woods and marshes. Call ahead to check departure times.

Lövånger, 50km south of the town by the E4, has a pretty medieval **church** with separate bell tower, and a well-preserved **church village**. Some houses have doors big enough to admit a horse and carriage, as well as the church-goers. Buses run roughly hourly from Skellefteå. Part of the church village is an STF hostel (see below).

Sleeping

Stiftsgården (☎ 72 57 00; stiftsgarden.skelleftea@svenskakyrkan.se; dm Skr200, s from Skr490, guesthouse s/d from Skr650/1000) Just behind the old church on Brännavägen, this idyllic, church-run place is home to the **STF hostel** and a guesthouse, both of which offer bright, comfortable rooms inside the tastefully restored, but not over-modernised, church cottages. Most rooms have a fireplace, TV and private bathroom.

Hotel & Café Viktoria (☎ 174 70; Trädgårdsgatan 8; s/d Skr660/850) Near the tourist office, this place offers simple but more than adequate rooms in a small hotel above a café.

First Hotel Statt (☎ 141 40; Statonsgatan 8; s/d from Skr1000/1200) Around the corner, and a step up in standard, is the First Hotel Statt, with good service and upmarket amenities.

Skellefteå Camping & Stugby (☎ 188 55; low/high season sites Skr90/130, d Skr245/270, cabins from Skr300) This is a large camping ground with excellent, family-friendly facilities off the E4 1km just north of town.

Eating & Drinking

Kriti (☎ 77 95 35; Kanalgatan 51; lunch Skr75, meals Skr80-210) This is a fun, friendly restaurant serving hearty, authentic Greek dishes – lots of meat and fish, plus pasta, pizza and moussaka. It has a nice bar section and outdoor seating in summer.

Monaco (☎ 177 10; Nygatan 31; meals Skr65-150) offers good pizza and pasta dishes, and the pretty, nearby **Café Lilla Mari** (☎ 391 92; Nygatan 33) offers sandwiches from Skr35, hot lunches from Skr60 and an array of sweet temptations served in a small, leafy courtyard.

You can get all the usual fast food on the main square in town. **Mr Greek** is a comfortable, dark-wood-and-brass pub next door to Kriti, with a casual setting and bar food on offer.

There's an outlet of the 'Irish' pub chain **O'Learys** (☎ 73 93 08; Kanalgatan 31) in practically every town in Norrland, but this is one of the better representatives, with a rooftop beer garden and a slightly upscale restaurant on the ground floor.

Getting There & Away

Bus 100 leaves every two hours on the Sundsvall–Umeå–Skellefteå–Luleå route (some buses continue as far north as Haparanda). Skellefteå's nearest train station is Bastuträsk and bus 27 connects there three times daily.

NORRBOTTEN

PITEÅ

☎ 0911 / pop 22,500

Northern Sweden's main beach town, Piteå, gives the impression that it would really like to be more like the equally pastel but somehow less crass French resort town Nice. Depending on your tastes, it may be the perfect holiday hangout. Piteå's warm coastal waters draw thousands of Norwegian sun soakers in summer.

Piteå has all the usual services and a **tourist office** (☎ 933 90; www.pitea.se; Bryggargatan 14; 9am-7pm Mon-Fri, 10am-4pm Sat & Sun summer, 8am-5pm Mon-Fri winter) in a pretty yellow building next to a hopping beer garden, right by the busy bus station. You can rent bikes here for Skr30 per day.

In nearby Öjebyn, 5km north of town, there is an interesting early 15th-century **church**, a **church village** with many houses perched on rocks, and a **museum** (admission free; Jun-Aug). The 16th-century **church**, off Sundsgatan in central Piteå, is one of the oldest wooden churches in Norrland. It escaped being burned by the Russians in 1721 because they were using it as their headquarters. There are several interesting wooden buildings on Storgatan, including a **rådhuset** (town hall), which now houses the **Piteå Museum** (☎ 126 15; admission free; Mon-Sat in summer).

The beachside **Pite Havsbadet** (☎ 327 00; info@pite-havsbad.se) area, about 8km south of Piteå itself and connected by frequent bus 1, is the summer destination of choice for many holidaymakers. It's huge and has an expensive **camping area** (sites Skr175), lots of **cabins** (from Skr450), an enormous and rather characterless **hotel** (summer s/d from Skr800/1000), a conference centre, restaurant, café, pool, minigolf, Imax theatre and some other family-focused activities – plus it hosts summer concerts and events – all behind a prisonlike fence with a discouraging front gate.

If that doesn't sound like your cup of tea, you may be better off in town at the central **STF Vandrarhem Piteå** (☎ 158 80; Storgatan 3; dm Skr200), in an old hospital set in a pretty park, or the more upmarket **Piteå Stadshotell** (☎ 197 00; info@piteastadshotell.com; Olof Palmesgata 1; s/d from Skr1200/1400), an elegant old hotel with lots of good facilities.

At the Stadshotell, you'll find both **Restaurang Röda Rummet** (mains Skr165-250), probably the finest restaurant in town (how does gin-flambéed reindeer fillet sound?), and the **Cockney Pub**, with a more casual atmosphere and menu to match (pasta, baked potatoes etc for less than Skr100).

Bus 100 runs between Umeå and Luleå via Piteå every one to three hours.

LULEÅ

☎ 0920 / pop 45,049

A very pretty town to approach by road, Luleå doesn't let up with the charm. It has a pedestrian thoroughfare that's pleasant to stroll along, full of shops and restaurants. The area around the marina is attractively sculpted, with parks and fountains here and there. The capital of Norrbotten, the town was granted its charter in 1621, but was later moved to its present location in 1649 because of the falling sea level (9mm per year) which is due to postglacial uplift of the land. An extensive offshore archipelago contains some 1700 large and small islands, many decorated with classic red and white Swedish summer cottages.

Information

Forex (Storgatan 46) Currency exchange.
Interpress (Storgatan 17) For newspapers and magazines.
Library (Kyrkogatan) Internet access is available free of charge in this awesome old stone building.
Naturkompaniet (Kungsgatan 17) Sells all sorts of outdoor equipment.
Tourist office (☎ 29 35 00; www.lulea.se; Storgatan 42; mid-Jun–mid-Aug, Mon-Sat rest of yr) Can help with inquiries (there is also a small office at Gammelstad).

Sights & Activities

Norrbottens Museum (☎ 24 35 00; Storgatan 2; admission free; Tue-Sun) is worth a visit just for the Sami section, but there are also exhibits about

GAMMELSTAD

During the 13th century the pope increased the number of fast days, during which only fish could be eaten. This resulted in the rich Gulf of Bothnia fishing grounds becoming of great interest to the rest of Europe, and meant profit for whoever controlled the area.

With the northern border between Sweden and Russia insecure after the Treaty of Nöteborg in 1323, the Swedish crown secured control of northern Bothnia by handing over its river valleys as fiefs to noblemen from central Sweden. In 1327, Luleå was named for the first time in connection with such an enfeoffment and, in the 1340s, the region became a parish of its own, with separate chapels in Piteå and Torneå.

By the end of the 14th century, Luleå Old Town (today's Gammelstad) was the centre of a parish stretching from the coast to the mountains along the Lule and Råne rivers. The Luleå farmers prospered during the economic boom of the Middle Ages and a stone church was built in the 15th century.

In 1621, Luleå was granted a town charter, but its development progressed very slowly. This proved to be rather fortunate because by 1649 the previously navigable channel from the archipelago had become too shallow and it was necessary to move the whole city to a better harbour, the present northern harbour of the current Luleå City. The church, the church village and the surrounding buildings became Luleå Old Town (Gammelstad).

Gammelstad church is the largest medieval church in Norrland and the only one with a reredos worthy of a cathedral and choir stalls for a whole consistory.

The church village developed because parishioners had to travel considerable distances to attend church, and required overnight accommodation. Today, Gammelstad is the largest church village in Sweden.

There are two historical walks around Gammelstad – the church walk and the town walk – which can each be done in approximately one hour.

the Swedish settlers. **Konstens Hus** (☎ 29 40 80; Smedjegatan 2; admission free; ⏰ Tue-Sun) is a modern art gallery. The neo-Gothic **Domkyrka** (⏰ Mon-Fri summer) dates from 1893 and has an unusual altarpiece.

Teknikens Hus (☎ 492201; adult/child Skr50/30; ⏰ mid-Jun-Aug, Tue-Sun rest of yr), within the university campus 4km north, is a museum with hands-on exhibitions of technological phenomena (take bus 17 or 35).

The most famous sight in Luleå is the Unesco World Heritage–listed **Gammelstad** (www.lulea.se/gammelstad), or 'Old Town', which was the medieval centre of northern Sweden. The stone church (from 1492), 424 wooden houses (where the pioneers stayed overnight on their weekend pilgrimages) and six church stables remain. Many of the buildings are still in use, but some are open to the public. Guided tours (Skr30) of the site leave from the Gammelstad **tourist office** (☎ 25 43 10; worldheritage.gammelstad@lulea.se; ⏰ 9am-6pm mid-Jun–mid-Aug, 10am-4pm Tue-Thu rest of yr) frequently between 10am and 4pm, mid-June to mid-August. The open-air museum, **Hägnan**, the old shop, **Lanthandeln**, and a nature reserve are nearby, and there are craft shops and a number of cafés in the area to rest weary sightseeing legs. Take bus 32 (hourly) from Luleå to the area.

A programme of **boat tours** of the archipelago with M/S *Laponia* and M/S *Favourite* depart from Norra Hamnen daily between June and August; typical prices are around

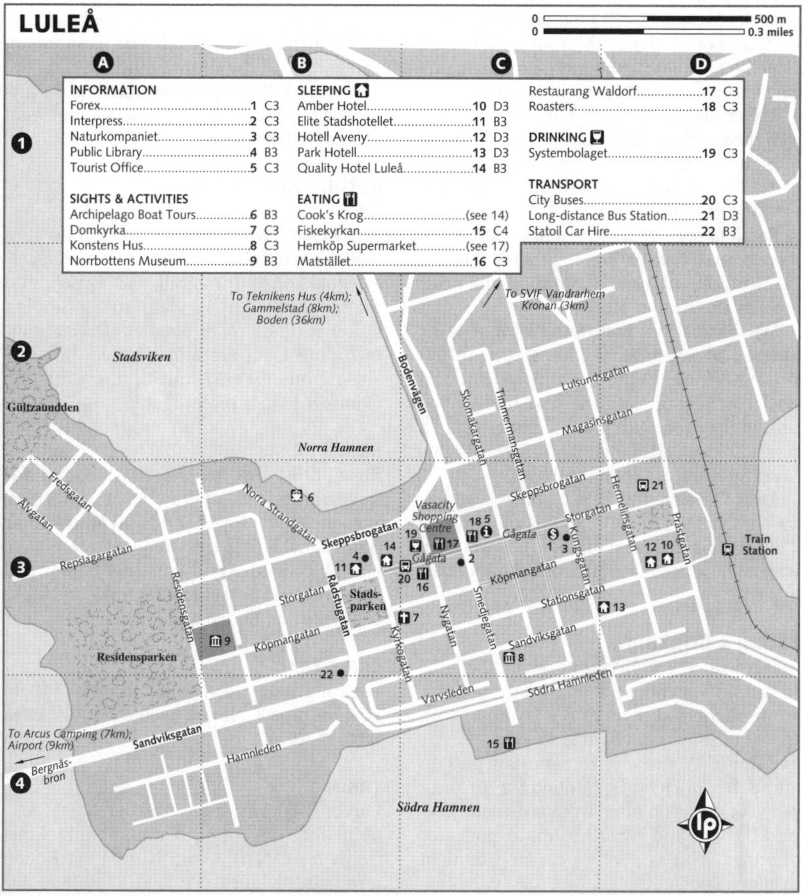

Skr150. Evening cruises are also popular; inquire at the tourist office.

Sleeping

The town's two finest hotels are neighbours at the eastern end of Storgatan – both have upmarket facilities, restaurants and bars, as well as nightclubs, and prices are identical: singles/doubles from Skr1200/1500, with the usual hefty seasonal discounts.

Elite Stadshotellet (☎ 670 00; stadhotellet@lulea.elite.se; Storgatan 15) This hotel has old-world class and elegance, and a charming glassed-in restaurant-pub called Tallkatten.

Quality Hotel Luleå (☎ 20 10 00; lulea@quality.choicehotels.se; Storgatan 17) A more modern place with business-grade rooms and a pool.

Park Hotell (☎ 21 11 49; hotellet@parkhotell.se; Kungsgatan 10; s/d from Skr490/690) One of a number of midrange options near the train station, Park Hotell offers pleasant rooms (some have private bathrooms and cost a little extra).

Amber Hotel (☎ 102 00; hotel.amber@telia.com; www.amberhotell.nu; Stationsgatan 67; s/d Skr790/950) Similar to the Hotell Aveny, but a step up, is the Amber Hotel, with rooms in a pretty, wooden guesthouse.

Hotell Aveny (☎ 22 18 20; www.hotellaveny.com; Hermelinsgatan 10; s/d Skr795/965) This hotel offers comfortable rooms at about the same price level as the Amber Hotell.

SVIF Vandrarhem Kronan/Luleå (☎ 43 40 50; www.vandrarhemmetkronan.se in Swedish; Kronan H7; dm Skr160) A bit out of the way, this year-round hostel is nevertheless the best budget option in the area, with good facilities set in a forested location. To get here, take any bus heading toward Kronanområdet.

Arcus Camping (☎ 43 54 00; camping@lulea.se; low/high season sites Skr110/140, chalets from Skr480/540) This place is 7km west of town, in a wooded, waterside setting not far from the E4 (take bus 6).

Eating & Drinking

Fiskekyrkan (☎ 22 02 01; Södra Hamnen; meals Skr50-170) In an old warehouse at the south harbour, atmospheric Fiskekyrkan is a favourite with the locals, and its not hard to see why – there's live music Wednesday to Saturday, plus an affordable lunch buffet (around Skr70) and a range of meals on offer, from fast-food cheapies (kebabs and pizzas) to more 'gourmet' offerings. This is a very popular late-night drinking spot.

Cook's Krog (☎ 21 18 00; Storgatan 17; meals Skr80-250) At the Quality Hotel, this is a cosy place specialising in steaks and other meat and fish from the charcoal grill.

Restaurang Waldorf (☎ 22 26 16; Storgatan; lunch Skr65, meals Skr85-175) Inside the Vasacity shopping centre, this is a busy place, especially at lunchtime. It has a bizarre menu featuring almost every known cuisine, from Italian to Chinese, and including Japanese and Swedish dishes.

Matstället (cnr Nygatan & Storgatan; meals Skr40-60) This bright, modern place is a cut above most fast-food outlets, with an appealing interior and a great selection of food (pizzas, kebabs, burgers, pasta, Tex-Mex and Asian dishes) at kiosk prices.

Roasters (☎ 888 40; Storgatan 43; lunch from Skr65) A good café with great coffee and an interesting menu of trendy café fare. It shares an entrance with the tourist office.

There's a **Hemköp supermarket** (Vasacity shopping centre, Storgatan); to purchase alcohol, visit nearby **Systembolaget** (Storgatan 25).

Getting There & Around

AIR

The **airport** (☎ 24 49 00) is 9km southwest of the town centre. SAS/Skyways fly regularly to Stockholm, Sundsvall and Umeå, and Malmö Aviation flies daily to Stockholm. Other airlines serve smaller destinations, including Gällivare and Kiruna. Take the airport bus (Skr45) outside the Elite and Comfort Hotels on Storgatan.

BUS

Bus 100 is one of the most useful for travellers – it runs between Haparanda, Luleå, Skellefteå, Umeå and Sundsvall at least four times daily. Bus 28 runs frequently to Boden, bus 21 goes to Arvidsjaur (via Boden and Älvsbyn), and bus 44 to Jokkmokk and on to Gällivare (via Boden and Vuollerim).

CAR & TAXI

For car rental you should call **Statoil** (☎ 186 22; Stationsgatan 30). If you need a cab, call **Luleå Taxi** (☎ 100 00).

TRAIN

Direct Tågkompaniet trains from Stockholm and Göteborg run at night only. Most trains from Narvik and Kiruna via Boden terminate at Luleå.

BODEN

☎ 0921 / pop 20,000

Until quite recently closed to foreigners, Boden is Sweden's largest military town. It's surrounded by forts, built between 1901 and 1998 to defend the country from the Russians. It has a surprisingly inviting (if small) city centre that is good for strolling.

Boden has all facilities, including a friendly **tourist office** (☎ 624 10; www.upplevboden.nu; Kungsgatan 40; Jun-Aug, Mon-Sat rest of yr), in the middle of the town centre.

Rödbergsfortet (☎ 48 30 60; tours adult/child Skr90/60; late-Jun–mid-Aug), south of the centre, is the only fort remaining from Boden's old defences. It's open to guided tours only – these run every half-hour from 10am to 4pm. **Pansarmuseet** (☎ 681 56; adult/child Skr30/free; 11am-4pm Mon-Fri, noon-4pm Sat & Sun mid-Jul–mid-Aug), 3km towards Jokkmokk, is a museum of tanks and armoured cars. On the southwestern edge of town, **Garnisonsmuséet** (☎ 683 99; Sveavägen; admission free; 11am-4pm Mon-Fri, noon-4pm Sat & Sun mid-Jul–mid-Aug) faithfully re-creates living conditions for the troops in the past.

Western Farm (☎ 151 00; www.western-farm.com; Buddbyvägen 6; adult/child Skr50/30; Jul–mid-Aug), 3km north of the station, is an unexpected find in this part of the world – it's a small Wild West town, complete with staff dressed up as native Americans and cowboys, with regular events and entertainment.

Luleå has a better selection of places to stay and eat, but there are a few options here. In the heart of town is **Quality Hotel Bodensia** (☎ 177 10; Kungsgatan 47; s/d Skr895/1130, discounted to Skr595/790), with comfortable, well-equipped rooms and good discounted rates. There's no shortage of pizzerias, grill bars and other eateries in town. **Hanssons** (☎ 544 84; Drottninggatan 9) is a pleasant café, right in the town centre, with a good selection of lunchtime snacks.

HAPARANDA

☎ 0922 / pop 4700

Haparanda was founded in 1821 as a trading town to replace Sweden's loss of Tornio (which is now in Finland) to Russia. These days the two border towns almost function as one entity (both the krona and euro are accepted at most places in both towns; Tornio is an hour ahead of Haparanda).

Haparanda's main **tourist office** (☎ 120 10; www.haparanda.se/turism; Torget 7; 8am-4pm Mon-Fri) is in Stadshotellet. There is another, joint, Haparanda–Tornio tourist office located on the 'green line'.

There are few sights in Haparanda, and the ugly church looks exactly like a grain silo, but one noteworthy attraction is the unique golf course. The **Green Zone Golf Course** (☎ 106 60) lies right on the border of the two countries, and during a full round of golf the border is crossed exactly four times. You will need to book in advance if you want to play under the midnight sun.

Full-day **boat tours** (☎ 133 95) of the archipelago sail on Wednesday and Thursday in July (adult/child Skr450/350), and include a visit to **Sandskär**, the largest island in Haparanda Skärgård National Park. Inquire at the tourist office about **white-water rafting** trips on the Kukkolaforsen rapids.

The scenic **Kukkolaforsen rapids**, on the Torneälv 15km north of Haparanda, run by at three million litres per second. In summer, you can watch locals fishing for whitefish using medieval dip nets. Also well worth a visit is the excellent tourist village here, which includes a **camping ground and cabins** (☎ 310 00; sites Skr150, 4-bed cabins from Skr500), plus a restaurant, café, fish smokehouse, saunas and a museum.

The comfortable, waterfront **STF Vandrarhem Haparanda** (☎ 61171; info@haparandavandrarhem.com; Strandgatan 26; dm from Skr120; yr-round) is nicely placed at the edge of a park close to the town centre. There's a kitchen, but meals are also available in the attached café-bar, which has a great patio open in summer.

The large, once-grand **Stadshotellet** (☎ 614 90; Torget 7; s/d from Skr1100/1400; summer budget beds Skr200) is the architectural focus of the town, and its pub-restaurant, **Gulasch Baronen**, offers a great range of reasonably priced meals (from Skr65).

Tapanis Buss (www.tapanis.se in Swedish; ☎ 129 55) runs express coaches from Tornio to Stockholm twice a week (Skr480, 15 hours). A regular local bus service connects Haparanda and Tornio. There are regional buses from Luleå (Skr121, 2½ hours, three daily) and towns further south. Daily bus 53 travels north along the border via the scenic Kukkolaforsen rapids, Övertorneå (Skr80, one to 1½ hours, three daily) and Pajala (Skr166, 3½ hours to 4½ hours, three daily), then continues west to Kiruna (Skr280, six hours, three daily).

THE INTERIOR

The northern parts of Norrbotten are dominated by forest and wandering reindeer, and there are numerous small towns to use as pit stops for further exploration.

The first major town you'll encounter if you head north from Haparanda, following the Torneälven river that marks the border with Finland, is the rather unremarkable **Övertorneå**. There's a bridge across the river to Finland here, and a tourist office by the bridge.

West of Övertorneå is **Överkalix**, a much better option. It's located at a scenic river junction on the Kalixälv, and has little hills nearby. The area is popular for **angling**; ask for permits at the small but very accommodating **tourist office** (☎ 0926-103 92; www.overkalix.se in Swedish; Storgatan 27). Take the winding road up to the top of the nearby hill, **Brännaberget**, for a fine view; there's a kiosk and little café here, as well as an amphitheatre for live music and stage productions. **Sirillus**, about a kilometre from the northern end of the bridge, is a beautiful Russian Orthodox church with an octagonal tower. **Martingården**, 5km north on road No 392, is a 17th-century **farm museum** with 'Överkalix paintings' on a cupboard and bed. There are a couple of eateries in the town, mostly grill bars.

There's a sign to mark the crossing of the Arctic Circle on road No 392. About 12km north of here is **Jockfall**, an impressive waterfall with a nearby **camping ground** (☎ 0926-600 33; sites from Skr65, cabins from Skr500), shop and a **café-restaurant** (meals from Skr45) serving locally caught salmon. This scenic area is a paradise for fishing folk.

Pressing on further north, **Pajala** (population 7300) has the world's largest **circular sundial** and a helpful **tourist office** (☎ 0978-100 15; www.pajalaturism.bd.se) located near the bus station. Other things worth a look are **Laestadius pörtet**, the mid-19th-century home of Lars Levi Laestadius, a local vicar and founder of a religious movement, and **Kengis Järnbruk**, a 17th-century iron foundry.

Bykrogen (☎ 0978-712 00; Soukolovägen 2; s/d Skr650/850) offers comfortable and newly renovated hotel rooms in Pajala. There's a wide range of food available at the attached restaurant, **Linkan** (meals Skr60-200), an attractive dining room done up in chic modern design, with a hopping evening beer garden in summer. There are a couple of other eateries in town, as well as a camping ground that doubles as a youth hostel and two more hotels. At the camping ground you can rent bikes, canoes and boats.

Bus 55 runs from Luleå to Pajala via Överkalix (Skr260, five hours, twice daily direct), while bus 53 runs between Haparanda and Kiruna (Skr280, six hours, three daily) via Övertorneå and Pajala. From Pajala, you can press on southwest to Gällivare (bus 46, Skr139, two hours, three daily), or northwest to Vittangi (bus 51 or 53, Skr106, two hours, twice daily direct), and from Vittangi you can journey through the wilderness, north to Karesuando (bus 50), or west to Kiruna (bus 53, Skr80, one hour, three daily).

JÄMTLAND

ÖSTERSUND

☎ 063 / pop 58,000

If you're lucky you'll catch a glimpse of Östersund's favourite tourist attraction, the monster called Storsjöodjuret, which usually stays hidden in the waters of Storsjön lake. Even if you're not that lucky, the town is worth a day or two of exploration. Many of its attractions lie on the adjacent island of Frösön, where there's a winter-sports centre. Östersund is also noteworthy as the starting point of the St Olavsleden pilgrim route to Trondheim in Norway.

A huge four-day music festival, Storsjöyran, is usually held over the last weekend in July, when the town centre gets sealed off in the evenings. Some 50,000 people attend the festival, but it's very expensive, with admission costing up to Skr350 per evening. Accommodation prices also shoot up at this time.

Information

The **tourist office** (☎ 1440 01; www.turist.ostersund.se; Rådhusgatan 44; ⏰ mid-Jun- Aug, 9am-5pm Mon-Fri rest of yr) is opposite the town hall; ask about the **Östersund Card** (adult/child Skr140/55), which gives discounts or free entry to many local attractions between June and mid-August.

The large library, opposite the bus station, has free Internet access. The town has all facilities, including banks, supermarkets and shops selling outdoor gear, primarily on Prästgatan.

Sights & Activities

Don't miss **Jamtli** (☎ 15 01 00; adult/child Jun-Aug Skr90/25, rest of yr Skr60/20; ⌚ Jun-Aug, Tue-Sun rest of yr), a kilometre north of the town centre. This museum is the highlight of Östersund, combining the lively exhibitions of the regional museum and a large museum village with staff wearing period clothing in summer. The regional museum exhibits the curious **Överhogdal Tapestry**, a Christian Viking relic from around 1100 which features lots of animals, people, ships and buildings (including churches). It's one of the oldest of its kind in Europe and may even predate the famous Bayeux tapestry.

The **Stadsmuseum** (☎ 12 13 24; adult/child Skr30/free; ⌚ Jun-Aug, Tue-Sun rest of yr), across the street from the tourist office, contains items of local historical, cultural and topographical interest. The adjacent **Gamla Kyrkan** is the old town church, completed in 1846. The impressive brick building with a cupola and tiled roof is the **rådhus** (town hall).

Activities include **lake cruises** (Skr65-95; ⌚ Jun-early Sep) on the old S/S *Thomée* steamship. There are also **sightseeing coach trips** (adult/child Skr100/50), **town walks** (from Skr65) and **elk-spotting safaris** (from Skr185) at least once weekly from June to August. Book any of these at the tourist office. Canoes and fishing gear can be rented from **Badhusparkens Uthyrningscenter** (☎ 13 38 38; Sjötorget) which also rents bikes (for about Skr65/250 per day/week).

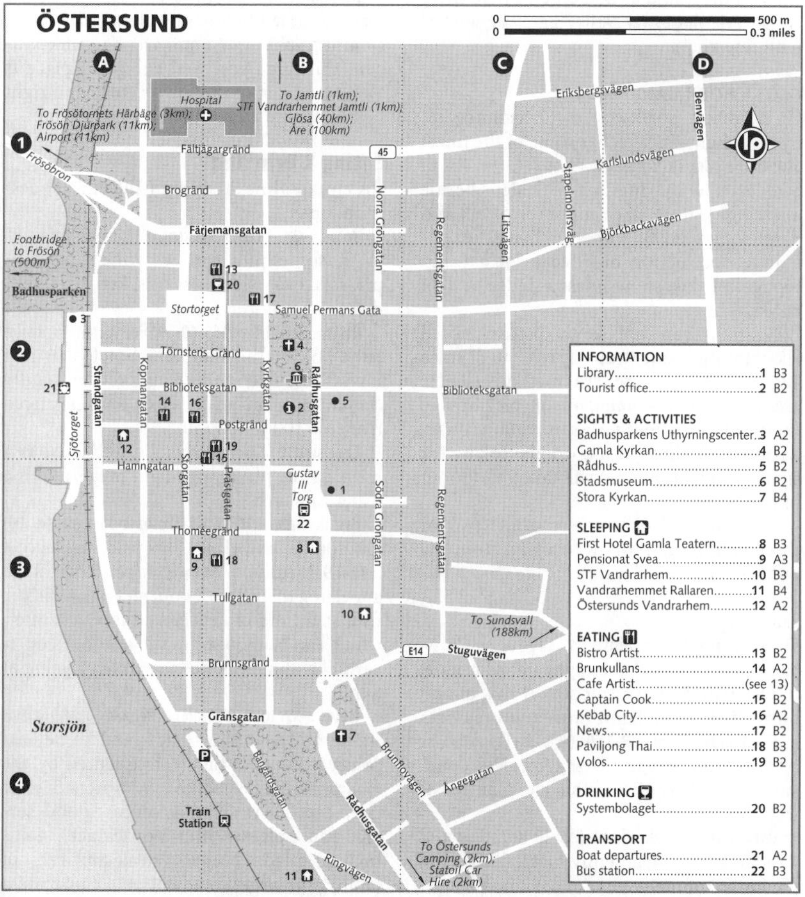

FRÖSÖN

This island is reached by road or footbridge from the middle of Östersund (the footbridge is from the pleasant Badhusparken – nearby you can rent bikes, inline skates and canoes). Just across the footbridge, outside Landstingshuset and near the Konsum supermarket, there's Sweden's northernmost **rune stone**, which commemorates the arrival of Christianity in 1050.

Also featured on the island are the animals at **Frösöns Djurpark** (☎ 51 47 43; adult/child/senior Skr140/70/100; mid-Jun–mid-Aug; bus 5) as well as the restored, late-12th-century **Frösöns kyrka** (8am-8pm in summer, Mon-Fri rest of yr; bus 3), with its distinctive separate bell tower. If you are a skier there are both slalom and nordic ski runs on the island at Östberget, where there is also a **viewing tower** (Skr10; mid-May–mid-Sep) with fine views.

GLÖSA ROCK CARVINGS

Glösa, 40km northwest of Östersund and by the Alsensjön lake, has some of the finest **Stone Age rock carvings** (admission free; 24hr) in Sweden. The carvings, on rock slabs beside a stream, feature large numbers of elk and date from 4000 BC. There's also an excellent reconstruction of a **Stone Age hut** and replicas of skis, snowshoes, a sledge and an elk-skin boat.

Nearby, there are some displays about elk-hunting using traps (prohibited since 1864) and more modern methods. There are roughly 13,000 *fängstgropar* (pit traps) in Jämtland, set in lines across migration routes; a short walk through the woods (follow the sign saying *Fornminne*) will take you to four of them.

Take bus 533 from Östersund (two or three daily), then follow the sign from the public road (500m walk).

Sleeping

STF Vandrarhemmet Jamtli (☎ 12 20 60; dm Skr140-160) You can spend the night in the middle of Östersund's big attraction at this quaint hostel, inside the Jamtli museum precinct.

STF Vandrarhem (☎ 13 91 00; Södra Gröngatan 36; dm from Skr165; late Jun–early Aug) A second, summer-only option is this clean and central hostel.

Östersunds Vandrarhem (☎ 10 10 27; Postgränd 4; dm Skr145) A conveniently located hostel in the centre of town.

Vandrarhemmet Rallaren (☎ 13 22 32; Bangårdsgatan 6; dm Skr140) This is next to the train station.

Frösötornets Härbäge (☎ 51 57 67; Utsiktsvägen 10; dm from Skr130; May-Oct) This place has hostel beds in wonderful turf-roofed huts at the viewing tower on Frösön.

Pensionat Svea (☎ 51 29 01; pensionat svea@spray.se; Storgatan 49; s/d from Skr450/550) A cosy place close to the heart of town; prices include breakfast.

First Hotel Gamla Teatern (☎ 51 16 00; bokning@gamlateatern.se; Thoméegränd 20; s/d from Skr900/1200) An elegant place in an old theatre. The budget rooms are reasonably priced in summer; better standard rooms cost Skr200 to Skr250 more.

Östersunds Camping (☎ 14 46 15; ostersundcamping@ostersund.se; sites from Skr100, hostel d from Skr280, cabins from Skr300; bus 2, 6 or 9) Off Krondikesvägen, this large and well-equipped place is 2km southeast of the town centre and right beside a large adventure swimming pool.

Eating & Drinking

Restaurants line Prästgatan, the main pedestrian street.

Volos (☎ 51 66 89; Prästgatan 38; meals Skr60-170) With something for everyone's tastes – pizzas, pasta, nachos, salads, kebabs, Greek dishes and more.

Bistro Artist (☎ 55 60 10; Prästgatan 16; mains Skr100-215) At the Radisson hotel, this is a lovely restaurant offering predominantly Italian fare, including pasta dishes priced from Skr100 to Skr140.

Café Artist The adjacent Café Artist is a more casual place, with light meals and the usual café fare.

Brunkullans (☎ 10 14 54; Postgränd 5; mains Skr100-200) Popular and classy, this place has a great late-19th-century atmosphere. There's an appealing menu, with gourmet pasta dishes, fish, steak and other classic dishes on offer, which can be enjoyed in the outdoor courtyard. The lunch buffet is excellent value at Skr70.

News (☎ 10 11 31; Samuel Permans gata 9; mains Skr110-280) News is a slick – and somewhat pricey – bar and bistro, frequented by the fashionable set who like to be watched while they eat. There's trendy décor, good service and a pleasant outdoor terrace. Mains include salads, burgers, steak and rack of lamb, plus vegetarian options. Lunch is a more casual affair, with bagels and *ciabatta* sandwiches from Skr45.

Paviljong Thai (☎ 13 00 99; Prästgatan 50B; lunch from Skr60, dishes Skr60-150) This place serves good-sized portions of great Thai cuisine, with all the favourite noodle, curry and seafood dishes on the menu.

Captain Cook (☎ 12 60 90; Hamngatan 9; meals Skr50-150) This is an Australian-themed pub with a good menu of bar food, ranging from light snacks to more hearty fare, and a selection of imported and local beer to wash it down.

Kebab City (☎ 13 70 22; Storgatan 31) Kebab City serves burger, kebab and falafel meals for around Skr50. It's one of many interchangeable kebab houses in town.

For alcohol, head to **Systembolaget** (Kyrkgatan 66, 10am-7pm Mon-Fri, 10am-3pm Sat).

Getting There & Around

The **airport** (☎ 193000) is on Frösön, 11km west of the town centre, and the airport bus leaves regularly from the bus terminal (Skr50). SAS flies several times daily to Stockholm.

The train station is a short walk south from the town centre, but the main regional bus station is central on Gustav III Torg; local buses usually run to both. Local buses 1, 3, 4, 5 and 9 go to Frösön (Skr15, or free with the Östersund Card).

Bus 45 runs south to Mora twice a day; in summer the Inlandsbanan train runs once daily, to Gällivare or Mora. Bus 156 runs west to Åre; bus 63 runs twice daily northeast to Umeå.

Direct trains run from Stockholm via Gävle, and some continue to Storlien (from where you can catch trains to Norway). You can also catch a train east to Sundsvall.

For car hire, contact **Statoil** (☎ 12 39 75; Krondikesvägen 97). Bikes and inline skates can be hired from **Badhusparkens Uthyrningscenter**, see p293. There are also **taxis** (☎ 51 72 00).

ARÅDALEN & PERSÅSEN

This seldom-visited part of Jämtland is a favourite spot for trekkers. Its lonely landscapes make you feel like you're really in the middle of absolutely nowhere – and pretty happy to be there. In spring, keep your eyes trained on the marshy ground for signs of reddish-yellow cloudberries (*hjortron*) – the rest of the year your only company may be reindeer and a few wild birds.

The rustic, 18-bed **STF Vandrarhem Arådalen** (☎ 0687-140 54; dm Skr130; mid-Jun–Aug) is an excellent hiking base and probably the best place in the area to get regional information. Ask the helpful staff about a 5km hike to **Östra Arådalens fäbod**, a well-preserved Sami farm that once produced cheese and is still in use for part of the year.

The barely-there village of Persåsen, now essentially confined to the large and modern museum/shop/hotel/restaurant complex that is the **Persåsen Hotell & STF Vandrarhem** (☎ 0643-44 55 50; www.persasen.se; Persåsen 3370, Oviken; dm from Skr130, cabins from Skr390, hotel s/d from Skr795/1195), was home to inventor John Ericsson (1803–89) for several years while he served in the military. Ericsson invented the caloric engine and the propeller while here, and the museum displays an intriguingly conflicted exhibit about his life. The shop acts as more of a crafts museum, with an astounding array of fine woodwork, textiles and other traditional handcrafted gifts from the region.

ÅRE & AROUND

☎ 0647 / pop 9692

Arguably Sweden's top mountain-sports destination, the **Åre area** (www.skistar.com/are) has 45 ski lifts that serve some 100 pistes and 1000 vertical metres of skiable slopes, including a superb 6.5km downhill run. The skiing season is from November to mid-May, but conditions are best from February, when daylight hours increase, and Easter is a hugely busy time. Unfortunately, Åre gets far too busy in winter and you can hardly move, let alone park your car. **Duved** is quieter.

The Åre **tourist office** (☎ 177 20) is in the train station. Most facilities are around the main square, which you reach by walking through the park opposite the station.

There are also excellent cross-country tracks in the area, and other winter activities, such as dogsledding, snowmobile safaris and sleigh rides (which are horse- or reindeer-drawn!) are available too. Åre also offers great summer outdoor recreation, including hiking, kayaking, rafting and fishing, as well as good mountain biking. The area west of Åre is popular among fell-walkers and there is a network of STF wilderness huts and lodges here for enthusiasts.

Sleeping & Eating

Things fill up quickly in winter, so it's best to book accommodation and skiing packages via **Åre Resor** (☎ 177 00; reservations@areresort.se).

Åre Camping (☎ 500 54; sites from Skr150) is a good summer option. **Park Villan** (☎ 177 33; Parkvägen 6; dm Skr170), the yellow house in the park opposite the train station, offers good backpacker accommodation outside of the ski season. The **STF Vandrarhem Åre** (☎ 301 38; brattlandsgarden@spray.se; dm Skr130) is 8km east of Åre; daily buses connect it to town.

Not all hotels stay open in summer, but those that do offer great bargains. The huge ski lodge and resort **Åre Fjällby** (☎ 136 00; reception@arefjallby.com; summer self-contained apt from Skr550), for example, often has off-season specials and discounts.

Like the hotels, the majority of restaurants are closed in summer, but there are still some very good choices, primarily on the main square. Typical Swedish fast food is available at **Åre Kiosk & Grill**, but nearby **Liten Krog** (dishes around Skr70) and **Werséns** (dishes around Skr70) have more style. **Villa Tottebo** (mains from Skr145), opposite the train station, is a classy establishment open year-round, and there's an inviting bar upstairs with a stellar view. There's a Konsum supermarket on the square.

Getting There & Away

Regional bus 156 runs from Östersund and connects Åre to the nearby winter-sports centre of Duved (much quieter and more family-oriented than Åre). Regular trains between Stockholm and Storlien, via Östersund, stop at Åre. Storlien is the terminus for SJ trains; change here for Norwegian trains to Hell and Trondheim.

STORLIEN & AROUND

☎ 0647

The area west of Åre is justly popular among fell-walkers, particularly around Sylarna, one of the finest mountains for trekking and climbing in Sweden. There's a very good network of STF wilderness huts and lodges along the trails, with meals available in most of them. Reservations aren't possible, but you're guaranteed a place to sleep (though it may be on the floor). Most hikers in this area seek out the **Jämtland Triangle** just north of Sylarna; ask at the Storlien tourist office or any STF lodge for details.

Storlien, near the Norwegian border, has a popular downhill skiing area (the Swedish king himself has a winter chalet here), as well as a supermarket and a **tourist office** (☎ 705 70; www.storlienfjallen.com in Swedish; 🕑 summer) at the train station.

The excellent **STF Vandrarhem Storvallen/Storlien** (☎ 700 50; dm Skr150-170), 600m off the E14 and about 5km east of Storlien, offers top-quality accommodation, good meals, friendly service and good hiking advice.

Le Ski (mains Skr50-150), in the village at Hotel Storlien, has a daily buffet, plus a good menu of reasonably priced meals like pizza, meatballs, salmon and steak.

HÄRJEDALEN

This is the least populated of Sweden's counties, but that just means fewer people to get in the way of its spectacular views. Härjedalen is a wilderness of forest, lake and mountain in the west, and forest, lake and marsh in the east. The rugged mountain scenery in the far northwest is breathtaking. There aren't many towns in the region worth visiting, but, after all, the reason you come to a place like this is to get far away from city life.

FUNÄSDALEN & AROUND

☎ 0684 / pop 2000

Dominated by the impressive peak **Funäsdalsberget**, Funäsdalen and the surrounding area is a favourite among hikers, skiers and other outdoor sports enthusiasts.

The **tourist office** (☎ 164 10; www.funasdalsfjall.se; Rörosvägen 30; 🕑 mid-Jun- mid-Aug, Mon-Fri rest of yr) is at the Fjällmuseum, and all the main tourist facilities are on Rörosvägen, the main road through town.

Sights & Activities

Härjedalens Fjällmuseum (☎ 164 10; adult/child Skr60/free) has displays covering the Sami, local farmers and miners, and includes the **Fornminnesparken** outdoor section. A **golf course**, one of Sweden's finest, can be found in Ljusnedal, just east of town.

There's an office of the forest agency **Naturum** (☎ 242 00; 🕑 Jun-Aug & Dec-Apr) 15km south at Tännäs Fiskecentrum, with information on the **Rogen Nature Reserve**, including details about the moraine ridges and the local musk ox. Excellent hiking can be found in the reserve, but it's better accessed from Grövelsjön in Dalarna. **Högvålen**, about 30km south of Tännäs on road No 311, is Sweden's highest village (830m).

Ramundberget, over 20km north of Funäsdalen, and **Tänndalen** (12km west), have excellent downhill and nordic **ski areas**. There are 24 ski lifts and 75 runs, and the 300km of cross-country trails constitute the longest ski system in the world. The profile of the mountain **Stor-Mittåkläppen** (1212m), as seen from Hågnvallen (4km east of Ramundberget), is most impressive.

Ljungdalen, about 40km north of Funäsdalen, is close to **Helagsfjället** (1797m), the highest peak in the area. There's good hiking and skiing here; the 12km one-way hike from Kläppen (north of Ljungdalen) to the STF cabin at Helags goes via some old **summer farms** and is reasonably easy. There is also a small **ski area** as well as a **tourist office** (☎ 0687-200 79).

Sleeping & Eating

There are a few STF hostels in the area, including one at **Ljungdalen** (☎ 0687-203 64; Dunsjögården; dm Skr120) and **Tänndalen/Skarvruet** (☎ 0684-221 11; Skavruets Fjällhotell; dm Skr145-175). Both are open year-round.

Hotel Funäsdalen (☎ 214 30; info@hotell-funasdalen.se; summer hostel beds Skr175, s/d Skr550/800) Off the main road in Funäsdalen is this large, well-equipped hotel, with a range of accommodation options plus a good restaurant.

Wärdshuset Gyllene Bocken (☎ 210 90; info@gyllenebocken.se; summer s/d from Skr450/700) This is a lovely old inn opposite the fine golf course in Ljusnedal, with a good restaurant attached. Rooms with private facilities are also available. The staff can organise golf for guests, plus other activities in the area.

Veras Stekhus & Pub (☎ 215 30; lunch around Skr85, mains Skr145-215) In the heart of Funäsdalen, near the tourist office, this is a relatively upmarket steakhouse with a great view from its outdoor terrace and a comprehensive menu of steak, reindeer and other meats (though there's not much to please vegetarians).

Not far away is **Café Loftet** (☎ 291 49; 🕑 lunch), with good café fare such as baguettes, quiche and salads from Skr30, plus more of that scenic panorama from its veranda.

Getting There & Away

Härjedalingen (www.harjedalingen.se in Swedish) runs buses between Stockholm and Funäsdalen (Skr380), via Gävle and Järvsö, several days a week; on Saturday buses also connect with Tänndalen and Ramundberget (Skr400). Contact the tourist office for information and bookings.

Local bus 622 and 623 run from Funäsdalen to Ramundberget and Tänndalen, respectively; there are also daily ski buses during winter. There is not a direct connection with Ljungdalen; take the once-daily bus 613 from Åsarna (which has an Inlandsbanan train station), about 100km east. Bus 164 runs from Funäsdalen via Åsarna to Östersund once or twice daily.

LAPPLAND

KARESUANDO (GÁRRASAVVON)

☎ 0981 / pop 350

This is the northernmost village in Sweden, and it feels that way. Directly across the bridge from the Finnish town of Kaaresuvanto, the tiny village is more interesting for what it takes to get there than for anything you can find in it. The main attractions here are natural ones: from late May to mid-July, there's a 90% chance of observing the midnight sun, while in winter temperatures drop to –50°C.

There's a fairly professional **tourist office** (☎ 202 05; www.karesuando.com in Swedish; 🕑 May-Sep) on the bridge to Finland. Inside there's regional information, souvenirs and a café serving drinks and cakes. There are no banks in the village, but there are a couple of convenience shops and fuel stations; eating options are very limited.

Items of interest in Karesuando are an **octagonal school** (1993); **Vita Huset** (🕑 8am-4pm), a folk museum with mainly Norwegian items from WWII; and **Sámiid Viessu**, a Sami art and handicraft exhibition and museum.

Treriksröset, about 100km northwest of the village, is the point where Norway, Sweden and Finland meet; ask the tourist office for details of boats leaving from Kilpisjärvi (on the Finnish side of the border) to visit this hard-to-access area.

There's a small **STF Vandrarhem** (☎ 203 30; dm Skr140; 🕑 mid-May–mid-Sep) up here, about a kilometre before you reach the bridge

ARCTIC PHENOMENA

Aurora Borealis

There are few sights as mesmerising as an undulating aurora. Although these appear in many forms – pillars, streaks, wisps and haloes of vibrating light – they're most memorable when they take the form of pale curtains, apparently wafting on a gentle breeze. Most often, the Arctic aurora appears faint green, light yellow or rose-coloured, but in periods of extreme activity it can change to bright yellow or crimson.

The visible aurora borealis, or northern lights *(norrsken)*, are caused by streams of charged particles from the sun and the solar winds, which are diverted by the earth's magnetic field towards the polar regions. Because the field curves downward in a halo surrounding the magnetic poles, the charged particles are drawn earthward here. Their interaction with atoms in the upper atmosphere (about 160km above the surface) releases the energy creating the visible aurora (in the southern hemisphere, the corresponding phenomenon is called the aurora australis). During periods of high activity, a single auroral storm can produce a trillion watts of electricity with a current of one million amps.

Although science dismisses it as imagination, most people report that the aurora is often accompanied by a crackling or whirring sound. Don't feel unbalanced if you hear it – that's the sort of sound you'd expect to hear from such a dramatic display, and if it's an illusion, it's a very convincing one. The best time of year to catch the northern lights in Sweden is from October to March, although you may well see them as early as August in the far north.

Midnight Sun & Polar Night

Because the earth is tilted on its axis, the polar regions are constantly facing the sun at their respective summer solstices, and are tilted away from it in the winter. The Arctic and Antarctic Circles, at latitudes 66°32'N and 66°32'S respectively, are the southern and northern limits of constant daylight on the longest day of the year.

The northern one-seventh of Sweden lies north of the Arctic Circle, but even in central Sweden, the summer sun is never far below the horizon. Between late May and mid-August, nowhere north of Stockholm experiences true darkness; in Umeå, for example, the first stars aren't visible until mid-August. Although many visitors initially find it difficult to sleep while the sun is shining brightly outside, most people get used to it.

Conversely, winters in the far north are dark and bitterly cold, with only a few hours of twilight to break the long polar nights. During this period, some people suffer from SAD (seasonal affective disorder) syndrome, which occurs when they're deprived of the vitamin D provided by sunlight. Its effects may be minimised by taking supplements of vitamin D (as found in cod liver oil) or with special solar spectrum light bulbs.

and tourist office. It's operated jointly with the **Hotel Karesuando** (☎ 203 30; s/d Skr550/650), across the road, with en suite rooms and a restaurant serving good, simple meals.

KIRUNA (GIRON)

☎ 0980 / pop 23,407

There's not much to Kiruna, but it's the major town this far north – in fact it's the northernmost town in Sweden. The surrounding district includes Sweden's highest peak, **Kebnekaise** (2111m), and some of the country's best national parks and hiking routes; see p301 for suggestions on tackling them.

This far north, the midnight sun lasts from 31 May to 14 July, and there's a bluish darkness throughout December and the New Year period. Many people speak Finnish, and Samis are a small minority – there are local radio stations that broadcast in both languages.

The helpful and efficient **tourist office** (☎ 188 80; www.kiruna.se, www.lappland.se; Lars Janssonsgatan 17; 8.30am-9pm Mon-Fri, 8.30am-6pm Sat & Sun Jun-Aug, Mon-Sat rest of yr) is next to the Scandic Hotel and has loads of excellent brochures, as well as a row of computers for Internet access. Staff can arrange various activities, including rafting, dogsledding and snow scooter trips, although these can be quite expensive.

Banks and other facilities can be found along Lars Janssonsgatan, and the library,

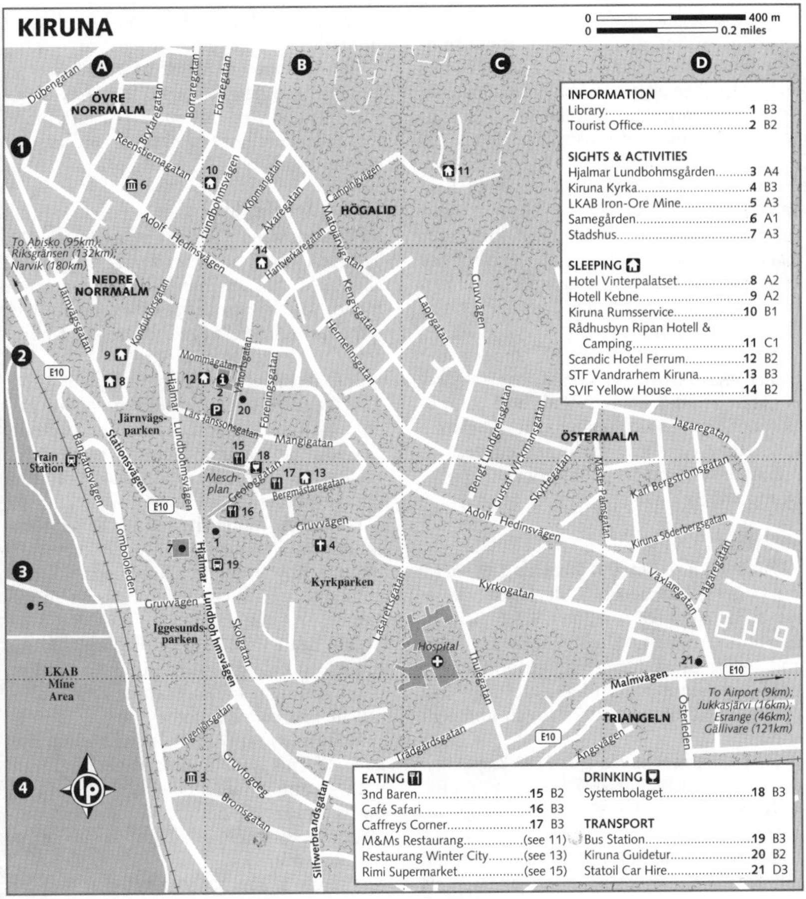

behind the bus station, offers free Internet access.

Sights & Activities

A visit to the depths of the **LKAB iron-ore mine**, 540m underground, is recommended – many of the facts about this place are mind-boggling. Tours depart from the tourist office regularly from mid-June to mid-August (adult/child Skr220/50), though tours in English happen only a few times a week; make bookings through the tourist office.

Kiruna kyrka (Gruvvägen; 10am-9pm summer) looks like a huge Sami *kåta* (hut), and it's particularly pretty against a snowy backdrop. Another landmark, firmly at the opposite end of the aesthetics spectrum, is the **Stadshus** (town hall; ☎ 705 21; Hjalmar Lundbohmsvägen; 9am-6pm), which, despite its grim façade, is actually very nice inside and has a free slide show on the hour, and free guided tours.

Hjalmar Lundbohmsgården (☎ 701 10; Ingenjörsgatan 1; adult/child Skr30/10; 8am or 10am-6pm Mon-Fri summer) is the former home of the first LKAB director and is now a museum. **Samegården** (☎ 170 29; Brytaregatan 14; adult/child Skr20/free; 10am-5pm Mon-Fri summer) has displays about Sami culture and an expensive handicrafts shop.

As well as the famous Ice Hotel, tiny **Jukkasjärvi**, 18km east of Kiruna, is home to a **church** (8am-10pm summer), which has a modern Sami painting behind the altar. Near the church is **Gárdi** (adult/child Skr60/30; tours 10am-6pm mid-Jun–mid-Aug), a reindeer yard that you can tour with a Sami guide to learn about reindeer farming and Sami culture. Also in this area is the **Hembygdsgård**, a typical open-air homestead museum. Regular bus 501 runs between Kiruna and Jukkasjärvi (Skr26, 30 minutes, several daily).

Some 23km further out is the space base **Esrange**, which researches the northern lights *(norrsken)* – see p298. Detailed four-hour **tours** (adult/child Skr390/200) of the facility are offered to enthusiasts in summer, but must be arranged in advance; inquire at the Kiruna tourist office.

Held in the last week of January, the **Kiruna Snow Festival** (www.kiruna.com/snowfestival) is based around a snow-sculpting competition. The tradition started in 1985 as a space-themed snow-sculpture contest to celebrate the launching of a rocket *(Viking)* from Esrange.

Sleeping

Rådhusbyn Ripan Hotell & Camping (☎ 630 00; ripan@kiruna.se; Campingvägen 5; sites Skr100, hotel s/d from Skr650/750, 4-bed cabins from Skr650;) In the northern part of town, this is a large and well-equipped camping ground with a good restaurant-pub. It has hotel-standard chalets in addition to its caravan and tent sites.

STF Vandrarhem Kiruna (☎ 171 95; Bergmästaregatan 7; dm Skr150-180, s/d from Skr290/380; yr-round) This central hostel has good facilities and an adjacent Chinese restaurant.

SVIF Yellow House (☎ 137 50; yellowhouse@mbox301.swipnet.se; Hantverkaregatan 25; dm from Skr150, s/d Skr300/400) There are more excellent facilities here, including a sauna, kitchen and laundry, a TV in each room, and a nice, quiet enclosed garden.

Kiruna Rumsservice (☎ 195 60; krs@kiruna.se; Hjalmar Lundbohmsvägen 53; d from Skr350) Another good option, especially for small groups. It offers rooms and apartments with a varying number of beds. Breakfast is additional.

Scandic Hotel Ferrum (☎ 39 86 00; ferrum@scandic-hotels.com; Lars Janssonsgatan 15; s/d Skr1212/1410, discounted to Skr690/840) Near the tourist office, this is a town landmark. It offers the finest rooms in town and has excellent facilities, including a café, restaurant and nightclub on the premises.

Hotel Vinterpalatset (☎ 677 70; vinterp@kiruna.se; Järnvägsgatan 18; s/d from Skr750/900) This pretty hotel is near Hotel Kebne and has pleasant upmarket rooms.

Hotell Kebne (☎ 681 80; info@hotellkebne.com; Konduktörsgatan 7; s/d from Skr950/1200) Ask about seasonal and weekend specials at this place, which has comfortable rooms and a good central location.

Eating & Drinking

M&Ms Restaurang (Campingvägen; meals Skr95-225). This restaurant at the camping ground (of all places) has an interesting and creative menu, which includes tortillas, beef fillets, reindeer, salmon, veggie dishes and burgers. The lunch buffet is Skr75.

3nd Baren (Föreningsgatan 11; meals Skr85-240) This is a popular, moderately priced restaurant and lively drinking spot of an evening. Try local specialities, such as reindeer or arctic char (fish); there are also vegetarian selections.

Restaurang Winter City (☎ 109 00; Bergmästaregatan 7; lunch Skr65, meals Skr55-140) This eatery, at the STF hostel, offers a lunch special, plus a range of pizzas, as well as classic Chinese and other Asian dishes.

Café Safari (☎ 174 60; Geologsgatan 4) This is the nicest café in town with good coffee, cakes and light meals, such as sandwiches, quiche and baked potatoes.

Caffreys Corner (☎ 611 11; Bergmästaregatan; meals Skr75-185) This is an unremarkable restaurant with a comprehensive menu, but the cosy bar is an inviting place, and there's an outdoor terrace where you can take advantage of good weather.

There's a **Rimi supermarket** (Föreningsgatan) near 3nd Baren, and the **Systembolaget** (Geologsgatan 7) is also central.

Getting There & Around

The small **airport** (☎ 680 00), 7km east of the town, has two to three daily nonstop flights to Stockholm with SAS, and to Umeå (weekdays only) with Skyways. The **airport bus** (☎ 156 90) connects with most flights (Skr45).

Regional buses to and from the **bus station** (Hjalmar Lundbohmsvägen), opposite the Stadshus, serve all major settlements around Norrbotten. Bus 10 runs twice daily to Gällivare (Skr121) and Luleå (Skr260), and 92 goes two to four times daily to Nikkaluokta (Skr71) for the Kebnekaise trail head. To reach Karesuando and Finland, take bus 50 (Skr162, not Saturday). Bus 91 runs two or

THE ICE HOTEL

If you're up this far north at the right time of year, don't miss the chance to visit to the fabulous **Ice Hotel** (www.icehotel.com), a unique and super-cool experience – if you'll pardon the pun.

Every winter at Jukkasjärvi, 18km east of Kiruna, an amazing structure is built from hundreds of tonnes of ice, taken from the frozen local river. This custom-built 'igloo' has a chapel (popular for weddings – giving new meaning to the expression 'cold feet'!), plus a bar – you can enjoy a drink (preferably vodka) from a glass made purely of ice – and exhibitions of beautiful ice sculpture by international artists. It also has 50 'hotel rooms' where guests can stay, on beds covered with reindeer skins and inside sleeping bags guaranteed to keep you warm despite the –5°C temperatures (and in winter that's nothing, outside the hotel it can be as low as –30°C).

There are numerous activities for guests to pursue here, and staff can arrange pursuits such as snowmobile safaris, skiing, ice-fishing or dogsledding.

All this can be quite pricey for a budget traveller, but anyone can go to the hotel for a **day visit** (adult/child Skr100/50), which is highly recommended. If you do visit, ask the bartender where the stereo is being kept – chances are it's in the fridge, as it's warmer there!

Even after the Ice Hotel has melted away in summer, visitors can still experience a little of the magic. Inside a giant freezer warehouse, called the **Ice Hotel Art Center**, at a temperature of –5°C, there are a few of the Ice Hotel features: a bar, ice sculptures and even small igloos where guests can stay overnight. Day visitors are welcome (the entry fee is the same as in winter and warm clothing is supplied). A recent exhibition featured sculptures based on the artwork of John Bauer, who illustrated many of the classic Swedish fairy tales.

Rooms inside the hotel in winter cost from Skr2800 for two. There are also stylish hotel rooms (heated – and *not* made of ice), three-bed cabins with skylights enabling you to watch the northern lights in winter, and chalets (with kitchen) sleeping up to four. These are all available year-round – summer prices are quite reasonable. See the website for more details and a list of seasonal rates.

three times daily to Riksgränsen via Abisko (Skr130).

Trains connect Kiruna with Luleå, Stockholm and Narvik (Norway). Trains to Narvik call at Abisko and Riksgränsen.

Contact **Statoil** (☎ 143 65; Växlaregatan 20) for car hire.

Standard bicycles are available for hire from **Kiruna Guidetur** (☎ 811 10; Vänortsgatan) for Skr75/295 per day/week. Mountain bikes are also available (Skr125/495).

ABISKO (ABESKOVVU)

☎ 0980

An exceptionally inviting and rewarding place to hike, the 75-sq-km **Abisko National Park** spreads out from the southern shore of scenic Lake Torneträsk. It's less rugged than either Sarek or Padjelanta, and easier to get to, being well served by trains, buses and the scenic mountain motorway between Kiruna to Narvik.

Abisko is the driest place in Sweden, with only 300mm of rainfall per year, which creates an interesting landscape, quite distinct from its surroundings. One of the most renowned mountain profiles in Lappland, **Lapporten**, can be seen from Abisko.

Sights & Activities

The popular **Kungsleden** trail follows the Abiskojåkka valley and day trips of 10km or 20km are no problem from Abisko. Kungsleden extends 450km south from Abisko to Hemavan, with STF huts serving most of the trail. Other hikes include the overnight trip to the STF hut at **Kårsavagge** (west of Abisko, 15km each way), the four-hour return trip to rock formations at **Kärkevagge**, with **Rissájávrre** the 'Sulphur Lake', and a four-hour return hike to **Paddus**, a former Sami sacrificial site, 4km south of Abisko Östra train station. There's also a route around **Abisko canyon** and a 39km-long **Navvy Trail** to Riksgränsen, alongside the railway line. Use the map *Fjällkartan BD6* (available at the STF lodge or at Naturum). For more information on the Kungsleden trail see p49.

Naturum (☎ 401 77; ⏲ Jul–mid-Sep) has an office and exhibition space next to STF Abisko

Turiststation; it provides some good information to help you prepare for the hikes described above, plus many others.

The **Linbana chair lift** (one-way/return from Skr70/95) takes you to 900m on **Njulla** (1169m), where there's a **café** (9.30am-3pm summer).

In Björkliden, 8km northwest of Abisko, you will find **Hotell Fjället** (641 00; www.bjorkliden.com) which offers various summer and winter activities, including hiking and caving (spelunking). The STF also organises great hikes for groups of all sizes; both places offer outdoor gear for hire or for sale.

The unique **Björklidens golf course** (0980-641 00; info@bjorkliden.com; 8am-4:30pm Apr-Sep), which was rated in the Top 100 by *Golf World* magazine, is the world's northernmost golf course – and as a result has a fairly short season (it is covered in snow for most of the year).

Sleeping & Eating

Abisko Fjällturer (401 03; www.abisko.net; dm per person Skr150) Just behind the town, this is a backpacker's delight. The small hostel has basic comfortable accommodation and a wonderful wooden sauna, but the treat is in the reasonably priced activities on offer, especially in winter. Owner, Tomas, and his father keep a large team of sledge dogs; one package includes a night's accommodation plus the chance to drive your own sled, pulled by dogs, for about 10km. There are also very popular week-long sled trips (around Skr8000), which include all of your meals and accommodation – you will need to book very early for these. During summer you can take mountain walks with the dogs. To find the place, follow signs to the 'Dog Hostel – Vandrarhem'.

STF Abisko Turiststation (402 00; info@abisko.nu, www.abisko.nu; dm from Skr190) This is another excellent option, kept to the usual high STF standards. Trekking gear can be hired here, there's a variety of guided tours, a shop with basic groceries, and breakfast/lunch/dinner available for Skr70/75/205. A packed lunch costs Skr70, and there's a pub in the basement that often has live music.

Hotell Fjället (641 00; info@bkorkliden.com; sites from Skr75, cabins from Skr600, s/d from Skr650/1000) This is a well-equipped resort about 8km northwest of Abisko in Björkliden, offering camping and cabin accommodation, as well as rooms in a large hotel. There are loads of facilities, including a restaurant, bar, equipment rental (ski gear in winter, bicycles and golf, fishing and hiking gear in summer), organised activities, and even a nine-hole golf course. Prices vary wildly depending on the season, and it's best to book ahead at any time of year.

Låktatjåkko (641 00; dm from Skr425) Nine kilometres further west of Hotell Fjället this is the highest place to stay in Sweden, at 1228m, and you'll have to hike into the hills to reach it. It has good facilities for weary hikers, such as a sauna and restaurant, and breakfast is included in the tariff.

Self-service **STF huts** (bed Skr160-220, nonmembers additional Skr50) along Kungsleden are spread at 10km to 20km intervals between Abisko and Kvikkjokk; you'll need a sleeping bag. Day visitors/campers are charged Skr25/45.

If you can invest the time, there's a great highly recommended 100km trek from Abisko to Nikkaluokta that runs via the STF lodge **Kebnekaise Fjällstation** (0980-550 00 info@kebnekaise.stfturist.se; dm spring/summer from Skr190/280; Mar-Apr & mid-Jun–mid-Sep). Meals are available here, and guided tours to the summit of Kebnekaise are offered.

Lapporten Stormarknad (8am-10pm), in Abisko village, is a grocery store that also carries a range of outdoor supplies, such as batteries, candles, bug spray and basic camping gear.

Getting There & Away

In addition to trains (stations at Abisko Östra and Abisko Turiststation) between Luleå and Narvik, bus 91 runs from Kiruna to Abisko (Skr997, one hour 20 minutes).

RIKSGRÄNSEN

0980

One of the most spectacular drives in this part of the country goes between Abisko village and Riksgränsen, a microscopic frontier settlement (Riksgränsen translates as 'National Border'). If you have a hankering to ski into Norway and back at midnight in June, this is the place to do it. Rental of downhill gear costs from Skr210 per day and day lift passes start around Skr250.

There's not much to the tiny settlement here, but you can visit Sven Hörnell's gallery to view his **wilderness photography exhibition** (431 11; admission free; Feb-Sep, show 3pm daily Jun-Aug). There's an excellent audiovisua show; the commentary is in Swedish, but you don't have to understand it to appreciate the stunning photography.

The historical **Navvy Trail** walkway follows the railway line and takes you to Abisko (39km) or Rombaksbotn, Norway (15km). **Katterjåkk Turiststation** (☎ 431 08; katterjakk@kiruna.frilufts.se; summer dm from Skr170; ⌚ Feb-Sep) is a well-run hostel 2km east of Riksgränsen. **Riksgränsen** (☎ 400 80; info@riksgransen.nu; summer/winter accommodation from Skr425/800 per person) dominates the hillside, this is a large resort which is popular with skiers in winter and converts to an 'alpine spa' retreat in summer. There are lots of organised wilderness activities in both seasons (also open to non-guests), and you can rent outdoor gear, including mountain bikes and canoes. There's also a café and restaurant here.

Getting There & Away

From Kiruna, bus 91 (Skr130, two hours, two or three daily) goes to Riksgränsen, via Abisko. Riksgränsen is the last train station in Sweden before the train rushes through tunnels and mountain scenery back to sea level at Narvik in Norway; three daily trains run on the Luleå–Kiruna–Narvik route.

GÄLLIVARE (VÁHTJER)

☎ 0970 / pop 19,500

Gällivare and its northern twin, Malmberget, are surrounded by forest and dwarfed by the bald Dundret hill. After Kiruna, Malmberget is the second-largest iron-ore mine in Sweden.

The helpful **tourist office** (☎ 166 60; www.gellivare.se; Storgatan 16; Internet access per 15 min Skr10; ⌚ 8am-6pm daily mid-Jun–mid-Aug; Mon-Fri rest of yr) is near the church in the town's centre, and staff can organise a number of activities and wilderness excursions. The town has all the main facilities, including banks and supermarkets, primarily on Storgatan. The **library** (Hantverkargatan) also has free Internet access.

Stora Sjöfallet National Park

This wild area of mountains and lakes lies over 115km west of Gällivare, but transport links are good. At the eastern end of the park, you can cross the Stora Lulevatten lake on the STF ferry to Saltoluokta lodge, and climb **Lulep Gierkav** (1139m) for the best views.

There's an interesting **Sami church** and inexpensive **handicraft outlet** at Saltoluokta, and the **Kungsleden trail** runs north and south from here. **Stora Sjöfallet** is now dry, due to the hydroelectric schemes, and many of the local lakes have artificial shorelines. Take the bus to the end of the road at the Sami village **Ritsem**, where there's an STF lodge, and you can cross by ferry to the northern end of the **Padjelantaleden trail**. Ask for details, maps and road conditions at the tourist office, or at any STF in the area.

Other Sights

The **Hembygdsmuseum** (admission free; ⌚ 11am-3.30pm daily mid-Jun–mid-Aug, Mon-Fri rest of yr), above the tourist office, has a cute collection of local artefacts. The 1882 **church** (⌚ summer) is also worth a look. The old church near the train station dates from 1755.

The **hembygdsområde** (⌚ summer), by the camping ground, has pioneer and Sami huts in a small open-air museum.

Dundret (821m) is a nature reserve with excellent views, and you can see the midnight sun here from 2 June to 12 July. In winter there are four nordic courses and 10 ski runs of varying difficulty, and the mountaintop resort rents out gear and organises numerous activities.

In Malmberget, 5km north of Gällivare, **Kåkstan** (admission free) is a historical 'shanty town' museum village, dating from the 1888 iron-ore rush. Contact the Gällivare tourist office for details of the **LKAB iron-ore mine tour** (Skr150; mid-Jul–late Aug). And if you like that, you'll love the **Gruvmuseum** (⌚ 2-5pm Tue-Thu mid-Jul–late Aug), covering 250 years of mining. Bus 1 to Malmberget departs from directly opposite the Gällivare church.

The Gällivare tourist office also runs tours of the **Aitik copper mine** (adult/child Skr150/75; ⌚ Mon-Fri late Jun-early Aug) if there's enough demand.

Sleeping & Eating

STF Vandrarhem (☎ 143 80; Barnhemsvägen 2; dm Skr150-160; closed May & Oct) This rural retreat is just across the footbridges from the train station; bike hire is available, and there's a good cycle path leading here from the town centre.

Quality Hotel Gällivare (☎ 550 20; gallivare@quality.choicehotels.se; Lasarettsgatan 1; s/d Skr1090/1450, discounted Skr690/890) This is a large, modern hotel opposite the train station. It has comfortable rooms and a good restaurant-pub.

Dundret (☎ 145 60; info@dundret.se; summer s/d Skr750/895, cabins from Skr550) At the top of Dundret hill, this is a large resort offering hotel and cabin accommodation, as well as a restaurant, outdoor gear rental and lots of activities – especially in winter. Prices are considerably higher in winter.

Gällivare Camping (☎ 100 10; Hembygdsområdet; sites Skr100, 2- & 4-bed cabins from Skr300; Jun-early Sep) This campground occupies a lovely spot beside the river; the cabins are set up more like apartments, with excellent, modern facilities. A short, well-marked footpath leads to an ICA supermarket.

Dining choices are pretty limited. Your best bet for anything other than fast food is the **Vassara Pub** (Lasarettsgatan 1; lunch Skr60-80, meals Skr70-220) inside the Quality Hotel, offering good-value lunch options and a decent selection of à la carte dishes.

The eastern part of Storgatan is home to two good restaurants: at No 17, **New Delhi** (☎ 169 60; lunch around Skr65) serves a range of Indian meals, while **Restaurang Peking** (☎ 176 85; lunch around Skr65) at No 21, has Chinese and Thai dishes on offer.

Getting There & Away

Regional buses depart from the train station. Bus 45 runs daily to Östersund (via Jokkmokk and Arvidsjaur, bus 93 serves Ritsem and Kungsleden in Stora Sjöfallet National Park (mid-June to mid-September only), buses 10 and 52 go to Kiruna, and bus 44 runs to Jokkmokk and Luleå.

Tågkompaniet (☎ 0771-44 41 11; www.tagkompaniet.se in Swedish) trains come from Luleå and Stockholm (sometimes changing at Boden), and from Narvik in Norway. More exotic is the **Inlandsbanan** (☎ 0771-53 53 53; www.inlandsbanan.se), which terminates at Gällivare.

JOKKMOKK (DÁLVADDIS)

☎ 0971 / pop 5633

Jokkmokk is the home of perhaps the best museum devoted to Sami culture in the entire country, and the village is worth a stop just for that. Jokkmokk also serves as a base for those visiting the **Laponia World Heritage site**; ask for information on the site at the tourist office or the Ájtte museum (below). Just north of the Arctic Circle, it can be reached by Inlandsbanan. Started as a Sami market and mission, Jokkmokk has been home (since 1605) to the **Sami winter fair** – a three-day event which attracts some 30,000 people and starts on the first Thursday in February – during which you can shop seriously for Sami *duodji* (handicraft).

The **tourist office** (☎ 121 40; www.turism.jokkmokk.se; Stortorget 4; 10am-6pm Mon-Fri yr-round, plus 10am-4pm Sat & Sun mid-Jun–mid-Aug) can help with information, and has Internet access. There are banks and other facilities in the small town centre.

For daily weather reports and forecasts, call ☎ 0980-113 50.

Sights & Activities

The welcoming and illuminating **Ájtte Museum** (☎ 170 70; Kyrkogatan 3; adult/child Skr50/free; 9am-6pm mid-Jun–mid-Aug, 10am-4pm Mon-Fri rest of yr) is the highlight of a visit to Jokkmokk; it gives the most thorough introduction to Sami culture anywhere in Sweden, including Sami dress, silverware and an interesting display of 400-year-old shamans' drums. Look out for replicas of sacrificial sites, and a diagram explaining the significance of various reindeer entrails. There are extensive notes in English. The museum also has a very practical section, with information on Lappland's mountain areas, including detailed maps, slides, videos and a reference library.

Naturfoto (☎ 557 65; Jun-Aug), at the main Klockartorget intersection, exhibits and sells work by local wilderness photographer, Edvin Nilsson. The beautiful **wooden church** (Storgatan; Jun-Aug), near Naturfoto, is worth a visit if you have time. The 'old' octagonal church on Hantverkargatan has been rebuilt, as the original was burned down in 1972.

Jokkmokks Fjällträdgård (adult/child Skr25/free), by the lake, introduces mountain trees and other local flora, and there's a **homestead museum** just across the road. **Jokkmokks Stencenter**, with lapidary and mineral exhibits, is reached from Borgargatan. These attractions are all open daily in summer, but keep irregular hours the rest of the year; check with the tourist office for details.

About 7km south of Jokkmokk you will cross the **Arctic Circle** on road No 45. There is a café and campsite at the site that awards cute but corny certificates to those interested in having proof that they have travelled this far north.

HIKING

Kvikkjokk (Huhttán), around 100km west of Jokkmokk, is on the **Kungsleden** and **Padjelantaleden** trails. There are several fantastic day walks from the village, including climbs to **Sjnjerak** (809m, three hours return), a steeper ascent of **Prinskullen** (749m, three hours return), and **Nammatj** (662m, two hours, but this hike requires taking a boat to the quay on the southern side of Tarraänto).

The best hiking in this area, at least for experienced and well-outfitted trekkers, is in **Sarek National Park** (☎ 0920-962 00). Sarek is full of sharp peaks and huge glaciers, and its largest valley, Rapadalen, is lush with birch and willow trees. The Kungsleden trail dips briefly into Sarek, at the southeastern corner of the park. Trekking here is certainly not for the casual walker, and hikers must be prepared for very rugged conditions. Major trails are often washed out or in poor repair, and the extremes of terrain make for volatile weather conditions. There are no tourist facilities within the park, so be sure to check with an STF lodge or the National Park office before setting out. For more information on hiking in these regions see p48.

Sleeping & Eating

Jokkmokks Camping Center (☎ 123 70; camping center@jokkmokk.com; sites Skr120, d hostel rooms Skr300, cabins from Skr510) This is 3km southeast of town and is popular in summer.

Gula Villan (☎ 550 26; Stationsgatan; s/d from Skr150/225) This is the diminutive yellow guesthouse with the sign advertising 'rum' as you exit the train station; rooms are simple but adequate.

STF Vandrarhem Åsgård (☎ 559 77; asgard@jokkmokkhostel.com; Åsgatan 20; dm Skr120-160; yr-round) The STF hostel is a clean, comfortable place behind the tourist office, surrounded by green lawns and trees.

Hotell Gästis (☎ 100 12; Herrevägen 1; s/d from Skr700/900) This place has very pleasant rooms, although it doesn't look too promising from the outside. There's also a good restaurant here, with lunch specials and à la carte dinners.

There is an unexpected surprise at the park located near the tourist office: a caravan where you can actually buy authentic takeaway **Laotian food** (around Skr55 for lunch).

> **SAMI CHURCH VILLAGES**
>
> Lappstaden, in Arvidsjaur, is the best-preserved Sami church village and has been at its present location since the 1820s, although the first church was built nearby in 1607. Sami people and settlers stayed overnight in such villages during major religious festivals, when they had probably travelled a long way from home. The buildings in Lappstaden are in distinct areas – one for church cottages and settlers' stables, another for market traders' cottages and a third for Forest Lapps' tents and storehouses. Forest Lapps were Sami people who lived in forest regions – they didn't keep reindeer like the Mountain Lapps, but were hunters and also fisherfolk.

At the **Ájtte museum restaurant** (lunch specials Skr65-80) you can try unusual regional dishes, local fish or perhaps a reindeer sandwich.

Café Piano (☎ 104 00; Porjusvägen 4; dinner mains Skr80-100) This is another good choice, with a grand piano inside, a large garden seating area outside and an extensive menu that features pasta and wok meals (around Skr65 at lunch).

For self-caterers, there's a **Konsum supermarket** (Storgatan) in town.

Getting There & Away

Buses arrive and leave from the bus station on Klockarvägen. Buses 44 and 45 run twice daily to and from Gällivare (Skr97, three to six hours), and bus 45 goes to and from Arvidsjaur once a day (Skr146, two to three hours). Bus 94 runs to Kvikkjokk (Skr121, three hours) twice daily.

Inlandsbanan trains stop in Jokkmokk. For main-line trains, take bus 94 to Murjek via Vuollerim (Skr171, up to six times daily) or bus 44 bus to Boden and Luleå (Skr162). Another alternative is bus 36 to Älvsbyn via Bredsel (Skr130), where you can visit the amazing 82m Storforsen, Europe's greatest cataract falls (best May–June).

ARVIDSJAUR

☎ 0960 /pop 6948

The small settlement of Arvidsjaur, on Inlandsbanan, was established as a Sami marketplace. The **tourist office** (☎ 175 00; www.arvidsjaur.se/turism/; Östra Skolgatan 18C; 9.30-6pm summer,

8.30am-4.30pm Mon-Fri rest of yr) is behind the park by the main square, and can provide useful information for seeing the area. There are facilities such as banks and supermarkets on Storgatan, the main road through town.

Lappstaden (admission free; 10am-7pm), a well-preserved Sami church village, contains almost 100 buildings as well as forestry and reindeer-breeding concerns. Guided tours cost Skr25 and leave at 5pm (July only). From early July to early August, an old **steam train** makes return evening trips to Slagnäs on Friday, and Moskosel on Saturday. Also in summer is the opportunity for **white-water rafting** (adult/child Skr350/175) on the nearby Piteälven.

Arvidsjaur is bustling in winter, when test drivers from around Europe put cars through their paces in the tough weather conditions, and there are excellent cold-weather activities available, including dog-sledding. Inquire at the tourist office for more details of all activities.

Friendly, cosy **Lappugglans Turistviste** (124 13; Västra Skolgatan 9; per person Skr150) and the small, stylish **Rallaren** (070-682 32 84; Stationsgatan 4; per person Skr150; summer only), both near the train station, have excellent hostel accommodation.

Kaffestugan (126 00; Storgatan 21) is a popular café by the main square, with good daily lunch specials (Skr60), plus an assortment of cakes, sandwiches and light meals. There's also **Athena** (105 95; Storgatan 10; mains Skr65-90), offering pastas, salads and grill dishes.

The daily bus between Gällivare and Östersund (No 45) stops at the bus station on Storgatan. Bus 200 runs daily between Skellefteå and Bodø (Norway) via Arvidsjaur. The Inlandsbanan train can take you north to Gällivare via Jokkmokk, or south to Mora via Östersund.

SORSELE

0952 / pop 2981

Sleepy Sorsele, on Inlandsbanan, has the small but sincere **Inlandsbanemuseet** (adult/child Skr20/free; summer) at the train station – a must for train enthusiasts. The adjoining **tourist office** (140 90; turist@vindelalven.se; 9am-5pm Mon-Fri, noon-5pm Sat & Sun), at the Inlandsbanemuseet, has details of local activities, including fishing and canoe tours. Internet access is available (Skr10 per 10 minutes). Sorsele has all facilities, including a bank, supermarket and public library (with Internet access).

The local **Hembygdsgård** (1-8pm Jun-Aug) has a good café with home-made food. Also out this way is the **STF Vandrarhem** (100 48; dm Skr120, cabins per person Skr140), 500m west of the train station. Reception is at the nearby **camping ground** (101 24; sites Skr75, 4-bed cabins from Skr295;), which has bikes and canoes for hire.

The Inlandsbanan train stops here, and bus 45 runs daily on the Gällivare–Jokkmokk–Arvidsjaur–Sorsele–Storuman–Östersund route.

TÄRNABY & AROUND

0954

A skiing capital in the Swedish lake district, Tärnaby, 125km northwest of Storuman on

SAMI CULTURE & TRADITIONS

Sami life was originally based on hunting and fishing, but, sometime during the 16th century, the majority of reindeer were domesticated and the hunting economy transformed into a nomadic herding economy. While reindeer still figure prominently in Sami life, only about 16% of the Sami people are still directly involved in reindeer herding and transport by reindeer sled, and only a handful of traditionalists continue to lead a truly nomadic lifestyle.

A major identifying element of Sami culture is the *joik* (or *yoik*). This is a rhythmic poem composed for a specific person to describe their innate nature, and is considered to be owned by the person it describes. Other traditional elements of the culture include the use of folk medicine, shamanism, artistic pursuits (especially woodcarving and silver smithing) and striving for ecological harmony.

The Sami national dress is the only genuine folk dress that's still in casual use in Sweden, and you'll readily see it on the streets of Jokkmokk, especially during the winter fair. Each district has its own distinct fashion, but all include a highly decorated and embroidered combination of red and blue felt shirts or frocks, trousers or skirts, and boots and hats. On special occasions, the women's dress is topped off with a crown of pearls and a garland of silk hair ribbons.

the E12, has gorgeous views of the nearby lakes. The village has most facilities and a **tourist office** (☎ 104 50; www.tarnaby.se; 🕑 8.30am-7pm Mon-Fri & 10am-6pm Sat & Sun mid-Jun–mid-Aug, weekdays only rest of yr). The tourist office dispenses coffee and cakes, stamps, fish cards and snow-scooter licenses. It also organises various talks and tours in summer, including Sami culture evenings, fishing, hiking, and cave and glacier tours.

Mountain biking is a warm-weather activity growing in popularity in the region. There's a very popular winter **ski area** here, and many of Sweden's champion skiers hail from the area – ask at the tourist office if the planned museum dedicated to them and their achievements has opened. Take the time to hike to the top of **Laxfjället** (820m) for great views of the lakes.

Samegården (☎ 104 40; Tärnafors; adult/child Skr30/15; 🕑 Mon-Fri summer), 5km east of the tourist office, has exhibits about the Sami and their lifestyle.

Hemavan, 18km north of Tärnaby, has a larger **ski area** and a summer **chairlift** (adult/child one way Skr65/50, return Skr75/60; 🕑 10am-5pm Jul-Aug), plus basic facilities. The southern entry to **Kungsleden** (Sweden's finest hiking route) is here, but most people doing just this section start in Ammarnäs.

The **STF Vandrarhem Tärnaby/Åkerlundska gården** (☎ 300 02; dm Skr160-180, s/d from Skr320; 🕑 Mar-May & mid-Jun–Sep) is a wonderful place, perched halfway up the hillside with killer views across the valley, comfortable bunks in cosy, rustic rooms, and modern facilities. There's a restaurant on the ground floor that serves meals, including a vast breakfast buffet for around Skr65.

The friendly **Hotell Sånninggården** (☎ 330 00; bjarne@sanninggarden.com; B&B/full board per person from Skr395/695), 6km north of Hemavan, has good-value, cosy accommodation, and an acclaimed **restaurant** (lunch buffet Skr99, dinner mains Skr130-260) serving regional specialities like herb-fried reindeer in Madeira, and *ripa* baked in berry sauce. If you're out this way, it's well worth stopping in for a unique meal – the extensive menu includes well-prepared elk, game birds, Arctic char and even the occasional bear. There are vegetarian options for those uncomfortable with consuming the local wildlife, and the magnificent desserts will please everyone – try the delectable arctic raspberry and cloudberry parfait.

UMNÄS

☎ 0951

Slightly off the beaten trail is this quirky tourist 'village'. **Umnäs Skoterhotellet** (☎ 520 20; frihet.i.lapland@telia.com; dm Skr150, s/d Skr650/850) is a friendly place, about 6km off the scenic E12 road (also known as the Blå Vägen, or Blue Hwy), 64km northwest of Storuman. There's a hotel with bar and **restaurant** (meals Skr35 to Skr185), a hostel and self-contained cabins are available, plus there's the opportunity for some great activities in the vicinity – including guided or self-guided snowmobile safaris (best February to April). But the main attraction on the premises is the unique **snow scooter museum** (admission Skr40), which contains some 70 vehicles from the 1960s right up to the present, as well as a separate **museum** (admission Skr20) of local history.

The **Silent Way** (☎ 520 43; www.silent-way.com) is also based in Umnäs, near the hotel (and run by another family member). This company offers guided **dogsledding tours** from December to May, with various trips possible, from a half-day excursion to a 16-day safari. Appropriate cold-weather gear can be rented, and food and accommodation in cabins is included in the cost. These trips are extremely popular, so book well ahead. The website has comprehensive information, as well as options, schedules and prices.

Buses between Storuman and Tärnaby stop at Slussfors on the E12, about 8km from Umnäs.

STORUMAN

☎ 0951 / pop 6595

Storuman, on Inlandsbanan, has an interesting location at the southern end of the 56km-long lake with which it shares a name. The very scenic **Strandvägen** road links the centre with a series of islands, including **Luspholmen**, with a small outdoor museum. Follow the road Utsiktsvägen (across the E12 from the train station) for 1.5km to the viewpoint at **Utsikten**; sunsets over the lake are magnificent. Sweden's largest **wooden church** is at **Stensele**, about 3km from Storuman towards Umeå on the E12.

The **tourist office** (☎ 333 70; entrelappland@swipnet.se; Järnvägsgatan 13; 🕑 Jun-Aug, Mon-Fri rest of yr) is at Hotell Luspen, near the station, and the town has most facilities.

Hotell Luspen (☎ 333 80; luspenhotell@swipnet.se; hostel s/d from Skr200/300, hotel s/d Skr600/720) is a friendly place by the train station, offering accommodation to suit most budgets. The helpful tourist office is also here, and you can rent bikes for exploration for Skr60 per day.

Eating options in the village are basically limited to fast food. There's an ICA and a Konsum supermarket on the main drag (E12), both open daily.

Bus 45 runs every day on the Gällivare–Jokkmokk–Arvidsjaur–Sorsele–Storuman–Östersund route. Buses between Mo i Rana (Norway) and Umeå also run daily, via Storuman and Tärnaby, and the **Lapplandspilen** (☎ 333 70) buses run overnight three times weekly from Hemavan to Stockholm, via Storuman. In summer, Inlandsbanan trains stop here.

FATMOMAKKE & AROUND

The southern areas of Lappland have some of the finest mountain scenery in Sweden, particularly around the mountain **Marsfjället** (1590m); you can hike up and back from Fatmomakke, but it's a long day (28km, 10 hours). The trek through the mountains to the village **Kittelfjäll** (where the scenery is even more impressive), via the wilderness cabin **Blerikstugan**, is best over two days (32km).

The late-18th-century **Sami church village** at Fatmomakke has an exhibition, *kåtas* (huts) and other old buildings. Silver shamanistic Sami jewellery was found here in 1981.

Klimpfjäll is about 20km west from here, and **Saxnäs** – a small village set in a scenic spot between lakes, and considered a paradise for fishing folk – is about 25km east.

The journey from Fatmomakke into Jämtland, close to the Norwegian border, offers some stunning scenery (mountains, plateaus and small lakeside settlements), and is highly recommended – although it's only possible with your own transport.

Directory

CONTENTS

ACCOMMODATION

Accommodation in Sweden is generally of a high standard; you'd have to be very unlucky to stay in a dump! Our Sleeping entries are categorised by price and then listed by preference, with favourites appearing first. 'Budget' options cost Skr500 or under, 'Midrange' options range from Skr500 to Skr1100, and 'Top End' places come in at over Skr1100.

Cabins & Chalets

Swedes are all for the outdoors, and cabins and chalets *(stugor)* are everywhere, either on campsites or scattered liberally through the countryside. Most contain four beds, with two- and six-person cabins sometimes on offer too. They're particularly good value for small groups and families, costing between Skr300 and Skr800 per night. In peak summer season, many are rented out by the week (generally for between Skr800 and Skr5000).

The cheapest cabins are simple, with bunk beds and little else (you share the

PRACTICALITIES

- Use the metric system for weights and measures.
- Watch out for the Swedish word *mil*, which Swedes may translate into English as 'mile' – a Swedish *mil* is actually 10km!
- Some shops quote prices followed by '/hg', which means per 100g.
- Use the PAL system for video recorders and players.
- Plug appliances into the round, continental-style two-pin sockets for (220V, 50Hz AC) power supply.
- Domestic newspapers (including the Göteborg and Stockholm dailies and evening tabloids) are Swedish-only. A good selection of English-language imports is sold (for a price) at major transport terminals, Press Stop, Pressbyrån and tobacconists – even in small towns.
- On the Internet, Sweden Globe (www.swedentimes.com) has English-language articles about Sweden.
- Radio Sweden International (www.sr.se/rs) broadcasts programmes nationally and to Europe on 1179kHz (89.6FM in Stockholm): check the website for a full list of frequencies and schedules.
- Try National Swedish Radio (Sveriges Radio) on channel P2 (96.2FM in Stockholm) for classical music and opera, and channel P3 (99.3FM in Stockholm but variable around the country) for pop and rock.
- National TV channels TV1 and TV2 broadcast mainly about local issues, in Swedish only. TV3, TV4 and TV5 have lots of shows and films in English.

bathroom and kitchen facilities with campers or other cabin users). Chalets are generally fully equipped with their own kitchen, bathroom and even living room with TV. Bring your own linen and clean up yourself to save cleaning fees of around Skr500.

Pick up the brochure *Campsites & Cottages in Sweden: Greater Freedom* from any tourist office, or check out the website www.stuga.nu.

Camping

Camping is wildly popular in Sweden, and there are hundreds of grounds all over the country. Most open between May and August only. The majority are extremely busy family holiday spots with fantastic facilities, like shops, restaurants, pools, playgrounds, canoe or bike rentals, minigolf, kitchens and laundry facilities. Lots of them also have cabins or chalets.

Camping prices vary (according to the season and facilities) from Skr90 for a small site at a basic ground, to Skr240 for a large site at a multistarred ground. Slightly cheaper rates may be available if you're a solo hiker or cyclist. If you're on the move, look out for grounds offering a Quick Stop reduction: where you get a discount if you arrive after 9pm and leave by 9am the following day.

You must have a Camping Card Scandinavia to stay at Swedish campsites. Apply for one at least a month before your journey by writing to **Sveriges Camping & Stugföretagares Riksorganisation** (fax 0522-64 24 30; info@scr.se; Box 255, SE-45117 Uddevalla) or fill in the form on the website www.camping.se; otherwise pick up a temporary card at any Swedish campsite. The card itself is free, but the annual validation sticker costs Skr100 and is stuck on your card at the first campsite you visit. One card covers the whole family.

Primus and Sievert supply propane gas for camping stoves, and containers are available at petrol stations. *T-sprit Röd* (methylated spirit; denatured alcohol) for Trangia stoves can be bought at petrol stations and *Fotogen* (paraffin; kerosene) is sold at paint shops such as Fargtema and Spektrum.

See p54 for information on free camping in Sweden.

Hostels

Sweden has well over 450 hostels *(vandrarhem)*, usually with excellent facilities. Outside major cities, hostels aren't backpacker hangouts but are used as holiday accommodation by Swedish families, couples or retired people. A related oddity is the frequent absence of dormitories, meaning you often have to rent out a room rather than a bed. Some hostels also have singles and doubles with en suite bathrooms that are almost of hotel quality, for very reasonable rates. About 50% of hostels open year-round; many others open from May to September, while some open only from mid-June to mid-August.

Be warned, Swedish hostels are virtually impossible to enter outside reception opening times, and these hours are frustratingly short (except in Stockholm and Göteborg): generally between 5pm and 7pm, occasionally also between 8am and 10am. The secret is to prebook by telephone – reservations are highly recommended in any case, as hostels fill up fast.

Sleeping bags are usually allowed if you have a sheet and pillowcase; bring your own, or hire them (Skr50 to Skr65). Breakfast is sometimes available (Skr45 to Skr65). Before leaving, you must clean up after yourself; cleaning materials are provided. Most hostels are affiliated with either the STF or SVIF (see below), but there are other non affiliated hostels also with high standards of accommodation.

STF

Some 315 hostels are affiliated with **Svenska Turistföreningen** (STF; ☎ 08-463 21 00; www.svenskaturistforeningen.se), part of Hostelling International (HI). STF produces a free detailed guide to its hostels, but the text is in Swedish only (the symbols are easy to understand). All hostel details on its website are in English.

Holders of HI cards can stay at any STF hostels for between Skr28 and Skr100; children under 16 pay about half price. Nonmembers can pay Skr45 extra, or join up at hostels (see p314 for membership costs). In this book we quote prices at STF hostels for members.

All STF hostels have kitchens.

SVIF

Around 191 hostels belong to STF's 'rival', **Sveriges Vandrarhem i Förening** (SVIF; ☎ 0413-55 34 50; www.svif.se). No membership is required and rates are similar to those of STF hostels. Most SVIF hostels have kitchens, but you sometimes need your own utensils. Pick up the free guide at tourist offices or SVIF hostels.

Hotels

Private, family-owned hotels with individuality are few and far between as the big hotel chains (with comfortable but often rather bland rooms) monopolise hotel accommodation options.

Sweden is unusual in that hotel prices tend to *fall* at weekends and in summer (except in touristy coastal towns), sometimes by as much as 40% or 50%. Rates usually include a breakfast buffet. Ask at tourist offices for the free booklet *Hotels in Sweden* or visit the website www.hotelsinsweden.net.

Travellers on a budget should investigate the two cheapest hotel chains, both with flat rates for rooms. **Formule 1** (www.hotelformule1.com) has four hotels, in Göteborg, Jönköping, Malmö and Stockholm; the small but functional rooms (Skr330) have shared facilities and can sleep up to three people. **Ibis** (www.ibishotel.com) hotels offer simple rooms (Skr600 to Skr700) with private facilities. Breakfast is additional at both chains.

The following hotels are the most common midrange and top-end chains:

Best Western (www.bestwestern.se in Swedish)
Choice (www.choicehotels.se)
Countryside (www.countrysidehotels.se)
Ditt Hotell (www.ditthotell.se)
Elite (www.elite.se)
First (www.firsthotels.com)
Radisson SAS (www.radisson.com)
Scandic (www.scandic-hotels.com)
Sweden Hotels (www.swedenhotels.se in Swedish)

Radisson SAS and Elite are the most luxurious. The top-end Countryside Hotels chain has the most characterful rooms, in castles, mansions, monasteries and spas.

Mountain Huts & Lodges

Most mountain huts *(fjällstugor)* and lodges *(fjällstationer)* in Sweden are owned by STF. There are about 45 huts and nine mountain lodges, usually spaced at 15km to 25km intervals, primarily in the Lappland region. Reception hours are quite long as staff members are always on site. Basic provisions are sold at many huts and all lodges, and many lodges have hiking equipment for hire.

STF huts have cooking and toilet facilities (none have showers, but some offer saunas). Bring your own sleeping bag. Huts are staffed during March and April and also from late June to early or mid-September. You can't book a bed in advance, but no-one is ever turned away (although in the peak of summer this may mean you sleep on a mattress on the floor). Charges for STF or HI members vary depending on the season, and range from Skr190 to Skr275 (children Skr75), with the highest charges on northern Kungsleden. Nonmembers pay Skr100 extra. You can also pitch a tent in the mountains, but if you camp near STF huts you are requested to pay a service charge (Skr60/80 for members/nonmembers), which gives you access to any services the hut may offer (such as kitchen and bathroom facilities).

At the excellent STF mountain lodges, accommodation standards range from hostel (with cooking facilities) to hotel (with full- or half-board options), and overnight prices range from Skr200 to around Skr800. There are often guided activities on offer for guests, plus they usually have a restaurant and shop.

Private Rooms, B&Bs & Farmhouse Accommodation

Many tourist offices have lists of rooms in private houses, which is a great way of finding well-priced accommodation and getting to meet Swedish people. Singles doubles average Skr200/300.

Along the motorways (primarily in the south), you may see *'Rum'* or *'Rum & frukost'* signs, indicating inexpensive informal accommodation (*frukost* means that breakfast is included) from around Skr200 to Skr300 per person. Kitchen facilities are often available and those who bring their own sheets or sleeping bags may get a discount.

The organisation **Bo på Lantgård** (☎ 035-12 78 70; www.bopalantgard.org) publishes a free annual booklet on farmhouse accommodation (B&B and self-catering), available from any tourist office. B&B prices average about Skr275 per person in a double room. Prices for self-catering range from Skr400 to Skr850 per night, depending on the time of year, facilities and number of beds.

BUSINESS HOURS

General opening hours are listed below, but there are variations (particularly in the largest cities where opening hours may be longer).

Banks Open 9.30am to 3pm; some city branches open 9am to 5pm or 6pm once a week.
Department stores Open 10am to 7pm Monday to Saturday (sometimes later), noon to 4pm Sunday.
Government offices Open 9am to 5pm Monday to Friday.
Museums Generally museums have short opening hours, even in July and August; see individual destinations for more details.
Restaurants Open for lunch from 11.30am to 2pm, and dinner between 6pm and 10pm; often closed on Sundays and/or Mondays.
Shops Open 9am to 6pm Monday to Friday, 9am to 1pm Saturday.
Supermarkets Open 8am or 9am to 7pm or 9pm.
Systembolaget (state-owned alcohol stores) Open 10am to 6pm Monday to Friday, 10am to 2pm Saturday, sometimes with extended hours on Thursday and Friday evenings.
Tourist offices Usually open daily Midsummer to mid-August, 9am to 5pm Monday to Friday mid-August to Midsummer; however, see individual destinations for specific hours.

CHILDREN

If you've got kids, you're guaranteed an easy ride in Sweden as it's very family-centric. In general, get the kids involved in your travel plans: if they've helped to work out where you're going, chances are they'll still be interested when you arrive! Remember, don't try to cram too much in. Lonely Planet's *Travel with Children,* by Cathy Lanigan, is a useful source of information.

Practicalities

Hotels and other accommodation options often have 'family rooms' that sleep up to two adults and two children for little more than the price of a regular double. Campsites have excellent facilities and are overrun with ecstatic, energetic children. They get very busy in summer, so book tent sites or cabins well in advance.

Highchairs and cots (cribs) are standard in most restaurants and hotels. Swedish supermarkets offer a relatively wide choice of baby food, infant formulas, soy and cow's milk, disposable nappies (diapers) etc. There are nappy-changing facilities in most toilets (men's and women's) and breast-feeding in public is not an issue.

Car rental firms hire out children's safety seats at a nominal cost, but it's essential that you book them in advance. Long-distance ferries and trains, hotels and some restaurants may even have play areas for children.

Sights & Activities

Swedes treat children very well, and domestic tourism is largely organised around children's interests. Many museums have a kids section with toys, hands-on displays and activities, and there are numerous public parks for kids, plus theme parks, water parks and so on. Most attractions allow free admission for young children – up to about seven years of age – and half-price (or substantially discounted) admission for those up to about 16. Family tickets are often available.

Liseberg amusement park (p204) in Göteborg is Sweden's largest; other major places for kids include Junibacken, Skansen and Gröna Lund Tivoli (p76) in Stockholm; Göteborg's Universeum (p204) and Astrid Lindgrens Värld (p132) in Vimmerby.

CLIMATE CHARTS

Sweden has a mostly cool temperate climate, but the southern quarter of the country is

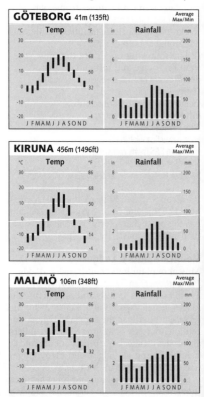

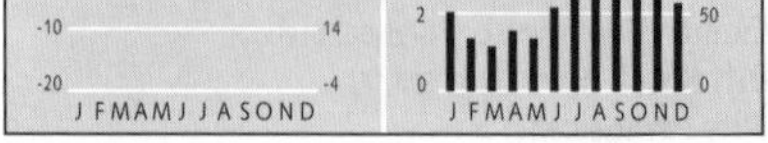

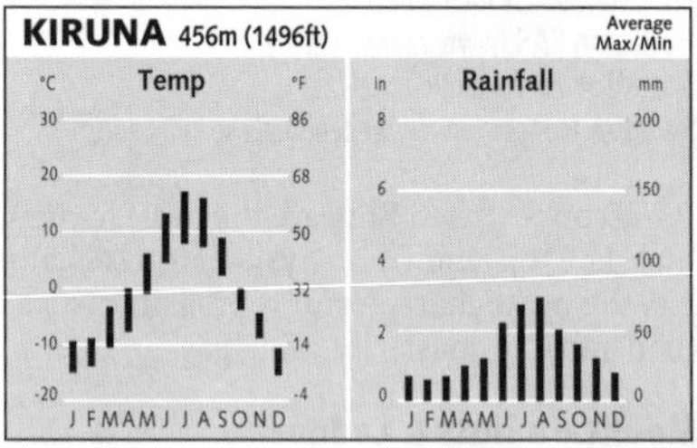

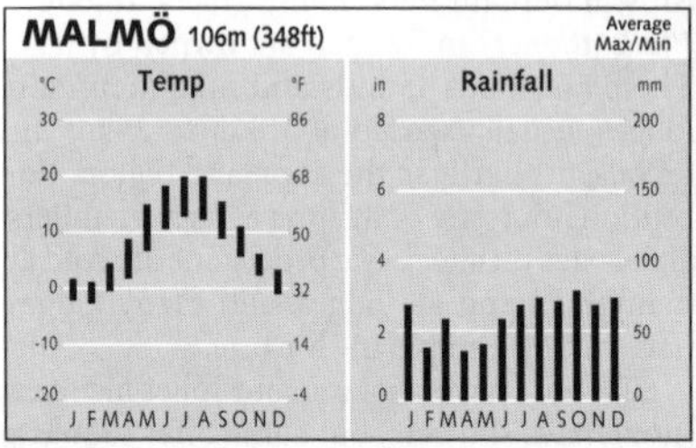

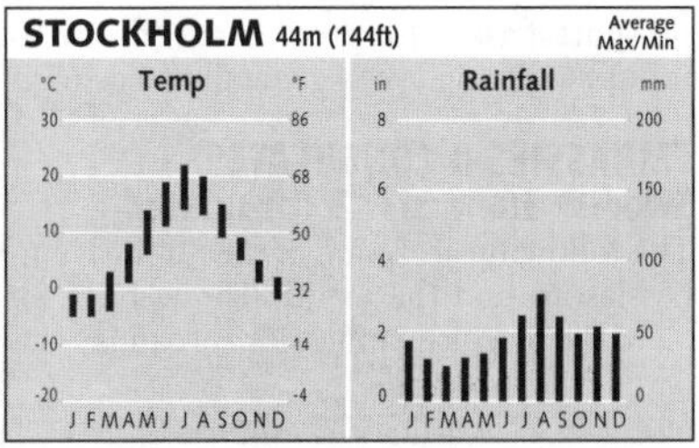

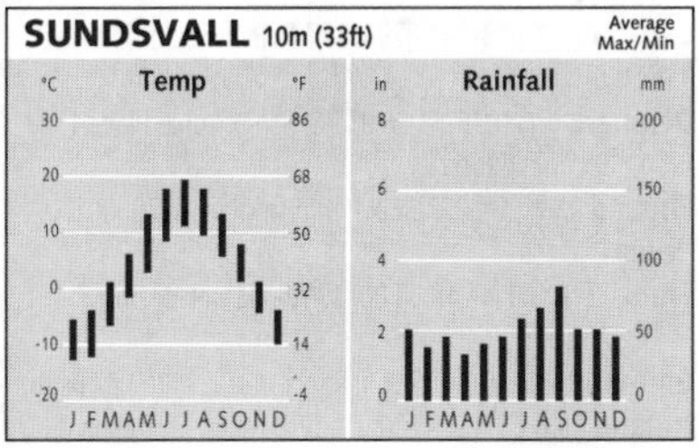

warmer. Norway's mountains act as a rain break, so yearly rainfall is moderate.

Swedish summers are generally fairly sunny with only occasional rainfall, but August can be wet. The average maximum temperature for July is 18°C in the south and around 14°C in the north. Long hot periods in summer aren't unusual, with temperatures soaring to over 30°C.

The harsh Lappland winter starts in October and ends in April, and temperatures can plummet as low as –50°C. Snow can accumulate to depths of several metres in the north, making for superb skiing, but snow depths in the south average only 20cm to 40cm. It usually rains in winter in the far south (Skåne).

The west coast is warmer than the east, thanks to the warming waters of the Gulf Stream.

For for information see the When to Go section on p17.

CUSTOMS

Duty-free goods can only be brought into Sweden from non-EU countries and Åland. Tobacco products and alcoholic drinks can only be brought into Sweden duty-free by those over 18 and 20, respectively.

Duty-free alcohol allowances for travellers from outside the EU are: 1L of spirits, 2L of fortified wine, 2L of wine and a quantity of beer that must be included within the Skr1700 limit. The tobacco allowance is 200 cigarettes, 50 cigars or 250g of smoking tobacco.

The limits on goods brought into Sweden with 'tax paid for personal use' from within the EU are more generous: 10L of spirits, 20L of fortified wine, 90L of wine (but no more than 60L of sparkling wine) and 110L of beer. The tobacco allowance is 800 cigarettes, 400 cheroots, 200 cigars or 1kg of tobacco.

Going through customs rarely involves any hassles, but rules on illegal drugs are strictly enforced; you may be searched on arrival, especially if you're travelling from Denmark. Live plants and animal products (meat, dairy etc), from outside the EU, and all animals, syringes and weapons must be declared to customs on arrival. For the latest regulations, contact **Swedish Customs** (☎ 0771-23 23 23; www.tullverket.se).

DANGERS & ANNOYANCES

Opening Hours & Queuing

It's difficult for foreigners to understand why some tourist offices aren't open at weekends, not to mention why museums open at 11am and close by 4pm (even in July), and hostels (and some hotels) only have reception for two or three hours in the afternoon. Don't even think of going to a liquor store in the evening or for most of the weekend – it will be closed.

Queuing by number is a national pastime in Sweden, hunt down the ticket machine as soon as you enter shops, post offices, liquor stores, offices, police stations etc. Don't miss your turn, or you'll have to go back to the end of the queue.

Road Hazards

Motorists should be alive to the risks posed by elk and reindeer; see p332.

Theft

Sweden is fairly safe, but petty crime is on the increase. In Stockholm, Göteborg, Malmö and Linköping, ask locally for the latest advice on areas to avoid before wandering around at night. Beware of pickpockets and bag-snatchers in crowded public places.

DISABLED TRAVELLERS

Sweden is one of the easiest countries to travel around in a wheelchair. People with disabilities will find transport services with adapted facilities, ranging from trains to taxis, but contact the operator in advance for the best service.

Public toilets and some hotel rooms have facilities for disabled people; **Hotels in Sweden** (www.hotelsinsweden.net) indicates whether hotels have adapted rooms. Some street crossings have ramps for wheelchairs and audio signals for visually impaired people, and some grocery stores are wheelchair accessible.

For further information about Sweden, contact the national association for the disabled, **De Handikappades Riksförbund** (☎ 08-685 80 00; www.dhr.se; Katrinebergsvägen 6, Box 47305, SE-10074 Stockholm).

Also, contact the travel officer at your national support organisation; they may be able to put you in touch with tour companies that specialise in disabled travel. The disability-friendly website www.allgohere.com has an airline directory that provides information on the facilities offered by various airlines.

DISCOUNT CARDS

City Summer Cards

Göteborg, Malmö, Stockholm and Uppsala have worthwhile summer cards that get you into their major attractions, and offer parking, travel on public transport and discounts at participating hotels, restaurants and shops; see the individual city chapters for details.

Hostel & Student Cards

A Hostelling International (HI) card means cheaper accommodation in STF hostels, mountain-stations and mountain-cabins. You can join the STF at hostels and many tourist offices while in Sweden (membership costs Skr285 for adults, Skr110 for those aged 16 to 25, Skr25 for six- to 15-year-olds and Skr410 for families).

The most useful student card is the International Student Identity Card (ISIC), which provides discounts on many forms of transport (including some airlines, international ferries and local public transport) and on admission to museums, sights, theatres and cinemas.

Seniors

Seniors normally get discounts on entry to museums and other sights, cinema and theatre tickets, air tickets and other transport. No special card is required, but show your passport if asked for proof of age (the minimum qualifying age is generally 60 or 65).

EMBASSIES & CONSULATES

Swedish Embassies & Consulates

The following are some of the Swedish embassies around the world. The website for all of the Swedish embassies abroad is www.swedenabroad.com.

Australia (☎ 02-6270 2700; 5 Turrana St, Yarralumla ACT 2600)
Canada (☎ 613-244 8200; 377 Dalhousie St, Ottawa K1N 9N8)
Denmark (☎ 045-33 36 03 70; Sankt Annæ Plads 15A, DK-1250 Copenhagen K)
Finland (☎ 09-6877 660; Pohjoisesplanadi 7B, 00170 Helsinki)
France (☎ 01-44 18 88 00; 17 rue Barbet-de-Jouy, F-75007 Paris)
Germany (☎ 030-505 060; Rauchstrasse 1, 107 87 Berlin)
Ireland (☎ 01-474 4400; 13-17 Dawson St, Dublin 2)
Netherlands (☎ 070-412 0200; Jan Willem Frisolaan 3, 2517 Den Haag)
New Zealand (☎ 04-499 9895; 13th fl, Vogel Bldg, Aitken St, Wellington)
Norway (☎ 24 11 42 00; Nobelsgate 16, NO-0244 Oslo)
UK (☎ 020-7917 6400; 11 Montagu Place, London W1H 2AL)
USA (☎ 202-467 2600; 1501 M St NW, Suite 900, Washington DC 20005-1702)

Embassies & Consulates in Sweden

The diplomatic missions listed here are in Stockholm; some neighbouring countries have additional consulates in Göteborg, Malmö and Helsingborg.

Australia (Map p103; ☎ 08-613 29 00; www.sweden.embassy.gov.au; 11th fl, Sergels Torg 12)
Canada (Map p103; ☎ 08-453 30 00; www.canadaemb.se; Tegelbacken 4)
Denmark (Map p103; ☎ 08-406 75 00; www.ambstockholm.um.dk in Danish; Jakobs Torg 1)
Finland (Map pp68-9; ☎ 08-676 67 00; www.finland.se/fi in Finnish & Swedish; Gärdesgatan 9-11)
France (Map p103; ☎ 08-459 53 00; www.ambafrance-se.org in French & Swedish; Kommendörsgatan 13)
Germany (Map pp68-9; ☎ 08-670 15 00; www.stockholm.diplo.de in German & Swedish; Skarpögatan 9)
Ireland (Map pp68-9; ☎ 08-661 80 05; irish.embassy@swipnet.se; Östermalmsgatan 97)
Netherlands (Map p103; ☎ 08-556 933 00; www.netherlands-embassy.se; Götgatan 16A)
New Zealand (☎ 070-346 9324; nzemb@xs4all.nl; Carnegielaan 10; 2517 KH The Hague) No representation in Sweden: closest embassy is in the Netherlands

Norway (Map pp68-9; ☎ 08-665 63 40; emb.stockholm@mfa.no; Skarpögatan 4)
UK (Map pp68-9; ☎ 08-671 30 00; www.britishembassy.se; Skarpögatan 6-8)
USA (Map pp68-9; ☎ 08-783 53 00; http://stockholm.usembassy.gov; Dag Hammarskjöldsväg 31)

FESTIVALS & EVENTS

Nearly all Swedish towns and cities have special summer festivals and concerts, usually between May and September. The main ones are covered in the relevant chapters, and in the Festivals & Concerts boxed text, below.

For books on Swedish festivals, try *Sweden (Festivals of the World)* by Monica Rabe, or *Maypoles, Crayfish and Lucia – Swedish Holidays and Traditions* by Jan-Öjvind Swahn (Swedish Institute).

April

Valborgsmässoafton (Walpurgis Night; 30 April) Celebrates the arrival of spring with bonfires and choral singers. Upper-secondary-school leavers wearing white caps are a common sight. The festivities developed from a combination of traditional bonfires on May Day eve, and student celebrations at Lund and Uppsala.

May

Första Maj (May Day; 1 May) Traditionally a workers' marching day in industrial towns and cities, and observed with labour-movement events, brass bands and marches.

June

Nationaldag (National Day; 6 June) Commemorates Gustav Vasa's election as King of Sweden on 6 June 1523, but surprisingly it isn't a public holiday. The distinctive Swedish flag (blue, with a yellow cross) is unfurled and hauled aloft at countless flagpoles around the country.

FESTIVALS & CONCERTS

Staggering numbers of festivals are staged in Sweden. The warm summer months are a particularly popular time, with everyone taking advantage of long daylight hours. Visitors should also look out for outdoor summer concerts and theatre productions staged at atmospheric venues like Dalhalla (p264) in Rättvik, or many of the country's fine castles. While some street festivals and concerts are free, others have admission prices (often quite high). The following is just a small sample of events on offer. Visit www.musikfestivaler.se or www.festivalfakta.com for details of many more Swedish music festivals.

Rock & Pop

Large, annual, three-day summer rock festivals are held around **Sölvesborg** (www.swedenrock.com) in early June, **Hultsfred** (www.rockparty.se) in mid-June, and **Arvika** (www.arvikafestivalen.se in Swedish) in mid-July. Towns hosting large rock concerts in their central areas include Sundsvall (early July), Östersund (late July) and Skellefteå (late June); see town websites for information.

Jazz, Opera & Folk

Well-respected jazz festivals are held in **Stockholm** (www.stockholmjazz.com) in mid-July and **Umeå** (www.botniamusik.se in Swedish) in late October.

The Lake Siljan area buzzes with events: **Musik vid Siljan** (www.musikvidsiljan.se) is a week-long event in early July with something to suit most tastes, including chamber, jazz and traditional folk music; the stunning Dalhalla venue in Rättvik hosts an **opera festival** (www.dalhalla.se) in early August and Falun has a popular folk and **world-music festival** (www.falufolk.com) in mid-July.

Other Annual Events

Stockholm Pride (www.stockholmpride.org) Gay and lesbian festival held in the capital in early August.
Medeltidsveckan (Medieval Week; www.medeltidsveckan.se) Staged in Visby on Gotland, also in early August.
Kiruna Snow Festival Europe's largest snow festival is held in late January and features snow-sculpting competitions and reindeer-sled racing, with Sami traditions also emphasised.
Jokkmokk Winter Market (www.jokkmokksmarknad.com) Another event highlighting Sami culture in early February.

Midsommardag (Midsummer's Day) This is *the* festival of the year, celebrated towards the end of the month. Decorating, raising and dancing round the Midsummer pole are traditional activities on Midsummer's Eve. For the folk touch, the Dalarna region is a good place to celebrate, but folk costumes, singing, music, dancing, pickled herring, *snaps*, strawberries and cream, and beer drinking are common everywhere.

August–September

Kräftskivor (Crayfish parties; late August) Swedes celebrate the end of summer by wearing bibs and party hats while eating lots of crayfish and drinking *snaps*. In the north similar parties take place but with *surströmming* (strong-smelling fermented Baltic herring), while in the south similar gatherings in September feast on eels and *snaps*.

December

Luciadagen (Lucia Festival; 13 December) Wearing a crown of candles, Lucia leads a white-clad choir in the singing, and *glögg* (a hot alcoholic punch) is drunk. Oddly, this celebration seems to merge the folk tradition of the longest night and the story of St Lucia of Syracuse.
Christmas markets (December) Held in many towns.
Julafton (Christmas Eve; 24 December) The night of the *smörgåsbord* and the arrival of *jultomten*, the Christmas gnome, carrying a sack of gifts. This is the biggest celebration at Christmas time.

FOOD

Our Eating entries are categorised by price and then preference, with favourites appearing first. 'Budget' options cost Skr75 or under, 'Midrange' options are between Skr75 and Skr185, and 'Top End' places come in at over Skr185. For in-depth information on Swedish cuisine, see p58.

GAY & LESBIAN TRAVELLERS

Sweden is a famously liberal country and allows gay and lesbian couples to form 'registered partnerships' that grant general marriage rights, with a few exceptions (such as not allowing access to church weddings). In 2002 the Swedish parliament voted in favour of allowing gay couples to adopt.

The national organisation for gay and lesbian rights is **Riksförbundet för Sexuellt Likaberättigande** (RFSL; ☎ 08-457 13 00; Sveavägen 59, Box 350, SE-10126 Stockholm), with an attached bookshop, restaurant and nightclub. Gay bars and nightclubs in the big cities are mentioned in this book, but ask local RFSL societies or your home organisation for up-to-date information. The *Spartacus International Gay Guide*, published by Bruno Gmünder Verlag (Berlin), is an excellent international directory of gay entertainment venues, but it's best used in conjunction with more up-to-date listings in local papers; as elsewhere, gay venues in the region can change with the speed of summer.

Another good source of local information is the free monthly magazine *QX*. You can pick it up at many clubs, stores and restaurants in Stockholm, Göteborg, Malmö and Copenhagen (Denmark). The magazine's website www.qx.se has excellent information and recommendations in English.

One of the capital's biggest parties is the annual **Stockholm Pride** (www.stockholmpride.org), a five-day festival celebrating gay culture, held between late July and early August. The extensive programme covers art, debate, health, literature, music, spirituality and sport.

HOLIDAYS

There's a concentration of public holidays in spring and early summer. In particular, Midsummer brings life almost to a halt for three days: transport and other services are reduced, most shops and smaller tourist offices close, as do some attractions. Some hotels close between Christmas and New Year, and it's not uncommon for restaurants in larger cities to close during July and early August (when their owners join the holidaying throngs at beach or lakeside areas).

School holidays vary from school to school, but in general the kids will be at large for Sweden's one-week sport's holiday (February/March), the one-week Easter break, Christmas, and from June to August.

Many businesses close early the day before and all day after official public holidays, including the following:

Nyårsdag (New Year's Day) 1 January
Trettondedag Jul (Epiphany) 6 January
Långfredag, Påsk, Annandag Påsk (Good Friday, Easter Sunday & Monday) March/April
Första Maj (Labour Day) 1 May
Kristi Himmelsfärds dag (Ascension Day) May/June
Pingst, Annandag Pingst (Whit Sunday & Monday) Late May or early June
Midsommardag (Midsummer's Day) First Saturday after 21 June
Alla Helgons dag (All Saints' Day) Saturday, late October or early November
Juldag (Christmas Day) 25 December
Annandag Jul (Boxing Day) 26 December

Note also that **Midsommarafton** (Midsummer's Eve), **Julafton** (Christmas Eve; 24 December) and **Nyårsafton** (New Year's Eve; 31 December) are not official holidays, but are generally nonworking days for most of the population.

INSURANCE

Insurance is important: it covers you for every thing from medical expenses and luggage loss to cancellations or delays in your travel arrangements – depending on your policy.

If you do need health insurance, remember that some policies offer 'lower' and 'higher' medical-expense options, but the higher one is chiefly for countries such as the USA that have extremely high medical costs. Everyone should be covered for the worst possible case, such as an accident requiring an ambulance, hospital treatment or an emergency flight home. You may prefer a policy that pays healthcare providers directly, rather than you having to pay on the spot and claim later.

In Sweden, EU citizens pay a fee for all medical treatment (including emergency admissions), but showing an EHIC form will make matters much easier. Inquire about the EHIC well in advance at your social security office, travel agent or local post office. Travel insurance is still advisable, however, as it allows treatment flexibility and will also cover ambulance and repatriation costs.

See p334 for health insurance details.

INTERNET ACCESS

If you plan to carry your notebook or palmtop computer with you, remember that the power-supply voltage in Sweden may vary from that at home. To avoid frying your electronics, buy a universal AC adaptor and a plug adaptor, which will enable you to plug in anywhere. Also worth purchasing is a 'global' or 'world' modem, as your PC-card modem may not work outside your home country. For comprehensive advice on travelling with portable computers, visit the World Wide Phone Guide at www.kropla.com. Teleadapt (www.teleadapt.com) sell all the gizmos you'll need. Most hotels have wireless LAN connections, and some even have laptops you can borrow.

Nearly all public libraries offer free Internet access, but often the half-hour or hour slots are fully booked for days in advance by locals, and facilities may occasionally be blocked. Many tourist offices also offer a computer terminal for visitor use (sometimes for free).

Internet cafés are rare outside big cities, as most Swedes have Internet access at home. Where Internet cafés do exist, they're full of teenage lads playing computer games. They typically charge around Skr1 per online minute, or Skr50 per hour.

Also see the Internet Resources section on p19.

LEGAL MATTERS

If arrested, you have the right to contact your country's embassy, who can usually provide you with a list of local lawyers. There is no provision for bail in Sweden. Sweden has some of the most draconian drug laws in western Europe, with fines and possible long prison sentences for possession and consumption.

MAPS

Tourist offices, libraries and hotels usually stock free local town plans.

The best maps of Sweden are published and updated regularly by Kartförlaget, the sales branch of the national mapping agency, **Lantmäteriet** (☎ 026-63 30 00; www.lantmateriet.se; SE-80182 Gävle). Maps can be bought at most tourist offices, bookshops and some youth hostels, service stations and general stores.

Motorists planning an extensive tour should get *Motormännens Sverige Vägatlas* produced by Kartförlaget for Skr270, with town plans and detailed coverage at 1:250,000 as far north as Sundsvall, then 1:400,000 for the remainder.

The best tourist road maps are those of Kartförlaget's *Vägkartan* series, at a scale of 1:100,000, available from larger bookshops. Also useful, especially for hikers, are the *Fjäll kartan* mountain series (1:100,000, with 20m contour interval); these are usually priced around Skr100 apiece and are available at larger bookshops, outdoor equipment stores and mountain stations operated by **Svenska Turistföreningen** (STF; ☎ 08-463 21 00; www.svenskaturistforeningen.se).

To buy maps in advance, try online at Lantmäteriet's website, which has a good mail-order service, or at **Kartbutiken** (☎ 08-20 23 03; www.kartbutiken.se; Kungsgatan 74, SE-11122 Stockholm).

MONEY

Sweden uses the krona (plural kronor) as currency. One krona is divided into 100 öre. The country has recovered well from an economic slowdown in 2002 and the krona is stable. See the Inside Front Cover for exchange rates, and p17 for typical costs.

Cash & ATMs

The simplest way to get money in Sweden is by accessing your account using an ATM card from your home bank. 'Bankomat' ATMs are found adjacent to many banks and around busy public places such as shopping centres. They accept major credit cards as well as Plus and Cirrus cards. Note that many ATMs in Sweden will not accept PINs of more than four digits; if your PIN is longer than this, just enter the first four and you should be able to access your account.

Credit Cards

Visa, MasterCard, American Express and Diners Club cards are widely accepted. You're better off using a credit card since exchange rates are better and transaction fees are avoided. Credit cards can be used to buy train tickets but are not accepted on domestic ferries, apart from on sailings to Gotland. Electronic debit cards can be used in most shops.

If your card is lost or stolen in Sweden, report it to one of the following appropriate agencies.

American Express (☎ 336-393-1111)
Diners Club (☎ 08-14 68 78)
MasterCard (☎ 020 79 13 24)
Visa (☎ 020 79 56 75)

Moneychangers & Travellers Cheques

Banks around the country exchange major foreign currencies and accept international brands of travellers cheques. They may, however, charge up to a rather steep Skr60 per travellers cheque, so shop around and compare service fees and exchange rates before handing over your money.

Forex (☎ 0200-22 22 20; www.forex.se) is the biggest foreign money exchange company in Sweden, with good rates and branches in major airports, ferry terminals and town and city centres; these are noted where appropriate in the destination chapters. They charge a service fee of Skr15 per travellers cheque exchanged.

Tipping

Service charges and tips are usually included in restaurant bills and taxi fares; a common practice is to round up a restaurant bill to the nearest Skr10. There's certainly no problem if you want to reward good service with an extra tip (or round up the taxi fare, particularly if there's luggage).

PHOTOGRAPHY & VIDEO

Print and slide film are readily available, but prices (including developing costs) are fairly high. It's better to bring your own film and develop your photos or slides back home. Expert, a chain of electrical goods shops, sells a wide range of film, and camera equipment can be bought or repaired there.

It's particularly important to ask permission before taking photos of people in Sami areas, where you may meet resistance. Photography and video is prohibited at many tourist sites, mainly to protect fragile artwork. Photographing military establishments is forbidden.

The clear northern light and glare from water, ice and snow may require use of a UV filter (or skylight filter) and a lens shade. ISO 100 film is sufficient for most purposes. In winter, most cameras don't work below –20°C. Lonely Planet's book *Travel Photography* contains some handy hints.

POST

In 2001–02, the Swedish postal service **Posten** (☎ 020-23 22 21; www.posten.se) was radically reorganised: in a cost-cutting bid, it closed many post offices and instead opened up a network of 3000+ counter services in shops, petrol stations and supermarkets across the country. Look out for the yellow post symbol on a pale blue background, which indicates that postal facilities are offered.

Most Swedes now buy their stamps and post letters while going about their grocery shopping. If your postal requirements are more complicated (such as posting a heavy parcel), you'll have to track down one of the original post offices as the post-office-lite counter services can't deal with them.

Postal Rates

Mailing letters or postcards weighing up to 20g within Sweden costs Skr5.50; it's Skr9.50 to elsewhere in Europe, and Skr9.70 beyond Europe. The *ekonomibrev* (economy post) option takes longer to reach its destination and costs marginally less (Skr5, Skr8.50 and Skr8.70, respectively). Airmail will take a week to reach most parts of North America, perhaps a little longer to Australia and New Zealand.

A package weighing 2kg costs Skr200 by airmail within Europe, and Skr235 outside Europe. The *ekonomibrev* option here is roughly Skr20 cheaper, but postage time may take up to a month.

Sending & Receiving Mail

Receiving poste restante mail under the new postal system is more difficult for travellers, as many of the old-style post offices have closed down. Poste restante mail must be sent to a Postcenter, now generally only found in larger towns. The person sending you mail will need to specify which Postcenter you will be collecting from, using the specific address (and postal code) for that Postcenter. You can find Postcenter addresses by visiting the website www.posten.se, and clicking on *'Öppettider hos Posten'* in the menu. Under *'Vad vill du göra'*, click on 'Postcenter', then in the box to the right type the town where you intend to send mail. A list of Postcenters in the area will pop up (this information isn't available on the English section of the website so you'll have to wade through the Swedish). Alternatively, telephone ☎ 46 8 23 22 21 and request assistance.

SHOPPING

In Sweden, there's no shortage of the gorgeous furniture and interior design for which the country is famous. Head to **DesignTorget** (www.designtorget.se), which showcases the work (usually quite affordable) of established and new designers. There are branches in Stockholm, Täby, Göteborg and Malmö.

Souvenirs, handicrafts and quality Swedish products in glass, wood, amber, pewter

FLATPACK FURNITURE TAKES OVER THE WORLD

If you're a few billion dollars poorer than you'd like to be, the Ikea success story is one that you should study closely. From humble beginnings selling pens, watches and nylon stockings from a shed in Älmhult, Småland, Ikea's creator-god Ingvar Kamprad has turned himself into one of the world's richest men. Today his personal fortune is reputed to be around US$32 billion (although Ikea's business structure is notoriously secretive).

The Ikea name (a combination of Kamprad's initials and those of the farm and village he grew up in) was officially registered in 1943. Furniture was added to the company's products four years later, gradually evolving into the Ikea-designed flatpack creations so familiar today. There was almost an early end to the Ikea empire when the first Stockholm shop and all its stock burned down in 1970. But, besides his devotion to work and obsession with cost-cutting, Kamprad also seems to thrive on adversity. Ikea bounced back, and today has over 200 stores; branches first opened in Australia in 1975, Saudi Arabia in 1983, the US in 1985, Britain in 1987, China in 1998 and Russia in 2000.

The company sells a look and lifestyle that seems to be craved universally; shoppers are offered clean, cleverly designed Scandinavian style at prices that sometimes seem too cheap to be real. It's estimated that 10% of Europeans were conceived in an Ikea bed!

However, the company is worshipped and criticised in equal measures, and is a mine of paradoxes. There's an emphasis on good design, yet its blue-and-yellow stores mar landscapes worldwide. Products are created with sustainability in mind, but we're all encouraged to throw away serviceable non-Ikea furniture and buy new. The clean-cut company was rocked in 1994 by revelations that Kamprad had had links with the Nazis. Ikea also seems to induce mass hysteria: a stampede in Jeddah left three people dead; and UK readers will recall the fighting crowds, evacuation of wounded people, and cars abandoned on the North Circular when the Edmonton shop opened in London. Cheap and innovative designs are great, but what is the price of individuality when every house in the land has Billy bookshelves and a Klippan sofa?

Still, like it or loathe it, Ikea is here to stay. Kamprad has taken a back seat, with control over his empire now divvied up among his three children, more new stores are planned and 160 million copies of the 2006 Ikea catalogue have just plopped through letterboxes all over the world. You'd better develop a taste for meatballs...

or silver are relatively expensive, but tend to be a lot cheaper when bought directly from the manufacturer; some places will organise shipping for you. The best souvenirs include glassware (such as bowls, jugs, vases and ornaments) from Glasriket (p127), Swedish painted wooden horses from Dalarna (p267), wooden toys and jewellery made from amber and silver. Some foodstuffs, such as *hjortronsylt* (cloudberry jam) and *sill* (pickled herring), are also well worth taking home. Sale prices in shops are advertised with the word *rea;* for discounts or special offers look for *lågpris, extrapris, rabatt* or *fynd.*

Handicrafts carrying the round token *Svensk slöjd,* or the hammer and shuttle emblem, are endorsed by Svenska Hemslöjdsföreningarnas Riksförbund, the national handicrafts organisation whose symbol is found on affiliated handicraft shops. Look out for signs reading *hemslöjd,* indicating handicraft sales outlets.

If you're interested in Sami handicrafts, look for the *Duodji* label (a round, coloured, authenticity token) and, if possible, go to a Sami village and make your purchase there. Be careful of some town shops that may have fakes on the shelves. Some typical Sami handcrafts include ornately carved sheath knives, cups, bowls, textiles and jewellery. Reindeer bone, wood (birch), reindeer hide and tin are commonly used materials.

Tax-Free Shopping

At shops that display the 'Tax Free Shopping' sign, non-EU citizens making single purchases of goods exceeding Skr200 are eligible for a VAT refund of up to 17.5% of the purchase price. Show your passport and ask the shop for a 'Global Refund Cheque', which should be presented along with your unopened purchases (within three months) at your departure point from the country (before you check in), to get export validation. You can then cash your cheque at any of the refund points, which are found at international airports and harbours. The *Tax Free Shopping Guide to Sweden* is available from tourist offices free of charge, or call ☎ 020-74 17 41 for more information.

Bargaining

Bargaining isn't customary, but you can get 'walk-in' prices at some hotels and *stugby* (chalet parks).

SOLO TRAVELLERS

Travelling in Sweden poses no particular problems for lone travellers, apart from it can be tricker than most other countries to meet people. Hostel dormitories aren't common, except in cities, and quite often you'll end up stuck in a room on your own, surrounded by families. Female solo travellers should obviously take care at night in the cities, and check with locals about which dodgy areas to avoid.

TELEPHONE & FAX

Swedish phone numbers have area codes followed by varying digits. Look for business numbers in the **Yellow Pages** (www.gulasidorna.se in Swedish). The state-owned telephone company, Telia, also has phone books, which include green pages (for community services) and blue pages (for regional services, including health and medical care).

Public telephones are usually to be found at train stations or in the main town square. They accept phonecards or credit cards (although the latter are expensive). It's not possible to receive return international calls on public phones.

For international calls dial ☎ 00 followed by the country code and the local area code. Calls to Sweden from abroad require the country code ☎ 46 followed by the area code and telephone number (omitting the first zero in the area code).

Mobile phone codes have ☎ 010, ☎ 070, ☎ 073, ☎ 0730. Toll-free codes include ☎ 020 and ☎ 0200 (not from public tele phones or abroad).

Directory assistance (☎ 118 119) International.
Directory assistance (☎ 118 118) Within Sweden.
Emergency services (☎ 112) Toll-free.

Fax

Fax is not a common form of communication in Sweden, and is difficult for on-the-road travellers to access. Many post offices used to offer a fax service but don't any longer, so your best bet is to ask at the local tourist office or your place of accommodation. Faxes can still be received at most hotels for free and you can often send a fax for a moderate charge.

Mobile Phones

It's worth considering bringing your mobile phone from your home country and buying a Swedish SIM card, which gives you a Swedish mobile number. Vodafone, for example, sells a local SIM card for Skr95, which you then need to load with at least Skr100-worth of credit. You can then purchase top-ups at many stores, including petrol stations. Your mobile may be locked onto your local network in your home country, so ask your home network for advice before going abroad.

Phonecards

Telia phonecards *(telefonkort)* for public phones cost Skr50 and Skr120 (for 50 and 120 units, respectively) and can be bought from Telia phone shops and newsagents.

You can make international telephone calls with these phonecards, but they won't last long! For international calls, it's better to buy one of a wide range of phonecards (such as a Star phonecard) from tobacconists that give cheap rates for calls abroad. These are generally used in public phone boxes *in conjunction with* a Telia card: so you might have to put the Telia card into the phone, dial the telephone number shown on the back of your cheap international phonecard, then follow the instructions given. International collect calls cannot be made from pay phones.

TIME

Sweden is one hour ahead of GMT/UTC and is in the same time zone as Norway and Denmark as well as most of Western Europe. When it's noon in Sweden, it's 11am in London, 1pm in Helsinki, 6am in New York and Toronto, 3am in Los Angeles, 9pm in Sydney and 11pm in Auckland. Sweden also has daylight-saving time: the clocks go forward an hour on the last Sunday in March and back an hour on the last Sunday in October.

Timetables and business hours are quoted using the 24-hour clock, and dates are often given by week number (1 to 52).

TOILETS

Public toilets in parks, shopping malls, museums, libraries, and bus or train stations are rarely free in Sweden; some churches and most tourist offices have free toilets. Except at larger train stations (where there's an attendant), pay toilets are coin operated, and usually cost Skr5.

TOURIST INFORMATION

Local Tourist Offices

Most towns in Sweden have centrally located tourist offices *(turistbyrå)* that provide free street plans and information on accommodation, attractions, activities and transport. Brochures for other areas in Sweden are often available. Ask for the handy booklet that lists addresses and phone numbers for most tourist offices in the country; the website of **Swedish Tourism Associated** (www.turism.se) also has this information.

Contact details for regional tourist offices are given at the beginnings of the destination chapters.

Most tourist offices are open long hours daily in summer; during the off-season (mid-August to mid-June) a few close down, while others have shorter opening hours – they may close by 4pm, and not open at all at weekends. Public libraries or large hotels are good alternative places for information.

Tourist Offices Abroad

The official website for the **Swedish Travel and Tourism Council** (www.visit-sweden.com) contains loads of excellent information in many languages, and you can request for brochures and information packs to be sent to you.

The following tourist offices can assist with enquiries and provide tourist promotional material by phone, email or post (most don't have a walk-in service). In countries without a designated tourist office, a good starting point for information is the Swedish embassy (see p314).

France (☎ 01-70 70 84 58; servinfo@suede-tourisme.fr; Office Suédois du Tourisme et des Voyages, 11 rue Payenne, F-75003 Paris)

Germany (☎ 069-22 22 34 96; info@swetourism.de; Schweden-Werbung für Reisen und Touristik, Michaelisstrasse 22, DE-20459 Hamburg)

UK (☎ 020-7108 6168; info@swetourism.org.uk; Swedish Travel & Tourism Council, 5 Upper Montagu St, London W1H 2AG)

USA (☎ 212-885 9700; usa@visit-sweden.com; Swedish Travel & Tourism Council, PO Box 4649, Grand Central Station, New York NY 10163-4649)

VISAS

Citizens of EU countries can enter Sweden with a passport or a national identification card (passports are recommended) and stay up to three months. Nationals of Nordic countries (Denmark, Norway, Finland and

Iceland) can stay and work indefinitely, but nationals of other countries require residence permits *(uppehållstillstånd)* for stays of between three months and five years; there is no fee for this permit for EU citizens.

Non-EU passport holders from Australia, New Zealand, Canada and the US can enter and stay in Sweden without a visa for up to three months. Australian and New Zealand passport holders aged between 18 and 30 can qualify for a one-year working-holiday visa (see the following section).

Citizens of South Africa and many other African, Asian and some Eastern European countries require tourist visas for entry. These are only available in advance from Swedish embassies (allow two months); there's a nonrefundable application fee of Skr315. Visas last up to three months, and extensions aren't easily obtainable.

Non-EU citizens can also obtain residence permits, but these must be applied for before entering Sweden. An interview by consular officials at your nearest Swedish embassy is required – allow up to eight months for this process. Foreign students are granted residence permits if they can prove acceptance by a Swedish educational institution and are able to guarantee that they can support themselves financially.

Migrationsverket (☎ 011-15 60 00; www.migrationsverket.se; SE-60170 Norrköping) is the Swedish migration board and it handles all applications for visas and work or residency permits.

WORK

Non-EU citizens require an offer of paid employment prior to their arrival in Sweden. They need to apply for a work permit (and residence permit for stays over three months), enclosing confirmation of the job offer, completed forms (available from Swedish diplomatic posts or over the Internet), two passport photos and their passport. Processing takes six to eight weeks, and there's a nonrefundable application fee of Skr1000.

EU citizens only need to apply for a residence permit (free) within three months of arrival if they find work, then they can remain in Sweden for the duration of their employment (or up to five years).

Australians and New Zealanders aged 18 to 30 years can now qualify for a one-year working holiday visa. Full application details are available online through **Migrationsverket** (www.migrationsverket.se).

Work permits are only granted if there's a shortage of Swedes (or citizens from EU countries) with certain skills, and speaking Swedish may be essential for the job. Students enrolled in Sweden can take summer jobs, but can be hard to find and such work isn't offered to travelling students. No seasonal work permits were to be granted for 2006.

Helpful information is available online from the **Arbetsförmedlinga** (AMV; Swedish National Labour Market Administration; www.ams.se).

Transport

CONTENTS

GETTING THERE & AWAY

Sweden is a mostly hassle-free destination, for visa requirements see p321.

AIR

Airports & Airlines

The main airport is Stockholm Arlanda, which links Sweden with major European and North American cities. Göteborg Landvetter is Sweden's second biggest international airport. Stockholm Skavsta (actually 100km south of Stockholm, near Nyköping) and Göteborg City both act as airports for the budget airline Ryanair.

Göteborg Landvetter (code GOT; ☎ 031-94 10 00; www.lfv.se)
Göteborg City (code GSE; ☎ 031-92 60 60; www.goteborgcityairport.se)
Stockholm Arlanda (code ARN; ☎ 08-797 60 00; www.lfv.se)
Stockholm Skavsta (code NYO; ☎ 0155-28 04 00; www.skavsta-air.se)

For travelling between international airports and city centres, see the Getting Around sections in the relevant chapters.

Scandinavian Airlines System (SAS) is the regional carrier with a good safety record.

Airlines Flying to & from Sweden

Most of the usual airlines fly into Sweden including the following:

Air France-KLM (airline code AF; ☎ 08-5199 9990; www.airfrance.com; hub Charles de Gaulle, Paris)
Blue1 (airline code KF; ☎ 0900-102 5831; www.blue1.com; hub Helsinki-Vantaa, Finland)
British Airways (airline code BA; ☎ 0200-770098; www.britishairways.com; hub Heathrow Airport, London)
City Airline (airline code CF; ☎ 0200-250500; www.cityairline.com; hub Göteborg)
Finnair (airline code AY; ☎ 0771-781100; www.finnair.com; hub Helsinki-Vantaa, Finland)
Icelandair (airline code FI; ☎ 08-690 9800, ext 2; www.icelandair.net; hub Keflavík, Iceland)
Lufthansa (airline code LH; ☎ 08-611 5930; www.lufthansa.com; hub Frankfurt, Germany)
Ryanair (airline code FR; ☎ 0900-202 0240; www.ryanair.com; hub Dublin, Ireland)
SAS (airline code SK; ☎ 0770-72 77 27; www.scandinavian.net; hub Stockholm Arlanda)
Skyways (airline code JZ; ☎ 0771 95 95 00; www.skyways.se; hub Stockholm Arlanda)

Tickets

Most airline websites list special offers, and there are good online ticket agencies that will compare prices for you (such as www.travelocity.co.uk and www.deckchair.com). However, dealing direct with a travel agent can furnish extra details, like which airlines have the best facilities for children, or which travel insurance is most suitable for you.

If you're planning on visiting the south, flights to Copenhagen airport, just across the Öresund bridge from Sweden, may be cheaper than flights to Malmö.

THINGS CHANGE...

The information in this chapter is particularly vulnerable to change. Check directly with the airline or a travel agency to make sure you understand how a fare (and the ticket you may buy) works and be aware of the security requirements for international travel. Shop carefully. The details given in this chapter should be regarded as pointers and are not a substitute for your own careful, up-to-date research.

Departure tax is included in the ticket price.

Australia & New Zealand

Airlines such as British Airways, Lufthansa, Thai Airways, Malaysia Airlines, Qantas Airways and Singapore Airlines can get you heading in the right direction, but you'll have to change planes at least once in Singapore, Bangkok, Paris or London. The following are major agencies for cheap fares:

Flight Centre Australia (☎ 133 133; www.flightcentre.com.au); New Zealand (☎ 0800 243 544; www.flightcentre.co.nz)

STA Travel Australia (☎ 1300 733 035; www.statravel.com.au); New Zealand (☎ 0508 782 872; www.statravel.co.nz)

Continental Europe

SAS offers numerous direct services between Stockholm and European capitals (including Amsterdam, Berlin, Brussels, Dublin, Geneva, Helsinki, Moscow, Oslo, Paris and Prague); many are routed via Copenhagen or Frankfurt. It also has routes from Göteborg to Copenhagen and Frankfurt.

Finnair has direct flights from Helsinki (which Swedes call Helsingfors) to Stockholm (around 15 daily) and Göteborg (up to four daily). Blue1 has regular daily flights from Stockholm to Helsinki, Oulu, Tampere, Turku (known as Åbo in Swedish) and Vaasa, and from Göteborg to Helsinki.

Skyways has several flights daily from Copenhagen to Swedish regional centres Karlstad, Linköping, Norrköping and Örebro.

The budget airline Ryanair has frequent flights from Stockholm Skavsta to Barcelona, Brussels, Düsseldorf, Frankfurt, Hamburg, Milan, Paris, Riga and Rome.

Across Europe many travel agencies have ties with **STA Travel** (www.statravel.com), where cheap tickets can be purchased.

UK & Ireland

London is Europe's major centre for discount fares. Budget airline Ryanair flies from London Stansted to Stockholm Skavsta, Göteborg City and Malmö Sturup; Glasgow Prestwick to Stockholm Skavsta and Göteborg City; London Luton to Västerås; and Shannon to Stockholm Skavsta.

Between London (Heathrow) and Stockholm Arlanda, several commercial airlines have regular daily flights, including SAS, British Airways and Finnair. Prices start at around UK£120.

From Sunday to Friday, SAS has one flight per day from Stockholm Arlanda to Manchester and Dublin. British Airways shuttles between Manchester and Stockholm Arlanda four times weekly.

SAS also flies daily between London (Heathrow) and Göteborg.

City Airline has two flights weekly from Göteborg (Landvetter) to Birmingham and Manchester.

The following are some recommended travel agencies and online ticket sites:

Flightbookers (☎ 0870 814 0000; www.ebookers.com)

STA Travel (☎ 0870 160 0599; www.statravel.co.uk)

USA & Canada

Thanks to the large ethnic Swedish population in Minnesota, North Dakota and Wisconsin, you may find small local agencies in those areas specialising in travel to Scandinavia and offering good-value charter flights.

Icelandair flies from Baltimore-Washington, Boston, New York, Minneapolis and Orlando via Reykjavík to many European destinations, including Stockholm. Twice per week between mid-May and mid-October, you can also fly from/to San Francisco.

If you're planning on flying within Scandinavia, SAS offers a Visit Scandinavia/Europe Air Pass to its transatlantic passengers. SAS's North American hub is New York City's Newark Airport, with direct daily flights to/from Stockholm.

From Canada, there are no direct flights; connect through one of Icelandair's US hubs or through Copenhagen or London.

Discount travel agents are known as consolidators in the USA; track them down through the *Yellow Pages* or the major daily newspapers. The following are travel agencies recommended for online bookings:

STA Travel Canada (☎ 1 888 427 5639; www.statravel.ca); US (☎ 1 800 781 4040; www.sta.com)

Expedia Canada (☎ 1 888 397 3342; www.expedia.ca); US (☎ 1 800 397 3342; www.expedia.com)

Travelocity Canada (☎ 1 877 282 2925; www.travelocity.ca); US (☎ 1 888 709 5983; www.travelocity.com)

LAND

Border Crossings

Customs and immigration posts on border crossings between Sweden and Denmark, Finland or Norway are usually deserted,

RAILWAYS & FERRIES

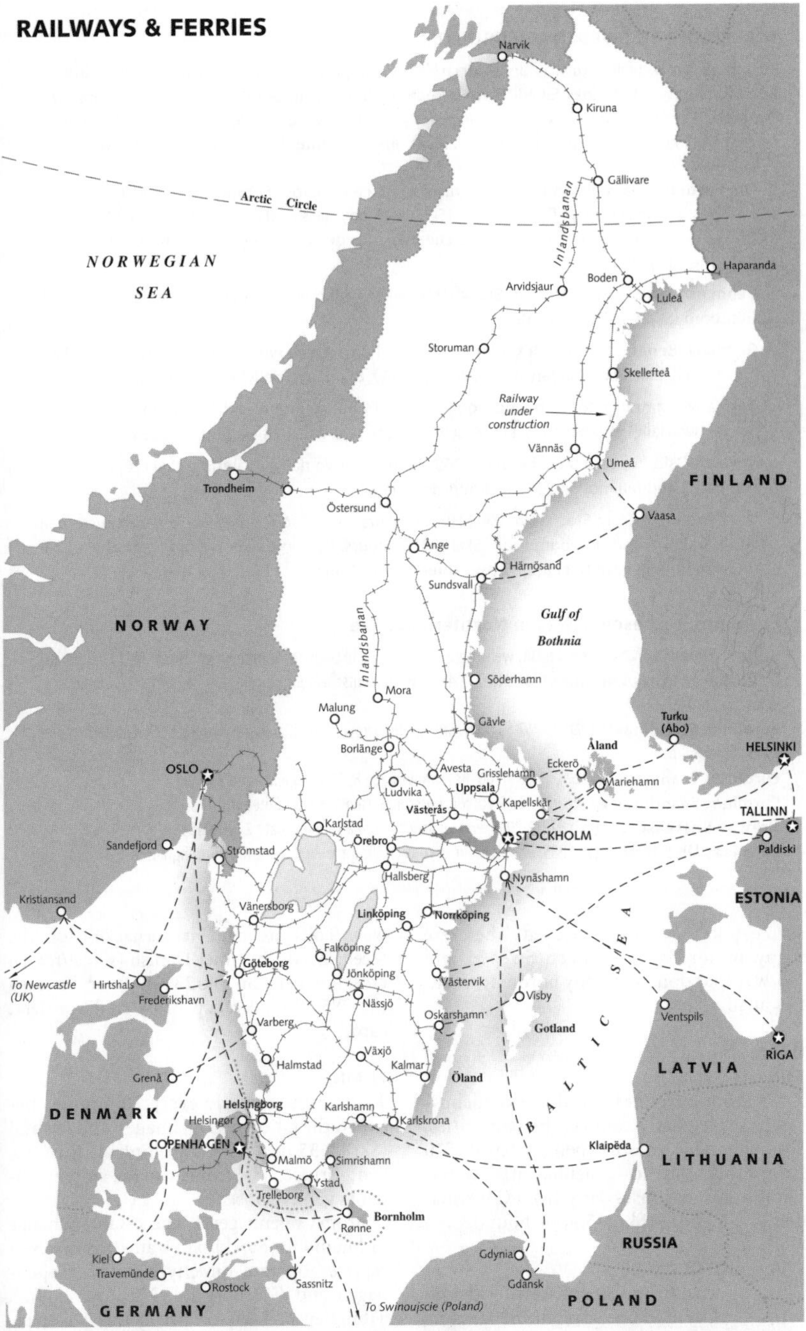

TRAVELLING TO SWEDEN BY EUROLINES

Eurolines (www.eurolines.com) is an association of companies forming Europe's largest international bus network. It links Swedish cities such as Stockholm, Göteborg and Malmö directly to Denmark, Germany and Norway, and indirectly to cities all over Western and central Europe. Advance ticket purchases are compulsory. Most buses operate daily in summer and several times per week in winter.

The **Eurolines Pass** allows unlimited travel to 35 cities across Europe. From mid-June to mid-September, and around late December, a 15-/30-/40-day pass costs €325/435/490 (€275/355/420 for those under 26 years or over 60; it's cheaper outside these months). Some popular routes include the following:

- Denmark (Copenhagen) to/from Stockholm (Skr248, nine hours, at least three per week) and Göteborg (Skr205, 4½ hours, daily).
- Germany (Berlin) to/from Stockholm (Skr590, 17 hours, three weekly), Göteborg (Skr610, 12 hours, daily) via Copenhagen, and Malmö (Skr500, 8½ hours, daily) via Copenhagen.
- Germany (Hamburg) to/from Stockholm (Skr648,14 hours, four weekly), Göteborg (Skr568, 11 hours, two daily) and Malmö (Skr388, seven hours, two daily) all via Copenhagen.
- Norway (Oslo) to/from Stockholm (Skr260, 7½ hours, two daily), Göteborg (Skr176, four hours, two daily) and Malmö (Skr260, 7½ hours, two daily).
- UK (London) to/from Stockholm (Skr1198, 30 hours, one to four times weekly) via Amsterdam and Hamburg, and Göteborg (from Skr1098, 35 hours; five times weekly). For both these routes you may have to change buses three or four times.

Eurolines Representatives in Northern Europe

Bayern Express (☎ 030 8609 6211; www.berlinlinienbus.de in German; Mannheimer Str. 33/34, 10713 Berlin)
Deutsche Touring/Eurolines (☎ 040-280 4538; www.deutsche-touring.com; Am Römerhof 17, 60486 Frankfurt am Main)
Eurolines Scandinavia (☎ 08 762 59 60; www.eurolinestravel.com; Klarabergsviadukten 72, City Terminalen, 11164 Stockholm)
Eurolines Scandinavia (☎ 033 88 70 00; Reventlowsgade 8, 1651 Copenhagen V)
Eurolines Scandinavia (☎ 031 10 02 40; Nils Ericssonplatsen 5, 41103 Göteborg)
Norway Bussekspress (☎ 02217 2000; www.nor-way.no; Karl Johans gate 2, NO-0154 Oslo)
Eurolines UK (☎ 0207 259 9285; www.eurolines.co.uk; 4 Vicarage Rd, Edgbaston, Birmingham B15 3ES)

so passports are rarely checked. There are many minor roads between Sweden and Norway that don't have any border formalities at all.

Denmark

BUS

Apart from Eurolines, see above, Säfflebussen buses regularly connect the same cities, although they're more expensive (eg Skr510 from Stockholm to Copenhagen). Swebus Express has five buses daily from Copenhagen to Göteborg (Skr225, four hours).

CAR & MOTORCYCLE

You can drive from Copenhagen to Malmö across the Öresund bridge on the E20 motorway. Tolls are paid at Lernacken, on the Swedish side, in either Danish (single/return crossing per car Dkr235/470) or Swedish (Skr285/570) currency, or by credit or debit card.

TRAIN

Trains run regularly every 20 minutes between the cities of Copenhagen and Malmö (Skr87, 35 minutes), travelling via the Öresund bridge. The trains usually stop at Copenhagen Airport.

From Copenhagen, it's necessary to change in Malmö for Stockholm trains. Six or seven services operate directly between Copenhagen and Göteborg (Skr373, four hours). Trains every hour or two connect Copen-

TRANSPORT

hagen, Kristianstad and Karlskrona. X2000 high-speed trains are more expensive.

Germany

BUS

See the Eurolines boxed text, opposite.

TRAIN

Hamburg is the central European gateway for Scandinavia, with direct trains daily to Copenhagen and a few on to Stockholm.

There are direct overnight trains running every day between Berlin and Malmö via the Trelleborg–Sassnitz ferry. The journey takes nine hours and a couchette/bed costs €88/125 (approximately Skr820/1170). See www.berlin-night-express.com for details.

Finland

BUS

Frequent bus services run from Haparanda to Tornio (Skr10, 10 minutes) and on to Kemi (Skr45, 45 minutes). buses link Boden and Luleå with Haparanda, and Tornio/Kemi with Oulu (Finland). **Tapanis Buss** (☎ 0922-129 55; www.tapanis.se in Swedish) runs express coaches from Stockholm to Tornio via Haparanda twice a week (Skr480, 15 hours).

Länstrafiken i Norrbotten (☎ 020 47 00 47; www.ltnbd.se) operates buses as far as Karesuando, from where it's only a few minutes' walk across the bridge to Kaaresuvanto (Finland). There are also regular regional services from Haparanda to Övertorneå (some continue to Pello, Pajala and Kiruna) – you can walk across the border at Övertorneå or Pello and pick up a Finnish bus to Muonio, with onward connections from there to Kaaresuvanto and Tromsø (Norway).

CAR & MOTORCYCLE

The main routes between Sweden and Finland are the E4 from Umeå to Kemi and No 45 from Gällivare to Kaaresuvanto; five other minor roads also cross the border.

Norway

BUS

Säfflebussen runs from Stockholm to Oslo (Skr380, 7½ hours, fives times daily) via Karlstad, and from Göteborg to Oslo (Skr220, four hours, seven daily). Swebus Express has the same routes with similar prices.

In the north, buses run once-daily from Umeå to Mo i Rana (eight hours) and from Skellefteå to Bodø (nine hours, daily except Saturday) are run by **Länstrafiken i Västerbotten** (☎ 0771-10 01 10; www.lanstrafikeniac.se) and **Länstrafiken i Norrbotten** (☎ 0771-10 01 10; www.ltnbd.se), respectively.

CAR & MOTORCYCLE

The main roads between Sweden and Norway are the E6 from Göteborg to Oslo, the E18 from Stockholm to Oslo, the E14 from Sundsvall to Trondheim, the E12 from Umeå to Mo i Rana, and the E10 from Kiruna to Bjerkvik. Many secondary roads also cross the border.

TRAIN

The main rail links run from Stockholm to Oslo, from Göteborg to Oslo, from Stockholm to Östersund and Storlien (Norwegian trains continue to Trondheim), and from Luleå to Kiruna and Narvik.

Trains run daily between Stockholm and Oslo (Skr642, six hours), and there's a night train from Stockholm to Narvik (Skr500 not including couchette, from 20 hours). You can also travel from Helsingborg to Oslo (Skr590, seven hours), via Göteborg. X2000 high-speed trains are more expensive.

UK

BUS

See the Eurolines boxed text, opposite.

TRAIN

The Channel Tunnel makes land travel poss ible between Britain and Continental Europe. From Brussels, you can connect to Hamburg, a main gateway to Scandinavia.

From London, a 2nd-class single ticket (including couchette) costs around UK£220 to Stockholm. For reservations and tickets, contact **Deutsche Bahn UK** (☎ 08702 435 363; www.bahn.co.uk).

Transport Operators

Services across Swedish borders are operated by the following:

Eurolines (☎ 08-762 5960; www.eurolines.com) See also the boxed text, opposite.

Säfflebussen (☎ 0771-15 15 15; www.safflebussen.se in Swedish, Norwegian & Danish) Long-distance buses within Sweden and to Oslo (Norway) and Copenhagen (Denmark).

Swebus Express (☎ 0200 21 82 18; www.swebusexpress.se) Long-distance buses within Sweden and to Oslo (Norway) and Copenhagen (Denmark).

Sveriges Järnväg (SJ; ☎ 0771-75 75 99; www.sj.se) Train lines in the southern part of the country, with services to Copenhagen (Denmark).

Tågkompaniet (☎ 0771-44 41 11; www.tagkompaniet.se in Swedish) Trains in the north of the country, with services to Narvik (Norway).

SEA

Ferry

Ferry connections between Sweden and its neighbours are frequent and straightforward. Most lines offer substantial discounts for seniors, students and children, and many rail-pass holders also get reduced fares. Most prices quoted in this section are for single journeys at peak times (weekend travel, overnight crossings, mid-June to mid-August); at other times, fares may be up to 30% lower.

DENMARK

Helsingør–Helsingborg

This is the quickest route and has frequent ferries (crossing time around 20 minutes).

HH-Ferries (☎ 042-19 80 00; www.hhferries.se) 24-hour service. Pedestrian/car and nine passengers Skr22/265.

Scandlines (☎ 042-18 63 00; www.scandines.se) Similar service and prices.

Sundsbussarna (☎ 042-38 58 80; www.sundsbussarna.se in Swedish) Regular passenger-only ferries to Helsingør from around 7am to 8pm daily. Pedestrian/bicycle Skr22/11).

Göteborg–Fredrikshavn

Stena Line (☎ 031-704 00 00; www.stenaline.se) Three-hour crossing. Up to six ferries daily. Pedestrian/car and five passengers/bicycle Skr210/1195/155.

Stena Line (Express) Two-hour crossing. Up to three ferries daily. Pedestrian/car and five passengers/bicycle Skr278/1495/215.

Varberg–Grenå

Stena Line (☎ 031-704 00 00; www.stenaline.se) Four-hour crossing. Three or four daily. Pedestrian/car and five passengers/bicycle Skr210/1195/155.

Ystad–Rønne

BornholmsTrafikken (☎ 0411-55 87 00; www.bornholmstrafikken.dk) Conventional (1½ hours) and fast (80 minutes) services, two to nine times daily. Pedestrian/car and five passengers/bicycle from Skr204/1192/21.

EASTERN EUROPE

To//from Estonia, **Tallink** (☎ 08-666 6001; www.tallink.ee in Estonian) runs the routes Stockholm–Tallinn and Kapellskär–Paldiski.

To/from Latvia, **Riga Sea Line** (☎ 08-5100 1500; www.rigasealine.lv) operates Stockholm–Riga night ferries. **Scandlines** (☎ 08-5206 02 90; www.scandlines.dk) operates Ventspils–Nynäshamn ferries around five times per week.

To/From Lithuania, **Lisco Line** (☎ 0454-33680; www.lisco.lt) runs daily between Karlshamn–Klaipėda.

To/From Poland, **Polferries** (☎ 040-121700; www.polferries.se) and **Unity Line** (☎ 0411-556900; www.unityline.pl) have daily Ystad–Swinoujscie crossings. Polferries also runs Nynäshamn–Gdańsk. **Stena Line** (☎ 031-704 0000; www.stenaline.se) sails Karlskrona–Gdynia.

FINLAND

Helsinki is called Helsingfors in Swedish, and Turku is Åbo.

Stockholm–Helsinki and Stockholm–Turku ferries run daily throughout the year via the Åland islands (exempt from the abolition of duty-free within the EU, making them a popular outing for Swedes). These ferries have minimum age limits; check before you travel.

Stockholm–Helsinki

Silja Line (☎ 08-22 21 40; www.silja.com) Around 15 hours. Car and up to five passengers/bicycle Skr700/95, ticket and cabin berth from Skr590.

Viking Line (☎ 08-452 40 00; www.vikingline.fi) Operates the same routes with slightly cheaper prices.

Stockholm–Turku

Silja Line (☎ 08-22 21 40; www.silja.com) Eleven hours. Car/bicycle Skr515/95, day/night ticket Skr215/330, cabin berth from Skr335. From September to early May, ferries also depart from Kapellskär (90km northeast of Stockholm): connecting buses operated by Silja Line are included in the full-price fare.

Viking Line (☎ 08-452 40 00; www.vikingline.fi) Operates the same routes with slightly cheaper prices. In high season it offers passage from both Stockholm and Kapellskär.

RG Line (☎ 090-18 52 00; www.rgline.com) runs the routes Umeå–Vaasa and Sundsvall–Vaasa.

Stockholm–Åland Islands (Mariehamn)

Besides the Silja Line and Viking Line routes above, two companies offer foot passenger-only overnight cruises. Prices quoted are for return trips.

Birka Cruises (☎ 08-702 72 00; www.birkacruises.com) A 22 hour round-trip. One or two daily. Berth from Skr350. Prices include supper and breakfast.

Eckerö Linjen (☎ 0175-258 00; www.eckerolinjen.fi) runs to the Åland Islands from Grisslehamn.
Ånedin-Linjen (☎ 08-456 22 00; www.anedinlinjen.com in Swedish) Six hours, daily. Couchette Skr50, berth from Skr235.

GERMANY

Trelleborg–Sassnitz

Scandlines (☎ 042-18 61 00; www.scandlines.se) A 3¾ hour trip. Two to five times daily. Pedestrian/car and up to nine passengers/passenger with bicycle Skr125/965/185.

Trelleborg–Rostock

Scandlines (☎ 042-18 61 00; www.scandlines.se) Six hours (night crossing 7½ hours). Two or three daily. Pedestrian/car and up to nine passengers/passenger with bicycle Skr210/1285/225.
TT-Line (☎ 0410-562 00; www.ttline.com) Operates the same as Scandlines, with similar prices.

Trelleborg–Travemünde

TT-Line (☎ 0410-562 00; www.ttline.com) Seven hours. Two to five daily. Pedestrian/car and up to five passengers/passenger with bicycle Skr240/1700/280. Berths are compulsory on night crossings and cost from Skr215 per person.

Göteborg–Kiel

Stena Line (☎ 031-704 00 00; www.stenaline.se) Fourteen hour. One crossing nightly. Pedestrian/car and up to five passengers Skr790/2190. Berths are compulsory, and cost from Skr190 per person.

NORWAY

There's a daily overnight **DFDS Seaways** (☎ 031-65 06 80; www.dfdsseaways.com) ferry between Copenhagen and Oslo, via Helsingborg. Passenger fares between Helsingborg and Oslo (14 hours) cost Skr1048, and cars Skr450. DFDS also sails from Göteborg to Kristiansand (Norway), three days a week (from seven hours); contact them for prices.

A **Color Line** (☎ 0526-620 00; www.colorline.com) ferry between Strömstad (Sweden) and Sandefjord (Norway) sails two to six times daily (2½ hours) year-round. Tickets cost Skr180 (rail passes get 50% discount); bicycles cost Skr40 and cars Skr195.

UK

DFDS Seaways (www.dfdsseaways.com) Göteborg (☎ 031-65 06 50); UK (☎ 08705-33 30 00) There are two crossings per week between Göteborg and Newcastle via Kristiansand (Norway). The trip takes 25 hours. Fares start from £33 per person including economy berth; cars cost £75 and bicycles are free.

GETTING AROUND

Public transport is heavily subsidised and well organised. It's divided into 24 regional networks *(länstrafik)*, but with an overarching Tågplus (www.tagplus.se) system, where one ticket is valid on trains and buses. The three-part *Rikstidtabellen* gives timetables for all domestic services: buy it at railway stations or large newsagents for Skr80. Handier local timetables are available free of charge or for a nominal fee from tourist offices or the operators.

Holders of International Student Identification Cards (ISIC) will get discounts with some operators – it pays to ask.

AIR

Airlines in Sweden

Domestic airlines in Sweden tend to use **Stockholm Arlanda** (code ARN; ☎ 08-797 60 00; www.lfv.se) as a hub, but there are 30-odd regional airports. Flying domestic is expensive on full-price tickets (usually between Skr1000 and Skr3000 for a single ticket), but substantial discounts are available on Internet bookings, student and youth fares, off-peak travel, return tickets booked at least seven days in advance or low-price tickets for accompanying family members and seniors. It's worthwhile asking about stand-by fares.

The following is a small selection of Sweden's internal flight operators and the destinations they cover. Skyways has the best offers.

FlyMe (airline code SH; ☎ 0770-79 07 90; www.flyme.com; hub Göteborg Landvetter) Stockholm to Göteborg, Ängelholm (near Helsingborg), Malmö and Östersund.
Malmö Aviation (airline code TF; ☎ 040-660 29 00; www.malmoaviation.se; hub Stockholm Bromma) Göteborg, Stockholm and Umeå.
Scandinavian Airlines System (SAS; airline code SK; ☎ 0770-72 77 27; www.scandinavian.net; hub Stockholm Arlanda) Arvidsjaur, Borlänge, Gällivare, Göteborg, Halmstad, Ängelholm–Helsingborg, Hemavan, Hultsfred, Jönköping, Kalmar, Karlstad, Kiruna, Kramfors, Kristianstad, Linköping, Luleå, Lycksele, Norrköping, Malmö, Mora, Örnsköldsvik, Oskarshamn, Oskersund, Skellefteå, Stockholm, Storuman, Sundsvall, Sveg, Torsby, Trollhättan, Umeå, Vilhelmina, Visby, Västerås and Örebro.

Skyways (airline code JZ; ☎ 0771 95 95 00; www.skyways.se; hub Stockholm Arlanda) Arvidsjaur, Borlänge, Göteborg, Halmstad, Hemavan, Jönköping, Karlstad, Kramfors, Kristianstad, Linköping, Lycksele, Norrköping, Mora, Skellefteå, Stockholm, Storuman, Sundsvall, Trollhättan, Vilhelmina, Visby and Örebro.

Air Passes

Visitors who fly SAS to Sweden from Continental Europe, North America or Asia can buy tickets on a **Visit Scandinavia Air Pass**, allowing one-way travel on direct flights between any two Scandinavian cities serviced by SAS, Skyways and other operators. When you buy your international ticket, you buy up to eight coupons, each of which can be used on one domestic flight and is valid for three months. A coupon for use within Sweden costs €69 (except Stockholm–Kiruna, which is €122); international flights between Sweden, Denmark, Norway and Finland cost €80. They can be purchased after arriving in Sweden if you have a return SAS international ticket. For the latest information, call SAS or check their website.

BICYCLE

Cycling is an excellent way to see Sweden and a very common mode of transport for Swedes. Most towns have separate lanes and traffic signals for cyclists. For more information see p53.

BOAT

Canal Boat

The canals provide cross-country routes linking the main lakes. The longest cruises, on the Göta Canal from Söderköping (south of Stockholm) to Göteborg, run from mid-May to mid-September, take at least four days and include the lakes between.

Rederiaktiebolaget Göta Kanal (☎ 031-15 83 11; www.gotacanal.se) operates three ships over the whole distance at fares from Skr9995/15,990 per single/double for a four-day cruise, including full board and guided excursions. For shorter, cheaper trips on the canal, contact tourist offices in the area.

Ferry

An extensive boat network and the 16-day Båtluffarkortet boat passes (Skr420) open up the attractive Stockholm archipelago (see p108). Gotland is served by regular ferries (see p157) from Nynäshamn and Oskarshamn, and the quaint fishing villages off the west coast can normally be reached by boat with a regional transport pass – enquire at the Göteborg tourist offices (p204).

BUS

You can travel by bus in Sweden on any of the 24 good-value and extensive *länstrafik* networks (contact details are given at the beginning of each chapter), or on national long-distance routes.

Express Buses

Swebus Express (☎ 0200 21 82 18; www.swebusexpress.se) has the largest network of express buses, but they only serve the southern half of the country (as far north as Mora in Dalarna). **Svenska Buss** (☎ 0771-67 67 67; www.svenskabuss.se in Swedish) and **Säfflebussen** (☎ 0771-15 15 15; www.safflebussen.se in Swedish, Danish & Norwegian) also connect many southern towns and cities with Stockholm; prices are often slightly cheaper than Swebus Express, but services are less frequent.

North of Gävle, regular connections with Stockholm are provided by several smaller operators, including **Ybuss** (☎ 0771-33 44 44; www.ybuss.se in Swedish) which has services to Sundsvall, Östersund and Umeå.

You don't have to reserve a seat on Swebus Express services. Generally, tickets for travel between Monday and Thursday are cheaper, or if they're purchased over the Internet, or more than 24 hours before departure. If you're a student or senior, it's worth asking about fare discounts; however most bus companies will only give student prices to holders of Swedish student cards (the exception is Swebus Express, where you can get an ISIC discount).

Regional Networks

The *länstrafik* bus networks are well integrated with the regional train system, with one ticket valid on any local or regional bus or train. Rules vary but transfers are usually free within one to four hours. Fares on local buses and trains are often identical.

In remote areas, taxis may have an arrangement with the county council to provide a reduced-fare taxi trip to your final destination. These fares are only valid when arranged in advance (they cannot be bought from the taxi departure point). Ask the regional bus company for details.

Bus Passes

Good-value daily or weekly passes are usually available from local and regional transport offices, and many regions have 30-day passes for longer stays, or a special card for peak-season summer travel.

CAR & MOTORCYCLE

Sweden has good roads, and the excellent E-class motorways don't usually have traffic jams.

Automobile Associations

The Swedish national motoring association is **Motormännens Riksförbund** (☎ 020-21 11 11; www.motormannen.se).

Bring Your Own Vehicle

If bringing your own car, you'll need your vehicle registration documents, unlimited third-party liability insurance and a valid driving licence. A right-hand drive vehicle brought from the UK or Ireland should have deflectors fitted to the headlights to avoid dazzling oncoming traffic. You must carry a reflective warning breakdown triangle.

Driving Licence

An international driving permit isn't necessary, your domestic licence will do.

Hire

To hire a car you have to be at least 20 (sometimes 25) years of age, with a recognised licence and a credit card.

Fly-drive packages may save you money. International rental chains (such as Avis, Hertz and Europcar) are more expensive but convenient; all have desks at Stockholm Arlanda and Göteborg Landvetter airports and offices in most major cities. The best car hire rates are generally from larger petrol stations (like Statoil and OK-Q8) – look out for signs saying *biluthyrning* or *hyrbilar*.

Avis (☎ 0770-82 00 82; www.avisworld.com)
Europcar (☎ 020-78 11 80; www.europcar.com)
Hertz (☎ 0771 211 212; www.hertz-europe.com)
Mabi Hyrbilar (☎ 08-612 60 90; www.mabirent.se) National company with competitive rates.
OK-Q8 (☎ 020-85 08 50; www.okq8.se in Swedish) Click on *hyrbilar* in the website menu to see car-hire pages.

ROAD DISTANCE (KM)

	Gävle	Göteborg	Helsingborg	Jönköping	Kalmar	Karlstad	Kiruna	Linköping	Luleå	Malmö	Skellefteå	Stockholm	Sundsvall	Umeå	Uppsala	Örebro	Östersund
Gävle	---																
Göteborg	514	---															
Helsingborg	672	227	---														
Jönköping	431	149	162	---													
Kalmar	536	346	248	262	---												
Karlstad	322	245	385	467	234	---											
Kiruna	1078	1577	1653	1735	1494	1603	---										
Linköping	333	278	291	369	129	225	212	---									
Luleå	752	1251	1327	1409	1168	1277	1041	333	---								
Malmö	701	281	136	60	271	284	504	1764	398	---							
Skellefteå	619	1118	1194	1276	1035	1144	908	460	941	133	---						
Stockholm	173	478	497	575	335	411	313	1251	207	925	552	---					
Sundsvall	221	720	796	878	637	746	510	858	543	532	186	399	---				
Umeå	490	989	1065	1147	906	1015	779	589	812	262	365	129	663	---			
Uppsala	102	455	431	612	372	447	289	1180	244	854	481	721	72	323	---		
Örebro	231	283	359	441	200	338	117	1294	113	968	1305	604	907	1176	641	---	
Östersund	379	775	869	951	717	874	538	815	659	582	835	197	437	706	172	987	---

Statoil (☎ 08-429 63 00; www.statoil.se/biluthyrning in Swedish) Click on *uthyrningsstationer* to see branches with car hire, and on *priser* for prices.

Road Hazards

In the north, elk (moose) and reindeer are serious road hazards, particularly around dawn and dusk; around 40 people die in collisions every year. Look out for the signs saying *viltstängsel upphör*, which means that elk may cross the road, and for black plastic bags tied to roadside trees or poles – this is a Sami signal that they have reindeer herds grazing in the area. Report all incidents to police – failure to do so is an offence.

Beware of trams in Göteborg and Norrköping, which have priority; overtake on the right.

Road Rules

In Sweden, you drive on and give way to the right. Headlights (at least dipped) must be on at all times when driving. Use of seat belts is compulsory, and children under seven years old should be in the appropriate harness or child seat.

The blood-alcohol limit is a 0.02% – one drink will put you over the limit. Maximum speeds are: motorways (signposted in green and called E1, E4 etc) 110km/h; highways 90km/h; narrow rural roads 70km/h; built-up areas 50km/h. The speed limit for cars towing caravans is 80km/h. Police using hand-held radar speed detectors can impose on-the-spot fines of up to Skr1200.

On many major roads broken lines define wide-paved edges, and a vehicle being overtaken is expected to move into this area to allow faster traffic to pass safely.

HITCHING

Hitching is never entirely safe in any country, and we don't recommend it. Travellers who decide to hitch should understand that they are taking a small but potentially serious risk; consider travelling in pairs and let someone know where you're planning to go.

Hitching isn't popular in Sweden and very long waits are the norm. It's prohibited to hitch on motorways.

LOCAL TRANSPORT

In Sweden, local transport is always linked with regional transport *(länstrafik)*. Regional passes are valid both in the city and on the rural routes. Town and city bus fares are around Skr15, but it usually works out cheaper to get a day card or other travel pass.

Swedish and Danish trains and buses around the Öresund area form an integrated transport system, so buying tickets to Copenhagen from any station in the region is as easy as buying tickets for Swedish journeys.

Stockholm has an extensive underground metro system, and Göteborg and Norrköping run tram networks. Göteborg also has a city ferry service.

Beware of getting ripped off in taxis. It's best to agree to a fare before the trip. In Stockholm, flag fall is around Skr32, then Skr7 per km; most taxis in the capital will take you to Arlanda airport for between Skr350 and Skr450.

TOURS

Recommended tours appear throughout this book and include those run by the following companies:

Svenska Turistföreningen (STF; Swedish Touring Association; ☎ 08-463 21 00: www.svenskaturistforeningen.se; Box 25, SE-10120 Stockholm) Offers scores of events and tours, mostly based on outdoor activities (eg kayaking and hiking).

Sweden Booking (☎ 0498-20 33 80; www.swedenbooking.com; Östervåg 3A, SE-62145 Visby) Can organise rail tickets as well as interesting package trips, like a traditional Christmas in Dalarna or canoeing in Värmland.

TRAIN

Sweden has an extensive and reliable railway network and trains are certainly faster than buses. However, many destinations in the northern half of the country cannot be reached by train alone.

Train Operators

Sveriges Järnväg (SJ; ☎ 0771-75 75 75; www.sj.se) National network covering most main lines, especially in the southern part of the country. Its X2000 fast trains run at speeds of up to 200km/h.

Tågkompaniet (☎ 0771-44 41 11; www.tagkompaniet.se in Swedish) Operates excellent overnight trains from Göteborg and Stockholm north to Boden, Kiruna, Luleå and Narvik, and the lines north of Härnösand.

There are some smaller regional train operators, but they tend to cooperate closely with SJ.

In summer, almost 25 different tourist trains offer special rail experiences. The most notable is **Inlandsbanan** (☎ 0771-53 53 53; www.inlandsbanan.se), a slow and scenic 1300km route from Kristinhamn to Gällivare, one of the great rail journeys in Scandinavia. Several southern sections have to be travelled by bus, but the route proper starts at Mora. It takes seven hours from Mora to Östersund (Skr347) and 15 hours from Östersund to Gällivare (Skr697). A pass allows two weeks' unlimited travel for Skr1195.

Costs

Travel on the super-fast X2000 services is much pricier than on 'normal' trains. Full-price 2nd-class tickets for longer journeys are expensive (around twice the price of equivalent bus trips), but there are various discounts available, especially for booking a week or so in advance *(förköpsbiljet)*, or at the last minute (for youth and pensioner fares). Students (with a Swedish CSN or SFS student card if aged over 26), and people aged under 26, get a 30% discount on the standard adult fare.

X2000 tickets include a seat reservation. All SJ ticket prices are reduced in summer, from late June to mid-August. SJ trains don't allow bicycles to be taken onto trains (they have to be sent as freight).

Station luggage lockers usually cost between Skr20 and Skr30 for 24 hours.

Train Passes

The Sweden Rail Pass, Eurodomino tickets and international passes, such as Inter-Rail, Eurail and ScanRail, are accepted on SJ services and most regional trains.

ScanRail (www.scanrail.com) has a flexible rail pass covering 2nd-class travel in Denmark, Finland, Norway and Sweden. Buy it outside Scandinavia, otherwise you'll face restrictions. There are three versions:

Flexi 5-day For travel on any five days within a two-month period, UK£171 (travellers under 26 UK£119, over 60 UK£152).

Flexi 10-day For travel on any 10 days within a two-month period, UK£229 (under 26 UK£160, over 60 UK£203).

Consecutive For unlimited travel during 21 consecutive days, UK£266 (under 26 UK£185, over 60 UK£235).

ScanRail passes are valid on state railways in Denmark, Finland, Norway and Sweden. They're also valid on most Swedish *länstrafik* trains – but *not* on Stockholm (SL) local trains, or on certain Länstrafikken trains in Värmland, Upplands Lokaltrafik (UL) and Östgötatrafiken trains. They're valid on two privately operated Swedish lines, the Arlanda Express (from Arlanda Airport to Stockholm) and the Connex night trains between Stockholm/Göteborg and upper Norrland.

The pass does *not* cover the Flåm line in Norway or Inlandsbanan in Sweden.

Pass holders also get discounts on cabins, and cheaper prices (up to 50% off) on the ferry services in the following table.

Route	Operator
Frederikshavn–Göteborg	Stena Line
Grenå–Varberg	Stena Line
Stockholm–Helsinki	Viking or Silja Line
Stockholm–Turku	Viking or Silja Line
Travemünde–Trelleborg	TT Line
Rostock–Trelleborg	TT Line
Nynäshamn–Visby	Destination Gotland
Oskarshamn–Visby	Destination Gotland

X2000 trains require all rail-pass holders to pay a supplement of Skr65 (including the obligatory seat reservation).

Health

CONTENTS

You're unlikely to encounter serious health problems in Sweden. Travel health depends on your predeparture preparations, your daily health care while travelling and how you handle any problem that does develop.

BEFORE YOU GO

Before departure, obtain travel insurance with good medical coverage. If you wear glasses or contact lenses take a spare set and a copy of your optical prescription. If you require a particular medication, carry a legible copy of your prescription from your doctor. Most medications are available in Sweden, but brand names may be different, so you'll need the generic name.

RECOMMENDED VACCINATIONS

Immunisations aren't necessary for travel to Sweden, unless you've been travelling somewhere where yellow fever is prevalent. Ensure that your normal childhood vaccines (against measles, mumps, rubella, diphtheria, tetanus and polio) are up to date. You may also want to have a hepatitis vaccination, as exposure can occur anywhere.

IN SWEDEN

AVAILABILITY & COST OF HEALTH CARE

There's no general practitioner service in Sweden, but pharmacies *(apotek)* sell non-prescription (and prescription) medicines, and give advice on how to deal with everyday ailments and conditions.

For emergencies and casualty services, g to a local medical centre *(vårdcentral)* or hospital *(sjukhus* or *lasarett)*, where dut doctors are standing by. There are centre in all districts and main towns, listed b area under municipality *(kommun)* in th local telephone directory. EU citizens wit an EHIC form are charged around Skr12 to consult a doctor and up to Skr300 for visit to casualty; hospital stays cost Skr9 per day (free for patients under 16 years Non-EU citizens should have adequate trav insurance or be prepared to face high cost although some countries (such as Australia have reciprocal health-care agreements wit Sweden.

Dentists *(tandläkare)* charge about Skr70 for an hour's treatment.

For general emergencies, including th ambulance service, call ☎ 112.

TRAVELLER'S DIARRHOEA

Simple things such as a change of wate food or climate can cause mild diarrhoea and a few rushed toilet trips with no othe symptoms do not indicate a major problem Stomach upsets are as possible in Sweden a anywhere else. Occasionally, cooked meat displayed on buffet tables may cause prob lems. Also, take care with shellfish (cooke mussels that haven't opened properly aren' safe to eat), unidentified berries and mush rooms.

Dehydration is the main danger wit any diarrhoea, particularly in children o the elderly. Under all circumstances flui replacement (at least equal to the volum being lost) is the most important thing t remember. With severe diarrhoea a rehy drating solution to replace lost minerals an salts is preferable. Commercially availabl oral rehydration salts can be added to boile or bottled water. In an emergency, add solution of six teaspoons of sugar and a hal teaspoon of salt to a litre of boiled water.

Gut-paralysing drugs such as loperamid or diphenoxylate can be used to bring relie from the symptoms, although they do no cure the problem. Use these drugs only i you do not have access to toilets, eg if yo *must* travel. Do not use these drugs for chil ren under 12 or if the person has a high ever or is severely dehydrated.

iardiasis

tomach cramps, nausea, a bloated stomach, vatery foul-smelling diarrhoea and frequent as are all symptoms of giardiasis, which an occur several weeks after you have been xposed to the parasite. The symptoms may isappear for a few days and then return; his can go on for several weeks.

NVIRONMENTAL HAZARDS

ypothermia

his condition occurs when the body loses eat faster than it can produce it and the core emperature of the body falls. It's surprisingly asy to progress from very cold to dangerusly cold due to a combination of wind, vet clothing, fatigue and hunger, even if the ir temperature is above freezing. It's best to ress in layers; silk, wool and some of the ew artificial fibres are all good insulating naterials. A hat is important, as a lot of heat s lost through the head. A strong, waterproof uter layer (and a space blanket for emergencies) is essential. Carry basic supplies, ncluding food containing simple sugars to enerate heat quickly, and fluid to drink.

The symptoms of hypothermia are exhausion, numb skin, shivering, slurred speech, rrational or violent behaviour, lethargy, tumbling, dizzy spells, muscle cramps and violent bursts of energy. Irrationality may ake the form of sufferers claiming they are varm and trying to take off their clothes.

To treat mild hypothermia, first get the erson out of the wind and/or rain, remove heir clothing if it's wet and replace it with ry, warm clothing. Give them hot liquids not alcohol) and some high-calorie, easily igestible food. Do not rub victims; instead, allow them to slowly warm themselves. This should be enough to treat the early stages of hypothermia. Early treatment of mild hypothermia is the only way to prevent severe hypothermia, which is a critical condition.

Insect Bites & Stings

Mosquitoes, blackflies and deerflies are common from mid-June to the end of July, and fly swarms in northern areas are horrific. To avoid bites, completely cover yourself with clothes and a mosquito head net. Any exposed areas of skin, including lower legs (and even underneath trousers), should be treated with a powerful insect repellent containing DEET (although frequent application of DEET isn't recommended). Calamine lotion, a sting relief spray or ice packs will reduce any pain and swelling.

Sunburn

In high northern latitudes you can get sunburnt surprisingly quickly, even through clouds, and especially when there's complete snow cover. Use sunscreen, a hat, and a barrier cream for your nose and lips. Calamine lotion or commercial after-sun preparations are good for mild sunburn. Protect your eyes with good quality sunglasses, particularly if you'll be near water, sand or snow.

Water

Tap water is safe to drink in Sweden, but drinking from streams may be unwise due to the presence of farms, old mine workings and wild animals. The clearest-looking stream water may contain giardia and other parasites. If you don't have a filter and can't boil water it should be treated chemically; iodine is effective and is available in liquid and tablet form.

Language

CONTENTS

The national language of Sweden is Swedish, a Germanic language belonging to the Nordic branch that is spoken throughout Sweden and in parts of Finland. Swedes, Danes and Norwegians can make themselves mutually understood, and most Swedes speak English as a second language.

Since they share common roots, and the Old Norse language left sprinklings of words in Anglo-Saxon, you'll find many similarities between English and Swedish – albeit with different pronunciations. There are three letters at the end of the Swedish alphabet that don't exist in the English version, namely **å**, **ä** and **ö**.

Swedish verbs are the same regardless of person or number: 'I am, you are' etc are, in Swedish, *jag är*, *du är* and so on. There are two genders, common (non-neuter) and neuter. Gender is reflected in the articles *en* and *ett* (a/an). The definite article (the) is added to the ends of nouns, eg *ett hus* (a house), *huset* (the house). Unfortunately there are no set rules for determining gender – it's something that has to be learnt word by word.

PRONUNCIATION

Sweden is a large country with considerable dialectal variety. There are sounds in Swedish that don't exist in English, so in the following pronunciation guides we've tried to give the closest English equivalents. In terms of dialect, we've gone with the version you'll hear in Stockholm. If you follow the pronunciation guides and listen to the way the Swedes themselves speak the language, you'll soon start getting the hang of it. The first thing you'll need to master is the songful rise and fall that is so characteristic of Swedish and Norwegian.

ACCOMMODATION

hotel
hotell — ho·*tel*
guesthouse
gästhus — *yest*·hoos
youth hostel
vandrarhem — vaan·dra·*hem*
camping ground
campingplats — kam·ping·*plats*

Where is a cheap/good hotel?
Var är ett billigt/bra hotell?
vaa air et *bil*·ligt/braa ho·*tel*
What's the address?
Vilken adress är det?
vil·ken *aa*·*dres* air det?
Could you write the address, please?
Kan du skriva ner adressen?
kan doo *skree*·va neer a·*dre*·sen?
Do you have any rooms available?
Finns det några lediga rum?
fins de *nor*·gra *le*·di·ga room?
How much is it per person/night?
Hur mycket kostar det per person/natt?
her *moo*·ket *ko*·sta det

I'd like ...
Jag skulle vilja ... — ya *skool*·le *vil*·ya ...
a single room
ha ett enkelrum — haa et *en*·kel·*room*
a double room
ha ett dubbelrum — haa et *doo*·bel·*room*
a room with a bathroom
ha ett rum med bad — haa et room med baad
to share a dorm
bo i sovsal — boo ee *soov*·*sal*

for one night
en natt — en nat
for two nights
två nätter — *tvo*·a *ne*·te
Does it include breakfast?
Inkluderas frukost? — in·kloo·*dair*·ras *froo*·kost?

May I see the room?
Kan jag får se rummet? kan ya for *se*·ya *room*·met?
Where is the bathroom?
Var är badrummet? vaa air baad·*room*·*met*?

CONVERSATION & ESSENTIALS

Hello.
Hej. hay
Goodbye.
Adjö/Hej då. ai·yer/hay·*dor*
Yes.
Ja. yaa
No.
Nej. nay
Please.
Snälla. *snel*·la
Thank you.
Tack. tak
That's fine.
Det är bra. de air braa
You're welcome.
Varsågod. *var*·sha·good
Excuse me.
Ursäkta mig. ur·*shek*·ta may
I'm sorry. (forgive me)
Förlåt. for·*lort*
May I/Do you mind?
Får jag/Gör det något? for yaa/*yer* de *nor*·got?
What's your name?
Vad heter du? vaa *he*·te doo?
My name is ...
Jag heter ... ya *he*·te ...
Where are you from?
Varifrån kommer du? *vaa*·re·fron *ko*·mer du?
I'm from ...
Jag kommer från ... ya *ko*·mer fron ...

DIRECTIONS

Where is ...?
Var är ...? vaa air ...?
Can you show me on the map?
Kan du visa mig på kartan? kan du *vee*·sa may poor *kar*·tan?
Go straight ahead.
Gå rakt fram. gor *rakt* fraam
Turn left.
Sväng till vänster. *sveng* til *ven*·sta.
Turn right.
Sväng till höger. *sveng* til *her*·ga
near
nära *nair*·a
far
långt lorngt

SIGNS

Ingång	Entrance
Utgång	Exit
Information	Information
Öppen	Open
Stängd	Closed
Förbjuden	Prohibited
Polisstation	Police Station
Lediga Rum	Rooms Available
Toalett	Toilets
Herrer	Men
Damer	Women

beach
strand strand
castle
slott slot
cathedral
domkyrka *dom*·sher·ka
church
kyrka *sher*·ka
main square
huvudtorg hoo·vood·*toy*
monastery
kloster *kloo*·sta
old city
gamla stad *gam*·la staad
palace
palats pa·*lats*

HEALTH

Where is the ...?
Var är ...? vaa air ...?
chemist/pharmacy
apoteket a·poo·*te*·ket
dentist
tandläkaren tan·*lair*·ka·*ren*
doctor
läkaren *lair*·ka·ren
hospital
sjukhus *shoo*·koos

I'm ill.
Jag är sjuk. ya air shook
My friend is ill.
Min vän är sjuk. (m/f) min ven air shook

I'm ...
Jag är ... ya air ...
asthmatic
astmatiker ast·ma·*tee*·kair
diabetic
diabetiker de·a·*be*·tee·ker

EMERGENCIES

Help!
Hjälp! yelp!
Call a doctor!
Ring efter en doktor! ring *ef*·ter en dok·*toor*
Call the police!
Ring polisen! ring poo·*lee*·sen
Call an ambulance!
Ring efter en ambulans! ring *ef*·ter en am·boo·*lants*
Go away!
Försvinn! fer·*shvin*
I'm lost.
Jag har gått vilse. ya har got vil·*se*

I'm allergic to antibiotics/penicillin.
Jag är allergisk mot antibiotika/penicillin.
yaa air a·ler·*gisk* moot an·tee·bee·*yo*·tee·ker/pen·ne·see·*len*

I need medication for ...
Jag behöver ett medel mot ... ya bee·her·ver et me·del moot ...
I have a toothache.
Jag har tandvärk. ya haar tand·*vairk*
I'm pregnant.
Jag är gravid. ya air *gra*·*veed*
antiseptic
antiseptisk an·tee·*sep*·tisk
condoms
kondomer kon·*do*·mer
diarrhoea
diarré dee·a·re·a
medicine
medicin me·de·*seen*
nausea
illamående il·la·*mo*·en·de
stomachache
ont i magen oont e *maa*·gen
sanitary napkins
dambindor *dam*·bin·dor
tampons
tamponger tam·*pong*·er

LANGUAGE DIFFICULTIES

Do you speak English?
Talar du engelska? *ta*·la du *en*·gel·ska?
Does anyone here speak English?
Finns det någon här som talar engelska? fins de non hair som *ta*·la *en*·gel·ska?
I (don't) understand.
Jag förstår (inte). ya fer·*stor* (in·*te*)
Could you speak more slowly, please?
Kan du vara snäll och tala lite långsammare? kan du *va*·ra snel ok *ta*·la *lee*·te *long*·sa·ma·rer?

NUMBERS

0	*noll*	nol
1	*ett*	et
2	*två*	*tvo*·a
3	*tre*	tree
4	*fyra*	few·*ra*
5	*fem*	fem
6	*sex*	sex
7	*sju*	shoo
8	*åtta*	ot·*ta*
9	*nio*	*nee*·ye
10	*tio*	*tee*·ye
11	*elva*	*el*·va
12	*tolv*	tolv
13	*tretton*	*tre*·ton
14	*fjorton*	*fyoo*·ton
15	*femton*	*fem*·ton
16	*sexton*	*sex*·ton
17	*sjutton*	*shoo*·ton
18	*arton*	*ar*·ton
19	*nitton*	*nee*·ton
20	*tjugo*	*shoo*·go
21	*tjugoett*	*shoo*·go·et
30	*trettio*	*tre*·tee
40	*fyrtio*	*fyor*·tee
50	*femtio*	*fem*·tee
60	*sextio*	*sex*·tee
70	*sjuttio*	*shoo*·tee
80	*åttio*	*ot*·tee
90	*nittio*	*nee*·tee
100	*ett hundra*	et *hoon*·dra
1000	*ett tusen*	et *too*·sen
1,000,000	*en miljon*	en mil·*yoon*

SHOPPING & SERVICES

I'm looking for ...
Jag letar efter ... yaa *lee*·ta ef·ta
a bank
en bank en bank
the city centre
centrum sent·*room*
the ... embassy
... ambassaden ... am·ba·*sa*·den
the market
marknaden mark·*naa*·den
the museum
muséet moo·*zee*·et
the post office
posten *pos*·ten
a public telephone
en offentlig telefon en o·*fent*·lig tel·le·*foon*
a public toilet
en toalettkiosk en toa·*let*·she·osk
the tourist office
turistinformationen too·*rist*·in·for·ma·*shoo*·nen

LANGUAGE

What time does it open/close?
Hur dags (öppnar/stänger) de? hur daags (*erp*·na/*steng*·er) det?
Could I please have ...?
Kan jag få ...? kan ya for ...
How much is it?
Hur mycket kostar den? her *mi*·ke *kos*·ta den?

bookshop
bokhandel *book*·han·del
camera shop
fotoaffär fo·*to*·a·*fair*
clothing store
modebutik *mood*·boo·*teek*
delicatessen
delikatessaffär del·li·*kaats*·a·*fair*
laundry
tvätt tvet
newsagency
pressbyrå/tabaksaffär pres·*bew*·ro/ta·*bak*·sa·*fair*
souvenir shop
souveniraffär soov·ven·*nee*·ra·*fair*
stationers
pappershandel pa·pairs·*haan*·del

TIME & DATE

What time is it?
Vad är klockan? vaa air *klo*·kan?
today
idag ee·dag
tonight
i kväll ee kvel
tomorrow
imorgon ee·mor·*ron*
yesterday
igår ee·*gor*
morning
morgonen moo·ron·*nen*
afternoon
efter middagen ef·ter mid·da·gen
night
natt nat

Monday
måndag *mon*·dag
Tuesday
tisdag *tees*·dag
Wednesday
onsdag *ons*·dag
Thursday
torsdag *torsh*·dag
Friday
fredag *fre*·dag
Saturday
lördag *ler*·dag

SAMI LANGUAGES

Sami languages are related to Finnish and other Finno-Ugric languages. Five of the nine main dialects of the Sami language are spoken in Sweden, with speakers of each varying in number from 500 to 5000.

Most Sami speakers can communicate in Swedish, but relatively few speak English. Knowing some Sami words and phrases will give you a chance to access the unique Sami culture.

Fell (Northern) Sami

The most common of the Sami languages, Fell Sami is considered the standard variety of the language. It's spoken in Sweden's far north around Karesuando and Jukkasjärvi.

Written Fell Sami includes several accented letters, but it still doesn't accurately represent the spoken language – even some Sami people find the written language difficult to learn. For example, *giitu* (thanks) is pronounced 'geech-too', but the strongly aspirated 'h' isn't written.

Hello. *Buorre beaivi.*
Hello. (reply) *Ipmel atti.*
Goodbye.
(to person leaving) *Mana dearvan.*
(to person staying) *Báze dearvan.*
Thank you. *Giitu.*
You're welcome. *Leage buorre.*
Yes. *De lea.*
No. *Li.*
How are you? *Mot manna?*
I'm fine. *Buorre dat manna.*

1 *okta*
2 *guokte*
3 *golbma*
4 *njeallje*
5 *vihta*
6 *guhta*
7 *cieza*
8 *gávcci*
9 *ovcci*
10 *logi*

Sunday
söndag *sern*·dag

January
januari yan·u·*aa*·ree
February
februari fe·broo·*aa*·ree

March
mars mars
April
april a·*preel*
May
maj may
June
juni *yoo*·nee
July
juli *yoo*·lee
August
augusti o·*goos*·tee
September
september sep·*tem*·ber
October
oktober ok·*too*·ber
November
november no·*vem*·ber
December
december de·*sem*·ber

TRANSPORT

Where is the ...?
Var är ...? vaa air ...?
bus stop
busshållplatsen boos·hol·*plat*·sen
train station
tågstationen torg·sta·*shoo*·nen
tramstop
spårvagnshållplatsen *spor*·vaags·hol·*plat*·sen

What time does the ... leave/arrive?
När avgår/kommer ...? nair *av*·gor/*ko*·mer ...?
boat
båten bor·ten
bus
bussen *boos*·sen
tram
spårvagnen spor·*vaagn*
train
tåget *tor*·get

I'd like ...
Jag skulle vilja ha ... ya *skoo*·le *vil*·ya haa ...
a one-way ticket
en enkelbiljett en en·*kel*·bil·*yet*
a return ticket
en returbiljett en re·*toor*·bil·*yet*

1st class
första klass *fer*·shta klas
2nd class
andra klass *an*·dra klas
left luggage
effektförvaring e·*fekt*·fur·*vaa*·ring
timetable
tidtabell tee·ta·*bel*

Where can I hire a car/bicycle?
Var kan jag hyra en bil/cykel? vaa kan ya *hee*·ra en beel/en see·*kel*

Glossary

You may encounter some of the following terms and abbreviations during your travels in Sweden. See also the Language chapter and Food & Drink chapter.

Note that the letters *å, ä,* and *ö* fall at the end of the Swedish alphabet, and the letters *v* and *w* are often used interchangeably (you will see the small town of Vaxholm also referred to as Waxholm, and an inn can be known as a *värdshus* or *wärdshus*). In directories like telephone books they fall under one category (eg *wa* is listed before *vu*).

aktie bolaget (AB) – company
allemansrätt – literally 'every person's right'; a tradition allowing universal access to private property (with some restrictions), public land and wilderness areas
ank – arrives, arrivals
apotek – pharmacy
atelje – gallery
avg – departs, departures
avgift – payment, fee (seen on parking signs)
avhämtning – takeaways

bad – swimming pool, bathing place or bathroom
bakfickan – literally 'back pocket', alow-profile eatery usually associated with a gourmet restaurant
bankautomat – cash machine, ATM
barn – child
bastu – sauna
bensin – petrol, gas
berg – mountain
bibliotek – library
bil – car
billjet – ticket
billjetautomat – ticket machines for street parking
biluthyrning – car hire
bio, biograf – cinema
björn – bear
bokhandel – bookshop
bro – bridge
bruk – factory
bryggeri – brewery
buss – bus
busshållplats – bus stop
butik – shop
båt – boat

campingplats – camping ground
centrum – town centre
cykel – bicycle
dag – day
dagens rätt – daily special, usually on lunchtime menus
dal – valley
diskotek – disco
domkyrka – cathedral
drottning – queen
dubbelrum – double room
duodji – Sami handicraft
dusch – shower
dygn – a 24-hour period
dygnet runt – around the clock
dygnskort – a daily transport pass, valid for 24 hours

ej – not
enkelrum – single room
exkl – excluded
expedition – office

fabrik – factory
fest – party, festival
fika – verb meaning to meet friends for coffee and cake
fjäll – mountain
fjällstation – mountain lodge
fjällstugor – mountain huts
fjärd – fjord, drowned glacial valley
flod – large river
flyg – aeroplane
flygbuss – airport bus
flygplats – airport
folkdräkt – folk dress
folkhemmet – welfare state
fr o m – from and including (on timetables)
friluft – open-air
frukost – breakfast
fyr – lighthouse
fågel – bird
färja – ferry
färjeläge – ferry quay
fästning – fort, fortress
förbjuden – forbidden, prohibited
förbund – organisation, association
förening – club, association
förlag – company

galleri, galleria – shopping mall
gamla staden, gamla stan – the 'old town', the historical part of a city or town
gammal, gamla – old
gatan – street (often abbreviated to just g)

gatukök – literally 'street kitchen'; street kiosk/stall/grill selling fast food
glaciär – glacier
grotta – grotto, cave
grundskolan – comprehensive school
gruva – mine
gränsen – border
gymnasieskolan – upper secondary school
gård – yard, farm, estate
gästgiveri – guesthouse
gästhamn – 'guest harbour', where visiting yachts can berth; cooking and washing facilities are usually available
gästhem, gästhus – guesthouse

hamn – harbour
hav – sea
hembygdsgård – open-air museum, usually old farmhouse buildings
hemslöjd – handicraft
hiss – lift, elevator
hittegods – lost property
hotell – hotel
hund – dog
hus – house, sometimes meaning castle
husmanskost – homely Swedish fare, what you would expect cooked at home when you were a (Swedish) child
hytt – cabin on a boat
hällristningar – rock carvings
hälsocentral – health clinic
höst – autumn

i – in
i morgon – tomorrow
idrottsplats – sports venue, stadium
inkl – included
inte – not
is – ice
ishall – ice hockey stadium

joik – see *yoik*
jul – Christmas
järnvägsstation – train station

kaj – quay
kanot – canoe
kanotuthyrning – canoe hire
kart – map
Kartförlaget – State Mapping Agency (sales division)
klockan – o'clock, the time
klocktorn – bell tower
kloster – monastery
kommun – municipality
konditori – baker and confectioner (often with an attached café)
konst – art
kontor – office
kort – card
kreditkort – credit card
krog – pub, restaurant (or both)
krona (sg), kronor (pl) – the Swedish currency unit
kulle (sg), kullar (pl) – hill
kung – king
kust – coast
kväll – evening
kyrka – church
kyrkogård – graveyard
kåta – tepee-shaped Sami hut
källare – cellar, vault
kök – kitchen

lagom – sufficient, just right
landskap – region, province, landscape
lavin – avalanche
lilla – lesser, little
linbana – chairlift
lo – lynx
loppis – secondhand goods (usually junk)
län – county
Länstrafiken – public transport network of a *län*

magasin – store (usually a department store), warehouse
mat – food
medlem – member
Midsommar – Midsummer's day; first Saturday after 21 June (the real celebrations take place on Midsummer Eve)
miljö – environment, atmosphere
MOMS – value added tax (sales tax)
morgon – morning (but *i morgon* means tomorrow)
museet, museum – museum
mynt – coins
mynt tvätt – coin-operated laundry (rare in Sweden)
målning – painting, artwork

natt – night
nattklubb – nightclub
naturcamping – camping site with a pleasant environment
naturistcamping – nudist colony
naturreservat – nature reserve
Naturum – national park or nature reserve visitor centre
Naturvårdsverket – Swedish Environmental Protection Agency (National Parks Authority)
nedre – lower
norr – north
norrsken – aurora borealis (northern lights)
ny – new
nyheter – news

obs! – take note, important
och – and
ordning och reda – orderliness

palats – palace
pendeltåg – local train
pensionat – pension, guesthouse
P-hus – multistorey car park
polarcirkeln – Arctic Circle, latitude 66°32'N
polis – police
pris, prislista – price, pricelist
på – on, in
påsk – Easter

raukar – limestone formations
ren – reindeer
resebyrå – travel agent
restaurang- restaurant
riksdag – parliament
rum – room
RFSL – Riksförbundet för Sexuellt Likaberättigande (national gay organisation)
rådhus – town hall
rökning förbjuden – no smoking

SAS – Scandinavian Airlines Systems
simhall – swimming pool
sjukhus – hospital
självbetjäning – self-service
sjö – lake, sea
skog – forest
skål! – cheers!
skärgård – archipelago
slott – castle, manor house
smörgås – sandwich
smörgåsbord – Swedish buffet
snabbtvätt – quick wash (at laundrette)
snö – snow
sommar – summer
sovsal – dormitory
spark – kicksledge
spårvagn – tram
stark – strong
statsminister – prime minister
STF – Svenska Turistföreningen (Swedish Touring Association)
stor, stora – big or large
stortorget – main square
strand – beach
stuga (sg), stugor/na – hut, cabin
stugby – chalet park; a little village of chalets
städning – room cleaning
sund – sound
svensk – Swedish
Sverige – Sweden
SVIF – Sveriges Vandrahem i Förening
Systembolaget – state-owned liquor store
säng – bed
söder – south

t o m – until and including
tandläkare – dentist
teater – theatre
telefon kort – telephone card
tid – time
tidtabell – timetable
toalett – toilet
torg, torget – town square
torn – tower
trappe – stairs
trädgård – garden open to the public
tull – customs
tunnelbana, T-bana – underground railway, metro
turistbyrå – tourist office
tåg – train
tågplus – combined train and bus ticket
tält – tent

uteservering – outdoor eating area
uthyrningsfirma – hire company

vandrarhem – hostel
vattenfall – waterfall
vecka – week
vik – bay, inlet
vinter – winter
vuxen – adult
vår – spring
vårdcentral – hospital
väg – road
vänthall, väntrum, väntsal – waiting room
värdekort – value card; a travel pass that can be topped up at any time
värdshus – inn
väst – west (abbreviated to v)
västra – western
växel – switchboard, money exchange

wärdshus – inn

yoik – Sami 'Song of the Plains' (also referred to as *joik*)

å – stream, creek, river
år – year

älg – elk
älv – river

ö – island
öl – beer
öppettider – opening hours
öst – east (abbreviated to ö)
östra – eastern
övre – upper

Behind the Scenes

THIS BOOK

This 3rd edition of *Sweden* was written and updated by Becky Ohlsen and Fran Parnell, based on the 2nd edition, which was written by Carolyn Bain and Graeme Cornwallis. This guidebook was commissioned in Lonely Planet's Melbourne office, and produced by the following:

Commissioning Editors Sam Trafford, Tashi Wheeler, Michala Green
Coordinating Editor Emma Gilmour
Coordinating Cartographer Barbara Benson
Coordinating Layout Designer Yvonne Bischofberger
Managing Editor Martin Heng
Managing Cartographers Mark Griffiths, Adrian Persoglia
Assisting Editors Diana Saad, Louisa Syme, Pat Kinsella
Assisting Cartographer David Connolly
Assisting Layout Designers Wibowo Rusli, Jacqui Saunders, Liz White, Christine Wieser
Cover Designer Jane Hart
Colour Designer Laura Jane
Indexer Nancy Ianni
Project Manager Fabrice Rocher, Rachel Imeson
Language Content Coordinator Quentin Frayne

Thanks to Sally Darmody, Adriana Mammarella, Kate McDonald, Emma Koch, Gabbi Wilson, Celia Wood. The health chapter was adapted from text by Dr Caroline Evans.

THANKS

BECKY OHLSEN

Heartfelt thanks, *stor kram* and *tusendubblingar* to my parents, Joel and Christina Ohlsen; Morfar Arne and Mormor Elisabeth Odeen; Natalie and Karl Ohlsen; Kristina Björholm and Captain Joe; Madeleine and Lars-Olof Ödlund; Jennifer Sjöberg; Tatiana Holmström-Lundgren; Roy Valve; the Dukes of Hazzard; and, as ever, the Sang-Froid Riding Club of Portland, Oregon, and its associates.

FRAN PARNELL

A huge thank you to everyone who helped me on the road. I'm grateful to all the tourist office staff who assisted, particularly Gabrielle at Askersund, Stina at Sunne, Eva at Torsby, Johanna at Lysekil, Lena at Håverud, and Ana Nilsson at Trollhättan.

For their enthusiasm, sharing of information, and saintly deeds, my thanks to Caroline Darnfors at the Kanalmuséet, Håverud; Anna from Germany (a huge Inspector Wallander fan); Peter the Scribe at Foteviken; Nils for the windsurfing tips (good luck with those waves); Stefan for doing his utmost to fix my broken-down car; and the friendly gentleman who let me nosey round his hotel room in Fjällbacka.

Thanks also to the people back home: Sam, for extreme patience and understanding; Mark Griffiths for the map pep talk; for 'Boing' texts and Nelson's Column, love to Billy; for helping sort out the postfire mess and putting up with mighty hysteria, love (and apologies) to Stuart.

OUR READERS

Many thanks to the travellers who used the last edition and wrote to us with helpful hints, useful advice and interesting anecdotes:

May Ahlen, Trygve Anderson, Stephen Arkell, Peter Baker, Amoroso Blanco, Stefano Blanco, Yaroslav Blanter, David Breen, Catherine

THE LONELY PLANET STORY

The story begins with a classic travel adventure: Tony and Maureen Wheeler's 1972 journey across Europe and Asia to Australia. There was no useful information about the overland trail then, so Tony and Maureen published the first Lonely Planet guidebook to meet a growing need.

From a kitchen table, Lonely Planet has grown to become the largest independent travel publisher in the world, with offices in Melbourne (Australia), Oakland (USA) and London (UK). Today Lonely Planet guidebooks cover the globe. There is an ever-growing list of books and information in a variety of media. Some things haven't changed. The main aim is still to make it possible for adventurous travellers to get out there – to explore and better understand the world.

At Lonely Planet we believe travellers can make a positive contribution to the countries they visit – if they respect their host communities and spend their money wisely. Every year 5% of company profit is donated to charities around the world.

Brinkley, Clare Carmody, John Carmody, Maria Castillo-Stone, Jan Delvert, Corinne Francois Deneve, Ylva Drougge, Sandra Engelhardt, Richard Folley, Pontus Forslund, Hilde Gerhardt, Jo Goodman, Flora Hajdu, Carina Hansen, Petter Hellstrom, Lykke Jensen, Tore Jungnelius, Christoph Kalthoff, Jaime & Soon Keat, Mary Ellen Kitler, Queenie Lau, Richard & Liz Lower, Brian McConaghy, Michael Mcguire, Adam Micha, Vincent Mifsud, Judith Miller, Jennifer Mundy, Gustaf Myrsten, Michael Nacke, Sarah Nortcliffe, Monika Obfolter, Henrik Ohrn, Mark Pearce, Aase Popper, Aljaz Prusnik, Urska Prusnik, Gabi Reischmann, Eva Rexach, Tariq van Rooijen, Hans Rossel, Marieke de Ruijter, Bruce Rumage, Claudia Schulte, Michelle Seltzer, Oxana Shveykina, Michael Spencer-Smith, Robert Stagg, Yael Straver-Lerys, Tibor Szabo, David Szylit, Nozomi Tamura, Kerstin Thorn-Seshold, Anders Thorsell, Fredrik Tukk, Jackie Wilson, Stina Wollenius, Fernando Zaidan

ACKNOWLEDGMENTS

Many thanks to the following for the use of their content:

Globe on back cover ©Mountain High Maps 1993 Digital Wisdom, Inc.

Stockholm Metro Map © Storstockholms Lokaltrafik 2002

Göteborg Tramlines Map © Göteborgsregionens Lokaltrafik 2002

SEND US YOUR FEEDBACK

We love to hear from travellers – your comments keep us on our toes and help make our books better. Our well-travelled team reads every word on what you loved or loathed about this book. Although we cannot reply individually to postal submissions, we always guarantee that your feedback goes straight to the appropriate authors, in time for the next edition. Each person who sends us information is thanked in the next edition – and the most useful submissions are rewarded with a free book.

To send us your updates – and find out about Lonely Planet events, newsletters and travel news – visit our award-winning website: **www.lonelyplanet.com/feedback**.

Note: We may edit, reproduce and incorporate your comments in Lonely Planet products such as guidebooks, websites and digital products, so let us know if you don't want your comments reproduced or your name acknowledged. For a copy of our privacy policy visit www.lonelyplanet.com/privacy.

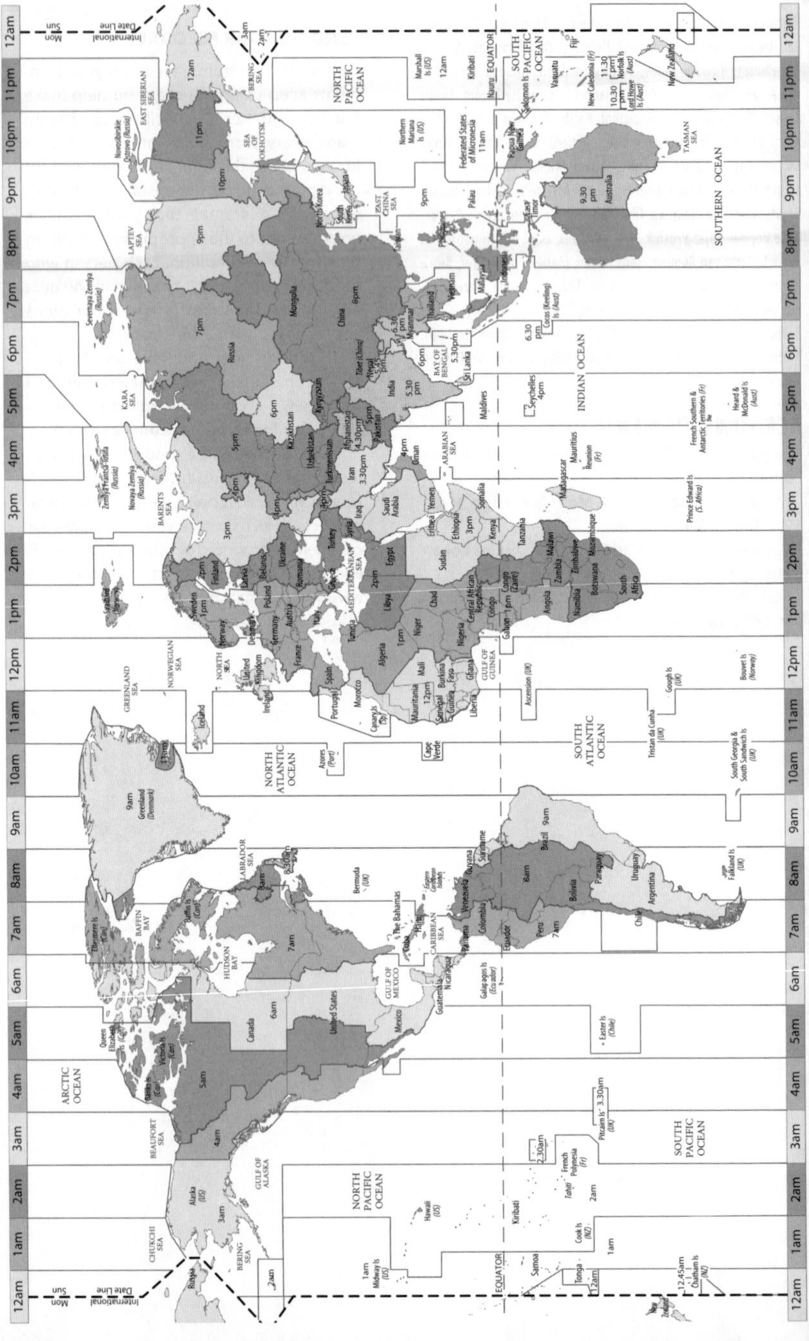
12am
1am
2am
3am
4am
5am
6am
7am
8am
9am
10am
11am
12pm
1pm
2pm
3pm
4pm
5pm
6pm
7pm
8pm
9pm
10pm
11pm
12am
International Date Line
Mon
Sun
ARCTIC OCEAN
NORTH PACIFIC OCEAN
SOUTH PACIFIC OCEAN
NORTH ATLANTIC OCEAN
SOUTH ATLANTIC OCEAN
INDIAN OCEAN
SOUTHERN OCEAN
EQUATOR
CHUKCHI SEA
BERING SEA
BEAUFORT SEA
GULF OF ALASKA
HUDSON BAY
BAFFIN BAY
LABRADOR SEA
GULF OF MEXICO
CARIBBEAN SEA
GREENLAND SEA
NORWEGIAN SEA
NORTH SEA
BARENTS SEA
KARA SEA
LAPTEV SEA
EAST SIBERIAN SEA
SEA OF OKHOTSK
EAST CHINA SEA
MEDITERRANEAN SEA
ARABIAN SEA
BAY OF BENGAL
GULF OF GUINEA
TASMAN SEA
Alaska (US)
Canada
United States
Mexico
Greenland (Denmark)
Iceland
Russia
China
Mongolia
India
Australia
New Zealand
Brazil
Argentina
Chile
Peru
Bolivia
Colombia
Venezuela
Algeria
Libya
Egypt
Sudan
Chad
Niger
Mali
Nigeria
Ethiopia
Kenya
Tanzania
Angola
Namibia
Botswana
South Africa
Madagascar
Saudi Arabia
Iran
Iraq
Turkey
Kazakhstan
Afghanistan 4.30pm
Pakistan
Nepal 5.45 pm
India 5.30 pm
Sri Lanka 5.30pm
Myanmar 6.30 pm
Iran 3.30pm
Australia 9.30 pm
Hawaii (US)
Tahiti
French Polynesia (Fr)
Pitcairn Is (UK) 3.30am
Chatham Is (NZ) 12.45am
Lord Howe Is (Aust) 10.30 pm
Norfolk Is (Aust) 11.30 pm
Newfoundland 8.30am

Index

NOTE
The Swedish letters å, ä and ö fall at the end of the alphabet.

000 Map pages
000 Photograph pages

000 Map pages
000 Photograph pages

000 Map pages
000 Photograph pages

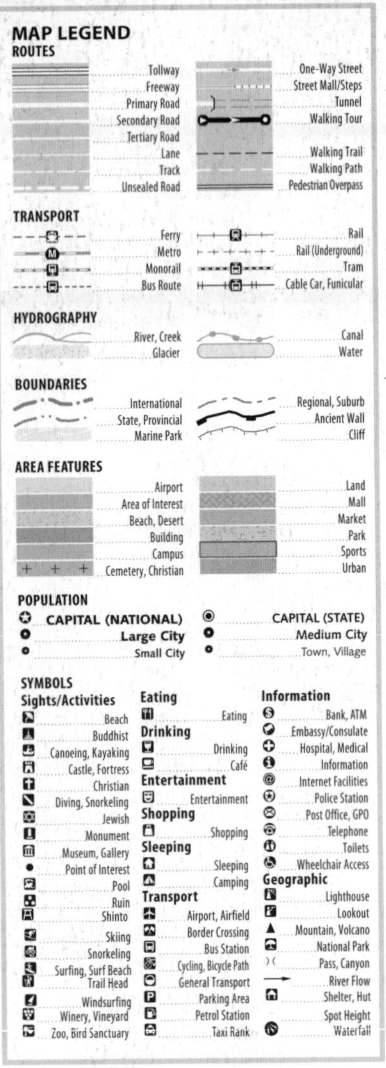

LONELY PLANET OFFICES

Australia
Head Office
Locked Bag 1, Footscray, Victoria 3011
☎ 03 8379 8000, fax 03 8379 8111
talk2us@lonelyplanet.com.au

USA
150 Linden St, Oakland, CA 94607
☎ 510 893 8555, toll free 800 275 8555
fax 510 893 8572
info@lonelyplanet.com

UK
72–82 Rosebery Ave,
Clerkenwell, London EC1R 4RW
☎ 020 7841 9000, fax 020 7841 9001
go@lonelyplanet.co.uk

Published by Lonely Planet Publications Pty Ltd
ABN 36 005 607 983

Cover photographs: Ice Hotel in Jukkasjärvi, Peter Grant/Image Bank Sweden (front); Millesgården in Stockholm, Ernest Manewal/Lonely Planet Images (back). Many of the images in this guide are available for licensing from Lonely Planet Images: www.lonelyplanetimages.com.

Printed through Colorcraft Ltd, Hong Kong.
Printed in China